RUM & REGGAE'S
HAWAI'I

Rum&Reggae's
HAWAI'I

by

Jonathan Runge

RUM & REGGAE GUIDEBOOKS, Inc.
Prides Crossing, Massachusetts
2001

While
every effort
has been made
to provide accurate
information, prices, places,
and people do change rather
frequently in Hawai'i. Typographical
errors also occasionally occur. Thus, please
keeping mind that there may be discrepancies between
what you find and what is reported here. In addition, some of
the recommendations have been given by individuals interviewed by the
authors and may not represent the opinion of the author or of Rum & Reggae Guidebooks, Inc. The reader assumes all responsibility when participating in the activities or
excursions described in this book.

This work was originally published in different form by St. Martin's
Press, New York in 1989 .

ISBN: 1-893675-01-7
LIBRARY OF CONGRESS CATALOG CARD NUMBER: 00-101142

Book design by Betsy Sarles and Scott-Martin Kosofsky
at The Philidor Company, Cambridge

Cover design by Betsy Sarles

Cover Illustration by Eric Orner

Maps by Manoa Mapworks, Inc. of Honolulu, Hawai'i

Printed in Canada on recycled paper

Enlighten with Aloha

CONTENTS

Introduction xi

Acknowledgments xiii

Before You Go xv

O'ahu 3

Maui 97

The Big Island 191

Kaua'i 293

Lana'i 383

Moloka'i 397

Hawai'ian Words 425

Index 441

Rum & Reggae Contact Info 451

About the Author 452

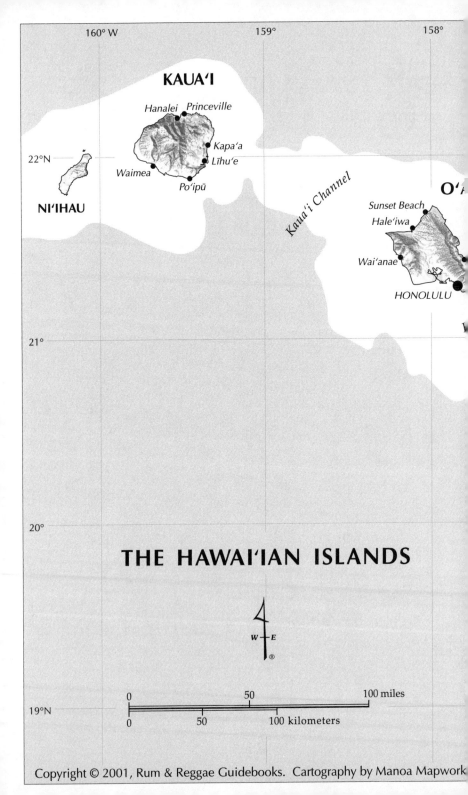

160° W   159°   158°

KAUA'I

Hanalei   Princeville

Kapa'a

Līhu'e

Waimea

Po'ipū

22°N

NI'IHAU

Kaua'i Channel

O'

Sunset Beach

Hale'iwa

Wai'anae

HONOLULU

21°

20°

THE HAWAI'IAN ISLANDS

W — E

®

| 0 | 50 | 100 miles |

| 0 | 50 | 100 kilometers |

19°N

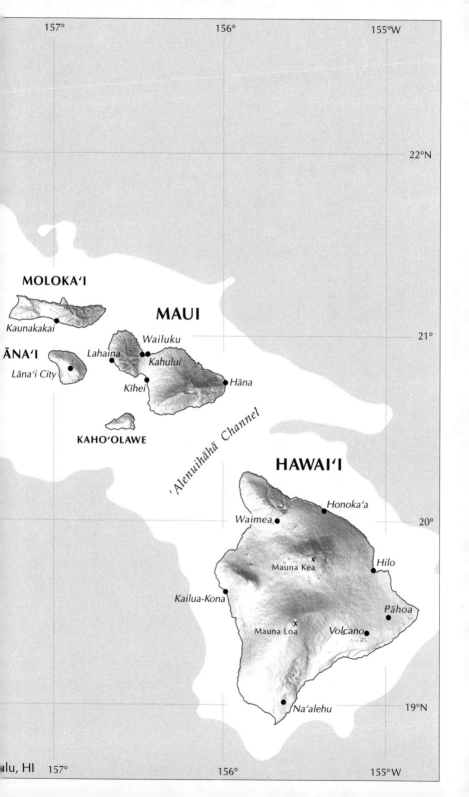

Introduction

"*OUR MIDDLE NAME IS BITCH.*" [TM] That's how we describe our distinct point of view. *Rum & Reggae's Hawai'i* is not your typical tourist guidebook to the Aloha State. We like to say that the *Rum & Reggae* series is written for people who want more out of a vacation than the standard tourist fare. Our reader is more sophisticated and independent. He's also more active—be it scuba diving, windsurfing, kitesurfing, hiking, sailing, golfing, playing tennis, or exploring. Or she's more particular, in search of places that are secluded, cerebral, spiritual, or très branché (if you have to ask what the latter means, those places are not for you).

This book differs from other guidebooks in another way. Instead of telling you that everything is "nice"—nice, that is, for the average Joe—*Rum & Reggae's Hawai'i* offers definitive opinions. We will tell you what's fantastic and what's not, from the point of view of someone who loathes the tourist label and the other bland travel books whose names we won't mention. Those branded books remind us of the ditty "Stranded, stuck on the toilet bowl, What do you do when you're stranded and you haven't got a roll." Get the picture?

We'll take you to all six major islands in the Hawai'ian chain and give you our recommendations of where to go (and where not to). More important, we filter out all the crap for you so you can *enjoy* reading the book *and* enjoy your vacation and keep the decision-making to a minimum. We wish *we* had this book when we were doing our research. It would have made our job a helluva lot easier. We would have had more time to kick back and get sand between our toes.

So mix yourself a stiff Mai Tai (don't forget the dash of orgeat

syrup), put on some Hawai'ian-slack key, and sit back and let *Rum & Reggae's Hawai'i* take you on your own private voyage to the land of aloha.

Acknowledgments

CONTRARY TO WHAT YOU MIGHT THINK, travel writing is not very glamorous. We often find the best part of the job is answering the "So what do you do?" question at cocktail parties. It's all downhill from there. We did not spend our days on the beach or by the pool sipping a Mai Tai. Well, okay, *sometimes* we did. But most of the time we were running around checking out this or that and complaining. Try changing hotels at least thirty times (don't forget the packing and unpacking and chronic laundry crises) and you'll begin to know what we mean.

Fortunately, some wonderful people in Hawai'i helped us out along the way. We'd like to take this opportunity to graciously thank those who did. In no particular order, they are: Eva and Jim Tantillo, Carolyn Barnes, Roy Ventner, Sharon Murotzune, Merideth Desha, Gail Mejia, Rob Devaraturda, Dara Fujimoto, Sandy Yara, Charlene Kaihane, Laura Aquino, Marni Reynolds, Babs Harrison, Gigi Valley, Caroline Witherspoon, Richard Koob, Ken Fujiyama, Michelle Wilhelm, and Connie Wright. If we overlooked your name, we are very sorry, but please accept our thanks for your help!

Back on the East Coast, finishing this book was, to us, like finishing the Boston Marathon. About three quarters of the way through the race comes Heartbreak Hill, a long, steady incline that makes or breaks the runner. We hit Heartbreak Hill both literally and figuratively. But, with great exertion and a lot of support, we made it up the Hill and to the finish line. Our deepest thanks to those who kept cheering us on at the moments we didn't think we could go on. We will never forget you! A huge thank-you to our wonderful copy editor, Kathie Ness, our fabulous book designers, Betsy Sarles and Scott-Martin Kosofsky, our very talented illustrator and future animation mega-star, Eric Orner, our amazing indexer, Judith Antonelli, our superb Web specialist, Michael

Carlson, our new publicist, Maryglenn McCombs, our understanding printer, Ed Catania, and finally our beyond-patient distributor, Mid-Point Trade Books, and our point people there, Chris Bell and Gail Kump.

There were also several people who helped in other ways. *Mahalo* to Duncan Donahue and Tom Fortier, Nan Garland, Carlos Meléndez and Sean Martin, Gedy Moody, Elvis Jiménez-Chávez and Christopher Lawrence, Alvaro Ortiz, Tina Vasserot Merle, Tomas Jonsson, Steve Parks, and Saffron Parker.

Finally, thank-you to my parents, Eunice and Albert Runge, without whom this book never would have happened. As for my business partner, Tony Lulek, who kept the ship on course through some very rough seas, this book is dedicated to you.

Oh yes, and thanks to my cat, Jada, for being my guardian angel.

To all who helped, *mahalo nui loa!*

Jonathan Runge
Prides Crossing, Massachusetts
September 4, 2001

Before You Go

*A **note about this guide**:* We have used a number of symbols and terms to indicate prices and ambience. Here are the code breakers.

Lodging Rates

☞ Lodging in the Aloha State is not cheap! You will find very few establishments in the **Dirt Cheap** category (camping, anyone?). Most big resorts fall into the **Wicked Pricey** and up range for standard rack rates (the published rate). Look for packages, corporate discounts and discounts, offered to organizations like AAA, the government, and AARP. Also, frequent flyer and credit card awards programs can save you bundles.

☞ Rates are for *high season* unless otherwise noted.

☞ Rates are for a double room, European Plan, unless otherwise noted. Rates for singles are the same or slightly less.

☞ Expect Hawaii State Excise and Hotel Room Occupancy Taxes of 11.42 %. Ouch!

☞ Although almost every establishment accepts major credit cards, be sure to ask when making reservations at smaller establishments, especially if you intend to use American Express.

Dirt Cheap	under $50
Cheap	$51–$100
Not So Cheap	$101–$150
Pricey	$151–$200
Very Pricey	$201–$300
Wicked Pricey	$301–$400
Ridiculous	$401–$500
Beyond Belief	$501 and up!

Restaurant Prices

Prices represent per-person cost for the average meal from soup to nuts.

$	$0–$10
$$	$11–$20
$$$	$21–$30
$$$$	$31–$40
$$$$$	over $40

Meal Codes

EP   (European Plan) — No meals included

CP   (Continental Plan) — Continental breakfast (or sometimes a more extensive breakfast) included

MAP (Modified American Plan) — Full breakfast and dinner included

FAP (Full American Plan) — Full breakfast, lunch, and dinner included (sometimes with an afternoon tea or snack as well)

ALL-INCLUSIVE — All meals, beer, wine, and well drinks (house brands) are included.

Touristo Scale Key

(1)

What century is this? Not of the First World.

(2)

Tiny or no airport: uh, this is a state, remember.

(3)

A nice, unspoiled yet civilized place.

(4)

Still unspoiled, but getting popular.

🐷🐷🐷🐷🐷 (5)

A popular place, but still not too developed.

🐷🐷🐷🐷🐷 (6)

Busy and booming; this was very quiet not long ago.

🐷🐷🐷🐷🐷🐷 (7)

Well-developed tourism and lots of tourists;
fast-food outlets conspicuous.

🐷🐷🐷🐷🐷🐷🐷 (8)

Highly developed and tons of tourists.

🐷🐷🐷🐷🐷🐷🐷🐷 (9)

Mega-tourists, and tour groups;
fast-food outlets outnumber restaurants.

🐷🐷🐷🐷🐷🐷🐷🐷🐷 (10)

Swarms of tourists and total development. Run for cover!

Climates of Hawai'i

The weather in the Aloha State is about as close to perfect as anywhere on Earth (we say this about the Caribbean in *Rum & Reggae's Caribbean*; now we *really* mean it for Hawai'i). The temperature rarely dips below 65° or climbs above 90° Fahrenheit (at sea level). The reasons for this ideal climate are the constant temperature of the ocean—about 75°F year-round—and the steady trade winds from the northeast. It does get cooler at night in the upcountry and in the mountains on some of the islands, making it ideal for sleeping. There is a "rainy season"—usually in December and January. When the trade winds are up, rainfall almost always occurs on the windward side of the islands, where the mountains catch the clouds. It comes in the form of brief, intense cloudbursts, quickly followed by sunshine. When the trades stop blowing and *go kona* (come from the south), it almost always means bad weather. This is when the weather can be iffy because mid-Pacific storms can stall, and it can be cloudy and or rainy for days (even a week). Hawai'i can get hit by furious hurricanes too. Due to its western location, Kaua'i seems to be especially vulnerable, having recently suffered direct hits by Category Four and Five (Five being the strongest) tempests named Iwa (1982) and Iniki (1992).

While the slopes of Mauna Kea on the Big Island contain 11 of the Earth's 13 climate zones, at sea level there are three basic climate categories: arid (hot and dry), lush (hot, somewhat humid, with lots of rainfall), and those areas in between that have a little of both (the windward side being the wetter and greener) or that fall somewhere in the middle. August and September, while only about five degrees hotter than winter, feel much warmer due to the increased humidity and decreased wind. The one constant is the sun. It is *always* strong and will swiftly fry unprotected pale faces—and bodies—to a glowing shade of lobster red.

Building a Base for Tanning

Since the advent of "fake 'n bake" (tanning machines) and pretanning accelerators, there is absolutely no reason to get burned on your first day out in the tropical sun. With some advance attention, you can stay outside for *hours* on your first day—and let's face it, what you want to do when you step off the plane is hit the beach.

Just about every town has a tanning center, often sporting a ridiculous name. Most health clubs have one or two tanning "coffins" lying around, beckoning pasty skins to look healthier and more attractive in a matter of minutes. Ultraviolet tanning is fairly safe when used properly, because the rays of the UVB light aren't as harmful as in earlier sun lamps or, of course, the sun.

Many of these tanning centers have tanning-prep packages: You start with about 5 minutes of "sunning" and work up to 20 or 30. Spread out over the two weeks prior to your departure, this should give you an excellent head start on a great Hawai'ian tan.

Pretan accelerators, available from a wide variety of manufacturers, chemically stimulate the manufacture of melanin, the pigment that darkens your skin. (Normally it takes direct exposure to the sun to start its production.) A pretan accelerator doesn't change your color or dye your skin like the QT of yesteryear (whoops, we're dating ourselves!). Rather, it prepares the skin with extra melanin so that you tan the first time out rather than burn, and much faster too.

What to Wear and Take Along

Less is more. That's the motto to remember when packing to go to Hawai'i (or anywhere). Even with luggage-on-wheels, bring only what you can carry or pull for ten minutes at a good clip, because you'll often be schlepping your luggage for at least that length of time, and we've learned that the worst thing is being luggage-impaired or luggage-challenged. If you haven't already done so, invest in a piece of luggage with wheels.

What you really need to take along is a bathing suit, shorts, T-shirts or tanks, sweatshirt or cotton pullover, a pair of sandals, sunglasses, and a Discman or Walkman. After all, you *are* on vacation. Plan to by a pair of flip-flops (what the locals call "slippers") at the local ABC or Long's when you arrive, and a quality aloha shirt during your stay. Since this is the 21st century and people tend to dress up for no reason, you may want to bring some extra togs to look presentable at the dinner table. To help you be totally prepared (and to make your packing a lot easier), we've assembled a list of essentials for a week.

The Packing List

Clothes

bathing suit (or two)

T shirts (4) — You'll end up buying at least one.

tank tops — They're cooler and show off your muscles or curves.

polo shirts (2) — Don't forget, those alligators (Lacoste/IZOD shirts) are in again

shorts (2)

nice, compatible lightweight pants (you can wear them on the plane)

sandals — Those that can get wet, like Tevas, are best.

cotton pullover or sweatshirt

undergarments

sneakers (or good walking shoes) or topsiders (for boaters)

If you must have them, wear the following (with appropriate shoes) on the plane:

Men: lightweight jacket

Women: lightweight dress

Essentials — Don't panic if you forget something, you can find it in most locations here.

toiletries

sunscreens (SPF 15+, 8, 4 [oil], and lip protector)

moisturizers (aloe gel for that sunburn)

some good books—We have found that it is best to bring the reading materials you want *with* you. Finding a worthwhile read at your destination may mean hopping in a car and heading to the nearest Border's—usually in a mall.

Cutter's or Woodsman's insect repellent, or Skin So Soft (oh, those nasty bugs)

sunglasses!

hat/visor!

Hardware/Lingerie (Just kidding about the lingerie thing! Actually, come to think of it…)

Walkman/Discman/mini disc player and tapes/CDs

camcorder or pocket camera (Disposables are essential for the beach. Sand has ruined many a camera)

Sports Accessories (where applicable)

tennis racquet

golf clubs

hiking shoes

fins, mask, snorkel, wetsuit, BC, regulator, and C-card

Paperwork

ATM card/credit cards

driver's license

Inter-Island Travel Deals

Both Aloha Airlines/Aloha Islandair and Hawai'ian Airlines have inter-island deals that ease the cost of traveling between islands. While there is limited ferry service between a few of the islands, we wouldn't think of using them due to the frequency of flights and the rough open-ocean seas.

At press time, Aloha/Islandair offered a coupon book of six anywhere/one-way/inter-island tickets for $377 (good for one year). Aloha also has a $321, seven-consecutive-days pass that is good for unlimited inter-island travel. Hawai'ian Airlines has 8- and 30-consecutive-day commuter passes available for $350 and $1,299 respectively. Hawai'ian also offers a coupon book of six anywhere/one-way/inter-island tickets for $391.50. Please note that airline prices and deals shift with the wind. Even so, there is no reason to forego exploration of the islands.

Other Airfare Tips

Be sure to check the Internet; deals are always available there. Always shop around to secure the lowest possible fare to your destination. Ask for the lowest fare, not just a discount fare. If you're adventurous, wait until your departure date draws nearer, and call again—additional low-cost seats may have become available. Or investigate the major travel tour companies for a charter flight.

Island/Activities Matchup

Looking for the best island for diving, golf, restaurants, or gay nightlife? This helpful chart will give you some suggestions.

Beaches
O'ahu
Kaua'i
Maui
Moloka'i
Privacy
Lana'i
Moloka'i
Big Island

Scuba
Big Island
Maui
Lana'i
Nightlife
O'ahu
Cerebral Stuff
O'ahu
Big Island

Food
  O'ahu
  Maui
  Big Island
  Kaua'i
Golf
  Big Island
  Maui
  Kaua'i
  Lana'i
Nature
  Kaua'i
  Big Island
  Moloka'i

Quiet
  Moloka'i
  Lana'i
Windsurfing
  Maui
  O'ahu
Gay Nightlife
  O'ahu
Nude Beaches
  Maui
  Big Island

Hawai'i Superlatives

The following is a *completely* subjective list which we *relished* creating. Let us know your favorites by e-mailing us at aloha@rum-reggae.com.

Best Beach — **Polihale,** Kaua'i
Best Nude (& Gay) Beach — **Little Beach,** Maui
Best Island for Beaches — **O'ahu**
Best Place for Sun — **Maui**
Best Luxury Hotel/Resort — **Mauna Kea Beach Hotel,** Big Island
Best Hotel Spa – **Hyatt Regency Kaua'i,** Kaua'i
Best Hotel — **W,** O'ahu
Best Hotel/Resort for Kids — **Hilton Waikaloa Village,** Big Island
Best Romantic Hotel — **Hotel Hana-Maui,** Maui
Best Small Inn — **Shipman House,** Big Island
Best B&B — **What a Wonderful World B&B,** Maui
Best Alternative Lodging — **Kalani Eco-Resort,** Big Island
Best Mountain Lodging — **Kilauea Lodge,** Big Island
Best Room with a View — **Princeville Hotel,** Kaua'i
Best Luxury Hotel/Resort — Kaua'i — **Hyatt Regency Kaua'i**
Best Luxury Hotel/Resort — O'ahu — **Kahala Mandarin Oriental**
Best Luxury Hotel/Resort – Moloka'i — **The Lodge at Moloka'i Ranch**

Best Luxury Hotel/Resort – Lana'i — **The Lodge at Ko'ele**
Best Luxury Hotel/Resort – Maui — **Four Seasons Wailea**
Best Luxury Hotel/Resort – Big Island — **Mauna Kea Beach Hotel**
Best Hawai'ian Regional Restaurant — **Merriman's**, Big Island
Best Continental Restaurant — **Chef Mavro**, O'ahu
Best Romantic Restaurant — **Hau Tree Lanai**, O'ahu
Best Japanese Restaurant — **Furasato**, O'ahu
Best Thai Restaurant — **Keo's Thai Cuisine**, O'ahu
Best Vietnamese Restaurant — **A Saigon Café**, Maui
Best Vietnamese Take-Out — **Ba-Le**, O'ahu
Best Plate Lunch — **Ka'a'awa Grinds**, O'ahu
Best Pizza — **Brick Oven Pizza**, Kaua'i
Best Island for Food — **O'ahu**
Best Restaurant – Kaua'i — **A Pacific Café**
Best Restaurant – O'ahu — **Indigo**
Best Restaurant – Moloka'i — **Lodge at Moloka'i Ranch**
Best Restaurant – Lana'i — **Formal Dining Room at the Lodge
    at Ko'ele**
Best Restaurant – Maui — **i'o**
Best Restaurant – Big Island — **Merriman's**
Best Mai Tai — **Royal Hawai'ian Hotel**, O'ahu
Best Place for a Sunset Cocktail — **Outrigger Canoe Club**,
    O'ahu (you need to be a guest of a member)
Best Nightclub — **Indigo**, O'ahu
Best Gay Nightclub — **Angles**, O'ahu
Best Place For Nightlife — **O'ahu**
Best Place For Gay Nightlife — **O'ahu**
Best Place to Get High — **Little Beach**, Maui
Best Place to Be for New Year's — **Honolulu**, O'ahu
Best Festival — **Merrie Monarch**, Big Island
Best Cerebral Experience — **Kalaupapa**, Moloka'i
Best Meditative Spot — **Byodo-In Temple**, O'ahu
Best Diving — **Big Island**
Best Snorkeling — **Maui**
Best Surfing – **North Shore**, O'ahu
Best Body-Surfing – **Makapu'u**, O'ahu
Best Camping — **Kaua'i**
Best Mountain Biking — **Moloka'i**

Best Golf Course — **Mauna Kea Course**, Big Island
Best Hike — **Kalalau Trail**, Kaua'i
Best Tennis — **Kapalua**, Maui
Best Windsurfing — **Maui**
Best Heli-touring — **Kaua'i**
Best Shopping — **Waikiki**, O'ahu
Best Aloha Shirt — **Sig Zane Designs**, Big Island/Maui
Best-Kept Secret — **Hawi**, Big Island

R&R's Top Ten Favorite Places to Stay in Hawai'i

Mauna Kea Beach Hotel, Big Island
It's the Buddha at night and that Rockefeller taste that make this place so wonderful.

Hotel Hana-Maui, Maui
Ah, Hana, how we love thee and this perfectly small resort.

Hanalei Colony Resort, Kaua'i
The sound of the surf and the moonrise over the bay left an indelible impression on us.

Shipman House, Big Island
Authentic restorations don't come any better than this jewel of a Victorian.

W, O'ahu
Just *so* groovy-cool and a welcome addition to the Hawai'ian lodging scene, we want one on every island!

Lodge at Moloka'i Ranch, Moloka'i
Newish, friendly, small, and peaceful are more than enough reasons to stay here.

Kahala Mandarin Oriental, O'ahu
Outside of the madness that is now Waikiki, this classic hotel has been spruced and goosed.

Hyatt Regency Kaua'i, Kaua'i
The spa alone is a reason to go here, as is one of the most stunning entrances anywhere (and we're all about entrances).

Lodge at Ko'ele, Lana'i
Lovely Lana'i City, towering Cook pines, fab architecture, and an Executive Putting Course next door make the Lodge our Lana'i fave.

Four Seasons Wailea, Maui
That Four Seasons panache and the resort's proximity to Little Beach give it the thumbs up from us.

Hawai'i's Top Ten Luxury Resorts

Mauna Kea Beach Hotel — Big Island
Mauna Lani Bay Hotel — Big Island
Four Seasons Hualalai — Big Island
Kahala Mandarin Oriental — O'ahu
Hyatt Regency Kaua'i — Kaua'i
Four Seasons Wailea — Maui
The Princeville Hotel — Kaua'i
Lodge at Ko'ele — Lana'i
Hotel Hana-Maui — Maui
Halekulani — O'ahu

Trash (and we're not talking about you!)

Many of Hawai'i's best beaches are on undeveloped parcels of private land, which people use anyway. This is fine, but some people don't pick up after themselves, so inevitably there are piles of trash or litter on or near the beach. The woods surrounding the beaches are particularly hard-hit. In addition, trash from Japan and California, or from other islands, can wash up on the shore. This happens everywhere. This is not to say that Hawai'ian beaches are dirty—just messy in places. As you will notice, Hawai'i *is* a fairly clean state.

The state and county beaches fare a lot better because they are cleaned up regularly. But the private ones aren't so lucky. So don't be surprised when you see the bane of modern civilization spoiling an otherwise perfect scene. Don't worry, though— there's usually plenty of room to avoid it. And, of course, carry out what you bring in.

The Top Ten Beaches in Hawai'i

Polihale, Kaua'i
   Sand dunes, no people, tons of sun, and faboo sunsets makes Polihale our favorite beach in the Aloha State.

Little Beach, Maui
   The most fun beach on Maui, this is our choice for the island's and state's best nude and gay beach.

Sunset Beach, O'ahu
   The Big Daddy of surfing venues in the world during the winter, Sunset is home to Hawai'i's biggest waves, including Waimea Bay and the Banzai Pipeline.

Red Sand Beach, Maui
   Located in one of our favorite places *on Earth*, this beach, carved out of a volcanic cinder cone and with red cinder pebbles for sand, is a de facto nude/gay beach.

Sandy Beach, O'ahu
   Body-surfing central and a great place to watch the local scene, just a 20-minute ride from Honolulu.

Makapu'u, O'ahu
   A stunning setting with great body-surfing. Note the lighthouse peeking out to the east.

Big Beach, Maui
   The big sister of Little Beach, this is a much longer strand with plenty of room to spread out.

Kehena, Big Island
   The prettiest black-sand beach in Hawai'i is also the Hilo side's nude/gay beach.

Hanalei Bay, Kaua'i
   With the spectacular backdrop of the Na Pali coast, the long and protected crescent is within walking distance of groovy Hanalei Town.

Papohaku, Moloka'i
   Looking for miles of deserted beach? This is da place, brah. Watch the currents!

Mai Tai High

Hawai'i's most famous drink is a concoction of various substances, particularly rum. It is reputed to have been invented at the Royal Hawai'ian Hotel in Waikiki. So, courtesy of the hotel, here is that wonderful recipe:

crushed ice
1 ounce light rum
1 ounce dark rum
1/4 ounce orange curaçao
dash orgeat syrup
dash rock-candy syrup
juice of 1/2 lime
orange juice

Fill a tall glass with crushed ice. Add everything except the orange juice and 1/4 ounce of the dark rum. Then fill up with OJ and top off with the rest of the dark rum. Garnish with a pineapple wedge, orchid, sugarcane stalk, or mint leaf.

Whew! Now sit back and enjoy the sunset!

ALOHA!

O'AHU

Touristo Scale:

🐷🐷🐷🐷🐷🐷🐷🐷🐷🐷 (10)

MOST OF THE IMAGES of Hawai'i that have been seared into our minds over the years come from O'ahu. From Pearl Harbor, to *Hawaii Five-O*, to Waikiki and Diamond Head; from *Magnum P.I.* and the Banzai Pipeline to Don Ho and the *Baywatch Hawaii* babes; all come from the isle whose name means "the gathering place."

Whoever named this island must have been psychic. Seventy-five percent of the state's 1,190,000 people live here, most in the greater Honolulu (pronounced ho´-no-loo-loo) area. The city, Hawai'i's capital, is the crossroads of the Pacific. People and businesses representing the entire Pacific Rim reside here. This makes for a very interesting mix of cultures, evident in everything from ethnic/racial variety and architectural styles to restaurant cuisines and the extraordinary number of karaoke clubs (very popular with Asians). Honolulu is also a metropolis of high-rise buildings, Hawai'i's only freeways, and pretty, well-tended houses— all in one of the most spectacular natural settings in the world. Behind the city rises the Ko'olau Range—towering, sculpted peaks of green crowned with clouds. The calm, protected waters of Pearl and Honolulu harbors shimmer below. Diamond Head, the very photogenic extinct volcano that is Honolulu's landmark, sits just to the east of Waikiki. These natural splendors, in combination with the incredible mix of people, make Honolulu and O'ahu a magical destination.

Those contemplating a quiet, low-key kind of vacation may want to choose one of the neighbor islands, as the focus on O'ahu is a-c-t-i-o-n. Scores of popular beaches, all kinds of recreation and activities, restaurants, bars, and clubs make both day and night pulsate with life. While it's great to be out of doors on any of the Hawai'ian islands, wilderness options are not O'ahu's forte. This is definitely a people place. The beach is where it's at, and O'ahu has some of the nicest, and definitely the hottest, beaches in the state. To be sure, there are other worthwhile outdoor options—good hikes, great surfing and kayaking (island favorites), windsurfing, kiteboarding, and golf—that will keep those who aren't already on the beach, in the waves, or at the bar very busy.

A Not-So-Brief History

The third largest in the Hawai'ian chain (608 square miles/1,575 square kilometers), the island was formed about two and a half million years ago by volcanoes on the magma hotspot that's now under both the southeast coast of the Big Island and the Lo'ihi sea mount (currently about 3,000 feet below sea level). The last volcanic eruption on O'ahu occurred about 12,000 years ago. There are no active or dormant volcanoes left on the island. Such landmarks as Diamond Head and Koko Crater are all extinct volcanoes.

Originally settled by migration waves from the Marquesas and Society islands—first in the 8th and then in the 12th and 13th centuries—the Hawai'ian Islands remained isolated from the outside world until Captain Cook's expedition landed at Kaua'i in 1778. At that time the islands shared the same language and customs, but contact was limited to periodic conquests, defeats, and occasional trading. O'ahu was ruled by the adopted son of Kahekili, the powerful chief of Maui. Within a year of Cook's first contact on Kaua'i, diseases brought by the Europeans, especially venereal diseases, had spread to all of the islands.

In 1786 O'ahu was conquered by the ruthless Kahekili, already the ruler of Maui, Moloka'i and Lana'i. His greed for territory and power led him to kill his adopted son, "sacrificing" the body to the war god Ku and then torturing the lesser O'ahu chiefs to death.

O'AHU

Nice guy, huh? Kahekili ruled from O'ahu and formed an alliance with his half-brother Ka'eokulani, the ruler of Kaua'i. Concurrent with all this warring, both Kahekili and Kamehameha, the chief of the Big Island (Hawai'i), were tapping into the white man's technology, making deals for guns and support from various British and American traders and mercenaries. This trade would greatly alter the outcome of the battles. The more guns and cannons a chief had in his forces, the more success he would have.

On O'ahu, the English merchant captain William Brown "discovered" the excellent anchorage at Pearl Harbor and bartered an alliance with Kahekili. Various intrigues and rivalries ensued until Kahekili died of natural causes in 1794. He left his half-brother Ka'eokulani and his son Kalanikupule in charge of his empire. Of course, egos clashed and to make a long story even longer, Kalanikupule prevailed. Unfortunately, Kalanikupule made a grave error in judgment when he killed William Brown and tried to commandeer his ships and men to go to the Big Island and fight the menacing chief, Kamehameha. Unsuccessful and humiliated, he was now without the white man's guns and support. In 1795 Kamehameha, sensing weakness, invaded from the Big Island, conquered Maui, Lana'i, and Moloka'i, and headed for Waikiki to do battle. One of Kamehameha's chiefs, Kai'ana, deserted him on the trip over (he had been sleeping with Kamehameha's favorite wife, Ka'ahumanu, and feared for his life). Upon arriving on O'ahu's shores, Kai'ana joined forces with Kalanikupule. They were no match for Kamehameha's warriors, guns, and cannons and were pushed inland to the 1,000-foot cliffs at Nu'uanu Pali. Kamehameha's army forced Kai'ana and most of the O'ahu forces to jump to their deaths off the cliff. Kalanikupule escaped but was later captured and killed. After this battle, O'ahu became part of the Hawai'ian Kingdom under the rule of Kamehameha the Great.

In the ensuing decades, O'ahu and its wonderful sheltered harbor in Honolulu became increasingly important in both commerce and politics. Missionaries and entrepreneurs from New England reinforced O'ahu's prominence in Hawai'ian affairs. Finally, in 1845, King Kamehameha III moved the capital and seat of government of the Hawai'ian Kingdom from Lahaina on Maui to Honolulu. Since then, Honolulu has dominated the affairs of the islands.

Palaces and estates were built by later kings and queens. In 1893 American sugar barons in Hawai'i, looking to circumvent U.S. tariffs on Hawai'ian sugar, staged an armed coup and overthrew Queen Lili'uokalani. She was placed under house arrest, and the Republic of Hawai'i was formed in 1894. The new government petitioned President Grover Cleveland for formal annexation, but Cleveland, who was a friend of the Queen's, refused. When McKinley won the election in 1898, the Republic petitioned again and the president, seeing the strategic value of the islands, gladly accepted. In 1900 the Hawai'ian Islands became a Territory of the United States. The sugar barons had beaten the tariffs.

With the construction of the Moana Hotel in 1901, Honolulu and its fabled Waikiki beach became a celebrated holiday destination of the rich and famous. Passenger ships would arrive bearing the fabulous, their entourages, and in later years, even their autos. The Halekulani was opened in 1907, and then the very glitzy Royal Hawai'ian in 1927. Fashionable tourism continued until the morning of December 7, 1941, when the Japanese conducted two surprise attacks on Pearl Harbor and the Schofield Barracks, the headquarters of the U.S. Pacific Fleet. We all know the rest. Remarkably, the U.S. military had almost fully recovered from the devastating attacks by the summer of 1942. O'ahu's importance in the War of the Pacific was repeatedly demonstrated in the years that followed. Honolulu was the center of activity, and its Chinatown became a legendary red-light district for sailors on leave. It wasn't until the end of the Vietnam War that this infamous part of the city finally began to fade in notoriety. O'ahu, however, remains the headquarters of the Pacific Command.

After World War II the push for statehood began, culminating in Hawai'i becoming the 50th state in 1959, with Honolulu as its capital. Today, three quarters of the state's population—an estimated 900,000 people—lives on O'ahu, making it the most populous Hawai'ian island by far. Honolulu continues to gain importance as the financial, commercial, and political heart of the state, and as a key player in the Pacific Rim.

O'ahu: Key Facts

LOCATION:	Honolulu: Longitude 21°18' N, latitude 157° 52' W
SIZE	608 square miles/1,575 square kilometers
HIGHEST POINT	Mt. Ka'ala (4,020 feet/1,225 meters)
POPULATION	876,156 (2000 Census)
TIME	Hawai'i Standard (year-round): 2 hours behind LA, 5 hours behind NY, 10 hours behind London
AREA CODE	808
AIRPORTS	Honolulu International Airport
MAIN TOURIST AREAS	Waikiki
TOURISM INFO	Hawai'i Visitors & Convention Bureau 2270 Kalakaua Avenue, Suite 801 Honolulu, HI 96817 Local: 808-923-1811 Web site: www.Hawaii.org

Focus on O'ahu: The Beach Scene

O'ahu—the soothing name and the place where *pali* (mountains and/or cliffs), palm trees, and golden sand meet the people. The place where beach culture is at its finest. Southern California? Like, O'ahu is where it's at.

There's no doubt about it—O'ahu's beaches are beautiful. This fact alone is enough to explain why beach culture is so strong on O'ahu. Add 30,000 hotel rooms and almost 900,000 residents, and the beach becomes the place to mix and mingle. There are all kinds of beaches here—certainly more than on any other island in the state. Each side of O'ahu offers something different—high-surf beaches on the North Shore, calm lagoons and lush tropical strands on the windward side, dry and sunny surfing beaches on the leeward side, and, of course, Waikiki and Honolulu on the south.

With all the bodies and beauty about, the beach becomes a must on any visit to O'ahu. From the body shows at Waikiki's Royal Hawai'ian Hotel and Sandy Beach, to the big waves of Waimea and Sunset, to the relative solitude of the windward-side beaches, there's something for everyone here. The only thing you won't find

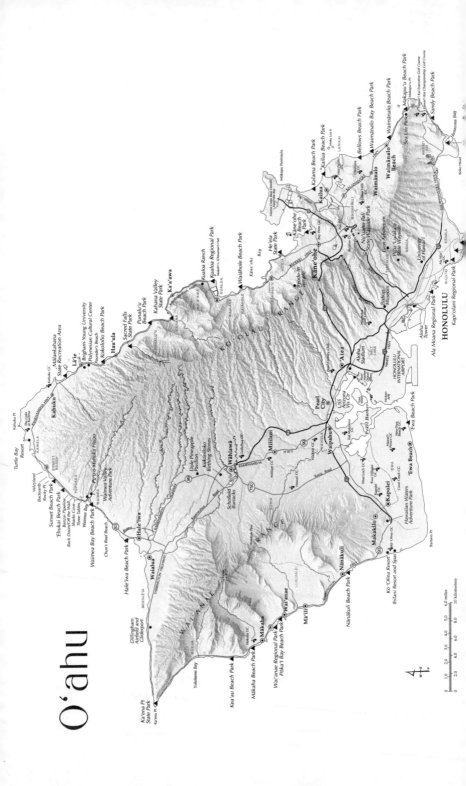

Oʻahu

Honolulu Street Map

TRAILS INDEX

1. Judd Trail
2. Nu'uanu Trail
3. Manoa Cliff Trail
4. Pauoa Flats Trail
5. Aihualama Trail
6. Manoa Falls Trail
7. Pu'u 'Ohia Trail
8. Makiki Valley Trail
9. Maunalaha Trail
10. Ualaka'a Trail
11. Wa'ahila Ridge Trail
12. Pu'u Pia Trail

Copyright © 2001, Rum & Reggae Guidebooks. Cartography by Manoa Mapworks, Inc. Honolulu, HI

To Hawai'i Kai, Hanauma Bay

Kahala Mandarin Hotel

Wai'alae Golf Course

Kahala Mall

Black Point

Kuilei Cliffs Beach Park

Diamond Head State Monument

22nd Ave

16th Ave

Ocean View

10th Ave

Wilhelmina Rise

Pālolo Ave

Kaimukī St

Kapi'olani Park

Natatorium

Aquarium

Sans Souci Beach

New Otani Kaimana Beach Hotel

Ala Wai Golf Course

Sheraton Moana Hotel

Waikīkī Beach

Queens Surf

Kūhiō Beach Park

Royal Hawaiian Hotel

Halekūlani

Ala Wai Blvd

Dole St

WAIKĪKĪ

Kapahulu Ave

Kalākaua Ave

Kalia Rd

Ka'iulani

Convention Center

Ala Moana Center

Magic I.

Ala Moana Beach Park

Pt. Panic

Wa'ahila Ridge St. Rec. Area

East-West Center

University of Hawai'i

MĀNOA VALLEY

University Ave

Manoa Rd

E. Manoa Rd

Lyon Arboretum

Manoa Falls

Ke'eaumoku St

McCully St

S. King St

Beretania St

H1

Punahou

Wilder Ave

Makiki St

Pi'ikoi St

Pensacola St

Ward Ave

Kapi'olani Blvd

Ward Centre

Ward Warehouse

Blaisdell Center

Restaurant Row

Ala Moana Blvd

Kewalo Basin

Contemporary Museum

Honolulu Academy of Arts

Punchbowl Cemetery

Roundtop Dr

Tantalus Dr

Round Top Dr

Honolulu Hale (City Hall)

Mission Houses

Iolani Palace

State Capitol

State Library

Bishop St

NU'UANU VALLEY

Queen Emma's Summer Home

Pacific Heights Rd

O'ahu Country Club

Foster Gardens

Nu'uanu Ave

Kuakini St

Vineyard St

Liliha St

School St

Chinatown

Aloha Tower Marketplace

Harbor

Honolulu Harbor

Sand Island

To Kailua

PALI HIGHWAY

KALIHI VALLEY

To Kāne'ohe

LIKELIKE HIGHWAY

Kamehameha Schools

Dole Cannery Square

N. King St

Houghtailing St

Kalihi St

Bishop Museum

Dillingham Blvd

NIMITZ HWY

Moanalua Gardens

Moanalua Cemetery

Pu'uloa Rd

Salt Lake Blvd

Ke'ehi Lagoon

Kalihi Lagoon Beach Park

Sand Island Access Road

NIMITZ HWY

Honolulu International Airport

Lagoon Dr

Palea St

0   .5   1 mi
0   1   2 km

is a totally deserted beach. But if that doesn't bother you, you'll love O'ahu. Here's the 411 on the island's main beaches:

Greater Honolulu and Vicinity

From Sandy Beach on the east to Pearl Harbor on the west, the greater Honolulu area has a coastline of over 25 miles. Given Honolulu's location on the lee side of the Ko'olau Range, the weather is usually sunny and warm, with gentler breezes and surf conditions than on the windward side. This, coupled with the reality that almost all visitors stay in this area, means mucho people. Luckily there are lots of beaches in that long span where you can find your own space.

Waikiki

If you love crowds, you will love Waikiki. The energy of thousands of vacationers seeking a good time permeates the gentle, caressing breezes, charging the air with a definite sexual tension. Ooooh! So start doing those sit-ups now and get that pretan accelerator going: This is intense body-watching territory.

Queen's Surf. Located on the Waikiki side of the Natatorium (an outdoor swim-meet arena), this is O'ahu's most popular gay beach. Swimming here is quite good from a tiny and packed golden sand beach. There is a spacious coconut-palm-and-banyan-shaded lawn, and a pavilion for relief from the heat. Restrooms/showers/picnic area/food concession.

Kuhio Beach Park. Set in front of Kalakaua Avenue and the Hyatt, this popular and crowded beach has just received a face-lift with new facilities, including a police station and sand pumped in from a couple of miles out in order to widen the strand. Restrooms/showers/concession.

The Royal Hawai'ian Beach. The widest part of Waikiki's strand is in front of this pink hotel, hence the name. Here the Waikiki body scene is at its best. The beach is packed with hard (and not so hard) bodies of all persuasions: military boys, models, flight attendants, and more. If you're more interested in a date than discourse, spread your towel here. To cool off, the swimming is

quite good. So is the patio bar at the Royal Hawai'ian, though frozen drinks are $7.75 a pop. Restrooms/shower/bar/restaurant/water sports.

Fort DeRussy. A former military fort that now exists for the R & R of the men and women in the U.S. armed forces, Fort DeRussy's grounds are open to the public. Ladies, if you like a man in uniform stripped down to a bathing suit, go no further. This is the place. And if you're a volleyball enthusiast, there are some great games going all the time. Restrooms/showers/picnic area.

Point Panic. Situated just west of Ala Moana Beach at the mouth of Kewalo Basin (at the end of Ahui Street), this spot is worth mentioning for experienced bodysurfers. During the summer months, nice sets come in and form perfect right tubes. These hit the seawall fronting the beach. Usually if you're bodysurfing, you will too—hence the name. Restrooms/shower.

Beyond Waikiki

Sandy Beach. Situated only 20 minutes from the hubbub of Honolulu is this wonderfully expansive beach, *the* place to see tanned muscled Hawai'ian surfer bodies. Hanging out by their pickup trucks at beachside (these parking spaces are premium—you've got to get here early for one), they watch and wait for the great waves or the *wahines* (girls) to arrive. And there are some very voluptuous *wahines*. It really is a scene, especially on weekends.

Like its neighbor Makapu'u, around the point on the windward side (see "The Windward Side," below), Sandy is a bodysurfing and boogie-boarding mecca, where the shore-breaking waves are locally called body whompers. Like those of its neighbor, these waves can be extremely dangerous to those not familiar with the technique. By all means, stay away from the right end of the beach, affectionately called the Gas Chambers (there's a reason for this nickname, i.e. *danger*).

Besides the terrific body-watching and bodysurfing, the beach itself, while crowded, is stunning. Set in the shadow of the Koko Crater, the panorama from the beach is one of the prettiest on O'ahu. Sandy Beach also benefits from its southern location. The weather is generally sunny here when clouds invade the windward beaches farther north, even Makapu'u. When the sun goes behind the *pali* at Makapu'u during the winter months, it will still be sunny at Sandy.

Sandy Beach is located on Route 72 about two miles north of the Hanauma Bay access road, along a gorgeous cliff drive where you can see Moloka'i on a clear day. On a crystal clear day, you can see Lana'i and Haleakala on Maui. Restrooms/ showers/picnic and terrific kite-flying areas.

Queens Beach. Located at the extreme northern end of Sandy Beach, this is a de facto nude and gay beach. In fact, there's not much of a beach here, just some low-lying dunes for privacy. An inlet provides a nice area for swimming, although it's a rather rocky entrance and exit. Occasionally dirt-bike enthusiasts will roar by and disturb the peace. Queens is reached by parking where Route 72 curves inland from Sandy Beach. (There will be other cars parked along the side of the road.) Be sure to pull your car well off the road. Follow the path toward the point. No facilities.

Hanauma Bay. If you could get here at sunrise, stay a few hours, and then leave, this would be an idyllic spot. Around 10 A.M., however, the flood begins, with tourists arriving by the busload and inundating the beach until late in the afternoon.

They come to enjoy this splendid cove, which is actually the remnants of an old crater—half of it submerged and now an underwater marine park. The beach is surrounded by cliffs on three sides, all of which are part of the park and protected from development. Indeed, if it weren't for the thousands of people at the beach, this would be one of the most beautiful places in Hawai'i.

We *do* recommend that you see it, though, preferably very early in the morning or very late in the afternoon, for two reasons. The first is to snorkel. We have never seen so many fish in one place in all of our travels. Even with hundreds of pairs of legs in only waist-deep water, there will be fish galore. This is because everyone feeds them and no one can fish here. Fish nirvana, we surmise. Anyway, buy some frozen peas (fish love 'em) and bring them along in a self-seal plastic bag. The fish will practically eat out of your hand. You needn't go outside the inner reef to see all

the fish. If you do want to go outside (to see turtles, rays, and eels), be very careful. The current rips out of the channels on either side of the bay, and it's possible to get sucked right out. Then you may get hit by the Moloka'i Express (a vicious current), and away you go into the deep blue sea. One way to see what's outside the inner reef in a somewhat safer manner is to walk over the reef, although there are menacing urchins and sharp coral to trip you up (make sure your fins protect your feet).

The second reason to visit Hanauma is for the "Toilet Bowl." While we cringe at the sound of it too, it actually is quite fun. Located at the end of a small cove (a short walk along a path around the northern point of the bay), the "Toilet" is a round pool about ten feet wide. It is connected to the sea by a lava tube. When a swell comes into the cove, it forces water into the tube, which in turn fills up the bowl, often to the point of overflowing. When the swell leaves, it sucks most of the water out of the bowl. Those adventurous enough to jump in will feel the fun effects of being flushed. It gets really exciting if the water's rough. Just be careful entering—jump in during the high flow, and hold on during the flush or you could get sucked out through the tube (not a pleasant experience and obviously very dangerous too!).

Be advised, Hanauma Bay is notorious for rental-car break-ins. Take everything out of the car, including whatever's in the trunk if possible. A shuttle will take you down the hill for 50¢ and back up for $1 (worth it to avoid the hot walk uphill). To get here, take H1 east from Honolulu, which turns into Kalaniana'ole Highway (Route 72). About one mile past the Koko Marina Shopping Center, you'll see signs to Hanauma Bay. Restrooms/showers/food concession/snorkel gear rental.

Wai'alae Beach County Park. For those who seek quiet refuge from the bustle of Waikiki but still want to be close to the action, Wai'alae may be the answer. Situated in the very tony suburb of Kahala, Wai'alae is adjacent to the Wai'alae Country Club and the Kahala Mandarin Oriental. The ranch houses you see on the main road here are worth at least a million dollars, due to the voracious appetite for Kahala property. The beach itself is very pleasant, with nice views of Koko Head and Maunalua Bay. Swimming is good in the reef-protected waters. Windsurfers are fond of this beach. Restrooms/showers/picnic area.

Diamond Head. There are actually two beaches here underneath the lighthouse. The first, accessed by the dead-end road off of Diamond Head Road just west of the lighthouse, is a small and rocky gay beach. Swimming here is not good due to numerous shallow coral reefs. The second, officially called Kuilei Cliffs Beach County Park, is accessed by a paved path from the parking lookouts east of the lighthouse. Surfers and expert windsurfers favor this area. The beach here is sandier than the first beach, but the swimming is pretty much the same. Shower.

Sans Souci Beach (Diamond Head). Tucked away between the renovated Natatorium and the New Otani Hotel (off Kalakaua Boulevard) is this small, quiet, but very pleasant golden sand beach. Great swimming and a bar at the New Otani make this a nice alternative to the crowds farther down. Restrooms/showers/bar-restaurant.

Ala Moana Beach and Magic Island. Located in Honolulu proper on Ala Moana Boulevard but within walking distance of the west end of Waikiki (just over the Ala Wai Canal, which separates Waikiki from the rest of Honolulu), this is probably the biggest natural lap pool we've ever seen. A coral breakwater along the length of the beach keeps the water very flat, ideal for long-distance swimming. After work, canoe clubs come out to practice, and on Wednesday evenings the Hawai'i Yacht Club has sailboat races. This is a great place to watch the sunset. The beach is fairly crowded with local residents, especially on weekends and at its eastern (left) end. The park bordering the beach is huge and shady, for some cool green relief from the sun.

Also at the eastern end of the beach is a peninsula that juts out along Ala Wai Harbor (home to hundreds of pleasure boats). Called Magic Island, this peninsula offers a small lagoon that's great for kids. Terrific views of Waikiki and Diamond Head are here, too. Restrooms/showers/picnic area/food concession/tennis/Ala Moana Shopping Center across the street from the park.

Honolulu Surf Shops and Surf Instruction

Blue Planet, 813 Kapahulu Avenue, Kaimuki, HI 96813. Local:

808-922-5444, fax 808-923-0214.
Web site: www.blueplanet-hawaii.com

Blue Planet has its own brand of clothing. Everything from surf wear to aloha shirts and accessories, all carrying the Blue Planet logo. They also have surf rentals here. Open Monday through Friday 10 A.M. to 6 P.M., Saturday and Sunday until 5 P.M.

Local Motion, 1958 Kalakaua Avenue, Waikiki, HI 96817. Local: 808-979-7873, fax 808-941-6382.
Web site: www.localmotioninc.com

Local Motion has their own line of surf wear and accessories, but in addition they design and build their own brand of surfboards. They also have rentals. Open daily from 9 A.M. to 10 P.M.

Hans Hedeman Surf School, 2947 Kalakaua Avenue, Waikiki, HI 96817. Local: 808-924-7778, fax 808-926-7779.
Web site: www.hhsurf.com

A surf shop with lots of accessories, but more famous for their surfing lessons. Open daily from 8 A.M. to 5 P.M. Lessons are daily at 9 A.M., 12 P.M., and 3 P.M., last about two hours, and range in price from $75 for small groups to $130 for private.

Turbo Surf Bodyboarders Headquarters, 870 Kapahulu Avenue, Honolulu, HI, 96816. Local: 808-738-8726, fax 808-739-5231.
Web site: www.turboworld.com

This shop offers everything from surf wear to t-shirts to boards, both for sale and for rent. Open daily from 10 A.M. to 9 P.M., Sunday until 5 P.M.

The Windward Side

The stunning beauty of O'ahu's windward side never ceases to amaze us. Fluted and richly green *pali* rise sharply from a narrow windswept plain, dense with coconut palms and banana trees. Kamehameha Highway takes you from end to end and is one of the must-dos for those staying on O'ahu. Just make sure you drive at the speed limit—slow drivers in rental cars aggravate locals. There are several excellent stops along the way for swimming, bodysurfing, windsurfing, sunning, and seclusion. Please keep in mind that the weather on this side of the island is wetter and cloudier than on other parts, especially during the winter months.

Makapu'u. About 20 minutes from Waikiki on Route 72 and a regular stop on The Bus (O'ahu's public transit), this exceptional cove offers some of the best boogie-boarding and bodysurfing on O'ahu. Set hundreds of feet below the highway and at the north side of a huge rock promontory, this natural surf bowl can serve up some challenging waves—especially for those who aren't used to mid-Pacific surf. These waves attract scores of body-boarders. While they can pose a threat to the uninitiated, the alert individual can avoid them by simply ducking into the waves. Frequently the board will pass right overhead. It sounds scary, but in reality it's not all that bad. Just be sure to duck!

Makapu'u is a popular spot, so don't expect a deserted beach. There will be plenty of people both on the beach and bobbing in the water. If your idea of a fun day at the beach includes people-watching, then you will find it very enjoyable here. Also enjoyable is the view from the left (north) side of the beach, where the top of the towering Makapu'u Lighthouse peeks out at you. Other photographic opportunities here include the uninhabited islands and bird refuges of Manana Island, better known as Rabbit Island, and Kaohikaipu Island. Restrooms/showers/limited parking. (If the lot is full, park on the side of the highway above the beach and walk down.)

Bellows Field Beach Park. Open to the public only on weekends, this gorgeous beach is part of the Bellows Air Force Station. While it is a county park, it can be accessed only through the base, from noon Friday until 6 A.M. Monday, and on holidays (6 A.M. to 6 A.M. the next day). The swimming is excellent, and the bodysurfing can be quite good too. The setting and the views of the Ko'olau Range are stunning. You should find plenty of beach to yourself on this mile-long strand of golden sand and ironwood pines. Located just north of Waimanalo on Route 72; the entrance is clearly marked. Restrooms/showers/picnic area.

Waimanalo Beach Park. Many O'ahu residents consider this beach the best on the island. Just a tad south of Bellows Beach, it is basically a continuation of the three-and-a-half-mile-long golden sand arc of Waimanalo Bay, making it the longest beach on the island. With all this space, there is bound to be plenty of room to call a spacious plot of sand your own. Please note: Do not leave any, repeat, any valuables in your rental car; this area is very notorious for rip-offs. Located on Route 72 just south of the center of Waimanalo. Restrooms/showers/picnic area.

Kailua Beach Park. Unknown to the hordes of tourists who bypass this well-to-do suburb on their round-the-island expeditions, this is one of the best beaches on the island. Locals love it for its very long crescent of golden sand, reef-sheltered water, and groves of ironwood pines. This is also the windsurfing capital of O'ahu. Trade winds blow in at an angle that's perfect for beach or water starts on a starboard tack. If you run into trouble, you'll just end up drifting onto the beach instead of out to sea. To get here, take the Pali Tunnel (Route 61) from the H1 freeway in Honolulu. When you reach downtown Kailua, take the right fork onto Kailua Road and follow it to the beach park. Restrooms/showers/picnic area.

Lanikai. Enclosed by the Keolu Hills, this very chic and tiny beach community is without a doubt one of the best places to live on O'ahu. Just south of the Kailua Beach Park on Kawailoa Road, Lanikai offers an eclectic mix of both people and architectural styles. Even better is its beautiful beach—a mile-long stretch of uncrowded golden sand. Reefs and the Mokulua islands keep the water calm and shallow. There are several public right-of-ways to the beach along Mokulua Drive (part of the main one-way loop). As you enter Lanikai, bear to the right on A'alapapa Drive, which will eventually turn into Mokulua. No facilities.

Kualoa Regional Park. A peninsula that juts out into Kane'ohe Bay, Kualoa is called Chinaman's Hat by most locals, for the distinctive shape of Mokoli'i Island just off its beach. At one time, Kualoa was sacred ground for the Hawai'ian royalty, or *ali'i*. Apparently they knew a great piece of real estate when they saw one. Today this is a very spacious park, with shade trees and an expanse of lawn for relaxing. The beach is very narrow, but the swimming is good and the views of "the Hat" and the mountains behind the park are wonderful. During low tide, you can wade out to the island. As with Malaekahana, be sure to wear a pair of old shoes or reef walkers for protection against the coral.

The park is right off Kamehameha Highway between Waikane and Ka'a'awa. Be sure to stop at the Ka'a'awa Grinds for lunch (the barbecued chicken is tops). Restrooms/showers/picnic area.

Malaekahana State Recreation Area. Slightly up the road past the Mormon community of La'ie is this delightful bay and the secluded Moku'Auia Island Bird Refuge (more commonly referred to as Goat Island). This small island offers privacy, particularly during the week, because to reach it you must negotiate a reef in waist-deep water—water that sends waves at you from two directions. (This maneuver can be very difficult for children and those afraid of water). For those who are intrepid or curious as to what natural wonders lie on the near shore, ford the crossing at the narrowest reach of water. Be sure to wear a pair of old shoes or reef walkers to protect your feet from the coral. Keep your eyes peeled for holes in the coral and rogue waves.

Once across, head to the left, over a small rocky point. Here you'll find a beautiful lagoon with a crescent of coral sand that provides the little island's best swimming spot. Being on the leeward side, there is only a slight breeze, so it can get rather hot. Fortunately, ironwood pines at the edge of the beach offer much-needed shade. Beaches on the windward side offer natural air conditioning from the trade winds, but not the protected swimming of the leeward lagoon. Please note that Goat Island is a designated refuge, so refrain from walking into the interior, as there are hundreds of nesting sites that shouldn't be disturbed (and camouflaged nesting holes that will twist unsuspecting ankles).

If you would rather stay on the "mainland," the beach to the right, while certainly not as private, is equally stunning, with good swimming, trade winds, and wonderful views of the Ko'olau Range to the south. Restrooms/showers/terrific picnic area with grills and tables.

Kokololio Beach Park. This is a spacious and attractive park with ample picnic tables, lawn, and parking. The beach is pretty and not at all crowded. Camping is also allowed here. Located just

south of Hau'ula on Kamehameha Highway. Restrooms/showers/picnic area with grills and tables.

Pounders. This beach, rarely crowded, offers what some feel are the most exquisite tropical views from any beach on the windward side of O'ahu, with the massive and verdant Ko'olau Range rising up from the churning turquoise sea. Located right off Kamehameha Highway, just past the 7-11 in Hau'ula; look for the parking lot just south of the bridge.

The North Shore

This is surfer heaven. The waves don't get any better. Home of the legendary Banzai Pipeline, the rest of Sunset Beach, and Waimea Bay, the North Shore is alive with surfing each winter. Huge swells from winter storms in the North Pacific track thousands of miles, sort themselves into neat but powerful sets, and hit the various reefs of this coast particularly well. When the northern hemisphere pivots toward the sun in summer, ocean storms move to the South Pacific. Without this turbulence to generate swells, the waves flatten out in April, and by summer the water here can be as calm as a lake. The surfing scene then switches to the leeward (Makaha) and Honolulu side, which gets smaller but still significant swells.

Sunset Beach. Made up of over two miles of beach on the coast north of Waimea Bay, this is the home of several of the world's most famous surf spots. In addition to the Pipeline, probably the most widely recognized big-wave break, the surf breaks of Sunset Beach, Velzyland, Backyards, Kammieland, Rocky Point, Gas Chambers, Back Doors, Pupukea, and Off the Wall dot this stretch of golden sand.

When there is a high-surf advisory, it's a good idea to stay out of the water and just watch (lifeguards will keep you out if necessary). At other times, swimming and bodysurfing can be fine here. The best spots to swim and watch the surfers are roadside at Sunset Beach proper and at Ehukai Beach Park (home of the Pipeline), which is just off Kamehameha Highway.

Sunset is also the land of *haole* (white, as in Caucasian) surfers, most of whom come from southern California. Locals tend to stick to the leeward side of the island, although there are certainly some local surfers here too. Pop into the Foodland supermarket around 6 P.M., where weathered types walk around in just baggies (bathing suits), and you can see for yourself. And Foodland, along with the beach, is where you can catch up on the latest in surf fashions. Of course the beach allows for great sunsets too (fun, especially with cocktails). Restrooms/showers at Ehukai and Sunset Beach.

Waimea Bay Beach Park. Where the *really* big ones are during high-surf advisories: the waves here crest over the deep reef at the mouth of the bay and can reach heights of 30 feet. This is definitely not kid stuff, but it's a great place to sun and watch. When the surf isn't up, the bodysurfing at the shore break is fabulous. A wide golden sand beach fits nicely between the Waimea River and the southern point of the bay, with just the right slope for comfortable viewing and sunbathing. Picnic tables and a lawn adorn a well-used but attractive park abutting the beach. Very popular with the military from Schofield Barracks, this beach can get crowded. Restrooms/showers/picnic area.

North Shore Surf Shops and Surf Instruction

Hale'iwa Surf & Sea, 65-595 Kamehameha Highway, Hale'iwa, HI 96712. Toll-free: 800-899-SURF (7873). Local: 808-637-DEEP (3337), fax 808-637-3008.
Web site: www.surfnsea.com
E-mail: surfnsea@lava.net
This shop has a large selection of new/used boards and instruction for all levels, and even has 24-hour ding repair (necessary if you wipe out on the Pipeline). They claim you can learn to surf in one lesson. Surf & Sea also has a full-service dive shop (North Shore diving is best in summer) and windsurf rentals and instruction. Located on the beach in Hale'iwa town. Open daily 9 A.M. to 7 P.M.

Hawai'i Surf and Sail, 66-214 Kamehameha Highway, Hale'iwa, HI 96712. Local: 808-637-5373, fax 808-638-9045.
Right in Hale'iwa, this is one of the North Shore's biggest surf shops, with an excellent selection of high-performance boards for

sale only. Open daily from 8:30 A.M. to 7:30 P.M.

North Shore Boardriders Club, North Shore Market Place, Hale'iwa, HI 96712. Local: 808-637-5026, fax 808-637-6138.

This is another good choice for surfboard purchases. Open daily from 9:30 A.M. to 8:00 P.M., Sunday to 7:00 P.M.

The Leeward Side

The leeward side of O'ahu has gotten a bad reputation from tourists. Being one of the last bastions for locals on the island, there have been many reports of hostility toward tourists (*haoles*). Understandably, many locals feel that they have been forced out of other parts of O'ahu by the tourist industry and the economic force it wields, so they are sensitive to any further encroachment. When you mention that you are going up by Wai'anae and Makaha, some people will caution you to be careful. Obviously these people haven't been to Times Square on New Year's Eve, which we feel is *much* scarier. True, there have been instances in the past of *haole*-heckling, and you are aware of yourself as just a visitor here, but if you stay cool and "do as the Romans do," you should easily go with the flow. Avoid driving obvious *malahini* (mainland) rental cars, like convertibles.

Why bother? Because this side of O'ahu is stunningly different from the rest of the island. It is much drier and more expansive, contrasting with the lush *pali* of the windward side. The light is intensely golden, and the sunsets are fabulous. The mountains that slope down to the Pacific turn wonderful colors as twilight approaches. So does the Makua Valley, facing inland toward Ka'ala, the highest point on O'ahu (4,020 feet), looking more like the colorful mountain valleys of northern New Mexico than a Hawai'ian valley.

Makaha Beach Park. One of the major surfing beaches on O'ahu and home to several surfing championships including tandem riding and the Makaha International, this is a long crescent of golden sand. Swimming is usually good. This is the most local crowd on O'ahu, so go with the flow. Located right off Route 93 in Makaha. Restrooms/showers/picnic area.

Yokahama Bay. One of the prettiest beaches on O'ahu happens to be at the end of the road (Route 93) and just shy of the western-most tip of O'ahu, Ka'ena Point. This is definitely beaching it, Hawai'ian-style. Pull your car up to the edge of the grass, back it in, open the tailgate, unfold the chairs and blanket, break out the cooler, pop the brewskis, and mellow out. We once spent a heavenly afternoon at Yokahama, watching the sun sink slowly into the sea, green flash (the green dot you see just as the top edge of the sun sinks into the ocean) and all. We highly recommend it. Yokahama is part of Makua-Ka'ena State Park. There is virtually nothing out this way except brown hills sweeping back and a huge radar dome on top of the ridge, looking like a giant golf ball waiting on its tee. The beach is a long expanse of golden sand, and the swimming is good on calm days. Restrooms/showers.

Other Things to Do

- ≈ **Windsurfing and kiteboarding**
- ≈ **Hiking**
- ≈ **Swimming with dolphins**
- ≈ **Kayaking**
- ≈ **Sailing**
- ≈ **Horseback riding**
- ≈ **Diving**
- ≈ **Golf**
- ≈ **Tennis**
- ≈ **Cerebral stuff**

Windsurfing and Kiteboarding

Windsurfers and kiteboarders (a new sport that lifts you into serious air time with a surfboard strapped to your feet) who crave the thrills of Waikiki and the generally charged atmosphere of Hawai'i's liveliest island will find O'ahu very satisfying. Certainly those interested in body-watching will adore it. All the tanned bodies of a multitude of races and persuasions give new meanings to the term "aloha spirit." And by the way, the windsurfing and kite-

boarding are pretty damn good, too.

There are three areas of focus on O'ahu for windsurfers and kite-boarders. The premier place is Kailua, the birthplace of Hawai'ian windsurfing. All the big shops and instruction schools are here, and Kailua Bay has something to offer for all levels. Expert wave-jumpers attack Backyards at Sunset on the North Shore. On the South Shore is Diamond Head, the scene of some fantastic wind-surfing during the summer months. La'ie on the windward side is an alternative for intermediate-level windsurfers.

Kailua. The cradle of Hawai'ian windsurfing and kiteboarding is located in the affluent bedroom community of Kailua, an 11-mile drive from Honolulu through the Pali Tunnel. This is one of the prettiest bays in the state, with miles of golden sand beach and many out-islands. Because of the opportunities for all abilities, it is also the hub of windsurfing on O'ahu. This is where the action is and the tourists aren't. Part of the bay—the area fronting the very tony community of Lanikai—is protected by a long reef. This is an ideal place to learn because the water is relatively flat. The trades blow perpendicular to the beach here, so the greatest dan-ger to the novice is being blown into the beach and having to walk a bit. The rest of Kailua Bay provides challenges for all lev-els—particularly for intermediates and advanced sailors in the summer, when the trades are up (on a good day they can blow 20 to 30 knots). There are several exciting reef breaks, including Zombies and Jump City, which offer great wave-jumping oppor-tunities. As with any windward beach, a *kona* (south) wind will make conditions here fairly lousy.

The windsurfing and kiteboarding scene is centered at Kailua Beach Park. There is a large grassy area on which to rig up and break down. The beach is only a few steps away. Almost all of the best windsurfing shops and schools are located near the beach, so the area is a buzz of activity. The beach is also popular with bathers. The beach park is at the end of Kailua Road. While most people stay in Waikiki, there are houses and cottages for rent in Kailua (see Where to Stay in this chapter or contact the surf shops—they put packages together).

Backyards. What Ho'okipa is to Maui, Backyards is to O'ahu. Lo-

23

cated on the eastern end of O'ahu's fabled North Shore high-surf area, this is where monster surf comes in winter. Backyards is actually part of the wave continuum called Sunset Beach. Reading like a who's who of celebrity surf breaks, this stretch of reef contains the famous breaks of Waimea Bay, Log Cabins, the Banzai Pipeline, Pupukea, Gas Chambers, Rocky Point, Sunset, Velzyland, and, of course, Backyards. While all the other breaks are the exclusive domain of surfers, Backyards is windsurfer territory. The waves here break big, clean, and hollow.

With wave heights that can reach almost 30 feet, you'd better know what you're doing. Obviously this is strictly expert terrain due to the wicked waves and the fluky, unpredictable gusty winds. Summertime, when the North Shore flattens out, is much mellower. Still, there will be good swells if the trades are up.

Backyards is located off of Kamehameha Highway, just east of Sunset Beach, and is accessed by any of the side roads *makai* (seaside) of the highway. Bring your binoculars and telephoto lens.

Diamond Head. Diamond Head is O'ahu's Empire State Building or Golden Gate Bridge—its universally recognized landmark. Sitting at the eastern end of Waikiki, the crater of this ancient extinct volcano rises majestically out of the water. At its base is some of the best summer windsurfing and wave-jumping in Hawai'i.

The conditions here exclude beginners. The sizable surf, offshore wind, and shallow reef make this intermediate and expert territory. The breaks are far offshore and traverse an inner shallow reef channel to the big stuff of Cliffs and Lighthouse. Some of the breaks on Diamond Head are also surfer territory, so stay clear.

Diamond Head is best in summer, when the southern swell comes up and the trades are strong. There are two lookout/parking areas just east of the lighthouse on the Diamond Head Road where you can watch the sets and the action before descending the long path to the beach.

Kahala. Just down Kahala Road from the intense scene at Diamond Head is Wai'alae Beach Park, a calmer setting well suited for windsurfing novices and intermediates. It's a stone's throw from the Kahala Mandarin Oriental and the Wai'alae Country Club.

The water of Maunalua Bay is protected by a long reef and is usually fairly flat. There is plenty of grass where you can rig up and break down. Parking is right next to the beach. Adding to the appeal of this beach is its lack of tourists.

La'ie. The home of the Mormons' Hawai'i Temple and the Polynesian Cultural Center (the best-selling attraction in the state) is also the scene of some superb and never-crowded trade-wind windsurfing and wave-jumping. Maleakahana, an extensive state park, provides ample parking, grass for rigging, and beach for launching. The best sailing is south of Goat Island, where a reef breaks some clean but small trade swells. Summertime, with its flatter water and the strong trades, is a speed-sailor's delight. Winter can bring large surf that has wrapped around Kahuku Point, so be careful. Beginners should stay between the reef and the beach.

Malaekahana State Park is just north of the village of La'ie. Park in the lot at the end of the road (the roof racks on other cars mean you're in the right lot). Be sure to visit Goat Island when you're tired of windsurfing (see the Focus on O'ahu section of this chapter).

Windsurfing and Kitesurfing Rentals, Equipment, and Instruction

Kailua is where you'll find the most options for windsurfing and kiteboarding, although there is also a good outfit in Hale'iwa. Here are your best bets:

Naish Hawai'i, Ltd., 155a Hamakua Drive, Kailua, HI 96734. Local: 808-262-6068, fax 808-263-9723.
Web site: www.naish.com

Naish Hawai'i, owned by the Naish family, Hawai'i's most famous windsurfing legends, designs its own line of famous custom windsurf boards as well as boards for Mistral (and is the sole distributor of Mistral on O'ahu). In 1990 the Naish family acquired Windsurfing Hawai'i and merged the two operations together. All rental equipment is available at Kailua Beach Park or at the Kailua retail store. The beginner daily rental is $30 and includes sail and rig, with harness option for $5.00. The intermediate and advanced daily rental is $40, which includes sail, rig, and harness (five-day and weekly rentals run between $160 and $225 and include two sails and soft rack). Half-day rentals, from 9:00 A.M. to 1:00 P.M. or 1:00 P.M. to 5:00 P.M., are between $30 and $40. Naish presently sells kiteboarding equipment ($750 to $1300) and provides instruction ($100/lesson). The store is open from 9:00 A.M. to 5:30 P.M. daily. Reservations for lessons should be made at least 24 hours ahead.

Kailua Sailboard & Kayaks, Inc., Kailua Beach Center, 130 Kailua Road, Kailua, HI 96734. Local: 808-262-2555, fax 808-261-7341. Web site: www.kailuasailboards.com

Kailua Sailboard & Kayaks, or KS&K, offers windsurfing equipment rentals and instruction as well as kayak rentals. In addition, KS&K now features kiteboarding instruction, including a one-and-a-half-hour introductory class for $99, with all equipment provided (Wipika, Flexifoil, and Mosquito Kites are featured). The class covers kite setup procedures and basic kite-flying techniques on trainer kites, safety rules and procedures, and an introduction to wind, takeoff, wind window orientation, and landing. Other classes include an introduction to power kite (a more intense board and kite) and advanced kiteboarding. Private instruction is also available at $79/hour. KS&K will drop off and pick up equipment right at Kailua Beach Park, so all you need to do is pay and sign forms at the shop and head for the beach. When you're done, just leave the board on the grass and hop in your car. The shop also offers Waikiki hotel pickup. Open daily 9 A.M. to 5 P.M.

Hawai'ian Watersports, 813 Kapahulu Avenue, Honolulu, HI 96815. Local: 808-255-4352, fax 808-734-6999. Web site: www.hawaiianwatersports.com

Located in Honolulu. Beginner classes are $45/person for one and a half hours of group instruction (four lessons are $160/per 1 1/2 hour). Private lessons (all levels) are $55 for 1 1/2 hours instruction, four lessons for $200. To rent equipment, experience and a deposit are required. A one-day beginner windsurf rental is $25, and a one-day advanced wave gear rental is $50. Open daily 9 A.M. to 9 P.M.

Hawai'i Surf and Sail, 66-214 Kamehameha Highway, Hale'iwa, HI 96712. Local: 808-637-5373, fax 808-638-9045.

Right in Hale'iwa, this is one of the North Shore's biggest surf and windsurfing shops with an excellent selection of high-performance boards (for sale only) to help you tackle the sets at Backyards. Open daily from 8:30 A.M. to 7:30 P.M.

Hiking

For most people, hiking in O'ahu means covering the distance between Fort DeRussy and the Natatorium in Waikiki. The natural wonders here are those adorned in swimwear. Of course you certainly want to see them; this walk is a must for all visitors to the island. However, O'ahu does offer some good hikes into the mountains that allow a beautiful view of just how geographically diversified the island is. All of these could be part of an all-day hike/beach expedition that explores different areas of the island.

Probably the best hike for the O'ahu visitor is to Kaliuwa'a Falls (Sacred Falls) on the windward side. It's an easy trek, will give you a pleasant glimpse of what tropical hiking can be, and will allow you to spend the afternoon cooling off on the splendid beaches at Goat Island, Pounders, Kualoa Point, or the groovy North Shore. The best time to do this hike is in the morning, as the weather tends to be sunnier in the mountains at this time and you don't have to worry about losing daylight. A morning hike also gives you the beach and the water to look forward to when you're hot, sweaty, and stepping through mud.

Sacred Falls State Park. Located on the windward side of O'ahu, Kaliuwa'a Falls (Sacred Falls) was one of the best hikes for the O'ahu visitor. This pleasant two-and-a-half-hour walk (one hour up, half an hour there, one hour down) took you through three types of vegetation zones to a large gorge and a 50-plus-foot waterfall cascading into a swimmable pool of cool water.

Tragically, on May 9, 1999 (Mother's Day), a section of rock sheered off the steep canyon wall about 500 feet above the fall's very busy swimming pool and observation area, sending tons of debris and boulders raining down on hikers and swimmers at speeds of up to 100 m.p.h. Eight people were killed and dozens

injured. Due to the fragile nature of the fall's geology and the potential for additional slides, the park has been closed indefinitely.
Honolulu Hikes. There are several hikes in greater Honolulu that we didn't do (we were too busy ogling at the beach) but which were recommended to us by others. The most popular hike is up the **Diamond Head** crater—especially true if you're staying in adjacent Waikiki. The inside of this extinct volcanic cone is a huge crater, a National Natural Landmark and a state monument. It is also the home of the Hawai'i National Guard and was heavily fortified during World War II. The walk takes you to the lookout at the top of the crater, with great views of the ocean, Waikiki, and Koko Head. While nature is evident here only in a historic sense (the crater is about 350,000 years old), this can still be fun. There are lots of bunkers and tunnels to explore. Bring a flashlight to aid exploration. It is open from 6 A.M. to 6 P.M. year-round. Admission is $1 per person.

There are other, more "natural" hikes close to Honolulu. These include **Tantalus,** also a very pleasant drive if you just feel like taking an "oooh cruise." It can be reached by taking the Punahou Street exit *mauka* (toward the mountains) off H1, turning left on Wilder and then right on Makiki. Bear left on Makiki Heights Drive, which will end at Tantalus Drive. Turn right; the drive will take you on a long and convoluted road through rain forest, with occasional stunning vistas of the city. There are several trails here worth hiking, including the **Manoa Cliff Trail** (six miles round-trip), the **Makiki Valley Trail** (a two-mile loop), and the **Pu'u Ohi'a Trail** (four miles round-trip).

In the Manoa Valley, next to Tantalus, there is the **Manoa Falls Trail** (about a mile and a half round-trip) that takes you to a refreshing and swimmable pool and waterfall. This is reached by going the length of Manoa Road and parking at the Lynn Arboretum. Also in the vicinity, at the crest of St. Louis Heights, is the **Wa'ahila Ridge Trail** (four miles round-trip). It provides some terrific vistas, excellent native vegetation, and privacy.

If you're going to check out the **Nu'uanu Pali Lookout,** be sure to take the time to hike the **Judd Trail.** This loop is just under a mile and a half long, is great for kids, and is a fine example of rain-forest vegetation. You can swim in the Jackass Ginger

Pool, and if it's been raining, do some sliding down the mud chutes nearby. Be prepared to get awfully muddy and potentially scraped and bruised. You might want to bring a straw beach mat for sliding—you can pick one up for a buck in the tourist traps of Waikiki (such as the omnipresent ABC Stores).

Other O'ahu Hikes. Two other hikes worth mentioning here are polar opposites. If you like it easy, manicured, and pampered, then why not cruise up to the North Shore, watch the surfers, and then head to **Waimea Valley Adventure Park** (808-638-8511)? This privately owned attraction is well maintained and recommended even though it is designed for tourists. All ages (great for kids) can walk up to the falls (or take a tram) and watch the cliff-diving show after observing some well-tended and well-labeled examples of Hawai'ian flora. You'll have to pay to get in ($24 for adults/$12 for kids aged 4–12!). The best time to go is during the week, late in the afternoon. The park is open every day from 10 A.M. to 5:30 P.M.

For those looking for challenge, there is the **Waimano Trail,** a rigorous all-day hike that is one of the hardest on the island. It is 14 miles round-trip, so only the really serious hiker should consider it. (Another difficult hike, the **Manana Trail,** is on the next ridge north.) It will bring you to the crest of the Ko'olau Ridge, as well as take you into the heart of windward O'ahu. Make sure you have plenty of daylight and wear long pants. Take Route 730 north from H1 and follow the signs to the Waimano Home. The trail starts across the street from the guardhouse.

Nature Tour Companies

Several companies offer hiking excursions with guides, transportation from your hotel, gear, and lunch/refreshments. These include:

O'ahu Nature Tours, P.O. Box 8059, Honolulu, HI 96830. Toll-free: 800-861-6018. Local: 808-924-2473, fax 808-924-5395. Web site: www.oahunaturetours.com

Guide and author Michael Walther is very knowledgeable and provides hiking tours of Diamond Head at sunrise, a rain-forest hike, and others. Prices range from $20 to $52.

Hike O'ahu with Hawai'ian Islands Eco-Tours, Ltd., 44-099 Keaalau Place, Kaneohe, HI 96744. Local: 808-236-7766, fax 808-234-1399.
Web site: www.hikeoahu.com

Geared toward the novice hiker, Hike O'ahu offers waterfall and rain-forest half-day hikes ($40 adults/$20 kids) as well as a full-day rain-forest/beach excursion ($80 adults/$40 kids). Bird-watching and custom hikes are also available.

Mauka Makai Excursions, Inc., 350 Ward Avenue, Suite 106, Honolulu, HI 96814. Toll-free: 877-326-6248. Local: 808-593-3525.
Web site: www.oahu-ecotours.com

Guide and co-owner Dominic Kealoha Aki grew up in Hawai'i and has a formidable knowledge of the Hawai'ian language and folklore, which he shares during the easy hikes. Trips take you to such varied places as King Kamehameha's summer palace and the Koko Head sea caves. Packages run from $35/ half day to $60 to $65/ full day for adults and $25/half day to $50/full day for kids, and include hotel pickup/drop-off, gear, bottled water, and a snack. Mauka Makai overbooked on the day we went, so one of us was left behind. Be sure to check ahead of time to ensure your plans are not spoiled.

Swimming with Dolphins

Many of us who grew up watching the TV series *Flipper* have always harbored fantasies about the relationship Bud and Sandy had with their finned friend. Now many resorts offer dolphin "encounter programs" where one can pet, kiss, feed, and commune with a trained dolphin. While you can't hold onto its dorsal fin for a ride (it can injure the animal because the fin is primarily cartilage, like that of a human ear or nose), the experience is worth the price.

On O'ahu, **Dolphin Quest** operates an excellent program in the Kahala Mandarin Oriental's inner lagoon. The program is 30 minutes long and allows you to really have a "close encounter" with this intelligent mammal, both in shallow water and in the deep with a mask and snorkel. Trainers get the dolphin comfortable with the guests, and within minutes they are petting and feeding him or her. (We had Hi'iaka—a very friendly Atlantic bottlenose. Her eyes were blue and very human-like, which surprised

us, and she watched us very carefully.) Prices are $95 for adults (hotel guests have preference) and $75 for kids aged 5–12 (shallow water only). Contact **Dolphin Quest**, Kahala Mandarin Oriental, 5000 Kahala Avenue, Honolulu, HI 96816. Local: 808-739-8918. Web site: www.dolphinquest.org

Ocean Kayaking

Ocean kayaking looks like a simple sport, something between canoeing and surfing. It is in fact very difficult. This is particularly true in the beginning, where learning to balance the tippiest "canoe" is an art. It is also great for your abs (abdominal muscles), as the constant tension required to balance the thing is always exercising the torso. Paddling, of course, does wonders for the back, chest, and arms. So we're looking at some serious exercise. Take a gander at some of the paddlers for the various canoe clubs, like the tony Outrigger Canoe Club or the prestigious Hui Nalu Surfing Club, and you'll see what we mean.

Besides being physical, kayaking can also be excitingly fast. When properly paddled, kayaks can move and catch waves much like a surfboard. Steering is by footpads, which are attached to cables that guide the rudder. As these boats are easily capsized, the first things you learn are how to extract yourself, right your boat, and get back in it—the hardest part. Once you get the hang of it, however, this gets to be a lot of fun and simply terrific exercise. This sport is not recommended if you are a klutz or if you just don't have a good sense of balance—you'll have a miserable time.

Kayaking Companies

For those with coordination, there are a few places that rent kayaks and provide instruction. We suggest:

Bob Twogood Kayaks Hawai'i, Inc., 345 Hahani Street, Kailua, HI 96734. Local: 808-262-5656, fax 808-261-3111.
Web site: www.aloha.com/~twogood

Located on the windward side in Kailua, this is a short hop from Honolulu through the Likelike Tunnel. As one of the foremost kayak shops on O'ahu, Twogood's is a good place to start the learning process or to buy a kayak. Open daily from 9 A.M. to 6 P.M., Saturday and Sunday open at 8 A.M.

Kailua Sailboard & Kayaks, Inc., Kailua Beach Center, 130 Kailua Road, Kailua, HI 96734. Local: 808-262-2555, fax 808-261-7341. Web site: www.kailuasailboards.com
Kailua Sailboard & Kayaks, or KS&K, offers kayak rentals and instruction as well as windsurfing equipment rentals. Open daily 9 A.M. to 5 P.M.

Kayak and Outrigger Events. For those lucky enough to be in Hawai'i at the right time, there are two kayak and outrigger events that shouldn't be missed. Both race across the wet and wild Kaiwi Channel between Moloka'i and O'ahu. In May over 50 kayakers compete in Kanaka Ikaiki. It begins at the Kaluako'i resort on Moloka'i and finishes at the Koko Marina Shopping Center (good views on the water side).

The premier event is the Moloka'i to O'ahu Outrigger Race. Held during Aloha Week in the early fall, this race is a very popular spectator happening and an international event. Over 50 teams from around the world compete. The canoes are from 40 to 50 feet long and hold a team of six men. The race begins at Moloka'i's Hale o Lono Harbor in the early morning and finishes in front of Fort DeRussy in Waikiki about five hours and over 40 miles later. Don't miss it if you're on O'ahu.

Sailing Charters

The waters surrounding the Hawai'ian Islands are anything but tranquil. The channels between the islands can be very turbulent as landmasses, wind, and sea merge to create a rather formidable Venturi effect (horizontally spiraling air currents). The islands' high peaks funnel wind through the channels, which in turn whips up the seas. When the trade winds blow, which is about 80 percent of the time, the Venturi effect makes the waters exceptionally rough for an upwind passage (from O'ahu to the Big Island, or from west to east). The ocean shelf between the islands, while deep, isn't anywhere as grand as the depth of the ocean around the Hawai'ian

chain. Thus the ocean currents speed up when they pass between the islands, adding motion to the surface seas. Because of conditions like these, the bareboat and crewed sailboat charter business is not as developed here as in the better sailing areas of the South Pacific or the Caribbean. Nevertheless, sailing here can be exhilarating for those who like it rough. A large number of private sailing yachts regularly make the trip from Honolulu and Kane'ohe to Maui and the Big Island. There are also a few charter operations for the avid sailor.

One of the best options when chartering is to sail the downwind leg only, which is a wonderful reach (and often an awesome ride) from the southeastern islands. The crew members deliver the boat to the departure port, such as Kona or Lahaina, where you join them for a great cruise around the islands until finally reaching O'ahu. You're guaranteed to experience some fabulous ocean sailing without the hassle of the pounding and soaking on the upwind beats. While there aren't a lot of natural harbors in which to anchor, there are enough places to make the cruise comfortable and interesting. A couple we spoke with while bouncing around the Waipi'o Valley in a Land Rover told us that their cruise was fantastic and well worth it. They were seasoned sailors who had cruised a lot, including the Caribbean and the Chesapeake, so their advice is well taken.

Here is one outfit that does charters:

Honolulu Sailing Company (Mike Mickelwait, Captain/Manager), Box 1500, Kaneohe, HI 96744. Toll-free: 800-829-0114. Local: 808-239-3900, fax 808-239-9718.

Horseback Riding

There are many stables on O'ahu, but most are for boarding and lessons only. A few do offer horses for hire. Such stables are of the guided-trail-ride genre; unfortunately, you aren't let loose with the horse to gallop away over the range. The rides will be on the tame side. Here are some choices:

Koko Crater Stables, 408 Kealahou Road, Honolulu, HI 96825. Local: 808-395-2628.

Situated in the southeast corner of O'ahu near the Koko Marina Shopping Center, this is a most convenient location for those staying in Waikiki. Instruction is offered, including lessons on hunters, jumpers, and dressage.

Kualoa Ranch & Activity Club, Inc., 49-560 Kamehameha Highway, (P.O. Box 650), Ka'a'awa, HI 96730. Toll-free: 800-231-7321. Local: 808-237-7321, fax 808-237-8925.

An ideal setting for horseback riding in one of the most scenic areas of O'ahu. Located on the windward side off Kamehameha Highway, about 45 minutes from Honolulu via the Likelike Tunnel. Rides range in length from 45 to 90 minutes ($28 to $45).

Correa Trails Hawai'i, 41-050 Kalanianaole Highway, Waimanalo, HI 96795. Local: 808-259-9005.

One-hour guided trail rides at the base of the Ko'olau Range, overlooking Waimanalo. Cost is $49.95 per person.

Turtle Bay Golf & Tennis Resort, 57-091 Kamehameha Highway, Kahuku, HI 96731. Local: 808-293-8811, fax 808-293-9147. Web site: www.turtlebayresort.hilton.com

One of the many perks of this resort is a well-maintained stable. Trail rides are 40 to 45 minutes long and cost $35/person. Evening rides are 90 minutes long and cost $65.

Diving

O'ahu is not a dive destination unto itself. One goes to O'ahu to have a ball, be it surfing, beaching, or bar-hopping. On a week's vacation, you might go diving once or twice, but you probably wouldn't go more than that. There's so much else to do!

There are some interesting dives, however, to keep enthusiasts entertained. Most year-round diving, as in all of Hawai'i, is done on the leeward side—from Hanauma Bay in the east to Makaha in the west. Some of the best dives on O'ahu are reached from the shore. This is particularly true in the summer off the North Shore, which is usually calm then and has some terrific underwater terrain. Winter on the North Shore is off-limits to divers due to the high surf. As there are a number of boat dives and even more possible shore

dives, it's a good idea to hook up with a dive operation for the best and safest diving experience.

Costs for an introductory dive for uncertified divers (all equipment included) are between $90 and $100. Ditto on costs for certified divers and a two-tank boat dive. For the latter, some dive shops also include equipment rental and transportation.

Here is a list of O'ahu's most popular dives:

Mahi. Probably the most popular boat dive on the island is to the wreck of the *M/V Mahi*—a 165-foot, 600-ton World War II navy minesweeper deliberately sunk in 1982 to form an artificial reef. It was going to be scrapped in the Hawai'ian deep, but South Seas Aquatics, a local dive shop, intervened and arranged to have it submerged close to shore. Located about a mile off the leeward coast near Waianae, in about 90 feet of water, this is also one of the best wreck dives in the state, partly due to its newness underwater and the care taken in sinking it. This dive is fully accessible; divers can swim into the wheelhouse and other parts of the ship if they so desire. Marine life has taken to this refuge, so you won't be the only creatures in the ship.

The Plane. Near the *Mahi* to the south is another wreck that was sunk as an artificial reef and is also intact and penetrable. Many divers like to dive the *Mahi* first and then head over by boat to the Plane, situated at a depth of about 70 feet, for their second dive. The fuselage is in good shape, a twisted prop attached to its bow. The cockpit is open, so you can get a gander at what's inside.

Makaha Caves and the Land of Oz. These two boat dives are on the leeward side of O'ahu, off Makaha. Makaha Caves is a series of lava formations—caves, arches, tubes, and ledges—in up to 50 feet of water, which harbor a variety of fish and crustaceans. The Land of Oz is a concentration of many lava tubes in a small area. Since it's close to the *Mahi*, it is a good second dive on a two-tank boat trip.

Hanauma Bay. This is undoubtedly the most popular dive site on O'ahu. Besides being a snorkeler's paradise, with its thousands of colorful, tame fish in waist-deep water, the area beyond the first shallow reef is also an excellent haven for marine life. This is because Hanauma Bay is a marine life conservation area, so the fish and coral feel quite at home here. Several sections of the bay have names that betray their nature: Witches Brew features swirling currents and eddies, which mix up the fish—and you, too, if you're not careful; the Slot is a channel through the inner reef of the bay where currents can sweep you in or out, depending on the tides. Fortunately an underwater cable has been laid down through the middle to help divers navigate and pull themselves in if necessary. (Ask the lifeguard for its location.) Many, if not all, of the Honolulu-based dive operations have daily tours here.

Maunalua Bay. The next bay west of Hanauma is Maunalua Bay, a much larger body of water that borders the oh-so-tony suburbs of Kahala and Koko Head and the sprawling development known as Hawai'i Kai. There are several dive sights here, including Turtle Canyon (30 to 40 feet), Big Eel Reef (40 to 55 feet), and Kahala Barge (another artificial reef in 80 feet of water). Heavy rains will affect visibility here, so be sure to check out the conditions before jumping in.

Shark's Cove. One of several summer shore dives on the fabled North Shore of O'ahu, Shark's Cove is probably the most heavily dived site on this side of the island. Its name is derived not from sightings of sharks in the area but from the jagged contours of the cove and its reef, which appear to have been bitten out by the mouth of a shark. Located at Pupukea Beach Park off Kamehameha Highway, the site consists of a string of caverns and caves that are fun to explore, especially when conditions permit night diving. Depths range from 15 to 45 feet. The shallower depths are good for snorkelers, too.

Three Tables. Also located at Pupukea Beach Park, just west of Shark's Cove, this is another popular shore dive. It's easy to find by the three small, flat lava beds that pop up from the surface just off the beach—hence the name Three Tables. From beach to the Tables it's mostly sandy, with depths ranging from about 15 to 20 feet— good for snorkelers. The coral and interesting lava formations are outside the Tables to a depth of about 45 feet. Fish are all over.

O'AHU

O'ahu Dive Operations

Here are a few of the plethora of dive shops:

South Seas Aquatics, 2155 Kalakaua Avenue, Suite 112, Honolulu, HI 96815. Local: 808-922-0852, fax 808-922-0853.

This is the shop responsible for the creation of the *Mahi* and Plane dive sites. *Mahalo* (thanks), South Seas, for that; they are a great asset to the O'ahu dive scene and a boon to business too, we're sure. South Seas is also the oldest dive shop in Hawai'i and focuses on diving on the leeward side of O'ahu. Open Monday through Saturday 10 A.M. to 9 P.M., Sunday open at 11 A.M.

Ocean Concepts Scuba, Inc., P.O. Box 1555, Aiea, HI 96701. Toll-free: 800-808-DIVE (3483). Local: 808-677-7975 or 808-682-2511, fax 808-682-1031.
Web site: www.oceanconcepts.com

With five locations all over O'ahu, including the windward and leeward sides, this is a five-star PADI operation with a host of options. Open from 9 A.M. to 8 P.M.

Hale'iwa Surf & Sea, 65-595 Kamehameha Highway, Hale'iwa, HI 96712. Toll-free: 800-899-SURF (7873). Local: 808-637-DEEP (3337), fax 808-637-3008.
Web site: www.surnsea.com

This is a full-service, five-star PADI dive operation (North Shore diving is best in summer). Surf & Sea can also teach you how to surf and windsurf with rentals and instruction. Located on the beach in Hale'iwa town. Open daily 9 A.M. to 7 P.M.

Windward Dive Center, 789 Kailua Road, Kailua, HI 96734. Local: 808-263-2311, fax 808-263-3302.
Web site: www.divehawaii.com

This is a full-service, five-star operation located in the tony suburb of Kailua. Open Monday through Friday 9 A.M. to 7 P.M., Saturday 7 A.M. to 6 P.M., and Sunday 8 A.M. to 5 P.M.

Aqua Zone, Sheraton Waikiki Beach Resort, 2255 Kalakaua Avenue, Honolulu, HI 96815-2579. Local: 808-366-7573, fax 808-396-2641.

Web site: www.aquazone.com

With a location right in the middle of things, this is convenient for those staying in Waikiki. Open daily 8 A.M. to 5 P.M.

Golf

The island with the most people naturally has the most golf options— over 30 of them in fact, when you include the private clubs and military bases. There are places to play on every side of the island, including the most heavily played course in the U.S., the public Ala Wai course bordering Waikiki. But the golf on O'ahu is not as stellar as what's available on neighboring islands, although the relatively new Ko Olina course on the west coast and the Links at Kuilima on the North Shore are excellent. Some of the best courses on the island—the Wai'alae, Mid-Pacific, and O'ahu country clubs—are private. You will have to know somebody or belong to a golf club with a reciprocal arrangement to play any of these courses. Check with your hotel's concierge or manager; they may be able to pull some strings. It wouldn't hurt to have your club send a letter of introduction in advance of your visit. But even if you don't get lucky, there is certainly enough variety among the courses that are open to the public to keep a duffer happy for a week.

The Private Clubs

Wai'alae Country Club, 4997 Kahala Avenue, Honolulu, HI 96816. Local: 808-734-2151, fax 808-734-4791.

The top private country club/golf course in the state, Wai'alae is a superbly maintained course worthy of discussion even though you are not likely to be able to play it. Home of the annual Hawai'ian Open, it sits adjacent to the Kahala Mandarin Oriental in the upscale suburb of Kahala.

The course is also known for its mammoth bunkers, wicked-fast greens, and unfavorable winds from the trades. The toughest hole is the first (the tenth during the Open—the course is reversed for the event), with its proximity to the Kahala Mandarin and an undulating green. Other toughies include a short but skillful par 3 fourth with its slender green, and some of the long par-5 holes. One must

be a guest of a member or have reciprocity to play at Wai'alae; otherwise the closest you will get to the course is the view from the bar at the Kahala Mandarin.

The O'ahu Country Club, 150 Country Club Road, Honolulu, HI 96817. Local: 808-595-6331, fax 808-595-3186.

The Mid-Pacific Country Club, 266 Kaelepulu Drive, Kailua, HI 96734. Local: 808-261-9765, fax 808-263-4369.

These are two more tony golf clubs with excellent courses. As with Wai'alae, they are worth the effort to try to play them. The O'ahu Country Club is located on the western end of the lush Nu'uanu Valley, north of downtown Honolulu. The Mid-Pacific Country Club is situated close to the beach in Kailua and adjacent to the very fashionable residential area of Lanikai.

Clubs (Courses) For the Rest of Us:
Here are some good recommendations for public play:

Ko Olina Golf Club, 92-1220 Ali'inui Drive, Kapolei, HI 96707. Local: 808-676-5300, fax 808-676-5100.
Web site: www.koolinagolf.com

> 18 holes—Par 72
> Championship Tee (blue): 6,867 yards, 72.8 rating
> Regular Tee (white): 6,450 yards, 71.0 rating
> Ladies' Tee (red): 5,361 yards, 71.3 rating

A welcome addition to the O'ahu golf scene, this great Ted Robinson–designed 18-holer is known for its water hazards and megabunkers as well as some superbly challenging par 3's, especially the 8th hole with its waterfalls and bunkers. The 18th hole, a par 4, is a real ball-buster with water everywhere. Greens fees are $145 ($98 for hotel guests).

The Links at Kuilima, 57-049 Kuilima Drive, Kahuku, HI 96731. Local: 808-293-8574, fax 808-293-9094.
Web site: www.kuilima.com

18 holes—Par 72
Championship Tee (blue): 6,795 yards, 73.2 rating
Regular Tee (white): 5,574 yards, 67.6 rating
Ladies' Tee (red): 4,851 yards, 64.3 rating

Opened in 1992 and part of the Turtle Bay Resort, this Arnold Palmer course is often compared to the traditional links courses of Scotland. Water hazards are abundant here, on 15 out of 18 holes. Greens fees are $125.

Turtle Bay Resort, 57-091 Kamehameha Highway, Kahuku, HI 96731. Local: 808-293-8574.

9 holes—Par 36
Championship (blue): 2,494 yards
Regular Tee (white): 2,771 yards
Ladies' Tee (red): 2,157 yards

This pretty course, set on the even prettier, windswept northeastern corner of O'ahu, is an excellent play. Designed by the Fazio brothers, Tom and George, the Turtle Bay offers high surf off the North Shore, steps away from the fairways. The course is essentially flat, with occasional mounding and some strategic bunkers and elevated greens. The trade winds provide the most challenge, as this corner of paradise is very exposed. Fortunately the rainy weather stays to the south, where it hits the abrupt *pali*. Generally the weather is quite good here.

While there are only two water hazards (on the second and eighth holes), the wind is the key factor. Probably the most famous hole on this 6,366-yard course is the sixth hole, a dogleg par 4 with the ocean and the surf as a backdrop. Rates for greens fees and shared carts are under $25 for 9 holes, $50 if you play twice. Call for tee times and reservations.

Hawai'i Kai Championship and Executive Golf Courses, 8902 Kalaniana'ole Highway, Honolulu, HI 96825. Local: 808-395-2358.

Championship Course
18 holes—Par 72
Championship Tee (blue): 6,614 yards, 71.4 rating

Regular Tee (white): 6,222 yards, 69.6 rating
Ladies' Tee (red): 5,591 yards, 72.7 rating

Executive Course (Par 3)
18 holes—Par 54
Men's Tee: 2,323 yards
Ladies' Tee: 2,108 yards

These two courses, located adjacent to Sandy Beach, one of the nicest beaches on O'ahu, provide some good golfing opportunities in the shadow of Koko Crater. The Championship Course is a well-respected play and caters heavily to the Japanese tourist (the property is owned by the Atsugi Kokusai Kanko Company). The club is only 20 minutes out of Waikiki and proves a lot more challenging than the Ala Wai municipal course in town. The Executive Course is all par 3s, with one exception, and may be advisable for novices and those in a rush.

There are four water hazards on the Championship Course, shared by the 2nd, 3rd, 7th, 8th, 9th, and 13th holes. Distance hitters will like this course, as it has four par 5s at 500 yards and over. The terrain is fairly flat, and there are six doglegs and 30 bunkers to keep you honest.

Rates for greens fees and shared cart are about $50. Call for tee times, and be sure to book well in advance; this is a popular course.

Pali Golf Course, 45-050 Kamehameha Highway, Kane'ohe, HI 96744. Local: 808- 296-PALI (7254).

18 holes—Par 72
Regular Tee (white): 6,494 yards, 70.0 rating
Ladies' Tee (red): 6,080 yards, 74.5 rating

This municipal golf course, run by the Honolulu Department of Parks and Recreation, is situated in one of the prettiest settings on O'ahu. The majestic and stunning *pali*. of the Ko'olau Range rise abruptly in an awesome display of nature's sculpting ability. Evidence of the windward side's lushness is pervasive–especially the weather, which can get rather wet and overcast. Nevertheless, this course is very popular; waiting lists of over a week are not uncommon during peak periods (weekends, holidays, and high-tourist seasons). And while the clubhouse and course could use an injection of capital to spruce things up a bit, this course is definitely worth a play.

The fairways are stacked next to each other, separated by stands of trees. Water hazards, besides what falls from the sky, factor in playing the 5th, 12th, 13th, and 14th holes. Power hitters will like the straight fairways. The ladies' tee is one of the longest in Hawai'i, at 6,080 yards. The rates for greens fees and cart are wonderfully low at $40.

Makaha Golf Club, P.O. Box 896, Wai'anae, HI 96792. Local: 808-695-9544.

> 18 holes—Par 72
> Championship Tee (blue): 7,077 yards, 73.2 rating
> Regular Tee (white): 6,414 yards, 70.6 rating
> Ladies' Tee (red): 5,856 yards, 73.9 rating

One of the highest-rated championship courses in the state sits off the beaten path on the leeward side of O'ahu, in the heart of "local land." Many *haole* tourists are terrified to venture into these parts. They are missing out, not only on great golf but on some terrific beaches and diving and surfing opportunities as well. The setting for this course, designed by William Bell, is gorgeous. Nestled at the foot of the Makaha Valley next to the mountains that rise to the north, the Makaha offers sweeping views up the valley to Mount Ka'ala, the highest point on O'ahu (elevation 4,020 feet) and down to the cobalt blue of the Pacific and the setting sun. There is very little development on the fairways, which is a definite plus and adds to the feeling of being "out there." The weather here is also the sunniest, driest, and warmest on the island.

While the fairways are long, they are also wide and thus forgiving. There are eight water hazards and 107 bunkers to provide the challenge, as well as seven doglegs and several undulating greens. Of particular note is the 18th hole, where the green is under siege by bunkers and water hazards. There are three fabulous distance holes—the 1st, 4th, and 14th, each well over 500 yards long.

Rates for greens fees and shared cart are under $100 for visitors and under $50 for guests of the resort. Call for tee times and reser-

vations. The nearby Makaha Valley Country Club (695-9578) has a 6,300-yard, par-71 course should you want more golf in this neighborhood.

Tennis

Oʻahu is not a tennis destination unto itself, but it has plenty of courts along with everything else for those who want to play. There are courts all over the island (181 public ones alone), including many within walk-ing distance of Waikiki. If tennis is your *raison d'être* and you want to be on Oʻahu, the Turtle Bay Hilton may be up your alley, although it's very quiet in these parts.

Tennis Centers

Turtle Bay Resort, 57-091 Kamehamea Highway, Kahuku, HI 96731. Local: 808-293-8811.

Two very good golf courses and the added attraction of all those surfers on the North Shore should be enough for the tennis buff to elect this quiet resort. There are ten Plexi-pave courts, four of which are lighted. An active tennis program with instruction, clinics, and round-robins highlights the organized side of tennis here. Rates are under $10 per person per day.

Recommended Public Courts

There are so many public courts on Oʻahu that it shouldn't be difficult to find a place to play. Those that tend to be really crowded are the ones in Waikiki, or just outside. Specifically, these include the Kapiolani Park Courts, Diamond Head Tennis Center, and Ala Moana Park. Listed below are your best bets. For a complete listing of the free city and county courts, call 808-971-7150 or 808-955-6696. Courts are available on a first-come, first-served basis.

Ala Moana Park, Honolulu. Local: 808-592-7031.
Ten hard courts, all lighted.

Diamond Head Tennis Center, Kaimuki Mey. Local: 808-971-7150.
Ten hard courts, none lighted.

Kapiolani Park Courts, Waikiki. Local: 808-971-2525.
Four hard courts, all lighted.

Koko Head District Park, Hawai'i Kai. Local: 808-395-3096.
Six hard courts, all lighted.

Ke'ehi Lagoon Courts, Honolulu. Local: 808-522-7031.
Twelve hard courts, four lighted.

Kailua Recreation Center, Kailua. Local: 808-266-7652.
Eight hard courts, all lighted.

Cerebral

One of the big advantages of almost any major metropolitan area is an abundance of options for the mind—museums, theater, music, historical societies, government offices, historic buildings of government, religious headquarters, schools, universities, and so on to provide a cornucopia of stimulation. This is true of Honolulu, a much-maligned city (due to the excesses of Waikiki) that has a lot to offer for its size (371,657 people).

Honolulu has been the focal point of the islands since the middle of the 19th century, when King Kamehameha III recognized its potential. He moved the capital of the kingdom from Lahaina, on Maui, to Honolulu to take advantage of its pleasant climate and excellent harbor. Since then, Honolulu and O'ahu have reigned supreme. Today about 75 percent of the 1.2 million people in the state live here. This concentration of people from all over the world creates an exotic mix of cultures—just being among them is exciting.

Based in Honolulu, you could keep busy for a long string of rainy days, or days when you just want to think. You can venture out of Waikiki to places like the Bishop Museum, the Honolulu Academy of the Arts, 'Iolani Palace, the State Capitol, the Arizona Memorial, the East-West Center, and more. You can also visit the University of Hawai'i's main campus at Manoa and pick up a catalog. Graduate school in Hawai'i may be just what your soul needs.

Museums

The Bishop Museum, 1525 Bernice Street, Honolulu, HI 96817.
Local: 808-847-3511, fax 808-842-4703.
Web site: www.bishopmuseum.org

As the foremost chronicler and force in the area of Hawai'iana, this is a definite must-see when on O'ahu. Located on Bernice Street at the junction of the Likelike Highway and the H1 freeway, it is Hawai'i's premier museum, containing the best display of Polynesiana in the world. There are several buildings on the grounds, many dating back to the 19th century. Made of stone in the neo-Gothic style, they give the museum the air of a venerable university.

The museum was founded by the Bishop Estate, one of the wealthiest trusts in the world. (It owns about 10 percent of all the land in Hawai'i.) The estate's funds are the legacy of Princess Bernice. Married to a Yankee named Charles Bishop, she was one of the last of the royalty to rule before Hawai'i's annexation to the United States. Upon her death in 1885, she bequeathed her entire fortune to her husband, who founded the Bernice Pauahi Bishop Estate. Her desire to establish a trust for the advancement of the Hawai'ian people and culture was faithfully executed by her husband, who commissioned the Bishop Museum in 1888 and also founded the Kamehameha Schools. A private secondary school for people of at least one-eighth Hawai'ian descent, it has one of the largest endowments of any private secondary school in the world.

Hawai'ian Hall, the main exhibition gallery, is a classic old-style museum space. Three stories high, it is ringed on each floor by balconies replete with arches, Corinthian pillars, and lots of dark koa wood. In this part of the museum are displayed most of the countless Hawai'ian artifacts collected by the princess and her family, as well as subsequent acquisitions. The first floor is the best; it houses the oldest and most prized items—feather capes, helmets, and other royal affectations, including the more westernized objects of the later Hawai'ian kings. There are also scores of artifacts, from spears and ceramic pots to wooden images of the gods, that highlight the islands' past. There is even room for a 50-foot sperm whale and a replica of a Hawai'ian house.

Several additional halls complement the main space. A planetarium show, held at 11:30 A.M., 1:30 P.M., and 3:00 P.M., simulates the voyage of the Polynesians to Hawai'i. The Hawai'ian Court displays various Hawai'ian artifacts and flora and explains their use. There is a daily exhibition of Hawai'ian crafts (we saw a quilting bee) in the Vestibule Gallery from 9 A.M. to 3 P.M., Monday through Saturday, as well as a music and dance performance at 2 P.M. For the more academic, there is an excellent research library (the Fuller Collection of Pacific Books and the Governor G. R. Carter Collection of Hawai'iana) and photo collection.

The museum is open every day except Christmas from 9 A.M. to 5 P.M. Admission is $14.95 for adults, $11.95 for ages 4 to 12 and Seniors. Free for children aged 3 and under.

Honolulu Academy of the Arts, 900 South Beretania Street, Honolulu, HI 96814. Local: 808-532-8701.
Web site: www.academyofarts.org

Whereas the Bishop Museum focuses on Hawai'iana, the Honolulu Academy of the Arts is Hawai'i's cultural link to the outside world. In addition to its resident collection of Asian art and Western styles, the Academy hosts exhibitions of all types of art forms from around the globe. The HAA also runs a terrific film program that brings in movies of distinction, from contemporary foreign films and independent cinema, to revival films and animation, to the latest in experimental video. This offers a welcome alternative to the very mainstream fare served up by the general Hawai'ian movie theaters (with the exception of the Varsity Theater near the UH-Manoa campus, which shows more artsy films).

Music thrives here too. Recitals—cellists, pianists, violinists, chamber music groups, and avant-garde musicians like the Kronos Quartet—are regularly featured in the Academy Theater. There is also a Camerata Series, which brings visiting symphony musicians to play chamber music with members of the Honolulu Symphony.

The Academy offers a regular lecture series on topics such as poetry, opera, and film as well as more esoteric subjects, such as metal-smithing and the art of the outrigger canoe. Occasionally Hawai'ian topics are featured; there are annual Hawai'ian crafts workshops called *Aha Hana Lima* (Gathering of Craftsmen).

The Academy is located on Beretania Street at Ward Avenue (across Beretania from Thomas Square). Be sure to stroll through the square, with its huge fountain and banyan trees. It is open Tuesday through Saturday from 10 A.M. to 4:30 P.M., Sunday from 1 to 5 P.M. Closed Monday, New Year's Day, July 4th, Thanksgiving, and Christmas. Walking tours are conducted at 11 A.M., except on Sundays, when they are held at 1:15 P.M. Admission is $7 for adults, $4 for seniors and students, and free for kids aged 12 and under.

The Mission Houses Museum, 553 S. King Street, Honolulu, HI 96813. Local: 808-531-0481.
Web site: www.lava.net/~mhm/main.htm

Located adjacent to the Honolulu Hale (City Hall), this complex of restored and replicated houses of the early missionaries, replete with artifacts on display for your review, is key for those interested in the early missionary period. Personally, we take a dim view of the prudish missionaries (the term missionary position, indicative of their creativity, wasn't coined for nothing!)—they set about to destroy the "savage" Hawai'ian culture, and they almost succeeded. Fortunately the intervention of King Kalakaua and the Bishop Estate has helped preserve such Hawai'ian traditions as the hula and founded a new pride in things Hawai'ian. The recent surge of interest in Hawai'iana should guarantee that it will survive in perpetuity. Still, the missionaries were integral in shaping the destiny of Hawai'i and its annexation to the United States. Their offspring became the sugar barons who eventually overthrew the monarchy for their own business interests.

The museum is open Tuesday through Saturday, from 9 A.M. to 4 P.M. Admission is under $8 for adults and free for kids under three. Tours, conducted frequently, include a walking tour of the neighborhood, too ('Iolani and Washington Palaces and the Capitol). The tour cost (including museum admission) is $15 and under for adults, free for children under three ($10 for the walking tour only). For more info, call 808-531-0481. Across the street is the coral stone Kawaiahao Church, one of Hawai'i's oldest (1842) and the church of some of the later Hawai'ian royals (Kamehameha IV and his queen, Emma, switched to the Anglican St. Andrew's Cathedral in the 1860s—again, to emulate the British).

The Contemporary Museum, 2411 Makiki Heights Drive, Honolulu, HI 96822. Local: 808-526-0232 or 808-526-1322. Web site: www.tcmhi.org

Located in a sprawling renovated house on three and a half acres in the hills above Honolulu, this museum offers exhibitions of Hawai'ian as well as renowned international artists. Open Tuesday through Saturday from 10 A.M. to 4 P.M., Sunday 12 to 4 P.M. Closed Monday and most major holidays. Admission is $5 for adults, $3 for seniors and students with I.D. and free for kids aged 12 and under. Every third Thursday of the month, admission is free to all. There is also a branch location downtown at the First Hawai'ian Center, 999 Bishop Street (open weekdays only).

Other Sights

Downtown Honolulu

In the downtown area there are several interesting sites within walking distance of each other: 'Iolani Palace, the State Capitol, the State Library, the Mission Houses (see above), Honolulu Hale, Kawaiahao Church, the botanic gardens, and Chinatown.

'Iolani Palace, P.O. Box 2259, Honolulu, HI 96804. Local: 808-522-0832. Built in the late 19th century for King Kalakaua, this palace represents the pinnacle of the Hawai'ian royal period and is the only royal palace in the United States. It was used by royalty for only about ten years. After the revolution of 1893 deposed the monarchy, it became the seat of the Provisional Government and later the legislature, until the new State House was finished in 1969.

The palace is a treasure trove of royal and republican memorabilia. The exterior is quite grand in the classic Victorian sense (especially the palace's beautiful parklike grounds) and reflects the Hawai'ian royalty's obsession with everything British (note the state flag with its Union Jack—once the flag of the monarchy). The only way to see the interior, resplendent in koa wood including the oh-so-grand koa balustrade, is on one of the guided tours, held Tuesday through Saturday from 9 A.M. to 2:15 P.M. Tours start every 15 minutes and last for 45. The tours are very

popular, so advance reservations are strongly suggested. You must purchase your tickets 30 minutes before your tour time at the Barracks Building on the palace grounds. Admission is $15 per adult and $5 for kids (children under five are not allowed). On Fridays, the Royal Hawai'ian Band gives free concerts at the ornate bandstand—the Coronation Stand for King Kalakaua at his most royal and arrogant (after that, it was all downhill).

Across King Street from the Palace is Ali'iolani Hale, originally built as the palace for Kamehameha V. Unfortunately for him, he died before it was completed, so it became the judicial and parliamentary headquarters during the latter days of the Hawai'ian monarchy. Today it still functions in the judicial service as the State Judiciary Building.

Hawai'i State Capitol. Located next to the 'Iolani Palace, on the same spacious grounds, this modern building was designed to reflect several things Hawai'ian. The bicameral chambers are cone-shaped, to resemble the volcanoes of the Big Island. The large reflecting pool represents the Pacific, and the outside columns were designed to look like royal palms. Above each of the entrances is a gigantic cast of the Hawai'ian state seal. The interior is filled with Hawai'i's trademark, koa wood. It is certainly worth a walk-through and is open Monday through Friday from 8 A.M. to 4:30 P.M. For more information, call 808-586-2211.

Hawai'i State Library. Located on the grounds of the 'Iolani Palace at 478 S. King Street, the library houses over 45,000 volumes of Hawai'iana and Pacific books for your edification. Tours are conducted Monday through Friday, 9 A.M. to 4 P.M., and last about one hour. For more information and reservations, call 808-586-3621.

Foster Botanic Gardens. This is Honolulu's botanical garden, a 15-acre park of manicured lawns and gardens at 180 N. Vineyard Boulevard, at Nu'uanu Street. It is a great place to meditate or maybe have a romantic interlude. Open daily from 9 A.M. to 4 P.M.; admission is $5 for adults and $1 for kids aged 6 to 12. Guided tours are available Monday through Friday at 1:00 P.M. and last for about 90 minutes (no charge). For more information, call 808-522-7065.

Web site: www.co.honolulu.hi.us/parks/hbg

Chinatown. Resembling other Chinatowns, this one is cleaner and more interesting because of its eclectic businesses, art galleries, and their patrons. At its heart are Hotel Street, the old red-light district, and the Chinese Cultural Plaza (the scene of a festival, with deafening firecrackers, during Chinese New Year). A stroll through these parts is certainly a mind-trip. Chinatown's perimeter is roughly the area between the Fort Street Mall on the Diamond Head (east) side, the river on the Ewa (west) side, N. Beretania on the *mauka* (mountain) side, and Nimitz Highway on the *makai* (ocean) side. Got that? Good.

Two groups conduct guided tours of Chinatown for a small fee. The Chinese Chamber of Commerce has a walk at 9:30 A.M. on Tuesdays for $5 per person; call 808-533-3181 for reservations. The Hawai'i Heritage Center runs a tour on Fridays at 9:30 A.M. for $5 per person; call 808-521-2749 for more information and reservations.

Beyond Downtown

Pearl Harbor. We all know about the legacy of Pearl Harbor and its place in world history. Today, as it was before December 7, 1941, the harbor is the headquarters of the U.S. Pacific Command and Fleet. The entire harbor, a huge bay of many inlets, is owned by the military. For the visitor and history buff on O'ahu, one site is a *must*—the U.S.S. *Arizona* Memorial.

USS *Arizona* Memorial, U.S. Dept. of the Interior, National Park Service, No. 1 Arizona Memorial Place, Honolulu, HI 96818. Local: 808-422-0561.

Web Site: www.nps.gov/usar
E-mail: azmemph@aol.com

Rarely have we been so moved as when we visited the *Arizona* Memorial. It consists of two parts—the Visitor's Center/Museum and the actual memorial structure itself, which spans the beam of the sunken battleship. When you arrive at the Visitor's Center, you receive a ticket bearing a group number for the interpretive program, which includes a talk by a park ranger; a short, fact-filled and excellent documentary, with actual footage taken by the Japanese; and the boat launch trip to the 184-foot white concrete shrine. While waiting for your number to be called, you can

check out the museum and, if you have time, the bookstore.

The shrine is set above the middle of the *Arizona*, and a viewing well allows you to look down on the rusting hulk. Sometimes a slick of diesel fuel is visible; the ship still leaks from time to time—a grim reminder that the tragedy didn't happen all that long ago. Over 1,100 men are entombed below, and the chapel at the far end of the structure has all their names inscribed in Vermont marble. Ironically, a large percentage of the visitors are Japanese. We will *never* forget the sight of young Japanese tourists casting flower blossoms into the viewing well. This is when we totally lost it. A visit here is a moving experience for people of all opinions.

The memorial is open (weather permitting) seven days a week, from 7:30 A.M. to 5 P.M., closed on Thanksgiving, Christmas, and New Year's Day. The interpretive program, a must-see, begins at 8 A.M. and goes until 3 P.M. It's very popular, so get here early to avoid a long wait (or in early afternoon, as most tour groups come in the morning). It is reached by taking the Kamehameha Highway (Route 99) west of Honolulu (about a 20-minute drive) or a ride on the #20 The Bus. Also, a company called the Arizona Memorial Bus Shuttle offers an express shuttle from Waikiki (839-0911). The parking lot is notorious for car break-ins, so don't leave any valuables.

University of Hawai'i–Manoa Campus, 2444 Dole Street, Honolulu, HI 96822. Local: 808-956-8111. Web site: www.uhm.hawaii.edu

Tired of subways and office cubicles? Or maybe just suffering from intellectual stagnation? One solution may be graduate school in paradise. The University of Hawai'i's main campus in Honolulu offers a variety of options. It's not small—17,000 full-time students share the 300-acre site. Besides the seven undergraduate colleges (Arts and Sciences, Business Administration, Continuing Education and Community Service, Education, Engineering, Health Sciences and Social Welfare, and Tropical Agriculture and Human Resources), there are nine graduate schools (Architecture, Law, Library Studies, Medicine, Nursing, Public Health, and Social Work, plus the Hawai'i Institute of Tropical Agriculture and the School of Travel Industry Management). Stop by the admissions office for a catalog and application, and check out the Student Center for goings-on about the campus and the superb bookstore.

While you're touring the campus, look for the **East-West Center,** at 1777 East-West Road (944-7111); it's definitely worth a visit. A Zen-like atmosphere permeates this multi-acre site within the university, dedicated to promoting mutual under-standing among the peoples of Asia, the Pacific, and the United States. The focal point of this federally and privately funded institute is Jefferson Hall, designed by I. M. Pei. Before you tour the grounds, which include the Thai Pavilion and the beautiful Center for Korean Studies, stop by Burns Hall to pick up a map and information on what's current at the center.

Punahou and Kamehameha Schools. These schools, located a few miles apart in Honolulu, are two of the top three private schools in the state. ('Iolani, situated just outside of Waikiki, is the other.) The campuses of the two schools are gorgeous. Punahou is the bastion of the rich *haole* and Kamehameha is the phenomenally well-endowed school for those of Hawai'ian ancestry.

Valley of the Temples. Just *mauka* (mountain side) of Kamehameha Highway (Route 83) in Kane'ohe, at the foot of the stunning Ko'olau Range, is this cemetery dedicated to the religions of all peoples. The jewel of the valley is the meditative **Byodo-In Temple,** a meticulous replica of the 900-year-old temple in Japan and a must-see. Gardens and carp ponds surround the temple, and a huge three-ton bell signals your presence to the temple and hopefully brings well-being. This is an excellent spot for medita-tion and contemplation.

Pu'uomahuka Heiau State Monument. Situated above Waimea Bay at the end of Pupukea Road on the North Shore, this is a wonderful spot for reflectiving, meditating, or watching the sun-set. Pu'uomahuka was a *luakini*, a temple of human sacrifice for the war god Ku.

Art Galleries

The Chinatown District is a very vibrant art scene these days. Indeed, many now dub it the Art District. Several times a year,

Nu'uanu Avenue has a block party/festival called Nu'uanu Nights, which is a good time to check out the galleries (consult with your concierge or pick up a copy of *Honolulu Weekly* for dates and times).

The Pegge Hopper Gallery, 1164 Nu'uanu Avenue, Honolulu (Chinatown), HI 96817. Local/fax: 808-524-1160.

Undoubtedly you will see a Pegge Hopper painting during your stay in Hawai'i (the reclining Hawai'ian woman is a favorite motif of hers). This is her gallery and well worth a stop. Tuesday through Friday, 11 A.M. to 4 P.M., Saturday to 3 P.M.

Roy Ventner Studio, 1160 Nu'uanu Avenue, Honolulu (Chinatown), HI 96817. Local: 808-381-3445.

Artist Roy Ventner has an eclectic array of pieces available for sale at very reasonable prices in his storefront studio. Hours are by appointment only. There is a rumor that he is opening a teaching studio as well. Ventner is a wealth of information about the happenings in Chinatown.

Salon 5, 1160A Nu'uanu Avenue, Honolulu (Chinatown), HI 96817. Local: 808-550-2855.

Right next to Roy Ventner's studio and two down from Pegge Hopper's is Salon 5, a two-level gallery featuring various local artists. Open Tuesday through Saturday, 12 to 8 P.M.

Artmosphere, 1109 Nu'uanu Avenue, Honolulu (Chinatown), HI 96817. Local: 808-255-9012.

Another Nu'uanu gallery with a great name and showcasing local talent, it's open Tuesday through Friday, 11 A.M. to 5 P.M., Saturday to 2 P.M.

Ramsay Galleries, 1128 Smith Street, Honolulu, HI 96817. Local: 808-537-2787.

This gallery features the permanent collection of Ramsay's crow-quill pen-and-ink drawings, as well as featured guest artists of Hawai'i. Open Monday through Friday, 10 A.M. to 5 P.M. and Saturday to 4 P.M.

Bookstores

There are loads of bookstores on O'ahu, including the large chains like Barnes & Noble and Border's. Many of the smaller stores are religion-oriented, but there are plenty of secular ones where you can find your favorite Jane Austen novel or Jackie Collins throbber. Among the best:

Art/Hawai'iana Books

The Academy Shop, Honolulu Academy of the Arts, 900 S. Beretania Street, Honolulu, HI 96814. Local: 808-532-8703.
   Open Tuesday through Saturday, 10 A.M. to 4:30 P.M., Sunday 1 P.M. to 5 P.M.

The Bishop Museum, 1525 Bernice Street, Honolulu, HI 96817. Local: 808-848-4158.
   Open daily 9 A.M. to 5 P.M.

Bestsellers Hawai'i, 1001 Bishop Street, 138 Pauahi Tower, Honolulu, HI 96813. Local: 808-528-2378.
Web site: www.hawaiibestsellers.com.
   Open Monday through Friday, 7:30 A.M. to 5:30 P.M., Saturday 9 A.M. to 4 P.M.

General Bookstores

Bestsellers Hawai'i, 1001 Bishop Street, 138 Pauahi Tower, Honolulu, HI 96813. Local: 808-528-2378.
Web site: www.Hawai'ibestsellers.com.
   Open Monday through Friday, 7:30 A.M. to 5:30 P.M., Saturday 9 A.M. to 4 P.M.

Barnes & Noble Booksellers, 4211 Wai'alae Avenue, Honolulu, HI 96816. Local: 808-737-3323.
   Open daily 9 A.M. to 11 P.M.

Border's Books & Music, 1200 Ala Moana Boulevard, Honolulu, HI 96814. Local: 808-591-8995.

Open Monday through Thursday, 9 A.M. to 11 P.M., Friday and Saturday until midnight and Sunday until 10 P.M.

Waldenbooks, Waikiki Shopping Plaza, Waikiki, 808-922-4154; Waikiki Trade Center, Waikiki, 808-924-8330; Kahala Mall, Kahala, 808-737-9550; Windward Mall, Kaneohe, 808-235-8044.
Open daily 9:30 A.M. to 9:30 P.M.

Rainbow Books and Records, 1010 University Avenue (at King), Honolulu, HI 96826. Local: 808-955-7994. Open 10 A.M. to 10 P.M.

Bookends in Kailua, 590 Kailua Road, Kailua, HI 96735. Local: 808-261-1996.
Open daily 9 A.M. to 8 P.M., Saturday and Sunday until 5 P.M.

Music Stores

There are loads of record stores on O'ahu where you can find both rock and Hawai'ian music. Among the best are the following:

Harry's Music Store, 3457 Wai'alae Avenue, Honolulu (Kaimuki), HI 96816. Local: 808-735--2866.
The best place for Hawai'ian music as well as musical instruments. Open Monday through Friday 9:30 A.M. to 5:30 P.M., Saturday 9 A.M. to 5 P.M., closed Sunday.

Tower Records, 611 Keeaumoku Avenue (across from the Ala Moana Center), Honolulu, 808-941-7774; 4211 Wai'alae Avenue, Kahala, 808-737-5088.
Everything, and it's open every day until 10 P.M.

Rainbow Books and Records, 1010 University Avenue (at King), Honolulu, HI 96826. Local: 808-955-7994.
Open daily 10 A.M. to 10 P.M.

Records Hawai'i, 2071B S. Beretania Street, Honolulu, HI 96826. Local: 808-955-8834.
Open Monday through Friday 12 P.M. to 6 P.M., Saturday 10 A.M. to 6 P.M., closed Sunday.

Hungry Ear Records and Tapes, 418 Ku'ulei Road, Kailua, HI 96734. Local: 808-262-2175.

Open daily 10 A.M. to 6:30 P.M.

Where to Stay

O'ahu is dominated by the metropolis of Honolulu, Hawai'i's capital and biggest city. Nestled in the middle of the southern coast at the foot of the Ko'olau Range, Honolulu is the engine that powers the state. For visitors, a lion's share of the hotels and resorts are in Waikiki, a familiar name to even the most provincial traveler. If you're looking for peace and quiet, do not stay in Waikiki. There are other parts of O'ahu, and Hawai'i, that will offer tranquility. If you like city life, then look no further. If you seek both, a great compromise is to stay just outside of Waikiki at the foot of Diamond Head, where it is much quieter yet within walking distance of the frenzy called Waikiki.

Note: Nonsmoking floors are a rarity in Hawai'i due to the voracious smoking habits of Asian tourists, the Japanese in particular. Nonsmoking rooms do exist, however, so be sure to request one if this is important to you.

Waikiki

Now for the big time—Waikiki! Over 90 percent of guest accommodations on O'ahu are jammed onto this narrow strip of land bordered by the Ala Wai Canal, Kapiolani Park, and the Pacific Ocean. Part of the city of Honolulu, Waikiki is one of the most famous resort areas in the world.

With every passing year, Waikiki becomes more like one huge shopping mall. Indeed, it is a shopping mall, and developers continue to add concrete and stories to this fabled spot. You will either love it or hate it. Singles and shoppers will love it. Honeymooners and families will probably loathe it. It's the perfect place for high-energy types who just can't get enough. For us, staying here for more than a few days can be oppressive due to the crowds and traffic. It's just not a relaxing place.

The key to enjoying Waikiki is to be in the right location, preferably a place on the beach or on a quieter side street. You'll need a refuge from all the commotion. Over 30,000 hotel rooms and a lot of other buildings, including high-rise apartments, are crammed together in an area only a half-mile wide and about two miles long. To escape, we recommend renting a car so that you can get out to the island's better beaches, hike, sightsee, and go to Chinatown at night—Hawai'i's *très branché* night scene.

Most people come to Waikiki on a package deal, and it shows. As much of the Waikiki clientele is budget-conscious, you'll see *very* mainstream and middle-of-the-road Americana, as well as a hefty dose of Japanese and others from Asian countries. Many of the "package" hotels are just adequate. Often the décor is very dated or haphazard, and right out of pastel hell. Most are places we wouldn't stay in unless they were so cheap that it was impossible to say no. There are many Waikiki hotels that we don't list here, mostly for reasons of space and because we wouldn't be caught dead staying in them. If all you want is a room on the cheap to change, nap, or sleep, one of the package hotels will probably do—but remember, you've been warned.

In this section we've tried to include the noteworthy, special, wonderfully situated, or unusual places. When booking your room or package, ask for one of the establishments listed.

Here are our recommendations:

The Halekulani, 2199 Kalia Road, Honolulu, HI 96815-1988. Toll-free: 800-367-2343. Local: 808-923-2311, fax 808-926-8004. Rooms and suites: 456.
Web site: www.halekulani.com

The Halekulani is a magnificent hotel. It remains one of the best in Hawai'i and co-stars on O'ahu with the Kahala Mandarin and W. By far, it is the best in Waikiki. It is also one of the most professionally run accommodations we've ever visited. Everything is well thought out, down to the last detail. Opened in 1984 on the site of the old Halekulani—a sorely missed low-key hotel of bungalows that was founded in 1907 and was known as the House Without a Key—this new high-rise maintains the old Halekulani's distinctive

sloping roof style, albeit with many more floors underneath. It features an interesting and attractive blend of Polynesian, Japanese, and American architectural styles. The main building of the old hotel, attached to the front of the central tower, is all that remains. It serves as the dining area and is a good place to rendezvous.

The best things about the Halekulani, besides its central location on a good swimming beach in Waikiki, are the rooms and the service. The thoughtfulness of the design and the tastefulness of the décor are among the best on Oʻahu. The rooms, decorated in seven shades of white with louvered shutters, large lanais, and at least a partial ocean view, are stunning. Almost minimalist in appearance, all the details have been addressed, from the electronic service/do not disturb indicators and door chain locks to the oversize tiled bathrooms with separate glass shower enclosures, large tubs, vanities with magnifying mirrors, and bathroom scales. But truly outstanding is the service: thoughtful, courteous, and efficient—just the way it should be.

The pool, with its surrounding fleet of padded chaises, is another extraordinary feature here. A huge tile mosaic of a blue orchid takes up two thirds of the pool. It's quite a sight when you look down from your room—particularly when someone attractive is floating in the water. Sunset cocktails are served on the lanai facing the pool, to the accompaniment of a Hawaiʻian band—an experience that shouldn't be missed. The hotel is also right in the middle of Waikiki's beach, so there is always a parade of people. There is a small beach in front, although a much better one is a few minutes' walk east along the beach to the Royal Hawaiʻian. For dining, the Halekulani's La Mer is one of the best restaurants in the state. It features two daily five-course prix-fixe dinners for $78 and $105 per person. Sunday brunch at Orchids is a Waikiki institution and a treat. The Halekulani has an added benefit for guests seeking cultural events: complimentary tickets to evening performances at the Honolulu Symphony Orchestra. In addition, the Halekulani offers a "For You, Everything" package, which includes complimentary tickets to Honolulu's finest museums, the Honolulu Academy of Arts and The Contemporary Museum.

Rates are **Wicked Pricey** and up.

The Sheraton Moana Surfrider, 2365 Kalakaua Avenue, Honolulu, HI 96815. Toll-free: 800-782-9488. Local: 808-922-3111, fax 808-
923-0308. Rooms and suites: 793.
Web site: www.moana-surfider.com

Officially named the Sheraton Moana Surfrider Hotel, this venerable hotel is universally known as just The Moana. Opened in
1901, it was the first hotel in Waikiki, and is built out of wood in
what is called the Hawai'ian colonial style. It is indeed a classic,
especially amidst the surrounding concrete jungle (it is wedged
between two towers on the beach). Kudos to the Japanese development company that bought the hotel (and Sheraton, the managa-
ment) for not demolishing it and building another monster tower in
its place. Instead, they spent over $50 million in a careful restora-
tion more than a decade ago. This includes the relaying of the
different woods used for each floor in the original building. Lovers
of the big, old wooden hotels should definitely check out the
Moana. Facing the ocean and shaded by a huge banyan tree
(planted in 1904 and protected by state law), the Banyan Court is a
great spot for lunch or a cocktail. A small pool on the side provides
a freshwater alternative to the beach in front.

The rooms have been authentically and tastefully renovated to
convey the feeling of the original décor. The woods used are the
original koa, mahogany, oak, cherry, and maple. High ceilings and
a mirror over the bed convey a feeling of space where the actual
square footage might be lacking. Large frame windows with louvered shutters let in ample light and views of the busy street or
beach below. Baths are small, tiled, and decorated with pretty Colonial wallpaper. Armoires have been designed to replicate the originals, though they now conceal the TV, bar, and fridge. Light
fixtures and controls, wall prints, Hawai'ian quilts, and the overall
décor reflect a very classic yet stylish taste. Be sure to request a
room in the main building; otherwise you'll end up in the adjoining
newer hotel towers which just don't have the charm. Beware of
rooms fronting noisy Kalakaua Avenue. It's best to pay more for a
room on the ocean side.

Rates are **Very Pricey** and up.

The Royal Hawai'ian Hotel, 2259 Kalakaua Avenue, Honolulu, HI 96815. Toll-free: 800-782-9488. Local: 808-923-7311, fax 808-924-7098. Rooms and suites: 527.
Web site: www.royal-hawaiian.com

Affectionately called the Pink Palace, this Moorish stucco hotel—painted in a vibrant shade of pink with green awnings over the windows and purple urns perched on the roof pediment—is as much a Waikiki landmark as is Diamond Head in the distance. Built in 1927 for four million bucks, it was *the* glamorous place to stay (movie stars and other swells loved it) until statehood changed both the look of Waikiki and the hotel industry. Today it sits in the shadow of the humongous Sheraton Waikiki— the latter one of the more serious crimes against architecture—trying to maintain its grandeur amid the chaos around it (the Royal Hawai'ian Mall is in front and the Moana is on the other side). Still, it's hard not to love The Royal Hawai'ian, for it is a relic in the current tide of hotel/resorts in Hawai'i. Fortunately, too, the Royal Hawai'ian is blessed with one of the nicest stretches of beach in Waikiki. If you want to be right in the hub, yet desire ambience and charm, then this might be the ticket.

The Royal Hawai'ian is managed by Starwood. There are 384 rooms in the original main building and another 193 in the much newer Royal Tower. Definitely stick to the main building for its style and character. Rooms here have tiny French balconies, pink and pastel accents, of course, canopy or four-poster beds, and Queen Anne–style desks and dressers. The Ocean and Deluxe Ocean rooms front the beach. There is 24-hour room service and a pool. On Mondays the hotel hosts the Royal Hawai'ian Luau, featuring the Royal Polynesian Extravaganza.

Rates are **Wicked Pricey** and up.

Hyatt Regency Waikiki Resort & Spa, 2424 Kalakaua Avenue, Honolulu, HI 96815. Toll-free: 800-233-1234. Local: 808-923-1234, fax 808-923-7839. Rooms and suites: 1230.
Web site: www.hyattwaikiki.com

Located near the west end of Kapiolani Park and across Kalakaua from Kuhio Beach Park, the Hyatt Regency Waikiki is a big hotel. Recognizable by its twin 40-story octagonal towers, the

hotel has the Hyatt's trademark atrium—this one open to the sky, with a large cascading waterfall and a 4,500-pound chandelier hovering over a jungle of foliage. There is also the standard high-priced shopping arcade (Gucci is here) sheathed in attractive woods.

The rooms are like Hyatts elsewhere—clean and comfortable, done in a muted earth-tone décor with blue linens, rattan furnishings, and wall-to-wall carpeting. Each has a narrow lanai and original artwork on the walls, plus the usual deluxe amenities. Try to get an oceanfront or ocean-view room up high, to minimize the noise from busy Kalakaua Avenue. As with other Hyatt properties in Hawai'i, there is a Regency Club—here occupying the top six floors of the Diamond Head Tower—where you can pay a lot more for use of a special elevator key, cocktail-hour bar and *pupus* (hors d'œuvres), continental breakfast, complimentary passes to 24 Hour Fitness (see the Gyms and Health Clubs secton) and the Honolulu Club, and concierge service. The hotel has several A.D.A. rooms available and designated nonsmoking floors. There is a rather small pool and two hot tubs on the third-floor terrace. A new 10,000-square-foot day spa, called Na Ho'ola, offers a variety of services to pamper the body. There are seven restaurants at the hotel and daily entertainment in the atrium. Camp Hyatt for kids is available daily from 6 to 10 P.M. during the summer months, and on Friday and Saturday during the rest of the year. Be advised that Hawai'i state law allows a child to attend adult-supervised activities at the hotel for up to only five and a half hours per week (and you thought you could leave 'em all week!).

Rates are **Very Pricey** and up.

Waikiki Parc, 2233 Helumoa Road, Honolulu, HI 96815. Toll-free: 800-422-0450. Local: 808-921-7272, fax 808-923-1962. Rooms: 298. Web site: www.waikikiparc.com

This midsize hotel is one of the best deals in Waikiki. Opened in 1987 by the same company that owns the Halekulani (across the street) and recently refurbished, it has many of the same tasteful touches that its big sister has—but at much more affordable prices. Twenty-two stories high, it has rooms decorated in shades of blue and white with rattan furniture. There are white ceramic-tiled floors and inlaid carpeting—something you don't usually see in hotels in this price range—as well as louvers instead of drapes. Rooms are all the same size and are available with king-size or two double beds, and almost all have writing desks. They also have cardkeys, electronic room safes, fridges and bars, two phones with data ports, and reading lamps. Feather pillows (we love them because they aren't as severe on our collagen-needy faces) are available on request. A.D.A. rooms are also available. There are laundry facilities and a small pool/deck on the premises. Our only complaint is that the rooms are on the smallish side. Since all the rooms are the same, the difference in price is for the view (the ocean-view side has lanais).

Rates are *Pricey* and up.

Radisson Waikiki Prince Kuhio, 2500 Kuhio Avenue, Honolulu, HI 96815-3696. Toll-free: 888-557-4422. Local: 808-922-0811, fax 808-921-5507. Rooms and suites: 625.
Web site: www.radisson.com

This 37-story tower located a block from the beach is a good value. Radisson took over the hotel, formerly the Outrigger Prince Kuhio, in 1999, establishing a presence on O'ahu. While the lanais on the dizzyingly high floors are not for acrophobes, the views are beautiful. The Prince Kuhio has a decent-size pool with Jacuzzi, a fitness room, a business center, room service, and a coin-operated laundry. Rooms are carpeted and decorated in pale tones with tropical furnishings and prints. All rooms have a lanai, cable TV, coffeemaker, fridge, voice-mail phone with dataport, safe, iron and board, and standard bath. Radisson offers the Kuhio Club on the top four floors, with enhanced amenities and a private lounge.

Rates are *Pricey* and up.

Aston Waikiki Beachside Hotel, 2452 Kalakaua Avenue, Honolulu, HI 96815. Toll-free: 800-922-7866. Local: 808-931-2100, fax 808-931-2129. Rooms: 79.
Web site: www.aston-hotels.com

Calling itself a "boutique hotel," which we feel is a generous use of the term (W, located in Diamond Head, is a true boutique hotel), this smallish accommodation is nevertheless a good option for Waikiki hotels in the deluxe category. We like its size, and the

rooms come with a variety of amenities, including TV/VCR with HBO (for the *Sopranos*/*Sex in the City* junkies among us), voice mail, mini-fridge, twice-daily maid service, and free continental breakfast. Also in the hotel's favor is its location, across the street from Kuhio Beach Park and close to Kapiolani Park. The décor is a tad nouveau riche–looking for us, but it is a nice change from the tropical pastel and rattan style that is so pervasive in Waikiki.

Rates are *Very Pricey* and up.

Sheraton Waikiki Beach Resort, 2255 Kalakaua Avenue, Honolulu, HI 96815-2579. Toll-free: 800-782-9488. Local: 808-922-4422, fax 808-923-8785. Rooms and suites: 1,852.
Web site: www.sheraton-waikiki.com

This is the Monster That Ate Waikiki. With almost 2,000 rooms and suites in a three-pronged, 31-story behemoth of a building, it overwhelms everything around—including the classic Royal Hawai'ian next door. There are over 39,000 square feet of convention space—you can guess where the hotel gets most of its business. The small lobby is always a beehive of activity; the rooms themselves are comfortable and standard Sheraton, with such amenities as a mini-bar/fridge, cable TV, phone, coffeemaker, and hair dryer. Most rooms have at least a partial ocean view and almost all have lanais. For the size of the hotel, you'd think it would have a huge pool (of course, as we all know, you can't always tell how big it is just from overall size), but it is located on the water, and the Royal Hawai'ian beach is just next door.

The hotel has almost completed a five-year, $20 million renovation and also offers the Keiki Aloha Club—the free kids' program, a baby-sitting service, a coin-operated laundry, room service, a fitness center, and a business center. This is a big package-deal hotel, so the price may make it worthwhile.

Rates are *Pricey* and up.

The Outrigger Hotels, 2375 Kuhio Avenue, Honolulu, HI 96815-2939. Toll-free: 800-OUTRIGGER (688-7444). Direct reservations: 303-369-7777, fax 303-369-9403. Local: 808-921-6600, fax 808-622-4852.
Web site: www.outrigger.com

We're bunching all of the Outrigger hotels together because there are five of them spread throughout Waikiki. In addition, the company's economy division, Ohana Hotels, has another 15 properties in Waikiki (see below). This combination, along with properties in Kaua'i, Maui, and the Big Island, makes it the largest hotel chain in the Aloha State as well as among the biggest to offer package deals. Given the numbers, there is quite a range of hotels and condos with a wide variation in amenities, depending on your budget. The company's founder, the late Roy Kelly, had a vision to make vacations affordable for average middle-class travelers and families. Indeed, the clientele we have seen staying at these hotels remain true to his philosophy.

On O'ahu, the flagship Outrigger resorts are the **Outrigger Waikiki on the Beach** and the **Outrigger Reef on the Beach**. Obviously they are waterfront properties. Both cater to a younger, very mainstream American/Canadian crowd. The Outrigger Waikiki has been newly renovated and sits adjacent to the Moana. The Outrigger Reef is wedged between the Halekulani and an Outrigger condo property, the Waikiki Shores. Of the two, we prefer the Outrigger Waikiki because the pool is on the beach and the beach itself is nicer (we'd feel a tad claustrophobic sitting around the crowded Reef pool, which is squeezed between two high-rise buildings). In addition, our bath at the Reef was the smallest and tightest we'd seen in the state, and it was an oceanfront Voyagers Club (premium-class) room.

As with so many Waikiki hotels, there is an attached shopping mall at the Outrigger Waikiki on the street side. Both hotels feature rooms decorated in relentless pastel shades with light wood and rattan furnishings. All have a lanai, air conditioning, safe, cable TV, fridge, coffeemaker, hair dryer, iron and board. Each hotel has a small fitness center, a coin-operated laundry, room service, and several restaurants and bars—including Duke's (the Waikiki) and the Shorebird (the Reef). Both offer the Voyagers Club, which, for more money, gives you use of a lounge with complimentary continental breakfast, early evening cocktails, light snacks, newspapers (including the *New York Times*, the *Los Angeles Times*, and the *San Francisco Chronicle*), and a computer with Internet access so you can check your e-mail.

The other Outrigger properties are the aforementioned **Waikiki Shores** (a condo high-rise on the beach next to the Reef and Fort DeRussy), the **Outrigger East** (a block from the beach), and the **Outrigger Islander Waikiki** (at the busy intersection of Kalakaua and Lewers, about three blocks from the beach). These are cheaper than the Waikiki and the Reef, with the Waikiki Shores the nicest of the three and the best option for families and groups because the rooms are fully furnished with kitchenettes or full kitchens.

Rates are *Very Pricey* and up for the Waikiki and the Reef, *Pricey* and up for the Shores, the East, and the Islander.

The Ohana Hotels, 2375 Kuhio Avenue, Honolulu, HI 96815-2939. Toll-free: 800-462-6262. Direct reservations: 303-369-7777, fax 303-369-9403. Local: 808-921-6600, fax 808-622-4852.
Web site: www.ohanahotels.com

If you're on a budget, you may want to opt for an Ohana hotel (there are 15). Part of the Outrigger group (they were Outrigger hotels until a name change in December 1999), the Ohana mantra is "Waikiki, clean and simple." Don't expect anything fancy, but the price is very reasonable. All rooms have air-conditioning, safe, cable TV with movie channels, and fridge (no fridges in the Waikiki Coral Seas). All Ohana hotels have some rooms with kitchenettes. The Ohana Waikiki Towers and the Ohana Waikiki Village are closest to the water.

Rates are *Not So Cheap* and up.

Hotel Honolulu, 376 Kai'olu Street, Honolulu, HI 96815. Toll-free: 877-922-3824. Local: 808-922-2824, fax 808-922-5514.

Situated in the throbbing heart of Waikiki and known for its "themed rooms," this is a three-story hotel where the accommodations come in three sizes: standard studios, deluxe studios, and one-bedroom suites. Under new ownership and management, the hotel has been completely redone. The studios have queen-size beds, small kitchenettes, ceiling fans, and lanais. The difference between the two is that the deluxe rooms are decorated with different themes, from French, Japanese, Chippendale, and Hollywood to—in the spirit of camp—the Joan Collins suite. A few of the deluxe studios also have daybeds for a third person. The one-bedroom suites also carry a décor theme and have a king-size bed and a fully furnished sitting area with large lanai. The rooms do not have phones or TVs (although the latter are available).

Rates are *Cheap* and up.

The Rest of O'ahu

If Waikiki is just too much for you, yet you still want to be on O'ahu, there are several wonderful alternatives—including the adjacent and much calmer Diamond Head and the very tony Kahala Mandarin Oriental. There are also accommodations that will feel far removed from Honolulu on the windward side, North Shore, and leeward side.

Diamond Head

W, 2885 Kalakaua Avenue, Honolulu, HI 96815. Toll-free: 877-W-HOTELS (946-8357). Local: 808-922-1700, fax 808-923-2249. Rooms and suites: 46.
Web site: www.whotels.com

Finally, a true boutique hotel arrives in Hawai'i. Located next to the tony and private Outrigger Canoe Club and the New Otani (and formerly the Colony Surf Hotel), W is the most stylish accommodation in the state. Small and out of the Waikiki hubbub, design reigns like a queen over this place. While the name immediately, and cleverly, makes us think of the fashion rag, it really stands for "whatever you want whenever you want it" or any derivation of the "who, what, when, where" saying and has no affiliation with the Fairchild magazine. Billed as a mixture of city chic and destination resort, the Feng Shui lobby is understated, with earth tones, large white marble tiles, simple yet grand floral arrangements, and lots of fashion and art books. A video of different Hawai'ian scenes plays in a framed installation in the wonderfully dimly lit and canopied elevator (although we question the appropriateness of the wood-carved, swastika-motif handrail—hopefully, good taste will prevail and a replacement will be installed by the time this is published).

The pastel-free rooms are truly the "f" word—fabulous—and feature lots of thoughtful touches, including dual-line cordless

phones, VCRs and CD players, chenille throws, 250-thread-count sheets, goosedown pillows, 24-hour room service, stocked mini-fridges, and Aveda products. The corporate floors also have fax/copier/scanner/printer machines and oversize desks. All have lanais and sensible marble baths.

While there is no pool, the hotel is steps away from Sans Souci beach, a great place to swim. There is also a health club next door at the New Otani, and Kapiolani Park is just across the street (tennis and jogging, anyone?). W has a beautifully designed restaurant, the Diamond Head Grill (by Steven Jones of the Wolfgang Puck establishments), and a curving martini bar. There is a small private dining room that seats ten or more, where the chef will work with you on planning a personalized menu. A small conference area can accommodate your company's Hawai'ian getaway.

Rates are **Wicked Pricey** and up.

New Otani Kaimana Beach Hotel, 2863 Kalakaua Avenue, Honolulu, HI 96815. Toll-free: 800-356-8264. Toll-free California: 800-273-2294. Local: 808-923-1555, fax 808-922-9404. Rooms and suites: 125. Web site: www.kaimana.com

Bordered to the north by the 500-acre Kapiolani Park and in the shadow of Diamond Head, the New Otani is one step removed from the frenetic pace and traffic of Waikiki. Built on the water in 1964 in classic '60s architectural style, it is a quiet, unassuming hotel with unusual (for Hawai'i) Art Deco rooms at fairly reasonable rates. At the New Otani you can get a corner room right on the water with an fabulous view of Waikiki for under $300 per night—something you can't get in hotels of similar quality in the heart of Waikiki. The superb and tranquil Sans Souci beach right at the hotel is popular with locals and swimmers, as the water is calm and protected.

As we said, the rooms have an Art Deco flair and appropriately are a symphony of pastels. Each has a fridge and mini-bar. Many of the rooms have etched smoked glass and wraparound lanais. Definitely book a room on the ocean; the Ocean Studio Superior or Deluxe rooms allow you to hear the waves. All rooms have lanais and such amenities as in-room safes and voice mail. There are two restaurants, the Hau Tree and the Mikayo, a bar, and a small health club on the premises. The hotel is small enough that the friendly staff gets to know you quickly, an *aloha* touch. Our only complaints concern the courtyard, which could use a decorator's warm touch, the small size of the standard rooms, the lack of a swimming pool, and the absence of room service after 10 P.M.

Rates are *Pricey* and up.

Diamond Head Beach Hotel, 2947 Kalakaua Avenue, Honolulu, HI 96815. Toll-free: 800-367-2317. Local: 808-922-1928, fax 808-924-1982. Rooms and suites: 57.
Web site: www.diamondheadbeach.com

Located on the water down the street from W and the New Otani and closer to Diamond Head, this pencil-thin, 14-story hotel is artfully wedged between two other buildings. While not as desirable as the New Otani, it nonetheless has fairly comfortable rooms with lanais and a haphazard, rather dated-looking, pastel-ish décor with bamboo furniture and wall-to-wall carpeting. The hotel also has suites with full kitchens. There is no pool, restaurant, or room service, but the units do have CD players—a plus. There is a small beach to the right of the hotel, and Kapiolani Park is on the other side of the street.

Rates are *Pricey* and up (CP).

Kahala

The Kahala Mandarin Oriental, 5000 Kahala Avenue, Honolulu, HI 96816-5498. Toll-free U.S.: 800-367-2525, Canada: 800-526-6566. Local: 808-739-8888, fax 808-739-8859. Rooms and suites: 371.
Web site: www.mandarinoriental.com

For people in the know and with the means, there are three places to stay on O'ahu: the Halekulani, W, and the Kahala Mandarin Oriental. Those who shun Waikiki and want a quiet stay at a spacious resort should opt for the Kahala Mandarin. For decades known as the Kahala Hilton, the hotel changed hands and reopened in 1996 after an extensive renovation (the old faded WASP look is gone). The private setting has made it a favorite of movie stars, celebrities, and heads of state over the years.

There is a reason for the Kahala Mandarin Oriental's continued

celebrity. It is the prettiest, most spacious, and calmest hotel/resort in Honolulu. The thrills and spills of Waikiki and downtown are a short drive around Diamond Head, yet on this side it's very quiet and very chi-chi. Kahala is one of the most desirable communities in Hawaiʻi (and one of the most expensive). Real estate prices here will make your head spin—a ranch house on a postage stamp can cost well over a million. Bordering the hotel grounds are the fairways of the Waiʻalae Country Club, the site of the annual Hawaiʻian Open. It is virtually impossible to book a room here during that week. The mountains of Maunalua Valley and Koko Head rise up in distant green splendor. Maunalua Bay, large and fairly calm, fronts the property. The Kahala Mandarin Oriental has its own beach, which although man-made, is ideal for swimming and features a complete water-sports center. There is also a 26,000-square-foot man-made lagoon where guests (and non-guests when space is available) are able to get very up-close-and-personal with Atlantic bottlenose dolphins (see the Swimming with Dolphins section earlier in this chapter).

The architecture of the hotel is classic early '60s and is uniquely distinctive. The main building, a ten-story structure, is the tallest structure in Kahala and is a landmark. Latticework designed to support cascades of bougainvillea envelopes the main building. As it turns out, the trade winds have prevented anything from growing. Rather than take down the lattice, the hotel decided to leave it up, and it has become the building's distinguishing feature. The lobby of the hotel is also vintage '60s and very elegant. There are three one-ton multicolored glass chandeliers hovering over wicker-furnished seating areas with parquet floors.

The parquet-floored and carpeted guest rooms are very comfortably furnished and nicely decorated in muted tones with white/tan linens and cottons. Furnishings are in the turn of the 19th century Hawaiʻian style (with four-poster beds) with Asian accents. The lanais are spacious, tiled, and feature Brown Jordan furniture (the least expensive rooms do not have lanais). All rooms have a dressing area, cable TV, safe, two-line phone with data port, clock radio/CD player, mini-bar, and spacious tiled bath with separate glass-enclosed shower, big tub with handheld shower, mahogany vanities, and separate loo with phone. Guests have the option of staying in the main building or choosing a room in the two-story Lagoon Terrace. Some of the rooms in the latter are right on the beach. Personally, we'd prefer being up high with a lanai in the main building.

Guests have use of the Maunalua Bay Club for tennis, and with a little effort and the help of the manager, you should be able to wrangle an introduction to one of the private country clubs for a round on the links. There is an oval pool for those who shun the beach. A fitness center with steam, sauna, and Jacuzzi is available on site. Several restaurants are on the premises, including Hoku's—one of the best on the island. There is nightly entertainment in the Honu Bar and Terrace.

Rates are *Very Pricey* and up.

Downtown Honolulu

"When you're alone and life is making you lonely you can always go . . . " Oops, sorry, Pet Clark's ditty pops into our mind whenever we think of that center-city term. So why would anyone want to stay downtown, you ask? Well, it's different, near lots of interesting historical sites, and also next to Chinatown and the Art District.

Aston at the Executive Centre Hotel, 1088 Bishop Street, Honolulu, HI 96813. Toll-free: 800-922-7866. Local: 808-539-3000, fax 808-523-1088. Rooms and suites: 116.
Web site: www.aston-hotels.com

Located in the heart of Honolulu's financial district on Bishop Street, this hotel caters to the business traveler. Set in a sleek glass high-rise, its views of the city and harbor are quite stunning. Its location next to the Chinatown/Art District and historic government buildings may appeal to some, as may its rates, which are lower than Waikiki. There is a 20-meter outdoor pool and a 24-hour fitness center, as well as a coin-operated laundry and 24-hour business center. All rooms come with three phones with voice mail and data port, cable TV, fridge, safe, whirlpool bath, iron and board, and coffeemaker. Executive Suites have a full

kitchen and washer/dryer.

Rates are *Not So Cheap* and up.

The North Shore

Turtle Bay Resort, 57-091 Kamehameha Highway, Kahuku, HI 96731. Toll-free: 800-203-3650. Local: 808-293-8811, fax 808-293-9147. Rooms, suites, and cabanas: 485.

Web site: www.turtlebayhotel.com

Set on 808 acres at Kuilima Point on the spectacular northeastern tip of O'ahu, this is the only resort (formerly the Hilton Turtle Bay Golf & Tennis Resort) on the North Shore. Sunset Beach and all its fabled surf breaks are just minutes away, At press time, the new owners are implementing a $35 million renovation, including an restoration/expansion of the golf courses and the addition of a full-service spa. At the moment, there are 27 holes of golf, including the 18-hole Arnold Palmer Course (designed by Arnold Palmer and Ed Seay and formerly called the Links at Kuilima), ten tennis courts, horseback riding, and two pools. Turtle Bay has its own protected beach—one of the safest places to swim on the North Shore—as well as two pools. As this is the windward side, be forewarned that although it's much drier than the coast farther south, during the winter it rains more here than in Honolulu.

The hotel, which will remain open during the renovation, has 485 rooms, suites, and cabanas (the latter have kitchen facilities). Rooms, suites and cabanas are being refurbished in phases with the last phase scheduled for completion in the fall of 2002. All have lanais, cable TV, coffeemaker, hair dryer, iron and board, mini-fridge, and phones. There is a coin-operated laundry, room service, baby-sitting service availability, seasonal children's program and an exercise room. ADA approved rooms are also available. The hotel has five restaurants/lounges, two of which will change their cuisine concepts during the renovation. For nightlife, Hale'iwa has Steamer's, a real surfer hangout, or the mellower scene at the hotel's Bay View lounge. Otherwise, it's early to bed or drive an hour and a half to get to Waikiki.

Rates are *Not So Cheap* and up.

The Windward Side

Paul Comeau's Condos at Pat's at Punaluʻu, (P.O. Box 589), 53-567 Kamehameha Highway, Kaʻaʻawa, HI 96730. Toll-free: 800-467-6215. Local: 808-293-2624, fax 808-293-0618. Rental units: 21.
Web site: turtlebaycondos.com/comeau

Pat's location, on what's probably the most beautiful part of Oʻahu, is the reason for staying here. Set right on the water, the building itself is hideous—the only high-rise on this otherwise bucolic seascape, where the verdant *pali* rise steeply from the beach. Be forewarned that this is one of the wettest parts of the island, and it is often cloudy or raining here when it's sunny in Honolulu, especially in the wintertime.

The studio, one-, two-, and three-bedroom units are basic condos and each is owner-decorated, so hope for everything and expect nothing. All units have fully equipped kitchens, cable TV, phones, and washer/dryer availability. Oceanfront units will guarantee the constant sound of waves and breezes from the trades. Units facing south will offer incredible views of the shoreline and the mountains. There is a small convenience store, a pool, a sauna, and a small gym on the premises.

Rates are **Cheap** and up.

Kailua

There are several "vacation rentals" available in this fashionable bedroom community and windsurfing center. Many of the surf shops offer packages or help in securing lodging in the area. Among the bigger listings are the following:

Kailuana: Kailua Beachfront Vacation Homes, (P.O. Box 841), 133 Kailuana Place, Kailua, HI 96734. Toll-free: 800-551-0948. Local and fax: 808-261-8903.
Web site: www.kailuana.com

There are only two units here: a one-bedroom cottage (sleeps up to four) and a three-bedroom, two-bath house (sleeps up to eight). Both are comfortable, well maintained, and come with a range of amenities, including washer/dryer, TV/VCR, stereo-tape player, hot outdoor shower, ceiling fans, and lots of books. There is no a/c, but the trades take care of ventilation. The property is located right on

the beach and is a nice way to stay in this chic suburb. If you're a windsurfer, this may be a terrific choice. Minimum stay is five days; maid service is available on request.

Rates are **Pricey** for the one-bedroom cottage and **Very Pricey** for the three-bedroom house.

Pat's Kailua Beach Properties, 204 S. Kalaheo Avenue, Kailua, HI 96734. Local: 808-262-4128 or 808-261-1653, fax 808-261-0893. Web site: www.10kvacationrentals.com/pats

With over 30 properties in Kailua/Lani Kai and more in neighboring Waimanalo, Pat's has a place for your budget and needs. There are beachfront homes, houses with pools, and cottages, all on or near the water. All units are fully furnished, have complete kitchens plus a variety of amenities, and can sleep anywhere from 2 to 15 people.

Rates are **Cheap** and up.

The Leeward Side

The leeward side is a part of Oʻahu that most tourists never see. This is really unfortunate, because it is one of the most stunning settings not only on Oʻahu but in all of Hawaiʻi. The weather here is the driest and sunniest on the island, and the beaches and sunsets are terrific. Why don't people see it? Because it is the land of the local—their last bastion. True, there are other pockets where pidgin predominates, such as Waimanalo and Hauʻula, but "Waianae Side" is the stronghold. And some of the tougher *mokes*, as hard-guy locals are called, don't like seeing *haoles* encroaching on their home turf—an understandable feeling. Stories of tourist harassment are rampant about this area, and incidents do occur. But an aware traveler who is sensitive to this resentment can certainly enjoy not only visiting here but staying here as well. It's just a case again of "when in Rome, do as the Romans do." Don't plan a champagne and caviar picnic on Makaha Beach with Vivaldi on the boom box—you're just asking for it. Rather, pull the car up to the beach, set up some beach chairs by the open trunk, pop a cold one, and enjoy a plate lunch (a Hawaiʻian favorite). Always avoid a group of big *mokes* drinking beer, which is common sense anywhere, and never take a local boy's wave ("Hoo, you like beef or whot?," meaning, "Do you wanna fight?").

J. W. Marriott Ihilani Resort and Spa, Ko'Olina Resort, 92-1001 Olani Street, Kapolei, HI 96707. Toll-free: 800-626-4446. Local: 808-679-0079, fax 808-679-0080. Rooms and suites: 387.
Web site: www.ihilani.com

The Ihilani Resort and Spa changed hands in 1999 and is now part of the Marriott chain. Built by a Japanese company and opened in 1993, its design and golf features reflect the Japanese affinity for white, stark atriums, pagoda-style roofs, and fairways along the ocean. Part of the 640-acre Ko'Olina Resort located on the dry southwestern tip of O'ahu, Ihilani's location is a tad removed, which should be a consideration if you want to be near Honolulu and Waikiki (about 45 minutes away). However, the Ihilani has a 35,000-square-foot spa with a slew of services including hydrotherapies, massage, herbal wraps, yoga, T'ai Chi, and a fitness center. Outside, there is an 18-hole, Ted Robinson–designed 6,867-yard championship golf course, a man-made lagoon with a large crescent beach, excellent for swimming (and several others farther south), a new 270-slip marina, a circular pool, and six tennis courts. Plans for the rest of the Ko'Olina Resort include a timeshare property at its southern end and condos/villas in the middle along the golf course.

Rooms and suites in the 15-story hotel are ample, with tan wall-to-wall carpeting, wicker and rattan furnishings, and a pleasant décor of pale greens, golds, tans, and creams. All have tiled lanais with cushioned teak furniture, and big marble baths with deep European tubs, separate glass shower enclosures, double vanities, and separate loos. Other amenities include cable TV, CD player, mini-bar/fridge, safe, and the highest-tech phones we've seen in the Aloha State. There is 24-hour room service, and there are four restaurants in the hotel.

Rates are **Wicked Pricey** and up.

Where to Eat

As you can well imagine, there is a tsunami of restaurants on O'ahu, as Honolulu is a major city and a meeting place of Pacific Rim, American, and world cuisines. The restaurants represent the cuisines of 21 nations and a range of lifestyles. Making a decision can be overwhelming.

Most of the best restaurants are outside of Waikiki and provide a great excuse to see the rest of Honolulu, which is a wonderful and attractive city in what must be one of the most beautiful settings in the world. The Downtown area is one of the most pleasant in the country, and Chinatown is a must-see and a happening place (much safer and more spruced-up than it used to be). Kaimuki, wedged between Waikiki, Diamond Head, and the mountains, has become one of Honolulu's hot restaurant districts.

While we love to dish out the dish on the places where we wouldn't be caught dead eating, space keeps a slight muzzle on our often sharp tongues. *Unless*, of course, we just *have* to let it loose. Suffice to say that if we haven't included a restaurant, don't bother. Of course we're not infallible, and we may miss a great spot or a new one that has opened after going to press. Please let us know if we have, or what you think of our recommendations, by e-mailing us at aloha@rumreggae.com. The listings below are in alphabetical order.

Downtown Honolulu

A Little Bit of Saigon, 1160 Maunakea, Downtown Honolulu, 528-3663. Delicious Vietnamese food (with great pho) for lunch and dinner. Open daily 10 A.M. to 10 P.M. $$

Ba-Le French Sandwich & Bakery, 150 N. King Street, Downtown Honolulu, 521-3973. When in Chinatown, be sure to visit this simple Vietnamese establishment for some fine sandwiches (the tuna is excellent) on crusty French bread, croissants, and French coffee with ice and condensed milk. Also great here are the shrimp rolls and the papaya salad. Ironically, this is one of the best places to buy baguettes, as they bake their own and have developed quite a reputation (the shop bakes around 1,500 loaves a day). The great news is that it is cheap and that there are almost 20 shops all over O'ahu! Open daily 6 A.M. to 5 P.M. $

Some Other Ba-le Locations

1019 University Avenue, Honolulu, 943-0507.

1450 Ala Moana Center, Honolulu, 944- 4752.

Kahala Mall, 4211 Wai'alae Avenue, Kahala, 735-6889.

Café Che Pasta, 1001 Bishop Street, Downtown Honolulu, 524-0004. Good fresh pastas in a gallery setting, popular with the lunch crowd. Evening performance art, cabaret, and DJ nights make it fun at night too. Open Sunday through Thursday 11 A.M. to 9 P.M., Friday and Saturday 9 A.M. to 2 A.M. $$

Chai's Island Bistro, Aloha Tower Marketplace, 1 Aloha Tower Drive, Downtown Honolulu, 585-0011. This is the second highly successful venture by Chai Chaowasaree, who brought us Singha Thai in Waikiki. But unlike Singha Thai, the cuisine here is Hawai'ian regional. Chai's is a happening spot with live entertainment nightly. Reservations suggested. Open daily 11 A.M. to 10 P.M. $$$$

Duc's Bistro, 1188 Maunakea Street, Downtown Honolulu, 531-6325. French-Vietnamese with panache and a fun atmosphere. Open for lunch Monday through Friday, 11:30 A.M. to 2 P.M., open daily for dinner 5 to 10 P.M. $$$

Indigo, 1121 Nu'uanu Avenue (at Hotel Street), Downtown Honolulu, 521-2900.We *love* this place! Not only is this high-tin-ceilinged restaurant one of the chic-est spots in town, right down to the attractive staff, but chef Glenn Chu's food is great too. Try the Tempura Ahi Roll—it's orgasmic. On Thursday and Friday nights, local DJs rock the house. The bar in the back is a fun hangout and features great Cosmopolitans. Every night is Martini Night ($2.75 each) from 5 to 6:30 P.M. Reservations suggested. Lunch is served Tuesday through Friday from 11:30 A.M. to 2 P.M., dinner Tuesday through Saturday from 6 to 10 P.M. $$$

Palomino Euro Bistro, Harbor Court, 66 Queen Street, Downtown Honolulu, 528-2400. This Mediterranean-style restaurant is actually part of a mainland chain. Nevertheless, this is a lively place with a bustling lunch scene and after-work crowd (the bar is large, the way we like our drinks) and eating here won't break the bank. Lunch is served Monday through Friday from 11:30

A.M. to 2:30 P.M. Dinner is served Sunday through Thursday from 5 to 10 P.M., Friday and Saturday to 11 P.M. $$$

People's Cafe, 1300 Pali Highway, Downtown Honolulu, 536-5789. This is the place to sample *ono* (delicious) Hawaiʻian food when you're downtown. Owned by the same Japanese family for generations. Open from 10 A.M. to 7:30 P.M., closed Sunday. $

Wong on Wong, 1023 Maunakea Street, Downtown Honolulu, 521-4492. It looks like a dump but the food is good and authentic Chinese. Open daily from 10:30 A.M. to 11 P.M. $$

Zaffron, 69 N. King Street, Downtown Honolulu, 533-6635. Surprisingly, there aren't many choices for Indian food in Honolulu, but this simple setting is probably your best bet. Open for lunch Tuesday through Friday from 11 A.M. to 2:30 P.M., dinner Thursday through Saturday from 6 to 9:30 P.M. $$

Honolulu

Alan Wong's, 1157 S. King Street, Honolulu, 949-2526. One of the most critically acclaimed restaurants in the state (and winner of the James Beard Award in 1996), Chef Wong's place has caused a sensation with its creative Hawaiʻian regional fare (with the accent on fresh seafood) and superb wine list. Reservations a must. Open daily from 5 to 10 P.M. $$$$

A Pacific Café, Ward Centre (2nd floor), 1200 Ala Moana Boulevard, Honolulu, 593-0618. This popular Hawaiʻian chain serves tasty Pacific Rim cuisine in an interesting, if somewhat odd, décor/space. Open for dinner nightly from 5:30 to 9:30 P.M. Free parking. Reservations suggested. $$$

Auntie Pasto's, 1099 S. Beretania Street, Honolulu, 523-8855. Big portions and a convivial atmosphere highlight this fun place (and Honolulu institution) for a bowl of pasta. Open Monday through Thursday 11 A.M. to 10:30 P.M., Friday 11 A.M. to 11 P.M., and Saturday 4 to 11 P.M. $$$

Chef Mavro, 1969 S. King Street (at McCully), Honolulu, 944-4714. Chef George Mavrothalassitis (formerly of La Mer and the Four Seasons Maui) creates a fusion of Hawaiʻian and French cuisines, and is the talk of the town. Reservations suggested. Open Tuesday through Sunday 6 to 9:30 P.M. $$$$$

Columbia Inn, 645 Kapiolani Boulevard, Honolulu, 596-0757. A local hangout and a local institution. Open Sunday through Thursday 6 A.M. to 11 P.M., Friday and Saturday to midnight. $

Down to Earth, 2525 S. King Street (at University Avenue), Honolulu, 947-7678. This is natural fast food that is both very tasty and good for you, within a great health-food store. Open from 7:30 A.M. to 10 P.M. daily. $

Garden Cafe, Honolulu Academy of the Arts, 900 S. Beretania Street, Honolulu, 532-8734. This is a very civilized and peaceful setting in which to have lunch. Reservations are recommended. Open Tuesday through Saturday, from 11:30 A.M. to 2 P.M. $$

John Dominis, 43 Ahui Street (at Kewalo Basin), Honolulu, 523-0955. John Dominis is probably the most famous (and expensive) seafood restaurant in Honolulu. With great views of the harbor and a reputation for *fresh* fish (and fresh service), this is a very popular place with tourists and locals alike—so reservations are a must. Open Sunday through Thursday 6 to 9 P.M., Friday and Saturday 5:30 to 9:30 P.M. $$$$

Kincaid's Fish Chop and Steakhouse, Ward Warehouse, 1050 Ala Moana Boulevard, Honolulu, 591-2005. This is a superb seafood restaurant with an excellent selection of fresh island fish prepared any way you want it (and don't forget the steaks, too). A lunch favorite, it's also open for dinner. Reservations suggested. Open daily for lunch from 11 A.M. to 2:30 P.M., dinner 5 to 10 P.M. $$$

Mariposa, Neiman Marcus, Ala Moana Center, 1450 Ala Moana Boulevard, Honolulu, 951-3420. With a fabulous view of the harbor from the store's third floor and all those ridiculously priced clothes to try on afterwards, chef Douglas Lum's restaurant offers a fusion of Pacific Rim and Texas cuisines that is certainly different, refreshing, and needless to say, expensive. Open for lunch and afternoon tea (Monday through Saturday), dinner (nightly), and Sunday brunch. Open for lunch 11 A.M. to 3 P.M. daily, dinner Monday through Saturday 5 to 10 P.M., Sunday to 9 P.M. Reservations suggested. $$$$

Mekong, 1995 S. Beretania Street, Honolulu, 591-8842.

Mekong 2, 1726 S. King Street, Honolulu, 941-6184. These restaurants offer the same delicious food as Keo's Thai Cuisine (the

Mekongs are owned by Keo), but it's decidedly cheaper here. The difference is that Keo's atmosphere is much more festive and glitzy. Mekong is the original, and many feel it has more intimacy and atmosphere than the newer Mekong 2. Open for lunch Monday through Friday 11 A.M. to 2 P.M., daily for dinner from 5 to 9:30 P.M. $$

Yanagi Sushi, 762 Kapiolani Blvd., Honolulu, 537-1525. This is a terrific sushi/sashimi bar and restaurant. Yum! Open daily for lunch from 11 A.M. to 2 P.M., dinner from 5:30 P.M. until 2 A.M. except on Sundays, when they close at 10 P.M. $$

Zippy's, Well known for its chili, this Denny's- or Friendly's-gone-Hawai'ian serves a good plate lunch as well. Open 24/7. $

Some Honolulu locations:

1725 S. King Street, Honolulu, 973-0880.

3345 Wai'alae Avenue, Kaimuki, 733-3722.

601 Kapahulu, Kaimuki, 733-3725.

1222 S. King Street, Makiki, 594-3720.

Ala Moana Center, Honolulu, 973-0870.

Koko Marina Shopping Center, Honolulu, 396-6977.

Kaimuki

3660 On The Rise, 3660 Wai'alae Avenue, Kaimuki, 737-1177. Serving acclaimed Pacific Rim cuisine in a crowded and lively place, chef Russell Siu's restaurant is very popular. Open Tuesday through Thursday 5:30 to 9 P.M., Friday and Saturday to 10 P.M., closed Monday. $$$

Boston's North End Pizza, 3506 Wai'alae Avenue (at 10th Avenue), Kaimuki, 734-1945. This is a chain with several locations that locals seem to love (and being Bostonians, we know about North End pizza). Open Sunday through Thursday 11 A.M. to 9 P.M., Friday and Saturday to 10 P.M. $$

Champa Thai, 5432 Wai'alae Avenue (at 9th Avenue), Kaimuki, 732-0054. With two other locations, including Kailua on the windward side, this is Kaimuki's best Thai fare. Open daily 5 to 9:30 P.M. $$

Hale Vietnam, 1140 12th Avenue (at Wai'alae Avenue), Kaimuki, 735-7581. Great and cheap Vietnamese food. Open daily 11 A.M. to 10 P.M. $$

Hee Hing, 449 Kapahulu Avenue, Kaimuki, 735-5544. Dim sum and a local fave for Cantonese and Szechuan. Open daily 10:30 A.M. to 9:30 P.M. $$

Irifune, 563 Kapahulu Avenue (at Campbell), Honolulu, 737-1141. This is a local Japanese favorite offering great food and sushi in a modest atmosphere and at very reasonable prices. Open Tuesday through Saturday for lunch from 11:30 A.M. to 1:30 P.M., dinner 5:30 to 9:30 P.M., closed Sunday and Monday. $$

Jose's Mexican Restaurant, 1134 Koko Head Avenue, Kaimuki, 732-1833. Good Mexican fare that's popular with local residents. Open daily 11 A.M. to 10 P.M., Sunday till 9 P.M. $$

Leonard's, 933 Kapahulu Avenue, Kaimuki, 737-5591. Wonderfully light and chewy *malasadas* (portuguese donuts)—you could easily eat several—plus sweet breads, pastries, and an assortment of standard bakery pies and cakes. Open daily 6 A.M. to 9 P.M., Friday and Saturday until 10 P.M. $

Ono Hawai'ian Foods, 726 Kapahulu Avenue, Kaimuki, 737-2275. This is a cheaper way to try Hawai'ian food in Honolulu. It's tiny, but the kalua pig and the lomi lomi salmon are so *ono* (delicious). The walls are plastered with photos of previous patrons and local talents. Open from 11 A.M. to 7:30 P.M., closed Sunday. $

Rainbow Drive-In, 3308 Kanaina Avenue, Kaimuki, 737-0177. This is the closest and best location for plate lunch near Waikiki. It has an old-fashioned drive-in atmosphere and great food too, although the macaroni salad is a little heavy on the mayo. Popular with locals. Open daily 7:30 A.M. to 9:30 P.M. $

SushiMan, 3036 Wai'alae Avenue, Kaimuki, 734-0944; 1471 Kapiolani Boulevard, Honolulu, 941-8383. This no-nonsense sushi bar chain offers sushi at about the best prices you'll find on the island. Open daily 10 A.M. to 10 P.M., Sunday 11 A.M. to 8 P.M. $

Waikiki

Most of the best dining options in Waikiki are fabulous *and* incredibly expensive. Those on a budget in search of good dining should head just north of Waikiki along King Street or to Kaimuki. Many of our Waikiki recommendations are Japanese restaurants.

Cheeseburger in Paradise, 2500 Kalakaua Avenue, Waikiki, 923-

3731. This chain is a good place for its namesake and always a hubbub of activity. Open for breakfast, lunch, and dinner daily, 8 A.M. to 11:30 P.M. $$

Furasato, Hyatt Regency Waikiki, 2424 Kalakaua Avenue, Waikiki, 922-4991. Incredible as it may sound, it's hard to find a really good sushi restaurant in Waikiki. This is an excellent choice, although it's not cheap. Open daily from 5:30 to 10:30 P.M. $$$

Hy's Steak House, Waikiki Park Heights Hotel, 2440 Kuhio Avenue, Waikiki, 922-5555. This decades-old local favorite is consistently ranked one of the best steak houses in the state. Reservations suggested. Open Sunday through Thursday 5:30 to 10 P.M., Friday and Saturday until 10:30 P.M. $$$$

Kacho, Waikiki Parc Hotel, 2233 Helumoa Road, Waikiki, 921-7272. This is an excellent Japanese restaurant with a serene atmosphere. Open daily from 5:30 to 10 P.M. $$$

Keo's Thai Cuisine, Ambassador Hotel, 2040 Kuhio Avenue, Waikiki, 951-9355. This is the offspring of the tony Thai restaurant once located on Kapahulu and often credited with introducing fancy Thai food to Honolulu. When the waiter asks what you'd like for a cocktail, try the Evil Princess, if only for its name (a delicious frozen rum drink of pineapple and coconut that sounds like a piña colada but is tart and tastier). After quaffing the Princess, try the Evil Prince, a creamy peanut-based dish. Reservations suggested. Open Sunday through Thursday from 5 to 10:30 P.M., Friday and Saturday until 11 P.M. $$$

Kobe Japanese Steak House, 1841 Ala Moana Boulevard., Waikiki, 941-4444. The Japanese version of surf n' turf, this is a teppanyaki restaurant with knife-tossing samurai chefs and a nice sushi bar. Open Sunday through Thursday from 5:30 to 10 P.M., Friday and Saturday until 10:30 P.M. (sushi bar open until 1 A.M.) $$$

La Mer, The Halekulani, 2199 Kalia Road, Waikiki, 923-2311. Under the direction of chef Yves Garnier, La Mer is one of the best French/continental restaurants in the state. The prix-fixe five-course dinner and the à la carte menu change monthly and will make you rave (the desserts are extraordinary). Located on the second floor in an oh-so-elegant muraled room in the old main hotel building with wonderful views of the water, this is an excellent splurge or special-occasion place, as the service is superb and the price tag is orbital. Dressy (jackets for men, dresses for women). Reservations required. Open daily from 6 to 10 P.M. $$$$$

Odoriko, King's Village, 2400 Koa Avenue, Waikiki, 926-7755. While the décor is beyond tacky, the kimono-clad waitresses, the all-Japanese clientele, and the best California roll in town make this a worthwhile sushi stop (try to ignore the turtles in the holding tank). Open 5:30 A.M. to midnight, closed Sunday. $$$

Orchids, The Halekulani, 2199 Kalia Road, Waikiki, 923-2311. While not as fancy or as expensive as La Mer and offering a more pan-Pacific menu, the Halekulani's other restaurant is still one of Waikiki's best. Sunday brunch (9:30 A.M. to 2:30 P.M.) is a Honolulu institution. Reservations suggested, especially for brunch. Open nightly from 6 to 10 P.M. $$$$

The Royal Luau, Royal Hawai'ian Hotel, 2259 Kalakaua Avenue, Waikiki, 923-7311. Held on Sundays at 6 P.M., the luau takes place on the lawn with sunset cocktails and mai tais (the Royal Hawai'ian is reputed to be the originator of the mai tai). Entertainment is provided by the Royal Polynesian Extravaganza. While not really as authentic as luaus on the neighboring islands, this is a good, if touristy, luau in the heart of Waikiki. $$$

Singha Thai, 1910 Ala Moana Boulevard, Waikiki, 941-2898. A consistently good Thai restaurant with a fun atmosphere. It's worth a stop. Open daily from 4 to 11 P.M. $$$

Diamond Head

Diamond Head Grill, W, 2885 Kalakaua Avenue (2nd floor), Diamond Head, 922-3734. While the space and the curved martini bar are *faboo* (designed by Wolfgang Puck's architect, Steven Jones), the food by new head chef, David Reardon, is over the top and lacks focus. There are just too many contrasting flavors, especially in the delicate opakapaka fish we had. Hopefully this place will find its groove soon. Reservations suggested. Open Sunday through Thursday from 5 to 10 P.M., Friday and Saturday 5:30 to 10 P.M. $$$$

Hau Tree Lanai, New Otani Hotel, 2863 Kalakaua Avenue, Diamond Head, 921-7066. With a fabulous view of the beach and Waikiki, a waterfront location, and the fabled hau tree and stars overhead, this al fresco dining location is a fabulous place to pop the question. Oh yes, the continental food is very good too. Reservations suggested. Open daily for breakfast from 7 to 10:45 A.M., lunch from 11:30 A.M. to 1:45 P.M., dinner from 5:30 to 8:45 P.M. $$$$

Michel's, Colony Surf Hotel, 2895 Kalakaua Avenue, Diamond Head, 923-6552. Try to ignore the fact that this was named the most romantic restaurant in the world in Robin Leach's *Lifestyles of the Rich and Famous*. Michel's is a wonderful place to dine on superb French/continental cuisine, and the view of Waikiki and Honolulu from this waterfront spot is fabulous. Yes, it is romantic too. Dressy (jackets for men). Reservations a must. Open daily from 5:30 to 9 P.M. $$$$

Miyako Japanese Restaurant, New Otani Hotel, 2863 Kalakaua Avenue, Diamond Head, 923-4739. A pleasant little restaurant serving lunch and dinner in a calm setting outside of Waikiki. Open daily from 5:30 to 9 P.M. $$$

Kahala and East Honolulu

Ba-Le French Sandwich & Bakery, Kahala Mall, 4211 Wai'alae Avenue, Kahala, 735-6889. Like the original in Chinatown, this simple establishment offers some fine sandwiches (the tuna is excellent) on crusty French bread, croissants, and French coffee with ice and condensed milk. Also great are the shrimp rolls and the papaya salad. Open daily 9 A.M. to 9 P.M. $

Bubbies Homemade Ice Cream, Kahala Mall, 4211 Wai'alae Avenue, Kahala, 739-2822. We all occasionally scream for ice cream, so scream over to this hot spot. Open daily 10 A.M. to 12 midnight. $

Hoku's, Kahala Mandarin Oriental, 5000 Kahala Avenue, Kahala, 739-8888. With beautiful views of Maunalua Bay, this multilevel restaurant is attractively decorated with natural woods, creamy colors, banquettes, and an open kitchen. The pan-Pacific and Hawai'ian regional cuisine has been an O'ahu favorite for several years. Reservations suggested. Open for lunch Sunday through Friday 11:30 A.M. to 2:30 P.M., dinner daily from 5:30 to 10 P.M. $$$$

Roy's, 6600 Kalaniana'ole Highway, Hawai'i Kai, Honolulu, 396-7697. Roy Yamaguchi is famous in the Aloha State, having made a reputation with this restaurant in Hawai'i Kai and now by hosting his own PBS show called *Hawai'i Cooks*. One of the pioneers of Pacific Rim/Hawai'ian regional cuisine when he opened this restaurant in 1988, he now has 17 restaurants on four Hawai'ian islands, around the Pacific Rim, and on the U.S. mainland. That said, this is a popular, lively place and is always packed. More important, the food lives up to its esteemed reputation. Open Sunday through Thursday from 5 to 9 P.M., Friday and Saturday 5:30 to 10 P.M. Reservations strongly advised. $$$$

Swiss Inn, 5370 Kalaniana'ole Highway, Niu Valley, 377-5447. Just minutes out of Waikiki is this cherished restaurant serving, of all things, wiener schnitzel and continental fare with veal accents. It's very popular with residents, so a reservation is a good idea, especially for Sunday brunch. Open Wednesday through Sunday for dinner from 6 to 9:30 P.M. Closed Monday and Tuesday. $$$

The Windward Side

Ahi's Punalu'u, 53-146 Kamehameha Highway, Punalu'u, 237-8474. Shrimp, cultivated just up the coast, is the specialty at this very casual joint in the heart of the windward side. Open for lunch and dinner 11 A.M. to 9 P.M., closed Sunday. Live entertainment on most nights. $$

Boston's North End Pizza, 29 Ho'olai Street, Kailua, 263-2253; 45-568 Kamehameha Highway, Kaneohe, 235-7756. This is a chain with several locations that locals seem to love. Open daily 11 A.M. to 9 P.M., Friday and Saturday until 10 P.M. $$

Buzz's Original Steak House, 413 Kawailoa Road, Kailua, 261-4661. A Polynesian atmosphere predominates in this cozy place where charbroiled steaks and seafood are served. There is a good salad bar too. Cash only! Open daily for lunch 11 A.M. to 2:30 P.M. and dinner 5 to 9 P.M. $$$

Champa Thai, 306 Kuulei Road, Kailua, 263-8281. This is the best

Thai option on the windward side. At press time they were in the process of moving, so call before heading over!

Giovanni's Aloha Shrimp, Kamehameha Highway (by the Kahuku Sugar Mill complex), Kahuku, 293-1839. Actually a graffiti-covered white truck, this is the best place to go for a quick shrimp cocktail, grilled shrimp, shrimp scampi, or hot and spicy shrimp plate. Giovanni's is the perfect touch after a day on the beach and for those with an acute case of the munchies. It's a popular hangout, so beware of tour buses. Open daily 10:30 A.M. to 6:30 P.M. $

Ka'a'awa Grinds, 51-480B Kamehameha Highway, Ka'a'awa (next to the 7-11), 237-1114. This small take-out counter has some of the best Teriaki barbecued chicken we've tasted, and the best plate lunch on O'ahu. Open 7:30 A.M. to 3:30 P.M., closed Wednesday. $

The North Shore

Cholo's Homestyle Mexican, 66-250 Kamehameha Highway, Northshore Marketplace, Hale'iwa, 637-3059. This is a cheap and cheerful taqueria serving breakfast, lunch, and dinner. Open daily 8 A.M. to 9 P.M. $

Hale'iwa Joe's Seafood Grill, 66-011 Kamehameha Highway, Hale'iwa, 637-8005. Right in town by the Rainbow Bridge with a nice view of the harbor. Popular choices at this seafood restaurant feature the fresh seared *ahi* and baked *ono*. This place also becomes a local surfer hangout after dinner. Open daily for lunch 11:30 A.M. to 4 P.M., dinner 5:30 to 9:30 P.M. $$$

Jameson's By the Sea, 62-540 Kamehameha Highway, Hale'iwa, 637-4336-. This is a North Shore institution and a very nice place to enjoy the sunset with a cocktail or some fresh fish dishes in the upstairs dining room overlooking Hale'iwa Bay. There are outposts of this restaurant in downtown Honolulu and on neighboring islands. Open daily 11 A.M. to 9 P.M., Saturday and Sunday open at 9 A.M. $$$

Kua'Aina Sandwich, 66-214 Kamehameha Highway, Hale'iwa, 637-6067. Renowned for its burgers, it's always crowded. There's an outpost in Honolulu now at the Ward Village Shops (1116

Auahi Street, 591-9133). No credit cards. Open daily 11 A.M. to 8 P.M. $

Pizza Bob's, Hale'iwa Shopping Plaza, Hale'iwa, 637-5095. Hand-rolled pizza in surfer heaven makes this a popular spot. Open daily 11 A.M. to 9 P.M., Friday and Saturday until 10 P.M. $

West O'ahu

Azul, J. W. Marriott Ihilani Resort and Spa, 92-1001 Olani Street, Kapolei, 679-0079. This is the leeward side's best restaurant, and its most expensive too. The cuisine is Mediterranean, prepared by chef Mark Adair, and the wine list is quite extensive. Reservations suggested. Open from 6 to 9 P.M., closed Sunday and Monday. $$$$$

Germaine's Luau, Ewa Beach, 949-6626 or 941-3338. Germaine's is acclaimed by many people as the best of the big luau extravaganzas, held on the beach in the southwestern corner of O'ahu, with free transportation by bus from Waikiki. Daily from 6 to 9 P.M. $$$

Going Out

With so much to do in the daytime, most people will want to crash at an early hour to rest up for the next day's activities. But there are those who live for the nighttime—to prowl the bars, hit the dance floors, go to a show or a movie, or simply stay up late for the hell of it. O'ahu won't disappoint the night owls. In fact, sometimes it's hard to keep up with all the action and still hit the beach for the prime sunning hours. While the bars in Hawai'i close at 2 A.M., many clubs in Waikiki stay open until 4 A.M. That's two extra hours to find that certain someone! Waikiki also is home to the big shows such as Don Ho and the Magic of Polynesia.

For the more culturally inclined among us, there are a variety of performing arts venues, depending on the season, including theater, the Hawai'i Opera, and the Honolulu Symphony. The Hawai'i Theater in downtown Honolulu is a wonderful beaux-arts building featuring a variety of performing arts companies.

The following pages provide the best options for O'ahu. Listings

are given in alphabetical order. We've tried to provide a spectrum of options, so every reader will find somewhere to have a good time. Please note that most bars and clubs hold Happy Hours, which are almost a ritual in Hawaiʻi and can often run for 12 hours! Drinks are routinely discounted and this is often the primo time to meet a potential playmate. Don't miss out.

Cosmic Cosmo

While Hawaiʻi is known for the Mai Tai (see Mai Tai High on page xxvii), who really drinks them? When we belly up to the bar, we want a martini—if only for the impractical (major spillage) but totally groovy glass in which it is served. A martini just looks so good in one's hand, versus a fruity drink with an umbrella in it. When the weather is chilly, a Grey Goose martini, straight up, with olives and parched (just wave the vermouth bottle over the shaker), is our choice. However, in a tropical clime, a little sweetness is appropriate. While some may say a Cosmopolitan is, like, so four years ago, we aren't ashamed to say we still love 'em. And we make a cosmic Cosmo. In the aloha spirit of sharing, here is our recipe (for two):

First, chill the glasses in the freezer. Fill a martini shaker with ice and pour about half full with Absolut vodka (from experience, we know Absolut makes the best Cosmos). Add about a full shot glass of cranberry juice. Add a half shot of triple sec and a splash of Rose's Lime Juice. Shake, shake, shake! Remove the glasses from the freezer and pour to the brim. The color should be a pale pink. Enjoy the aloha!

Bars and Clubs

Being the major metro area in the state, Honolulu has the most nightlife options of all of the islands. For tourists, Waikiki is full of nightspots. For the intrepid and chic, the downtown/Chinatown area has some very hip 'n happenin' watering holes. By all means be adventurous. We certainly are and relish being on the edge (and often at the edge too!). Be sure to pick up a copy of the latest *Honolulu Weekly* (www.honoluluweekly.com), as it will have the current listings for nightlife.

Waikiki

Acqua, Hawai'ian Regent Hotel (3rd floor), 2552 Kalakaua Avenue, Waikiki, 924-0123. This Mediterranean restaurant turns into the place for salsa and Latin music later in the evening, so slip on those cha-cha heels and get on down. Open until 1 A.M. $5 cover Thursday through Saturday, and Monday.

All Star Café, 2080 Kalakaua Avenue (at Lewers Street), Waikiki, 955-8326. The biggest sports bar in Waikiki should be carrying the event you want to see. It's open Sunday through Thursday until 11 P.M., until midnight on weekends. No cover.

Barefoot Bar, Hale Koa Hotel, 2055 Kalia Road, Waikiki, 955-0555. The beachfront bar at the military-only Hale Koa Hotel, this is where the G.I.s hang. Open daily 11 A.M. to 11 P.M., Friday and Saturday until midnight.

Banyan Court, Sheraton Moana, 2365 Kalakaua Avenue, Waikiki, 922-3111. A quiet outdoor bar under a huge banyan tree, nestled in the oceanfront courtyard of this stately old hotel, this is a great place to pop that question. Open until 12:30 A.M.

Breathless Nightclub, 2375 Kuhio Avenue, Waikiki, 926-6811. This tacky restaurant turns into a tackier nightclub featuring the latest dance music and tons of tourists. It gets going late, especially on weekends, and is open until 4 A.M. $8 cover.

Duke's Canoe Club, Outrigger Waikiki Hotel, 2335 Kalakaua Avenue, Waikiki, 922-2268. On the beach, this place is a popular tourist hangout. Open until 1 A.M. No cover.

Moose McGillicuddy's, 310 Lewers Street, Waikiki, 923-0751. It's a dance floor, it's a sports bar, it's loud, it's crowded, it's the Moose. A mix of military men, tourists, and locals frequent this Waikiki pickup institution. Open 7:30 A.M. to 4 A.M. $3 cover on Friday and Saturday, $5 on Tuesday.

Red Lion, 240 Lewers Street, Waikiki, 922-1027. This is a cramped, crowded, and rowdy basement dance dive, popular with military boys and those who adore them. Open until 4 A.M. daily with a $3 cover.

Wave Waikiki, 1877 Kalakaua Avenue, Waikiki, 941-0424. One evening we went here at 2 A.M. and discovered a line of people at the door, waiting to get in (the bar is open until 4 A.M.). This is

the place for live music (until 1:30 A.M.) and a younger (twenties) crowd. Even though the Wave is essentially one large room, the effect of the murals, mirrors, and huge video screens can be somewhat disorienting. Nonetheless, the bands are fantastic, the DJ mix on the dance-rock side, the dance floor packed, and the crowd rather buzzed and horny. It can be lots of fun, even for old farts in their forties (and Wednesday is Big Ass Beer Night). There is a small cover charge of $5, free before 10 P.M.

Honolulu

Anna Bannana's, 2440 S. Beretania Street (near U.H.), Honolulu, 946-5190. This is a big university hangout, although the drinking age is 21. It's always crowded, and the upstairs has a dance floor and live bands. Dance floor open 11:30 P.M. to 2 A.M. Cover $4 to $5.

Brew Moon, 1200 Ala Moana Boulevard, Ward Centre, 593-0088. We're putting in a plug here for Brew Moon as it's a Boston-based company, and hey, the beer's pretty good too. Live music and dancing on various nights. Open until 1:30 A.M. No cover.

Cafe Che Pasta, 1001 Bishop Street, Suite 108, Bishop Square, Downtown Honolulu, 524-0004. With a cabaret, DJs, and an eclectic variety of music, this restaurant turns in to a kinda' happenin' place later at night. Every Friday and the first Saturday of each month. Open until 2 A.M., cover $5.

Cafe Sistina, 1314 S. King, Honolulu, 596-0061. A stylish Italian-motif restaurant/bar with a stylishly dressed crowd, this is an interesting eclectic alternative to a rowdy, loud scene. Open until 10:30 or 11 P.M., depending upon the crowd. Cover $10.

Chai's Island Bistro, Aloha Tower Marketplace, Downtown Honolulu, 585-0011. Nightly entertainment, including the Brothers Cazimero on Wednesdays and Hapa on Thursdays, plus free valet parking (when regular parking can be tough), makes this a worthwhile destination. Open until 11 P.M. Cover $5.

Compadres Mexican Bar & Grill, 1200 Ala Moana Boulevard, Ward Center, 591-8307. Margaritas, an excellent tequila selection, nachos, and a college and young professional crowd (which can mean all types these days) make this a popular place.

There's an outdoor patio and a sports bar too. Live music on weekends from 9 to 12 P.M., no cover.

Diamond Head Grill, W, 2885 Kalakaua Avenue, Diamond Head, 922-3734. The sight of the S-curved martini bar and the fabulously designed room that's attached make it worth the trip just to have a quiet drink here. Open Sunday through Thursday until 11:30 P.M., Friday and Saturday until 12:30 A.M.

Duc's Bistro, 1188 Maunakea Street, Downtown Honolulu, 531-6325. A funky place in funky Chinatown for those who seek out these kind of places. Open until 2 A.M.

Gordon Biersch Brewery Restaurant, 1 Aloha Tower Drive, Suite 1123, Downtown Honolulu, 599-4877. Located in the thriving Aloha Tower Marketplace, this is a very popular restaurant/bar/club/microbrewery for the downtown work crowd. Live music, an outdoor bar lanai, and a highly rated brew add to the appeal. Open until 1 A.M.

Hank's Café Honolulu, 1038 Nu'uanu Avenue, Downtown Honolulu, 526-1410. This is a fun, tiny, and totally untouristy bar with art-covered walls and Hawai'ian or local music on weekends. If you're in Chinatown, by all means stop by. Open until 1 A.M., closed Sundays.

Havana Cabana, 1131 Nu'uanu Avenue, Downtown Honolulu, 524-4277. An attractive cigar bar with live jazz or blues, in Chinatown. You'd better like cigar smoke. Open until 1:30 A.M. daily.

Indigo, 1121 Nu'uanu Avenue, Downtown Honolulu, 521-2900. We have to say it again—we love this place! This high-tin-ceilinged restaurant and bar is one of the chic-est spots in town, especially on Thursday and Friday nights, when local DJs or live music rocks the entire house. The bar in the back is a fun hangout and features great martinis and cosmopolitans. A very attractive staff adds to the visual pleasure. Open Tuesday through Friday until 2 A.M., only open for dinner on Saturday.

Murphy's Bar and Grill, 2 Merchant Street, Downtown Honolulu, 531-0422. If you're looking for an Irish pub, you've found it. Set in a wonderful old building, it's open until 2 A.M. daily. St. Patty's Day here is big-time.

O'Toole's Irish Pub, 902 Nu'uanu Avenue, Downtown Honolulu, 536-6360. Another Irish pub, adjacent to Murphy's; it's fun to hop

between the two. Wednesdays are popular, with live music jams. Open Monday through Thursday until midnight, Friday through Sunday until 2 A.M., no cover.

The Pier Bar, 1 Aloha Tower Drive, Downtown Honolulu, 536-2166. This fun outdoor bar is also a venue for some of the best live music in Honolulu. Open until 2 A.M. Cover is $3 after 9 P.M.

Shipley's Alehouse & Grill, Manoa Marketplace (2nd floor), 2756 Woodlawn Drive, Honolulu (near U.H.), 988-5555. Live entertainment and DJs make this a popular place with the university crowd and locals too. Open until 2 A.M. Cover is $3 to $5.

Venus, 1349 Kapiolani Boulevard, Honolulu, 951-8671. This is a mixed (gay and straight) dance club tucked away in the parking garage of the Ala Moana Shopping Center. Open till 4 A.M. Cover $5.

Escort Services

If you're really desperate and are willing to pay for companionship, there are seven pages of listings in the Yellow Pages under "Escort."

Gay Bars and Clubs

Gay nightlife in Hawai'i has always been focused in Waikiki. With the demise of the original Hula's and Dirty Mary's (the owners of the property on which they sat sold the land to shopping mall developers), gay nightlife has never really been the same. True, there *is* a new Hula's at the eastern end of Waikiki facing Kapiolani Park. But not being able to sip a cocktail and schmooze under the fabled banyan tree has taken away a lot of the fun. The other two gay clubs, Angles and Fusion, may at times be crowded but also lack that certain magic. Indeed, the whole scene seems to be mostly tourists, as locals tend to stay away.

For lesbians there are even fewer options. Many hang out at Hula's, especially for Happy Hour (which is 11 hours long). Other options include The Black Garter Café (known as Café Che Pasta during the day), 1001 Bishop Street, Pacific Tower, 584-0004, Fridays only from 9 P.M. to 2 A.M., $5 cover; and Angles, 2258 Kuhio Avenue, Waikiki, 926-9760, where Womyn's Night is Sunday from 4 to 9 P.M.—it's a dirt-cheap barbecue.

Hula's Bar & Lei Stand, 134 Kapahulu Avenue, Waikiki, 923-0669. Web site: www.hulas.com. We miss the old Hula's! While parking is a lot easier here and you can see the ocean and Diamond Head from its second-floor open-windowed perch, it's just not the same. There is a small glass-enclosed and air-conditioned dance floor, but most hang out on the open-air window seats for the breezes and the sights below and beyond, or to watch the variety of videos played around the club. Happy Hour is popular here and runs from 10 A.M. to 9 P.M., one of the longest we've seen in the state! Open until 2 A.M. Cover is $2 between 10 P.M. and midnight.

Angles, 2258 Kuhio Avenue, Waikiki, 926-9760. Often referred to as "Ankles," this tiny second-floor club is always crowded late at night, probably due to its central Waikiki location. There is a small overheated dance floor and a covered outside lanai with a great view of the traffic on Kuhio Avenue. Open till 2 A.M. No cover.

Fusion, 2260 Kuhio Avenue, Waikiki, 924-2422. Virtually next door to Angles above Paradise BBQ, this second-floor dance club (why are the major gay bars in Waikiki all on the second floor?) is where everyone goes when the other places close—it's open until 4 A.M. $5 cover on weekends.

Michelangelo, 444 Hobrom Lane, Waikiki, 951-0008. Located on the western end of Waikiki and part of the Eaton Square "men's complex" (there's a male strip/heavy cruise joint called **P-10A,** 942-8536, and a "health club" known as **Max's,** 951-8232, in the same building), this is a hangout, sports-bar-type place with a pool table and cheap drinks. Open until 2 A.M. with no cover.

Shows

As these are always popular, make sure you make reservations.

Brothers Cazimero, Chai's Island Bistro, Aloha Tower Marketplace, Downtown Honolulu, 585-0011. The best Hawai'ian musicians of the Honolulu show circuit. Be sure to catch their show here on Wednesdays. Their voices and harmonies are extraordinary, and they are accompanied by hula dancers.

Frank DeLima, Captain's Table, Hawai'ian Waikiki Beach Hotel, Waikiki, 922-2511. Frank is probably the most popular comedian in Hawai'i. As he is Portuguese ("Port-a-gee") and those of Portuguese descent are the constant subject of ethnic jokes in Hawai'i (Portuguese jokes are a *really* big deal here), Frank is best known for *his* hilarious ethnic jokes, such as: "Did I tell you about the carload of Port-a-gees who went to the airport and saw a sign that said 'Airport left'? They turned around and went home." He performs on Friday and Saturday. Cover is $7 with two-drink minimum. He was on vacation at press time and there was a rumor that he wasn't coming back. Knowing Frank, this might be a joke on us. Check it out and let us know.

The Don Ho Show, Waikiki Beachcomber Hotel, 2300 Kalakaua Avenue, Waikiki, 923-3981. What can you say about the most famous Hawai'ian, Don Ho, who brought us "Tiny Bubbles" and "Lovely Hula Hands"? Well, he still does his show, now at the more intimate Waikiki Beachcomber five nights a week, Sunday through Thursday, replete with Vegas-style dancers, singers, and his daughter Hoku.

Gyms and Health Clubs

For the health-conscious and those who want a good pump before going out, hotel health clubs and exercise rooms often just don't cut it. Here are two places that do:

24-Hour Fitness, 2490 Kalakaua Avenue, Waikiki, 971-4653. As the name says, this place is open 24/7, and it's an excellent facility for both weights and cardio, all with a view of the ocean. Day passes are $20. Weekly passes are $52.

The Gym, 768 South Street, Honolulu, 533-7111. Located by the Restaurant Row/Ward Centers off of King Street and minutes from Waikiki, the 21,000-square-foot facility has just about everything. Open Monday through Friday, 5 A.M. to 11 P.M., Saturday 6 A.M. to 9 P.M., and Sunday 7 A.M. to 8 P.M. Day passes are $15, weekly passes are $35.

The Rest of O'ahu—Clubs and Bars

Buzz's Original Steak House, 413 Kawailoa Road, Kailua, 261-4661. A Polynesian atmosphere predominates at this cozy restaurant and bar. This is a nice place for a relaxing cocktail. Cash only. Open daily for lunch from 11 A.M. to 2:30 P.M., dinner from 5 to 9 P.M.

Ahi's Punalu'u, 53-146 Kamehameha Highway, Punalu'u, 237-8474. This is a fun local hangout with pickup trucks and bikes in the parking lot and live bands/music on most nights. Great shrimp *pupus* too! Open from 11 A.M. to 9 P.M., closed Sunday.

Hale'iwa Joe's Seafood Grill, 66-011 Kamehameha Highway, Hale'iwa, 637-8005. Right in town by the Rainbow Bridge with a nice view of the harbor, this place becomes a local surfer hangout after dinner, with surfer videos and live music on Fridays or Saturdays. Open until 2 A.M. Cover for the music events is $5 to $10.

O.K., You Asked for It. Here They Are!

While we don't fly all the way to paradise to shop, O'ahu and especially Waikiki are shopping bliss for the sun-weary, bored, or out to revenge a wayward or negligent spouse. Here are the places where you can max out the plastic with the latest from the world's fashion capitals and more. The majority of shops are located either at the Ala Moana Shopping Center or the Royal Hawai'ian Shopping Center at 2100 Kalakaua Avenue.

High Fashion and Accessories Boutiques

A/X Armani Exchange—2270 Kalakaua Avenue, 923-1663.
Agnes B.—Ala Moana, 947-5500.
Cartier—Ala Moana, 955-5533; Royal Hawai'ian, 922-7555.
Chanel—Ala Moana, 942-5555; Royal Hawai'ian, 923-0255.
Dior—Ala Moana, 943-6900; 2200 Kalakaua Avenue, 923-0925.
Emporio Armani—Ala Moana, 951-8475.
Ferragamo—Ala Moana, 973-6100; Royal Hawai'ian, 971-4255.
Givenchy—Royal Hawai'ian, 971-2950.

OʻAHU

Gucci—Ala Moana, 942-1148; 2424 Kalakaua Avenue, 923-2968.
Guess—Ala Moana, 951-0294.
Hermès—Royal Hawaiʻian, 922-5780.
Neiman Marcus—Ala Moana, 951-8887.
Prada—Ala Moana, 955-5226; Royal Hawaiʻian, 922-5731.
Prada Sport—2174 Kalakaua Avenue, 921-0200.
Tiffany & Co.—Ala Moana, 943-6677; 2365 Kalakaua Avenue, 922-2722.
Versace—Ala Moana, 947-2244; Royal Hawaiʻian, 922-5337.

Stuff You Can Wear Next Season

Banana Republic—Ala Moana, 955-2602; King Kalakaua Plaza, 955-7955.
The Gap—Ala Moana, 949-1933.
Liberty House—Ala Moana, 941-2345; 2314 Kalakaua Avenue, 941-2345.

Aloha Wear

Reyn's— Ala Moana, 949-5929; Sheraton Waikiki Hotel, 923-0331.
Island Collections— Ala Moana, 973-3280; Hyatt Regency, 922-1450.
Liberty House—Ala Moana, 941-2345; 2314 Kalakaua Avenue, 941-2345.

Don't Miss

USS *Arizona* Memorial—One of the most moving experiences we've ever had came at this very poignant memorial. An absolute must-see.
Dolphin Quest—Fulfill your fantasies of Flipper with the dolphin encounter program at the Kahala Mandarin Oriental.
Indigo Restaurant—A groovy and happening restaurant and nightspot and a refreshing relief from Waikiki, this in place in Chinatown is worth the detour.
Byoto-In Temple—With a setting to match this stunning re-creation of a 900-year-old Buddhist temple, a visit here will bring peace of mind.

The Windward Side—The amazing *pali* and incredible scenery of this side of O'ahu are a must-see.

The North Shore—The home of the Banzai Pipeline and Waimea Bay surf breaks, among others, this strand is surfing ground zero during the winter months.

The Bishop Museum—Probably the best collection of Hawai'iana anywhere, this museum should be a required stop on the itinerary.

Spring rolls and a tuna sandwich at Ba-le—What can we say but yum!

Sandy Beach and Makapu'u—Check out the bodysurfers, the body-boarders, and just the bodies at these two very pretty east O'ahu beaches.

A *malasada* **from Leonard's**—The Krispy Kreme of Hawai'i—no trip is complete without injesting at least one hot Leonard's *malasada* (Portuguese donut).

Dinner at the Hau Tree Lanai and a drink at W's Diamond Head Grill—A romantic and stylish treat one step removed from the hustle of Waikiki, this is a great last-night occasion.

Maui

Touristo Scale:

 (9)

T HERE IS A POPULAR SAYING on this island: *Maui no ka oi*—"Maui is the best." Well, we agree to a degree. Maui has some of the most magical places in the islands, Hana and Haleakala for example. It also has a relaxed pace and much to offer the visitor. Unfortunately, Maui also has experienced some wanton development *à la* O'ahu, which has ravaged the prime beachfront with a tsunami of condos, high-rise hotels, and huge resort properties. Today Maui's leeward coasts—the best sunny beaches—are packed with all of the above, and development is creeping up the slopes of Haleakala and the West Maui Mountains. The lack of a master plan offers a painful, and permanent, lesson that the islands of Kaua'i and Moloka'i have taken to heart with zoning regulations and long-term planning.

This is not to say that Maui has been ruined. *Au contraire*, most of the island is rugged, wild, and fun to explore. Haleakala, the 10,023-foot (3,055 meters) dormant volcano that dominates both the land and the life of Maui, is a National Park with miles of hiking trails and an aura all its own. The lush and verdant north and east coast from Pa'ia to Kipahulu is stunning, as is the rugged and dry south coast at Haleakala's base. Upcountry Maui near the towns of Kula and Makawao is beautifully pastoral, the elevation providing refreshingly cooler temperatures, breezes, and amazing views.

Maui is divided into four sections: Central, South, West, and East. Central Maui consists of the isthmus between Haleakala and the West Maui Mountains, historically a huge sugarcane-growing area. Today it still has miles of cane fields and is also the home of Kahului and Wailuku, the commercial and political hubs, respectively, of the island and county (the county includes the islands of Moloka'i and Lana'i). South Maui sits on the leeward coast of the towering Haleakala, keeping it hot and sunny. It runs from Ma'alaea Bay to Makena and includes the overdeveloped Kihei, the Wailua development, several golf courses, and Maui's finest beaches, Big and Little Beaches. West Maui is a peninsula featuring scenic mountains, a sunny and dry climate on its leeward side, and Lahaina, once the political and whaling capital of the Hawai'ian Kingdom. One of Maui's largest resort areas, Ka'anapali, is located here as are some of the island's best surfing beaches. East Maui is our personal favorite. At the easternmost tip sits Hana, one of our most cherished places on the planet. East Maui is the windward side of the island and is incredibly lush from the frequent rain showers swept in off the Pacific by the trade winds. It is also relatively undeveloped and retains the magic of a tropical paradise.

A Not-So-Brief History

The second-largest island in the Hawai'ian chain (729 square miles/1,881 square kilometers), Maui was formed about 1 million years ago by volcanoes when it sat on the magma hotspot now under the southeast coast of the Big Island and the Lo'ihi sea mount (currently about 3,000 feet below sea level). There are no active volcanoes on Maui, however Haleakala is dormant—its last eruption occurred 200 years ago.

Originally settled by migration waves from the Marquesas and Society (Tahiti) islands—first in the 8th and then in the 12th and 13th centuries—the Hawai'ian Islands remained isolated from the outside world until Captain Cook's expedition landed at Kaua'i in 1778. At that time Maui, ruled by the powerful chief Kahekili, shared the language and customs of the other Hawai'ian Islands, but contact was limited to periodic conquests, defeats, and occasional trading. Within a year of Cook's first contact on Kaua'i, diseases brought by the Europeans, especially venereal diseases, had spread to all of the islands.

In 1786 the ruthless Kahekili, already the ruler of Moloka'i and

Lana'i, conquered O'ahu. His quest for territory and power went as far as killing his adopted son (then the ruler of O'ahu), sacrificing the body to the war god Ku, and then torturing the lesser O'ahu chiefs to death. Kahekili moved to O'ahu and ruled from there, forming an alliance with his half-brother Ka'eokulani, the ruler of Kaua'i. Concurrent with all this fighting, both Kahekili and Kamehameha, the fearsome ruler of the Big Island, were tapping into the white man's technology, making deals for guns and support from various British and American traders and mercenaries. This trade would greatly alter the outcome of future battles. The more guns and cannons a chief had in his forces, the more success he would have. But it wasn't until 1787, incredibly, that a white man set foot on Maui—almost ten years after Captain Cook's "discovery" of the islands and his untimely death that same year. It was a Frenchman, Captain Jean-François de Galaup de La Perouse, who stepped ashore at Makena (a bay there is named after him). Even more incredible, La Perouse bucked Louis XVI's order and did not claim the island for France. Oops!

Various intrigues and rivalries ensued until Kahekili died of natural causes in 1794. He left his half-brother Ka'eokulani and his son Kalanikupule in charge of his empire. Of course egos clashed, and to make a long story even longer, Kalanikupule prevailed. However, Kalanikupule made a grave error in judgment when he killed former ally William Brown (an English merchant captain holed up in Honolulu's Pearl Harbor) and tried to commandeer his ships and men to go to the Big Island and fight Kamehameha. Unsuccessful and humiliated, he was now without the white man's guns and support. In 1795 Kamehameha, sensing weakness, invaded from the Big Island and conquered Maui, then Lana'i and Moloka'i, and headed for Waikiki to do battle. More intrigues and ruthless battles ensued, with Kamehameha the victor and now unifier of the Hawai'ian Islands (the ruler of Kaua'i read the writing on the wall and basically capitulated to Kam's terms).

Kamehameha the Great, as he liked to be called, made Lahaina the seat of government in 1802, where it stayed until it was moved to Honolulu in 1845 by King Kamehameha III. Whaling ships arrived from New Bedford, Massachusetts, in 1819, and whaling became a big business in Lahaina. Missionaries, also from New

Honokōhau Bay
ancient paved trail
Honolua Bay
Mokulēʻia Bay
Honokahua Bay
Kapalua Bay Hotel
Nāpili Bay
Ritz Carlton
Kapalua Bay GC
Kapalua
Nāpili Kai
Beach Club
Kapalua
Village GC
Kapalua
Plantation GC
HONOKŌWAI
Embassy
Suites
Sheraton
Maui
Kāʻanapali
Beach Hotel
Royal Lahaina
Resort
Westin Maui
Royal Kāʻanapali GC
Hyatt Regency
KĀʻANAPALI
KAPALUA–
WEST MAUI
AIRPORT
HONOKŌHAU
HONOKAHUA
KAHAKULOA
Kahakuloa Bay
Hakuheʻe Pt
30
**WEST MAUI
MOUNTAINS**
Waiehu
GC
Kahului Bay
Waiheʻe
Waiehu
Kanaha
Beach Park
Haleki'i-Pihana Heiau
State Monument
Maui Arts &
Cultural Ctr
KAHULUI
AIRPORT
SPRECKELSVILLE
*Hoʻokipa
Beach Park*
36
Low
Pāʻ
Pāʻ
Wailuku
Lahaina
Plantation Inn
*Iao Valley
State Park*
Iao Str.
Kahului
The Dunes at
Maui Lani GC
Maui
CC
37
HĀ
HALEAKALĀ HWY
HONOAPIʻILANI HWY
Waikapū
Maui Tropical
Plantation
Sandalwood
GC
Puʻunēnē
KŪ IHELANI HWY
Pulehu Rd
Puka
Maui
Ocean
Center
MOKULELE HWY
MĀʻALAEA
*Puamana
Beach Park*
30
OLOWALU
Māʻalaea Beach
Ukumehame Beach Park
Papawai Pt
Māʻalaea
Mai Poina
ʻOe la'u Park
LĪPOA
Kīhei
31
Silversword GC
Maʻalaea Bay
Kalama Park
What a Wonderful
World B&B
Kēō
Kamaʻole Parks I, II, III
Wailea Coastwalk
KEAWAKAPU
Wailea Blue GC
KULA HWY
Renaissance Wailea
Grand Wailea Resort
Kea Lani Hotel
Four Seasons
WAILEA
PIʻILANI HWY
*Wailea Emerald
& Gold GC*
MĀKENA
ʻULUPALA
RANC
Maui Prince Hotel
Puʻu ʻŌlaʻi
Tedeschi
Little Beach
Big Beach
Mākena North
& South GC
Molokini Island
ʻĀhihi Bay
Cape
Kīnaʻu
La Pérouse Bay

N
W   E
S
®

| 0 | 2.0 | 4.0 | 6.0 miles |
| 0 | 2.0 | 4.0 | 6.0 | 8.0 | 10 kilometers |

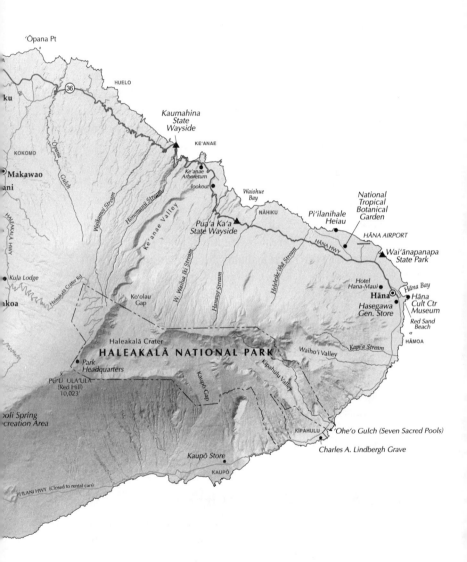

Maui

'Ōpana Pt

HUELO

36

ku

KOKOMO

Kaumahina
State
Wayside

KE'ANAE

Makawao

ani

Ke'anae
Arboretum

lookout

Waiohue
Bay

National
Tropical
Botanical
Garden

NĀHIKU

Pi'ilanihale
Heiau

HĀNA AIRPORT

HALEAKALA HWY

Honomanu Stream

Ke'anae Valley

Pua'a Ka'a
State Wayside

HĀNA HWY

Wai'ānapanapa
State Park

Kula Lodge

W. Wailua Iki Stream

Hanawi Stream

Heleleike'ōhā Stream

Hotel
Hana-Maui

Hāna Bay

koa

Haleakalā Crater Rd

Ko'olau
Gap

Hāna

Hāna
Cult Ctr
Museum

Hasegawa
Gen. Store

Red Sand
Beach

HĀMOA

Haleakalā Crater

HALEAKALĀ NATIONAL PARK

Waiho'i Valley

Kapi'a Stream

Park
Headquarters

PU'U ULA'ULA
(Red Hill)
10,023'

Kaupō Gap

Kipahulu Valley

oli Spring
creation Area

KIPAHULU

'Ohe'o Gulch (Seven Sacred Pools)

Kaupō Store

Charles A. Lindbergh Grave

KAUPŌ

PI'ILANI HWY (Closed to rental cars)

England, arrived in 1823 and engaged in an ongoing power struggle in Lahaina. Five years later, Maui's first sugar mill opened. In the ensuing decades, as petroleum replaced whale oil for fuel on the mainland, the sugar barons gained tremendous power and helped topple the monarchy in Honolulu in 1893, leading to the eventual annexation of the islands to the United States. One of the barons, Dwight Baldwin, introduced pineapples on Maui, and that industry took off. For the first half of the 20th century, agriculture was the economy of sleepy Maui. It really wasn't until the late 1960s that tourism became a force (the Hotel Hana-Maui, opened in 1946, was the island's first resort). Now that force has become a hurricane, with no signs of ever losing strength.

Maui: Key Facts

LOCATION	Kihei: Longitude 20°47' N, latitude 156° 28' W
SIZE	729 square miles/1,881 square meters
HIGHEST POINT	Heleakala (10,023 feet/3,055 meters)
POPULATION	117,644 (2000 Census)
TIME	Hawai'ian Standard (year-round): 2 hours behind LA, 5 hours behind New York, 10 hours behind London
AREA CODE	808
AIRPORTS	Kahului (main), Kapalua (West Maui), and Hana
MAIN TOURIST AREAS	West Maui—Lahaina, Ka'anapali, Kahana, Kapalua, South Maui—Kihei, Wailea, Makena, Upcountry—Kula, Makawao, Hana
TOURISM INFO	www.visitmaui.com/808-244-3530

Focus on Maui: Windsurfing

Wind and surf—these two elements come together on Maui to create optimal conditions for that sport called windsurfing. Windsurfing is the combination of sailing, wave-jumping, and surfboarding. The windsurfer takes the board out from the beach, jumps a wave, sails outside, tacks or jibes, cruises back in, rides the

wave to the whitewater, tacks or jibes, and heads back out again.

The Valley Isle is a windsurfing mecca, the Woodstock of wind, waves, boards, and sails. This is the foremost and most fashionable place for windsurfers of all abilities to gather—it's where the action is. Ironically, Maui's best windsurfing spots are virtually in the wind blast zone of the jumbo jets that roar in and out of Kahului Airport. However, it's not the jet engines that make this part of the island one of the world's windsurfing capitals. Rather, it is Maui's unique geography. An isthmus connects the 10,000-plus-foot Haleakala with the 5,000-plus-foot West Maui Mountains, creating a vortex that accelerates the trade winds and makes for very strong and steady wind velocity. On this isthmus sits Kahului and the groovy, hippyish town of Pa'ia, forming the axis of Maui's windsurfing industry.

The winds are the strongest and most consistent on the shores of the isthmus, just perfect for propelling the boards toward the lips of incoming breaks and launching them several feet into the air before they land in the trough of the next wave. Because of the land's configuration, some locations have wind when others are calm. Wave heights, while not as big as those on O'ahu's North Shore, are big enough at times for the hotshots to do loop-de-loops. These are flips where the entire board, rig, and helmsman do a somersault, the top of the mast clearing the water while upside down! Even more amazing is the fact that the sailboarder will land right side up and continue on his or her way with the casual aplomb of a water-skier jumping a boat wake. Fortunately for those who aren't quite so confident or skilled, there are other locations on Maui to suit every type of windsurfer.

Ho'okipa Beach Park, on the north shore near Pa'ia, is to wind-surfers what O'ahu's Pipeline and Waimea Bay are to surfers—the best and the biggest, the domain of the experts and hotshots. Waves at these breaks have been known to reach 30 feet! Spectators often sit on the bluff overlooking Ho'okipa, watching and admiring the waves and the windsurfers. However, the big boys' (and girls') stuff isn't the only game around. There are other, tamer places to catch some air—Kanaha and Spreckelsville, to name a couple. Together these make Maui the windsurfing mecca of the world, with opportunities for all levels as well as excellent locations for slalom sailing and just general cruising. While there is some terrific windsurfing to be found on O'ahu (see that chapter) and an ongoing argument about which island has the better sailing—both have outstanding locations, conditions, and support services—most windsurfers, if asked where they would prefer to go, would choose Maui. Opportunities on Kaua'i and the Big Island just don't hold up to those on Maui or O'ahu.

Knowledge Is Power

Before you plan to attack the Maui windsurfing scene, there are a few things you should know about the winds and seas of the Land of Aloha. First, there is something called the Pacific anticyclone. It is responsible for the trade winds. This weather phenomenon is the result of a semistationary high-pressure system that covers about half of the northern Pacific. The location of the Hawai'ian Islands, about 1,000 miles southwest off the system's center, ensures a steady flow of unimpeded air from the northeast—the direction of the wind as the Pacific anticyclone circulates clockwise over thousands of miles. In the summer, when the trades blow 90 percent of the time and with greater velocity, the anticyclone is usually centered about 1,000 miles west of the coast of northern California. In the winter, the system weakens and moves south, until its center is off the coast of Baja California. In winter, trades blow only about 50 percent of the time; the rest of the time there are variable winds, no wind at all, or *kona* (southern) winds. *Kona* winds are associated with storms and fronts where the wind comes from the south-southwest. They usually mean bad or unsettled weather. Trade winds mean consistent tropical weather. So in planning your trip, be aware of the seasonal wind patterns. If you want guaranteed high winds, then the summer months are the time to go. Once on the island, familiarize yourself with the peculiar wind patterns of various windsurfing spots. Due to the varying shape of the land, there can sometimes be a five- to ten-knot difference in wind speed within just a few miles.

You'll also want to bone up on waves and currents. Situated in the middle of the deep-blue Pacific, the Hawai'ian Islands are subjected to ocean swell from thousands of miles in all directions.

Most of the time, the swell originates in the middle-latitude storms of the North and South Pacific. In the winter the swell comes from storms to the north. Because the storms are closer to the islands, the winter swell and surf is the biggest. When the swell hits the protective reefs of the islands' northern shores, the result is monster surf, like that on the North Shore of O'ahu. In the summer the swell is generated from storms raging in the South Pacific and affects the southern coasts of the islands. Because it has to travel farther to reach Hawai'i, the southerly swell is smaller. When there is little swell from the north or the south, strong trades create their own swell. Wave-break characteristics—e.g., tubes, lefts, rights—are determined by the depth and shape of the coral reefs. When you hear a wave report, keep in mind that in Hawai'i a wave is measured from its back side. The front side, the side you face from the beach, will be a lot higher. Windsurfers measure most big breaks in terms of parts of the rig. *Logo-high* means the waves are as high as the logo on a sail (usually about a quarter of the way down from the top of the sail). *Mast-high* means the waves are as high as or higher than the top of the mast, and so on.

Finally, there are currents to contend with. Generally, most beaches or reefs have channels that siphon out all the water that comes crashing in. These provide flatter exits on a board. They can also be deadly, sweeping you and your board out to sea. If you get caught in one, paddle or swim to the side, perpendicular to the current. Eventually you will drop out of it. Don't try to swim against it, because you will rapidly exhaust yourself, and by all means don't panic. Always determine where the currents and channels are before getting on your board. Ask somebody who sails there regularly to fill you in—people are friendly.

Once you get farther out, other, larger currents will come into play. These, too, can be very dangerous, as the distance from shore can be overwhelming. These currents, like the notorious Moloka'i Express on O'ahu, can carry a sailor to Tahiti. And remember, there are sometimes sharks in deeper water. *Never windsurf alone offshore.*

Equipment and Instruction

Unless you are terribly attached to your board and rig, leave it at home and rent the hardware in Hawai'i. The hassle of schlepping a board, mast, boom, and sails by air will be physically taxing and will cost almost as much as renting. Also, the equipment you rent in Hawai'i is designed for conditions there. Not only will you have gear that is tailored for the experience, you may actually save your own equipment from damage. You can change rented boards and rigs as conditions or your expertise changes, so you won't need to bring three boards, three masts, and so on thousands of miles. Most shops offer custom performance boards and production boards (floaters and sinkers), rigs, and sails, and will be able to outfit you according to your level of experience. Be forewarned, though: Most shops do *not* carry an insurance waiver. Therefore you are responsible for the repair or replacement cost of damaged equipment (beyond the normal wear and tear). Be sure to ask about this before signing on the dotted line. You may prefer to rent from a shop that carries "collision" insurance.

Once you have your equipment straightened out, it's a good idea to get some instruction on the unique windsurfing conditions in Maui. Besides, lessons never hurt anyone. It's very likely that you haven't been out on the board for a while, so the brush-up will be good for you. Instruction levels begin with uphaul classes and progress to water starts, through speed and jibing techniques, and on to performance tactics and wave-jumping. Those who have little or no experience in the sport will begin with uphauling, the fundamental technique for getting the board underway. It means standing on the board, pulling the mast and sail out of the water, filling the sail, and moving forward. Often this is the most frustrating and exhausting part of the sport, as inevitably the first tries mean falling in the water repeatedly—especially if it is windy. After a while your lower back begins to feel it. That's why it's definitely a pleasure to learn how to water start—where you lie in the water and let the wind do the work of pulling you up. Like slalom water-skiing, the ease of water starting is similar to the ease of skiing on one ski— once you do it you'll never go back. All you need is a steady wind. Next on the agenda are classes on tacking and jibing (turning the

board), followed by performance techniques.

For those who are competent but have little experience in windsurfing, taking a wave—especially a big wave—is harder than it looks. A pro will be able to keep you from making a fool of yourself. Several good windsurfing schools offer packages, clinics, and courses for those wanting to improve. Many shops also provide individual instruction.

The windsurfing/wavejumping craze has become big business on Maui, and to a lesser extent on Oʻahu. As a result, there are a lot of decent choices for both renting and purchasing equipment and for instruction and courses. Many of these businesses will arrange your accommodations or offer packages that include them. Most packages will put you up at nearby condos. Be sure to ask before signing up—a lot of these packages are designed for younger folk, so the accommodations may not be up to your expectations. If you don't mind, however, you can save some money by going this route. Be sure to book both rentals and instruction as far in advance as possible to ensure that you'll get what you want. Reservations are always a good idea, even if you're going the same day.

Windsurfing Operations

There are several excellent windsurfing shops that offer rentals, equipment, instruction, and kiteboarding. Special vans equipped to handle windsurfing equipment are available from most major car-rental companies.

The Maui Windsurf Company, 22 Hana Highway, Kahului, HI 96732. Toll-free: 800-872-0999. Local: 808-877-4816, fax 808-877-4696.
Web site: www.maui-windsurf.com

The Maui Windsurf Company has over 200 boards for hire, including beginner, slalom, and asymmetrical boards. It also has full-batten sails and surf masts, and changes in rigs are permitted. If you like, you can rent boards and masts separately. Equipment is for sale and there is a repair shop. Rental rates (including full gear and roof racks) are $45 per day. The shop is open seven days, 8:30 A.M. to 6 P.M., and is affiliated with Vela Sports.

Hi-Tech Surf Sports, 425 Koloa Road, Kahului, HI 96732. Local: 808-877-2111, fax 808-871-6943.

Web site: www.htmaui.com

Now in a new 6,200-square-foot store in downtown Kahului, this shop rents well over 300 Hi-Tech custom and production boards, which have been developed and tested on Maui's north shore. You get the same equipment as the Hi-Tech competition team, so many experts prefer to rent here. Each rental includes a Hi-Tech custom or production board (slalom, asymmetricals, wave, and speed), a Simmer or North/Ezzy sail (full-batten and RAF), a Hi-Tech rig, a Hi-Tech or Ampro mast, and a roof rack. Changes in boards and rigs are permitted. Components may also be rented, and there is a repair shop. In addition, equipment is available for sale. Rates are $46 per day, with discounts for multiple days. Hours are from 9 A.M. to 6 P.M. daily.

Hawai'ian Island Surf and Sport, 415-A Dairy Road, Kahului, HI 96732. Toll-free: 800-231-6958. Local: 808-871-4981, fax 808-871-4624.

Web site: www.maui.net/hisurf

This is one of Maui's largest and most complete rental centers, with over 200 boards and sails for hire. In operation since 1983, they never run out of equipment. It is also Hawai'i's largest retail outlet and the exclusive home of Jimmy Lewis custom boards—the fastest boards in the world. Hawai'ian Island carries Tiga, F2, Mistral, Windsurfing Hawaii, Winsure, Rainbow fins, Simmer Style, Gaastra, Neil Pryde, DaKine Hawaii, and Ampro. It's the high-wind test center for Mistral, Tiga, and F2. Jimmy Lewis custom boards available for rent include round pin, wave, asymmetrical, minislalom, and slalom. Production boards include Mistral, Tiga, F2, Hifly, and Seatrend. Rigs consist of Ampro masts, Windsurfing Hawaii booms/bases, and Windsure booms. Your options for sails are Simmer Style, Gaestra, and Neil Pryde. You can change equipment as often as you like. Equipment is also available for sale. Rental rates (full rig and roof rack) are $45 per day. Open daily from 8:30 A.M. to 6 P.M.

Second Wind Sail and Surf, 111 Hana Highway, Kahului, HI 96732. Local: 808-877-7467, fax 808-877-0091.
Web site: www.maui.net/~secwind

In business for over 16 years, Second Wind has more than 150 boards and sails for rent, with many options available. Cost for complete rental of all gear is $43 per day. Open daily from 9 A.M. to 6 P.M.

Neil Pryde Maui, 425 Koloa Street, Suite 100, Kahului, HI 96732. Toll-free: 800-321-7443. Local: 808-877-7443, fax 808-877-2149.
Web site: www.neilprydemaui.com

The legendary Neil Pryde windsurfing company established a store on Maui in 1996. It is also home of the Neil Pryde Test Center, where you can try out new equipment. They have 75 boards and 200 sails/rigs for rental. Rates are $46 per day for everything you need. Open daily from 9 A.M. to 6 P.M.

Maui Windsurfing

There are five superb sites where prevailing conditions are the best spots for tacks, jibes, and jumps: Hoʻokipa, Spreckelsville, Kanaha, Maʻalaea, and Kihei. After sailing, everyone converges on Paʻia Town—known as the Aspen of windsurfing—where the action is off the water. Competitions are held regularly here from April through October. By all means, plan to spend some time here—it's well worth it. Besides excellent sailing, you will most assuredly meet other people who are semiserious to serious about the sport, and you might get a date out of it too. For the latest on wind conditions, check out the Maui Windcam at www.windcam.com.

Hoʻokipa Beach Park. This is really the big time—the premier beach for windsurfing and wave-jumping. You know you have arrived into the hallowed halls of windsurfingdom when you can handle Hoʻokipa. Its location on the Hana Highway, combined with the bluffs and parking area that overlook the beach, makes it one of the best attended and hottest shows on Maui. Sailors are guaranteed an audience to witness their wildest wave-jumping fantasies . . . and nightmares.

Ho'okipa is so very popular among experts and spectators because of the often ideal wind and surf conditions that allow for incredible jump heights and the famous loop-de-loops within a stone's throw of the beach. The best days are when the trades are stiff and there is some winter swell (usually in winter, spring, or fall—the summer brings high trades and its accompanying trade swell). Only experts and the well informed should attempt this beach. The reef is very sharp and shallow, and the surf and currents are dangerous. If you're not up to it, you will totally stand out. Not only will you be run out of the water by the other sailors whose cuts and turns you're screwing up, you will also look like a total fool to the watching throngs. Even if you're not good enough to attempt the water, be sure to spend a few hours in the gallery. Watching the pros hit the waves is really thrilling.

The primary show is to the left and center of the beach, where three wave breaks, Lanes, H'Poco, and Middles, serve up the surf for the daredevils. Close in on the left (west) side of the beach, right below the "grandstand," are the infamous rocks, where many a rig and board have been puréed by the raging surf-the trades and the current sweep everything toward them. On the far right side of the beach is another off-limits area, Pavilions, which is surfer territory. Woe to the ignorant soul who sails over there.

To reach Ho'okipa, take the Hana Highway east of Pa'ia and look for the sails on the water. Park in the area just above the rocks on the left side of the beach. The entrance to the beach is clearly marked and the traffic flow is one-way to avoid accidents on the blind-curved west exit. Be sure to bring refreshments— the show is great with cocktails (alcohol-free for the driver, of course) and pupus. We've heard that it's easy to find something to smoke here, but being the responsible, upright citizens that we are, we wouldn't have actually investigated this. What did we just say? Can't remember, but man do we have the munchies, and where's that Visine!

Kanaha Beach Park. If there is one beach that is the "universe" of windsurfing in the Aloha State, it is Kanaha. We have never seen so many windsurfers in one place in all of our travels. The beach is a blanket of colorful sails and sand. If they're not on the

water, they're on the beach. There are opportunities for all levels here, from beginner to advanced sailors to those looking for a date-which is what makes it so special (of course, *we* never have to look). Other big pluses are the large grassy park, which makes rigging up and breaking down a breeze, and the shower facilities for rinsing off the salt.

There's a fairly sandy bottom here, and little shore break, so beach access is easy. The beach is long, with several different launch points. A large, long reef protects the inner bay. This calmer inside part is perfect for novices learning how to water-start and jibe. At the lower reef (on the western half of the beach), there is a very manageable clean break that is good for intermediates. The upper reef (the eastern half) has bigger swells and is the place for experts and jumpers when the winter surf is too much at Hoʻokipa. The best conditions exist in the spring and fall, when the trades are still strong and the winter swell is at its end and beginning. As at all north shore beaches when the trades are up, it is a starboard tack out (to jump) and a port tack in (to ride the waves). The only time when Kanaha is not great is during *kona* (southern) winds, when conditions are better in Kihei.

To reach Kanaha Beach Park, take the Airport Road (Keolani Place) toward the terminal and turn left on Koeheke Street, where you see the rental-car return stations. (There's small sign for Kanaha Beach Park.) Follow the road to the stop sign and turn right. The beach sits at the end of the runway. You'll get an up-close and personal view of the bellies of various aircraft. There are four entrances to the park; you can take any one, as they all connect. The best place for parking is the first left, where there is a large parking area and clean restrooms. The best place for launching is the last left, where you park among the trees and are steps away from the beach.

Spreckelsville. Situated between Kanaha and Paʻia is Spreckelsville, a tony residential neighborhood even though it's at the end of the major airport runway. Despite the noise and rumble, prices are high and homes are in demand here. Celebrities like to come to Spreckelsville because it is so low-key. The winds here are as high as the prices—this is one of the windiest spots on Maui. When there isn't much wind at Hoʻokipa or Kanaha, there will be about five knots more of it at Spreckelsville, commonly referred to as Sprecks. This is due to its location in relation to Haleakala: The trades, facing no obstructions, sweep straight down off the slope and make a direct hit here. The swell is also a lot bigger than at Kanaha, adding more challenge and making it a playground for wave-jumping intermediate to advanced sailors. In fact, several times a year the waves on the outer reef (Spartan Reef) are the north shore's biggest.

To get to Sprecks, take the Hana Highway east from Kahului and turn left at the pillars on Kealakai Place. Follow this road to Nonohe Place and park in the red-dirt parking lot.

Ma'Alaea Bay. The trades blow through Ma'alaea Bay, situated on the south side of the isthmus between the West Maui Mountains and Haleakala. Turbo'd by a venturi effect, they blow here with a vengeance. According to the *Guinness Book of World Records*, this is the windiest body of water in the world—the average wind speed is 24 knots! Only experts should venture out here to attempt what is some of the fastest windsurfing in the world. Less-than-experts will end up on the shores of Kaho'olawe. The exception to this rule is when the wind is blowing *kona* (from the south)—then the bay may be the best spot on the island. On the western end of the bay are some of the fastest wave breaks in Hawai'i, known as Freight Train Rights. But if there are surfers around, forget it.

Ma'alaea Bay is just off Route 30. Follow the signs to the Boat Harbor and head down the road that fronts the beach—you'll see the windsurfers' launch area.

Kihei. A screaming port tack across Ma'alaea Bay from the Boat Harbor will bring you to the relative calm of Kihei. Thanks to the flat water, this long stretch of beaches and condos is a great beginner's area, particularly in summer. Slalom and short boards are the favorites here. The most popular access is Mai Poina 'Oe la'u Beach Park (a.k.a. Ohukai), the first beach park on the South Kihei Road. Be forewarned: Winds are fluky and subject to gusts because of the slope of Haleakala. When *kona* winds kick up a southern swell, the area becomes more challenging, with some great wave-jumping, especially at the break opposite Ohukai, called Pavilions.

Kiteboarding

Kiteboarding is the latest mutation in the sport of windsurfing. Serious air time is captured with a specially designed "kite," control lines, a quick-release mechanism, and a surfboard strapped to your feet (what will they think of next, huh?). Due to the fact that Maui's best windsurfing areas are adjacent to Kahului Airport, this new sport is bumping heads with the Federal Aviation Administration. Be advised that the FAA has established a "no-fly" zone between Kanaha Beach Park and Tavaris Bay five miles to the east. This is to prevent hazards to aircraft, which usually take off right into the trades over this area. Kiteboarding launching is allowed just west of Kanaha and only after 11 A.M. (a compromise worked out with fishermen who don't want to be decapitated). Kiteboarders are also advised to avoid areas filled with windsurfers, as they tend to get wigged out by kiteboarders and their attached lines. As with any high-risk sport, it is strongly suggested that a significant amount of instruction be given before any individual attempts are made. Curious bystanders should be very careful around launch and landing sights, as the wind can be unpredictable and the projectile equipment is very hazardous.

Rules of the Road

Before you hop on the board and join the fray, there are some important rules of the road, both official and by consensus, that should be the framework for all windsurfing and wave-jumping experiences. In most instances, nautical and sailing rules apply. However, are some exceptions.

- Under all circumstances, swimmers and surfers have the right-of-way. Windsurfers must stay well away. Never trespass into the surfing breaks, especially when there are surfers out—you will be sorry later.
- Be courteous and helpful-everyone benefits from this. Try to learn the local hierarchy; knowing the strata can only help you.
- A starboard tack boat has the right-of-way over a port tack boat. (This is the basic rule of the road in yachting.)

- The windsurfer heading out from the beach to jump a wave has the right-of-way over the windsurfer riding a wave in. This is an instance where the starboard/port right-of-way does not apply.
- The first person to catch a wave owns it. Others should stay clear.

Those are the basics. Smooth sailing!

Other Things to Do

≋ **Golf**
≋ **Tennis**
≋ **Beaches**
≋ **Scuba**
≋ **Haleakala**
≋ **Hiking**
≋ **Biking**
≋ **Oooh cruise to Hana/'Oheo Gulch**
≋ **Whale watches (December 15 through April 15)**
≋ **Horseback riding**
≋ **Cerebral stuff**

Golf

One of the few positive aspects of the wanton development on Maui is the creation of some of the state's best and most beautiful golf courses—all within an hour's drive of each other. Both West and South Maui have some great golfing options, so regardless of where you're staying, you will always be close to the fairways. The only part of the island without easy access to 18 holes is Hana, where you will have to fly or drive to get to a course with anything more than three practice holes.

With 14 courses on the island, you should be able to get the tee time you want. Below are what we think are the best golfing opportunities on the island.

# MAUI

West Maui

Kapalua is West Maui's golf mecca and a major reason why guests check into the Ritz and the Kapalua hotels. All are under the umbrella of the Kapalua Golf Club.

The Kapalua Golf Club, 300 Kapalua Drive, Kapalua, HI 96761. Local: 808-669-8044 (Village and Bay Courses), 808-669-8877 (Plantation Course).

The Plantation Course
18 holes—Par 73
Championship Tee (blue): 7,263 yards, 75.2 rating
Regular Tee (white): 6,547 yards, 71.9 rating
Ladies' Tee (red): 5,627 yards, 73.2 rating

The Bay Course
18 holes—Par 72
Championship Tee (blue): 6,600 yards, 71.7 rating
Regular Tee (white): 6,051 yards, 69.2 rating
Ladies' Tee (red): 5,124 yards, 69.6 rating

The Village Course
18 holes—Par 71
Championship Tee (blue): 6,632 yards, 73.3 rating
Regular Tee (white): 6,001 yards, 70.4 rating
Ladies' Tee (red): 5,134 yards, 70.9 rating

The Plantation Course, Kapalua's premier course, was designed by Ben Crenshaw and Bill Coore and is ranked fourth in the world by *Golf Digest*. It is also the home of the annual PGA Tour Mercedes Championship, held in January. Bordered by the pineapple plantation that owns most of the land in Kapalua, the course has six par 5s and its layout is acclaimed as the best in the state. With a rating of 75.2, this is one of the hardest courses in Hawai'i.

Besides its length, the course has tons of very strategically placed bunkers to work anyone's nerves, making both power and placement key. There are no water hazards, although fab water views abound. The par 3 eighth hole is a very tough placement shot over a ravine onto a green surrounded by bunkers. The 18th hole is a whopping 663 championship yards and slight dogleg left.

The Village Course was designed by Arnold Palmer and Ed Seay and is certainly one of the most scenic golf courses in the state—a hilly highland links with stunning views. Two of the most beautiful holes anywhere are the fifth and sixth, set on a six-million-gallon lake stocked with grass carp. This is the "top" of the course, at 800 feet above sea level. From here the view sweeps past the lake to pineapple fields, the channel, and Moloka'i beyond.

The course begins with a steady uphill climb, reaching the summit at the fifth green. Then it's downhill for the remainder of the first nine. The 10th, 13th, and 17th holes on the undulating back nine are tough. Trade winds will make you ponder your driver on the 14th and 15th holes. There are two holes of about 500 yards or longer for power hitters, although this course emphasizes placement far more than power. Two water hazards at the aforementioned fifth and sixth holes, and one to the right side of the 18th, add to the beauty and challenge. There are four doglegs and 61 bunkers to test your control.

The Bay Course, designed by Arnold Palmer and Francis Duane, is tough. As at the Mauna Kea and the Mauna Lani courses on the Big Island, there is a raging surf water hazard here, where the tee and green are on opposite sides of a cove. The course has wonderful water views, although there is a lot more development around it, in the form of condos and villas, than there is at the more pastoral Plantation and Village Courses. The fairways on this course are longer and straighter, however, which power hitters may prefer. (There are four fairways of about 500 yards or longer.) There are two water hazards, four doglegs, and 68 bunkers to finesse or lose your ball.

Rates for greens fees and cart are $175 for visitors and $125 for resort guests. Call for tee times.

Ka'anapali Resort. Less chi-chi than faboo Kapalua, Ka'anapali's golf courses are as good as if not as glamorous as its northern neighbors. There are actually two 18-holers at Ka'anapali, the North and South courses. The North Course is the older, more scenic, and tougher of the two—designed and built in 1961 by Robert Trent Jones, Sr. (one of only two courses in Hawai'i designed by him). The South Course is shorter at 6,555 yards and

is a 1977 expansion by Arthur Jack Snyder of an executive course. Of the two, the North is better. Both straddle Route 30 and the resort.

Royal Ka'anapali North Golf Course, Ka'anapali Beach Resort, Lahaina, HI 96761. Local: 808-661-3691.
>18 holes—Par 71
>Championship Tee (blue): 6,994 yards, 72.8 rating
>Regular Tee (white): 6,136 yards, 70.0 rating
>Ladies' Tee (red): 5,417 yards, 71.1 rating

The North Course is full of doglegs (six), water hazards (five), and bunkers (89) to keep you honest. The 14th green sits steps away from the beach; a hook right will put your ball on a beach blanket. There are also a fair number of uphills, downhills, and straightaways. This course is a power hitter's dream, with the first hole 541 yards long.

Rates for greens fees and cart are about $140 for visitors and under $120 for guests staying at the Ka'anapali Resort. Call for tee times.

South Maui

The western slope of Haleakala has spawned some amazing golf courses in Wailea and Makena. There are five 18-holers, three in Wailea and two in Makena, that are in one of the best locations for golf in Maui. They sit in Haleakala's rain and wind shadow, so conditions are almost always ideal for duffers. The setting is just above the sea and allows some superb views of the Pacific and the mountains of West Maui.

Wailea Golf Club

Wailea Blue Course, 120 Kaukahi Street, Wailea, HI 96753-8493. Local: 808-875-5155.
>18 holes—Par 72
>Championship Tee (blue): 6,758 yards, 71.6 rating
>Regular Tee (white): 6,152 yards, 68.9 rating
>Ladies' Tee (red): 5,291 yards, 70.3 rating

Designed by Arthur Jack Snyder, the Blue is the oldest course in South Maui. It is a classic, with lots of water hazards and bunkers, but gentle and forgiving fairways (our type of course). There are only two parallel fairways, and all are lined with lots of flowering trees, making them quite lovely. Unfortunately, there is also a lot of development around the course in the form of homes, villas, and various resort buildings-including the tennis center—so the natural beauty sometimes extends only as far as the end of the fairway. There are four holes of 500 or more yards to challenge the power hitters. For accuracy, there are four water hazards, shared by the 2nd, 5th, 9th, 15th, and 18th holes.

For the Blue Course, greens fees are $90 for all Wailea Resort guests and $120 for the general public.

Wailea Gold and Emerald Courses, 100 Wailea Golf Club Drive, Wailea, HI 96753-4000. Toll-free: 888-328-MAUI (6284). Local: 808-875-7450.

Gold Course
18 holes—Par 72
Championship Tee (gold): 7,078 yards, 73.0 rating
Regular Tee (blue): 6,653 yards, 71.4 rating
Ladies' Tee (red): 5,442 yards, 70.3 rating

Emerald Course
18 holes—Par 72
Championship Tee (emerald): 6,825 yards, 73.0 rating
Regular Tee (blue): 6,653 yards, 71.4 rating
Ladies' Tee (red): 5,442 yards, 70.3 rating

These two courses, both designed by Robert Trent Jones, Jr., are markedly different. The Gold Course is South Maui's toughest, with an artful use of elevation, bunkers, doglegs, and obstacles like low-lying lava rock walls (*papohaku*—built by the early Hawai'ians and left in place) adding to the challenge. It also now hosts the Senior Skins Game and has received accolades from *Golf*, *Golf Digest*, and that arbiter of upscale attitude, *Condé Nast Traveler*. The course runs over 7,000 yards from the blue tee, and the emphasis is definitely on strategy and placement.

The Emerald Course is known for its beauty and the views from its fairways. It is also known as a course for golfers of all levels.

For the Gold and Emerald Courses, greens fees are $100 for all Wailea Resort guests and $125 for the general public. These are popular courses, so call ahead for reservations and tee times.

Makena Golf Courses, 5415 Makena Alanui, Makena, HI 96753. Local: 808-879-3344.

The Makena courses, both designed by Robert Trent Jones, Jr., are gorgeous and magnificently maintained. The grass is incredible, partly due to the fact that carts are prohibited on the fairway (a Japanese custom—and this resort caters to the Japanese).

North Course
18 holes—Par 72
Championship Tee (black): 6,914 yards, 72.1 rating
Regular Tee (blue): 6,567 yards, 70.4 rating
Ladies' Tee (white): 5,303 yards, 70.9 rating

The North Course was opened in 1993. With its spectacular setting and scenery as its focus, this is a course of both manmade hazards (bunkers, water hazards, low-lying lava rock walls) and natural hazards. This is a course for all types of golfers, providing challenge but also forgiving to those of us who are golfingly challenged. Among the toughest holes is the 14th, with a 200-foot drop in elevation between the tee and the green.

South Course
18 holes—Par 72
Championship Tee (black): 7,017 yards, 72.6 rating
Regular Tee (blue): 6,629 yards, 70.7 rating
Ladies' Tee (white): 5,529 yards, 71.1 rating

The South Course is a thinking person's course, with fast, undulating Bermuda grass greens, rolling fairways, and terrific ocean views. There are several really superb holes, including the 15th and 16th bordering the ocean (the 16th is one of the prettiest holes on Maui). The 514-yard, par 5 tenth hole is a down-the-middle drive with one water hazard on the right side of the fairway and another protecting the pin; it's one of the top driving holes in the state. The

13th hole is all carry-to-the-green, with a water hazard in between. There are seven doglegs and 65 bunkers—including one of the largest and deepest traps we've ever seen, guarding the green on the 15th hole.

Greens fees are $85 for Maui Prince guests and $140 for the general public.

Pukalani Country Club, 360 Pukalani Street, Pukalani, HI 96788. Local: 808-572-1314.

18 holes—Par 72
Championship Tee (blue): 6,945 yards, 72.8 rating
Regular Tee (white): 6,494 yards, 70.6 rating
Ladies' Tee (red): 5,612 yards, 71.2 rating

Pukalani lies on the leeward slopes of Haleakala about 1,500 feet above sea level, in a beautiful area known as Upcountry. The cooler air and the spectacular views of the West Maui Mountains and the blue Pacific make this a delightful place to spend some time on the fairways. This is a very low-key course, designed by Bob Baldock, and provides a refreshing alternative to the glitzy golf of the big resorts below.

Pukalani is a long, open course, with four 500-plus-yard, par 5 holes. There are eight doglegs, including a double on the fifth hole, and water hazards on the tenth and 18th holes. The constant wind here is always a challenge.

Rates for greens fees and shared cart are $50—a bargain.

Tennis

Maui gets the prize for being the tennis hub of Hawai'i. There are five top-notch tennis centers—the Wailea Tennis Club, the Makena Tennis Center, the Royal Lahaina Tennis Ranch, and the Kapalua Tennis Garden and Village Tennis Center—that offer everything a racquet freak desires. There are many more multicourt locations, both municipal and private, throughout the major populated areas (Kihei, Kahului, and West Maui).

South Maui

Wailea Tennis Club, 131 Wailea Ike Place, Kihei, HI 96753. Local: 808-879-1958.

Rated one of the top 50 U.S. tennis resorts by *Tennis* magazine, the Wailea Tennis Club offers visually beautiful and superbly maintained courts. The weather is perfect (warm and dry) for the game of loves and deuces. There are eleven Plexi-pave courts, three lighted for night play. Rates are $25 to $30 per hour. For refreshment, there is Joe's Bar & Grill.

Makena Resort Tennis Club, 5400 Makena Alanui, Makena, HI 96753. Local: 808-879-8777.

Six Plexi-pave courts (two lighted for night play) are available at Makena's Golf and Tennis Center. Operated by Peter Burwash International, rates are $18 to $20 per hour per couple or $12 per day per person for unlimited use.

West Maui

If we were to go to Maui with tennis as our numero uno priority, Kapalua would be our first choice. With two tennis centers and 20 courts, tennis is a big deal here. The Royal Lahaina Tennis Ranch in Ka'anapali is also a good tennis destination.

Kapalua Tennis Garden and Village Tennis Center, 100 Kapalua Drive, Kapalua, HI 96761. Local: 808-669-5677 (Tennis Garden), 808-665-0112 (Tennis Center).
Web site: www.kapaluamaui.com/tennis.htm

Another acclaimed top-50 tennis resort according to *Tennis* magazine, Kapalua has two tennis complexes and the largest tennis staff in the state. Twenty Plexi-pave courts (nine lighted) are situated in two locations at the resort. Rates are under $15 per person per day. Private lessons are available for under $60 an hour.

The tennis program here is very sophisticated. There are tennis tournaments, group and private instruction, organized round-robins, and matches on request. There is also the Kapalua Tennis Camp, which takes place several times throughout the summer.

Royal Lahaina Tennis Ranch, Ka'anapali Resort, Ka'anapali, HI 96761. Local: 808-661-3611.

A 4,000-seat stadium is the centerpiece of the third tennis center on Maui (and it can be rented). There are 11 Plexi-pave courts, six of which are lighted. The complex is under the guidance of Monnier Sports Enterprise Team. The instructional program here is excellent—it made a major difference in our serve in just one easy lesson.

A myriad of tennis programs and classes are available here. Due to its proximity to the big-hotel strip, the Royal Lahaina is both convenient and popular. Book well in advance. Rates are $10 per person per day.

Recommended Public Courts

For a complete listing of all the courts on Maui, call 808-243-7230.

South Maui

Kalama Park, Kihei
Two hard courts, lighted. Free.

West Maui

Lahaina Civic Center, Lahaina. Local: 808-661-4685.
Five Laykold courts, lighted. Free.

Malu'ulu O Lele Park, Lahaina.
Four hard courts, lighted. Free.

Central Maui

War Memorial Center, Kahului.
Five hard courts, lighted. Free.

Beaches

Lying on the beach in front of the Hyatt Regency Maui recently, we were marveling why such a beautiful, placid beach should be so empty. Here we were at the busy Ka'anapali Resort—a strip of big-time hotels and condos stretching north behind a narrow, golden, mile-long strand, and yet there was plenty of breathing space. So we took a walk up the beach, and lo and behold, there were the peo-

ple, the jet skis, the catamarans, and so forth. The beach buzzes with activity everywhere except in front of the Hyatt, where everyone seems to prefer the pool. Fortunately, the very best Maui beaches have been spared the dense development of Ka'anapali. They are either county or state parks or as yet undeveloped.

Like all of the Hawai'ian Islands, Maui does have some gorgeous beaches. While not as stunning as those on O'ahu and Kaua'i, they are some of the safest for swimming in the state. Due to the rapid development of West and South Maui, some of the best are found, surprisingly, near Maui's major airport in Kahului or south of Makena. All are easy to reach by car.

West Maui

West Maui's shoreline is a sprawl of development from Lahaina Town to the far reaches of Kapalua. High-rise hotels and condos proliferate alarmingly, as do shopping malls and fast-food chains. Traffic on Route 30, the only major road, can be bumper-to-bumper from Lahaina north to Honokowai when tourists and hotel workers hit the road at the same time (between 10 A.M. and 6 P.M.). To handle this traffic, sections of the road were widened in 2000.

With all that said, there are still good options for beaches on West Maui; the choices depend on the location of your hotel or the reliability of your rental car. Remember that all hotel beaches will have facilities you can use (restrooms, bar, food, and water sports for hire). Since it's pretty difficult to know who's who and all beaches are public, it's easy to use any hotel's pools, and lounge chairs too—all it takes is attitude. The only time you will need to identify yourself is if you try to get a towel.

West Maui's best bets are as follows:

Ka'anapali Beach. As mentioned earlier, the most enjoyable part of this beach is in front of the Hyatt, or slightly south of it at the Hanaka'o'o Beach Park, where the swimming is better. If you like a crowd and lots of activity, head up to the beach in front of Hula's Grill (in front of Whaler's Village—a great place for mai tais and sunset cocktails) and hang out. This stretch is Maui's toned-down version of Waikiki.

The beach is wider here than at the Hyatt, and there is certainly lots to watch. The Sheraton Hotel is located on the northern end of the beach at Black Rock—known in Hawai'ian as Pu'u Keka'a. This was a sacred burial ground and *heiau* of the Maui *ali'i* (royalty) before the Sheraton bulldozed it and relocated the remains. (They say you have vivid dreams if you stay there.) Around sunset, the Sheraton has a local man, dressed in a *lavalava* (a cloth worn in various ways to cover the torso) and carrying a torch, reenact the dive of the brave Maui king Kahekili off Black Rock.

Kapalua Beach. This is a lovely and protected sandy cove (meaning safe swimming) in front of a lovely and expensive hotel (one of the best on West Maui). Of course, all amenities are available on the beach, such as a bar, and lounge chairs (hotel guests only—remember what we said?). A grove of coconut palms and manicured grass fronts the beach, should you desire shade. This is the ultimate hotel beach on West Maui. Restroom/showers/hotel facilities/water sports.

Slaughterhouse. Some people feel this is the best beach on West Maui, especially for bodysurfing. Located on Mokule'ia Bay, Slaughterhouse can be treacherous in winter if the surf is up, so be advised. It is located off Route 30, just under a mile north of D.T. Fleming Beach Park, around mile marker 32. Look for the parked cars; the path to the beach is easy to find at the left of the lot. *Leave no valuables in your car.* No facilities.

Honolua Bay. Some surfers claim that Honolua offers the best surfing in the state. When the strong northwest winter swell is in, the sets form perfect tubes at three separate breaks. This can be fun just to watch, with a cocktail in hand. When the surf is down, the snorkeling here can be fantastic. The beach itself is rocky and not great for sunbathing. Located just north of Slaughterhouse Beach; look for the surfers and the car park on the cliffs above. *Leave no valuables in your car.* No facilities.

Central Maui

Some of the best beaches on Maui sit between the island's two great mountain ranges on the north side of this vast windswept

isthmus. This is windsurfer heaven. The trade winds rip across the lowland, and surf conditions can be anywhere from mild to big, perfect for different levels of board sailors. Even if you're not a windsurfer, all this activity can be great fun to watch. Some of these beaches can also be great for sunbathing and swimming.

Kanaha Beach Park. This is windsurfing central. The beach, a mile-long stretch of golden sand and ironwoods, is littered with sail-boards and sails of every color in the spectrum (great photo ops here). There is a reef out in the bay that keeps the water relatively flat for those learning to make water starts or for those who just want to swim and soak. It can get crowded here if the wind is up. Don't expect peace and quiet; the beach sits at the end of the Kahului Airport runway. To reach the beach, take the airport road and turn left at the car-rental return sign. (The small Kanaha Beach Park sign is hard to see.) Turn right at the stop sign and take the third turnoff to the park. Restrooms/showers/picnic tables.

Spreckelsville. This is *the* chi-chi neighborhood in Central Maui. Homes of the rich and famous are clustered on the former land of a sugar baron. Two beaches here are fairly secluded and pretty. One of the beaches fronts the Maui Country Club (private, natch). To get there from Kahului, take the Hana Highway east to Kealaki'ai Place. Turn left and then follow Nonohe Place to the beach.

H. P. Baldwin Beach Park. Named after one of Maui and Hawai'i's biggest scions of sugar and land, this is a pleasant beach with nice trade-wind breezes and good swimming. A reef protects the area. There is also a great view of the West Maui Mountains and their abrupt northeastern shore. A local favorite, this is a real Hawai'ian beach. We recommend it. It's located off the Hana Highway (Route 36) about three miles from the airport. Restrooms/showers/picnic area.

Ho'okipa Beach Park. This is probably the premier place on the planet to watch sailboard wave-jumping. The sport will keep you rapt for hours as you watch the best in the world do loop-de-loops off ten-plus-foot waves. This is particularly true when the wind is up-that is, blowing like crazy.

The swimming here is not terribly safe or comfortable. Sunning and watching are the order of the day, although surfers love the eastern end of the beach for its consistent and fine winter breaks (right and left). The two groups—windsurfers and surfers—tend to keep to themselves, windsurfers staying on the western side. To get here, drive east on the Hana Highway through Pa'ia (be sure to pick up a spinach-nut burger at Picnic's-so *ono*). About two miles out of town, you'll see Mama's fish House on your left and then the windsurfers. Follow the signs for parking (which is now a one-way affair after too many accidents). Still, *be careful* turning off. Restrooms/showers/picnic area.

South Maui

Resting at the foot of the dry western slope of Haleakala, this virtually continuous strand of golden beaches stretches from Ma'alaea in the north to Makena in the south. Both ends are wonderful; the middle section—Kihei—is for the most part overdeveloped. Our favorite beaches on Maui, the sister beaches of Big Beach and Little Beach in Makena, are located on the southern end. The Wailea Resort area has some pretty, well-kept beaches that everyone can use. The Ma'alaea Beach is very breezy, fairly deserted, and close to West Maui.

Big and Little Beaches. These beaches—hangouts, actually camps, for hippies in the early '70s (until they were kicked out by the county)—represent the last undeveloped large sandy stretch on the island. Big Beach, a long, wide crescent of golden sand and *kiawe* trees, is one of the prettiest beaches on Maui. Breathing space abounds, and there are often nice sets for bodysurfing. If only Maui had more beaches like this! A small cinder cone, Pu'a O Lai, separates Big Beach from Little Beach. You must climb up over its base (which is not difficult) to reach Little Beach. This is Maui's de facto nude beach and is just a small sandy cove that faces Molokini Island. Little Beach has great snorkeling off Pu'a O Lai. Occasionally there are good bodysurfing waves too.

To get here, from the entrance of the Maui Prince Hotel, drive exactly 1.2 miles on the main road. You will come upon several dirt roads to the right (you'll pass Makena Landing Road twice on your right). Take the main dirt road where you see all the cars, and park where you can. Bring refreshments, as there are no facilities, or stop at the Maui Rainbow Factory just before the turnoff.

Maluaka, Polo, Wailea, Ulua, and Mokapu Beaches. These wonderful little crescent beaches dot the Makena and Wailea coast in front of the upscale resorts and condos of the area. All offer excellent swimming and snorkeling. Coupled with the amenities of the various resorts (such as beach bars, restaurants, and pools/Jacuzzis), these beaches can make for a very relaxing afternoon. If you're not lucky enough to be staying at one of the resorts, by law there is public access and parking for a select number of cars (first come, first served) at each resort. Restrooms/showers/bars/restaurants.

Kamaole Beach Parks 1, 2, and 3. Overdeveloped Kihei has three parks with beaches that break the relentless building of the fastest-growing town on Maui. Of the three, Park 1 has the most greenery and space to spread out. However, we'd advise just getting in the car and going to Big or Little Beach unless you have small children, in which case the facilities here may be handy. Restrooms/showers/picnic area/parking.

Ma'alaea Beach. Situated on the southern end of the isthmus that connects the two sections of Maui, this is a narrow golden-sand strip of almost three miles. The views of both Haleakala and West Maui are fantastic. Summer brings big waves in perfect barrels that are nicknamed "freight train rights," making this a surfer favorite. Every day brings stiff breezes from the trade winds. Swimming is good when the sea is calm. This is not a tourist stop, so it doesn't get crowded. It is located just off Route 310. No facilities.

Hana

Red Sand Beach. Probably one of the few red-sand beaches in Hawai'i, this beautiful, secluded spot—officially known as Kaihalulu—is eastern Maui's nude beach. While nudity on any Hawai'i beach is still illegal and it's at your own risk, just about everyone was in the buff on our last visit. Red Sand is a wonderful and private place to enjoy, clothes or no clothes. The sand gets its hue from the presence of iron in the cinder cone of Ka'uiki Hill. Swimming and snorkeling are good close to shore due to the protection of some outlying rocks. Farther out, there are some strong rips, and there's no lifeguard on duty—so be careful. To get here, take Hau'oli Road down by the Sea Ranch Cottages, and follow the path to the left next to the fence that hugs the base of Ka'uiki Hill. Be careful; the cinders on the path can be slippery, and you could end up in the raging surf. This is not recommended for the clumsy or nervous. No facilities.

Hamoa Beach. This very pretty salt-and-pepper sand cove is a good bet for that much-needed beach break. Hamoa is maintained by the Hotel Hana-Maui, so it is clean and well kept. The swimming is good, and there is a lifeguard here, which is a rarity on this side of the island. A lunch concession is run by the hotel, and there is a water-sports center. Hamoa Beach is reached by taking the Haneo'o Road about two miles south of the town of Hana. Restrooms and showers for hotel guests only, plus picnic area/snack bar.

Wai'anapanapa State Park. For those who like the sexiness of black-sand beaches, this is your best option on Maui. There are natural lava tube arches and caves, too. The swimming and snorkeling can be good, depending on sea conditions. If you like, you can spend the night in one of the rustic, but clean, cabins for about $30 (see the Where to Stay—Hana section). The park is located about four miles north of Hana Town, off the Hana Highway, and is marked by signs. Restrooms/showers/picnic area/camping.

Scuba

Diving on Maui is a thriving big business, and for good reason. There is a wide diversity of dive sites, and the many big hotels, condo complexes, and resorts attract young, active people who love to scuba dive. The dive boats tend to be larger here, so the groups are larger. While this offers greater camaraderie and the ability to be more selective about potential conversation partners and dive

buddies, the intimacy of the small dive boats is lacking. The dives take a good part of the day because of the long but certainly interesting boat rides (with lots of humpback whales during the winter months) to and from the dive sites. Molokini and Lanaʻi are the most popular dive destinations here. Occasionally, when conditions are right, there are trips to the relatively uncharted depths off Molakaʻi. We wouldn't miss this opportunity if it is available. Most trips leave from the docks in Lahaina Town (the rest from the Maʻalaea Harbor/Kihei area), many at the uncivilized hour of 6:30 A.M. The rationale for this early departure time is that the trade winds blow stronger in the afternoon, affecting dive conditions for the worse and making for rougher channel crossings. But we'll tell you, it's pretty rough getting up in the dark at 5:30 A.M. and putting on a damp wet suit while the sun is rising. Ah, diving, like skiing, makes you do some fairly extraordinary things. Of course, once you're in the water, you forget about these inconveniences.

Due to the number of dive operations and the variety of sites available, divers have many options. Most divers will have heard of Molokini and probably will wind up there; except for the humpback whales nearby, however, we found it to be pretty unexceptional. The back side of Molokini is supposed to be more exciting, with a greater likelihood of seeing big fish. Even better than Molokini is Lanaʻi, where several southern dive spots provide some very good opportunities. Molokaʻi, especially along its northern side during the calm days of summer, can be fabulous. So is Kahoʻolawe (but stay away from anything that might look like an unexploded bomb). Finally, there are even some nice spots off West Maui, making travel time much shorter.

Here are the *no ka oi* (the best) of Maui's dive sites.

Molokini. The winner of the Maui dive—site popularity contest, this is an island with a bay formed by the collapsed side of an extinct volcano's crater. We think the diving here is overrated and overused. At least ten other dive boats, along with occasional (moving) whale-watching boats, were in the small bay when we were there. Beware of a strong current that sweeps by the deeper sections of a sloping reef (average depth for this dive is 50 feet; it drops off at about 90 feet): Swimming against it will use up a lot of oxygen. Schools of smaller fish can be seen close to shore; otherwise, the best thing about Molokini is the chance encounter with pelagic fish and whales. If you're leaving from Lahaina, be prepared to get up before dawn.

Kaho'olawe. Although the deeper waters around the U.S. Navy-owned island-turned-bombing-target are usually off-limits, they are sometimes opened on weekends to dive operations. This is a must-do if it's available-be sure to ask.

Hyatt Reef. This is a surprisingly good dive (to 50 feet) in the waters off the biggest resort strip on Maui (Ka'anapali). Sea turtles and octopi are often spotted here, the coral is quite good, and it's an easy shore dive from the beach off the Hyatt.

Cathedrals. The most popular of the dives off Lana'i, these two lava structures lie in about 70 feet of water. They are located within a few miles of each other, close to the southern shore of Lana'i. You can swim inside and poke around various "rooms" and ledges that make up the interior. The dives are interesting, although there isn't a great deal of marine life to be seen, besides schools of small fish. This dive is one of the early-morning numbers out of Lahaina.

Monolith. Another Lana'i dive just west of the Cathedrals, this 40-foot plateau drops off to over 100 feet. Good marine life is found here.

Honolua Bay. One of the prettiest bays in West Maui, and a famous surf break rated as one of the best winter surf spots in Hawai'i, the underwater scene here can be quite good too. An underwater marine park, which means abundant coral and uninhibited fish, this is a popular shallow shore dive for divers of all levels. The diving here is good only in summer. If there are surfers riding big waves, forget it—wrong season!

Grand Canyon. As its name implies, this is a large underwater canyon with depths to 100 feet, situated off the southernmost point of Lana'i. There are lots of colorful tropical fish, as well as turtles and rays.

Sharkfin Rock. Named after its resemblance to a huge shark's dorsal fin in the water, this is a sheer wall down to 90 feet with abundant marine life, particularly the butterfly fish in search of

MAUI

some frozen peas from a self-seal plastic bag. Located in a sheltered bay, this dive offers conditions that are almost always calm.

Dive Operations

Here are a few of the many good dive operations on Maui:

Lahaina/West Maui

Maui Dive Shop, Lahaina Cannery Mall, Lahaina, HI 96761. Local: 808-661-5388.
Web site: www.mauidiveshop.com
Maui Dive Shop has three boats: two that leave from the Kihei Boat Ramp and one that leaves from Ma'alaea Harbor. The Kihei boats hold a maximum of 6 divers and the Ma'alaea Harbor boat holds a maximum of 12 divers per trip. The cost for a two-tank dive is $120 per person. Their store is open daily from 6 A.M. to 9 P.M. They also have a shop in Kihei.

Lahaina Divers, 143 Dickenson Street, Lahaina, HI 96761. Toll-free: 800-998-3483. Local: 808-667-7496.
Web site: www.lahainadivers.com
E-mail: lahdiver@maui.net
Lahaina Divers, in operation for over 20 years, is a full-service PADI Five Star Gold Palm facility. They have two boats: the 50-foot *Endeavor* and the 43-foot *Reliant*. The *Endeavor* can carry a maximum of 24 divers, while the *Reliant* can carry a maximum of 18. They also rent equipment and offer resort and certification courses. The cost for a two-tank dive runs $115 per person. The shop is open daily from 6 A.M. to 8 P.M..

South Maui

Mike Severns Diving, P.O. Box 627, Kihei, HI 96753. Local: 808-879-6596.
Web site: www.mikesevernsdiving.com
A small but reputable dive operation, Mike Severns Diving has been in operation since 1979. They have one boat, the *Pilikai*, a 38-foot Munson Hammerhead, which can carry a maximum of 12

divers per trip (divided into two groups of six each). The cost for a two-tank dive is $105 per person without equipment, $120 per person with equipment. Your trip will be guided by one of four dive masters, either a biologist or a marine naturalist. All their dive packages offer healthy snacks and drinks. They also have an amazing safety record.

Maui Dive Shop, 1455 S. Kihei Road, Kihei, HI 96753. Local: 808-879-0843.
Web site: www.mauidiveshop.com

Maui Dive Shop has three boats: two that leave from the Kihei Boat Ramp and one that leaves from Ma'alaea Harbor. The Kihei boats hold a maximum of six divers, and the Ma'alaea Harbor boat holds a maximum of 12 divers per trip. The cost for a two-tank dive is $120 per person. Their store is open daily from 6 A.M. to 9 P.M.. They also have a shop in Lahaina.

Ed Robinson's Diving Adventures, P.O. Box 616, Kihei, HI 96753. Toll-free: 800-635-1273. Local: 808-879-3584.
Web site: www.mauiscuba.com

Ed Robinson has two boats, one 32-foot and one 30-foot. Dives are done in groups of four to six per dive master. He also offers equipment rental, certification, and resort-style courses. Cost of a two-tank dive, equipment included, is $110 per person.

Shaka Divers, 24 Hakoi Place, Kihei, HI 96753. Local: 808-250-1234.
Web site: www.shakadivers.com.

Specializing in open-water shore dives, this unique operation doesn't even have a storefront. It operates instead from a bus, called the Scubabus, which is pretty much a mobile dive shop. Dives are generally from 20 to 60 feet and can be off sandy beaches or rough, rocky cliffs and everything in between. Most of the dives are in the same locations the dive boats go to, but for about half the cost. Dives last about an hour, and the cost for a two-tank dive is $59, which includes everything you need.

Maui's Nature Options

Maui is dominated by Haleakala, the 10,023-foot dormant volcano that demands to be the center of attention. Every morning hundreds of tourists leave their hotels or condos at 4 A.M. to watch the sun rise over the crater on the summit. The crater and a sizable chunk of surrounding land were turned into a National Park in 1916 in order to preserve a fine example of a dormant volcano. Indeed, life on Maui revolves around Haleakala, physically and spiritually. The nature scene tends to do that, although West Maui's mountain range offers some great hikes too.

How do you "do" Haleakala? First, let's talk about the sunrise option. Personally, we wouldn't get out of bed at 4 A.M. for all the tea in China. We'd just have to stay up all night and try to sleep at the pool the next day. But either way, the sunrise experience, we are told, is heaven. It's about a two-hour drive from Lahaina, so be sure you know the weather forecast. Imagine driving all that way to be in the clouds, wind, and rain at sunrise! We'd rather be in REM sleep, thank you. Be sure to bring a blanket (and a Bloody Mary-though not for the driver, of course) and beat the crowd to breakfast at the Kula Lodge (a must!), about 25 miles down from the summit on a longer loop home.

There are three prerequisites in the nature category for passing the "I've done Maui" tourist course. The first is seeing sunrise on the summit of Haleakala, as just mentioned. The second is driving the road to Hana and beyond to see O'heo Gulch, commonly and improperly referred to as the "Seven Sacred Pools." Finally, there are the whale-watch excursions, where scores of boats go out daily from November to May in search of a close encounter with a humpback whale. There are also other things to do in the great outdoors, away from the madding crowd of West Maui and Kihei—from hiking, to helicopter and horseback rides, to biking down Haleakala.

Hiking

Hiking is probably the biggest outdoor activity on Maui, and for good reason. A considerable amount of the mountainous interior is federal or state property, and thus protected. Much of this is accessible to the public, providing some great hiking opportunities.

Haleakala National Park. Haleakala National Park has 36 miles of hiking trails to wander and ponder, most of which are overnight affairs. Two day-hikes into the crater, eight and twelve miles long respectively, are available for hardy souls. For pampered backpackers, there are three cabins on the crater floor: Holua, Kapala'oa, and Paliku. Holua is the closest at four miles in, Paliku the farthest at ten miles in. Each offers primitive but private accommodations (up to 12 per party) for those who want to hike in and spend the night—call 808-572-4400. Otherwise, a campground is located at both the Holua and Paliku cabins (permits are required). To maintain a wilderness atmosphere, camping is limited to 25 people per campground. Hikers are also asked to stay on the trail to prevent damage to the surroundings and to maintain a wilderness decorum—that is, keep it down. Quiet is the vogue here.

The three major trails in the park are Halemau'u, Sliding Sands, and the Kaupo Trail. The Halemau'u Trail provides the easiest access and exit from the crater and is about ten miles long. From the parking lot off the park road at the 8,000-foot marker, the trail goes for a mile over rolling terrain until it reaches the rim. Then it continues down a two-mile series of steep switchbacks to the crater floor. You are now at an elevation of about 6,600 feet. From here, the trail waltzes through cinder cones and volcanic pits, eventually ending at Paliku Cabin, where you'd better have a reservation. Sliding Sands Trail gets its name from the loose cinders that cover the trail; be careful—they can slip you up. It descends from the 10,000-foot summit, a four-mile precipitous hike down switchbacks to the crater floor. Climbing out on this trail is like going up a down escalator. In another four miles, the trail meets the Halemau'u Trail at Pu'u O'illi, passing the Kapala'oa Cabin at about the six-mile mark (again, reservations are necessary). For the really adventurous, the Kaupo Trail takes you down from 6,400 feet to sea level in nine miles. It goes through the lush and subtropical Kaupo Gap until it meets Highway 31 in the tiny village of Kaupo. All of these hikes require that you be in very good condition and well prepared. The elevation makes physical exertion harder on the body and causes

dramatic changes in the weather. One moment it can be 75° and sunny, the next 50°, windy, and raining. Hypothermia and sunburn are *real* problems here, so be sure to be prepared.

If you'd rather see Haleakala at a more civilized hour than dawn, two possible day-hikes will take you into the crater and have you back home in time for an eight-o'clock reservation at David Paul's. The first option takes you down the Halemau'u Trail to the Holua Cabin and back—an eight-mile round-trip. The second takes you down the Sliding Sands Trail and up the Halemau'u Trail—12 tough miles on those quads and hamstrings. We'd recommend the first option because it's easier and more convenient; you leave from and return to the same place.

For those looking for relief from the relentless tyranny of condo-land, you can backpack in and spend the night—certainly a memorable experience. If you'd like to do this (and we'd definitely recommend trying), your best bet is to reserve a cabin. It means you carry less in and have a bunk (*sans* pillow) on which to collapse. Each cabin has an outhouse-like toilet, a wood-burning or gas stove, a few cooking utensils, and just enough water and firewood to get you through the night. According to the Park Service, you should carry a map, sleeping bag, sunglasses, sunscreen and lip balm, food, water bottle, waterproof matches and fire starter, rain gear, jacket or sweater, extra dry clothes and socks, toiletries, first-aid kit, and flashlight and candles (the latter a must, if just for the effect) for the cabin. To reserve one, you—an adult 18 years or older, we hope—must write in at least 90 days before the time you plan to be there, indicating cabin and dates desired. Make sure you list your preferences, and be sure to list alternatives to enhance your chances. Cabin assignments are decided by lottery on the first day of every month for the period beginning two months hence. You are notified only if you win, and you can stay in the cabins for a total of three nights per month, with just two consecutive nights permitted in one cabin. If you are on-island and decide you want to stay in a cabin, call Monday through Friday between 1 and 3 P.M. to check for cancellations or no-shows. It's outrageously cheap—$40 (up to six people) or $80 (7 to 12 people) per night. You can't beat that. The address: Haleakala National Park, P.O. Box 369, Makawao, HI 96768.

If you really want to rough it , you'll have to schlep everything in and out. In addition to the essentials listed above, the Park Service recommends a waterproof tent with rain fly and a cookstove with fuel (no open campfires are allowed). Permits, which are limited, are necessary and may be obtained from the Park Headquarters.

Attention Day-Hikers:

Before you leave for Maui, be sure to pack a pair of good walking/hiking shoes that you don't mind becoming permanently discolored by Hawai'ian mud: Whatever shoes you take will never be the same. Good hiking boots or shoes with Vibram soles, for traction on slippery trails, are a good idea if you're thinking about doing some day-hikes.

Hike Maui. P.O. Box 330969, Kahului, HI 96733. Local: 808-879-5270, fax 808-893-2515.
Web site: www.hikemaui.com

Normally we wouldn't give such glowing reviews to a commercial operation that helps you do what you could easily do yourself, which is walk. But Hike Maui is hardly what you'd consider commercial. Founded in 1983 by Ken Schmidt, Hike Maui still is Ken Schmidt. When you pay the fee, you are hiring Ken (and his well-trained staff of seven other guides). Ken and company are authorities on the native habitat. They are qualified to tell you not only about which plants are edible on your hike (we pigged out on the thimbleberries—a sweeter version of the raspberry) but about virtually any subject. Ken has studied almost everything from botany and geology to religion, psychology, and ancient Asian philosophy, and he has imparted much of his knowledge to his guides (who come with their own special backgrounds). Half the fun of going on a hike with Hike Maui is listening to the guide. When we went, our group had an hour-long discourse on *kabuna* psychology, the spiritual philosophy of the ancient Hawai'ians. At times you lose track of the beauty around you because you're concentrating on the guide's commentary. They are willing to talk about anything, but they are especially helpful in describing what you're seeing. From the minute the trip begins, they are pointing out facts, flora, and fauna at a dizzying rate.

Hike Maui runs a variety of day-hikes all over Maui. There are

several hikes into the Haleakala crater, coastal and snorkel hikes, hikes to waterfalls and through redwood cloud forests and rain forests. We went on a five-hour hike into the West Maui Mountains and enjoyed it thoroughly. A wholesome lunch—the best veggie sandwich we've ever had—was provided by Picnics in Pa'ia. Considering what you gain in knowledge and experience, the cost of the hikes (average $85) is well worth the money and par with the cost of just about every activity on Maui. All hikes include the use of daypacks, rain ponchos, water bottles, health-food lunches, round-trip transportation from Ma'alaea Harbor, and most interestingly, "guidance in attuning to natural forces and energies."

Biking Down Haleakala

Another variation on the Haleakala trip is biking down the volcano. This is reputed to be the quickest 10,000-foot descent of any road in the country (38 miles are covered). It is almost all downhill, but there will be places where you will have to bike uphill. You will need good brakes, a rearview mirror, a windbreaker or poncho, and a helmet of course. Bike touring on Maui is not the best because of heavy traffic, poor roads on the windward sides, and the lack of a paved road circumnavigating the island. The Haleakala experience is probably your best biking bet here.

Nine companies provide bikes and guided descents. If you're a speed demon like us, you'll opt for a company called the Haleakala Bike Company (see below). Their philosophy is minimum pampering (no hotel pickup or lunch); they get you to the top of the volcano, offer an optional tour of the park in a van, give you your equipment, and set you free. We like that—a descent at your own pace. Their rates are also cheaper (between $49 and $69).

Otherwise, you'll find most of these guided trips torturously slow, despite the fact that the road is full of banked hairpin turns—just great for cruising. As a result, the trip is *very* frustrating. Insurance and liability, we are told, are the culprits. Also, there is always a slowpoke in the group whose idea of zooming is 15 m.p.h. on the straightaway. You are not allowed to pass anyone, and the slowest and wobblies go first, so the rest of the group suffers accordingly. But if you are the cautious, conservative type, then the trip's controlled pace may be just right for you. Maximum speeds are usually 20 m.p.h. A van takes you up to the summit with equipment either at sunrise or at midday. On the way up, you may be subjected to (tortured by) the guide's lobotomized chatter on a microphone—living proof that the airhead is alive and well and living on Maui. There is a breakfast or lunch stop along the way. The trip takes about six hours, start to finish. Costs for the guided trip range between $100 and $120.

Here are three options for biking down Haleakala:

Haleakala Bike Co., 810 Haiku Road, #120, Haiku, HI 96708. Toll-free: 888-922-2453. Local: 808-575-9575.
Web site: www.bikemaui.com

This company allows you to set your own pace and to not go in a group at all. To keep costs down, frills such as hotel pickup and breakfast and/or lunch are not included. All equipment and a ride to the top of Haleakala (some tours include a two-hour van tour of the park) are what you get. Costs are cheaper here, with the Express Tour (no park guided tour) only $49; the sunrise and summit tours run $69 and $59 respectively. You can also rent Gary Fisher Mountain Bikes for $19 per day.

Maui Downhill, 199 Dairy Road, Kahului, HI 96768. Toll-free: 800-535-BIKE (2453). Local: 808-871-2155, fax 808-871-6875.
Web site: www.mauidownhill.com

One of the oldest downhill bike operations on Maui, this outfit is also the largest, with over 60 employees, 300 bikes, and 15 vans. There are five different bike tours, including sunrise packages, ranging in price from $62 to $115. Hotel pickups are included.

Maui Mountain Cruisers, 15 S. Wakea Avenue, Kahului, HI 96732. Toll-free: 800-232-MAUI (6284). Local: 808-871-6014.
Web site: www.mauicruisers.com

Another guided downhill tour company, this is the cheaper by a few dollars. There are two tours daily for sunrise and lunch trips. Hotel area pickups are available. Costs are under $125.

Bike Rentals

To rent a mountain bike (and others), besides **Haleakala Bike Co.,** check out **West Maui Cycles** in Lahaina (808-661-9005 or www.maui.net/~wmcycles). It's open from Monday through Saturday from 8:30 A.M. to 6:00 P.M., Sunday from 10:00 A.M. to 3:00 P.M. Also try **South Maui Bicycles** in Kihei at 808-874-0068. They are open Monday through Saturday from 10 A.M.to 6 P.M. and Sunday from 10 A.M. to 2 P.M.

Oooh Cruises

The Road to Hana and the Seven Sacred Pools. Two things become clear on this tourist and honeymoon pilgrimage. First, there are 52 miles, 54 bridges, and 617 turns on the famous road to Hana from the Kahului Airport, and 11 twisting miles more to the pools. Every day hundreds of rental cars (almost 500,000 people a year) make the slow, winding journey. They go not necessarily to enjoy the view but to see the pools—only to be disappointed in them because the gulch looks similar to most of the scenery passed along the way. Charles Lindbergh's grave in nearby Kapahulu is a big attraction—even though local residents don't appreciate the publicity or the tourist traffic. Second, there are not seven sacred pools. The word "sacred" in the name has created some wildly exaggerated mystique, even though the pools aren't sacred and there are many more than seven (we think some savvy tour operator thought that one up). The correct name is the not-so-appealing 'Oheo Gulch. Most people will be disappointed with the "pools." It is a mistake to make the pools the destination at all. Rather, the actual drive itself should be.

The trip will take all day (unless, of course, you choose to stay in Hana). So why not plan to go to the beach to break things up a bit? There are three small but pretty beaches where you can catch some rays. Do keep in mind that Hana is on the windward side of Maui. This means that passing clouds and showers are very likely at any time, but bring your suit and towel—the water from the sky or the ocean will be very refreshing.

The road to Hana itself is spectacular and unique, particularly if you're lucky enough not to be the driver. It is a long haul, but we definitely recommend doing it—especially if you can arrange to fly back. Along the way, you will pass all kinds of rain-forest vegetation—ferns, monkeypod trees, African tulip trees, banyans, bamboo, eucalyptus—and constantly changing ocean views. It's a good idea to stop several times along the way—and a good remedy for getting stuck in one of the seemingly endless rental-car caravans that plague this narrow, twisting road. If you are a slow driver or in no rush, please allow the faster cars (usually local traffic) to pass. Compounding the traffic is the fact that most of the bridges are one-car affairs, which require that one direction or another has the right-of-way, thereby stopping traffic.

When renting a car for this trip, we'd recommend a standard stick shift to give you the power to pass the slowpokes in a very short space (second gear is a big hit on this road). Be sure to fill up before leaving Pa'ia, as there are no gas stations until you get to Hana. If you don't have the time or the inclination to drive all the way to Hana, turn around at Ka'enae; the road from there is just more of the same.

There are several waterfalls along the way, and they will keep on coming. After a while we began to OD on them. It might be a good idea to stop at one, walk in, and enjoy it; then you won't feel compelled to stop at every single damn one. The few noteworthy ones include Twin Falls (mile marker 2), Puohokamoa Falls (mile marker 11), Haipua'ena Falls (next after Puohokamoa), and Waikani Falls (mile marker 16). Do not miss the Ke'anae Peninsula (mile marker 18), where you drive down to sea level past a small pretty church, and a dramatic lava rock coastline, replete with crashing surf, cliffs, and a mountain vista laced with huge waterfalls. Other must-stops are Wailua Bay, the Pi'ilanihale Heiau (the largest in Hawaii), Wai'anapanapa State Park for its black-sand beach, and of course Hana. Once in Hana, definitely check out the Hotel Hana-Maui and plan to have a wonderful (and expensive) lunch there. You may want to beach it (see Beaches—Hana earlier in this chapter) or go horseback riding in the ranchland above the town (the Hana Ranch store will have info, or call 808-248-8261). For some reason, most people have to stop at Hasegawa's, the topsy-turvy general store crammed with a hodgepodge of just about everything. Residents of

New York City will feel as if they're in a messy version of the neighborhood bodega.

We really don't think it's worth the schlep to Oʻheo Gulch, as it will add at least two hours to your trip (the road gets worse) for just more of the same. It would be more fun to have a wonderful lunch at the Hotel Hana-Maui. And the misnamed Seven Sacred Pools are really 24 large pools and dozens of smaller ones carved out of the lava by the convergence of the Pipiwai and Palikea streams. They can be brimming with water or more reminiscent of puddles, depending on the water volume of the two rivulets that run through the gulch. If it's been raining recently (often in winter), the water will be high. If it's been raining heavily very recently, the water will be very high but also muddy. It will look more like Mississippi River water than that of a pristine tropical stream. If it has been dry, the pools can look pretty pathetic, although the water should be clearer.

If you do decide to go, rather than face the crowds who walk down to the pools, hike up to see Makuhiku and Waimoku Falls, an easy two-mile hike that surprisingly few people take. Waimoku Falls is 400 feet high in the center of a good example of a Hawaiʻian valley. The hike is not difficult but, as in all Hawaiʻian hikes on the wetter sides of the islands, it can be muddy. Don't wear white shoes. You will have to ford the stream once, but it's simple unless the water level is high. The hike itself will take you through native and exotic (i.e., foreign) forests, including a wonderful, quiet grove of bamboo that is *très* tropical.

Whale Watches

All right. You've "done" Haleakala and driven the road to Hana. One more activity, during mid-December through mid-April, will allow you to pass the "I've Done Maui" course. It is the whale watch. (Those of you visiting in the summer are excused.) If you scuba dive, chances are you will see whales off in the distance and get about as close as the excursion boats do. If you want to get closer, there are several pleasant ways to go out, hoist a few, and maybe see some of the world's biggest mammals.

Most boats leave from West Maui, either Lahaina Town or Kaʻanapali, or from Maʻalaea Harbor. They will ply about the waters of Au'au Channel in search of "thar she blows." Due to the danger of spooking the humpbacks and potentially harming them with boat hulls and propeller blades, state law requires that boats stay 100 yards away or turn off their engines and drift. Whales are intelligent creatures, and they know to keep their distance. Occasionally some will swim close by, but most of the time you will have to be content with seeing their small dorsal fins, huge tail flukes, the spouts, and glimpses of their backs. Let's face it, the whale-watch boats are familiar and hardly pique the whales' curiosity anymore. Pods with calves are particularly wary of the motorized spectator fleet.

Many, many boats do these excursions. We'd recommend a sailboat, as it's fun to sail. Also, with sailing there is less of the hobbyhorsing that comes with floating powerboats in ocean swells and, with luck, less chance for the motion-sensitive among you to get seasick. Catamarans, the double-hulled sailboats that you see off the beach, are fairly stable and spacious. Here are our choices:

Pacific Whale Foundation, 101 N. Kihei Road, Kihei, HI 96753. Toll-free: 800-942-5311. Local: 808-879-8860.
Web site: www.pacificwhale.org
We'd recommend using this non-profit organization, founded in 1980, because its goal is saving the world's whales from extinction. There are 15 cruises daily on four boats (two from Lahaina and two from Ma'alaea Harbor). As we're partial to sailing, we'd suggest taking the sailboat from Lahaina. Rates are $30 for adults and $15 for kids, and all profits go to the PWF. Reservations advised.

Trilogy Excursions, 180 Lahainaluna Road, Lahaina, HI 96761. Toll-free: 888-MAUI-800. Local: 808-661-4743.
Web site: www.sailtrilogy.com
Run by the Coon family, this smooth operation's specialty takes you to Lana'i on one of six catamarans 40 feet and over. Vans take you on a guided tour to Lana'i City (a refreshing and real Hawai'ian town) and through the miles of now fallow pineapple fields. Snorkeling and swimming are available off of Hulopo'e Beach. Trilogy also has an overnight excursion. The whale watches run twice daily and cost $39 per person, kids ages 3 to 15 are half price.

America II, P.O. Box 86, Lahaina, HI 96761. Local: 808-667-2195. Web site: www.galazymall.com/stores/reefdancer

This is your chance to sail aboard a real America's Cup champion. Successfully raced by Dennis Connor in the 1987 race in Fremantle, Australia, the boat is now berthed in Lahaina and is available for whale watches and sunset sails. There are four trips daily (in season, two are whale watches). Rates are $30 for adults and $15 for children 6 to 12 years old (younger children are discouraged unless experienced).

Club Lanaʻi. Don't bother.

Horseback Riding

High above the town of Hana, horseback riding is "da bomb." The rolling pastures of the Hana Ranch spread out before you like a lush green carpet, the cobalt blue of the Pacific creating that much-sought-after feeling of space. Cantering along past the fields of cattle is what riding, to those who romanticize the Old West, should be. If you plan to go to Hana, definitely consider going riding instead of going to Oʻheo Gulch (the "Seven Sacred Pools").

There are other places to ride, too, but none as invigorating as those hills above Hana. Pony Express Tours is a nice way to mosey through the Haleakala crater, but you will be slow-poking it. (It would be far better to walk through the crater because it's the silence, albeit occasionally shattered by the roar of chopper blades, that is truly wonderful.) You can also ride in Makena, Kula, and on West Maui. If you're on Maui during the July 4th weekend, don't miss the Makawao Rodeo and Parade—one of the best in the state (tickets to the rodeo run between $6 and $10). Here's who to contact for riding information.

Hotel Hana-Maui Stables, Hana, HI 96713. Local: 808-248-7238.

This is how to do it. Guided group rides and private rides are available. Rates are $30 per hour.

Pony Express Tours, P.O. Box 535, Kula, HI 96790. Local: 808-667-2200 or 808-878-6698, fax 808-878-3581.

Haleakala trail rides are the specialty here. Remember, this is not a gallop-and-canter trip, it's a trail ride—that is, slow. For some people, however, it sure beats walking.

Makena Stables, 8299-A S. Makena Road, Makena, HI 96753. Local: 808-879-0244.

This is an intelligent operation that limits groups to six and is adjacent to Big Beach—the best beach on Maui.

Other Riding Stables on Maui:

Adventures on Horseback, P.O. Box 1419, Makawao, HI 96768. Local: 808-242-7445 or 808-572-6211.
Web site: www.maui.net/~horses

Ironwood Ranch, Ltd., P.O. Box 10066, Lahaina, HI 96761. Local: 808-669-4991/4708, fax 808-669-4702.

Thompson Ranch, R.R.1, P.O. Box 203, Kula, HI 96790. Local: 808-878-1910.

Helicopter Rides

There is too much intrusion on nature on Maui as it is, and helicopters here certainly add to it. As you may already know, we think these machines should fly only in areas that are otherwise inaccessible, so as not to disturb hikers' (or residents') solitude and seclusion. As the geography of Maui doesn't really allow this, we don't recommend helicopters on Maui (the only islands where we do are Kaua'i and the Big Island). There are more than ten helicopter companies, however, and rides will run you between $70 and $250 per person.

Cerebral Stuff

Cerebral attractions are not one of Maui's strengths, and there are many other fine reasons to visit the island. But if you're going or are already there, there are enough thought-provoking stimuli around to augment the activities of Haleakala's island.

MAUI

The Art Scene

Maui's greatest appeal to the intelligentsia is the fairly new Maui Arts & Cultural Center (Maui Central Park, P.O. Box 338, Kahului, HI 96733, phone 808-242-2787, fax 808-242-4665, www.maui.net/~macc). Located here are two theaters, an amphitheater, a *pa hula* (an outdoor hula platform), an art gallery, and classrooms and meeting spaces. Opened in 1994 at a cost of over $32 million, the art center covers the spectrum of the art scene, from hula and the Maui Symphony Orchestra to Hawai'ian slack key guitar and Mark Morris or Tony Bennett and Cubanismo. Check out their Web site for the current calendar of events. This is a great alternative to the sometimes tedious Polynesian revues at the resorts and to the tackiness of parts of Lahaina and Kihei.

Visual Arts

The 1980s and '90s saw the commercialization of the art scene on Maui. Many artists hailed from the mainland and elsewhere, where freed from international trends of abstraction and theme, they created a free-for-all of style and form. What emerged was a hybrid of those black-lit posters we used to stare at for hours and scenes from a marine biology textbook. Today Maui is home to some very successful artists who have won acclaim—justified in some cases and exaggerated in others. However, one has to wade through scenes of leaping dolphins and humpback whales to find the more original local art. There is still no "Hawai'ian School" of art, although the work of artists like Pegge Hopper or those who interpret historical Hawai'ian images maybe the closest thing to it.

There are a number of ways to catch up on the Maui art world. Friday night, from 6 to 9 P.M., is Gallery Night at the many galleries of Lahaina Town and is a fun way to find out what's happening. Most of the big resorts, the Hyatt Regency and the Grand Wailea in particular, are mini-museums, although a lot of their art tends to be from the Far East and elsewhere. Some of the better-known artists, such as Wyland have their own gallery/studios.

Hui No'eau Visual Arts Center, 2841 Baldwin Avenue, Makawao, HI 96768. Local: 808-572-6560, fax 808-572-2750. Web site: www.maui.net/~hui

Occupying an old stucco mansion with spacious and lovely grounds, this center is a real must for art fans. Hui No'eau's focus is on education. Those planning an extended stay should check out their adult and child education programs. There are classes, workshops, and studios for painting, drawing, ceramics, weaving, paper and print making, batik, basket and quilt making (a Hawai'ian specialty), and jewelry making. The center also has almost constant exhibitions, as well as lectures, seminars, and film and slide presentations. It's a nonprofit organization—you, too, can become a patron and help the art cause on the island. Be sure to call in advance to determine the daily happenings and current exhibits. It is open from Tuesday through Sunday from 10 A.M. to 4 P.M.

Music and Book Stores

Need maps, the latest Stephen King thriller, or a book on *kahuna* psychology? Well, Maui isn't really a reader's paradise. There are a few bookstores that will probably have the printed pages you desire; most of the others are religion-oriented. Music-lovers will fare better.

Bookstores

Borders Books, Music & Cafe, Maui Marketplace, 270 Dairy Road, Kahului, 877-6160.

Open Sunday through Thursday from 9 A.M. to 10 P.M., Friday and Saturday until 11 P.M.

Waldenbooks, Lahaina Cannery Mall, 667-6172, and Kukui Mall, 874-3688.

The bookstore chain on Maui. Open daily from 9:30 A.M. to 9 P.M.

Paperbacks Plus, 1977 Main Street, Wailuku, 242-7135.

A good selection of new books; they also buy, sell, and trade used books. Open Monday through Friday 8:30 A.M. to 5:30 P.M., Saturday and Sunday 9 A.M. to 5 P.M.

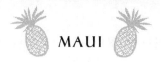

MAUI

CD Stores

Jukebox Music & Gifts, 21 Baldwin Avenue, Paʻia, 579-9885.
Open daily from 10:30 A.M. to 6 P.M.

Request, 10 N. Market Street, Wailuku, 244-9315, and 991 Lima-hana Place, Lahaina, 661-8855.
Open from 10 A.M. to 6 P.M., closed Sunday.

Tropical Disc, 2395 S. Kihei Road, Kihei, 874-3000.
Open Monday through Saturday from 9 A.M. to 8 P.M., Sunday 11 A.M. to 7 P.M.

Sacred Sites

Piʻilanihale Heiau. This is the largest *heiau* in the state, located just west of the Hana airport. It is 340 feet by 415 feet, with the highest part of the temple being 50 feet high (that's a lot of lava rocks!). The walls of the temple are eight to ten feet thick. Most historians believe it was built in the 15th century by Piʻilani, the king of Maui, for Ku, the war god. Thus it was probably the site of human sacrifice.

The property on which it sits is now part of the National Botanical Gardens, and tours are arranged through Kahanu Gardens; call 808-248-8912. The cost is $5 for self-guided tours and $10 for guided.

ʻIao Valley. Located just west of Wailuku in the West Maui Mountains, this is one of the most sacred valleys on the island. It is said that, like the Waipiʻo Valley on the Big Island, this one is filled with *mana*, or Hawaiʻian royal spirits. A drive up into the valley is well worth your time, although you should be prepared to meet the tourist buses at the end of the road. Even better is a hike starting at ʻIao Park, which will take you by the ʻIao Needle. The Needle is probably one of Maui's most recognized landmarks and is indeed photogenic. There are trail maps at the visitors' center (and lots of feral cats in the parking lot).

Where to Stay

Maui is consistently one of the most sought-after destinations in Hawai'i, and its popularity translates into a cornucopia of choices when it comes to accommodations. While the island is fairly large, virtually all are concentrated on the calm, sunny, dry coasts of South or West Maui. Unfortunately, both are beginning to resemble Southern California sprawl all too closely. Nevertheless, within some of these giant resorts, one can find a niche and certainly enjoy oneself. Best of all are the more remote areas like Hana, which, even though it rains more, is one of our favorite places in the world.

Maui is also condo heaven, with over 175 properties from which to choose. More condos are available to tourists on this island than on any other island in the state. If you prefer this mode of lodging, there are more than enough options. Accommodations on Maui are generally more expensive than on the other islands, particularly in the big resorts, so the condo route may be less costly. As always, look for package deals to save money.

We have grouped the lodgings in five areas: West Maui, South Maui, Upcountry, Central Maui, and Hana. As we said, almost all are located in West Maui or South Maui. West Maui accommodations are on a strip along the water that begins in the old whaling town of Lahaina and continues up through Kapalua, with the largest concentration in the Ka'ananapali Resort, just north of Lahaina Town. On West Maui, the prettiest area is Kapalua. On South Maui, the hotel-condo area runs along the coast from the overdeveloped town of Kihei and through the planned community of Wailea. It ends in Makena, at the wonderfully undeveloped Big and Little Beaches (the island's best). Above the South Maui coast is pretty and pastoral Upcountry Maui, which sits on the western slope of Haleakala at an elevation of 1,500 to 3,000 feet. Upcountry is much cooler and breezier, and obviously the sunset views are quite amazing. The beach, however, is at least 30 minutes away. Central Maui is the commercial hub of the island and offers Maui's best windsurfing opportunities and some very cheap accommodations. Hana, well, we just *love* Hana. It sits on the eastern end of Maui and is a magical place unto itself. If you're looking for a romantic or exotic locale, Hana is it! Remember—it is on the wind-

ward side, so it rains a lot more, which is why it is *so* green and verdant. We wish we were in Hana right now!

West Maui

Ka'anapali

Hyatt Regency Maui, Ka'anapali Beach Resort, Ka'anapali, HI 96761. Toll-free: 800-228-9000. Local: 808-661-1234. Rooms and suites: 806.

Web site: www.maui.hyatt.com

This is the hotel that pioneered the "super-resort" concept—the you-never-have-to-leave-the-grounds big hotel. Opened in 1980 on 40 acres and renovated in 1997, the Hyatt is fun, if you like big hotels, as there is always something to see or observe and always something going on. For those who want action and want to stay on the Ka'anapali strip, this is our favorite.

While the towers aren't interesting architecturally, the atrium is quite attractive. There is a multimillion-dollar collection of Asian and Pacific art that is well presented and interesting to view. The gardens, while done up in a major way—including macaws, a flock of pink flamingos, and even penguins!—are pleasant to stroll through after having a few cocktails. The pool is where the action is, because more people hang out here than on the terrific beach in front. The free-form pool covers half an acre and features several waterfalls, rock formations, a grotto you can swim through and have a drink at a pool bar inside, and a "secret" underwater cave with a breathing hole and a 150-foot water slide to assuage all those fantasies of sliding down water chutes into tropical pools watched by lovely hula maidens. The beach in front is very nice, uncrowded, and nicely sloped for optimal tanning. To keep in shape and soothe the body, a new 9,000-square-foot spa and fitness center opened in 2000. It features just about anything your body desires and is a state-of-the-art facility. There are also six tennis courts (not lighted) on the grounds and two 18-hole golf courses at the Ka'anapali Resort.

The rooms and suites at the Hyatt Regency Maui, while not large, are very tastefully appointed in shades of tan and green. All have wall-to-wall carpeting, rattan furnishings with tropical print fabrics, stuffed chairs or loveseats, attractive prints on the walls, cable TV, safe, and mini-bar/fridge. They also have a small lanai and some, like the corner rooms, have two. The Hyatt provides some of the best Japanese robes, called *yukatas*, in Hawai'i. (Unfortunately they are not complimentary-but you can buy one.)

Four restaurants (including the very good Cascade Grill and Sushi Bar), two bar/lounges, and the Drums of the Pacific luau are available to guests. Of course there is also the standard concourse of extremely upscale shops where you would never dream of buying anything.

Rates are **Wicked Pricey** and up.

The Westin Maui, 2365 Ka'anapali Parkway, Lahaina, HI 96761. Toll-free: 800-WESTIN-1 (937-8461). Local: 808-667-2525. Rooms and suites: 761.
Web site: www.westinmaui.com

The first thing you hear when you walk into the Westin Maui is the sound of water from the humongous water park that acts as the centerpiece of the hotel. A central waterfall, surrounded by a reflecting pond stocked with koi and black and white swans, is the first thing you see. This water world is a 650,000-gallon pool complex, featuring an 85,000-square-foot pool area spread out among five free-form pools and two water slides—one of which provides a thrilling 120-foot ride. You can even walk behind the waterfall via a passageway or swim up to a Jacuzzi tucked away in a "grotto." While the pink-shaded, 11-story towers with little crescent balconies are rather '60s looking, the public areas are elegant and appealing, with stone floors greatly enhancing the ambience (we found the hall carpets and room upholstery a tad tired). The beach in front offers the best swimming in Ka'anapali.

Rooms are on the small side, except for those in the Ocean View wing, where they are 30 percent larger. All come in shades of white and tan with wall-to-wall carpet, mirrored walls, lots of marble accents, light wood furnishings, feather pillows (a plus), dual-line data- and fax-port phones, coffeemaker, and iron and board. Baths are also on the smallish side, with tiled floors, separate loo, and single vanity. All rooms have lanais, which unfortunately have plastic furniture—a mistake, but the most of the views are commendable.

As with all resorts in this category, there are restaurants (six), lounges (three), activities, the Westin Kids Club, a business center, and a health club—a veritable city unto itself.

Rates are *Very Pricey* and up. Look for packages.

Maui Marriott Resort & Ocean Club, 100 Nohea Kai Drive, Lahaina, HI 96761. Toll-free: 800-228-9290. Local: 808-667-1200, fax 808-667-8181. Rooms and suites: 624.
Web site: www.marriott.com

With a much needed face-lift in 2000, the refurbished Maui Marriott has a new look. As with other Marriotts in Hawai'i, the resort is a combination (50/50) of hotel and time-share. While we loathe the idea of the latter (the time-share crowd conjures up images of matching sweatsuits and bad eyewear), Marriott is spending a ton to redo this place. A spruced-up entrance and atrium, enlarged water features including more pools, water slides, and grottos (all basically a standard feature at big Ka'anapali resorts), rooms and vacation suites with a more West Indian look (why that choice of décor in Hawai'i is an enigma to us), and new restaurants and bars are all included in the extensive renovation. All guest rooms have a sleeper sofa, mini-fridge, coffeemaker, iron/board, cable color TV, phones with voice mail and dataport. and lanai. Let us know what you think of the finished product.

Rates are *Very Pricey* and up. Look for packages.

Sheraton Maui, 2605 Ka'anapali Parkway, Lahaina, HI 96761. Toll-free: 800-782-9488. Local: 808-661-0031, fax 808-661-0458. Rooms and suites: 510.
Web site: www.sheraton-hawaii.com

With a premier location and a beach on 23 acres at Pu'u Keka'a at the northern end of the West Maui resort strip, the Sheraton, one of the original Ka'anapali resorts, received a $160 million renovation in 1997. While the outside architecture is still rather '60s looking, the interior has been brought up to speed (and the buildings don't exceed six stories). Central to its *au courant*-ness is a 142-yard freshwater swimming lagoon with various grottos and spas, a new fitness center, and updated room décor. Other amenities include three lighted tennis courts, coin-op laundry, three restaurants and three bars, a summer children's program, and daily room service (6:30 A.M. to 10 P.M.). Guests have privileges at the Ka'anapali Resort's golf facilities. A nightly torch-lighting and cliff-diving ceremony is a Sheraton Maui trademark.

Rooms and suites feature wall-to-wall carpeting and an earthtone décor. All come with cable TV/video games, Hawai'ian-style bedspreads and artwork, wicker/rattan and dark wood furnishings, iron/board, safe, phones with voice mail and dataports, and lanai. Suites also have microwaves. Baths have 100 percent cotton bath towels, height-adjustable showerhead, makeup/shaving mirror, and hair dryer. Over 80 percent of the rooms have ocean views, the best being in the Hale O Ka Moana wings.

Rates are **Wicked Pricey** and up. Look for packages.

Ka'anapali Beach Hotel, 2525 Ka'anapali Parkway, Lahaina, HI 96761. Toll-free: 800-227-4700. Local: 808-661-0011. Rooms and suites: 430.
Web site: www.kaanapalibeachhotel.com

This older resort on the Ka'anapali strip offers standard hotel fare in four low-rise buildings that form a horseshoe around the grounds and the beach. The décor is somewhere between tasteful and tacky, but certainly not unpleasant. All rooms have a Hawai'ian colonial décor with a neutral color scheme of tans and whites, with Hawai'ian quilt bedspreads and Hawai'ian prints on the walls. All also feature a lanai, wall-to-wall carpeting, safe, fridge, coffeemaker, and iron and board.

There is a good-size swimming pool, attractive grounds, and of course Ka'anapali Beach. The staff is required to attend Hawai'iana seminars—a thoughtful touch. There is also the "Aloha Passport for Kids" program, a good free program for children up to 12 years old. Probably the best reason to stay here, however, is the price—among the lowest of the Ka'anapali resorts.

Rates are **Pricey** and up. Look for packages.

Royal Lahaina Resort, 2780 Kekaa Drive, Lahaina, HI 96761. Toll-free: 800-227-4700. Local: 808-661-3611. Rooms and suites: 521.
Web site: www.hawaiihotels.com

The Royal Lahaina is one of the oldest properties in the Ka'anapali resort area. Built in 1962, rooms are spread out among 27 acres in a 12-story tower (newer) and several two-story "cottages" (the originals). It is located at the end of the resort area, so it's mellower and quieter than its neighbors in the heart of the strip. Keka'a Point separates the Royal Lahaina from the others, which helps keep it isolated. One of the best features of this hotel is its superb tennis facility (11 courts/6 lighted) and 3,500-seat tennis stadium-the Royal Lahaina Tennis Ranch. There are also three pools, and of course the beach in front. Three restaurants, two cocktail lounges, and a poolside grill are on the grounds for refueling and refreshment. There's also a nightly Polynesian revue/luau.

Rooms were last refurbished in 1993 and are pleasant enough and comfortable. All feature a tan décor with wall-to-wall carpeting, Hawai'ian colonial furnishings and Hawai'ian quilt bedspreads, cable TV, fridge, safe, iron and board, and room service. A free shuttle connects the resort to Whaler's Village (the commercial center of Ka'anapali) and Lahaina Town.

Rates are *Not So Cheap* and up. Look for packages (especially on the Internet).

Aston Ka'anapali Shores Resort, 3445 Honoapi'ilani Highway, Lahaina, HI 96761. Local: 808-667-2211, fax 808-661-0836. Units: 464.
Web site: www.aston-hotels.com

One of the better condo options on West Maui is the Aston Ka'anapali Shores. It is a well-run resort, and people who stay here love it. Located on the beach, its two pools and sunning area are the focal point and center of activity. There are also two jet spas, a fitness center, and three tennis courts. For refreshment, a restaurant and lounge are on the property.

There are studios, one- and two-bedroom units, and two-bedroom penthouses. The units we'd recommend are the oceanfront two-bedroom models with "01" in their room numbers. These are within inches, it seems, of the water. The corner-wrap lanais give you a bird's-eye view not only of the humpback whales out in the channel (during the winter months) and Moloka'i and Lana'i, but also of all the bodies basking in the sun around the pool. All units have a lanai, fridges in the hotel rooms and complete kitchens and washer/dryers in the suites, safe, and cable TV. There is daily maid service.

Rates are *Pricey* and up. Look for packages.

Embassy Suites Maui, 104 Ka'anapali Shores Place, Lahaina, HI 96761-9419. Toll-free: 800-535-0085. Local: 808-661-2000. Units: 413. Web sites: www.marcresorts.com

Located north of the Ka'anapali resort area is the Embassy Suites Maui, an all-suite property that should appeal to families and those who want more room(s) for their money. We found this 12-story structure to be a symphony in pink, both inside and out. This made us wonder why pink is such a popular color for tropical hotels. Unable to come up with a logical answer, we entered the breezy and simple lobby of pink coral stone floors, an atrium, and fish ponds loaded with *koi*. Outside, there is lots of green foliage (perhaps the pink and green color scheme is a subliminal preppy plot), a one acre pool with a water slide and a hot tub/jet spa for the older and younger at heart, and a kids' pool too. A fitness center, "Beach Buddies" kids' program, miniature golf, a beauty salon and spa, three restaurants, a concierge and activities desk, and a daily complimentary breakfast buffet and evening cocktail reception (beware any sales pitches for time-shares) round out the amenities.

The one- and two-bedroom suites we saw were huge, with a surprisingly tasteful décor of Hawai'ian colonial furnishings, red and green fabrics, a humongous entertainment center with a 35-inch TV/VCR/stereo with dual cassette player, wall-to-wall tan carpet with a green-tiled entryway, and pull-out sofa. Everything seems oversized here, including the white-tiled baths with glass-enclosed shower, separate tub and loo, and dual vanities. Most suites also come with something called a Maui kitchen, which we'd never heard of but is defined as a wet bar, fridge, and microwave. Some of the more deluxe suites have kitchenettes with fridge, dishwasher, toaster, and coffeemaker. There is daily maid service and room service.

Rates are *Wicked Pricey* and up. Look for packages.

Ka'anapali Ali'i, 50 Nohea Drive, Ka'anapali, HI 96761. Toll-free: 800-642-MAUI (6284). Local: 808-667-1400. Units: 264.

MAUI

Web site: www.classicresorts.com

As the *ali'i* name implies, these are royal-deluxe condos right in the middle of the Ka'anapali resort area. If you're looking for convenience, space, and luxury in Ka'anapali, then this is the place. In our opinion, for the money we'd opt for Kapalua, which is a much more appealing setting.

The very attractive and elegant units come in one- and two-bedroom sizes of 1,500 and 1,900 square feet, respectively, with such nice features as whirlpool bathtubs and two full baths. Décor is on the pastel and light wood side, with tropical fabrics. The cluster of four eleven-story towers surrounds swimming pools and sits on the beach next to the Westin Maui. Three lighted tennis courts, a fitness center, men's and women's saunas, grocery delivery, concierge, room service, and daily maid service round out the amenities.

Rates are **Wicked Pricey** and up.

Maui Eldorado Resort, 2661 Keka'a Drive, Ka'anapali Beach, Lahaina, HI 96761-1933. Local: 808-661-0021, fax 808-667-7039. Units: 101.

Web site: www.outrigger.com

Now part of the Outrigger group, the family-friendly Maui Eldorado is an attractive and unassuming series of two-story buildings situated on the seventh fairway of the Royal Ka'anapali golf course. Units come in spacious studio (750 square feet), one-bedroom (1,250 square feet), and two-bedroom (1,600 square feet) sizes, with a décor of beige and rattan furnishings sporting tropical print fabrics and wall-to-wall carpeting. All have cable TV, complete kitchen, washer/dryer, safe, coffeemaker, lanai, and daily maid service. Child-care referrals are available too. There are three swimming pools, shuffleboard, lawn bowling, and a beach cabana (this property is not on the beach) for guests' use, and guests have privileges at the adjacent golf and tennis facilities.

Rates are **Pricey** and up. Look for packages.

Kapalua/Napili

Kapalua Bay Hotel and Villas, One Bay Drive, Kapalua, HI 96761. Toll-free: 800-367-8000. Local: 808-669-5656. Units: 194 rooms and suites, 12 villa suites.

Web site: www.kapaluabayhotel.com

Once the only resort in this part of West Maui, progress has brought neighbors—including the Ritz-Carlton. The good news is that Kapalua is removed from the high-rises of Ka'anapali and Kahana to its south and basks in the breezes of the northwestern corner of West Maui. Set on 18 acres and bordered by a large pineapple plantation, the resort's views are magnificent and the beach is comfortable and protected. The hotel, opened in 1976, received a face-lift in 1999. This included remodeling the rooms, suites, and villas. Like the Mauna Kea Resort on the Big Island, Kapalua is low-key, and this attracts a sophisticated clientele. It also has one of the best tennis centers in the state, with 20 Plexi-pave courts in two complexes. Golf enthusiasts will love Kapalua's three 18-hole championship courses.

Arriving at the main entrance of the hotel, you find a very pleasant and airy lobby with wonderful views of the channel and Moloka'i in the distance. Lots of hanging vines accentuate a central skylight. Comfortable and tasteful lounge satellites in muted tones of tan and white, with white-tiled floors and bamboo/rattan furniture with pale-toned fabrics, orbit the central area. The lobby is shaded by louvers, and the color scheme is a symphony of cream brightened by various *objets d'art* on the walls. From the lobby you can see the restaurant on the floor below, replete with waterfall and fish pools. The grounds are well maintained, and the pool is great for sunning as it sits in an open spot with fab views and a steady breeze. At the pool, there is the Plumeria Terrace restaurant and bar.

There are two types of accommodations at Kapalua; the hotel and the villas. Both offer twice-daily maid service and full use of all resort and hotel facilities. Hotel rooms feature double-door entries, gold/tan wall-to-wall carpet, blond wood furnishings, and a décor in shades of white. Dark wood louvers lead out to the large white-tiled lanai with chaise and table and chairs. Nice touches here are the large window with screens—for the bug-phobic among us—and

feather pillows. The white-tiled bathrooms have a glassed-in shower, tub with a European hand shower, dual vanity, scale, and a window (rare these days in hotel baths). All rooms have a lanai, ceiling fan, cable TV, iron/board, and three phones in every room (two with dataports and one in the head).

The villas come in clusters: the Bay Villas, the Golf Villas, the Ridge, and the Ironwoods. Only the Bay Villas offer full use of the resort and hotel facilities; they are quite sumptuous. Accommodations for the Bay Villas can be arranged only through the Kapalua Bay Hotel (the other villa clusters are privately owned and managed by Kapalua Villas, 800-545-0018). All the villas are one- and two-bedroom units which are individually owned and decorated more or less in the same style as the hotel. All have fully equipped kitchens, laundry facilities, daily maid service, and room service. The most deluxe of the lot are the Ironwoods Villas, which are bigger and face Oneola Bay. The Bay and Ridge villas are located north of the hotel. The Golf Villas sit on the sides of the 10th and 18th fairways of the Bay Course. All villas can be rented on a weekly, monthly, or seasonal basis.

Rates are *Ridiculous* and up.

Ritz-Carlton Kapalua, One Ritz-Carlton Drive, Kapalua, HI 96761. Toll-free: 800-241-3333. Local: 808-669-6200, fax 808-665-0026. Rooms and suites: 548.
Web site: www.ritzcarlton.com

The only Ritz property in Hawai'i is here in Kapalua. Set on 50 sloping acres overlooking the Pailolo Channel and the island of Moloka'i, and surrounded by Captain Cook pines and ironwoods, the Dickey-style-roofed Ritz is an overt nod to luxury and service. Here a pineapple motif is interspersed with tray ceilings, crystal chandeliers, oil paintings of Hawai'i and tall ships, colonial furniture, chintz, stone floors, and Oriental carpets—quite a combo for tropical Hawai'i. While we find the Ritz a tad formal for our tastes, others seem to love its over-the-top luxury statement. A grand piano in the breezy lobby is often played by a professional or by a proficient guest (no "Chopsticks" allowed here). Kapalua's golf courses, a huge draw, border the property. There are three pools in the center of the U-shaped layout, all tiered so that they flow into each other. A golf cart shuttles guests to the beach at the bottom of the hill.

We found the guest rooms a tad small for the money. All have wall-to-wall carpeting, a lanai with louvers and curtains for privacy, rattan furniture with peach fabrics, Simmons Posturepedic king-size or double beds, feather pillows, CD player/alarm clock, safe, iron/board, and plush terry bathrobes. Eighty percent of the rooms have an ocean view. Baths are large white marble affairs, with doubly vanity, separate shower, loo, and makeup mirror. There is twice-daily maid service and 24-hour room service. In keeping with the emphasis on service, if a guest has a special need, the management has a $2,000-per-guest budget to procure that need. For example, if someone needs a DVD player in his suite, an employee will scurry away and buy one if necessary (unfortunately, the guest doesn't get to keep it).

For dining and drinking, the Ritz has four restaurants, an espresso bar, a pool bar, and a lounge in the lobby. Besides golf, there are the two ten-court Kapalua tennis centers, a putting green, a fitness center, a spa, and a business center. The Ritz Kids program, a free service if you are a guest at the hotel, is available daily from 9 A.M. to 4 P.M. for kids ages 5 to 12. There are half-day programs too. The program changes daily, covering nature, science, water, and other exciting topics.

Rates are **Wicked Pricey** and up. Look for packages.

Napili Kai Beach Club, 5900 Honoapi'ilani Road, Lahaina, HI 96761. Toll-free: 800-367-5030. Local: 808-669-6271. Rooms and suites: 163.
Web site: www.napilikai.com

Built in 1962, this is a pleasant waterfront complex of Polynesian-style buildings in a great setting—between two terrific beaches. It also sits adjacent to the tony Kapalua Resort, with its fabulous golf courses and tennis complex. There are four small swimming pools and two 18-hole putting greens, but the best feature is the calm-water beaches. These, combined with kitchen facilities in most units and the Napili Keiki Club (a kids' club, open during then summer months and holiday periods), make the Napili Kai a reasonably priced alternative for families, especially through package deals.

The rooms, studios, and suites are spread out among several two-story buildings, so it's manageable and mellow. All units have a pale-toned décor, rattan furnishings, wall-to-wall carpeting, color TV, safe, phone with dataport, kitchenette (except the hotel rooms, which have a fridge and coffeemaker). Note that not all the rooms have air conditioning, so if this is important, be sure to ask for it.

A bar and restaurant are on the grounds, as is an exercise room and a water-sports pagoda.

Rates are *Very Pricey* and up. Look for packages.

Napili Point Resort, 5295 Honoapi'ilani Road, Napili, HI 96761. Toll-free: 800-669-6252. Local: 808-669-9222, fax 808-669-7984. Units: 121.
Web site: www.napili.com
E-mail: napilipt@compuserve.com

If you want a waterfront location at a reasonable price, then these very pleasant condos are the answer. Units come in one- and two-bedroom floor plans, and are comfortable—although, as they are owner-decorated, they will vary in décor. All have washer/dryer, daily maid service, complete kitchen with icemaker (we *love* ice-makers), cable TV/VCR, safe, and private lanai. There are two pools on the property, plus barbecue facilities, and Napili Bay Beach is 200 yards away (the coast in front of the property is rocky). The views of Moloka'i and the sunset from here are wonderful.

Rates are *Pricey* and up. Look for packages.

Lahaina

Plantation Inn, 174 Lahainaluna Road, Lahaina, HI 96761. Toll-free: 800-433-6815. Local: 808-667-9225. Rooms: 19.
Web site: www.theplantationinn.com
433-6815

Sitting on Lahainaluna Road in the heart of Lahaina Town, the Plantation Inn looks as if it's been around since the whaling days of the 19th century. Inns of this nature, size, and appearance are rare in Hawai'i, so we feel it deserves special mention. The inn's name aptly reflects its architectural style. Like authentic Hawai'ian plantation houses, it reflects a curious hybrid of styles from both the

Southern (Charleston, with its twin-pillared verandas) and New England colonial heritages.

The rooms are very nice indeed. Tiffany lamps, lots of oak trim, all-brass fixtures, festive floral wallpaper, ceiling fans, hardwood floors, stained glass, overstuffed chintz chairs and sofas, and soundproofing are some of the features that set this hotel apart from other lodging on Maui. The furniture, while consistent with the style of the building, is different from room to room. This thoughtful design extends to the bathroom fixtures, where pull-chain loos and pedestal sinks lend a look from yesteryear. All rooms have a TV/VCR and central air, and most rooms have a lanai. Kitchenettes are available in a few of the units. Breakfast for two is included in the room rate.

Rates are *Not So Cheap* and up (CP).

Maui Islander, 660 Waine'e Street, Lahaina, HI 96761. Local: 808-667-9766, fax 808-661-3733. Units: 372.
Web site: www.aston-hotels.com

This is a decent lower-cost lodging on West Maui, in the heart of Lahaina Town. Formerly an apartment complex, there is no beach, but there are three tennis courts, some barbecue areas, and a small pool. The rooms in the several two-story buildings, are clean and comfortable enough. This is a great place if you don't plan to hang out in your hotel except to sleep. Hotel rooms, studios, and one-bedroom suites are available. The latter two have fully equipped kitchens. All have ceiling fans, safe, and cable TV. The best rooms are located upstairs, as they have high ceilings. Only the one-bedroom suites have a lanai. Be sure to get a room on the ocean side of the complex, or you'll hear the traffic on Route 30, the major road.

Rates are *Not So Cheap*. Look for packages (especially on the resort's Web site).

Pioneer Inn, 658 Wharf Street, Lahaina, HI 96761. Local: 808-661-3636. Rooms: 34.
Web site: www.bestwesternhawaii.com/maui/pioneer.htm

Built in 1901, the Pioneer Inn is a wooden architectural classic by the wharf in the heart of Lahaina Town. Now operated by Best Western, the place has been newly renovated and is no longer the

funky dive it used to be. That said, those in search of character in the hustle-bustle of downtown Lahaina should opt to stay in this lodging by the oldest banyan tree in the state. Rooms here are fairly simple, with Hawai'ian colonial furnishings, cable TV, lanai, tiled baths, and queen-size beds, and are now all air-conditioned. If you do stay here, request a quieter room, as the Inn's location is on the noisy side (and the rowdy Whaler's Saloon is in the building).

Rates are **Not So Cheap** and up. Look for corporate and AAA discounts.

House of Fountains, 1579 Lokia Street, Lahaina, HI 96761. Toll-free: 800-789-6865. Local: 808-667-2121, fax 808-667-2120. Rooms: 3. Web site: www.maui.net/~private/home.html

This bed-and-breakfast comes highly recommended by someone we trust. Run by a friendly German couple, Daniela and Thomas Clement, it sits up on a hill in a residential neighborhood of Lahaina. Outside there is a pool, Jacuzzi, barbecue, and lots of lanais. All rooms feature white-tiled floors, white rattan furnishings with tropical-print fabrics, TV/VCR, air conditioning, fridge, safe, and phone. Sunset views are pretty spectacular. Note that you must drive to get to the beach.

Rates are **Cheap** and up.

South Maui

Four Seasons Resort Maui at Wailea, 3900 Wailea Alanui, Wailea, HI 96753. Toll-free U.S.: 800-332-3442, Canada: 800-268-6282. Local: 808-874-8000, fax 808-974-6449. Rooms and suites: 380.
Web site: www.fourseasons.com

If you want to go the royal-deluxe luxury route in South Maui, then the Four Seasons is the place for you. Located cheek-by-jowl next to the Grand Wailea Resort Hotel & Spa, this 15-acre property is typical of all Four Seasons resorts, where an air of tastefulness and the desire to please permeates the place. A sensible, calm lobby of stone floors, pale tones, greenery and flora, and attractive wicker and peach seating areas greets the guest. Below the lobby is the pool area, with canopied cabanas, padded chaises, a small water slide, and a peculiar-looking fountain (it reminded us of an Olympic torch). Guest rooms are close to both the pool and the beach. There are three restaurants and a bar for refueling and refreshment. A complimentary daily activity program is available for kids ages 5 to 12. Baby-sitting is also provided for $12 an hour for one to two children of the same family (additional fees apply for more kids or for the hours of midnight to 6 A.M.).

Rooms and suites have an Asian sensibility about them, with wall-to-wall berber carpeting, rattan furniture with peach and green fabrics, yellow wallpaper (most resorts have painted walls), ceiling fans, white louvered shutters opening out to tan-tiled lanais with padded teak furniture and a drying rack, mini-bar and fridge, coffeemaker with fresh coffee beans and grinder, iron/board, two phones with dataport, CD/AM/FM clock radio ensemble, TV/VCR, safe, feather pillows, and good wood hangers (*no more wire hangers!*). We loved the baths, which are large with lots of marble and mirrors, dual vanities, separate glass shower, separate deep tub, separate loo, magnifying mirror, hair dryer, *and* music with six pre-set stations (bravo!). Eighty-five percent of the rooms offer ocean views and all come with twice-daily maid service.

Oddly, we were very impressed by the truly fab game rooms here, which we consider the best of any resort in Hawai'i. There are two pool tables, two Ping- Pong tables, an air hockey table (now we're talkin'), a Nintendo room with eight stations, shuffleboard, and foosball. Wow! Who needs to go to the pool or the beach? There's also a library with chess and checkers. Adjacent to all this fun is a spa and a fitness center with Cybex equipment and free weights, and an "al fresco" aerobics room under a canopy, with treadmills, elliptical machines, Stairmasters, and LifeCycles. All have their own TV sets with headphones. We wonder why more resorts can't follow the Four Seasons example!

Rates are **Wicked Pricey** and up.

What a Wonderful World Bed & Breakfast, 2828 Umalu Place, Kihei, HI 96753. Local: 808-879-9103, fax 808-874-9352. Rooms: 4. Web site: thesupersites.com/wonderfulworld

Nestled on a hillside in a residential neighborhood of Kihei is this little gem of a place. Hosted by Eva Tantillo, who is one of the nicest people we met in the Aloha State, this bed-and-breakfast is a refreshing alternative to the expensive super-resorts down the road in Makena. Fabulous views of West Maui, Moloka'i, and the Pacific are enjoyed from the breezy second-floor lanai. We saw humpback whales spouting away while we feasted on one of Eva's killer breakfasts. Eva's two Cavalier King Charles spaniels, Laka and Alu, are also part of the fun of staying here, and Eva is a wealth of information about Maui, its activities, and especially some secret places.

There are four very comfy rooms here, all with kitchen-type facilities. All have cable TV, VCR, private bath, air conditioning, and ceiling fans. There is a common patio area with gas grill and tables, and a laundry facility. Eva has snorkel equipment and body boards available for guests too. The beach is only a five-minute drive away, and Big and Little Beaches, Maui's best, are only a 20-minute drive away.

Rates are *Cheap* (full American breakfast).

Grand Wailea Resort Hotel & Spa, 3850 Wailea Alanui, Wailea, HI 96753. Toll free: 800-888-6100. Local: 808-875-1234, fax 808-874-2411. Rooms and suites: 780
Web site: www.grandwailea.com

The Grand Wailea goes out of its way to impress, and to a certain extent we were when we visited. Probably what impressed us most was the absolutely huge water complex in the middle of it all. Called the Wailea Canyon Activity Pool, it will take you hours to figure it all out. There are 770,000 gallons of water in nine separate pools—one with a "baby beach"—plus seven water slides, myriad waterfalls, grottos, rapids, Jacuzzis, a rope swing, and the world's first water elevator (which was very popular when we were there and operates on a water-lock system similar to a manmade canal but cylindrical in shape—you have to see it to really understand how it works). We were also impressed by the art collection on display, including some very unusual Botero sculptures in the main lobby area (but with all the other stuff around, who notices art?). There is the 50,000-square-foot Spa Grande, the state's largest, which offers every sort of body pampering known to man, including the Terme Wailea Hydrotherapy Circuit, a series of water therapies from around the world. There's also a 20,000-square-foot Camp

Grande for kids, which includes a snack bar, movie theater, Nintendo game room, computer learning center, pottery room, video game arcade, foosball, and Ping-Pong tables. For kids ages 5 to 12, Camp Grande has a staff for supervision. There's even a free-standing chapel on the grounds (you guessed it—lots of weddings). We wondered what they didn't think of—all we could come up with was the IRS and a funeral home. Finally, we were impressed by the number of families staying here. The water complex resembled a water park on a hot summer's day. If you want peace and quiet, we'd suggest the Hibiscus Pool (for adults), the beach, the spa, or another resort.

With all the above making us a tad dizzy, we found the rooms and suites to be in keeping with the "grande" scope of the resort. Guests have a choice between the Napua Tower, with the biggest and most luxurious rooms, and five other wings, each with its own look. All come with an eclectic décor that we'd best describe as nouveau riche (but then, we hail from New England): a melange of wicker, rattan, marble, hardwood, various Oriental rugs, and incongruous *objets d'art* here and there. It looks to us like Nieman Marcus did the decorating—you know that Texas oil-money look. Rooms are good- sized, as are the baths. All guest rooms contain either a king-size bed or two double beds. Each room features a private lanai, a marble bathroom with oversize bathtub and separate glass-enclosed shower, a sitting area, and a desk. In-room amenities include air conditioning, ceiling fans, color TV with cable, three telephones, mini-bar, safe, coffeemaker, and bathrobes.

Rates are **Wicked Pricey** and up. Look for packages.

Kea Lani Hotel Suites & Villas, 4100 Wailea Alanui, Wailea, HI 96753. Toll free: 800-659-4100. Local: 808-475-4100, fax 808-875-1200. Units: 450 suites and villas.
Web site: www.kealani.com

Sometimes we can't help ourselves. To us, the design of the Kea Lani resembles a giant soft-serve vanilla sundae—the attack of the seven-story Dairy Queen. The Kea Lani definitely has a different, look and either you'll love it or you'll hate it. This all-suite (and 37-villa) hotel opened in 1991 on 22 acres just south of the Four Seasons. While the architecture may be different, a main advantage of

the Kea Lani is that you get more room for your money. One-bed-room suites are 840 square feet, which is at least 50 percent larger than other hotel rooms in the same price range. Outside, there is the requisite water complex (two swimming lagoons connected by a 140-foot water slide) and an adult lap pool for serious swimmers (a big plus). Other resort features include a 24-hour fitness center, a spa, and a year-round children's program for kids ages 5 to 12. One of Maui's best restaurants, Nick's Fishmarket Maui, is on the premises (part of it is *al fresco*), as are three other restaurants and a lounge.

As we said, the suites are big, and are a symphony of creams and faux-crackled Louis XVI-style furnishings (hey, why not?). All have tan wall-to-wall carpet, sofa-beds, ceiling fans, CD/DVD players, cable Sony Trinitron TVs with HBO, VCR, and stereo receiver, marble-top wet bar, fridge, coffeemaker, microwave, iron/board, feather pillows on the bed, additional TV in the master bedroom, safe, and two phones with dataports. The baths are also large, with dual pedestal sinks, tub, separate tiled walk-in shower, separate loo, and makeup mirror. There are nonsmoking and ADA suites too.

Rates are **Very Pricey** and up. Look for packages.

Maui Prince Hotel, 5400 Makena Alanui, Makena, HI 96753-9986. Toll free: 800-228-3000. Local: 808-874-1111, fax 808-879-8763. Rooms: 310.
Web site: www.mauiprincehotel.com

While we've never been terribly fond of the architectural style of the Maui Prince, we're mad for the location—just down the road from Big and Little Beaches. As the only resort in Makena, this gives the Prince a distinct advantage for those who can't get enough of Maui's best beaches. The hotel itself is very Japanese in look and feel, with a rather stark lobby and atrium greeting the guest. The Prince lacks the water complexes of the bigger Wailea resorts up the road. We like this fact, since it makes the hotel quieter and more serene. There are only two small circular pools and, gasp, the beach for swimming (can you imagine?!). Makena's excellent golf courses and tennis facility are across the street.

The rooms are very pleasant if somewhat spare, with tan berber wall-to-wall carpeting, pretty rattan furnishings, dark wood accents, and large lanais. Actually, these are what hotel rooms used to look like before the past decade of hyper-wealth made them look like catalogs from strung-out decorators. All have a fridge, coffeemaker, cable TV/VCR, rollaway cot, safe, and iron/board. Baths are white-tiled and average in size, with a hair dryer. Three restaurants and two bars are on site for refreshment.

Rates are **Wicked Pricey** and up.

Renaissance Wailea Beach Resort, 3550 Wailea Alanui Drive, Wailea, HI 96753. Toll-free: 800-992-4532. Local: 808-879-4900, fax 808-879-6128. Rooms and suites: 345.
Web site: www.renaissancehotels.com

Situated on a 15-acre parcel in the middle of the sprawling Wailea Resort is this attractive if somewhat conventional deluxe hotel. The rooms and suites are in relatively low-rise buildings (seven stories) and the beach here is excellent. A tasteful and low-key lobby of cream-colored stone, neutral-toned seating areas, and floral arrangements and palms greets the visitor. The grounds are pretty and well maintained, with over 30 plant species identified for your edification. There are two pools, rather small for a resort this size, and two spacious Jacuzzis with superb water-jet action.

Rooms are comfortable, of good size, with wicker and rattan furnishings. The color scheme is a symphony of beige. All rooms have tan wall-to-wall carpet and a tiled private lanai oriented toward either the ocean or Haleakala. We prefer the ocean view, which faces west toward the setting sun. Rooms come with a king-size or matching double beds, fridge, cable TV/VCR, iron/board, two phones with dataport, safe, and coffeemaker. The white-tiled baths are ample and feature a large tub with European shower, double-sink marble vanity, and a makeup mirror. There are 26 oceanfront rooms in the Mokapu Beach Club. We have heard that the resort is upgrading the rooms with new carpet, bedding, and patio furniture.

Guests have full use of the Wailea Resort's facilities, including the three outstanding 18-hole golf courses and the tennis park. The Renaissance also offers room service, a complimentary health club, a massage clinic, two tennis courts, three restaurants, and Camp Wailea for kids ages 5 to 12.

Rates are **Wicked Pricey** and up.

MAUI

Makena Surf, 96 Makena Road, Kihei, HI 96753. Toll-free: 800-367-5246. Local: 808-879-1595, fax 808-874-3554. Units: 107.
Web site: www.drhmaui.com

This is the best (and most expensive) condo property on South Maui. Located in beautiful Makena, it sits in splendid isolation on a small private beach and is only minutes from the best beaches on Maui: Big and Little beaches. These are true luxury condos, interspersed throughout a series of red-roofed, three-story buildings. On the other side of the road are the fairways of the Makena Golf Course. There are four tennis courts (two lighted) and two good-size pools for sunning, should you get tired of the small beach on the property.

Units come in one-, two-, and three-bedroom sizes, and are very large and sumptuously appointed (remember that each unit is owner-decorated, so they will vary in décor). Views are fabulous as you're on the water. Units come with cable TV/VCR, CD player, fully equipped kitchen with microwave, washer/dryer, wet bar, and safe. Baths have Jacuzzi tubs. There is daily maid service.

Rates are **Wicked Pricey** and up.

Villas of Wailea, 3600 Wailea Alanui, Wailea, HI 96753. Toll-free: 800-367-5246. Local: 808-879-1595. Units: Over 240.
Web site: www.drhmaui.com

Five condo clusters—Wailea Elua Village, Wailea Ekahi Village, Wailea Ekolu Village, Wailea Grand Champions, and the Polo Beach Club—are spread out over the Wailea Resort and make it look very much like the planned residential development that it is. These clusters are very nice and line the fairways or the coastline. Wailea Ekahi overlooks Keawakapu Beach, Elua sits on Ulua Beach, Ekolu and Grand Champions sit high up on the slope above the Blue Course fairways (great if you're a duffer), while the Polo Beach Clubs sits right on its namesake. (The Ekolu, Grand Champions and Ekahi clusters are about the same in prices, while the Elua and Polo Beach Club condos are more expensive.) All of these condo clusters have pools and golf and tennis privileges at the Wailea Resort.

All buildings are two stories except the Polo Beach Club, which is an eight-story structure. There is a lanai in every unit (which come in studios and one-, two-, and three-bedroom floor plans). Units are attractive and spacious (remember that each unit is owner-decorated, so they will vary in décor). All have cable TV/VCR, CD player, fully equipped kitchen with microwave, washer/dryer, wet bar, and safe. Baths have Jacuzzi tubs. There is daily maid service.

Rates are *Pricey* and up.

Outrigger Wailea Resort, 3700 Wailea Alanui, Wailea, HI 96753. Toll-free: 800-367-2960. Local: 808-879-1922, fax 808-874-8176. Rooms and suites: 516.
Web site: www.outrigger.com

The former Aston Wailea Resort has been acquired by the Outrigger Group and, at press time, is undergoing an extensive renovation. Located just north of the Grand Wailea Resort, the $25 million project will feature a complete redo of guest rooms and baths and the addition of a new day spa, fitness center, and water complex.

Rates are *Very Pricey* and up. Look for packages.

Maui Hill, 2881 South Kihei Road, Kihei, HI 96753. Local: 808-879-6321,
fax 808-879-8945. Units: 140.
Web site: www.aston-hotels.com

Although the architecture makes it look more like a Saudi Arabian airport than a resort on Maui, this is a moderately priced and well-located condo property in South Maui. While it's across the main road from the beach, there is a tennis court, pool, Jacuzzi, putting green, and several barbecue facilities. The Makena/Wailea beaches aren't too far away.

Units come in one- to three-bedroom sizes and feature a lanai, ceiling fans, fully equipped kitchen with microwave and a wet bar, washer/dryer, cable TV/VCR with HBO (gotta keep up on *The Sopranos* and *Sex and the City*), and iron/board. Décor is standard tropical condo (remember, units are owner-decorated).

Rates are *Pricey*. Look for packages.

Upcountry

Kula Lodge, Haleakala Highway (Route 377), Kula, HI 96790. Local: 808-878-2517. Units: 5.
Web site: www.kulalodge.com

Located in scenic Upcountry Maui, this establishment has the air of a mountain lodge. Situated on the road to Haleakala, the lodge's restaurant does a booming breakfast and lunch business. The main building has a seating area with stone fireplace and a large dining room with a cathedral ceiling and a terrific view of the Maui isthmus and the Pacific. If you're hell-bent on seeing sunrise on Haleakala, you may want to stay here to make the journey more comfortable.

The lodging comes in the form of five pleasant and comfortable chalets, each with an eclectic décor and wall-to-wall carpet. Chalets 1 and 2 (ocean view) have a queen-size bed, Swedish fireplace, and sleeping loft with twin beds jimmied in. Chalets 3 and 4 are like 1 and 2 but without a fireplace. Chalet 5 is a studio with a double bed, but no loft. Each has wood paneling throughout, and all chalets come with a lanai. There are no phones or TVs.

Rates are *Not So Cheap* and up.

Silver Cloud Guest Ranch, RR2 Box 201, Kula, HI 96790. Toll-free: 800-532-1111. Local: 808-878-6101, fax 808-878-2132. Rooms: 12.
Web site: www.silvercloudranch.com

If you like the refreshing climate and pastoral beauty of Upcountry Maui, then you'll love the Silver Cloud bed-and-breakfast. Set on nine acres at an altitude of 3,000 feet, the views of West Maui, Lan'ai, Moloka'i, Kaho'olawe, and the setting sun over the Pacific are fab. There are three plantation-style buildings on the property, which borders the Thompson Ranch (great for horseback riding). The main building, Plantation House, houses a common kitchen, dining, and living area, and six rooms including the King Kamehameha and Queen Emma, which have their own private lanais with great views and king- and queen-size beds respectively. The Mauka Hale bunkhouse is actually a U-shaped building with five units, each with kitchen and private lanai. The Lana'i Cottage sits by itself and has a woodstove. All rooms have a private bath. A full breakfast is included. Those who want to do the Haleakala sunrise thing may want to spend a night or two here. Be forewarned that the beach is at least 30 minutes away and there is no pool.

Rates are *Cheap* and up.

Central Maui

Banana Bungalow, 310 North Market Street, Wailuku, HI 96793. Toll-free: 800-8HOSTEL (846-7835). Local: 808-244-5090, fax 808-244-3678.
Web site: home1.gte.net/bungalow/maui.html

This is a definitely funky option in the funkiest neighborhood on Maui. A hostel for budget travelers of all ages, Banana Bungalows' aim is to provide cheap, clean rooms for boardsailors, backpackers, or outdoors enthusiasts who just need a good bed to sleep in. It is very basic but very big in the camaraderie factor. Dorm rooms with four to six beds (bunk beds) or private rooms with two twins or queen-size beds are available (bed linens provided). Baths are shared. There is a large tropical garden with hot tub, hammocks, and a barbecue facility. Common kitchen facilities, a common room with cable TV, and even free Internet access is provided. A coin-op laundry is on the premises, and secure storage is provided for equipment. The Banana is nothing fancy, but it's wicked cheap. As the Banana caters to travelers, a return ticket is required at check-in (i.e., no long-term boarders).

Rates are *Dirt Cheap*.

Hana

Hotel Hana-Maui, P.O. Box 9, Hana, HI 96713. Toll-free: 800-321-HANA (4262). Local: 808-248-8211. Rooms and suites: 66.
Web site: www.hotelhanamaui.com

There aren't many places that have continually lived up to our expectations, but the Hotel Hana-Maui is one of them. Twelve years after our first visit, it still is our favorite place to stay in Hawai'i. It all begins with your arrival at this small but subtly grand hotel. Guests are greeted by their names and with a lei, and are handed a fruit punch (it used to be a mai tai, but these days all

hotels are very p.c. and offer alcohol-free drinks, much to our chagrin). This warm, personalized and aloha welcome sets the tone for the rest of your stay.

Passport Resorts of San Francisco has recently bought the hotel. They have plans to renovate the rooms, upgrade food service, and add a spa. They will continue the hotel's affliation with Small Luxury Hotels of the World. The hotel is situated on 66 acres in the heart of Hana. Indeed, to a great extent Hana *is* the hotel. It employs most of the people and is the center of activity in the town. Its location is part of its philosophy—to fit like a glove into the fabric of the community. That was the credo of founder Joseph Fagen and continues to be reflected in the attitude of the staff. Besides the quality of the accommodations, it is the staff that distinguishes the Hana-Maui from other luxury hotels. Service may not be as hurried or as attentive as at other luxury hotels, but the true hospitality and warmth that you feel makes it even better. One of the reasons for this aloha spirit is that most of the staff is in one way or another related, so it's one big family affair.

Unlike other luxury hotels, there is no over-the-top entrance drive and gatehouse, just a small circle with a koi pool and portico. However, the hotel (and the town) is surrounded by the 4,500-acre Hana Ranch, so there is lots of room to roam. The design of the common areas makes you feel as if you're on one continuous lanai. Many seating areas surround open-air pools and fountains, which let in the natural light and allow for cooling breezes. Huge arrangements of halegonias and locally grown flowers are everywhere. There is a well-stocked library, particularly with Hawai'iana books, along with a pleasant bar with fireplace (evenings can be cool in Hawai'i), a club room with the sole TV and VCR on the premises, and a dining pavilion that is airy and spacious.

Rooms and suites are tastefully appointed in pale and natural tones of tan and white with comfortable rattan and bamboo furniture, bleached hardwood floors, stone countertops, large lanais, lovely original artwork on the walls, Hawai'ian quilt bedspreads, fresh flowers and well-kept plants in the rooms, louvered windows and doors, plenty of closet space, excellent speed-controlled ceiling fans in every room, and wet bar with fridge and ice maker for that necessary cocktail. Even the bathrooms are superb. Glazed terra-cotta tiles surround a sunken tub. A walk-in shower is spacious and convenient. There is a private loo with phone so you can go about your business while someone else goes about his. The green, built-on-stilts Sea Ranch Cottages, our personal favorites, have fantastic ocean views, and many have a hot tub on the lanai. If you must have waterfront and the sound of waves, choose the Sea Ranch. No details have been forgotten, including plush terry robes, fresh Kona coffee beans (both regular and decaf), a Krups coffee mill and drip coffeemaker. There is even fresh cream in the fridge. Now that's thoughtful. All that is missing is *The New York Times* (the *Times Fax* is available).

The excellent dining room features Pacific Rim, American, and Asian cuisines, and there's a beach pavilion where luncheon is served daily. On Thursdays and Sundays, Hawai'ian music and hula are presented in the dining room by local musicians and a local *halau* (hula troupe). Another dining option is the Hana Ranch restaurant, which is open for dinner on weekends and has a Pizza Night on Wednesdays. For cocktails, the Paniolo Bar is a fun place to hang out.

For recreation, the hotel has two pools, including a wonderfully large pool for swimming laps next to the fitness center, two tennis courts surfaced with Roladek (so you can play right after it rains), a three-hole practice golf course, riding stables at the Hana Ranch (a real plus—the rides here are fabulous), and the semiprivate Hamoa Beach with facilities and barbecue lunches. The social desk is very helpful in arranging whatever you want to do and will also take care of menial tasks like car rentals and reservations. A short walk around the bend from the Sea Ranch Cottages is the Red Sand Beach, one of Maui's most dramatic locations (and a nude beach too).

Rates are **Wicked Pricey** and up.

Hana Kai Maui Resort, 1533 Uakea Road, (P.O. Box 38), Hana, HI 96713. Toll free: 800-346-2772. Local: 808-248-8426, fax 808-248-7482. Units: 12.
Web site: www.hanakaimaui.com

Tucked away on a side street in Hana Town is the seaside Hana Kai. This is a good alternative to the lovely but very expensive Hotel

Hana-Maui for those who would like to stay in Hana (which is one of our favorite places on earth). This unassuming property features condo units in studio and one-bedroom floor plans. On the grounds is a spring-fed pool (not for swimming) filled with koi, and barbecue facilities. For a dip, the black-sand beach in front is swimmable. While the décor of the rooms is nothing fancy and rather eclectic, we found them perfectly pleasant for the amount charged. Each comes with a fully equipped kitchen and private lanai facing Hana Bay. There are no TVs or phones, which many guests relish (those who need a link to the outside world can use their cell phones or the pay phone). As the Hana Kai is right in town, stores and the Hotel Hana-Maui's and Hana Ranch's restaurants are within walking distance.

Rates are **Not So Cheap** and up.

Hana Accommodations and Plantation Houses, P.O. Box 564, Hana, HI 96713. Toll free: 800-228-HANA (4262). Local: 808-248-7868, fax 808-248-8240. Units: 7.
Web site: www.hana-maui.com

Hana Accommodations and Plantation Houses is located three miles south of town in the midst of the Hana Ranch's pastures, along the craggy coast line and near a special swimming hole called Waioka Pool. Available in studio, two- and three-bedroom floor plans, these simple units feature tropical furnishings, TV, phone, ceiling fans, fully equipped kitchens, and large lanais—some with outdoor showers/tubs and private sunning areas. Barbecue facilities are also available. Host Tom Nunn will help you with any special needs as well as advice on Hana attractions and folklore.

Rates are **Cheap** and up.

Heavenly Hana Inn, 4155 Hana Highway, (P.O. Box 790), Hana, HI 96713. Local: 808-248-8442. Units: 3.
Web site: www.heavenlyhanainn.com

Located just a couple of miles north of Hana Town, this inn welcomes guests with an imposing Japanese gate with dual lions and Oriental lanterns. The grounds have a Japanese/Zen sense of order about them, as does the recently (1994) refurbished interior décor. There are three suites, two one-bedroom units, and one two-bedroom unit. All feature private bath and shower, queen-size bed, cable TV, fridge, iron and board, and their own private entrance. We've heard that this is one of those places where the owners don't really need the business and may close for a period of time to travel or just take a break, so be sure to call in advance.

Rates are **Pricey** and up.

Wai'anapanapa State Park. In Hana at the end of Wai'anapanapa Road off Hana Highway (Highway 360). Reservations are made through:

Division of State Parks, 54 South High Street, Suite 101, Wailuku, HI 96793. Local: 808-984-8109.

Web site: www.hawaii.gov/dlnr/dsp/maui.html

Very primitive cabins are offered in this pretty state park just north of Hana. All the basics are provided, including electricity, hot water, bathrooms, linens, and beds. Best of all, they can sleep six for under $50. But the price makes them popular, so book well in advance. You may want to bring some amenities to make it more comfortable.

Rates are **Dirt Cheap**.

Where to Eat

Maui has a slew of restaurants, the majority catering to the tourist trade and concentrated on West and South Maui. Given the clientele, dining out can be pricey, especially at the big hotels and resorts. Locals flock to Central Maui, where a score of Asian restaurants in Wailuku, Kahului, and Pa'ia are cheap, cheerful, and quite good. Upcountry Maui may not have a ton of eateries, but the ones there are worthwhile destinations. In keeping with its isolated location, Hana has fewer options than the fingers on one hand.

Here are our recommendations:

West Maui

Anuenue Room, Ritz-Carlton Kapalua, 669-6200. The premier restaurant at this premier hotel is a great place for that special-occasion dinner. The cuisine, by chef Virgile Brandel (of the Ritz

in St. Thomas), is a combination of French Provençal and Hawai'ian and shouldn't be missed. Try the Roasted Kona Ula (Kona lobster) or the Ahi (yellowfin tuna) in Spring Roll. Reservations recommended. Open Tuesday through Saturday from 6 to 10 P.M. $$$$$

A Pacific Café, Honokowai Marketplace, Honokowai, 667-2800. The newer of the two Maui locations, this is ultra-famous chef Jean-Marie Josselin's signature restaurant (there are four in Hawai'i) featuring Hawai'ian Regional cuisine. The "A Pacific Café" group has received accolades from all corners. Specialties include pan-seared mahi mahi with a garlic sesame crust and lime ginger sauce. Always packed; reservations are a must. Open for dinner nightly from 5:30 to 9:30 P.M. $$$$

Bay Club, Kapalua Bay Hotel and Villas, Kapalua, 669-8008. The Bay Club is a Kapalua institution, its popularity due to its wonderful setting on a lava rock promontory overlooking Moloka'i and to its fresh-fish/New American cuisine. The Bay Club's wine cellar is exceptional. Reservations advised for dinner. Open daily for lunch from 11:30 A.M. to 2:00 P.M. and dinner from 6:00 to 9:30 P.M. $$$$$

Cascade Grill and Sushi Bar, Hyatt Regency Maui, Ka'anapali, 661-1234. An excellent sushi bar is the star of this Hyatt eatery overlooking the resort's waterfalls and grottos. Open daily from 5:45 to 10 P.M. $$$

Chart House, 1450 Front Street, Lahaina, 661-0937. Locals like this place—part of the well-known chain—for the portions, price, and its position on the water's edge. Open for dinner daily from 5 to 10 P.M. $$$

Cheeseburger in Paradise, 811 Front Street, Lahaina, 661-4855. With the catchy name (and not owned by Jimmy Buffet), this very casual place is open for breakfast, lunch, and dinner like its counterpart in Waikiki. This is a better bet than hitting the fast-food joints. Open daily from 8 A.M. to 10 P.M. (midnight on busy evenings). $$

Chez Paul, One Olowalu Village, Highway 30, Olowalu, 661-3843. Located at a blink of an intersection on the highway between Lahaina and Ma'alaea, Chez Paul is a highly regarded and charming little restaurant specializing in excellent French cuisine. Slightly more casual than others in its class, this is the oldest French restaurant in the state. There are two seatings daily, at 6:30 and 8:30 P.M. $$$$

Compadres, Lahaina Cannery Mall, Lahaina, 661-7189. While it is part of a chain, there aren't many choices for *comida Mexicana* in West Maui. Great margarita selection too, and a fun happy hour makes it worth your while. Open for breakfast from 8 A.M. to noon and for lunch and dinner from 11 A.M. to 11 P.M. Bar closes at 1 A.M. $$$

David Paul's Lahaina Grill, 127 Lahainaluna Road, Lahaina, 667-5117. Acclaimed by locals and international epicurian alike, David Paul's has become a must-stop for diners on West Maui. Featuring a "New American" menu integrating local fish, meats, and produce, Chef Paul's art-crammed eatery is a treat. His Reconstructed California Roll and his Maui Onion-Crusted Seared Ahi with Vanilla Bean Rice and Apple Cider-Soy Butter Vinaigrette sent us into taste orgasms. Reservations strongly suggested. Open daily from 6 to 10 P.M., Friday and Saturday until 10:30 P.M. $$$$

Dollies, 4310 Lower Honoapiilani Road, Napili, 669-0266. Great, cheap food, excellent pizza, and a fun bar make this a local hangout. Open 11 A.M. to midnight daily. $$

Gerard's, Plantation Inn, 174 Lahainaluna Road, Lahaina, 661-8939. Of the *français* choices, the consensus is that Gerard's is the best in the taste department. Located on the veranda and front room of the Plantation Inn, it's a small but airy affair. The Island/French contemporary menu changes constantly, so there's lots of creativity coming out of Chef Gerard. Open 6 to 10 or 11 P.M. daily. Reservations required. $$$$

i'o, 505 Front Street, Lahaina, 661-8422. At probably the grooviest-looking restaurant on Maui (and Maui's trendiest by far), chef James McDonald's Pacific Rim menu makes i'o the hottest spot for dining on Maui. We loved the Silken Purse (steamed wontons stuffed with roasted peppers, mushrooms, macadamia nuts, and more, served with a jalapeño-scented tomato sauce and basil-yogurt purée), the Lemongrass Coconut fish, and the Foie Gras-Crusted Catch. Drooling yet? Open for dinner daily from 5:30 to 10:00 P.M. Reservations advised. $$$$

Kimo's, 845 Front Street, Lahaina, 661-4811. Kimo's is a Lahaina institution and one of the few places on Maui where you can eat on the water and hear it too (the restaurant sits on a pier). The décor features lots of old Lahaina memorabilia (although we immediately noticed a Nantucket flag in the vestibule). This restaurant is a tourist attraction and does a booming business. Kimo's specialty, the prime rib, sells out just about every night. Reservations are a must for dinner. Open daily for lunch from 11 A.M. to 3 P.M., dinner from 5 to 10:30 P.M. $$$

Lahaina Coolers Restaurant & Bar, Dickenson Square, Lahaina, 661-7082. When most of the local eateries have stopped serving but you're hungry, head to the Lahaina Coolers for pizza and other comfort food. Open from 8 A.M. to 2 A.M. (full menu until midnight). $$

Lahaina Fish Co., 831 Front Street, Lahaina, 661-3472. For fresh seafood served on the water at very reasonable prices, the Lahaina Fish Co.'s simply prepared fare may be to your liking. Open daily for lunch from 11:00 A.M. to 5:00 P.M., and dinner from 5 to 10 P.M., grill menu until midnight. $$$

Longhi's, 888 Front Street, Lahaina, 667-2288. Longhi's is probably the best-known restaurant in Lahaina. Today it's more of a tourist attraction than a fine dining experience. A small place on Front Street with black-and-white tiled floors, wicker-back chairs, ceiling fans, and French doors opening out onto the street, its menu is in the waiter's head. He/she recites a laundry list of choices, which change daily, all slanted to northern Italian fare. Someone told us that the staff used to be hired according to their astrological sign, but we're sure memory had something to do with it. The breakfast cinnamon rolls are still yummy. Reservations suggested for dinner. Open daily for breakfast, lunch, and dinner from 7:30 A.M. to 10 P.M. $$$

Maui Tacos, Lahaina Square, Lahaina, 661-8883, and Napili Plaza, Napili, 665-0222. Need a quick burrito or taco fix? This chain, started on Maui with locations around the state and on the mainland, should satisfy. Open daily from 9 A.M. to 9 P.M., Sunday until 8 P.M. $

Old Lahaina Luau, 1251 Front Street, Lahaina, 667-1998. This is Maui's best and most authentic luau, and you should not miss it if you've never been to a luau before. It also provides a good opportunity to sample Hawai'ian fare and be entertained with hula and some Polynesian flair at the same time. Mai Tais are served and mixed drinks are available. Open nightly, check-in is 5:30 P.M. and show and dinner are finished around 8:30 P.M. Reservations a must. $$$

Orient Express, Napili Shores Resort, Napili, 669-8077. For those up in Napili and Kapalua, Orient Express is a favorite restaurant featuring Thai and Chinese cuisine. Open daily for dinner until 9:30 P.M., early bird specials from 5:30 to 6:30 P.M. $$

Outback Steakhouse, Kahana Gateway Shopping Center, Kahana, 665-1822. This Australian chain is very popular for its beef and large portions. Open daily for dinner from 4 to 10 P.M. $$$

Pacific 'O, 505 Front Street, Lahaina, 667-4341. Across the way from i'o is chef James McDonald's first creation. While not as trendy as i'o, the Pacific Rim cuisine here is similar and won't disappoint, nor will the beachfront setting. Lunch is a bargain. Reservations advised. Open daily for lunch from 11 A.M. to 4 P.M. and dinner from 5:30 to 10 P.M. $$$$ (lunch $$).

Pizza Paradiso, Honokowai Marketplace, Honokowai, 667-2929. If you need a pizza pie north of Ka'anapali, check this place out. Open daily from 11 A.M. to 10 P.M. Free delivery. $$

Red Lantern, 1312 Front Street, Lahaina, 667-1884. Offering surprisingly good Chinese food, this is not only a good lunch or dinner choice but a must for late-night munchies. Open daily from 11 A.M. to 10 P.M. $$$

Roy's Kahana Bar & Grill, Kahana Gateway Shopping Center, Kahana, 669-6999.

Roy's Nicolina, Kahana Gateway Shopping Center, Kahana, 669-5000. Roy Yamaguchi is the superstar of Hawai'ian chefs. Starting with his first restaurant in Hawai'i Kai on O'ahu, he now has five restaurants in Hawai'i and more around the world. Roy pioneered Hawai'ian Regional cuisine, and those who dine at his restaurants are rarely disappointed. Always packed; reservations are advised. The two restaurants' menus are similar yet different enough to set them apart. Nicolina serves later in the evening, and the atmosphere there is mellower. If Roy's Kahana is packed, try Roy's Nicolina. Both are open daily from 5:30 to 10 P.M. $$

Ruth's Chris Steak House, 900 Front Street, Lahaina, 661-8815. This very popular steak house chain now has an outpost on Maui. While it's not cheap, the very ample portions served with an ocean view help soften the blow. Open daily from 5 to 10 P.M. $$$$

Sam Choy's Lahaina, 900 Front Street, Lahaina, 661-3800. This Hawai'ian chain has a unique combo of real Hawai'ian cuisine and Pacific/American touches for a different dining experience. Open daily for dinner from 5 to 9:30 P.M. $$$

Sansei Seafood Restaurant & Sushi Bar, The Kapalua Shops, Kapalua, 669-6286. Sansei has received absolute raves since it opened a few years ago, racking up the "best" awards from several publications. An excellent sushi bar and Asian/Hawai'ian fusion fare make this a must-stop when on West Maui. As an added bonus, there's karaoke on Thursdays and Fridays from 10 P.M. Open daily for dinner from 5:30 to 10 P.M., Thursday and Friday until 2 A.M. $$$

Sunrise Café, 693 Front Street, Lahaina, 661-8558. Tucked away on Front Street is the tiny Sunrise Cafe, which opens at 6 A.M. to serve the boats going out on charter. Besides breakfast, hot entrees are available to eat at the counter or to go for lunch and dinner. The coffee is wonderful and the croissants tasty, making it a good first stop before any kind of excursion. Open daily from 6 A.M. to 6 P.M. $

Thai Chef, Lahaina Shopping Center, Lahaina, 667-2814. This Lahaina Thai eatery is a good bet for curry dishes and Pad Thai. Open for lunch Monday through Friday from 11 A.M. to 2 P.M., daily for dinner from 5 to 10 P.M. BYOB. $$

Village Pizzeria, 505 Front Street, Lahaina, 661-8112. If you just want a pizza, this is a good option. Open daily from 11 A.M. to midnight. $$

Woody's Island Grill, 839 Front Street, Lahaina, 661-8788. Right on the water and next-door to Kimo's sits Woody's, brought to Maui by the Cheeseburger in Paradise people. Surf n' turf is the name of the game here. All entrées include Caesar salad, veggies, and rice or potatoes. Open daily for lunch and dinner from 11 A.M. to 9:30 P.M. $$$

South Maui

Annie's Deli, 2511 S. Kihei Road, Kihei, 875-8647. Superb sandwiches are the draw here. Open daily from 8 A.M. to 4 P.M. $

Antonio's, 1215 S. Kihei Road, Kihei, 875-8800. Many call this the best Italian restaurant on Maui, featuring daily fresh pastas. Their *osso buco* is pretty good too, as is the garlic bread. Open for dinner Tuesday through Sunday from 5 to 9:30 P.M. $$$

A Pacific Café, Azeka Place II, Kihei, 879-0069. The older of the two Maui locations, this is one of ultra-famous chef Jean-Marie Josselin's signature restaurants (there are four in Hawai'i) featuring Hawai'ian Regional cuisine. The "A Pacific Café" group has received accolades from all corners. Specialties include pan-seared mahi mahi with a garlic sesame crust and lime ginger sauce. Always packed; reservations are a must. Open for dinner nightly from 5:30 to 9:30 P.M. $$$$

Café Navaca, Kihei Kalama Market Place, 1945 S. Kihei Road, Kihei, 879-0717. There aren't many good Mexican choices in South Maui, but this is one of them, with a Southwestern slant—try the Seared Ahi Tacos. Open daily for breakfast, lunch, and dinner from 8 A.M. to 10 P.M. (late-night menu from 10 P.M. to 1 A.M.). $$$

Carelli's on the Beach, 2980 S. Kihei Road, Kihei, 875-0001. The beautiful seaside setting is about the best thing at this overpriced, see-and-be-seen place serving seafood *à la italiano*. Open daily from 5:45 to 10:30 P.M. Reservations advised. $$$$

Da Kitchen, Rainbow Mall, Kihei, 875-7782. This is the tastiest plate lunch in Kihei. Open daily from 9 A.M. to 9 P.M. $

Hakone, Maui Prince Hotel, Makena, 875-5888. If you're looking for *haute* Japanese cuisine and sushi, Hakone delivers with delicious food in an attractive space. While it's not cheap, it is good. Open from 6 to 9 P.M., closed Sunday. Reservations advised. $$$$

Hana Gion, Renaissance Wailea Beach Resort, 879-4900. Another fine Japanese restaurant, this is located at the Renaissance. It's expensive but so savory, especially the *intime* setting. Reservations suggested. Open from 5:30 to 9 P.M., closed Thursday. $$$$

Jacque's on the Beach, 760 S. Kihei Road, Kihei, 875-7791. The

menu here is surprisingly continental in our era of focused fusion. The daily fresh grilled fish with purple potatoes is the house specialty, and it comes at a low price that will make you pinch yourself. Open daily for dinner from 5 to 10 P.M. $$$

Kihei Café, 1945 S. Kihei Road, Kihei, 879-2230. Gotta hangover? Head for this place for your head. Open daily from 5 A.M. to 3 P.M., Sunday from 6 A.M. to 3 P.M. $$

Kihei Prime Rib & Seafood House, 2511 S. Kihei Road, Kihei, 879-1954. This surf n' turf palace is very popular with the locals, especially for the huge portions and the early bird special from 5 to 6 P.M. Open for dinner nightly from 5 to 10 P.M. $$$

Maui Rainbow Factory, Makena Road, Makena, 874-6050. This roadside food truck, located just before the Big and Little Beach turnoff, is a wonderful find. Veggie and regular sandwiches, roll-ups, plus lots of beach munchies and that all-important water (there are no food or water facilities at Big and Little Beaches). Open daily; just look for the truck. $

Maui Tacos, Kameole Beach Center, 2411 S. Kihei Road, Kihei, 879-5005. Need a quick burrito or taco fix? This chain, started on Maui with locations around the state and on the mainland, should satisfy. Open daily from 9 A.M. to 9 P.M. $

Nick's Fishmarket Maui, Kea Lani Hotel, Wailea, 879-7224. Nick's is a Honolulu institution, and its namesake now has a place on Maui. Spilling out onto a large lanai at the Kea Lani, overlooking the grounds and the Pacific, Nick's has been an instant hit—it's always packed. This is the finest high-end seafood restaurant in South Maui. Chef Kyle Yonashiro's Hawai'ian Regional/seafood (and meat) cuisine is really great, especially the Black and Blue Ahi with Cajun Spices or the Fresh Opah Seasoned with Basil and Citrus Aioli. Besides the food, Nick's has an extraordinary 2,000-bottle wine cellar. Open daily from 5:30 to 10 P.M., Friday and Saturday until 10:30 P.M. Reservations a must. $$$$

Prince Court, Maui Prince Hotel, Makena, 875-5888. If you're looking for a good Sunday brunch, and then possibly an afternoon at Little Beach, head for this brunch favorite featuring Pacific Rim fare. Reservations suggested. Open daily for dinner from 6 to 9:30 P.M., Sunday brunch is served from 9 A.M. to 12 P.M. $$$

Sandcastle Restaurant & Lounge, Kamaole Shopping Center, Kihei, 879-0606. Relatively cheap surf n' turf makes this popular with the Kihei crowd. Open daily for lunch from 11:30 A.M. to 3 P.M. and dinner from 5 to 10 P.M. $$

Thai Chef, Rainbow Mall, Kihei, 874-5605. This newcomer to South Maui (there's one in Lahaina) provides a welcome ethnic diversion (Thai food) from the surf n' turf places in Kihei and the pricey Japanese restaurants at the resorts. Open for lunch Monday through Friday from 11 A.M. to 2 P.M., daily for dinner from 5 to 10 P.M. $$

Central Maui

A Saigon Café, 1792 Main Street, Wailuku, 243-9560. Serving the best Vietnamese food on Maui, this is a real gem in a hard-to-find location (there is no sign—call for directions). Owner Jennifer Nguyen is everywhere, behind the bar, greeting diners, and "slingin' hash." The cold spring rolls, *pho*, and lemongrass chicken are superb. Open Monday through Saturday from 10 A.M. to 9:30 P.M., Sunday to 8:30 P.M. $$

Charley's, 142 Hana Highway, Pa'ia Town, 579-9453. Located in the hip windsurfing town of Pa'ia, Charley's is as well known for its bar as it is for the good and hearty fare (including breakfasts). This place is a lot of fun. Open daily 7 A.M. to 10 P.M., Friday until 1 A.M. $$

Fujiya Restaurant, 133 Market Street, Wailuku, 244-0206. The local favorite for Japanese cuisine, Fujiya features *nigiri* sushi. Located by the Wakamatsu Fish Market, and it's cheap. Open daily except Sunday, from 5 to 9 P.M. $$

Jacque's Bistro, 89 Hana Highway, Pa'ia, 579-6255. Like Jacque's in Kihei the menu here is refreshingly continental. The daily fresh grilled fish with purple potatoes is the house specialty, and it comes at a low price that will make you pinch yourself. Open daily for dinner from 5 to 10 P.M. $$$

Mama's Fish House, Hana Highway (1 1/2 miles east of Pa'ia town), Pa'ia, 579-8488. This was the first seafood restaurant on Maui, and some claim that it is still an excellent choice. Situated on the beach at Ku'au Cove within sight of the windsurfing hot-

shots at Hoʻokipa Beach Park, it's a good place to find fresh fish and an incredible setting in which to eat it, although it has become a tourist trap. Open daily for lunch from 11 A.M. to 2 P.M., extended lunch from 2:30 to 4:30 P.M., and dinner from 5 to 9 P.M. $$$$

Marco's Grill & Deli, 444 Hana Highway, Kahului, 877-4446. If you're looking for cheap and hearty Italian fare, as well as burgers and a great meatball parm sub, then dis is da place. The Vodka Rigatoni was just what we needed. Good breakfasts, too. Open daily from 7:30 A.M. to 10 P.M. $$

Maui Tacos, Kaʻahumanu Center, Kahului, 871-7726. Need a quick burrito or taco fix? This chain, started on Maui with locations around the state and on the mainland, should satisfy. Open daily from 9 A.M. to 9 P.M. $

Picnic's, 30 Baldwin Avenue, Paʻia, 579-8021. This is a must-stop for any road trip to Hana or when you're in Paʻia. Picnic's will pack picnics (hence the name) for outings but also has tables for eating in. Picnic's is a latter-day health-food restaurant—it acknowledges that humans love sweets and such and indulges you with the finest ingredients, and yet it also serves good-for-you foods. Breakfast includes an assortment of freshly baked pastries like macadamia nut sticky buns, pineapple-molasses bran muffins, and raisin scones. Lunch is even better. Not to be missed is the spinach-nut burger, truly to die for, or their plate lunch. Yogurt shakes and espresso/cappuccino round out the fare. Be sure to pick up *Picnic's Guide to Hana*; it's the best mile-by-mile description of the journey available, and it's free. Open from 7 A.M. to 5 P.M. daily. $

Siam Thai, 123 N. Market Street, Wailuku, 244-3817. This Thai restaurant is a local favorite. Everybody loves the food and the portions, served up in a simple but festive atmosphere. Open daily from 5 to 9 P.M. $$

Upcountry

Haliʻimaile General Store, 900 Haliʻimaile Road, Haliʻimaile, 572-2666. This Upcountry eatery, run by Bev and Joe Gannon, features an Asian/American fusion cuisine all its own and has proved popular with locals and visitors. It's set in a general store, of all places. Their Szechwan Salmon is a big hit. Open for lunch Monday through Friday from 11 A.M. to 2:30 P.M. and dinner nightly from 5:30 to 9:30 P.M.. Reservations advised. $$$

Kitada's Kau Kau Korner, 3617 Baldwin Avenue, Makawao, 572-7241. Kitada's is reputed to have the best *saimin* on Maui, so why not find out for yourself when you're in this neck of the woods? Open for breakfast and lunch every day except Sunday, from 6 A.M. to 1:30 P.M. $

Komoda's Store and Bakery, 3674 Baldwin Avenue, Makawao, 572-7261. Sweet-lovers should stop here and have one of Komoda's island-famous cream puffs. They also bake some terrific *malasadas* and breads. Open 7 A.M. to 5 P.M., Saturday until 2 P.M., closed Wednesday and Sunday. $

Kula Lodge, Haleakala Highway, Kula, 878-1535. This is the place to have breakfast after viewing the sunrise on Haleakala, or to stop for lunch on the way back. The setting is mountain lodge rustic, the view is great (at 3,200 feet), and the fare is decidedly American. Open daily for breakfast from 6:30 to 11:15 A.M., lunch from 11:45 A.M. to 4:15 P.M., and dinner from 4:45 to 9 P.M. $$

Makawao Steak House, 3612 Baldwin Avenue, Makawao, 572-8711. For some superb steaks and cowboy-size portions in an Upcountry atmosphere, don't miss this charming and popular place. This classic steak house is well worth the trip. Open daily 5:30 to 9:30 P.M. $$$

Polli's Mexican Restaurant, 1202 Makawao Avenue, Makawao, 572-7808. Polli's is a Makawao institution and very popular with the locals. That's because it serves the best Mexican food on Maui in a cozy Upcountry setting. Vegetarians will also like the wide selection of veggie dishes. Open daily for breakfast, lunch, and dinner from 7 A.M. to 10 P.M. Lunch $$, Dinner $$$

Pukalani Terrace, Pukalani Country Club, 360 Pukalani Street, Pukalani, 572-1325. The club's restaurant serves a terrific Hawaiian-style lunch daily (breakfast and dinner are served also). Open daily for lunch from 10:30 A.M. to 2:30 P.M. Lunch $

MAUI

Hana

Hotel Hana-Maui, Hana, 248-8211. In keeping with the exceptional taste and design of the Hotel Hana-Maui, the restaurant here is outstanding. Not only is the Hawai'ian Regional cuisine exquisite, the high-ceilinged main room overlooking Hana Bay makes the meal even more enjoyable. Twice-weekly hula programs add to the pleasure. If you're in Hana for the day, treat yourself to lunch here. Lucky enough to be in Hana overnight? Then dinner here is a must, as is breakfast on the lanai. Reservations required for dinner. Open daily for breakfast from 7:30 to 10 A.M., lunch from 11:30 A.M. to 2:30 P.M., and dinner from 6:15 to 9 P.M. $$$$

Hana Ranch Restaurant, Hana, 248-8255. The other, more casual option for dining in Hana is also owned by the hotel and is considerably cheaper. Open daily for breakfast from 8 to 10 A.M., and lunch from 11 A.M. to 3 P.M. Dinner is served only on Wednesday, Friday, and Saturday, from 6 to 9 P.M. $$

Going Out

Those who want to look nightlife right in the eye (and often see the dawn of the new day) should choose Honolulu on O'ahu as their destination. Although development has overwhelmed much of leeward Maui, nightlife has not kept pace-this island's nightlife is much tamer. While there is stuff to do, and there are some fun bars and clubs, the choices are limited. The most happening town on Maui is Lahaina, where there are a number of lively bars, followed by Kihei, Kahului, and Makawao. Another option is the major resorts, which have the standard assortment of lounges and rather unexciting hotel discos (except the Grand Wailea, which has the state-of-the-art Tsunami dance club).

Your best bet is to make the most of cocktail hour and sunset and be in bed fairly early, as mornings in Hawai'i are glorious. In addition, many full-day excursions begin at the crack of dawn. But night owls, don't despair. There's enough to keep you busy. Here are your better choices:

Bars and Clubs

West Maui

Lahaina Town

This is where the action is, almost all of it on Front Street. So bar-hopping is easy and totally walkable.

BJ's Chicago Pizzeria, 730 Front Street, 661-0700. Fantastic Hawai'ian music and jazz plus a second-floor lanai location on the water make this a great place for a cocktail and conversation. Open daily, with music from 7:30 to 10 P.M.

Cheeseburger in Paradise, 811 Front Street, 661-4855. While it is part of a chain, the seaside views, live music, and friendly staff make it a popular place. Music is nightly until closing, (between 10 P.M. and midnight).

Compadres, Lahaina Cannery Mall, Lahaina, 661-7189. Also part of a chain, this spot in the Lahaina Cannery has an amusing happy hour and great margaritas. Closes between 11 P.M. and 1 A.M., depending on the crowd.

Longhi's, 888 Front Street, 667-2288. On weekends, Longhi's second floor turns into a fun place for live bands and dancing. Friday only from 10 P.M. to 1:30 A.M. Cover is $5.

Maui Brews, 900 Front Street, 669-2739. This restaurant and night-club presents live and recorded music from around the world. Call for nightly acts. Entertainment is from 9 P.M. to 2 A.M. Cover charges range from free to $40.

Moose McGillicuddy's, 844 Front Street, 667-7758. Moose's, located on the second floor with a lanai overlooking Front Street, has always been one of the liveliest dance clubs in Lahaina. Rock 'n' roll and disco to a DJ, multi-flavored margaritas, and the mix of tourists and locals are the main attractions here. Open from 9:30 P.M. to 2 A.M. Cover charges range from $1 to $5 depending upon the entertainment.

Pioneer Grill & Bar, Pioneer Inn, 661-3636. Formerly the Old Whaler's Saloon, this institution within an institution (the Pioneer Inn), is worth stopping at for a cocktail just to see its nautical memorabilia. You enter through swinging doors to find a room filled with harpoons, 19th century shipping lists, and pictures and models of whaling ships. This is always crowded with

an eclectic mix of people and features nightly entertainment. Open nightly from 6 to 9 P.M. No cover.

The Rest of West Maui

Dollies, 4310 Lower Honoappiilani Road, Napili, 669-0266. Great, cheap food, excellent pizza, and a fun bar make this a local hangout. Open until midnight daily, no cover.

Hula Grill, Whaler's Village, 2435 Kaanapali Parkway, Ka'anapali, 667-6636. On the beach in Whaler's Village, this is the place for happy hour and casual drinks in Ka'anapali. Hula's is a great place to hear live Hawai'ian music too, daily from 3 to 5 P.M. They also have Hawai'ian music and dancing (weather permitting) in the evenings from 6:30 to 9 P.M.

Sansei Seafood Restaurant & Sushi Bar, The Kapalua Shops, Kapalua, 669-6286. Great karaoke on weekend nights after 10 P.M. makes a stop at Sansei worthwhile for those who don't want to schlep into Lahaina.

Luaus and Shows

There are two evening programs that we think are worth the time and money. For a more authentic luau and traditional hula show/revue than seen at most resorts in the state, the Old Lahaina Luau, now located across from the Lahaina Cannery Mall, is about as good as it gets. Shows are nightly and cost $69 for adults and $39 for kids ages 2 to 12. Of course, dinner is included with the show (duh, luau!). Call 667-1998.

Another show getting raves comes from the creators of Montréal's Cirque du Soleil and is presented in the state-of-the-art Maui Myth & Magic Theater at 878 Front Street in Lahaina Town. 'Ulalena is a combination of Hawai'ian legend, acrobatics, surround-sound traditional Hawai'ian music, lighting, wild costumes, hula, and modern dance. Anyone who has seen a Cirque du Soleil performance will have an idea of this kind of theater. For reservations, call 808-661-9913/toll-free: 877-688-4800. Tuesday through Saturday there are two shows nightly, at 6:00 and 8:30 P.M. Tickets are $40 for adults and $25 for kids ages 5 to 17. For more info, visit the 'Ulalena Web site at www.mauitheatre.com

South Maui

Café Navaca, 1945G S. Kihei Road, Kihei, 879-0717. No more Latin music on the weekend! Bummer! But they do have a DJ on Friday from 10 P.M. to 2 A.M. Cover is $5.

Hapa's Brew House, 41E Lipoa, Kihei, 879-9001. Everyone talks about Hapa's as the place to go in Kihei. When we went, it never seemed to happen (O.K., it *was* Sunday and karaoke night!). The best nights are Thursday through Saturday. Open from 5 P.M. to 1 A.M. Cover is $5 for DJ or live music nights. Entertainment varies, so call before heading over.

Life's A Beach, 1913E S. Kihei Road, Kihei, 891-8010. Although the name is, like, so '80s, this joint presents good old-fashioned rock 'n roll. Open 9 P.M. to 1 A.M., no cover charge.

Lobster Cove, 1000 Wailea Ike Drive, Kihei, 879-7677. Jazz and bossa nova are also on the emenu at this Wailea restaurant and bar. Open nightly from 9:30 P.M. to midnight, no cover.

Pizazz Café, Azeka Place Shopping Center, Kihei, 891-2123. We met a couple who just loved the jazz fest presented here on Tuesday through Sunday. Open 7:30 P.M. to midnight (sometimes later depending upon the crowd). Cover is $5 to $8.

Tsunami, Grand Wailea Resort, Wailea, 874-2355. If a state-of-the-art discotheque floats your boat, Tsunami is Maui's best with a great light and sound system and video screens galore. Open daily from 9 P.M. to 1 A.M. Sunday through Tuesday is sports bar with Top 40, Wednesday through Saturday is live DJ and the cover is $5.

Central Maui

Charley's, 142 Hana Highway, Pa'ia, 579-9453. This is the hangout in groovy and windsurfer-heavy Pa'ia Town. Open 10 P.M. to 1 A.M.

Sal's Place, 162 Alamaha, Pa'ia, 893-0609. With a different theme every night of the week (disco on Tuesdays, Latin music on Thursdays, live music on Saturdays, you get the picture), this is Kahului's hot spot and a local hangout. Open nightly until 2 A.M. Cover on Latin night only is $5.

MAUI

Upcountry

Casanova's, 1188 Makawao Avenue, Makawao, 572-0220. If you're upcountry, this is *da kine* place to go. It gets hot and crowded and presents different DJs/styles depending on the night. Open nightly 9 P.M. to 1 A.M. Cover is anywhere from free to $5.

Gay & Lesbian Nightlife

With the 1998 closing of Hamburger Mary's and the Lava Bar in Wailuku, there are no gay or lesbian bars at press time. Gay life revolves around the daytime scene at Little Beach, various organized events, and a few lame gay nights at local bars. For more gay and lesbian info, contact Both Sides Now at 808-244-4566 or www.maui-tech.com/glom.

Maui Health Clubs

Gold's Gym, three locations: Kihei 874-2844, Lahaina 667-7474, Wailuku 242-6851.

Full-service gym, with daily ($20) and weekly ($50) rates. Open from 5:30 A.M. to midnight Monday through Thursday, Friday until 10 P.M., Saturday from 7 A.M. to 9 P.M., and Sunday from 9 A.M. to 6 P.M.

Maui Muscle Fitness, 3445 Lower Honoapiiliani Road, Lahaina, 661-0844.

Complete gym; daily ($10) and weekly ($35) rates available.

Maui Muscle Sports Club Kahana, Lower Honoapiiliani Road, Kahana, 669-3539.

Full-service health club, open daily 5 A.M. to 11 A.M. Daily ($20) and weekly ($98) passes available.

24 Hour fitness, 150 Hana Highway, Kahului, 877-7474.

Full-service health club, open 24 hours a day. Daily ($20) and weekly ($52) rates are available.

Don't Miss

Little Beach, Makena—The best let-it-all-hangout beach on Maui, there are no condos or hotels around to spoil the view-just woods and sand in a cove where you can sun and swim in the buff if you like. On the way to the beach, stop by the Maui Rainbow Factory truck for a sandwich and bottled water.

Hana—This peaceful town at the eastern end of the island is one of the most beautiful places in the state. The two-hour drive from Kahului is rewarded with the magical serenity that is Hana and the stunning, clothing-optional Red Sand Beach.

i'o—The most talked about new restaurant on the island is both design and culinary trendsetter, located on the water in Lahaina.

Wavejumping at Ho'okipa—This beach park just east of Pa'ia is the place in winter to see some of the best wave-jumping and loop-de-loops (flips) by expert and dare-devil windsurfing—fun for the whole family!

The Plantation Course, Kapalua, Maui—With a 75.2 championship rating and a tough par 73, this course is rated fourth in the world by *Golf Digest*. Designed by Ben Crenshaw and Bill Coore and Surrounded by pineapple fields and the cobalt blue of the Pacific, it is the home of the annual PGA Tour Mercedes Championship.

Haleakala National Park—The huge dormant crater at 10,023 feet above sea level is an ethereal (and often chilly) place to hike or view sunrise.

A Saigon Café—One of Maui's best-kept secrets, this Vietnamese restaurant in Wailuku has delicious food and very reasonable prices.

'Ulalena—Staged by the creators of the famous Cirque du Soleil from Montréal (now based in Las Vegas) at a state-of-the-art theater in Lahaina, this dance, music, acrobatic, and light-show extravaganza tells the story of the first Hawai'ian settlers.

'Iao Needle at Twilight—The eerie light, the cloud mist, the empty parking lot, and all those feral cats make viewing this sacred pinnacle a transcending experience.

The Big Island

Touristo Scale:

🦜🦜🦜🦜🦜🦜🦜 (7)

THE HOME OF THE FIRE GODDESS PELE, Hawai'i, the Big Island, lives up to its name. This is the ultimate Hawai'ian island of superlatives. It's the largest island in the Aloha State (at 4,038 square miles, it is twice the area of all the other islands *combined*), the youngest island geologically (only 800,000 years old), and the fastest-growing (in both landmass and population). It has the tallest mountains, the only active volcano, the greatest number of climate zones, the biggest ranch, the largest coffee and macadamia nut producers, the most lava fields, the most deluxe resorts, and the best diving. It even has snow skiing for the intrepid during the winter months (yup, it's true). A trip to the Big Island is a must. While it sounds like a cliché, there *is* something for everyone here.

About the size of the state of Connecticut, the Big Island, from the visitor's perspective, is basically made up of the Kona (North and South) and South Kohala coasts, with Kailua-Kona acting as the main hub for activity on the island. North Kona and South Kohala are where some of the state's largest and most deluxe resorts are located (green oases amid massive black lava fields) as well as some of Hawai'i's best golf options. North Kohala is a mostly mountainous peninsula which until recently consisted of ridiculously scenic pastures (it was called Hawai'i's Swiss Alps); it is now scarred with ultra-rich developments. We adore the wonderfully idyllic town of Hawi, at the tip of the peninsula, which has so far resisted the carpetbaggers from beyond. The misty Parker

Ranch/cowboy town of Waimea, also in North Kohala, still has lots of character and cattle. The northeastern, windward side of the island is called the Hamakua Coast and is filled with deep river valleys (including the magical Waipi'o Valley), waterfalls, lush cane fields, and forests. At the eastern end of this coastline is Hilo, probably the only true and authentic Hawai'ian city in the Aloha State and home of the fabulous Merrie Monarch hula festival. It also gets over 120 inches of rain a year, which is why it has been able to escape the development of the sunny, leeward side. South of Hilo is Puna, another favorite of ours, with a rugged coast, lava flows and formations, verdant vegetation, black-sand beaches, some of the world's purest air, and better weather. Upslope from Puna (at 4,000 feet/1,219 meters) is Volcano, the Hawai'i Volcanoes National Park, and Madame Pele's lair. The south Ka'u district is mostly arid and unpopulated and frequently subject to vog (volcano-caused smog). In the middle of this massive island sit two of the world's largest landmasses and the North Pacific's highest mountains, Mauna Kea and Mauna Loa. With these mountains come 11 of Earth's 13 climate zones (from tropical rain forest to subarctic tundra). With that kind of diversity, it's easy to see why there are so many things to see and do outdoors. Hiking, skiing, biking, horseback riding, deep-sea fishing, and volcano watching are just some of the many options available. Not bad for one island, huh?

The Big History

The Big Island looms large in Hawai'ian history. It is the birthplace of Kamehameha the Great and the setting of Captain Cook's triumph and demise. From his base in Kohala and Kona, Kamehameha, aided by Captain Cook and his band of Englishmen with their guns and cannons, conquered the Hawai'ian Islands and formed the Kingdom of Hawai'i. Kamehameha ruled from Honolulu and then Lahaina, but always kept the Big Island as his identity. Indeed, he died here.

The largest island in the Hawai'ian chain (4,038 square miles/10,458 square kilometers), the island began forming less than one million years ago *and* is still growing courtesy of Madame Pele and her Kilauea volcano. A magma hotspot under the southeast coast of the Big Island is now shared by the Lo'ihi Seamount (currently about 3,000 feet below sea level).

Originally settled by two migration waves from the Marquesas and Society (Tahiti) Islands in the 8th and then the 12th and 13th centuries, the Hawai'ian Islands were left in isolation from the "outside" world until the arrival of Captain Cook's expedition in 1778 at Waimea on Kaua'i and at Kona on the Big Island. Within a year of Cook's first contact, disease—especially venereal diseases—brought by the Europeans had spread to all of the islands. But Captain Cook's legacy was felt most on the Big Island. Indeed, he lost his life in a brief (and many historians say superfluous) skirmish at Kealakekua Bay. A 27-foot-high white marble obelisk, erected on this site in 1884, honors Captain Cook.

Kamehameha was a smart and ruthless warrior. He tapped into the white man's technology, making deals for guns and and other support from various British and American traders and mercenaries. This negotiating ensured his eventual victories. After all, the more guns and cannons a chief had in his forces, the more success he would have. Kamehameha had the support of Captain Cook and the Englishmen who came after him. The latter recognized a winner and supported Kamehameha's ambitions with arms and ships in exchange for favors such as land and trading rights.

Various intrigues and rivalries ensued until in 1795 when Kamehameha, sensing weakness, set out from the Big Island and conquered Maui, Lana'i, Moloka'i, and O'ahu. Only the conquest of Kaua'i remained, but invasion attempts in 1796 and 1804 failed, defeated by foul weather during the crossing over the wide and dangerous Kaua'i Channel and by typhoid fever or cholera. Kaua'i's king, Kaumuali'i, aware that Kamehameha was hell-bent on conquering his island and would probably eventually win, entered into negotiations with Kamehameha, who was also getting tired of battle. Finally, in 1810, with the mediation of an American merchant named Nathan Winship, an agreement was reached and the islands united under Kamehameha the Great. Lahaina was established as the capital of the new kingdom—close enough for Kamehameha to visit his beloved home.

Kamehameha was also very smart when he married Ka'ahumanu, the daughter of Maui's (eventually defeated) chief. She

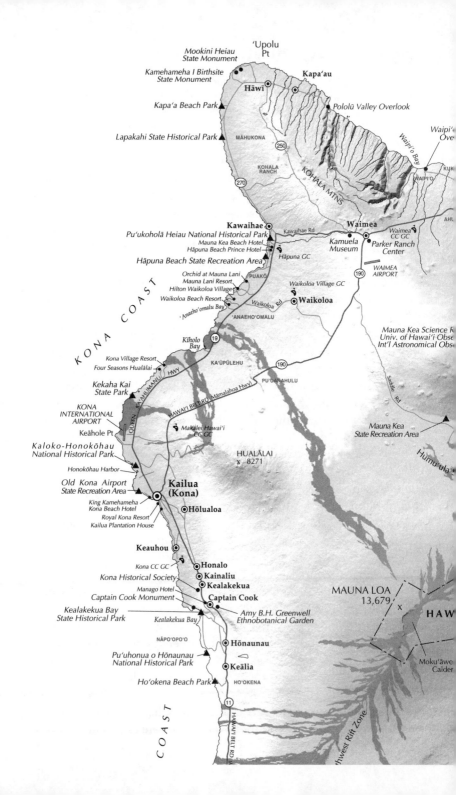

The Big Island
Northern Half

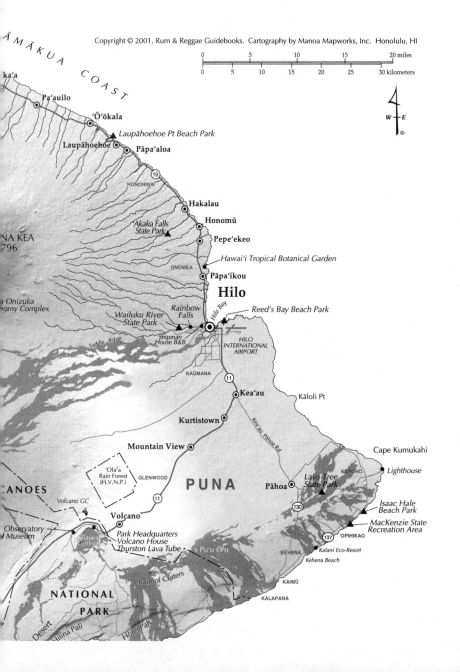

Copyright © 2001, Rum & Reggae Guidebooks. Cartography by Manoa Mapworks, Inc. Honolulu, HI

| 0 | 5 | 10 | 15 | 20 miles |
| 0 | 5 | 10 | 15 | 20 | 25 | 30 kilometers |

W — E

ĀMĀKUA COAST

ka'a

Pa'auilo

'Ō'ōkala

Laupāhoehoe Pt Beach Park

Laupāhoehoe — Pāpa'aloa

(19)

HONOHINA

Hakalau

Honomū

Akaka Falls
State Park

Pepe'ekeo

NA KEA
796

Hawai'i Tropical Botanical Garden

ONOMEA

Pāpa'ikou

Onizuka
omy Complex

Hilo

Wailuku River
State Park

Rainbow
Falls

Hilo Bay

Reed's Bay Beach Park

Shipman
House B&B

HILO
INTERNATIONAL
AIRPORT

Saddle Rd

KAŪMANA

(11)

Kea'au

Kāloli Pt

Kurtistown

Kea'au-Pāhoa Rd

Mountain View

Cape Kumukahi

'Ola'a
Rain Forest
(H.V.N.P.)

GLENWOOD

PUNA

Pāhoa

Lava Tree
State Park

KAPOHO

Lighthouse

ANOES

Volcano GC

(11)

(130)

POHOIKI

Isaac Hale
Beach Park

Observatory
Museum

Kilauea
Caldera

Volcano

Park Headquarters
Volcano House
Thurston Lava Tube

Pu'u O'o

(137)

'OPIHIKAO

MacKenzie State
Recreation Area

KEHENA

Kalani Eco-Resort

Chain of Craters

Kehena Beach

KAIMŪ

NATIONAL

KALAPANA

PARK

Desert

Hilina Pali

Hōlei Pali

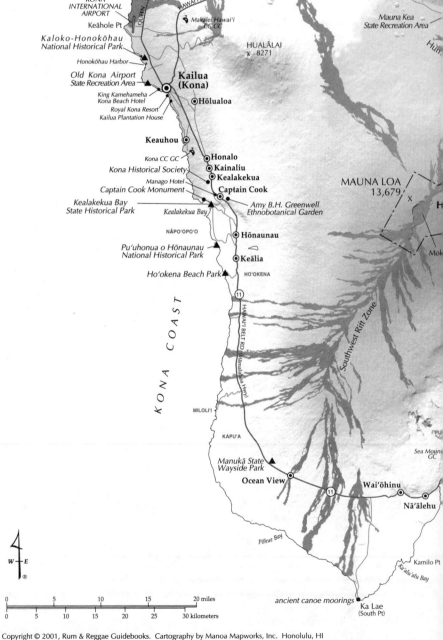

KONA
INTERNATIONAL
AIRPORT

Keāhole Pt

HAWAI'I BELT

Makalei Hawai'i
CC GC

Mauna Kea
State Recreation Area

Kaloko-Honokōhau
National Historical Park

HUALĀLAI
x 8271

Honokōhau Harbor

Old Kona Airport
State Recreation Area

Kailua
(Kona)

King Kamehameha
Kona Beach Hotel

Hōlualoa

Royal Kona Resort
Kailua Plantation House

Keauhou

Kona CC GC

Honalo

Kona Historical Society

Kainaliu

Kealakekua

Manago Hotel

Captain Cook Monument

Captain Cook

MAUNA LOA
13,679 x

Kealakekua Bay
State Historical Park

Kealakekua Bay

Amy B.H. Greenwell
Ethnobotanical Garden

NĀPO'OPO'O

Hōnaunau

Pu'uhonua o Hōnaunau
National Historical Park

Keālia

Ho'okena Beach Park

HO'OKENA

11

Southwest Rift Zone

HAWAI'I BELT RD (Māmalahoa Hwy)

K O N A   C O A S T

MILOLI'I

KAPU'A

Sea Mount
GC

Manukā State
Wayside Park

Ocean View

11

Wai'ōhinu

Nā'ālehu

Pōhue Bay

Kamilo Pt

Ka'alu'alu Bay

W   E

0   5   10   15   20 miles

0   5   10   15   20   25   30 kilometers

ancient canoe moorings

Ka Lae
(South Pt)

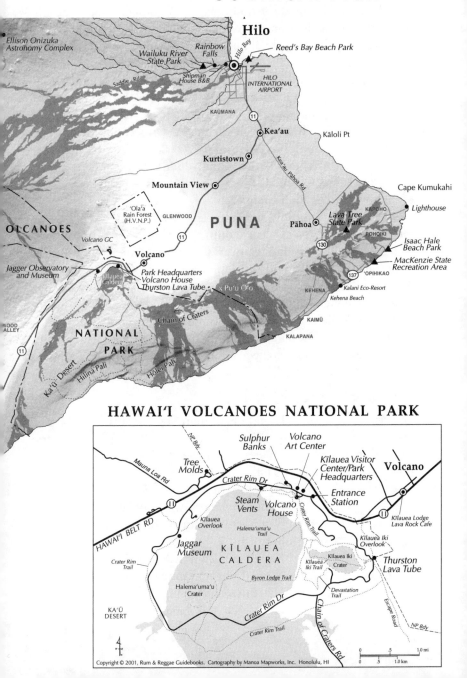

The Big Island
Southern Half

Ellison Onizuka
Astronomy Complex

Hilo

Rainbow Falls

Reed's Bay Beach Park

Wailuku River
State Park

Hilo Bay

Shipman
House B&B

HILO
INTERNATIONAL
AIRPORT

Saddle Rd

KAŪMANA

11

Kea'au

Kāloli Pt

Kurtistown

Kea'au Pāhoa Rd

Mountain View

Cape Kumukahi

'Ola'a
Rain Forest
(H.V.N.P.)

GLENWOOD

PUNA

KAPOHO

Lighthouse

OLCANOES

Volcano GC

11

Lava Tree
State Park

Pāhoa

POHOIKI

Jagger Observatory
and Museum

Volcano

Park Headquarters
Volcano House
Thurston Lava Tube

130

Isaac Hale
Beach Park

MacKenzie State
Recreation Area

x Pu'u Ō'o

'OPIHIKAO

137

KEHENA

Kalani Eco-Resort

Kehena Beach

Chain of Craters

WOOD
ALLEY

11

**NATIONAL
PARK**

Ka'ū Desert

Hilina Pali

Holei Pali

KAIMŪ

KALAPANA

HAWAI'I VOLCANOES NATIONAL PARK

NP Bdy

Sulphur
Banks

Volcano
Art Center

Kīlauea Visitor
Center/Park
Headquarters

Volcano

Mauna Loa Rd

Tree
Molds

Crater Rim Dr

Entrance
Station

11

Steam
Vents

Volcano
House

Crater Rim Trail

11

Kīlauea Lodge
Lava Rock Cafe

HAWAI'I BELT RD

Kīlauea
Overlook

Halema'uma'u
Trail

Kīlauea Iki
Overlook

Jaggar
Museum

KĪLAUEA
CALDERA

Kīlauea Iki
Trail

Kīlauea Iki
Crater

Thurston
Lava Tube

Crater Rim
Trail

Byron Ledge Trail

Devastation
Trail

Escape Road

KA'Ū
DESERT

Halema'uma'u
Crater

Crater Rim Dr

Chain of Craters Rd

NP Bdy

Crater Rim Trail

0   .5   1.0 mi

0   .5   1.0 km

became Hawai'i's first queen. Besides the obvious political alliance and benefits, Ka'ahumanu was somewhat of a feminist for her day. She abhored the *kapus,* the traditional codes of behavior, especially those that forbade women to eat with men. Ka'ahumanu was responsible, with the help of her son Kamehameha II and the New England missionaries, for abolishing the *kapu* system of *ali'i* (royal) privileges and the worship of Hawai'ian gods, and for converting Hawai'ian society to Christianity. In 1847 John Palmer Parker, of Massachusetts, founded the Parker Ranch in Waimea, presently the largest privately owned ranch in the United States (hard to believe, but it's true). It consists of over 225,000 acres. It made cattle a major industry on the Big Island, along with sugar cane grown on the Hamakua Coast. Hilo became the Big Island's center of government (it still is) and commerce.

Although the largest island in the Hawai'ian archipelago, the Big Island remained a sleepy locale until after Hawai'i became the 50th state in 1959. Tourism is a relatively recent newcomer, pioneered by Laurance Rockefeller and his Mauna Kea Beach Hotel in 1965. The Mauna Lani and Kona Village followed, and along with a slew of hotels and condos in Kailua-Kona and luxury resorts on the Kohala and North Kona coasts, made tourism the major economic force on the Big Island. Hawai'i Volcanoes National Park, with its on-going volcanic activity, has also been a big part of the growth of tourism.

The Big Island: Key Facts

LOCATION	Hilo: Longitude 19°44' N, latitude 155°5' W
SIZE	4,038 square miles/10,458 square kilometers
HIGHEST POINT	Mauna Kea (13,796 feet/4,205 meters)
POPULATION	143,848
TIME	Hawai'ian Standard (year-round): 2 hours behind LA, 5 hours behind New York, 10 hours behind London
AREA CODE	808
AIRPORTS	Kona International Airport (Kona/Kohala/Waimea) Hilo International Airport (Hilo/Puna/Volcano)
MAIN TOURIST	Kailua-Kona, Kohala Coast,

AREAS	Hawai'i Volcanoes National Park / Volcano
TOURISM INFO	www.bigisland.com

Focus on the Big Island: Pele and the Hawai'i Volcanoes National Park

> "Heaven has no rage like love to hatred turned,
>   Nor hell a fury like a woman scorned."

William Congreve, the 17th-century English dramatist, wrote this in his play *The Mourning Bride*. Over the centuries, this quotation has been modified and condensed into the saying "Hell hath no fury like a woman scorned." While many would argue that a man scorned can be equally vengeful (or worse), there's no doubt that the Hawai'ian goddess of fire, Pele, is an angry woman—a woman scorned. Just one look at her awesome power in Hawai'i Volcanoes National Park, where lava continuously spews forth from lava vents and occasionally wipes out downslope towns and subdivisions, will convince even the most skeptical. Well, okay, a little imagination will help too. Here's why she's so pissed off: According to Hawai'ian legend, her prettier younger sister, Hi'iaka, ran off with Pele's true love, Lothiau. Ouch! We don't blame her—a double betrayal is so harsh, and revenge *can* be so sweet. This happened on Kaua'i, and since then her fiery fury has progressed down the island chain (legend has it that she was chased from island to island by other gods). In any event, she is in full residence at the park and is also building a new home at the Lo'ihi Seamount (currently 3,000 feet below sea level) because inevitably her enemies will make her move on.

Besides the legacy of Madame Pele, the ocean, mountains, and the earth's core interact here in ways very rarely seen elsewhere on the planet. At the heart of this fusion is Pele's volcanism—the creation of land through volcanic activity. The Hawai'ian Islands, which extend from the Big Island in the southeast to the Kure Atoll over a thousand miles away to the northwest, were created over 25 million years ago by all of nature's energies working together. A magma spout below the ocean floor found its way through a crack in the earth's thin crust and began building up a shield volcano at the base of what is now known as the Kure Atoll. As the surrounding ocean was almost 20,000 feet deep, it took a very long time for the volcano to break through the surface of the ocean (in Mauna Loa's case, about 2 million years). Kure continued to build skyward until it was probably a considerable landmass. What prevented this volcanic island from piercing the stratosphere was another force, the movement of the earth's crust. The Hawai'ian Islands are located on the edge of the Pacific Plate. This plate is moving northwest at the rate of two to three inches a year. As it moved, the magma flow to Kure was effectively sheered off. Meanwhile, the magma spout (which is below the earth's crust and is therefore stationary) assumed a new location to the southeast. As the flow would begin again, it would start the process of island building once more. Without any new course of magma to continue building, the forces of wind, rain, and sea began the process of erosion, cutting away at Kure until all that remains of the huge shield volcano now is a coral reef.

This process is still at work in Hawai'i. From the visitor's perspective, the best example of it is the difference between Kaua'i and the Big Island—and the progression of change is exemplified in the islands in between. Kaua'i has long ago moved off the hot spot and been subjected to the forces of erosion. Evidence of this can be seen in the sculpted pali of the Na Pali coast and the deep erosion of Waimea Canyon. On the Big Island, Madame Pele is still working her magic—lava continues to flow daily, creating new land on the southeast side of the island. Someday this flow will stop and a new island of Lo'ihi will eventually rise out of the sea, although we certainly won't be around to see it.

Hawai'i Volcanoes National Park

This park is the big time in the world of volcanism—the Manhattan of magma. There is enough here to satisfy anyone's thirst for scenery and for knowledge about volcanoes. The Park Service has set up a variety of information outlets and many miles of hiking trails for the visitor's enjoyment. Call 808-985-6000 for more info and for current conditions, or visit the park's Web site at www.nps.gov/havo.

By far, the star (besides Madame Pele herself) of **Hawai'i Volca-**

noes National Park is the caldera of Kilauea—a huge (and we mean *huge*) crater. It is the focus not only of the park but also of the volcanic activity itself and has been the site of many large-scale eruptions. Today you are most likely to see mellower activity in the form of lava flows from downslope vents. Still, the idea of walking across the bottom of the crater, where beneath the thin crust lies a direct path to the earth's core, and of the potential of all that pressure exploding at your feet is certainly food for thought.

The Hawai'i Volcanoes National Park, like national parks everywhere, is a major tourist attraction, and rightfully so. Do expect busloads of tourists at **Volcano House** between the hours of 10 A.M. and 4 P.M. The **Crater Rim Drive** is also a parade of slow-moving rental cars, so keep that in mind and don't be in a rush.

Once at Volcano, at the crest of 3,980 feet, you'll find **Volcano Village.** The main gate to the park is about a mile farther up the road. Shortly thereafter you come to the park's **Visitor Center,** the **Volcano Art Center, Volcano House,** and the **Volcano Golf Course.** Due to the elevation, the temperature here is cooler than at the coast. Its windward location means the weather is frequently overcast and hazy. It rains often, usually in the evening or early morning. The average rainfall for Volcano is about 100 inches.

There are several things to explore here. First, there is the often missed but truly nifty **Volcano Village**. Here you'll find some classic Hawai'ian-style houses along the main village road and some general stores for sandwiches, beverages, gas, and groovy souvies, as well as accommodations like the Kilauea Lodge, and My Island Bed & Breakfast (see Where to Stay), several dining spots including the Kilauea Lodge, the Lava Rock Café, Surt's at the Volcano, and a couple of other luncheonette (see Where to Eat) for breakfast, lunch, and/or dinner.

Inside the park, the **Visitor Center** (open daily from 7:45 A.M. to 5 P.M.) is a must first stop for printed info, displays, lectures, and movies of Kilauea erupting (shown on the hour from 9 A.M. through 4 P.M.). There are rangers on duty to explain the park, and there's a bulletin board displaying the latest volcanic activity. If you are interested in overnight camping, you must check in here. A word of warning: Do *not*, we repeat, do *not* take *any* form of lava rock back home with you. It is a prescription for bad luck. Madame Pele is known to get very upset about anyone taking anything of hers (can you blame her after what her sister did). She will cast a spell on you if you leave with any of her belongings. The Visitor Center used to have a display case full of letters from unfortunate tourists who took some rocks and had catastrophically bad luck since. However, the display and the volume of returned rocks grew so large that they had to dismantle it due to lack of manpower and space and so as to not encourage others from mailing things back. We think this is unfortunate as it was the most interesting exhibit at the Visitor Center and some people we know get vicarious thrills from voyeurism.

The **Volcano Art Center** (open daily from 9 A.M. to 5 P.M., phone 808-967-7565) is next-door to the Visitor Center and worth a peek. It has some nice *objets d'art* for sale. The prices are rather high, but the Center supports local artisans who are working in the arts and crafts traditions of past and present Hawai'i (and they make great wedding presents). Across the road is **Volcano House** (see Where to Stay), a clapboard hotel that looks much better on the outside than on the inside and has the best view of the Kilauea crater from a hotel room we've seen here. It also is a nice place to be before 9 A.M. and after 5 P.M. At other times, there will be a constant crush of tourists traipsing through. Lunchtime is megabus buffet madness. Your best bet for Volcano House is to be here for sunrise and breakfast and then skedaddle. The **Volcano Golf and Country Club** offers 18 holes (see Golf in Other Things to Do) in Pele's backyard. (They say that she sometimes does peculiar things to the direction of your shots.) Adjacent to these links is the **Volcano Winery** (808-967-7479), home of the half-grape, half-tropical-fruit wines. The winery has three whites worth the stop, and unlike Napa, the tastings are free. Open from 10 A.M. to 5:30 P.M.

After exhausting the above options, head for the **Crater Rim Road.** If you're not going to hike into the crater, a drive with stops will allow you to get the gist of it all. Some stops offer short walks that are worthwhile and easy, even for those couch potatoes among us. We recommend stops at Steam Vents, the Jaggar Museum (no relation to Mick and open daily from 8:30 A.M. to 5 P.M.), the Halema'uma'u crater (Pele's inner lair) for an offering of a lei or flowers, the Thurston Lava Tube, and the Kilauea Iki Crater.

You can also drive down the **Chain of Craters Road** all the way to the coastal bluff, a 40-mile round-trip drive with a vertical descent/ascent of 3,700 feet. (There are no gas stations or convenience stores on this road, so be prepared.) This long drive will take you by gigantic pit craters, easily viewed after a short walk from the car. The road will end at the 1995 lava flow (that flow and the flows of the preceding 15 years wiped out the road, the Royal Gardens subdivision, and the village of Kalapana). There is a lookout here for an overview of the flow. Before driving all the way down, be sure to check with the rangers for current conditions and night viewing possibilities. There are also some fantastic petroglyphs to be seen when you reach the coast at Puʻu Loa. There is also a narrow, twisting road from the Chain of Craters Road to the Hilina Pali Lookout (about nine miles), great for a sportscar but not so great if you roar around a turn and meet somebody head on. (The road will barely allow two compact cars to pass each other, and you are often boxed in by lava.) Once there, however, the view is very expansive, looking out to the brown Kaʻu Desert, the cobalt-blue Pacific, and the dry *pali* to the shore—all the way to South Point. *Be careful not to breathe the volcanic fumes.* Also, *never* walk on lava where glowing red is visible through the cracks. The crust could break and you *will* be vaporized. Consult with the park rangers if you have any questions or doubts.

Hiking enthusiasts will delight in the number of well-maintained trails here. Besides the formidable Mauna Loa trail, there is an excellent variety of trails for both the intrepid and the inert hiker. Some of the best are as follows:

Halemaʻumaʻu Trail (3.2 miles one way). This is probably the most popular trail, running from the Visitor Center to the rim of the Halemaʻumaʻu Crater—said to be Pele's inner sanctum. The hike will take you down the steep bluffs of the Kilauea Caldera and onto its floor, where you will walk across the parched lava flows, many of them recent, to the Halemaʻumaʻu overlook. The perspective from the middle of the crater is something otherworldly. If you don't want to walk back (the only choice is same way you came), then arrange to be picked up at the overlook by a friend or by Volcano House (free to guests, available for a fee to others), or hitchhike back to your car (use discretion for the latter, of course!).

Kilauea Iki Trail (3.4-mile loop). Meaning "little Kilauea," this trail is similar to what you would see on Halemaʻumaʻu, but it is a shorter, and wonderful, walk. If you don't want the length or hassle of Halemaʻumaʻu, then this is your best bet. Park at the Kilauea Iki overlook. There is a 0.3-mile spur to the Thurston Lava Tube, which is recommended.

Thurston Lava Tube (0.3-mile loop). This is a good example of the lava tunnels that run throughout the Volcano, Kaʻu, and Puna districts, although it is certainly not as interesting as the Cave of the Flying Vagina over in Puna (see Kalani Oceanside Eco-Resort, in Where to Stay). This walk through the lighted tunnel is less than a half-mile total, so by all means get out of the car. As this is a popular stop and kids *will* scream once inside, try to go early in the morning or at dusk, when there are fewer tourists.

Bird Park (Kipuka Puaʻulu) (1.2 miles). A *kipuka* is an area left untouched by a surrounding lava flow—an island of green in a sea of blackness. Because the adjacent lava acts like a moat, these areas provide an excellent environment for native Hawaiʻian flora and fauna, protecting them from the ravages of introduced species. The Park Service maintains a path through the forest that is very easy to negotiate. Birds are abundant here, especially in the early morning (from dawn until 10 A.M.), and plants are labeled for your edification.

Halape Trail (14 miles round-trip). For the more serious backpacker, this trail leads down from the Kipuka Nene picnic area on the Hilina Pali Road to the beach at Halape. In 1975 an earthquake caused a tidal wave that wiped out the coconut grove at the shore, killed two campers, and left a golden sand beach in its place. This trail is a two-day affair—overnight camping is permitted at the Halape shelter. You must register at the Visitor Center to camp. This is a strenuous, hot, and dry hike. You should be well prepared before attempting it, and bring *plenty* of water.

Mauna Loa Trail (36.6 miles round-trip). This is the *really* big time—heavy-duty hiking to the summit of the largest mountain mass in the world (10,000 cubic miles). Due to the altitude, the trip will take a minimum of three days (two days up, one day down), but a four-day schedule is a much better idea. The hike begins at the end of the Mauna Loa Road at an elevation of 6,662 feet and ends 18 miles later at the summit cabin, elevation 13,250 feet. That's a vertical rise of 6,588 feet. There is a cabin about midway at Red Hill (after seven miles at 10,035 feet). The summit is in a subarctic climate zone—there is snowpack throughout most of the winter. At this elevation, altitude sickness, hypothermia, and sunburn are real problems. But the volcanic wilderness experience of this hike cannot be beat. Backcountry permits are required (contact the Visitor Center at 808-985-6000). Still, we'd rather sip a hot toddy by the fire at the Kilauea Lodge, thinking of the poor souls shivering in their sleeping bags and plagued by headaches, than actually *attempt* to climb Mauna Loa. But then again, we still enjoy the missionary position!

Other Things to Do

Being so *big,* the Big Island offers a lot to do besides reading the latest David Sedaris, sipping mai-tais by the pool, or getting a massage. Actually, the above doesn't sound bad to us at all. But if you are restless and, we hope, adventurous, the following are some options:

- ≈ **Golf**
- ≈ **Diving**
- ≈ **Beaches**
- ≈ **Mountain biking**
- ≈ **Horseback riding**
- ≈ **Deep-sea fishing**
- ≈ **Tennis**
- ≈ **Cerebral Stuff**
- ≈ **Hiking**
- ≈ **Helicopter tours**
- ≈ **Snow skiing**

Golf

Golfers will adore the Big Island, home to 19 courses—the most in the state. The premier fairways and greens are in Kohala and North Kona, not surprisingly at the luxury resorts. The first courses were built here—the incredible Mauna Kea course and the Mauna Lani North and South courses (originally one course, which morphed like an amoeba into two in 1991—the South Course is most like the original). The Four Seasons has made an impact with its Hualalai course. The Hilton Waikoloa Village has the King's Course, ranked in the top 25 by *Golf Digest*, and the Beach Course, a Scottish links-style course. All have been sculpted in lava flows, making the contrast of black and green very striking. Three other good courses are the two Waikoloa links and the Kona Country Club. There is also an 18-holer adjacent to the Kilauea Crater at Hawai'i Volcanoes National Park, along with an excellent municipal course in Hilo.

Mauna Kea Resort, Mauna Kea Beach Hotel, 62-100 Mauna Kea Beach Drive, Kamuela, HI 96743. Local: 808-882-7222.

> **Mauna Kea Course**
> 18 holes—Par 72
> Championship (black): 7,114 yards, 73.6 rating
> Tournament (blue): 6,737 yards, 71.9 rating
> Regular (orange): 6,365 yards, 70.1/75.7 rating
> Forward (white): 5,277 yards, 65.2/70.2 rating

Among the top-rated courses in the state, this is also one of the most beautiful. As with the other courses on the Kohala and Kona coast, the Mauna Kea was planted on an ancient and desert-like 'a'a (rough lava flow). The now mature plantings and landscaping (the course was completed in 1964) make that seem implausible, but it's true. As golf courses go, the beauty and maintenance of the Mauna Kea are stunning. Designed by Robert Trent Jones, Jr., and considered by many to be one of his finest courses, it is rated the number 2 course in Hawai'i by *Golf Digest* and rated number 72 in *Golf Digest's* "America's 100 Greatest" golf courses.

The course has some very special holes, including the famous six-tee third, which tees off on one side of a cove and greens at the other side—quite a water hazard. More than a few balls have been lost into the raging sea below on this par 3. The 11th (par 3) slopes downhill until the green drops off into the sea. This is a hilly course, with lots of uphill greens and undulating fairways. Views of Mauna Kea, Mauna Loa, the Kohala Mountains, and Hualalai round out some pretty incredible scenery. For power-hitter and low-number drivers, the 5th, 8th, 10th, and 17th holes are all over 500 yards long and par 5s. For finesse, the course has seven doglegs and 120 bunkers.

Rates for greens fees and cart are $110 for guests and $135 for visitors. Tee times are from 7 A.M. (eight minutes apart) until 4 P.M. Reservations for hotel guests can be made up to four days in advance; nonguests can make reservations only two days in advance. The available golf packages (minimum two nights) are definitely worth investigating if you're interested in staying here.

Hapuna Beach Prince Hotel, 62-100 Kauna'oa Drive, Kamuela, HI 96743. Local: 808-880-3000.

Hapuna Prince Course
18 holes—Par 72
Tournament (black): 6,875 yards, 72.5 rating
Championship (blue): 6,534 yards, 70.4 rating
Regular (orange): 6,029 yards, 66.8 rating
Forward (white): 5,067 yards, 64.4 rating

Opened in 1992 and designed by Arnie Palmer and Ed Seay, this course is a fine complement to the beauty and challenge of the Mauna Kea. It's known for the stingy width of its fairways. While it's not as stunning or as difficult as its sister course, duffers will enjoy the Hapuna links. The third hole is its signature hole, while the sixth hole has won awards for its design. The toughest holes on the course are the 14th and the 18th.

Rates for greens fees and cart are $110 for guests and $135 for visitors. Tee times are from 7 A.M. (eight minutes apart) until 4 P.M. Reservations for hotel guests can be made up to four days in advance; nonguests can make reservations only two days in advance.

Mauna Lani Resort, Golf Pro Shop, 68-1310 Mauna Lani Drive, Kohala Coast, HI 96743. Local: 808-885-6655.

The North and South Courses are among the best in Hawai'i and form an emerald necklace around the still faboo Mauna Lani Resort. In 1991 the outstanding Mauna Lani course was divided into North and South courses, utilizing nine holes of the original course and adding nine to each new one. The most popular is now the South Course, which many feel got the better half of the expansion.

The South Course
18 holes—Par 72
Championship (black): 6,926 yards, 72.8 rating
Tournament (blue): 6,453 yards, 70.5 rating
Middle (white): 6,059 yards, 68.3 rating
Forward (gold): 5,202 yards, 64.1 rating

A "Senior Skins" course, the South Course got the best ocean-view holes and play when it took nine holes of the original Mauna Lani course. Designed by Belt Collins & Associates, it is one of the toughest courses in the state, carved out of *a'a* lava in such a way as to be known as a ball-breaker and a ball-eater too. The greens almost look as if they are set on lava platforms, like the ancient Hawai'ian *heiaus*. And lava, not trees, separates the fairways. Hole 15 is extraordinary: Not only is it an ocean hole where there is a major water hazard over the raging surf to the green, but whale watching is incredible here during the winter months. There are also water hazards on the 4th, 11th, 15th, and 17th holes.

The North Course
18 holes–par 72
Championship (black): 6,913 yards, 73.2 rating
Tournament (blue): 6,601 yards, 71.7 rating
Middle (white): 6,086 yards, 69.4 rating
Forward (gold): 5,383 yards, 70.6 rating

The other jewel of Mauna Lani golf is the newer North Course, also designed by Belt Collins & Associates. While not as popular as the South Course, it's still a superb and tough play on fairways defined by lava fields and vegetation such as *kiawe* trees. Memorable holes are the fourth, with a gully that is an archeological preserve and two very large traps in front of the green, and the fifth, which is a pretty par 3 with a waterfall on the back of the green and a stream running along the side. Also memorable are the 10th, where the tee is on an island in a two-acre tidal pond, the 14th, which is a short par 3 with a 30-foot drop to the green, and the 17th hole, which is the course signature hole, a par 3 with an amphitheater in a deep lava bowl. Water hazards exist on the 5th, 6th, 9th, 10th, 14th, and 15th holes.

Rates for greens fees and shared carts are $95 for resort guests and $185 for visitors during the high winter season. Call for tee times.

Waikoloa Beach Resort

There are two courses within the Waikoloa Beach Resort:

Kings' Course, 600 Waikoloa Beach Drive, Waikoloa, HI 96738. Toll-free: 877-WAIKOLOA (924-5656). Local: 808-886-7888.

> **King's Course**
> 18 holes—par 72
> King's: 7,074 yards, 73.9 rating
> Championship: 6,594 yards, 71.3 rating
> Resort: 6,010 yards, 68.6 rating
> Forward: 5,459 yards, 71.0 rating

Designed by Tom Weiskopf and Jay Morrish, this 7,000-plus-yarder is a great challenge and a superb addition to the Big Island golf menu. There are nine acres of water, including six major lakes and 83 bunkers. This course is tough and has many Scottish-links-style fairways. The signature holes are the par-4 fifth and the seventh hole, a par 3 over a lake, with lava boulders and a fairway-length sand trap on the left side. Good luck.

Beach Course, 1020 Keana Place, Waikoloa, HI 96738. Toll free: 877-WAIKOLOA (924-5656). Local: 808-886-6060.

Beach Course
18 holes—Par 70
Championship: 6,566 yards, 71.5 rating
Resort: 5,958 yards, 68.6 rating
Forward: 5,094 yards, 69.4 rating

This course lives up to its namesake by allowing both play by the sea and great water views. Designed by Robert Trent Jones, Jr., this par 70 features petroglyph fields and an interesting lava/fairway configuration. More forgiving than the King's Course and with better water views, this course gets crowded, so plan ahead.

Rates for greens fees and shared carts are $105 for resort guests and $195 for visitors during the high winter season. Call for tee times.

Hualalai Golf Club, Four Seasons Resort Hualalai, 100 Ka'upulehu Drive, Ka'upulehu-Kona, HI 96740. Toll-free: 888-340-5662. Local: 808-325-8000.

Hualalai
18 holes—Par 72
Mahope (coconut): 7,117 yards, 73.7 rating
Championship (black): 6,632 yards, 71.5 rating
Regular (white): 6,032 yards, 68.9/74.0 rating
Mua – Forward (red): 5,374 yards, 66.3/70.4 rating

Four Seasons Resorts has never been a company that holds back on amenities, including the design and construction of its fabled golf courses. This Jack Nicklaus–designed course is a designated PGA tour facility through 2006. In keeping with the Four Seasons ultra-lux image, only Four Seasons guests and Hualalai residents can play this course. The signature hole is the par-3 17th, a raging surf play, especially at high tide. Hualalai also has a superb nine-acre driving range and practice facility, although we're not sure if the staff will spritz you with Evian there.

Rates for greens fees and carts $160 for resort guests and residents *only*. Call for tee times.

Waikoloa Village Golf Club, 1792 Melia Street, Waikoloa, Hawaii, 96738. Local: 808-883-9621.

18 holes—Par 72
Championship Tee (blue): 6,691 yards, 71.8 rating
Regular Tee (white): 6,230 yards, 69.2 rating
Ladies' Tee (red): 5,480 yards, 72.1 rating

Designed by Robert Trent Jones, Jr., this course is set up in the lava fields seven miles inland, at Waikoloa Village. The vantage point and elevation of this airy course give you a wonderful sense of perspective. Unfortunately there has been a lot of building around the fairways. The 18th hole ends with a green set on the other side of a large freshwater hazard. There are three over-500-yard holes at par 5, 11 doglegs, and 70 bunkers.

Rates for greens fees and carts are under $80 for visitors. Call for tee times.

Kona Country Club, 78-7000 Ali'i Drive, Kailua-Kona, HI 96740. Local: 808- 322-2595.

Ocean Course
18 holes—Par 72
Championship Tee (blue): 6,579 yards, 71.6 rating
Regular Tee (white): 6,155 yards, 69.7 rating
Ladies' Tee (yellow): 5,499 yards, 71.9 rating

Ali'i Mountain Course
18 holes—Par 72
Championship Tee (blue): 6,470 yards, 71.5 rating
Regular Tee (white): 5,841 yards, 68.7 rating
Ladies' Tee (yellow): 4,906 yards, 69.2 rating

This large golf complex, designed by William Bell, is on the water just south of Kailua-Kona. The Kona Country Club is accessible to most resorts and thus quite popular. The surrounding area is highly developed, but the slope of the property ensures good views of the ocean, especially from the Ali'i Mountain Course. The 3rd, 12th, and 13th holes of the Ocean Course front the ocean, including a blowhole. There are 3 water hazards, 6 doglegs, and 93 bunkers in 27 holes. The 6th and 11th holes on the Ocean Course, and the 4th and 6th holes on the Mountain Course, are over 500 yards.

Rates for greens fees and cart are $125 per person for the Ocean Course and $100 per person for the Mountain Course. Check for specials that include a day of golf on both courses and a free lunch. Call for tee times.

Volcano Golf and Country Club, P.O. Box 46, Volcanoes National Park, HI 96718. Local: 808-967-7331.

18 holes—Par 72
Championship Tee (blue): 6,547 yards, 70.8 rating
Regular Tee (white): 6,190 yards, 68.8 rating
Ladies' Tee (red): 5,567 yards, 70.7 rating

This is a fairly flat course set within a three-iron drive to the Kilauea Crater. It's shorter than the other recommended courses, but its unusual setting and cool elevation—at 4,000 feet—make it a change of pace and an alternative to exploring the park. The fairways are lined with *ohia* trees and lava, and the proximity to Madame Pele's lair has been rumored to do strange things to the flight paths of the balls. If you have a bad day here, you know you did something to offend her. If your score is great, she likes you—consider yourself blessed. There are seven doglegs and no fairways over 500 yards.

Rates for greens fees and shared cart are very reasonable at $60. Tee times are from 7 A.M. to 3:30 P.M. Lunch at the clubhouse is excellent and one of the best deals around.

Hilo Municipal Golf Course, 340 Haihai Street, Hilo, HI 96720. Local: 808-959-7711.

18 holes—Par 71
Championship Tee (blue): 6,325 yards, 70.4 rating

Regular Tee (white): 6,006 yards, 68.8 rating
Ladies' Tee (red): 5,034 yards, 69.1 rating

The only municipal course on the Big Island is one of the best of its genre in the state. Duffers staying on the windward side of the island or in Hilo should definitely not miss it. This is a very popular course, so be sure to book well in advance. There are no bunkers, but there are more than 12 water hazards. Wide fairways, lots of coconut trees, and elevated greens complete the picture. The fourth hole, with the wind against you, is a tough 400-yard power hit.

Rates for greens fees and shared cart are $20 on weekdays, $25 on weekends and holidays. Call for tee times and reservations.

Diving

The Big Island is one of our favorite places in Hawai'i, even without its superb diving—which happens to be the best in the state. Even better, the great diving is within a half-hour's boat ride of Kailua-Kona, the island's major resort area. There are tons of excellent dive sites here, including:

Kaiwi Point. Just a few minutes by boat from Kailua-Kona, the point offers a wall and ledge that begin just below the water's surface and run to about 40 feet. White-mouth morays swim at you with mouths wide open, waiting for a handout. It's a bit disconcerting at first, but they don't actually bite, although one person on our dive had his ear nibbled. The wall is packed with orange cup coral. Due to its narrow shelf, this point is a hangout for large pelagic fish: whales, whale sharks, white-tipped sharks, hammerheads, rays, dolphins, and even humpback whales in the winter. The lava dome close to the surface is a gas to swim into. Stay close to the bottom and in the center; a slight surge will move you around a bit. This area is terrific for night diving, too.

Golden Arches. There used to be a turtle that lived here, whose nickname was "Miss Piggy," but we haven't seen her in three years. There have been a lot of harlequin shrimp around lately. There are some beautiful lava arches, and the visually stunning but awfully poisonous lionfish (do not touch!) are frequently seen here. Located near the National Energy Lab.

Pine Wreck Point. This is a must-dive for deep-dive enthusiasts. The depth is 115 feet, making first-dive bottom time at less than 20 minutes. The explorable plane is split in two and rests on a sandy bottom with lots of fish. Besides the plane wreck, a sunken boat nearby can be a fun second dive, depending on your bottom times.

Aquarium. This underwater state park, with lots of tame fish to feed, is a nice boat dive for novices—there are lots of pyramid and pennant butterfly fish. The coral here is quite lovely. It's located in scenic Kealakekua Bay—the general site of the demise of Captain Cook.

Chimney. This large, long lava tube is a good dive day and night. Night is particularly fun because of all the critters that love to hang out in the tube. It's about a 20-minute boat ride from Kailua-Kona.

Keahole Cove. This cove is located just north of the Kona Airport. It takes a little longer to get to but is worth the effort. The bottom drops off quickly, and there is a great lava pinnacle close to shore. Back in the '80s there was a resident white eel, dubbed "Hoover" because he virtually inhaled his food and was almost five feet long. Lately there have been sightings of a white eel, but we doubt it's the same one. Great site for night diving to see manta rays.

Other dives worthy of mention are **Pyramid Pinnacles, Fantasy Reef, Red Hill,** and **Hammerhead Point.** (Sounds like a fun place to dive, huh? Have you ever seen a hammerhead shark? It looks like a creature from the bar scene in *Star Wars*.) There are several advanced dive sites also worth mentioning: Au Au Canyon, Ule Rock, and Three Room Cave. Also Turtle Pinnacles and Turtle Heaven are great sites. You might want to try Suck 'Em Up Lava Tube, where you can often see a white-tip reef-shark swimming through the lit lava tube. Just ask your dive shop about these places. Some require a special trip.

The Diving Trousseau

Diving is certainly a gear-intensive sport, much like downhill skiing, which is probably why skiers take to diving so easily. New styles, colors, and innovations are constantly modifying "the diving look." There are even scuba fashion shows on national morning television. Fortunately for overburdened travelers to Hawai'i, you don't need to bring a lot of gear with you to go diving. Actually, you don't have to bring anything; it's all there waiting for you and is often included in the price of admission. Included are tanks, weights, BC, regulator, full wet suit (Farmer John overalls and a full jacket), mask, snorkel, fins, and light if necessary. Personally, we like having our own mask, snorkel, fins, BC, and regulator for reasons of comfort, fit, style, and safety. Experienced divers like having their own wet suits, too (you never know what people do down under when number one is necessary). When you cart all of this, however, you add an extra-large gear bag to your already heavy luggage. If you have never gone diving before, you may want to see how it goes before you invest in scuba equipment.

If you have an underwater camera, bring it. If the water clarity is good, you can sometimes get great photos. But a better bet is to hire one of the dive guides to take a video of you and/or your pals diving. Most dive operations in Hawai'i offer this service. We were thrilled with the quality and fun of Keller's video from Jack's Diving Locker. The picture quality is remarkably good, and you can hear the bubbles gurgling. It's worth the $60 or so for a truly groovy souvy.

Kailua-Kona Dive Operations

Jack's Diving Locker, 75-5819 Ali'i Drive, (P.O. Box 5306), Kailua-Kona, HI 96740. Toll-free: 800-345-4807. Local: 808-329-7585, fax 808-329-7588.
Web site: www.jacksdivinglocker.com
E-mail: info@jacksdivinglocker.com
Located in the Coconut Grove Marketplace, Jack's has always been our favorite dive operation in the Aloha State. With a full array of dive services and nine employees, Jack's offers morning and evening boat dives every day and a night dive three or four times a week. It also offers the Big Island's only introductory shore

dive, conducted twice a day and guaranteed to please, smack dab in the middle of Kailua-Kona, on the King Kamehameha Hotel's beach. Jack's boat dives are small—only six customers per dive—and friendly. The guides are there because they love what they do, and it shows. Owner Tina Clothier, the cover girl on the NAUI manual, feels this enthusiasm makes for more relaxed diving and encourages the guides to take the boat for a spin to whale watch or watch the sunset or just go for a ride. Also diving on one of our trips with Jack's was the late and great Jerry Garcia, who couldn't have been more excited about the underwater sites. Although we very rarely get star-struck, we were impressed at how friendly and down-to-earth he was. Then again, that's part of the Dead's legacy.

All equipment is included. Sandwiches, beverages, and cookies are provided on every two-tank dive. Open 8 A.M. to 9 P.M. daily. Dive packages, which include lodging and rental car, are available through the shop. Jack's is open from 8 A.M. to 9 P.M. (closed Christmas Day).

Kona Coast Divers, 75-5614 Palani Road, Kailua-Kona, HI 96740. Toll-free: 800-KOA-DIVE (562-3483). Local: 808-329-8802.
Web site: www.konacoastdivers.com
E-mail: divekona@kona.net

This is the largest dive operation on the Big Island. The new state-of-the-art dive boat, *Diver Two,* is very convenient and can hold up to 24 divers comfortably (Kona Coast also has a six-passenger dive boat). All dives have one dive guide to every six divers as well as someone who is always on the boat. There is an on-site training pool and dive shop with highly trained technicians and a friendly staff. Dive/lodging packages and multiday dive packages as well as full- and half-day private charters are available. Open Monday through Friday 7 A.M. to 6 P.M., Saturday and Sunday 8 A.M. to 5 P.M.

A Sea Paradise Scuba Inc., 78-7128 Kaleopapa Road, (P O. Box 5655), Kailua-Kona, HI 96745. Toll-free: 800-322-KONA (5662). Local: 808-322-2500.
Web site: www.seaparadise.com
E-mail: spscuba@interpac.net

Located south of Kailua-Kona on Keauhou Bay, this is another good full-service dive shop near the Kona Surf Hotel. Sea Paradise offers the usual array of dive services. Open daily from 7:30 A.M. to 5 P.M.

Aloha Dive Company, P.O. Box 4454, Kailua-Kona, HI 96745, Toll-free: 800-708-KONA (5662). Local/fax: 808-325-5560.
Web site: www.alohadive.com
E-mail: diveadc@kona.net
Although Aloha Dive Company doesn't have a store, it does pride itself on being able to reach any dive site on the entire island. It offers the standard dive services without lots of divers, which we like.

Kohala

Kohala Divers Ltd., Kawaihae Shopping Center, (P.O. Box 44940), Kawaihae, HI 96743. Local: 808-882-7774.
Web site: www.kohaladivers.com
E-mail: h2osport@kohaladivers.com
Kohala Divers has two boats for diving. One is a 36-foot Munson that holds a maximum of ten divers; the other is a 36-foot Topaz that is used for night dives and dive charters (six divers max). They offer resort-style courses as well as certification classes. The cost of a two-tank dive (equipment included) is $102.50. The store is open daily, Monday through Wednesday from 8 A.M. to 5 P.M. and Thursday through Sunday until 7 P.M.

Hilo

Nautilus Dive Center, 382 Kamehameha Avenue, Hilo, HI 96720.
Local: 808-935-6939.
Web site: www.nautilusdivehilo.com
E-mail: info@nautilusdivehilo.com
If you're on the Hilo side of the island, Nautilus is your best bet. Diving on the windward side, when the trade winds are down and the seas are calm, is a treat. It's also a mostly local business—a refreshing change from the Kona side. And it's cheaper! Open Monday through Saturday from 9 A.M. to 5 P.M.

Beaches

The Big Island is big—big enough to fit all of the other Hawai'ian islands inside it twice. Yet because it's so new (relative to the other islands), it hasn't had the time for wind and water to pulverize its lava into sand. Thus, proportionally, there just aren't as many good beaches as on the older islands. Not to worry, though; the beaches recommended in this section will keep even diehard beach buffs happy. Aficionados of black-sand beaches will be in heaven here, although there are plenty of golden-sand beaches, too (some helped along by imported sand).

Kailua/Kona

While most of the affordable hotels on the western side of the Big Island are located in Kailua-Kona and along Ali'i Drive south to Keauhou, there are virtually no beaches in this area. In Kailua-Kona proper, the King Kamehameha Hotel has a beach, but it's right in the harbor and hardly pristine. It is a good, calm place for kids, though, as well as being the beach used for the Ironman Triathlon. There is a better beach just north of the King Kam, as the hotel is called, at the site of the old airport runway. The rest of the coast south to Kealakekua is pretty much lava rock. There are four exceptions, however, one of which is highly recommended.

Old Airport State Park. Located just north of the King Kamehameha Hotel, this park is within walking distance (follow the path along the shore) and popular with locals. There isn't a lot of sand, and the bottom tends to be rocky, but this is the best alternative to Honokohau and very close to the center of Kailua-Kona. Stick to the southern end of the beach, where it is less crowded and sandier. To reach it by car from the King Kam, take Kaukini Road (the first left as you go uphill from the King Kam on Palani Road), and then take another left on Kaiwi Road. This will turn into a dirt road leading to the landing strip. Park on the runway. No facilities or lifeguard.

Honokohau. This is our favorite non-resort beach on the Big Island. A long crescent of salt-and-pepper sand, it is secluded and undeveloped. It is also the only nude beach (and gay-friendly beach) on the western side of the Big Island. As it borders private land of a sympathetic owner, you needn't worry about legal problems here. Obviously the people-watching (ahem) can be fun. You may feel awkward if you don't take off your suit—at least to swim.

The beach is long enough to give you plenty of breathing space. The swimming is good, although the water is shallow and the bottom can be rocky and coral-strewn in spots. An added plus is a brackish pond bordering the middle of the beach where you will find Queen's Bath (on the northern end of the beach—follow the path inland just a bit). This is a good spot to rinse away the salt. Honokohau is also a great place to see turtles. We saw four swimming in the sea and two sunning themselves on the beach. Remember—it can get hot here, so be sure to bring lots of water and refreshments.

Honokohau can be reached by taking the road to Honokohau Harbor off Route 19. The turnoff is clearly marked and about three miles north of Kailua-Kona. Follow the road to the harbor, and take your first right. This will lead you past various marinas on your left. Go to the end of the road and park—other cars will be there. The path to the beach begins in the dip over the stone wall on the right side of the road. There may or may not be a sign saying "Beach," but there is one saying "Use at Your Own Risk." (There are actually several signs of this type as you walk toward the beach.) Basically, just keep following the signs and bearing right. You will eventually come to the water. Turn right and keep walking—the beach is about another 200 yards down. The sand can be hot, so be sure to wear sandals. Bring plenty of water to drink. No facilities or lifeguard.

Disappearing Sands. Officially known as White Sands County Park, this is a small cove of golden sand that is a favorite of boogie boarders and bodysurfers if there is a southern swell. It's not at all spacious—hence the name—so it can get crowded. Ali'i Drive is very close by. Restrooms/showers/picnic area/lifeguard.

Kahalu'u Beach Park. The next beach south of Disappearing Sands on Ali'i Drive, this small salt-and-pepper-sand beach also gets crowded. Restrooms/showers/picnic area/food concession/lifeguard.

Kohala

Kohala is the area north of the Kona Airport all the way to Hawi town, on the northern end of the Kohala peninsula. As far as beaches are concerned, Kohala really stretches from the Outrigger Waikoloa Beach Resort to the Mauna Kea Beach Hotel. Some of the loveliest beaches on the island are found here. Naturally, the deluxe resorts have built on them. But by law all beaches are open to the public, so don't be intimidated by guards and gatehouses. South of the Outrigger, there is a pretty gray-sand beach at the Kona Village Resort (actually in North Kona), but it's small and crowded with hotel guests and their children. The Four Seasons has a nice man-made beach. The best beaches in this area, however, are 'Anaeho'omalu Bay (the Outrigger's beach), Hapuna Beach, and Kauna'oa Beach (the Mauna Kea's beach).

'Anaeho'omalu Bay. Since this is considered by many to be the most idyllic setting on the Big Island, it is unfortunate that Sheraton built such an uninspiring hotel on its perimeter (the hotel is now part of the Outrigger chain). Here you'll find golden sand, coconut groves, excellent swimming, and a tranquil bay for a day of leisure. You may also find a lot of people. Full of historic artifacts, this area was a retreat of the Hawai'ian *ali'i*—the fish ponds on the bay were exclusively for royal use. To get here, follow the "Beach Access" signs after entering Waikoloa Road (the one heading *makai*—toward the sea) from Route 19. Restrooms/showers/picnic area/bar-restaurant/water sports at the Outrigger/lifeguard.

Hapuna Beach State Park. One of the most popular beaches on the Big Island, until recently this was one of the few Kohala beaches without some kind of development surrounding it. Now, however, the massive and heavy-looking Hapuna Beach Prince sits at the northern end of the beach. With golden sand, great views of Maui, ample parking, and the promise of a semi-unspoiled retreat, it can get very crowded here. But Hapuna is very pretty and well maintained, with good summer swimming. There are lifeguards, but you should still exercise caution during heavy surf and use fins. (We've heard that Hapuna, due to the undertow, has the dubious distinction of having the most drownings in the state.) Restrooms/showers/picnic area/camping/no lifeguard. The park does have shelters for rent—very simple rustic A-frames for $20 a night. Call 808-587-0311 for more information.

Beach 69. Another beach around Kanekanaka Point at Wai'alea Bay, this is more secluded than Hapuna Beach. Popular with locals, there is great snorkeling around the northern end of the beach. No facilities.

Mauna Lani. Situated on Makaiwa Bay, the golden-sand beach of this star-studded resort is quite a pleasant place to spend the day (and public access is not a problem here). The man-made beach echoes the V shape of the front of the hotel. It is studded with palm trees and sprinkled with sumptuous chaises sporting retractable awnings. A beach bar and cafe are next to a busy, social pool. Swimming here is good, too, when the sea is calm. Restrooms/showers/bar/restaurant/water sports/lifeguard.

Kauna'oa Beach. Most people refer to this as Mauna Kea Beach, as it is enveloped by the Mauna Kea Beach Resort. This is our favorite beach in Kohala. Why? Quite simply, it is spacious, very well maintained, and particularly scenic due to the superb landscaping of this former RockResort (now managed by Prince Resorts). Two lava rock points jut out from either end of this half-moon-shaped and wide golden-sand cove, making the swimming here excellent under most conditions (and safer than Hapuna). There are lifeguards on duty here. A beach bar and very casual outside cafe, good for cocktails and lunch, are just steps away from the water. If you desire shade, a delightful manicured lawn and a coconut grove of very tall and stately palm trees border the beach. The one glitch in this pretty picture is public access. If you are not a guest of the resort, there is very limited parking available. Restrooms/showers/bar/beach cafe/water sports at the hotel/lifeguard.

Hamakua Coast

Due to the vicious currents and surf that rip and pound at this exposed coastline from Hawi to Hilo, there are very few beaches with sand on the Hamakua Coast. More important, *swimming here is not advised.*

Hilo and Puna

Welcome to the land of black sand. This is where Madame Pele is still working her magic, creating beachfront that will someday go for top dollar (when the lava stops flowing for good). This east-side stretch is a sensuous coast—the inner sanctum of this tempestuous volcano goddess. The black sand evokes the black satin sheets that would shroud her waterfront boudoir. Where are we going with this? Um, we don't know, but the imagery is true. From Hilo in the north to Kehena in the south, the coastline can be spectacular—especially the drive along Route 137. However, only three recommended beaches are good enough for both sunning and swimming—two in the Hilo area and one sensational spot in Puna.

Hilo

Richardson Ocean Beach Park. The nicest place to swim and snorkel in Hilo, this beach is part of a cooperative marine center run by the county, the University of Hawai'i-Hilo, the Hoaaloha'O Waiuli Coastal Trail Committee, and the Leleiwi Community Association. Besides the great views of Hilo and Mauna Kea, the two small black-sand beaches are very safe for swimming and several reefs offer some superb snorkeling. The center maintains a nature trail that takes you by at least 30 different kinds of tropical vegetation and a replica of a Hawai'ian fish pond—pointed out in an informative trail guide (available at the center). The center periodically offers interesting programs. Richardson's is easy to reach. Just follow Kalaniana'ole Avenue (Route 137) east of the junction of Route 11 for four miles, until you pass the Mauna Loa Shores condos. Look for signs soon after on the left. Restrooms/shower/picnic area/visitor center/lifeguard.

Reeds Bay Beach County Park. Within walking distance of the Banyan Drive hotels, this is a very pleasant park with safe swimming and views of the harbor. It is particularly scenic when the ocean liners are in. The water here is colder, though, due to freshwater springs. Restrooms/shower/picnic area/lifeguard.

Puna

Kehena Beach. Located on Route 137, this is one of the most beautiful black-sand beaches in Hawai'i. Divided in two sections by a lava finger that juts out from impressive black lava cliffs, Kehena is also the east side's nude/gay beach (Honokohau being the west side's). It is tucked into one of the most rugged coasts in the state, where lava still flows into the ocean less than five miles away.

Exercise caution swimming here, and use fins; the currents can be strong, and the bottom falls off quickly. When the water is calm, which is fairly often, the snorkeling can be interesting off the north point. Just be careful not to get too close to the end of the point, or off you go! If you don't swim, there is ample shade from a grove of ironwood trees and a semi-secluded cave for an afternoon nap or delight. Remember to bring water, as black sand gets much hotter than the other varieties. Occasionally tiny red ants can be a nuisance.

The beach is off Route 137, just north of the hamlet of Kehena, at the small paved lookout on the *makai* side of the road (one and a half miles south of the Kalani Oceanside Eco-Resort). There are usually cars parked on the side of the road (a giveaway to a secluded beach). The path to the beach is about 50 feet north of the lookout. It is rather rough in spots, and the lava rock is *sharp*, so wear shoes. As it descends fairly steeply, you must be at least moderately limber to attempt it. No facilities.

The South

Loosely defined as the area following Route 11 south from Captain Cook on the west coast, around Mauna Loa to Hawai'i Volcanoes National Park, the South offers three beaches that may be of interest, although the Big Island's best have already been discussed.

Ho'okena Beach County Park. Just five miles south of the access road for Pu'uhonua'o Honaunau National Historic Park and two and a half miles from Route 11, this is the best beach in the south district, with great swimming and bodysurfing. The gray- and black-sand beach itself is quite lovely, with coconut palms, large lava cliffs, and a quaint village nearby. Bring something to drink—there is no drinking water available. While in the area, be sure to check out the picturesque village of Miloli'i, about 15 miles south of the Ho'okena access road. Restrooms/showers/ picnic area/no lifeguard.

Green Sand Beach. As its name implies, the sand here is actually a shade of olive green, derived from olivine in the area's lava. Officially known as Papakolea Beach, this is the only green beach in the state. The problem here is access—you must hike in at least an hour (two and a half miles) from South Point to reach it. It will, however, be secluded. Also, swimming here can be treacherous—so use common sense. No facilities or lifeguard.

Punalu'u Beach County Park. This is a pretty and isolated (although somewhat developed) cove on the southeastern side of the island with a nice black-sand beach. As it is only a mile off Route 11, Punalu'u has for years been a standard stop on the tour-bus trip from the west coast hotels to Volcano. Swimming is okay, but use caution. Restrooms/showers/picnic area/lifeguard/snack shops nearby.

Mountain Biking

Serious mountain bikers will adore the Big Island because there is so much spectacular terrain to explore. The trails are as varied as the island, from beginner to extreme. All along the way there are stunning vistas, for the Big Island can be like a Hawai'ian version of Montana—this is Big Sky country too. There are trails dispersed around the island featuring rolling pastures, wild orchids, single tracks, steep climbs, sand, and of course volcanoes. The Big Island Mountain Bike Association, with the dubious acronym BIMBA, promotes the sport, trail access and development, and safety among other things. Contact the association at 808-961-4452 or www.interpac.net/~mtbike.

Some outfits that provide both equipment and tours are:

Mauna Kea Mountain Bikes, Inc., Toll-free: 888-682-8687, local: 808-883-0130, www.bikehawaii.com.

Lawrence Lambino, Local: 808-967-8291.

Hilo Bike Hub, Local: 808-961-4452, www.gtesupersite.com/hilo-bikehub.

Hawai'ian Pedals, Local: 808-329-2294, www.hpbikeworks.com.

Backroads Bicycle Touring, 1516 5th Street, Berkeley, CA 94710. Toll-free: 800-462-2848. Local: 510-527-1555.

They offer eight-day bike trips where you stay in motels, and also a five-day bike/camping trip.

Horseback Riding

If there is one place on the Big Island that conjures up images of horses, it is Waimea. Home of the Parker Ranch, the largest privately owned ranch in the U.S. at 225,000 acres, Waimea offers miles and miles of grassy fields and pastures just begging for a spirited canter. This is the spiritual home of the *paniolo* (Hawai'ian cowboy). While the Parker Ranch is private, there are several recommended stables in the grassy Kohala Mountains and in the Waipi'o Valley for all levels of riders. These areas are unbelievably scenic.

Kohala Na'alapa Stables, Kamuela, HI 96743. Local: 808-889-0022.

They offer two rides a day: a morning ride for $75 per person lasting two and a half hours, and an afternoon ride for $55 per person lasting one and a half hours. They are open seven days a week.

Waipi'o Na'alapa Stables, P.O. Box 437-185, Kamuela, HI 96743. Local: 808-775-0419.

They offer two rides a day into Waipio Valley, at 9 A.M. and 1 P.M. The cost is $75 per person and the rides last two and a half hours.

Deep-Sea Fishing

Sport fishing on the Big Island is big time. The shelf off the Kona coast drops off from 20 feet to over 6,000 feet in nine short miles.

This means that big pelagic fish will cruise close to the coast, making the deep-sea fishing off Kona some of the best in the world. You won't have to travel very far at all to do it. Blue marlin and yellowfin tuna are favorite catches here. And there have been some incredible prizes caught here in the islands. In 1984 a 1,649-pound blue marlin was hauled in off of Kona. The largest Pacific blue marlin caught on rod and reel was 1,806 pounds, off of O'ahu. (The official world record for a marlin, according to the International Game Fish Association is 1,365 pounds. The rules for this are pretty strict, that is why the bigger fish didn't qualify; either there was more than one angler or other help was used, thereby disqualifying the catch.)

There are scores of boats that go out in search of the big one. Chartering a boat is expensive. A boat for you and a party of no more than six people, costs upwards of $450 for a half-day, which includes only tackle, equipment, and ice. You must bring your own lunch and beverages. If you book 24 hours in advance, you can charter on a shared basis, which is considerably cheaper, at around $110 per person for a half-day. This makes more sense if your party is just you and yours.

Most of the boats are based in Honokohau Harbor, just north of Kailua-Kona. **Gentry's Kona Marina** (call 808-329-7896) is where the boat action is. Captains and crew hang out at **Harbor House** (808-326-4166) for burgers and brew. The fishing is best when the seas are calm, so the summer months—especially August—are considered the finest time to go. In winter, you'll have to check weather and sea conditions before booking.

Check out www.hawaiifishing.com for information on charters, sea conditions, and much more. Here is one charter that we recommend:

Kona Charter Skippers Association, Captain Pete (he was there when the 1,649-pound blue marlin was caught), 74-857 Hualani Place, Kailua-Kona, HI 96740. Toll-free: 800-762-7546. Web site: www.konabiggamefishing.com

Tennis

Kohala

Mauna Kea Beach Hotel, 62-100 Mauna Kea Beach Drive, Kamuela, HI 96743. Local: 808-882-7222.

Besides having the best golf course in Hawai'i, the Mauna Kea maintains its high standards with its Tennis Park — rated one of the 50 greatest tennis resorts in America by *Tennis* magazine since 1981. The reasons for this high rating are 13 Plexi-pave courts (none lighted), video instruction, shower/changing facility, bar, fully stocked pro shop (including stringing of racquets), and seasonal tennis packages on a 13-acre complex. The Mauna Kea is also the biggest tennis center on the Big Island.

The only downside of the Tennis Park is that you must be a hotel guest or a member of the Club at Mauna Kea to play here. But if you're avid about the game and have the bucks to stay at one of Hawai'i's top resorts, then why not? Court times are from 7 A.M. to sunset. Reservations may be made up to 24 hours in advance. The staff (including three tennis pros) will pair you with a partner of similar skill if you are without one. Occasionally non-guests can play—just call ahead to see if any courts are open. The cost is $12 per person per day.

Orchid at Mauna Lani, One North Kaniku Drive, Kohala Coast, HI 96743. Local: 808-885-2000.

There are ten Plexi-pave courts (seven lighted) here, plus instruction and a pro shop. The Orchid's tennis facility is also among *Tennis* magazine's top 50 courts in the U.S. Fees for the general public are $15 per person per day. Resort guests are charged $12.50 per day per person. There is a clinic every morning at 9 A.M.

Tennis at the Mauna Lani

There are two tennis complexes within the Mauna Lani Resort area:

Racquet Club at Mauna Lani, 68-1400 Mauna Lani Drive, Kohala Coast, HI 96743. Local: 808-885-7765.

The Racquet Club has six Plexi-pave courts (three lighted), a locker room, instruction available,and a pro shop. The club is open from 6:30 A.M. to 7 P.M. Fees are $20 per court per hour.

Tennis Garden at Mauna Lani, 68-1400 Mauna Lani Drive, Kahala Coast, HI 96743. Local: 808-885-1485.

Ten Plexi-pave courts (none lighted), locker rooms, instruction and a pro shop make the Garden a favorite at the resort. Open from 7 A.M. to 6 P.M. daily. Fees are $20 per court per hour.

Hilton Waikoloa Village, 425 Waikoloa Beach Drive, Waikoloa, HI 96738. Local: 808-886-1234.

The Hilton Waikoloa has eight Plexi-cushioned courts (none lighted). Cost is $25 for a full day. Open from 7 A.M. to dusk.

North Kona

Four Seasons, 100 Ka'upulehu Drive, Ka'upulehu-Kona, HI 96740. Local: 808-325-8000.

The Four Seasons has eight Rubberized-Remembrance courts (four lighted). Cost is $15 per person per day. Open from 7 A.M. to 8 P.M.

Royal Kona Resort, 75-5852 Ali'i Drive, Kailua-Kona, HI 96740. Local: 808-334-1093.

Four hard courts (three lighted) are available at the Royal Kona. Fees are $15 per couple per day. Open from 8 A.M. to 8 P.M.

Island Slice Tennis, Keahou Beach Hotel, 78-6740 Ali'i Drive, Kailua-Kona, HI 96740. Local: 808-322-6112.

Six hard courts (two lighted) and instruction are offered here. Fees are $10 per day per person. Open from 7 A.M. to 9 P.M.

Municipal Courts

There are 43 around the island. For a complete listing of public courts (county and municipal), call 808-961-8313.

Kona

Kailua Park, Old Kona Airport, Kailua—Kona
Four hard courts/lighted/free.

Kohala

Kamehameha Park, Kapaʻau
Two hard courts/lighted/free.

Waimea Park, Lindsey Road
Two hard courts/lighted/free.

Hilo

Hoʻolulu Tennis Park, Kalanikoa Street. Local: 808-961-8720.
Three indoor lighted courts (it rains a lot in Hilo). Fees are much cheaper on this side of the island—only $2 per hour from 8 A.M. to 4 P.M. and $4 per hour from 4 to 10 p.m. Four outdoor courts can be reserved; the cost is $25 per court per day. Otherwise, outdoor courts are free on a first-come first-served basis, by the hour. The Tennis Park includes the enclosed Edith Kanakaʻole Tennis Stadium (home of the Merrie Monarch hula festival).

Lincoln Park, Kinoole/Ponahawai Street.
Four hard courts/two lighted.

Puna

Shipman Park, Volcano Highway.
Two hard courts/not lighted.

Cerebral Stuff

The Big Island's sheer size and energy provide stimuli for a variety of imaginative pursuits. From the excitement of the Merrie Monarch Festival to the authenticity of Hilo to the solitude of the Waipiʻo Valley, the Big Island has much to offer the knowledge-thirsty soul.

The Merrie Monarch Festival

Hula is a dance of beauty, harmony, and emotion. Once a sacred and valuable means of communicating heritage and traditions (the pre-contact Hawaiians did not read or write), it has developed into a distinct and beautiful art—a Hawai'ian marriage of opera and ballet. The combination of the cool grace of the hands, the warmth of the hip movements, the expressiveness of the face, and the *mele* (chants) or music is hypnotic.

However, when most people think of hula, they think of smiling girls in grass skirts swaying to the strums of the ukulele. You certainly can see hula danced this way, but when you do, you're probably just witnessing entertainment for tourists. You can experience a different and uplifting perspective on hula when you see it danced seriously by those who regard it as a cherished Hawai'ian birthright. For the *haole*, there is no better way to learn about hula—and take in a heady dose of Hawai'ian culture—than to attend the annual Merrie Monarch Festival.

Merrie Monarch is a true celebration of Hawai'iana, for there is nothing more Hawai'ian than the hula. It is a showcase of all the best in dance, chants, and music. Held in Hilo, on the Big Island, usually during the first week in April, it is also incredibly fun.

For four nights, hula is danced under the arched roof of the Edith Kanaka'ole Tennis Stadium in Ho'olulu County Park. It's a small arena, not unlike the ones where high-school hockey is played (except that the end walls are open to the breezes of the night), so you will be able to see everything. With the exception of the rows on either side of the stage, where the television lights glare (the final two evenings are telecast live), there is not a bad seat in the house. Be advised that seats are limited and they are definitely in demand, so you will have to reserve tickets well in advance. Also, be sure to buy a program—it will make everything you are about to see much clearer, and it's a nice, authentic souvenir.

Officially, the festival begins on Sunday with an exhibition of hula and music at Mokuola (Coconut Island). Then there are lunchtime programs at Waiakea Villas, in Hilo, on Monday and Tuesday. But the festival really gets rolling on Wednesday, at the stadium, with an exhibition noted for the *keikis* (children's) performance, followed by three nights of competitions.

Two types of hula are performed in these competitions: *kahiko* and *'auana*. The *kahiko*, or ancient hula, is danced to the drumming of a large gourd called the *ipu*, the rattle of the *uliuli* (a gourd with stones inside), and the chanting of the *kumu hula* (hula master). The costumes, made of leaves, flowers, and island materials, are stunning. This is what most aficionados call the "real" hula, as it closely resembles the state of hula before the missionaries arrived. Even if you don't speak Hawai'ian, you'll find it fairly easy to understand the story just from the pantomime. The inflections in the chanting also give you an idea of the emotions being depicted. This contrasts markedly with the 'auana, or modern hula. Probably the biggest difference between 'auana and kahiko is the use of music. Hawai'ian music is very melodious and upbeat, featuring falsetto vocals and such instruments as the ukulele, bass fiddle, and steel guitar.

Thursday is the Miss Aloha Hula Contest, in which more than 15 wahines present both kahiko and 'auana hulas (sorry, guys, no bathing suit competition here). By the time the awards are presented and Miss Aloha Hula has been "crowned" (figuratively speaking—she doesn't actually wear one), it's been a long evening. The kahiko segment, the most interesting, comes first. If you want to catch it all, plan on being there around 6 P.M. and staying for about six hours. It's touching to see the finalists awarded—they've worked very hard and the emotion of the moment is contagious. For a hula dancer and a Hawai'ian, this is indeed a high honor.

Of course, part of the fun of any festival is the audience. It's amusing to watch the flow of people on the concourse outside the stadium, where various groups gather to chat and see who else is there. You'll never see more flora-bedecked people than here, and also you'll never see more antees (aunt-like women)—the robust, mature, and lovable Hawai'ian da kine (type) that is the hallmark of every Hawai'ian family. Inside the arena, even subtle hula moves will bring roars and screams from the knowledgeable audience. The house is really brought down, however, when the kane (men) come on stage—especially during the kahiko program, where they often wear practically nothing. The shrieks and squeals may remind you of teenage girls at 'NSYNC concerts.

The final two nights of the festival are the highlights of Merrie Monarch. Each night is devoted to one of the two hula styles; there are winners in each category as well as an overall winner. Over 30 halau (hula troupes), both male and female, compete each night. They come from all over Hawai'i, with sizable contingents also traveling from California and even a show-biz group from Vegas. All of the *halau* practice throughout the year for these two nights, and the importance they place on this event is evident. At one point, when we were standing against a wall at the top of the arena, we turned around to check out the action on the concourse and saw the Halau Mohala 'Ilima getting ready for their turn at the *'auana* program. The girls were lined up side by side, gently swaying to the strumming of the guitar by Haunani Apoliona and Olomana, their stellar musicians. Heads were bowed and there was no talking. The *kuma hula* Maupana de Silva brushed the girls' hair, starting from the back of the line and working forward, so that each dancer would look and feel beautiful before her entrance. It was a very peaceful scene, and yet the complete silence of the dancers testified to the importance of the next few minutes on stage.

Friday night is the *kahiko* program. If you can only see one event, this should be it. Beginning at 6 P.M., the evening is a spectacle of swiveling hips, swishing skirts, and stomping feet. *Kahiko* was and is a sacred tradition, a devotion to the goddesses Laka and Hi'iaka. Hula was a very important ritual—dancers used to be like nuns, even taking vows of celibacy. And while the latter certainly isn't practiced anymore, the solemnity of the event is reflected in the dancers' expressions. Entrances and exits are made with hands on the hips. Eyes are straight ahead, framed by high cheekbones and by the maile leis that sit on the dancers' heads like crowns. The stage itself is a sea of maile, ti leaves, and blossoms; between that and the leis and flora nearly everyone is wearing, the air is particularly fragrant. It's spellbinding.

Saturday night, the *'auana* program, is a different affair. The music sets the upbeat mood, and the dancing follows suit. Expressions change, too, from somber lips to smiles. The hula of the evening is more familiar to the average *haole:* this is the stuff of Hollywood and Don Ho Christmas specials, except that it's so much better. Styles of dancing vary more widely here, from rather prudish and stiff movements dating from the Victorian era to a more unabashed and suggestive motion that is a real crowd-pleaser. Costumes tend to be a little dowdy, mirroring the styles of the late 19th century, when *'auana* hula was nurtured by the kingdom's *ali'i* (ruling class), who emulated Victorian England. Some of the costuming, though, is a wonderful mix of past and present, accenting the curves and shapes that make the hula all the more mesmerizing. Even the audience is more dressed up—Hawai'ian society's toniest are out in full force. It is also on this night that some of Hawai'i's best musicians perform as backup, so you are guaranteed an audiovisual extravaganza.

Following the 'auana program is the presentation of the awards. This is really fun, especially if you have been judging on your own for both programs (make sure you bring a pen so you can keep score). Picking the winners isn't easy. Contestants are judged on expression, posture, precision, hand gestures, foot movements, interpretation, costumes (authenticity, coordination, and leis), and overall appearance. But it's the reactions of the halau that are worth the price of admission (which, by the way, is $10 each night). Upon being selected as one of the five finalists, even as fourth runner-up, the chosen halau goes wild. Apparently, being included as among the best is virtually as important as being the winner. It sounds trite—"everyone's a winner"—but it's a nice way to end a contest.

So what do you do when the show's over? By all means head for the Homalimali Bar at the Naniloa Hotel (on Banyan Drive). It's one of the highlights of the festival, and drinks are cheap. The crowd is a mix of divergent types of people who'd never assemble in one room under other circumstances. Everyone is having a great time watching others make the scene. And this is the scene in Hilo once the evening's festivities have concluded. Besides the groovy crowd, the music also makes it—an excellent Hawai'ian band plays until three in the morning with few breaks. They play requests, and frequently the more mature 'auana dancers in the room will get up on stage and dance with the sort of grace and skill that come only from years of experience. And you can tell they're having a great time, making the most of the opportunity to dance once more in front of a crowd.

Festive Terms to Know

halau: A hula troupe, either all men or all women. The word is both singular and plural.

kumu hula: The teacher or hula master of a halau.

kahiko: The ancient style of Hawai'ian hula, danced to chants (*mele*).
'auana: the modern hula with music.
wahine: female.
kane: male.
ami: The rotating pelvic gyration that is a hula crowd-pleaser.
kaholo: The side step that is the keystone of hula.
mele: merry.
keikis: kids.

To get tickets and more info about the Merrie Monarch Festival, write or call: **Merrie Monarch Festival,** c/o Hawaii Naniloa Resort, 93 Banyan Drive, Hilo, HI 96720. Local: 808-935-9168.

Art Galleries

Like everything else on this dynamic island, the art scene holds its own. There are several excellent venues in which to see what's happening all around the island. Among the best:

The Volcano Art Center, Hawaii Volcanoes National Park, HI 96718-0104. Local: 808-967-7179/7511.
Occupying the original Volcano House (built in 1877), this is one of the state's premier art galleries and one of the most interesting sites at Volcanoes National Park. The building is an unassuming one-story, brown-shingled house with a red tin roof and a lanai running the length of its front. It houses prints, wood carvings, ceramics, jewelry, carved whale and walrus ivory, and Hawai'iana books. Nothing here is really inexpensive. A nice-size koa wood bowl will run around $500, and prices skyrocket to a couple of g's. But there are things for less.
Inside the lanai is the gallery's main lobby, where you'll find jewelry, information and sales, and a working fireplace. Windham Hill–ish music wafts through this charming structure. The main exhibits are through a door on the left side of the lobby. Usually these are shows by local artists; they change periodically. Everything on display at the gallery is local and almost everything is for

sale, so bring credit cards. In several small rooms off to the right of the lobby there are lots of books on Hawai'i—art, nature, hiking, history, crafts, music, and so on.

The Volcano Art Center is adjacent to the Hawai'i Volcanoes National Park Visitor Center. It's open daily from 9 A.M. to 5 P.M. It also sponsors classes, workshops, special events, concerts, seminars, and retreat conferences (a calendar is available). If you'd like, you can become a member of the Friends of the Volcano Art Center (it's a nonprofit organization—and a very worthy cause, too). For info, call or write to the address and phone number above.

Holualoa Town. Perched above Kailua-Kona on Route 180 is a village that is small in size but large in its importance to the art world on the Big Island. There have been a number of changes to the art scene here. There is now the Holualoa Foundation in addition to the Kona Art Center and a number of galleries.

Kona Art Center, P.O. Box 272, Holualoa, HI 96725. Local: 808-322-7997.

Operated by Carol Rodgers (Bob passed away a few years ago), now in her eighties, the Kona Art Center still inhabits an old coffee mill. It's a fun stop even if you just want to browse and chat with the Carol about Hawai'ian artists. The center runs classes where visitors are welcome and operates the Little Church Gallery across the street. Here you'll find the works of local artists as well as a weaving studio.

The Holualoa Foundation for Arts and Culture, P.O. Box 169, Holualoa, HI 96725. Local: 808-322-336.

One of the newest additions to the Hawai'i art scene is the Holualoa Foundation, a nonprofit corporation that seeks to bring an understanding of culture and all art media to persons of all ages. They offer "hands-on weekend workshops" hosted by local as well as visiting artists. Workshops include everything from watercolor classes to jewelry, and from creative writing to woodworking. They also have a special event called Project Art in February or March which lasts for two days, is totally free, and offers more than 20 different art media to choose from. Give Peggy Chestnut, the president of the foundation, a call for complete details.

Studio 7 Gallery, P.O. Box 153, Holualoa, HI 96725. Local: 808-324-1335.

This excellent gallery and showcase of local artists features wood pieces. Prices are reasonable and several of the items can make great wedding gifts. There are lots of wood bowls (mainly koa and milo) by Jack Straka, hand-carved *objets d'art* by Scott Hare, curly koa mirrors, small furniture pieces and jewelry boxes by Marcus Castaing, paintings by Herb Kane, and plenty more. Nadine, the friendly manager, will be glad to show you around. It's open Tuesday through Saturday from 10 A.M. to 4 P.M., closed Sunday and Monday.

Other Galleries in Holualoa:

Holualoa Gallery, 76-5921 Mamalahoa Highway, 322-8484.

Ululani Group Gallery, 322-7733.

Chestnut and Company, 76-5942 Mamalahoa Highway, 324-1446.

Hale 'O Kula Gallery, 324-1688.

Country Frame Shop & Gallery, 324-1590.

Hilo

Cunningham Gallery, 116 Keawe Street, Hilo, 808-935-7223

Waipi'o Valley

Waipi'o Valley Artworks, Kukuihaele, HI 96727. Local: 808-775-0958.

Open daily from 8 A.M. to 6 P.M. Café from 8:30 A.M. until 5 P.M.

Waipi'o Valley

The Waipi'o Valley is a magical place. It's the cradle of Hawai'ian civilization, the "Valley of the Kings," and it is truly enchanted; filled with the karma of almost a thousand years of Hawai'ian spirits. Much has been written about the valley, and while it's undeniable that travel writers tend to get carried away and embellish, in this case much of what's written is true. It is the largest valley on the Big Island, and its lack of development and intense lushness make it one of the most stunning settings in Hawai'i. Steep *pali* rise up almost 2,000 feet on either side. Cliffs frame the mile-wide valley mouth where it meets the raging surf with a long black-sand beach. The Wailoa Stream empties out through the beach, providing some marvelous freshwater swimming before it enters the ocean. Inland, there are twin waterfalls at one end. The far end funnels seven miles into the high Kohala Mountains.

Taro farming was the primary industry in the valley; it once supported over 10,000 people. Indeed, the valley was one of the most fertile producers in all the islands. But as the Hawai'ian kingdom grew and contact from the outside increased, the valley's importance diminished. Then in 1946, a tsunami crested at 46 feet and wiped out much of the remaining community. Amazingly, no lives were lost (the spirits were watching). Now only isolated taro fields exist. The rest is overgrown and wild, adding to the valley's sense of isolation.

The valley is accessible only by foot, horseback, or four-wheel-drive vehicle. If you walk, be prepared to pay for it with stiff legs for the next couple of days. The mile-long road down is notoriously steep and narrow—relentless on leg muscles. We walked down, which really had our thighs screaming for mercy. If you are not in training, we recommend taking the Waipi'o Valley Shuttle in and out. Unless it has four-wheel-drive, your rental car will not make it. The shuttle uses vintage Land Rovers. And while they may not be very comfortable, they do add to the sense of adventure—and they get you there in one piece.

There are a couple of different ways to see Waipi'o. One option is an hour-and-a-half tour of the valley, run by the Waipi'o Valley Shuttle people. Local drivers will take you into the middle of the valley, fording streams and pausing to explain the history, folklore, and vegetation you are seeing and to pick edible fruit (we had grapefruits). Then you head to the beach to look at a thick cluster of trees that evidently was the major *heiau* but is now totally overgrown. Far more interesting is the river. It is wide, slow-moving, and refreshing for a dip. We went in and loved it. You'll drive around a little more, but that's about it. If you want to see the falls or more of the valley, see it by foot. Or tour it on horseback, through the stables in the valley.

The valley is the subject of great legends, including several stories that made our hair stand on end. All of the spirits of legends come out at night. Of particular interest is the alleged existence of a "door to the dead" at the beach. Stories abound of occasional night marches, where the royal spirits conduct a procession through the valley, walking a foot off the ground. Yikes! Then there's Nenewe, the shark man, and the white dog that changes size—we look at all light-colored dogs carefully when we're in Waipi'o.

The story of the 1,300-foot Hi'ilawe Falls (the twin falls) is more spiritual than spooky. Apparently Lono, the god of wind, harvest, and fertility, was looking for a bride when he found the beautiful Hi'ilawe by the waterfall. So that the two could be lovers forever, they changed into waterfalls, hence the pair.

Pu'uhonua O Honaunau National Historic Park, P.O. Box 129, Honaunau, HI 96726. Local: 808-328-2288.
Web site: www.nps.gov/puho/

One of the most interesting aspects of Hawai'ian cultural history is the existence of the place of refuge. The *pu'uhonua,* as it is called in Hawai'ian, was sacred ground that provided sanctuary and redemption for a member of an enemy tribe or anyone in trouble with the law. In those days, being in trouble meant that you had broken a *kapu* and were literally running for your life. *Kapus* were a strict code of conduct for the common people (not the *ali'i,* or ruling elite). They were the rules of life, the Hawai'ian constitution. Such things as letting your shadow fall on the chief's palace grounds or harvesting out of season were violations of the *kapu* and were punishable by death. To break a *kapu* was to offend the gods, who would show their anger violently in the form of tidal waves, earthquakes, volcanic eruptions, and famine. So the offender had to go, and fast. If you were caught, it was curtains. But if you could reach the temple, usually by swimming in or by outsmarting your pursuers, you were free. After being blessed by the *kahuna* (high priest), you were free to go back into society, just like that! (We wish we had *pu'uhonuas* for parking tickets.)

Pu'uhonuas existed all over Hawai'i. The best example of one is here, along with the adjacent royal grounds. Once again, the National Park Service has done a super job of restoring and managing the site and providing informative displays and materials. During the day, there are several local craftsmen "on display," simulating the way things were done before the *kapu* and Hawai'ian gods were outlawed in 1819 by King Kamehameha II. While they are interesting, by far the best time to visit Pu'uhonua o Honaunau is at twilight, when the crowds have gone and there is virtually no one around. The light at sunset casts an ethereal glow upon the walls, statuary, and the stone platforms of the *heiau*. Reflections off the tidal pools add to the spiritual feeling of this place. Watching the sunset and the sky redden from a contemplative spot is healing. The setting is one of the best places in Hawai'i for meditation. Above all, it is peaceful.

There are actually two parts to the park. The first is a restoration of the royal chief's "palace" grounds. Replicas of several thatched buildings are scattered within a beautiful stand of coconut palms. At the center is a tiny crescent beach that was the royal canoe landing (it's also a great, although rather busy and public, spot for a swim). A long stone wall separates the royal grounds from the *pu'uhonua*. At the seaside end is the Hale o Keawe *heiau*, which has been strikingly reproduced, complete with wooden statuary. The temple was originally built in the 17th century, a hundred years after the Great Wall and the huge stone *heiau* platform inside the *pu'uhonua* were constructed. The temple housed the bones of 23 chiefs. Their collective *mane*, or spirits, provided protection for the *pu'uhonua*.

The *pu'uhonua* itself is a very evocative place—oddly a visualization of Brian Eno's "Music for Airports"—a barren lava field framed on two sides by the wall and surrounded on the other two sides by tidal pools and a rocky beach. Dominating the plain is a large stone platform near the entrance and a grove of coconut palms at the far (ocean) side. Otherwise, there is little else but rocks. The stark beauty and simplicity of the sacred grounds are very spiritual. It's clear that this was no Garden of Eden—not even a very hospitable-looking place. Yet it was the only hope for many desperate people. Undoubtedly places like this saved countless lives. This knowledge, combined with the unworldly setting and the rays of twilight, make a visit here a mind-blowing experience.

The Park Service has a marvelous brochure about the history and the grounds that is a must-read. The visitors' center, open during the day, has plenty of parking. A beach and picnic area at the southern end of the park is a great place for a barbecue before or after sunset. Those who want to see the park while it's open may want to arrive around 3:30 P.M., tour the grounds, have a picnic, and then return to the *pu'uhonua* for sunset and meditation. (Sunset in Hawai'i is generally between 6 and 8 P.M., depending on the season.)

Before you visit the park, we highly recommend stopping in Captain Cook, a funky and granola-esque town that is very refreshing after the relentless tourist development that has engulfed Kailua-Kona. Here you can get supplies for a wholesome picnic in the park. From there, continue on to Kealakekua Bay to see a rather large *heiau* and the Captain Cook Monument (this is where he met his demise). The drive down from Captain Cook is one of the most scenic in Hawai'i. There are expansive vistas of the Pacific as you meander through coffee orchards and fields. On the lower part of the road is the Royal Kona Coffee Mill and Museum (808-328-2511), which is open for tours and a cup of coffee. Once you've seen the sights at the black-sand beach, go straight on the road directly south. It runs for four miles through the remains of old lava flows and deposits you right at the park. It's a narrow and rolling straightaway (a great road for a sports car) so you may want to turn on your headlights.

Lyman Museum and Mission House, 276 Haili Street, Hilo, HI 96720. Local: 808-935-5021.
Web site: www.lymanmuseum.org

This is the foremost museum on the Big Island and one of the top three in the state (the Bishop Museum on O'ahu and the Kaua'i Museum are the other two). It houses the largest mineral, shell, and geologic collection in the Pacific and is among the best in the world.

The museum, a modern building constructed in 1973, has two

floors. The ground floor is the Island Heritage Gallery. This has an extensive collection of Hawai'ian artifacts, implements, and clothing, as well as some from the variety of ethnic groups that have flowed into the islands since 1778. Among the Hawai'ian exhibits are an authentic pill grass house, prized *kapa* cloth, and feather leis and *kahilis* (feather staffs) used by the royalty. Displays from other ethnic groups include a Buddhist altar and kimonos from Japan, as well as items from the Portuguese, Chinese, Filipino, and Korean populations. Each exhibit includes an explanation of its significance.

The second floor is the Earth Heritage Gallery. Here you'll find a thorough explanation of Madame Pele's doings in Hawai'i, with exhibits and displays of everything you always wanted to know about volcanoes but were afraid to ask. Also in the gallery is the mineral collection, with over 26,000 specimens that will delight geologists and offer pleasant browsing for the rest of us. Far more interesting to the layman is the gallery's collection of shells—the most extensive in the Pacific.

The Mission House was built in 1839 by the Lymans, missionaries who first arrived on the Big Island in 1832. The house has been restored to its original appearance and contains artifacts and memorabilia of the missionary period. You will notice that the Mission House, as with the architecture of other mission homes in Hawai'i, resembles the New England colonial period with Hawai'ian touches. This is because the first missionaries were Yalies from Connecticut, and they brought with them the Yankee style as well as the Congregational faith. Tours of the house are given hourly, starting at 9:30 A.M.

The museum has an excellent lecture series and special exhibit program. Be sure to call when you arrive to see what's scheduled. There is a gift shop where you can find some thoughtful Hawai'ian souvenirs as well as books and educational materials (great for the kids). The museum is open Monday through Saturday from 9 A.M. to 4 P.M. The cost of admission is $7 for adults, $3 for kids aged 6 to 18.

General Sights

Kealakekua Bay (Kealakekua). The site of the Hikiau *heiau*, the Captain Cook Monument, and several other *heiaus*, this scenic bay is where Captain Cook met his demise.

Puʻukohola Heiau National Historic Sight (Kawaihae). Built by Kamehameha the Great for his war god Ku, this is a large *heiau* on a hill overlooking the Pacific at Kawaihae. You really can't see much of it; the walkway through is closed to the public because the temple is crumbling from years of earthquakes and neglect. But the site is magical, and the pamphlet distributed by the Park Service is the most interesting thing of all. It's worthwhile to make the trip just so you can say that you were on Kamehameha's home turf. It is open from 7:30 A.M. to 4 P.M. For more info: P.O. Box 4963, Kawaihae, HI 96743. Local: 808-882-7218.

Moʻokini Heiau (Hawi). Located on the tip of the Kohala Peninsula in a beautiful setting, this is one of the most striking and oldest *heiaus* in Hawaiʻi, dating back to A.D. 480. It was used only by the *aliʻi* and was dedicated to Ku, the war god. Legend has it that the temple was built in one night by a chain of 18,000 warriors passing smooth lava stones hand to hand from the Pololu Valley. Just down the road is Kamehameha's birthplace. Late afternoon and sunset here are the best times to visit.

University of Hawaiʻi—Hilo. This pleasant little campus offers a number of events and programs for the general public, including excellent concert (the Hawaiʻi Concert Series) and dance programs. Theater is also an option. Call 808-961-9310 or 808-961-9518 for information about tickets and activities, respectively.

Hawaiʻi Tropical Botanical Garden (Hilo). Situated at Onomea Drive, this is one of the most accessible and splendidly scenic settings on the Big Island. It's been designated a nature preserve and sanctuary, and it is supported by a nonprofit organization. Even its semi-tourist atmosphere doesn't take away from the stunning beauty that's around. There is an admission charge (under $10) and you must ride the minibus (fare is covered by admission) to the trailhead. There are over 1,000 plant species here, including heliconias, gingers, bromeliads, and groves of coconut palms, mangos, and monkeypods. Plants are labeled for identification The garden is a very tranquil setting, a nice place for a walk or to work things out. You can spend all day here if you wish. The garden is open from 9 A.M. to 5 P.M. daily and is located just north of Hilo off Route 19. Turn off at the blue "Scenic Route" sign and turn in at the Old Yellow Church, which is the registration office (you can reserve tickets here) and gift shop.

Hulihe'e Palace / Moku'aikaua Church / Ahu'ena Heiau. Smack dab in the middle of Kailua-Kona's waterfront are these three different historic sites. All can be seen fairly quickly and offer relief from the general oppressiveness of Kailua-Kona. Hulihe'e Palace (808-329-9555) is a good example of how the 19th-century Hawai'ian royalty emulated the English in style and design, although there are also some interesting and genuine Hawai'ian artifacts, such as Kamehameha the Great's spears, on display. It's open from 9 A.M. to 4 P.M. daily; admission is under $5. Moku'aikaua Church is a fine example of early missionary architecture and is said to be the oldest operational church in the state. It's open daily from 7 A.M. to 5 P.M. Ahu'ena *heiau is* a restored temple that was dedicated to the god Lono (fertility) and now sits on the grounds of the King Kamehameha Hotel. Ahu'ena was rebuilt in 1813 by Kamehameha the Great and became his last residence. The *heiau* is open daily during daylight hours with tours conducted at 1:30 P.M., except on Friday, when the tours are held at 3 P.M. It's hard to believe, looking at Kailua-Kona today and considering all the other stunning options on the Big Island, that this is where the king wanted to be.

Parker Ranch (Waimea). Two tours are available to see parts of this 225,000-acre ranch (the largest privately held ranch in the U.S.). The Paniolo Country Tour costs around $40 and operates daily except Sunday. The shorter Paniolo Shuttle Tour costs $15 and runs daily except Sunday. For more info, call 808-885-7655.

Hiking

With twice the area as all the other islands combined, the Big Island naturally offers lots more hiking opportunities, in the sense of greater, harder, and longer hikes. Some of the most challenging hikes in the Hawai'ian Islands are found here. The

Mauna Loa Trail is the prime example of these several-day, mountain-climb hikes. The climate at the summit will be subarctic, so this is serious stuff even for the serious hiker, and possibly a little more than the reader of this book will care to get into (for info on this trail, see the section on Hawai'i Volcanoes National Park earlier in this chapter).

For the more leisurely among us, there are plenty of easier walks and hikes. One outfit that offers interesting guided adventures is Hawai'i Forest & Trail. They conduct half- and full-day tours, with van pickup at selected locations and refreshments/nourishment and gear included. For more info call: 800-464-1993 or 808-331-8505 or check out their web site: www.hawaii-forest.com. Rates range rom $85 on up to $145. For self-motivators, two of the best walks/hikes are as follows:

Lava Trees State Monument. Putting new meaning into the term phallic symbol is this small but evocative park set in one of the lushest and most sensual places we have ever been. The "lava trees" are actually the lava casts of tree trunks. They were formed by a sudden drop in the lava level, caused by a fissure or earthquake. The lava on the trunks was cooled by the trees themselves, and what's left are these freestanding monuments, many in the most provocative outlines possible.

As you pull into the park, you'll notice giant earpod trees towering skyward to about 100 feet. Wrapped in ivy and vines, they create a canopy high above the ground. All the stones and roots are moss-covered and bathed in green. The effect is like being in a huge, enclosed botanical garden. There is a short loop walk around the park to see the lava trees. Don't forget your camera.

To get here, take Route 11 south from Hilo or north from Volcano and turn off on Route 130 at Kea'au. When you get to Pahoa Town, go straight on Route 132, which will lead you to the entrance to the park. Route 132 is one of the prettiest drives in Hawai'i, so don't miss it.

Waipi'o Valley. See Cerebral Stuff, above.

Helicopter Tours

Here we go again: What to do about those noisy, intrusive machines that also allow you to see things you would never normally see? Well, as we have stated previously, we wish that choppers would go only where people can't, so as not to disturb the peace of hikers and residents. But at the moment, they go wherever the hell they want. So the decision is up to you. Note that there is a quieter, fixed-wing alternative: **Big Island Air** flies Cessna 402s and conducts two-hour circle-island tours, something that the helicopters don't do. The planes fly at an altitude of 500 to 1,500 feet, so you can see the sights as well as you would in a helicopter.

Here is a listing of air sightseeing operations. All offer tours of Volcanoes National Park and the Waipi'o/North Kohala coastline. Prices start around $80 per person and go up, depending on the length and breadth of the tour. As mentioned, Big Island flies fixed-wing aircraft. All the other services use helicopters.

Big Island Air, P.O. Box 1476, Kailua-Kona, HI 96745. Toll-free: 800-303-8868. Local: 808-329-4868.
   The cost of a one-and-a-half tour is $199 per person.

Hilo Bay Air, P.O. Box 4278, Hilo, HI 96720. Local: 808-969-1545/1547.

Kona Helicopters, 75-6160 Ali'i Drive, Kailua-Kona, HI 96740. Local: 808- 329-0551.

Mauna Kea Helicopters, P.O. Box 1713, Kamuela, HI 96743. Local: 808- 775-9515 or 885-7596.

Orchid Isle Helicopters, Inc., P.O. Box 1320. Pahoa, HI 96778. Local: 808-969-6664.

Papillon Hawai'ian Helicopters, P.O. Box 339, Hanalei, HI 96714. Toll-free: 800-367-7995, in Hawai'i 800-635-9336. Local: 808-885-4197.

Volcano Heli-Tours, P.O. Box 626, Volcano, HI 96785. Local: 808-967-7578.

Snow Skiing

Huh? When we first heard about snow skiing in Hawai'i, we thought the idea sounded ludicrous too. Imagine, skiing in the tropics! But when you think about it, it is very possible. Two mountains on the Big Island peak at almost 14,000 feet above the Pacific. At those altitudes, anything can happen, especially cold weather. And we've done it (to *say* we've done it). Personally, we'd choose Vail any day.

So it goes on Mauna Kea, which in Hawai'ian means "White Mountain." It stands 13,796 feet above sea level and 29,671 above the ocean floor, making it the world's tallest mountain—just beating Everest in a back-to-back height contest. It is also a dormant shield volcano—Madame Pele's whims having moved south to Mauna Loa and Kilauea. Snow can fall from December to April, with the best ski-able terrain usually happening in January. We say "usually" because the conditions here are predictably unpredictable. Don't plan to come to Hawai'i on a ski vacation; you'll probably have better conditions in North Carolina, not to mention an easier time breathing (the 13,000-plus-foot altitude provides about one-third less oxygen than you are accustomed to breathing). When we skied here, the ski conditions, as they say, "sucked." It was rutted and wind-rippled boilerplate, although the sun was beginning to soften it up when we left (about 3 P.M.). It took all of our Vermont know-how to ski it. The others with us, from the West Coast, had a rough time. Sometimes, we were told, it can be heavenly corn snow. Unfortunately, our day on the mountain was not as blessed, although it couldn't have been sunnier. This is not meant to discourage you. For the *experience*, this gig can't be beat. You can be the first one on your block to say you've skied in Hawai'i—always a hit at cocktail parties (and we do crave attention).

There used to be a few outfits, based in Waimea, that would take skiers up Mauna Kea in four-wheel vehicles. These operations, however, were as unpredictable as the snow. We think insurance and lack of interest (and snowmaking?) did them in. The originator, Ski Shop Hawai'i, is long gone. But things change, so ask your hotel concierge if there is a company that does this. Ski Guides Hawaii (808-885-4188) is one that we have heard of. Also check out www.hawaiisnowskiclub.com for great information. Otherwise, you'll need to schlep your ski equipment to Hawai'i (which is oddly *très chic*).

Here's how it went for us: We left around 10 A.M. from Waimea and traveled through several climate zones to the summit. We'd say this was heavy-duty scenery. The Saddle Road on the way up is stunning. It climbs through the pastures and tree stands of the Parker Ranch, past the polo fields of Waiki'i and into the *a'a* and *pahoehoe* (rough and smooth) lava fields. The lava sweeps to the feet of Mauna Kea to the north and Mauna Loa to the south—a truly extraordinary sight. The barrenness of the surroundings makes it apparent why no one lives here except the military. You will pass the Mauna Kea State Park (elevation 6,500 feet), where cabin rentals are possible (call 808-974-6200). Once off the Saddle Road, the road climbs steeply up the volcano in a series of grueling(on the engine) uphills and switchbacks. At 9,000 feet, there is a restroom and the crew headquarters of the ten-plus observatories on the summit. The pavement also ends at this complex. It's four-wheel-drive, electronic-fuel-injection from here on up. It's also wicked dusty, and air conditioning was one of the amenities that was not on the menu on our trip. So we had to roll up the windows, making the six of us jammed together feel entombed in the dust. But the landscape was so unreal that we could deal.

The drive to the summit is truly not of this world. This is terrain one would expect to see on pictures sent from a space probe. Indeed, the lunar module was tested here. There are boulders and rocks strewn everywhere on a stark, very dusty landscape. We saw no vegetation from our vantage point, although we hear there are some hardy plants that are able to survive. One of the people on our trip, while wandering through the rocks because the skiing was just not her cup of tea, found a human skeleton. That news created a sensation among us, although when we returned with her to find it, she couldn't remember where it was (high-altitude disorientation, we suppose).

The summit, when covered with ski-able snow (dubbed "Pineapple Powder"), can provide a variety of treeless ski terrain. Cinder cones and bowls have been named in the ski tradition à la Hawai'i. A trail map, which reads like a U.S. Geological Survey—striations

247

ticking off the altitude—reveals the names and locations of the ski-able terrain: Pele's Parlor, Warrior's Run (both of which we skied), Poi Bowl, King Kamehameha's Run, Keiki Bowl, The Tunnel, Ono Trail, Ali'i's Run, and so on. Ideally, you will be able to ski the sunnier south side. The bowls here (Poi Bowl, Keiki Bowl, and King Kam's Run) are large and easily accessed from the top of the road. In addition, the snow gets warmed by the sun faster on this side, making the likelihood of corn snow skiing better. However, if there hasn't been a lot of snow, the south side will be bare. This leaves the north side the closest option, and reaching it can be exhausting. A traverse and climb—particularly on the way back—is a real chore when there is 33 percent less oxygen in the air. When we went, there was a 750-foot portable rope tow running up the slope. Unfortunately, the necessary permits to run it did not exist, so the state made them take it down. It would have been a lot more convenient. A snowmobile could have taken us about half the distance (a real nuisance because you have to take off your skis), but its clutch burned out, so that was that for skiing unless we wanted to walk up—which is never an easy task with ski equipment. But it was the walk back, when we thought we'd never reach the car, that made us wonder why we were doing this. The best reason we could muster was to say that we had skied in Hawai'i.

Where to Stay

Accommodations here are in keeping with the Big Island's status as the most diverse island in the Hawai'ian chain. The range is amazing. From some of the classiest resorts in Hawai'i, to a five-room hotel without electricity, to a resort with pseudo-Venetian vaporettos and a subway-like tram, to a New Age retreat on the lush Puna coast, there truly is something for everyone here.

There are accommodations all over the island, although they are concentrated in four primary areas: Kailua-Kona, the Kohala coast, Hilo, and Volcano. By far the poshest resorts are in Kohala, the cheapest lodgings in Hilo, and the widest choice in Kailua-Kona. Remember that the Big Island is huge in comparison to the other Hawai'ian Islands. It will take you two to two and a half hours to drive from Kailua-Kona to Hilo at highway speeds. But

Kailua-Kona, in the Kona district, and the Kohala coast, in the Kohala district just north of Kona, are where most of the tourist accommodations are.

Situated on the dry western side of the island, Kailua-Kona was once a sacred site and is the final home of Kamehameha the Great. Over the past two decades, it has been developed to resemble a Southern California tract town, replete with shopping plazas and fast-food chains. Fortunately, this is only a corner of the Big Island and is easy to escape. If possible, we would avoid staying here. With all the space on the island, it's almost criminal to let yourself be cramped up in a rather characterless community. On the other hand, the lodging here will be cheaper than the deluxe resorts of the Kohala coast just to the north, and the desire to get out will force you to see more than you would if you were sequestered away in luxury (although that doesn't sound so bad to us). One other advantage to staying in Kailua-Kona is the broad choice of restaurants and nightlife.

The Kohala Coast is where the very deluxe resorts are located. Straddling two districts (North Kona and Kohala) and hugging the coast like an emerald necklace (thanks to golf courses, irrigation, and mega-landscaping) at the edge of massive black lava fields, this is where the Mauna Kea, the Mauna Lani, the Fours Season Hualalai, the Kona Village Resort, the Orchid at the Mauna Lani, the Hapuna Beach Prince, the Outrigger Waikoloa Beach, and the Big Island's biggest resort, the Hilton Waikoloa Village (village is a misnomer—it's more like a mini-city), are located. The island's best beaches (with the exception of Puna's Kehena black-sand beach) can be found here too.

An area that is often overlooked as a tourist destination is Hilo, the Big Island's metropolis (pop. 40,759). Hence the prices in Hilo are much lower. Of course, there are reasons for this. It does rain a lot here, to the tune of 120-plus inches a year. The hotels in this area are just that—not the mega-resorts that are becoming increasingly common to the vacation scene in Hawai'i. Personally, we like Hilo a lot, because it is far removed from the tourist scene and is a genuine Hawai'ian town. We also love the Shipman Inn, a beautifully restored Victorian mansion in a residential neighborhood there. An added plus is that the treasures of the eastern side of the

island—the Puna district and Hawai'i Volcanoes National Park—
are easily accessed from Hilo.

Another area that has seen a lot of growth over the last
decade in the small inn / B&B category is Volcano Village. Perched
in the cool and often misty clime of 4,000 feet, there are several
places here that we recommend for both lodging and dining. Its
location at the edge of Hawai'i Volcanoes National Park is a big
asset too, and we like the idea of a glowing fire and a hot toddy at
night and a T-shirt and shorts in the daytime.

There are several other places that are definitely worth considering. These include Captain Cook and Waimea. Perhaps you might
want to bounce around the island and experience the different
areas yourself. In any event, here are our recommendations to help
you make up your mind.

Kohala and North Kona

Resort and golf lovers, look no further. Created out of the biggest
stretch of lava we've ever seen, these resorts come in all shapes and
sizes, so there should be one that tickles your fancy. Our favorites
are the Mauna Kea, the Mauna Lani, and the Four Seasons
Hualalai. We'd be ecstatic to stay at any one of the three. We love
the Mauna Kea Beach Hotel and feel the Hapuna Beach, while situated on a gorgeous beach and a nice hotel in its own right, is not
on the same level as its older and much more distinguished sister.

The Mauna Kea Beach Hotel, 62-100 Mauna Kea Beach Drive,
Kamuela, HI 96743. Toll-free: 800-774-6234. Local: 808-882-7222,
fax 808-880-3112. Rooms and suites: 310.
Web site: www.maunakeabeachhotel.com
E-mail: mkrres@maunakeabeachhotel.com

Built by Laurance Rockefeller and opened in 1965 as the star of
his RockResorts hotels, this architectural gem is now under the
management of Prince Resorts Hawai'i. Unfortunately, since the
Prince Resorts just took over on February 1st, 2001, we are not sure
what their plans are for the hotel (still no word of any changes).
Westin, the former management, had decided not to ruin a good
thing and has kept the Mauna Kea much the same as it was under

the Rockefellers. It is still magnificent and one of the classiest places to stay in Hawai'i. Many companies have tried to copy it, but none of the knockoffs can pull it off like the original. The Mauna Kea is a masterpiece of understatement, from the architecture and décor to the carefully chosen and well-displayed art collection. The lobbies, open and airy with koi ponds and palm trees, are a statement of proper proportion. Nothing looks wrong here—everything's just so well done. We just love it!

Besides its status as a bastion of good taste, there are other reasons for staying here. It has one of the best, most beautiful, and hardest golf courses in the state (see the Golf section earlier in this chapter). The Mauna Kea's Tennis Park (see Tennis) is outstanding and is the most complete tennis facility on the island. Its beach is the nicest on the Kohala coast (and a natural one, too, not man-made like many of the beaches at the other resorts)—in fact, it's one of the best on the Big Island. Art lovers will appreciate its collection—more than a thousand pieces reflecting the cultures of the Pacific. Of special note is the Buddha, beautifully displayed at the summit of a long staircase that seems to have been built just for the statue (another thoughtful Rockefeller touch). It is particularly moving at night, when the viewing is enhanced by strategic lighting and landscaping.

Some people say the Mauna Kea isn't what it used to be. They feel the change in management from RockResorts to Westin caused a slide in the level of service and the physical condition of the property. Worst of all, according to the detractors, the stiff competition among the upper echelon of resorts has brought in less sophisticated clientele and groups—the bane of the distinguished traveler. While there may be a degree of truth in what they say, we remained impressed on our return visit. Let's face it, the jumbo jet has changed the caliber of tourism in the islands—Hawai'i now is a mass destination—so not every woman will be wearing a black cocktail dress with a single strand of pearls at dinner. That said, the Mauna Kea is still wonderful.

The rooms, on eight floors, are spacious, and the Asian décor is somewhat masculine and muted. The wicker and willow furniture is very attractive, and there are wonderful details, such as koa wood desks with brass inlays and Buddha lamps. The floors are terra-cotta tiles covered with berber-style area rugs, and lots of richly colored wood (including louvers instead of curtains) makes the rooms comfortable and harmonious. Soft, paler tones of tans and white complement the wood, as do the original Teruo Miyake prints on the walls (matching postcards are on the desk for you to take home), and the tan and muted pastel bedspreads and cushions add just enough zest to keep the décor from being too sedate. Bathrooms are large tan marble affairs, with a separate loo and double vanity (although we would lose the fluorescent lighting—so unhealthy for one's ego). Each room has a large tile-floor lanai and a ceiling fan along with the standard deluxe amenities. The lack of large TVs in the rooms is another very welcome Rockefeller touch (there are small TV/VCR units in each room, and they can be removed upon request). The TVs just don't go with the mood of the place. Another plus: The rooms have sliding screens framed in wood to keep out the bugs.

If money is really no object, consider the Villas and Fairways homes on the resort's grounds. The Villas, situated between fairways, are quite lovely two-bedroom homes with private pools and Hawai'ian koa wood throughout. The Fairways are three- to four-bedroom homes, some with pools, that are privately owned (and decorated) and sit on the highest part of the resort near the highway. Both are fantastically expensive, but private, and none are "on the water."

In keeping with the understated tone of the resort, it is fairly quiet here at night (and room service ends at midnight). During the day, however, there is a slew of activities, besides the golf and tennis, and a fitness center in the Beach Front building will help to maintain your muscle tone. The hotel's small circular pool is a reminder of resorts past. Four restaurants, including the Batik, which features excellent Pacific Rim cuisine, provide a variety of expensive but good culinary options. A luau, hosted by fabulously talented *kumu hula* (hula teacher) Nani Lim Yap (of the singing Lim family) with her *hula halau* (hula troupe) and superb musicians in tow, is held weekly on the grounds by the beach. Guests at the Mauna Kea Beach Hotel can use the facilities throughout the Mauna Kea Resort, which included the Hapuna Beach Prince Hotel and golf course.

Rates are **Wicked Pricey** and up. Look for packages.

Mauna Lani Bay Hotel and Bungalows, 68-1400 Mauna Lani Drive, Kohala Coast, HI 96743-9796. Toll-free: 800-367-2323. Local: 808-885-6622, fax 808-885-1484. Units: 350 rooms and bungalows. Web site: www.maunalani.com
E-mail: maunalani@maunalani.com

The Mauna Lani is the other classic Big Island resort. We love the Mauna Lani too. Although newer than the Mauna Kea (it was built in 1983), it has a distinctive design and a reputation built on years of excellent service and happy customers. A prominent staircase with twin pools and cascades on each side descends from the hotel's entrance and is the focus of the huge and breezy atrium, ensuring that you are the center of attention when you glide down from the main lobby to the ground floor and beach (and we just love dramatic entrances). At the ground level are blue-tiled terraces with seating areas, koi ponds, and 75-foot palm trees. The great thing about this space is that it all works, *feng shui* in a Big Island resorts.

The Mauna Lani is also a lively place while still being very relaxing. Activities are available throughout the resort, but the lobby remains almost serene and Zen-like. On certain evenings the beautiful voice of Nani Kim Yap, of the singing Lim family, can be heard floating through the atrium.

The guest rooms are spacious and very tastefully appointed. The décor of whites, dark wood, area rugs, and contemporary furnishings is soothing and pretty. Beds are comfy and have feather pillows—a plus. Most rooms have a view of the water. Each has a lanai, ceiling fan, bar/fridge, and the standard deluxe amenities—including a TV. Sliding wooden louvers replace drapes—a welcome touch. Baths have two vanities opposite each other (one with a makeup mirror) and a shower/tub combination. The floors are made of Jerusalem tile, as is the shower/tub area. The counters are white marble, and the mirrors are framed in teak wood.

Like all resorts on the Kohala Coast, the Mauna Lani was carved out of a lava flow. With almost two decades of manicuring and pampering, the grounds are gorgeous. Part of the Mauna Lani's appeal too is two superb golf courses and the Tennis Garden (see Golf and Tennis, earlier in this chapter). While man-made, the beach is quite nice, and the double-hooded chaises are a wonderful amenity. The large free-form pool is the place to hang out and sip Mai Tais while watching the scene. There are also four restaurants, including the highly regarded Canoe House and the Bay Terrace for breakfast and Sunday brunch. There are more restaurant options at the Orchid (see below), which shares the amenities of the Mauna Lani resort.

Rates are **Wicked Pricey** and up. Look for packages.

Four Seasons Hualalai, 100 Ka'upulehu Drive, Ka'upulehu-Kona, HI 96740. Toll-free: 888-340-5662. Local: 808-325-8000, fax 808-325-8100. Units: 243 rooms and suites.
Web site: www.fourseasons.com

Opened in 1996 and Hawai'i's only Four Seasons resort, the Hualalai, like the Four Seasons Nevis in the Caribbean, has made a very favorable impression in a short amount of time. With service as its *raison d'être,* the Four Seasons Hualalai has become a huge hit among the money-is-no-object crowd. There is no large high-rise here, just 36 two-story bungalows and a low-key but very pretty reception building of bamboo, dark stone floors, salmon colored fabrics, rough marble tables, and beautiful floral arrangements. A fab spa with a 25-meter lap pool and all those body treatments is on the grounds. Those in search of true luxury should look no further.

We love the commitment to Hawai'iana that the Four Seasons has demonstrated. All artwork and artifacts are from the islands. You won't find Asian ceramic vases or art here, as you do at other major resorts. From the impressive lava rock walls at the entrance and the lovely Hawai'ian prints to the lava rock cove/pool and bamboo furniture, no detail has been omitted (oops, are we gushing?).

The standard room is over 600 square feet, with walk-in closets and a very pleasant lanai with sumptuous lanai furniture. The décor is in keeping with the Hawai'iana motif, with lots of teak and rosewood trim, stone floors with tan berber carpeting, rattan furnishings, Hawai'ian quilt bedspreads, canopy beds, and wooden-louvered shutters leading out to private gardens. Baths have dual sinks, granite countertops, tubs with a European-style hand-held shower, and separate loo with phone. Lower units have an indoor/outdoor shower setup: You walk out of a glassed-in shower to a bamboo-canopied outdoor shower. All rooms have TV/VCR,

CD player/alarm clock, fridge, safe, ceiling fan, two phones in the living/dining area with dataport plus a separate Internet/fax connection, iron/board, coffeemaker, and both terry and light cotton robes for lounging. There is twice-daily housekeeping, same-day laundry service, and a coin-op laundry facility.

On the activities side, the Four Seasons doesn't disappoint. We never heard of a resort in Hawai'i offering complimentary scuba lessons—but this one does. There's also a complimentary "Kids for All Seasons" program (ages 5 to 12) and free shoeshine *and* sandal repair! Golfers have an 18-hole Jack Nicklaus–designed course, and there is an eight-court tennis complex—four lighted (see Golf and Tennis earlier in this chapter). But the *pièce de résistance* is the three oceanfront pools with chilled towels and Evian spritz service (just a little more on my legs, please!). Don't forget the full-service Hualalai Sports Club and Spa with so many features that you could spend a week just pampering your body and never make it to the beach. Three restaurants and 24-hour room service provide nourishment and refreshment.

Rates are **Ridiculous** and up. A few packages are available.

The Hapuna Beach Prince Hotel, 62-100 Kaunaoa Drive, Kohala Coast, HI 96743. Toll-free: 800-774-6234. Local: 808-880-1111, fax 808-880-3112. Units: 350 rooms and suites.
Web site: www.hapunabeachprincehotel.com

Opened in 1994 on the northern end of Hapuna, one of Hawai'i's finest beaches, the Hapuna Beach Prince Hotel is the bookend to the Mauna Kea Beach Hotel, as it sits on the southern end of the Mauna Kea Resort. Management may claim that this to fulfills Laurance Rockefeller's dream of a second hotel to complement his original, but we feel the builders misinterpreted his vision when they plopped down a behemoth on this beautiful stretch of natural beach. While the Hapuna Beach is a nice hotel in itself, it just doesn't have the balance and harmony of its sister to the north. That said, it is on a gorgeous beach, the pool is significantly bigger than the Mauna Kea's, and guests have privileges throughout the Mauna Kea Resort (this includes the Mauna Kea Beach Hotel and golf course).

Rooms are comfortably sized, with wall-to-wall berber carpeting, blond wood, tan walls, fridge, TV (VCRs available on request), three phones, Internet hookup, safe, iron/board, and coffeemaker. Baths have marble floors, dual vanities with granite top, separate glass-enclosed showers, separate tubs with hand-held showers, and separate loo. Louvered wood shutters open out onto a big slate-tiled lanai. All rooms have an ocean view.

The hotel's opening also created another 18-hole golf course for the Mauna Kea Resort, this one designed by Arnold Palmer and Ed Seay (see Golf earlier in this chapter). Tennis buffs have the use of the 13-court Tennis Park at Mauna Kea. A state-of-the-art fitness center is located at the Hapuna Golf Clubhouse, and the resort has its own stables in Waimea (12 miles up the road). There are four restaurants, including the signature Coast Grill and the excellent Hakone Japanese restaurant, and two bars. Room service is available 24 hours a day.

Rates are **Wicked Pricey** and up. Look for packages.

The Orchid at the Mauna Lani, One North Kaniku Drive, Kohala Coast, HI 96743. Toll-free: 800-845-9905. Local: 808-885-2000, fax 808-885-8886. Units: 586 rooms and suites.
Web site: www.orchid-maunalani.com

Originally built as a Ritz-Carlton in 1990 (the blue-tiled roof is the giveaway), but part of the Starwood Group's Luxury Collection since 1996, the Orchid shares the amenities of the 3,200-acre Mauna Lani Resort. The Ritz imprint is still apparent in the two six-story wings where the guest rooms and suites are located. What do we mean by that? Well, there are the dark halls with Oriental carpets and floral wallpaper, the mahogany furnishings and chintz fabrics, the crown moldings, the white marble baths—you know.

Guest rooms feature colonial furniture, wall-to-wall tan carpeting, a large tiled lanai, and a soothing décor of pale green walls, framed floral prints, and white louvered shutters. All have mini-bar/fridge, TV with Lodgenet, safe, and iron/board. White-tiled marble baths have dual vanities, separate shower, tub and loo (the latter with phone), hair dryer, and makeup mirror. There is twice-daily maid service plus 24-hour room service.

Outside, there is a 10,00-square-foot swimming pool, two lava-enhanced whirlpools, jogging and walking trails, and ten tennis courts (seven lighted). For duffers, the Mauna Lani resort has 36 holes of golf (see Golf, earlier in this chapter). Baby-sitting and a children's program are available. The Orchid has three restaurants and two lounges, and guests have privileges at the Mauna Lani Bay Hotel next door.

Rates are **Wicked Pricey** and up. Look for packages.

Hilton Waikoloa Village, 425 Waikoloa Beach Drive, Waikoloa, HI 96738. Toll-free: 800-HILTONS (445-8667). Local: 808-886-1234, fax 808-886-2901. Units: 1,240 rooms and suites.
Web site: www.hilton.com/hotels/KOAHWHH

Costing $360 million to build in 1988 and opened as a Hyatt, this remains one of the most over-the-top resorts in Hawai'i and a fine example of the 1980s excess—in this case, by developer Chris Hemmeter and his "fantasy" resorts. If this place were our fantasy, we'd be very worried. Those who like their accommodations to be low-key, authentic, or relaxed will loathe this place.

Carved out of a 62-acre lava field, proportions are out of scale, with grand flagstone staircases, massive lagoons, vast colonnades, and three huge seven-story towers. Twelve 24-passenger Disney-engineered Venetian canal boats shuttle guests over a mile of waterways or they can take a monorail tubular tram to their building—that's right, a monorail! There's even a mile-and-a-half-long underground tunnel for employees to zip around to various parts of the resort. Note that there is no ocean beach (a man-made "lagoon" beach is the surrogate).

Other features of the resort include the DolphinQuest Learning Center, where guests can hop in the water and swim with tame Atlantic bottlenose dolphins (fantasies of Flipper) under the supervision of staff trainers for around $115 a pop. The Hilton's main pool is three-quarters of an acre, with the requisite waterfalls, water slides (including one that is 175 feet long), three Jacuzzis, and a sandy-bottom kids' pool. There are two more pools at the Ocean Tower, one featuring water slides and a river current; the other a smaller pool for adults. A four-acre saltwater lagoon is filled with tropical fish (for snorkeling). There are nine restaurants and eight lounges/bars. To lure the convention business, there are 50,000 square feet of indoor meeting space and 100,000 of outdoor meeting space. There are two 18-hole golf courses (see Golf, earlier in this chapter) and an 18-hole seaside putting course. There's also a $5 million collection of Asian, Oceanic, and Western art (seen in four self-guided art tours or by scheduled tours offered by the resort), and the 25,000-square-foot Kohala Spa. Oddly, there are only eight tennis courts (we guess people who go here don't play a lot of tennis). Red Sail Sports is on campus and provides a host of water sports. On the guest activity list are tai chi, yoga, and stress management.

Rates are **Ridiculous** and up. Look for packages.

Kona Village Resort, P.O. Box 1299, Kailua-Kona, HI 96745. Toll-free: 800-367-5290. Local: 808-325-5555, fax 808-325-5124. Units: 125 *hale* (thatch-roofed bungalows).
Web site: www.konavillage.com

Located next to the Four Seasons Hualalai but light-years apart in approach and tone is the all-inclusive (Full American Plan), family-oriented Kona Village Resort. Casual is the buzzword here. Opened in 1965 on 82 acres at the edge of a lava flow, it was designed to resemble a Polynesian village, and it really does deliver. It's visually very interesting, as all of the architecture and décor recall the ancient styles of the various Pacific archipelagos. Nine groups are represented: Hawai'i, Fiji, Maori, the Marquesas, New Caledonia, Palau, Somoa, New Hebrides, and Tahiti. Features of a specific group will be incorporated into a house, and each style is different, including the shape of the house and its interior layout. Our favorites are the Royal Ocean Front New Hebrides and the Sand Marquesan *hale*; both have large lanais and are on the water. Many of the *hale* are on the ocean; the best are on a sandy beach on the southern end of the property. All have thatch roofs and primitive-looking exteriors. Inside, they are tasteful and sumptuous in a very simple way. In keeping with the feeling of isolation, there are no room phones, no radios, and no TVs, but all rooms include a private lanai, miniature refrigerator (stocked with complimentary beverages and mixers), coffeemaker, safe, ceiling fan, and daily maid service. There is no air conditioning. Twenty-three of the *hale* have Jacuzzis on their lanai.

The casual atmosphere extends to the strict anti-dress code at dinner that forbids coats and ties (but women must wear dresses or muumuus and men pants and shirts with collars) and the lack of locks on the doors—guests check their valuables upon arrival or use the room safe.

The resort does have amenities, however. There is a fitness center with massage, three lighted tennis courts, sailboats, outrigger canoes, snorkeling gear, and assorted beach games for the guests' use. The salt-and-pepper beach is pleasant; it's one of the few natural beaches on the Kona Coast. The Shipwreck Bar is a fun place for a drink (it's fashioned out of a real boat) and a view of the goings-on at the pool. Meals are served in Hale Moana and Hale Samoa. The Kona Village Luau, the most authentic on the Big Island, is held on Fridays at Hale Ho'okipa and is open to the public.

It should be noted that the Kona Village welcomes children, so this resort does have a high percentage of young families. If the idea of screaming kids at the pool and beach disturbs you, think twice about coming here. The resort also offers Honeymoon, Anniversary, and Wedding Packages.

Rates are *Ridiculous* and up (FAP). Look for packages and AAA discounts.

Outrigger Waikoloa Beach, 69-275 Waikoloa Beach Drive, Waikaloa, HI 96738-5711. Toll-free: 800-OUTRIGGER (688-7444). Local: 808-886-6789, fax 808-886-7852. Units: 545 rooms and suites. Web site: www.outrigger.com

Formerly the Royal Waikoloan, Outrigger bought this resort several years ago and has poured $25 mil into renovations. Reopened in October 1999, this is Outrigger's premier Big Island property. Remember, the Outrigger brand is geared toward the mainstream; this may be a good choice for families who don't want to spend a fortune. The resort is located on 15 acres just to the south of the Hilton Waikoloa Village, and guests here have privileges at the two Waikoloa courses, King's and Beach. The hotel is on 'Anaeho'omalu Bay, with its very pretty golden-sand crescent beach (there's a small walk past tidal pools to access the beach). The six-story hotel consists of two blockish wings centered by one airy sandstone lobby. Paler tones prevail.

Rooms are comfortable and feature blond rattan/wicker furnishings, wall-to-wall carpeting, and a décor of off-white, tan, and teal. All come with cable TV with Internet access, dressing alcove, private lanai, dataport phones with voice mail, blackout drapes, coffeemaker, Yukata robes, iron/board, hair dryer, safe, fridge, and standard-size baths with tub/shower and granite vanity.

The Outrigger renovation included the installation of an "action" pool (waterfalls, slide, kids' pool, and hot tub), which families will love. A beach activities center offers snorkeling, kayaking, windsurfing, dive trips, and other ocean activities. There are six Plexipave courts and a tennis pro for the Williamses among us. There are two restaurants and two bars/lounges for refueling and refreshment. A spa/health club, business center, the Voyager's Club, and the Cowabunga Kids Club (ages 5–13) round out the amenities.

Rates are **Wicked Pricey** and up. Look for packages and internet specials.

Puako Beach Apartments, 3 Puako Beach Drive, Kamuela, HI 96743. Toll-free: 888-72ALOHA (722-5642). Local: 808-882-7711. Units: 38.
Web site: www.hawaiioceanfront.com
This is probably one of your best bets for condos in Kohala in terms of location (it's right in the middle and near the Waikoloa complex) and price (very reasonable). There's even a nice beach that is off the beaten path. Units are owner-decorated and simple in décor. They come in one- to four-bedroom apartments. There is a pool and twice-weekly maid service.

Rates are **Not So Cheap** and up.

Kailua-Kona

Kailua Plantation House, 75-5948 Ali'i Drive, Kailua-Kona, HI, 96740. Toll-free: 888-357-4262. Local: 808-329-3727, fax 808-326-7323. Rooms: 5.
Web site: www.kphbnb.com
We love the Kailua Plantation House and feel it's the best and most chic place to stay in Kailua-Kona. Built right on the ocean in 1990, there are only five rooms, which gives it a welcome feeling of intimacy. Yet look out the back and the crashing surf is right there.

Run by Donna Stonerock and John Strach, the KPH is less than a mile south of the town of Kailua-Kona. Three rooms are oceanfront and two are streetside (definitely try to get the oceanfront rooms). A tile-floor common living area has comfy sofas, area rugs, and ceiling fans and is a great place to catch up on reading. It is here that breakfast is served. A common lanai is the place to watch the amazing sunsets. Sticking like a dagger out into the lava coast are a plunge pool and Jacuzzi (this is obviously a couple's/honeymooners' delight).

Each of the five rooms has a different décor. All have private bath, lanai, cable TV, phone, fridge, sound reduction between rooms, and daily maid service. We love the soothing blues and bamboo furniture of the Pilialoha ground-level ocean front room. The bath is huge, with a double vanity, glass-block shower, Jacuzzi tub, separate loo/bidet, and big walk-in closet. No children under 12 are allowed (we single adults applaud—this place is too small for screaming kids).

Rates are *Pricey* and up.

King Kamehameha's Kona Beach Hotel, 75-5660 Palani Road, Kailua-Kona, HI 96740. Toll-free: 800-367-6060. Local: 808-329-2911, fax 808-922-8061. Rooms and suites: 457.
Web site: www.konabeachhotel.com

The King Kamehameha occupies the sacred turf of King Kamehameha the Great. A reconstruction of the 'Ahu'ena *heiau* is the grounds. It was at this *heiau* that, after the death of the king in 1819, Queen Ka'ahumanu broke one of the cardinal *kapus* and ate with men. This act ended ancient Hawai'ian society as we know it.

So it is with an aura of history that this attractive and spacious property sits in the midst of all the hubbub of Kailua-Kona. It's bigger than it looks at first glance, and is a great location for bar-hoppers and lounge lizards. The lobby, lined with portraits of Hawai'ian royalty and dotted with unusual square chairs, is very interesting. The room décor, while unexceptional, is comfortable, handsome, and adorned with Hawai'ian prints by local artists. Each room is a decent size, with a vanity separate from the bathroom—a welcome convenience—and cable TV, digital phone with dataports and voice mail, iron/board, fridge, safe, and dark wooden louvers opening onto a private lanai.

The mini shopping mall on the premises is both convenient and a nuisance (it attracts crowds). The hotel's location is about as central as one can get in Kailua-Kona. Virtually everything is within walking distance, including a host of restaurants and bars/clubs. If you like being in the center of the action, then you will love the King Kam, as it is called locally. The pool is big and sensibly shaped, with enough room to do laps. There is a cute little beach, where the swimming is excellent. Unfortunately it's right in the harbor, which for us is a little too close for comfort. Fortunately, a wonderful beach is just a short walk away at the old airstrip (see Beaches, earlier in this chapter). The hotel also has lots of daily activities, including four tennis courts (two lighted).

Rates are *Not So Cheap* and up. Look for packages.

Uncle Billy's Kona Bay Hotel, 75-5739 Ali'i Drive, Kailua-Kona, HI 96740. Toll-free: 800-367-5102. Local: 808-329-1393, fax 808-935-7903. Rooms: 145.
Web site: www.unclebilly.com

Owned and operated by a Hawai'ian family (which in the hotel business is very rare), the Kona Bay is one of two pleasant, unpretentious small hotels that are reasonably priced and centrally located (the other is in Hilo—see Uncle Billy's Hilo Bay Hotel). The Kona Bay is located in the heart of the busiest part of Kailua-Kona and is not on the water. However, at these prices (under $100), you can't be too choosy.

The blue and white décor is disarmingly tacky. Rooms feature wall-to-wall carpeting, cable TV, fridge, lanai, and ceiling fan (all rooms have air conditioning). There are two pools on the property (one for kids) and its smack-dab-in-the-middle-of-Kailua-Kona location allows for scores of eating and drinking options.

Rates are *Cheap* and up. Look for Internet specials.

Kona Tiki, P.O. Box 1567, Kailua-Kona, HI 96745. Local: 808-329-1425. Rooms: 17.

Now here's a real bargain find on the water in Kailua-Kona. Located just south of town on Ali'i Drive, there is absolutely no pretense about this place—just clean, dependable accommodations for under $40 per night. The décor is classic tacky, but all rooms face the ocean and have a lanai. You can hear the water at night—usually impossible at that price. Some rooms come with kitchenettes, and all have refrigerators. With only 17 rooms, they are understandably booked way in advance, so call early.

Rates are *Cheap* (three-day minimum/no credit cards).

Royal Kona Resort, 75-5852 Ali'i Drive, Kailua-Kona, HI 96740. Toll-free 800-222-5642. Local: 808-329-3111, fax 808-329-9532. Units: 452 rooms and suites.
Web site: www.rkona.com

Architecturally, the Royal Kona (formerly the Kona Hilton) is an interesting hotel with its '60s air (it was built in 1968). Its sloping, full-balconied sides are unusual. Indeed the ocean side looks like an Olympic ski jump. Apparently it's supposed to resemble a sloping waterfall. It's also big—11 acres with three multi-story buildings.

Inside, the décor is nowhere as inspiring. As a matter of fact, it's borderline tacky. However, if you can stomach it, the rooms can be rather cheap for such a central, oceanfront Kona location. Each room has two double beds, cable TV, fridge, coffeemaker, safe, lanai, and dual vanity in the bathrooms. The hotel has a decent-size round pool, a man-made saltwater lagoon, and four tennis courts (three lighted). There's also a nightly Polynesian Dinner Show (don't forget your Instamatic)!

Rates are *Cheap* and up. Look for packages, especially on the Royal Kona's Web site.

Ohana Keauhou Beach Resort, 78-6740 Ali'i Drive, Kailua-Kona, HI 96740. Toll-free: 800-922-7866. Local: 808-322-3441, fax 808-322-3117. Units: 311 rooms and suites.
Web site: www.aston-hotels.com

Probably the best thing about the Keauhou Beach Resort is its location. Set on ten acres, it's slightly out of the hubbub (three miles south of Kailua-Kona) and next to one of the better beaches in the area, Kahalu'u Beach Park. Each room has an ocean view, small lanai, coffeemaker, phone with dataport, safe, and a fridge. The rooms have been recently remodeled, much to our relief. There are six tennis courts (two lighted). Fortunately they have also updated the pool. The area used to have an indoor-outdoor green carpeted surface, but now is surrounded by marble stone.

Rates are *Pricey* and up. Look for packages and internet specials.

Kona Bali Kai, 76-6246 Ali'i Drive, Kailua-Kona, HI 96740. Toll-free: 800-535-0085. Local: 808-329-9381. Rooms: 154.

The only worthwhile units here are the oceanfront ones. The others are right on busy Ali'i Drive. The former, however, put you very close to the water, so you can hear the waves on the lava below. The lanais are fairly private, too. The condo units are individually decorated, so you've got to hope for everything and expect nothing. A small pool doesn't help matters. At least the lobby is pleasant.

Rates are *Pricey* and up. Look for packages.

Outrigger Royal Sea Cliff Resort, 75-6040 Ali'i Drive, Kailua-Kona, HI 96740. Toll-free 800-922-7866. Local: 808-329-8021, fax 808-326-1887. Units: 154.

While we find this condo property to be too impersonal and geometric for our taste, some people may like it, even though it's about as un-Hawai'ian-looking as you can get. At press time the hotel was turned over to Outrigger Hotels. We have been told that they are planning a facelift in the near future, and boy does it need it. We suggest calling before you make any plans to stay here. The building, a white concrete affair, is very long; it stretches from the road to the ocean. Thus there are few oceanfront units here. However, the place is well maintained and the units are nicely furnished, even if they are a tyranny of pastels. Your options range from studios to one- and two-bedroom units. The fully equipped kitchens have microwaves and washer/dryers—a nice convenience. There are small but pleasant pools, one of which is saltwater (there is no beach). There is also a tennis court, Jacuzzi, and sauna.

Rates are *Pricey* and up. Look for packages and Internet specials.

Captain Cook/South Kona

Manago Hotel, P.O. Box 145, Captain Cook, HI 96704. Local: 808-323-2642, fax 808-323-3451. Units: 64 rooms (42 with private bath). Web site: www.managohotel.com

Still one of the cheapest places to stay on the Big Island and a place that everybody seems to love, the Manago Hotel is an institution here. Built in 1917, it's been run by the same family since then (the third generation is now in charge). Situated at an elevation of 1,400 feet in the hip town (oops, we used the "h" word) of Captain Cook, where health-food stores and authentic Hawai'ian architecture abound, everything about this hotel is funky, right down to the ancient reception desk and what looks like original décor. While the interior is light-years from *Elle Décor*, what it lacks in taste is balanced by tons of character and a reputation for offering very cheap accommodations. We applaud the idea and effort.

Our favorite room—and the most expensive at a whopping $59 per night—is the Japanese Room, with a futon, mats, screens, and a Japanese bath. If you can't get it, be sure to get a room facing the ocean in the new wing. These have lanais and private baths. There is a local/American restaurant and cocktail lounge on the premises. Definitely a fun place to stay, even for only a couple of nights.

Rates are **Dirt Cheap** and up. We rarely get to use that term in the Aloha State!

Hale Aloha Guest Ranch, 84-4780 Mamalahoa Highway, Captain Cook, HI 96704. Toll-free/fax: 800-897-3188. Local/fax: 808-328-8955. Units: 4 rooms.
Web site: www.halealoha.com
E-mail: vacation@halealoha.com
Set on a five and half acres, all the guest rooms here have a private entrance, shared bath and kitchen, and a view of the ocean. Rooms come with either a queen-size or a king-size bed. The Master Suite includes a private bathroom with shower and Jacuzzi tub, refrigerator, a large private covered lanai with an ocean view, a television and VCR, an antique king-size bed, and an additional room with a full-size bed. This suite also includes a queen-size bed (with a mosquito net) on the lanai, for a sleeping experience out in nature, yet still safe and comfortable. A great breakfast of home-grown fruits and juices, Kona coffee, homemade pancakes and omelets, breads and pastries is served every day, either on your private lanai or in the main lanai.

Rates are **Cheap** and up.

Waimea

Waimea Country Lodge, 65-1210 Lindsey Road, Kamuela, HI 96743. Toll-free: 800-367-5004. Local: 808-885-4100, fax 808-885-6711. Units: 21 rooms.
Web site: www.castleresorts.com/WCL

Formerly the Parker Ranch Lodge, the Waimea Country Lodge resembles a motel more than a lodge. It was originally used to house guests and workers at the Parker Ranch—still the largest privately owned ranch in the U.S. at 225,000 acres (all the land you see surrounding Waimea, and more). Now part of Castle Resorts and Hotels, this is a simple accommodation if you need to stay in often-misty Waimea (elevation 2,500 feet) for ranch business, looking at real estate in the Kohala peninsula, or if you're big-time into horseback riding. Otherwise, you'll wonder why you came all this way to stay in a motel without a pool. Rooms are comfortable and feature pine furnishings, cable TV, telephone with dataport, and private bath. Studios with kitchenettes are available.

Rates are **Cheap** and up. Look for Internet specials.

Waipi'o Valley

The Waipi'o Valley is a mystical place in Hawai'ian folklore (see Cerebral Stuff). There used to be two places to stay here for the intrepid and spiritual, but at press time both seem to be closed. The Waipi'o Treehouse has closed permanently, and we have a funny feeling Tom Araki's is not open any more either (no one answers the phone). Both of these places offered the unique experience of spending the night in the "Valley of the Kings." We will keep you posted if we hear of anything opening in the valley itself.

Hilo

Shipman House Bed & Breakfast Inn, 131 Ka'iulani Street, Hilo, HI 96720. Toll-free: 800-627-8447. Local/fax: 808-934-8002. Units: 5 rooms.
Web site: www.hilo-hawaii.com

By far the nicest accommodation on the Hilo side of the Big Island and indeed one of our favorite accommodations in all of

Hawai'i, Shipman House is a carefully restored, huge Victorian mansion sitting on five and a half incredibly lush hillside acres. Hawai'i's last queen and Jack London have both been guests here. It's been in the Shipman family since 1901 and is now owned by W. H. Shipman's great-granddaughter, Barbara-Ann Andersen, and her husband Gary. Built in 1899, it was bought by W. H. to surprise his wife, Mary (who adored the house), for $13,000, which was *mucho dinero* in those days. While we have no idea what the Andersens paid for it (they bought the house from relatives), we do know that they must have spent a bundle restoring it. Just one look at the honey-colored Douglas fir floors and the woodwork and you'll agree. Equally gorgeous is much of the original furniture, including a grand piano (guests may play) and a koa wood dining table that made us drool. Pretty Oriental rugs blend beautifully with the period furniture. A library with impressive koa mantel and bookshelves is also available for guests. Continental breakfast is served on the lanai.

There are three guest rooms in the main house and two in an adjacent cottage. All have 10- to 12-foot ceilings, fridges, cotton kimonos, and fresh flowers. Each of the guest rooms has a private bath with pedestal sinks, marble and mahogany vanity, tiled shower, and large tiled or claw-foot tub. Auntie Clara's Shell Room, on the second floor of the main house, seems to be the most popular room. It has a queen-size bed and a view of Hilo Bay. This is a no smoking accommodation.

Rates are *Pricey* (CP).

The Naniloa, 93 Banyan Drive, Hilo, HI 96720. Toll-free: 800-367-5360. Local: 808-969-3333, fax 808-969-6622. Units: 325 rooms and suites.
Web site: www.naniloa.com

The Naniloa was once the most deluxe big hotel in Hilo, but it's looking a tad long in the tooth these days. That said, it has that distinctive '60s architectural style. Looking at it, you get the same feeling as you would from, say, looking at Lincoln Center in New York City. It's an embodiment of an era of angles and curves. The lobby is particularly beautiful, with a sweeping view of Hilo Bay greeting you as you enter. The grounds are manicured in the Japanese-style with a kidney-shape swimming pool as the focal point. Several tidal pools provide an opportunity to take a dip in the bay. The Naniloa is the hotel to stay at during the Merrie Monarch Festival each spring and is always booked well in advance for that week (which we highly recommend).

Last renovated in 1991, the rooms are the average big-hotel sort, of adequate size with king or twin beds and small bathrooms. The pastel décor is the standard kind of tacky, but the rooms are clean and have cable TV, phones, and small lanais, and the staff is really friendly. Keeping in mind that rates here are around $100 per night (and this is Hilo's best big hotel), you can forgive the uninspiring rooms and décor. If you want inspiration, stay at the Shipman House. However, the views from the upper floors, of the bay and Mauna Kea in the distance, are exceptional. There are two restaurants and a lounge/nightclub on the premises.

Rates are *Not So Cheap* and up. Look for Internet specials.

Hilo Hawai'ian Hotel, 71 Banyan Drive, Hilo, HI 96720. Toll-free: 800-367-5004. Local: 808-935-9361, fax 808-961-9642. Units: 286 rooms and suites.
Web site: www.castleresorts.com/HHH

Now the best big hotel in Hilo (but do not assume it's like a Kohala resort, or you'll be very disappointed), the recently renovated Hilo Hawai'ian faces Coconut Island (a park), Hilo, and the gradual slope of Mauna Kea way the hell in the distance. The grounds are well kept and include tidal pools and a koi pond, and there's a small pool. There is also the Queen's Court Dining Room (featuring a very popular Sunday brunch), the Wai'oli Lounge, and a coin-op laundry at the hotel.

The good-size guest rooms are a symphony of warm whites and beige. The higher floors have outstanding views in both directions, of either the bay or the formal Japanese garden across Banyan Drive. Each room has cable TV, telephone, and fridge and is very clean. Most rooms have a small lanai.

Rates are *Not So Cheap.* Look for Internet specials.

Uncle Billy's Hilo Bay Hotel, 87 Banyan Drive, Hilo, HI 96720. Toll-free: 800-367-5102. Local: 808-935-0861, fax 808-935-7903. Units: 143 rooms.

The sister of Uncle Billy's Kona Bay Hotel, this Hawai'ian family-owned hotel—a rarity—is situated next to the Naniloa on Banyan Drive, with a small but pleasant courtyard and koi ponds separating the hotel's two wings. There is a seaside pool.

Rooms feature a disarmingly tacky blue and white décor with wall-to-wall carpeting, cable TV, fridge, lanai and ceiling fans (all rooms have air conditioning too). While the units are clean and comfortable, this is not the kind of hotel where you'd want to hang out all day. You should stay here only for a decent place to crash.

Rates are **Cheap** and up. Look for Internet specials.

Dolphin Bay Hotel, 333 Illi'ahi Street, Hilo, HI 96720. Local: 808-935-1466, fax 808-935-1523. Units: 18 rooms.
Web site: www.dolphinbayhilo.com

Situated a few blocks up from downtown Hilo, the Dolphin Bay is clean and cheap. Those on long visits often stay here (weekly and monthly rates are available). Rooms have a kitchenette, private baths, and are simple, with a table fan for a little breeze, but no phone, cable TV (just local TV), room service, or swimming pool. The place is lovable, local, and certainly as untouristy as you can get. It's more like a European guest house. Outside, there is lots of shade and tropical flora to enjoy.

Rates are **Cheap.**

Puna

Kalani Oceanside Eco-Resort, RR2 Box 4500, Pahoa-Beach Road, HI 96778. Toll-free: 800-800-6886. Local: 808-965-7828. Units: 32 rooms/plus 3-acre camping area.
Web site: www.kalani.com

Founded in 1975, the Kalani Oceanside Eco-Resort is the premier holistic mecca in the state. Situated on 113 verdant acres of the sparsely developed Puna coast and less than five miles from the lava flow, the resort is located in one of the prettiest, lushest, and most fascinating areas of the Big Island. It is a simple yet attractive place with spacious and peaceful grounds. Come here to experience the spirit of the late '60s in the 21st century.

There are three two-story buildings, or *hale*, which are designed with communal living in mind. There is a fully equipped kitchen on the first floor and a large, open studio space on the second. Each floor has four rooms with fairly simple wicker furnishings: twin beds, a night table, and a desk. The nicest rooms, with high ceilings that open up onto the studio space, are on the second floor. However, none of the second floor rooms have private baths; the shared bath is downstairs. (Some of the rooms on the first floor do have private baths, but they are definitely less pleasant although the floors are tiled.) The real problem with the second floor is evident when there is a program scheduled in your building. It will mean a commotion in the studio space all day. This can be a real drag if the program involves one of the self-help groups conducting a "yay-me" session—where everyone applauds each other as though each member had just won the Nobel Prize. To prevent yourself from being driven to distraction, reserve a room in one of the *hale* not being used for a program and away from the noisy water pumps. If you want privacy (the walls are paper- thin), consider renting one of the cottage units that is separate from the other buildings. Be advised that the power generator shuts off at 11 P.M., and an converter may or may not keep power going after that in all of the accommodations. The generator is turned on at 6 A.M. Bring one of those Itty-Bitty book lights if you want to read at night.

Somewhat in contrast to the granola accommodations is a surprisingly nice Olympic-size swimming pool—great for laps. Next to the pool is a Japanese teahouse structure where the wood-burning sauna and massage rooms are located. Two Jacuzzis are adjacent to the pool. Clothing is optional after 7 P.M., although on our last visit everyone was naked at 1 P.M. (we felt overdressed). Also on the grounds are five assembly spaces, including the tented Rainbow Room with has a suspended wood floor, and a newly resurfaced tennis court. For dining there is the Hale Makani, where three meals are served daily ($27 per person per day or meals can be purchased separately). The cuisine tends to be on the vegan/vegetarian side and is served cafeteria-style. If you feel like having a hamburger, forget it. A store with essential sundries and some excellent hand-painted *pareo* is adjacent to the cafe. Otherwise, the closest supermarket is about a half-hour drive away in Pahoa Town.

The holistic aura of Kalani is augmented by its setting. In addition to the dense tropical vegetation on its perimeter, there are several other natural wonders close by. A little over a mile down the road is the clothing-optional Kehena Beach, the most splendid black-sand beach on the Big Island, if not the state (see Beaches, earlier in this chapter). Within a ten-minute drive is the Kalapana lava flow, so Madame Pele is very much your neighbor. In between are lava tubes, including the Cave of the Flying Vagina (named after a remarkable natural relief of the female anatomy), thermal springs, crater lakes, and steam vents.

Kalani has some extraordinary programs. The diversified curriculum runs the gamut of alternative, holistic, and mainstream offerings. One recurring theme is dance; two of the original principals in this operation were professional dancers. Included in the dance program are an informative and fun hula program that coincides with the Merrie Monarch Festival in nearby Hilo (tickets for all events are included in the cost of tuition), as well as Trancedance, Water Dance, and Healing Dance. Yoga is studied here with a passion. Seminars on Iyengar, Astanga, Hatha, and Piedmont yoga, and Watsu (underwater shiatsu) are probably the most comprehensive on the Big Island if not in all of Hawai'i. Other topics include several gay and lesbian programs/retreats, t'ai chi, various self-help and therapy sessions, and spa weeks. Anyone is eligible to sign up for any program. If you have any sense of spiritual adventure, there should be something on the schedule that will appeal to you. Seminars vary in length; many are seven days/six nights. Fees and full room and board for these sessions are between $780 and $940 per person (for single occupancy, add $300).

Rates for rooms only are *Cheap* and up.

Volcano Village

Volcano Village is one of the neatest communities in Hawai'i. Situated at 4,000 feet above sea level, the temperature is much cooler here. Indeed, at night it often drops into the 40s (5 to 8° degrees C). Many lodgings have fireplaces, which are a welcome place to warm your toes at night. It also rains a lot, with over 180 inches annually. Many of the houses are classic Hawai'ian bungalows, built earlier in the century, with spacious yards. It's totally authentic and fortunately gets missed by most of the tour buses, as it is off the main road just before you reach Volcanoes National Park.

There are now a lot more options for staying in Volcano Village. Most are bed-and-breakfasts and quite reasonable. The village has a few good restaurants too (see Where to Eat). We recommend at least one or two nights in Volcano as an interesting diversion for a Big Island vacation. Note that Volcano House and the Namakani Paio Cabins are the only lodgings within the park.

Kilauea Lodge, P.O. Box 116, Volcano Village, HI 96785. Local: 808-967-7366, fax 808-967-7367. Units: 13 rooms.
Web site: www.kilauealodge.com

Built in 1938 as a YMCA, the lodge was restored by Albert and Lorna Jeyte in 1987 and is now the most luxurious place to stay (and has the best restaurant) in Volcano. This small and charming yellow clapboard tin-roofed inn actually consists of the original Y building plus the newer Hale Aloha, The Cottage, and Tutu's Place (which is down the street). A large and very attractive dining room and parlor features a huge stone fireplace; a full breakfast, included in the room rate, is served here, as is dinner.

The rooms are all non-smoking and have central heat (now we've never noted *this* in Hawai'i before!). Most of the rooms have wood-burning fireplaces. The Honeymoon Deluxe Room, nicknamed the "Robert Redford Room" after he stayed there, has a fireplace and dual shower heads in the bathroom. Many rooms also have four-poster beds, lanai, and high ceilings. All baths have heated towel racks! Guests have use of the common room in Hale Aloha, which is filled with rattan furnishings, chintz upholstery, books, and games, and has a VCR and a big fireplace.

Rates are **Not So Cheap** and up (full breakfast).

My Island Bed & Breakfast Inn, P.O. Box 100, Volcano Village, HI 96785. Local: 808-967-7216, fax 808-967-7719. Units: 6 rooms and a 3-bedroom house
Web site: www.hawaiinetdirectory.com/myislandbnb.html

We were delighted to discover this wonderful B&B. Host and native Gordon Morse provides a wealth of information about the area and, along with his wife, Joann, and daughter Ki'i, runs a very warm and welcoming establishment. The seven acres of grounds are beautifully landscaped, with an abundance of flowers planted so there's something blooming every month and grown to adorn the guest rooms. The quaint main house was built in 1886 as the Lyman missionary home; a full breakfast is served here each morning between 7 to 8:30 A.M. by the woodstove. It also houses three guest rooms with shared and private baths and has a well-stocked library, an information center, and a TV.

There are three more rooms with separate entrances in a garden building as well as the Deck House, which has three bedrooms, two baths, a full kitchen, and a comfortable, rather eclectic décor—great for a group. We feel the rooms in the main house have much more character. Rooms are furnished with a variety of antiques, simple furnishings, and Hawai'iana. While they are not fancy, neither is the price. There are plans underway to build another building and three more rooms (including a fully wheelchair accessible room). My Island is a hop, skip, and a jump from four Volcano restaurants.

Rates are **Dirt Cheap** and up (full breakfast). No credit cards (but personal checks are okay).

Volcano House, P.O. Box 53, Hawai'i Volcanoes National Park, HI 96718. Local: 808-967-7321. Units: 42 rooms.

This is a truly unique lodging experience in a most unnerving location—on the rim of the world's most active volcano. You are right at Madame Pele's doorstep, and believe us, you'll feel her energy (people are said to have phenomenal sex here). The view from the deck (or your room) at sunrise is otherworldly. Vents spout columns of steam out of the crater as the sun rises up from the Pacific behind them. That scene alone is worth the ticket. The exterior of the wooden buildings has the same pleasing, rustic red look as it did in the 19th century.

The registration desk is vintage—it looks like an old Western Union clerk's counter. There is a huge stone fireplace (which is said to have been going continuously for the past 100 years) and a pleasantly worn-in, comfortable sitting area. The rooms are small and could use a spruce-up as the décor is very eclectic—nothing really matches. We liked the big padded rocker in the little alcove facing the crater and found it a nice place to read or just look at the view. Rooms don't have TVs or radio but do have a phone. The bathrooms have a transom window, so anyone walking down the hall will hear you taking a shower, etc. Be advised that the walls are paper-thin. We heard a couple, obviously married for years and years, nagging each other at 5:30 in the morning: "Harry, where did you put my cigarettes? Yes you *did* have them last!" The hotel does not offer non-smoking rooms. This disturbance (and the cigarette smell) caused us to rise and get in our car to experience sunrise in the park, which was wonderful and the *raison d'être* for being here anyway. When making your reservations, be sure to ask for a room facing the crater. The hotel also operates cabins a few miles away (see below).

Even more unfortunate disturbances are the busloads of tourists who descend on the hotel around 10 A.M. for the endless buffet seatings and don't finally clear out until around 4 P.M. It is impossible to enjoy the hotel during the day. If you're going to stay here, be sure to arrive late in the afternoon and be out and about by 9 A.M. The hiking and exploring here are enough to keep you busy for a few days. The Ka Ohelo Dining Room serves three meals a day and a snack bar operates in Uncle George's Lounge until 4:30 P.M. The Lounge serves drinks until 9 P.M.

Rates for the crater view rooms are **Pricey**. Other rooms are **Cheap** and up.

Volcano Country Cottages, P.O. Box 545, Volcano Village, HI 96785. Toll-free: 800-967-7969. Local: 808-967-7960, fax 808-967-7960. Units: 2 cottages.
Web site: www.volcanocottages.com

Nestled among towering *tsugi* trees and chirping birds are these two rustic, quaint, and well-tended cottages on the grounds of one of the village's oldest homes. The Artist's House has two bedrooms, a fully equipped kitchen, bath, and a wood-burning stove and can sleep up to eight with the fold-out bed and futon in the living area. Artist's supplies are available for you to use when inspired. The Ohelo Berry Cottage is a studio with kitchenette, bath, and lanai with rocking chair. Breakfast (baked goods, tropical fruits, juice, and coffee) is left in the cottages every evening so that guests can help themselves whenever they want—maybe as a late night snack instead. The village's four restaurants are a short walk away.

Rates are **Cheap** and up (CP).

Chalet Kilauea/The Inn at Kilauea, Box 998, Volcano Village, HI 96785. Toll-free: 800-937-7786. Local: 808-967-7786, fax 808-967-8660. Units: 6 rooms and suites.
Web site: www.volcano-hawaii.com

Frankly, we were a tad surprised by the shade thrown by this place. Here was attitude galore in the lovely, unpretentious Volcano Village. Case in point: a gourmet breakfast served *by candlelight!* We don't know where the hosts come from, but in these parts candles are used only at dinner. Maybe breakfast is served before dawn and is considered a very fashionably late dinner? Who knows? We do know that at the prices charged we'd steer you to the Kilauea Lodge.

There are six themed rooms and suites with names like "Out of Africa" and the "Continental Lace Suite." Hmm. All have marble baths with Jacuzzis as well as TV/VCRs. There is a Jacuzzi perched in a gazebo off the main building. Oh yes, afternoon tea is also served here. We weren't surprised.

Rates are **Not So Cheap** and up (full breakfast).

Carson's Volcano Cottages, P.O. Box 503, Volcano, HI 96785. Toll-free: 800-845-LAVA (5282). Local: 808-967-7683, fax 808-967-8094. Units: 6 rooms and 3 cottages.
Web site: www.carsonscottage.com

With a variety of rooms and cottages on this property south of Route 11 (but still within walking distance of Volcano Village's restaurants), this rather cute and eclectic property has something for everyone. We like the Storybook Cottages for their imagination and Nick's Cabin for its rustic appeal. All cabins have a woodstove and all rooms and cabins have private baths. Some of the rooms have cable TV. Some of the rooms/cabins have private hot tubs, and there is a communal one among giant ferns. A full breakfast is served by the fireplace in the main dining room.

Rates are **Not so Cheap** and up (full breakfast).

Volcano Inn, P.O. Box 490, Volcano Village, HI 96785. Toll-free: 800-997-2292. Local: 808-967-7293, fax 808-985-7349. Units: 5 rooms and 4 cottages.
Web site: www.volcanoinn.com

We found this clean and well-kept lodging a bit too cutesy for our taste (the décor was full of tchotchkes and all-too-dear affectations). However, the hostess is very nice, so even if the furnishings aren't out of a decorator's showcase, this could be a viable option for some. All rooms and cottages except one have TV/VCR (a plus) and fridge (two of the cottages have kitchen facilities). A full breakfast is served at the Inn from 7 to 8 A.M.

Rates are *Cheap* and up (full breakfast).

Namakani Paio Cabins, Volcano House, P.O. Box 53, Hawai'i Volcanoes National Park, HI 96718. Local 808-967-7321. Units: 10 cabins.

If you want to rough it like the pioneers of yore, the Namakani Paio Campground, located three miles up the road at the 4,000-foot elevation, has ten cabins that are managed by Volcano House (the campground also has tent sites). Each cabin has one double and two single bunk beds, with a maximum occupancy of four. There is an electric light, but leave your blow dryer at home—there are no outlets. For cooking, there is an outdoor barbecue grill, but you'll have to bring your own charcoal and cooking utensils. The cabin rate includes a "linen bag" that has sheets, pillows, pillow cases, towels, soap, and one blanket for two (who are presumably going to keep each other warm in the double bed). Additional "bags" are five bucks per person. Since it gets chilly and damp at this elevation, the management advises that you bring extra blankets or a sleeping bag. Shower and bath facilities are in a separate building.

Rates are *Dirt Cheap.*

South District

Colony One at Sea Mountain Resort, P.O. Box 70, Pahala, HI 96777. Toll Free: 800-488-8301. Local: 808-928-8301, fax 808-928-8008. Units: 75.
Web site: www.seamtnhawaii.com

And now for something completely different, there are these

condos on the Ka'u Coast—about as far away from everything as you can get on the Big Island. Set downslope from Mauna Loa and Kilauea, both active volcanoes, the surrounding terrain, as you can imagine, is volcanic. It's also dry grassland, so the area is very sunny—take note, sun worshippers. Also note that the pretty black-sand beach is a regular tour-bus stop. But the Aspen Institute–Hawai'i is located here, and it's is a great place to stay if you want to hike the Ka'u and Volcano districts.

The condos, in Polynesian-style architecture, are comfortable one- and two-bedroom units. All have full kitchen, washer/dryer, and a tropical rustic décor. There are four Laykold tennis courts, a Jacuzzi, and an 18-hole Snyder golf course.

The hotel discounts rates $3 for singles (gee, thanks).

Rates are **Not So Cheap** for studios and **Pricey** for the one- and two-bedroom units (two-night minimum).

Shirakawa Motel, P.O. Box 467, Na'alehu, HI 96772. Local: 808-929-7462. Units: 13 rooms.

If you want to stay in the Ka'u district (the southeast side of the Big Island), this is the much cheaper alternative to the Sea Mountain resort. Its claim to fame is that it's the southernmost lodging in the United States. Made up of 13 motel units, it's very basic—but then again, it's clean and cheap. For food, there's a general store and coffee shop in Na'alehu or the more gourmet facilities at Sea Mountain, about ten miles up the road.

Prices are **Cheap.**

Where to Eat

Navigating the restaurant scene on the Big Island is not very difficult. Most of the dining options are in the big resort areas of Kohala and Kailua-Kona, with the best (and most expensive) restaurants not surprisingly at the best and most expensive resorts. Don't be discouraged, though, as there are many excellent and affordable options spread out throughout the island. Kailua-Kona has a huge variety for the palate. Misty Waimea offers Merriman's, which many consider the Big Island's best, and several grill rooms.

Both the Hilo and Volcano areas have seen the opening of several very good bistros and eateries. Bon appetit!

Kohala

Bamboo Restaurant & Gallery, Highway 270, Hawi, 889-5555. Hawi is one of our favorite spots on the Big Island, and this is the place to eat in Hawi. Occupying an old wooden building, Bamboo serves excellent Hawai'ian Regional cuisine and is known for its lilikoi (passion fruit) margaritas. Open for lunch from 11:30 A.M. to 2:15 P.M., dinner from 6 to 8:30 P.M. Closed Monday. Reservations suggested. $$$

Batik, Mauna Kea Beach Hotel, Kohala Coast, 882-7222. The signature restaurant of this wonderful hotel has long been a star in Kohala. A fusion of Pacific Rim and Continental cuisines with a Provencal accent, Batik also has a beautiful décor. Open 6:30 to 9 P.M. Closed Tuesday and Saturday. Reservations strongly advised. $$$$$

Bay Terrace, Mauna Lani Bay Hotel and Bungalows, Kohala Coast, 885-6622.Breakfast and Sunday brunch are a must at this lush restaurant with seating available outside. Dinner has a seafood focus, and there's a popular buffet on weekends. Open daily for breakfast from 6:30 to 10:30 A.M., and for dinner from 6 to 9 P.M. Reservations for dinner suggested. $$$

Brown's Beach House, Orchid at Mauna Lani, Kohala Coast, 885-2000. Having achieved raves about its Hawai'ian Regional cuisine with a faboo ocean-side setting, this restaurant is a popular Kohala dining spot now with chef Roy Basilio at the helm. Open daily for lunch from 11:30 A.M. to 2 P.M., dinner from 6 to 9:30 P.M. Reservations for dinner suggested. $$$$

Café Pesto, Kawaihae Harbor Highway, Kawaihae, 882-1071. A refreshing change from the Kohala resorts' high prices, this is imaginative Italian fare with an attitude. Pizzas are superb. Definitely worth a stop. Café Pesto has a sister restaurant in Hilo. Open daily from 11 A.M. to 9 P.M. (weekends until 10 P.M.). Reservations suggested. $$$

Canoe House, Mauna Lani Bay Hotel and Bungalows, Kohala Coast, 885-6622. The Mauna Lani's top restaurant is also one of the Big Island's best, with chef Pat Saito serving up Pacific Rim cuisine in a beautiful and elegant setting. Try to eat here if you can (make it, afford it, or both). Open daily from 5:30 to 9:30 P.M. Reservations strongly advised. $$$$$

Coast Grille, Hapuna Beach Prince Hotel, Kohala Coast, 880-1111. Huge portions are served beachside at this Hawai'ian Regional bistro. Specialties include an oyster bar and New England lobster, the latter raised locally at a cold-water aqua-farm. Open daily from 6 to 9:30 P.M. Reservations advised. $$$$$

Donatoni's, Hilton Waikoloa Village, Waikoloa, 886-1234. This is surprisingly good Northern Italian cuisine in a restaurant that attempts to re-create the splendor of Venice with its lanai overlooking the Hilton's gondola rides. Fortunately, the food holds up its end of the bargain. Open for dinner from 6 to 10 P.M. Closed Sunday and Monday. Reservations advised. $$$$

Grand Palace Chinese Restaurant, Kings' Shops, Waikoloa, 886-6668. Some say this is the best Chinese on the island and we certainly feel it's worth a stop, especially for lunch. Open daily from 11 A.M. to 9:30 P.M. $$$

The Grill, Orchid at Mauna Lani, Kohala Coast, 885-2000. Another fine resort grill room with a excellent surf 'n turf menu. Open for dinner from 6:30 to 9:30 P.M. Closed Sunday, Monday, and Thursday. Reservations advised. $$$$$

Hakone, Hapuna Beach Prince Hotel, Kohala Coast, 880-1111. The best Japanese food in Kohala, but also the most expensive. Great sushi. Open 6 to 9 P.M. Closed Tuesday and Wednesday. Reservations suggested. $$$$

Imari, Hilton Waikaloa Village, Waikoloa, 886-1234. This teppan yaki and sushi restaurant is very good and very popular. Open daily from 6 to 9:30 P.M. Reservations advised. $$$$

Kamuela Provision Company, Hilton Waikoloa Village, Waikoloa, 886-1234. Pacific Rim and American cuisines are the focus of this more casual, family-oriented restaurant at the Hilton. Open daily from 5:30 to 10:30 P.M. Reservations suggested. $$$

Kawaihae Harbor Grill, Kawaihae Center, Kawaihae, 882-1368. This reasonably priced restaurant is worth a stop if just for the Waimea Tomato and Feta with fresh basil vinaigrette. Open daily for lunch from 11:30 A.M. to 2:30 P.M., dinner from 5:30 to 9:30 P.M. Reservations suggested. $$$

Pavilion, Mauna Kea Beach Hotel, Kohala Coast, 882-7222. A fantastic breakfast buffet and an American/Continental dinner menu are the main offerings of this airy indoor and outdoor restaurant. Open daily from 6:30 to 11 A.M. and 6 to 9:30 P.M. $$$$

Roussel's at Waikoloa Village, 68-1792 Melia Street, Waikoloa, 883-9644. The Big Island's Cajun place will satisfy most multi-alarm taste buds. Located up the slope at the Waikoloa Village Golf Club. Open Tuesday through Saturday from 11 A.M. to 9 P.M.; dinner only on Sunday and Monday, from 5 to 8:30 P.M. Reservations suggested. $$$

Roy's Waikoloa Bar & Grill, King's Shops, Waikoloa, 886-4321. Roy has the magic touch and his Pacific Rim restaurants are a hit wherever they are. Roy Yamaguchi is the godfather of this cuisine and its presentation, and this particular restaurant is wildly popular and noisy. Open daily for lunch from 11:30 A.M. to 2 P.M., dinner from 5:30 to 9:30 P.M. Reservations strongly advised. $$$$

Tres Hombres Beach Grill, Kawaihae Shopping Center, Kawaihae, 882-1031. With an unusual décor of Mexico-goes-to-Polynesia, this is Kohala's sole Mexican outpost. Great margaritas. Open daily from 11:30 A.M. to 9 P.M., Friday and Saturday until 10 P.M. $$$

North Kona

Hualalai Club Grille, Fours Seasons Hualalai, North Kona Coast, 325-8000. A surprisingly affordable Pacific Rim/grill room at the not surprisingly expensive Four Seasons—check it out. Located at the 18th hole of the Four Seasons golf course. Open daily for lunch from 11 A.M. to 3 P.M., dinner from 5 to 9 P.M. Reservations suggested. $$$

Harbor House, Honokohau Harbor, Honokohau, 326-4166. Located at the man-made boat basin a few miles north of Kailua-Kona, this is a simple but fun place for lunch or an after-the-nude-beach burger and brewski. Great boat and boat-crew watching. Open daily from 11 A.M. to 7 P.M., Sunday until 5:30 P.M. $$

Kona Village Luau, Kona Village Resort, North Kona Coast, 325-5555. This is the best and most authentic luau on the Big Island, set, appropriately, in a very Polynesian-looking village. If you've been waiting for an opportunity to sample Hawai'ian food, especially the *kalua* pig roasted in the *imu,* this will give you the whole gestalt of this cherished Hawai'ian tradition and a chance to see this wonderful resort, too. The luau is held on Friday only starting at 5 P.M. and finishing around 9 P.M. Reservations required. $$$$

Pahu I'a, Four Seasons Hualalai, North Kona Coast, 325-8000. Imaginative world cuisine is the focus of this very elegant beachfront restaurant, the Four Seasons premier choice. Open daily for breakfast from 6 to 11:30 A.M., dinner from 5:30 to 10 P.M. $$$$$

Kailua-Kona / Keauhou

Bianelli's Gourmet Pizza & Pasta, Pines Plaza (Nani Kailua Road), Kailua-Kona, 326-4800. A great place for pizza and simple pastas. Open Monday through Friday from 11 A.M. to 10 P.M., Saturday and Sunday from 5 to 10 P.M. $$

Denny's, Crossroads Center, Kailua-Kona, 334-1313. The only 24/7 option in Kona. $

Don's Chinese Kitchen, Kona Coast Shopping Center, Kailua-Kona, 329-3770. Cheap but good Cantonese food. Open daily from 10 A.M. to 9 P.M. $

Edward's at the Kanaloa, 78-261 Manukai Street, Keauhou, 322-1434. A Kona institution and a favorite spot for that romantic dinner by the sea. Go more for the mood than the Mediterranean fare, as the service is sometimes wanting. Open daily for breakfast, lunch, *pupus,* and dinner from 8 A.M. to 8:30 P.M. Reservations for dinner advised. $$$$

French Bakery, 74-5467 Kaiwi, Kailua-Kona, 326-2688. Get your croissants and baguettes here. Adjacent to Golden Chopstix. Open Monday through Friday from 5:30 A.M. to 3 P.M., Saturday until 2 P.M. Closed Sunday. $

Golden Chopstix Chinese Restaurant, 74-5467 Kaiwi Street, Kailua-Kona, 329-4527. In the same complex as the French Bakery, this is a great place for plate lunch. Open Monday through Saturday for lunch from 11 A.M. to 2:30 P.M., daily for dinner from 4:30 to 9 P.M. $$

Huggo's, 75-5828 Kahakai Street (at Ali'i Drive), Kailua-Kona, 329-1493. A Kona landmark known for its dramatic and stunning ocean-front setting, this Hawai'ian Regional surf 'n turfer is a popular touristo hangout. Open daily for lunch from 11:30 A.M. to 2:30 P.M., dinner from 5:30 to 9:30 P.M. Reservations for dinner advised. $$$

Island Lava Java, Ali'i Sunset Plaza, Kailua-Kona, 327-2161. A good place for that morning Joe. At press time they were closed due to a storm in November 2000. They are set to open in May 2001.

Jameson's by the Sea, Ali'i Drive (White Sands Beach), Kailua-Kona, 329-3195. Part of the Hawai'ian restaurant chain. Go for the sea-side ambience and Hawai'ian music more than the food. Open Monday through Friday for lunch from 11 A.M. to 3 P.M. Dinner is daily from 5 to 9 P.M. Reservations suggested. $$$

Jennifer's Korean Barbecue, 74-5605 Luhia Street, Old Industrial Area, Kailua-Kona, 326-1155. This dive in an industrial park offers the best Korean food on the island. Open from 11 A.M. to 9 P.M. Closed on Sunday. $$

King Kamehameha Luau, Hotel King Kamehameha, Kailua-Kona, 329-2911. Another good luau, held on Kamehameha's sacred grounds. This is a fine option if you are unable to make it to Kona Village. The Polynesian show can be entertaining and there is an open bar. Held every night except Monday and Saturday from 5:30 to 8:30 P.M. $$$

Kona Brewing Co. & Brewpub, 75-5629 Kuakini, Kailua-Kona, 334-2739. Local brewskis and burgers make this a fun hangout. Open daily from 11 A.M. to 10 P.M., Friday and Saturday until 11 P.M. $$

Kona Inn Restaurant, 75-5744 Ali'i Drive, Kailua-Kona, 329-4455. The remnants of the old and historic Kona Inn can be seen at this New American eatery-by-the-sea. It's a good place to go with kids. Open daily for lunch from 11:30 A.M. to 2:30 P.M., dinner from 5:30 to 9:30 P.M. $$$

Kona Ranch House, 75-5653 Ololi Street (Highway 11), Kailua-Kona, 329-7061. Open for breakfast, lunch, and dinner, this is a fam-ily-style restaurant with good portions for not too much money. The island beefsteak is a sure bet, as are their delicious break-fasts. Open daily from 6:30 A.M. to 9 P.M. $$$

La Bourgoyne, Kuakini Plaza (Highway 11), Kailua-Kona, 329-6711. Seemingly no bigger than a shoebox, this is the only real French restaurant on the Big Island. Superb food. Open Tuesday through Saturday from 6 to 10 P.M. Reservations required. $$$$

Ocean Seafood Chinese Restaurant, 75-5626 Kuakini (Highway 11), Kailua-Kona, 329-3055. Very good Chinese in a simple space. Open daily from 10:30 A.M. to 9 P.M. $$

Ocean View Inn, 75-5683 Ali'i Drive, Kailua-Kona, 329-9998. The dinosaur of Kona restaurants (it's been open over 60 years and it looks it), this is a good place to try some local dishes like poi, lomi lomi salmon and plate lunch, as well as ample breakfasts. Open for breakfast from 6:30 to 11 A.M., lunch from 11 A.M. to 2:45 P.M., dinner from 5:15 to 8:45 P.M. Closed Monday. No Credit Cards. $$

Oodles of Noodles, Cross Roads Shopping Center, Kailua-Kona, 329-9222. Don't let the hokey name fool you—this is a surprisingly good and cheap noodle joint with a Pacific Rim twist. It's worth the schlep to this shopping center. Open daily from 11 A.M. to 9 P.M. $$

Sam Choy's, 73-5576 Kauhola Street, Kaloko Light Industrial Area, Kailua-Kona, 326-1545. Sam Choy's is a renowned Hawai'ian chain of restaurants (this one is the original) known for its comfort food with local twists, huge portions and funky décor. Always crowded and noisy, it can be hard to find (call for directions). Open for breakfast and lunch from 6 A.M. to 2 P.M., dinner from 5 to 8:30 P.M. Closed Sunday and Monday. BYOB. $$$

Sibu Café, Banyan Court Mall (Ali'i Drive), Kailua-Kona, 329-1112. The only Indonesian cuisine on the island—what it lacks in ambience is made up in taste. Open daily for lunch from 11:30 A.M. to 3 P.M., dinner from 5 to 9 P.M. No credit cards. $$

Thai Rin, 75-5799 Ali'i Drive, Kailua-Kona, 329-2929. A very good Thai choice right on the main drag. Open for lunch from 11 A.M. to 2:30 P.M. (except Sunday); dinner daily from 5 to 9 P.M. $$$

Captain Cook / South Kona

Aloha Theater Café, Highway 11, Kainaliu, 332-3383. A groovy and funky place in an old theater building where the emphasis is on good-for-you food, the Aloha is a local fave. The specialty is their homemade pastries and desserts, and their veggie options. Open Monday through Thursday from 8 A.M. to 3 P.M., Friday and Saturday 8 A.M. to 9 P.M., Sunday 8 A.M. to 2 P.M. $$

Manago Hotel Restaurant, Highway 11, Captain Cook, 323-2642. The funky and cool Manago Hotel has an equal in its restaurant, serving local and diner food with an accent on the sea. Open for breakfast from 7 to 9 A.M., lunch from 11 A.M. to 2 P.M., and dinner from 5 to 7:30 P.M. Closed Monday. $$

Teshima, Route 11, Honalo (on the way to Captain Cook), 322-9140. Good Japanese fare at very reasonable prices. Open daily from 5 to 9 P.M. No credit cards. $

Waimea / Hamakua Coast

Akaka Noodle Shop, Route 220, Honomu, 963-6701. Coconut shells dangling from the porch roof of this false-storefront shop spell out A-L-O-H-A and beckon you to come in. Once inside, you'll find a wonderfully vintage-looking place with relics from the plantation days of Honomu, including old school desks where you can eat your excellent plate lunch and saimin. This establishment's specialty is its shave ice, made from an antique machine that creates magic from a huge block of ice. It's open from 9 A.M. to 5 P.M. Closed Wednesday. No credit cards. $

Aioli's, Opelo Plaza Center, Kamuela, 885-6325. Going to Volcano for the day and want a picnic? Stop here for excellent take-out. Open daily from 5 A.M. to 8 P.M. $

Edelweiss, Highway 19, Waimea, 885-6800. An old favorite with a very friendly staff serving Swiss/Austrian cuisine (lots of veal and creamy sauces). It's still very popular. Open daily for lunch from 11:30 A.M. to 1:30 P.M., dinner from 5 to 8:30 P.M. Reservations accepted for dinner. $$$

Koa House Grill, Highway 19, Kamuela, 885-2088. This grill serves a New American menu and has a fun bar too. Open daily for lunch from 11:30 A.M. to 2 P.M., dinner from 5 to 9 P.M. $$$

Maha's Café, Waimea Shopping Center, Waimea, 885-0693. A cute and cheap place that serves a delicious breakfast or lunch. It's set in an old missionary house marooned in the middle of a shopping center parking lot. Open from 8 A.M. to 4 P.M. Closed Tuesday and Wednesday. $$

Mamane Street Bakery & Café, Route 240, Honoka'a, 775-9478. If you're going to Waipi'o Valley Lookout or the valley itself, stop here for some yummy breads and pastries. Open daily from 6 A.M. to 5 P.M. Closed Sunday. $

Merriman's, Opelo Plaza, Route 19, Kamuela, 885-6822. An upbeat, casual establishment, Merriman's has been one of the best Big Island restaurants for over a decade. Chef Peter Merriman has maintained his creative flair with his Hawai'ian Regional cuisine and use of local produce. It's a great (and cheap) place for lunch too. Open for lunch Monday through Friday from 11:30 A.M. to 1:30 P.M., for dinner daily from 5:30 to 9 P.M. Reservations advised. $$$$

Parker Ranch Grill, Parker Ranch Center, Highway 19, Kamuela, 887-2624. A great place to try some Parker Ranch beef by a roaring hearth. Steak aficionados shouldn't miss this one. Recently Remodeled. $$$

Tex Drive-In and Restaurant, Highway 19, Honoka'a, 775-0598. This is the home of the best *malasadas* (a type of Portuguese donut) on the Big Island. Served warm with Kona coffee, they hit the spot. Tex's also serves fast but hearty breakfasts, lunches, including plate lunch, and dinners in a too-bright and sterile-looking room. Open daily from 6 A.M. to 8:30 P.M. Next door is a convenience store for beer, cigarettes, and aspirin. $

Waimea Coffee & Co., Parker Square (Highway 19), Waimea, 885-4472. Need a cup of Joe for a trek to the Hilo side (or vice versa)? Then stop here for some "fuel." Open Monday through Friday from 7 A.M. to 5 P.M., Saturday 8 A.M. to 4 P.M., closed on Sunday. $

Hilo

Café 100, 969 Kilauea Avenue, Hilo, 935-8683. All over Hawai'i you'll see something on the menu called "loco moco." It all started here in WW II. This is the home of this distinctly Hawai'ian stick-to-your-ribs dish of rice, hamburg patty, gravy, and eggs. Open daily from 6:45 A.M. to 8:30 P.M., Friday until 9:30 P.M. No credit cards. $

Café Pesto, 308 Kamehameha Avenue, Hilo, 969-6640. The original Café Pesto (the newer sister is in Kawaihae), this is imaginative Italian fare with an attitude. Pizzas are superb. Definitely worth a stop. Open daily from 11 A.M. to 9 P.M. (weekends until 10 P.M.). Reservations suggested. $$$

Don's Grill, 485 Hinano Street (at Kekuanaoa Street), Hilo, 935-9099. Good cheap eats Hawai'ian style—locals love this place. Open Tuesday through Thursday 10:30 A.M. to 9 P.M., Friday until 10 P.M., Saturday and Sunday from 10 A.M. to 9 P.M. $$

Harrington's, 135 Kalaniani'ole Highway (Reed's Bay), Hilo, 961-4966. Many people recommend this restaurant as a pretty and romantic place to have a surf 'n turf dinner and a few cocktails. Open for lunch Monday through Friday from 11 A.M. to 2 P.M.; dinner served daily from 5:30 to 9:30 P.M. Reservations suggested. $$$

Honu's Nest, 270 Kamehameha Avenue, Hilo, 935-9321. Japanese fare plain and simple makes this a popular little eatery with locals. Open Monday through Saturday from 10 A.M. to 4 P.M. No credit cards $$

Ken's House of Pancakes, 1730 Kamehameha Avenue, Hilo, 935-8711. It's 2 A.M. and you're hungry. Where do you go in Hilo? Ken's is the only show in town that's open 24/7. $

New China Restaurant, 510 Kilauea Street, Hilo, 961-5677. Remember Cantonese cuisine (egg rolls, fried rice, pork strips, chop suey)? Well, this is a good place to chow down on some chow mein. Open from 10 A.M. to 9 P.M. Closed on Monday. $$

Pescatore, 235 Keawe Street, Hilo, 969-9090. A rival to Café Pesto with a much more Italian menu and ambience, Pescatore is a welcome addition to the downtown Hilo dining scene. Open daily for breakfast, lunch, and dinner from 7:30 A.M. to 9 P.M. $$$

Royal Siam, 70 Mamo Street, Hilo, 961-6100. The best Thai food in Hilo Town is served here. Open Monday through Saturday for lunch from 11 A.M. to 2 P.M., dinner from 5 to 8:30 P.M. $$

Seaside, 1790 Kalaniani'ole Highway, Hilo, 935-8825. A Hilo institution, the specialty here is not seafood or the décor but freshwater fish served local-style (the whole shebang). Most are raised in the ponds outside the window (the salty ones on the menu come from the big Pacific pond). Open from 5 to 8:30 P.M. Closed on Monday. $$$

Puna

The Godmother, Route 130 (the main street), Pahoa, 965-0055. Traditional southern Italian fare and a full bar make this an option in quirky Pahoa Town. Open daily for breakfast and lunch from 7 A.M. to 2:30 P.M., dinner from 3:30 to 9 or 10 P.M. $$$

Liquin's Mexican Restaurant, Route 130 (the main street), Pahoa, 965-9990. Cheap and good Mexican fare in a funky storefront on the main street. This is a fun place, especially with a few margaritas. Open daily from 11 A.M. to 9 P.M. $$

Kalani Oceanside Eco-Resort, Route 137, Kehena, 965-7828. If you're looking for vegan or vegetarian fare, or just plain healthy natural foods, and are planning to visit Kehena's beautiful black-sand nude beach, stop here to have breakfast, lunch, or dinner and check out this unique place. Open daily for breakfast from 7:30 to 8:30 A.M., lunch from 12 to 1 P.M., dinner from 6 to 7:30 P.M. $$

Paolo's Bistro, Route 130 (the main street), Pahoa, 965-7033. Tuscan cuisine by chef Paolo Bucchioni uses local and Italian produce and ingredients to offer a more refined dining experience in the frontier-ish Pahoa Town. Open Tuesday through Saturday from 5:30 to 9 p.m. $$$

Volcano Village

Kilauea Lodge & Restaurant, Old Volcano Road, Volcano Village, 967-7366. Volcano's premier restaurant is set in an old YMCA lodge with a large hearth. Chef Albert Jeyte offers a Continental menu with some local touches. Open daily for dinner from 5:30 to 9 p.m. Reservations advised. $$$$

Volcano's Lava Rock Café, Old Volcano Road, Volcano Village, 967-8526. This is a fun little bistro with a full bar, good entertainment, and a nice mix of locals and visitors. The eclectic menu is a mixed bag of comfort food, stir-fry, and flame-broiled entrées. The Lava serves a delicious breakfast too. Open daily for breakfast from 7:30 to 11 A.M., lunch from 11 A.M. to 5 P.M. Dinner is served Tuesday through Saturday from 5 to 9 P.M. $$

Surt's at the Volcano, Old Volcano Road, Volcano Village, 967-8511. With a sister restaurant on Kaua'i, chef Surt Thamountha fuses

Asian and French cuisines into a very savory result and a much-needed addition to the Volcano dining options. Curry lovers will be thrilled. Open daily for lunch from 11:30 A.M. to 4 P.M., dinner from 4 to 9:30 P.M. They serve wine and beer. Reservations suggested. $$$

Thai Thai Restaurant, Old Volcano Road, Volcano Village, 967-7969. This fairly simple Thai restaurant offers a rather uninspired menu of pad Thais, curry dishes, and stir-fry. Open daily from 5 to 9 P.M. $$

Volcano Golf & Country Club, Hawai'i Volcanoes National Park, 967-8228. Locals say this is the best lunch deal in Volcano. Open daily from 8 A.M. to 2:30 P.M. $$

Volcano House, Hawai'i Volcanoes National Park, 967-7321. With one of the most remarkable views on the planet (of the Kilauea crater), try to have breakfast here (both breakfast and lunch are buffets) before the tour buses arrive with the lunchtime hordes. Dinner is much calmer—à la carte and, unfortunately, viewless. Open daily for breakfast from 7 to 10:30 A.M., lunch from 11 A.M. to 2 P.M., dinner from 5:30 to 9 P.M. Reservations required for dinner. $$

Going Out

Nightlife on the Big Island is not like Honolulu or even Maui. If you're looking for lots of action when the sun goes down, you won't find it here. However, there are some good options that will make for a fun evening out, especially in Kailua-Kona. With everything else the Big Island has to offer during the daylight hours, who's got the energy anyway?

Kona

Billfish Bar, King Kamehameha Hotel, 329-2911. A centrally located, low-key bar with cheap drinks. Open 11 A.M. to 9:30–10 P.M. No cover.

Durty Jake's, 75-5819 Ali'i Drive, Kailua-Kona, 329-7366. Belly dancing from 7 to 10 P.M. on Thursday nights packs this indoor/outdoor local hang in K.K. If nothing's happening here (or after last call), you can always head upstairs to Lulu's. Open daily until midnight. No cover.

Flashbacks Bar & Grill, 75-5699 Ali'i Drive, Kailua-Kona, 326-2840. An oldies-music, mostly touristo hangout for the kid in you. Open daily until 11:30 P.M. No cover.

Hard Rock Café – Kona, 75-5815 Ali'i Drive, 326-7655. No need to explain this one with its second-floor bar/lanai overlooking Kailua Bay across the street. Open daily until 11 P.M. No cover.

Huggo's on the Rocks, 75-5828 Kahakai Street, Kailua-Kona, 329-1493. A Gen Y mix of locals and touristos pack this seaside and outdoor watering spot. Open daily until 11 P.M. No cover.

Kona Brewing Co., 75-5629 Kuakini Highway, Kailua-Kona, 334-2739. Kona's premier microbrewery is a fun pub, especially on weekends. Open Monday through Thursday until 10 P.M., weekends until midnight, Sunday until 9 P.M. No cover.

Korner Pocket Bar & Grill, Haleki'i Street, Kealakekua, 322-2994. This Captain Cook dive with billiards and sports TV is a fave local hangout. Open daily until 2 A.M. No cover.

Lulu's, 75-5819 Ali'i Drive, Kailua-Kona, 331-2633. Billiards and good drinks attract a menagerie of locals and touristos to this casual second-floor joint above Durty Jake's. Open daily until 1 A.M.

Mask Bar & Grill, 75-5660 Kopiko Road, Kailua-Kona, 329-8558. The Big Island's premier gay and lesbian bar sits in the middle of a shopping plaza. The small dance floor is packed on weekends. Open daily until 2 A.M. No cover.

The Other Side/The Edge, 74-5484 Kaiwi Street, Kailua-Kona, 329-7226. It's only rock 'n roll, but we like it at this decent-size place in the old industrial area. Adjoining the bar is a dance space called The Edge. Open daily until 2 A.M. No cover.

The Office, 95-12562 Kuakini Highway, Kailua-Kona, 329-2525. As its name implies, this tiny local hangout looks like an old-style office space, complete with office furniture. Open daily until 2 A.M. No cover.

Kohala

Honu Bar, Mauna Lani Bay Hotel, Kohala Coast, 885-6622. This fun and stylish bar at the chic Mauna Lani has nightly live entertainment, billiards, table games, cigar bar, and sports TV. Drinks aren't cheap, but if you have to ask. . . Open daily until midnight. No cover.

The Paniolo Lounge, Orchid at Mauna Lani, Kohala Coast, 885-2000. Chic cowboys and horses (and polo ponies) are the themes of these two bars. One's a mellow bar (Polo) and the other features mellow late-night entertainment (Paniolo). Open daily 5 P.M. to midnight. No cover.

Roussels at Waikoloa Village, Waikoloa Village Golf Course, Waikoloa, 883-9644. Live bands rock Roussel's on Fridays. Open until 2 A.M. Thursday and Friday. No cover.

Second Floor, Hilton Waikoloa Village, Waikoloa, 885-5737. The big dance club/disco in Kohala is located at the Hilton. Also billiards and sports TV. Open daily until 1 A.M. No cover except for special events.

Hilo

Breakwater Nightclub, Naniloa Hotel, 93 Banyan Drive, Hilo, 969-3333. The dance spot in Hilo is the place to be on weekends. Open 10 P.M. to 3 A.M. Cover is $5. Strict designated-driver program.

Cronies, 11 Waianuenue Avenue, Hilo, 935-5158. Located in a former drugstore, this is a happening bar with good music and entertainment and a young crowd. Open 11 A.M. to 2 A.M. Cover on Thursday $3 to $5.

Shooter's, 121 Banyan Drive, Hilo, 969-7069. Looking for military men and the like? Check out this macho bar. Open 2 P.M. to 2 A.M. Cover on live music nights is $3 to $5.

Volcano

Volcano's Lava Rock Café, Old Volcano Road, Volcano Village, 967-8526. A fun and friendly place with cheap drinks and good entertainment—and, hey, this is Volcano, not Kona. Live entertainment Thursday and Saturday 6:30 to 8 P.M.

Don't Miss

Hawai'i Volcanoes National Park and Volcano Village—No visit to the Big Island should omit the impressive and awe-inspiring Kilauea Caldera, the world's most active volcano. Be sure to pay your respects to Madame Pele, the Hawai'ian goddess of fire, with an offering of flowers at the Hale'uma'u Caldera, her current home. Be sure to visit Volcano Village with its vintage Hawai'ian-style architecture.

Puna—We adore Puna. It is so lush and has some of the world's cleanest air (when the trade winds blow). Check out funky Pahoa Town, the scenic drives on Poho'iki Road and Route 137, and Kalani Eco-Resort.

Shipman House, Hilo—This extraordinary Victorian mansion and estate in this most Hawai'ian of Hawai'ian cities has been wonderfully restored and is now a bed-and-breakfast. Don't miss this!

Sig Zane Designs, Hilo—For the best aloha wear in the Aloha State, check out Sig's original boutique at 122 Kamehameha Avenue, 808-935-7077.

Merrie Monarch Festival, Hilo—This magical competition, with its superb presentation of hula and Hawai'ian music, is one of our favorite events in Hawai'i. Held annually in early April. Call well in advance for tickets and accommodations (808-935-9168).

A Hot Malasada at Tex's, Honoka'a—Renowned throughout the Big Island for decades, Tex's hot *malasadas* (Portuguese sugar-dusted donuts–sort of) and a cup of java make for a yummy, fattening, and welcome respite on the popular northern cross-island drive.

Waipi'o Valley—Once the home of thousands of Hawai'ians and dubbed the "Valley of the Kings," it now is virtually uninhabited—by *living* humans, that is. The valley is known for its spirits, said to come out at night.

Merriman's, Waimea—Located in the often misty town that is home to the Parker Ranch, Merriman's, with chef Peter Merriman's innovative Hawai'ian Regional cuisine, is our favorite restaurant on the Big island.

Hawi Town and the Kohala Mountain Road (Route 250)—Hawi has been left untouched (at press time) by the tourism tsunami of the western side of the Big Island. Its tranquility is a reflection of the "old" Big Island. There are some fun cafés and galleries to check out. Then take Route 250 *south*, not north, for an incredibly scenic ride.

The Mauna Kea Beach Hotel at night—Laurance Rockefeller's Hawai'ian vision is a masterpiece of architecture, art, and taste left relatively undisturbed by subsequent owners. But it's at night when it really shines, especially the stairway to Buddha—an incredible sight.

Nani Lim (Yap)—Part of the famous singing Lim family of Kamuela, Nani Lim is a singer and entertainer *extraordinaire* of Hawai'ian music and hula. Her shows rotate nightly at various Kohala resorts. We love her and highly recommend her talent.

Honokohau Beach, Kailua-Kona—The west side's unofficial nude and gay beach is a great place to sun and strut.

Diving with Keller at Jack's Diving Locker, Kailua-Kona—Our favorite dive shop takes you to Hawai'i's best diving, and Keller makes it so much fun. Call 800-345-4807 to schedule a dive.

Kaua'i

Touristo Scale:

🐷🐷🐷🐷🐷🐷🐷 (7)

EVERYBODY LOVES KAUA'I. We second that emotion. We've always said that Kaua'i is what you imagine Hawai'i to be if you've never been there, like Hollywood's version of a South Pacific island (over 50 movies have been filmed on Kaua'i, *including* South Pacific). While Kaua'i is really in the *North* Pacific, it is truly spectacular—a unique place of dramatic contrasts. Fluted, verdant *pali* (spire-shaped mountains), sculpted by eons of surf, wind, and rain, rise majestically from the cobalt-blue sea. Red rock canyons carve their way toward coconut groves and strands of sand. A cloud-crowned volcanic peak collects more rain than anywhere else on earth. Yet a few miles away, only 19 inches of rain falls every year.

Kaua'i may have been the first landfall when the canoes arrived from the Marquesas and Society Islands over a thousand years ago. Due to the elements of nature, the forces of time, and the "discovery" of the islands by Europeans, there are no remains or records to prove which island was settled first. This we do know: It is the birthplace of hula, the great oral history tradition of the Hawai'ian people. Today Kaua'i is a wonder of the tourism world. One of the best golf resorts in the state, Princeville, sits on a bluff overlooking some of the most gorgeous scenery in the world. A vast hiking network in two state parks beckons the nature enthusiast. Stunning beaches, some top-notch accommodations and restaurants, and a quiet, peaceful demeanor make Kaua'i a great place to go to relax, honeymoon, or just enjoy the company you keep.

Cannons

Hāʻena Beach Park

Hāʻena State Park

Limahuli Gardens

Hanalei Colony Resort

Kaulupaoa & Kauluolaka Heiaus

Kēʻē Beach

Tunnels Beach

Maniniholo Dry Cave

Hanakāpīʻai Beach

Waikanaloa & Waikapelaʻe Wet Caves

WAINIHA

N Ā P A L I   C O A S T

Nāpali Coast State Park

Kalalau Beach

Waniha River

Kalalau Valley

Hanapu Valley

Kalalau Lookout

Saʻalolo Valley

lookout

Miloliʻi Valley

Kuʻia NAR

Kōkeʻe Lodge

Kōkeʻe State Park

Alakaʻi Swamp

lookout

Waimea

Polihale Heiau

Barking Sands Beach

Canyon

Polihale State Park

State

lookout

Park

Waimea Canyon Dr

Waimea River

Pacific Missile Range Facility

MĀNĀ

Kōkeʻe Rd

W a i m e a   C a n y o n

550

Kekaha Beach Park

Kekaha

Waimea

Waimea Plantation Cottages

Captain Cook Monument

Russian Fort Elizabeth State Historical Park

Waimea State Recreation Pier

Lucy Wright Beach Park

50

KAUMUALIʻI HWY

Hanapēpē

ʻEleʻele

540

PORT ALLEN

Salt Pond Beach Park

Hanapēpē Bay

W E

0   2.0   4.0   6.0 miles

0   2.0   4.0   6.0   8.0   10. kilometers

Kaua'i

A Brief History

The fourth-largest island in the Hawai'ian chain (550 square miles/1,425 square kilometers), Kaua'i appeared about 6 million years ago when it formed on the magma hotspot that is now under the southeast coast of the Big Island and the Lo'ihi sea mount (currently about 3,000 feet below sea level). There are no active or dormant volcanoes on the island, which has been beautifully sculpted by the elements over the millennia.

Originally settled by migration waves from the Marquesas and Society Islands—first in the 8th and then in the 12th to 13th centuries—the Hawai'ian Islands remained isolated from the outside world until Captain Cook's expedition landed at Kaua'i in 1778. At that time the islands shared the same language and customs, but contact was limited to periodic conquests, defeats, and occasional trading. O'ahu was ruled by the adopted son of Kahekili, the powerful chief of Maui. Within a year of Cook's first contact on Kaua'i, disease brought by the Europeans, especially venereal diseases, had spread to all of the islands.

In 1786 O'ahu was conquered by the ruthless Kahekili, already the ruler of Maui, Moloka'i, and Lana'i. Kahekili ruled from O'ahu and formed an alliance with his half-brother Ka'eokulani, the ruler of Kaua'i. Meanwhile, Kamehameha, the powerful chief of the Big Island, was massing his army to invade Maui and overthrow his longtime nemesis, Kahekili. Concurrent with all this plotting, both Kahekili and Kamehameha were tapping into the white man's technology, making deals for guns and support from various British and American traders and mercenaries. This trade would greatly alter the outcome of the battles. The more guns and cannons a chief had in his forces, the more success he would have.

Various intrigues and rivalries ensued until Kahekili died of natural causes in 1794. He left his half-brother Ka'eokulani of Kaua'i and his son Kalanikupule of O'ahu in charge of his empire. Of course egos clashed, and to make a long story really shorter, Kalanikupule survived and became the ruler of Kaua'i. However, Kalanikupule made a grave error in judgment when he killed his English ally William Brown and commandeered his ships and men to go to the Big Island and fight Kamehameha. Unsuccessful at the

attempt and humiliated by the loss of support, he was now also without the white man's guns. In 1795 Kamehameha, sensing weakness, invaded from the Big Island, conquered Maui, Lana'i, and Moloka'i, and headed for O'ahu to do battle and won. Only the conquest of Kaua'i remained, but two invasion attempts, in 1796 and 1804, were foiled, respectively, by foul weather during the crossing over the wide and dangerous Kaua'i Channel and by typhoid fever or cholera. Kaua'i's king, Kaumuali'i, aware that Kamehameha was hell-bent on conquering his island and would probably eventually win, entered into negotiations with Kamehameha, who was also getting tired of battle. Finally, in 1810, with the mediation of an American merchant named Nathan Winship, an agreement was reached and the islands united under Kamehameha.

In the ensuing decades, Kaua'i was a quiet backwater of the kingdom and a significant sugar producer. In 1893 American sugar barons with interests in Hawai'i, looking to circumvent U.S. tariffs on Hawai'ian sugar, staged an armed coup and overthrew Queen Lili'uokalani in Honolulu. She was placed under house arrest, and the Republic of Hawai'i was formed in 1894. The new government petitioned President Grover Cleveland for formal annexation, but Cleveland, who was a friend of the Queen's, refused. When McKinley won the election in 1898, the Republic petitioned again and the president, seeing the strategic value of the islands, gladly accepted. In 1900 the Hawai'ian Islands became a Territory of the United States. The sugar barons had beaten the tariffs.

After World War II the push for statehood began, culminating in Hawai'i becoming the 50th state in 1959, with Honolulu as its capital. With the decline of the sugar industry, Kaua'i's main industry today is tourism.

Kaua'i: Key Facts

LOCATION	Lihue: Longitude 21°59' N, latitude 159°22' W
SIZE	550 square miles/1,425 square kilometers
HIGHEST POINT	Mt. Kawaikini (5,243 feet)
POPULATION	58,303 (2000 Census)
TIME	Hawaii Standard (year-round): 2 hours behind LA, 5 hours behind New York, 10 hours behind London

AREA CODE	808
AIRPORTS	Lihu'e Airport, Princeville Airport
MAIN TOURIST AREAS	Coconut Coast, Hanlei/Princeville, and Po'ipu
TOURISM INFO	Kaua'i Visitors Bureau
	4334 Rice Street, Suite 101
	Lihu'e, HI 96766
	Local: 808-245-3971, fax 808-246-9235
	Web site: www.kauaivisitorsbureau.org

Focus on Kaua'i: Nature

The natural splendors of Kaua'i are wonderfully accessible to the visitor, be it by foot, boat, car, horseback, or helicopter. Experiencing nature is a must for any stay in Kaua'i, and the options are so many that there is no excuse not to venture out. Whatever you decide, a helicopter tour is highly recommended (see the Helicopter Tours section, below).

There are three major state parks on the island: Na Pali, Waimea Canyon, and Koke'e. All offer excellent hiking opportunities. Na Pali is almost an environmental opposite of Waimea Canyon and Koke'e. Na Pali is a rugged, mountainous coastline with numerous valleys and beaches. Waimea Canyon and Koke'e combined are like a miniature Grand Canyon. Na Pali gets lots of rain, the latter two very little. We strongly suggest seeing all.

The Na Pali Coast

This is the premier wilderness experience in Hawai'i. Tucked away on the northwest coast of Kaua'i, it is made up of five valleys of rugged, fluted *pali*. The area is so stunning that the term "God's country," however clichéd, aptly describes this setting. It is beyond spectacular.

The Na Pali coast begins where the road (Route 560) ends, at Ha'ena Beach Park, and extends to the sand dunes of Polihale and Barking Sands. All of this beauty is now owned by the state and is, thankfully, a state park. There are no roads; the precipitous terrain

precludes that possibility. There is only one path, the Kalalau Trail, which follows an ancient Hawai'ian trail. Built in the 1800s and consisting of 11 miles of uphills and downhills, the Kalalau Trail is frequently muddy and meets the ocean only twice, at Hanakapi'ai Beach and at Kalalau. The trail starts at Ke'e and ends abruptly at Kalalau. The valley's sheer vertical and magnificent *pali* prevent travel farther down this wild coastline. The entire hike is considered strenuous due to both its length and the unpredictability of the weather and trail conditions. Once you are there, the rewards are incredibly satisfying. If you are thinking about hiking, be prepared to rough it. And if you don't mind slumming it with nature, this *is* paradise.

There are several ways to appreciate this beauty, depending on just how adventurous you want to be. You can hike partway or the whole 11 miles, you can Zodiac (be transported by large motorized inflatable rafts) in and out, Zodiac in and hike out, or you can helicopter over, see it all, and go back to the comfort of your hotel or condo in a fraction of the time.

Hiking the Na Pali Coast

If you are going to hike, the trail is divided into three parts: Ke'e to Hanakapi'ai, Hanakapi'ai to Hanakoa, and Hanakoa to Kalalau. The entire hike, if you're in good shape and are wearing good hiking shoes, will take you between five and six hours, with a few brief stops. Obviously it will take you all day if you take your time and go easy, so plan accordingly, and make sure that weather and daylight are in your favor.

If you have no intention of hiking all the way to Kalalau, the first section, Ke'e to Hanakapi'ai, is ideal for a day-trip. It will take you about an hour to hike the two miles in and another hour to hike the distance back. It's not hard, but it will take you up and down terrain that will make you sweat. The trail will bring you to a lovely though not very secluded beach (see the Beaches section, below) and will get you back in plenty of time to play a few sets of tennis or make happy hour at Bamboo Bamboo in Hanalei. If it has been raining at all, the trail will be muddy, so leave your brand-new Tevas or Nikes in the hotel room. Along the way, you will pass all kinds of leafy green vegetation: palms, *hale* trees, Chinese ivy, fiddlehead ferns, and much more. You will also notice that there are two kinds of hikers: the serious hikers, who will have backpacks and that granola-and-grass look about them; and the day-trippers (many of them honeymooners – you know what they look like). If you don't feel like hiking to Hanakapi'ai, then the first half mile of the trail (about 10 to 15 minutes from the trailhead) will give you some of the best views of the entire Kalalau Trail—great visuals with little hassle. Now that's not asking too much, is it?

Past Hanakapi'ai, the hike becomes much tougher, with four miles of switchbacks climbing to the elevated Hanakoa Valley (800 feet above sea level). You will walk through the Hono'onapali Natural Area, which contains the two smallest "hanging valleys" of the park. A stream cuts through the Hanakoa Valley, where a camping area on abandoned farming terraces offers relief for those who feel the next and longest section can wait until tomorrow. The biting bugs here, especially the mosquitoes, can be ferocious. Be sure to bring strong repellent.

The final section is five miles long and brings you down to Kalalau beach (see the Beaches section). It is drier here; the rainfall in each valley diminishes as you travel south, to the point where ten miles can mean a difference of 100 inches in annual rainfall. The land opens up to stunning vistas, affording views of the magnificent gothic-looking peaks of the Kalalau Valley, and unfortunately little relief from the sun and heat. Just before the trail descends into the valley, there is a great spot to rest and enjoy the expansiveness of this side of paradise. The valley itself is two miles deep and one mile wide, and is the largest of the Na Pali valleys. For over 1,000 years this valley was an isolated and thriving community of *taro* farmers, communicating and trading only with their coastal neighbors by means of canoes. The last of the original inhabitants, who left in 1919, lived in thatched *hales*, growing *taro* and fishing with nets just as their ancestors had done. For a number of years after that, the valley was used for cattle ranching, but the government found that the cattle were damaging to the ecosystems. In the '60s, facing an onslaught of hippies and squatters, the government was forced to take action to protect the land and thus created the Na Pali Coast State Park.

KAUA'I

If you're just not into hiking all that way, there are other ways to see Kalalau. Rather than hike the 11-mile trail twice, why not Zodiac in (see below) and walk out? first, you get to see and experience the Na Pali coast from two perspectives—land and sea. Second, your backpack will be lighter walking out, as most edible supplies will gradually be used up. Third, you'll have a comfortable bed, a hot shower, and hopefully a Jacuzzi waiting for you at the end of the trail to soothe those positively aching muscles. Some people like to do the reverse—walk in and Zodiac out—so they will have walked to this magical place, its majestic peaks getting closer with each mile. We think the first choice probably makes more sense.

Want to do it? Then here is what you should do. Contact the Department of Land and Natural Resources well in advance of your arrival to reserve space. Specify the Na Pali coast, the dates, the number of people and their names (those under 18 must be accompanied by an adult). You are limited to five days of camping for each 30-day period; in addition, no two consecutive nights are allowed at Hanakapi'ai and Hanakoa. If you are planning a day hike beyond Hanakapi'ai, you will also need a day-hike permit. The address and phone number are as follows:

Department of Land and Natural Resources
Division of State Parks, Outdoor Recreation and Historic Sites
3060 Eiwa Street, Room 306
Lihu'e, HI 96766
Local: 808-274-3444
Web site: www.hawaii.gov/dlnr/Welcome.html

Upon arrival on Kaua'i, you and your party will have to stop by the Department's Lihu'e office in person to obtain your permit, which is free. (They will be charging for permits in the near future; the cost will be $10 per person.) The office is open Monday through Friday (except holidays), 8 A.M. to 4 P.M. Make sure you have proper ID. You can get permits by mail if you photocopy everyone's ID and make sure that the department receives them at least seven days before your departure for Kaua'i.

Official business done, you'll need some equipment. Serious backpackers, BYOB (bring your own backpack). But those who'd rather arrive with Tumi luggage may prefer to rent equipment. There are a couple of outfitters in Hanalei that have most of the gear you will need: Pedal & Paddle, Ching Young Village, Hanalei, HI 96714, 808-826-9069. Located in the Ching Young Village shopping center, P&P has tents, daypacks, backpacks, camp stoves, coolers, water-treatment tablets, and poncho blankets for rent. It also has a camping and hiking info center, maps, freeze-dried food, and other groovy paraphernalia for the hiking set. It's open daily from 9 A.M. to 5 P.M. There is also Kayak Kaua'i, in Hanalei, 808-822-9179. They have pretty much the same as Pedal & Paddle, minus the food supplies.

Remember that you'll be carrying everything—no porters here. So come prepared, but travel as light as possible. Food can be bought at the Foodland Supermarket in Princeville, the Big Save in Hanalei, and the Hanalei Natural Foods in the Ching Young Center. Check the weather conditions and forecast. Being caught for five days in a severe storm is not a great idea.

The Na Pali Coast by Boat

Those of you who will have nothing to do with muddy shoes, sweat, and bugs may want to consider a day-trip by boat, one of the most popular ways to see the Na Pali coastline. Sailboats, Zodiacs (huge inflatable, hard-bottomed rubber rafts with big twin outboards), high-speed catamarans, and other powerboats make this trip—usually during the calmer months of May to September and occasionally during the rest of the year (depending on sea conditions). Keep in mind that even the biggest boat will rock. Those with motion issues (we remember an ex who would hurl with the slightest bounce) should forego a water tour or take motion meds and opt for the power catamaran (less bouncy).

While we *love* sailboats and are very much sailors at heart, you may want to opt for a Zodiac when the seas are calm and the swell is minimal (generally in summer), because they can cruise close to shore. This can be fun as you go through lava arches and into huge caverns of lava rock sculpted by eons of surf. Zodiacs usually accommodate 16 passengers, plus the guides. The guides can be a mishmash of help and hindrance—they run the gamut from enter-

taining and articulate to annoying and not particularly knowledge-able. The trip will last five to six hours, depending on the seas. It can be the bumpiest ride, as Zodiacs are light and you sit on the pontoons. Pregnant women and those with back/neck problems are discouraged from making the voyage. The crew provides foul-weather gear, which is often wet and mildewed on the inside when you put it on—not a nice feeling. When we took this excursion, it poured like there was no tomorrow and everyone got drenched—and we mean soaked to the bone. But in retrospect, it was worth it, although we *certainly* didn't feel that way at the time. So anything can happen. Pray for a sunny, dry, calm day.

Most vessels used to depart from the Hanalei/Ha'ena area, but a swirling controversy pitting environmentalists against tour compa-nies ended with a governor's edict, which is still in effect. Now most of these boats leave from the South Shore, which is a drag, as the North Shore scenery is much prettier and the trip from there is shorter, too. However, there are still some boats that have permits to leave from the North Shore. If you do take the Zodiac, be sure to sit toward the stern (back) for a smoother and drier ride. From the Coconut Coast or the North Shore, sit on the starboard (right) side going out and the port (left) side going back so you face the coast each way. Do the opposite from the South Shore. Besides being incredibly scenic, this perspective gives your eyes something steady to focus on and will help motion-sensitive individuals from getting seasick.

Captain Zodiac, the originator of Zodiacking on Kaua'i, goes to Nu'alolo Kai State Park, a small *pali*-shrouded valley where rem-nants of a Hawai'ian community still exist. This is an interesting and secluded destination that's accessible only by boat, but it's not nearly as beautiful or serene as Kalalau. Still, the snorkeling is quite good on an extensive reef when the water visibility is clear. There is a historic trail but it is so overgrown that you can hardly see anything, let alone go from one end to the other. To see a bit of the ruins, walk down the beach to the wall with the big "X" on it—a freak of nature that the Hawai'ians took as a "no trespassing" sign from the gods—and you will see the foundations of some Hawai'ian dwellings, built next to the cliff for protection from the wind and rain. Lunch—a sandwich-and-potato-chip-type affair—is served here on some picnic tables. There is an outhouse *sans* door—for a better view of the flora and fauna. If the trade winds are up, the voyage home can be very wet. Again, be sure to sit in the aft (rear) section of the vessel unless you want to get soaked and shaken.

All boats totally pause for photo op's and historical or informative chats about what you are seeing. While boats are not permitted to land at Kalalau beach except to pick up and drop off passengers, some stop at the beaches and valleys to the west.

These outfits operate trips and are based in Hanalei, Port Allen, or Hanapepe.

Zodiacs

Captain Zodiac/Kaua'i Zodiac Inc., P.O. Box 456, Hanalei, HI 96714. Toll-free: 800-422-7824. Local: 808-826-9371/9192. Web site: www.planet-hawaii.com/zodiac

This is the original, and with that distinction comes a lot of experience and know-how. The Hanalei squabble (see above) has curtailed this outfit's business out of Hanalei Bay; trips now depart from the Coconut Coast. The operation is well run and well organized, and the trips run Monday through Friday (there is talk of running trips on Saturday), weather and sea conditions permitting. During the winter months, when conditions are too rough for the long trip, Kaua'i Zodiac runs whale-watch excursions and trips to deserted Kipukai Beach on the southeastern coast.

While we found some of the guides to be a tad deficient intellectually, they are quite competent in making the journey safely. And although the lunches are somewhat lacking in style, the tour itself is well worth it. There is currently only one option to Na Pali—a six- to six-and-a-half-hour trip, including snorkeling and lunch at Nu'alolo Kai. The cost is $150/adult and $125/child aged 4 to 12. Trips depart at 9 A.M. and return between 3 and 4 P.M. Snorkeling and damp foul-weather gear are provided. Reservations are a must.

Kaua'i Z – Tour Z, P.O. Box 1082, Kalaheo, HI 96741. Local: 808-742-6331, fax 808-332-9177. Web site: www.ztourz.com E-mail: ztourz@hawaiian.net

Kaua'i Z offers a trip to the Na Pali Coast on a 24-foot Zodiac that holds 16 people. Departure is from Kikiaola Harbor in Waimea. The tour lasts about five hours and covers all 17 miles of the Na Pali coastline. You will visit sea caves, waterfalls, snorkel at Nu'alolo Kai reef, and enjoy a deli-style lunch. The cost is $120/adult and $90/child aged 4 to 12. There are two departure times, 6 A.M. and 12 noon.

Na Pali Explorer, 9935 Kaunuali'i Highway, Waimea, HI 96796. Toll-free: 877-338-000. Local: 808-338-9999.
Web site: www.napali-explorer.com
Na Pali Explorer offers two trips to the Na Pali coastline aboard their 48-foot RIB (rigid inflatable boat). The Na Pali Snorkel Expedition leaves from Port Allen at 8 A.M. and consists of a trip up the entire Na Pali coast, with a stop at Nu'alolo Kai, where you will land on the beach, and possibly snorkel. The trip includes breakfast, deli-style lunch, and snacks, lasts about five hours, and costs $132/adult and $72/child. A second trip leaves at 2 P.M. There is no snorkeling on the late trip, and only snacks and beverages are provided. The cost is $77/adult and $44/child.

Power Catamarans

Napali Catamarans, P.O. Box 927, Hanalei, HI 96714. Local: 808-826-6853.
Web site: www.napalicatamarans.com
Departing from Hanalei Bay, Napali Catamarans offers a four-hour, 15-mile trip along the Na Pali coast on a 32-foot double-hulled catamaran that holds 15 passengers. The trip includes lunch and snorkeling. It runs Monday through Saturday, from 8 A.M. to 12 noon, and another from 12:30 to 4:30 P.M., and costs $125 per person.

Na Pali Coast Hanalei, P.O. Box 927, Hanalei, HI 96714. Local: 808-826-6114.
Web site: www.napalicoasttours.net
Na Pali Coast offers a three- to four-hour trip along 15 miles of the Na Pali coast. A light lunch and snorkeling gear are provided.

Departures are from Hanalei Bay at 8:30 A.M. or 1:30 P.M. Their boat, named the *U.F.O.*, is a 28-foot catamaran and holds 13 people. The cost is $120/adult and $90/child aged 4 to 11.

Liko Kaua'i Cruises, Inc., 9875 Waimea Road, (P.O. Box 18), Waimea, HI 96796. Toll-free: 888-SEA-LIKO (732-5456). Local: 808-338-0333, fax 808-337-1544.
Web site: www.liko-kauai.com
Departing from Kekaha, Liko Kaua'i runs a 49-foot power catamaran. They offer two trips a day to the Na Pali coast, at 7:30 A.M. and 12 noon. Both trips include a deli-style lunch, soft drinks, and snorkeling gear. The trips last about four hours each. The cost is $95/adult and $65/child aged 4 to 14. They also offer a sunset cruise featuring appetizers and nonalcoholic refreshments. Departure time is 4 P.M. and the cost is $45/person.

Captain Andy's Sailing Adventures, P.O. Box 876, Ele'ele, HI 96705. Local: 808-335-6833.
Web site: www.capt-andys.com
E-mail: fun@sailing-hawaii.com
Aboard the 65-foot catamaran *Spirit of Kaua'i,* the Ultimate Na Pali Coast Excursion leaves Port Allen at 8 A.M. While enjoying a gourmet breakfast, you will power up the Na Pali coast, hopefully catching sight of dolphins, and anchor for a catered lunch by Gaylords. Plenty of time for some great photo op's. State-of-the-art snorkeling gear and instruction will give you a chance to explore the reefs along the Na Pali coast. The trip runs until about 2:30 P.M. Cost is $139/adult and $99/child aged 7 to 12. They offer other trips like the Snorkeling/Barbecue which also includes breakfast and lunch, for a bit less that the Ultimate Excursion.

Sailboats

Captain Sundown, P.O. Box 697, Hanalei, HI 96714. Local: 808-826-5585, fax 808-826-5196.
Web site: www.captainsundown.com
E-mail: sundown@aloha.net
Using a 40-foot cat (short for catamaran), Captain Sundown

conducts a six-hour sail that departs at 9 A.M. from Hanalei Bay. You will have to paddle 200 yards out to the mooring in a Hawai'ian outrigger canoe, then sail along the north shore to the Na Pali coast and the snorkeling destination of Nu'alolo Kai. Cost is $135/person and includes lunch and snorkeling. Limited to 15 passengers.

Bluewater Sailing, P.O. Box 1318, Hanalei, HI 96714. Local: 808-828-1142, fax 808-828-0508.
Web site: www.sail-kauai.com
E-mail: bluwat@aloha.net
Departing from Hanalei Bay aboard a 42-foot Pearson Ketchrigger yacht named the *Lady Leanne II,* you will sail offshore for four to five miles off the north coast of Kaua'i, anchoring for lunch and some great snorkeling in a quiet cove. Summer departures are from Hanalei Bay, winter from Port Allen. The yacht carries 15 passengers. The trip lasts about half a day and cost $105/adult, $85/child aged 5 to 12.

Blue Dolphin, P.O. Box 869, Ele'ele, HI 96705. Toll-free: 877-511-1311. Local: 808-335-5553.
Web site: www.bluedophincharters.com
Sailing aboard a 62-foot catamaran or a 56-foot trimaran, you can take a five- to six-hour snorkeling/scuba trip up the Na Pali coast. The vessels carry a maximum of 49 passengers, though they are allowed to carry 98. The trip includes a continental breakfast, full deli-style lunch, and plenty of *pupus*. They also offer an assortment of beer, wine, and Mai Tais. Departure is from Port Allen at either 8 A.M. or 1:30 P.M. The cost is $109/adult for snorkeling, $134/adult for scuba diving, and $89/child aged 2 to 11. They also offer other trips to different parts of the island.

Waimea Canyon

Although only a few miles apart, the difference between the Na Pali coast and Waimea Canyon is like night and day. Reminiscent of Arizona and dubbed the "Grand Canyon of the Pacific" by Mark Twain, Waimea Canyon features the same stunning red and ochre that you'd see in Sedona but with the added contrast of the lush greens on the shaded valley floors. It's also hard to believe that just a few miles east of here is one of the wettest spots on earth, Mt. Wai'ale'ale. Such is the contrast of the "Garden Isle" of Kaua'i.

No trip to the island is complete without a visit to the canyon; it really *is* wondrous. If you decide to take a chopper ride (see the Helicopter Tours section, below), then you will definitely see it up close. If you don't, or if you just want to spend time at the canyon rim contemplating your next career move, impending divorce, or previous lives, you should definitely make the drive. There are several pull-offs along the way where you can carefully walk to the edge and sit, picnic, or whatever. Avoid the designated lookouts— where the tour buses stop and unload. Try to see it in the late afternoon, after the crowds have gone, when the light kicks beautiful shadows on the canyon walls. The tropical twilight in the canyon is magical. Even better: stay in one of the rustic and very cheap cabins at the Koke'e Lodge (see Where to Stay, below).

Hiking in Waimea Canyon

For the hiking enthusiast, there are miles of trails—45, in fact—in the canyon and Koke'e State Park. Some trails take you inside the canyon, some along the rim, and some to the edge of the Na Pali coast. Trail maps are available at the Koke'e Lodge Museum.

Probably the best hike starts just up the first dirt road on the right past the Koke'e State Park Headquarters, where you can park at the trailhead of the Kumuwela Trail. After walking just under a mile (eight tenths, to be exact), you will come upon Kumuwela Road. Turn right; in about a quarter of a mile you will bear right. This will take you to the Kumuwela Lookout, where the view runs right down through the canyon to the ocean. From here, the incredibly scenic Canyon Trail (1.4 miles) takes you along the canyon rim. You will cross the Koke'e Stream at the 800-foot Waipo'o Falls. After the falls, you can either take the short Cliff Trail spur (one tenth of a mile) to the Cliff Lookout or bypass it on the Black Pipe Trail (four tenths of a mile). The former will serve up more or less the same view that you've already been seeing on the Canyon Trail. The latter will take you through a *koa* forest with native hibiscus and *ili'au* plants. Both trails will connect you to a dirt road that leads to the Halemanu-Koke'e Trail (1.2 miles). This will bring you back through forests to the starting point. The entire hike should take you a leisurely three-and-a-half to four hours.

Another really gorgeous hike is the Awa'awapuhi Trail. About a six-and-a-half-mile round-trip with a vertical descent of almost 1,500 feet, it is a lot more strenuous than the Canyon Trail (especially on the way back). However, at the end of the trail you will be rewarded with a truly extraordinary vista of the Na Pali coast. The trail takes you along a densely forested ridge where the view doesn't open until the very end. But what a sight then—well worth the wait.

If you are into bird-watching, the Pihea Trail (past the Pu'u O Kila Lookout) is a favorite secret of the Audubon Society. Another pleasant nature hike through forests of redwood, *lehua*, *sugi* pine, and *koa* can be found on the Pu'u Kaohelo and Berry Flats Trails (two miles).

Helicopter Tours

In general, we are opposed to sightseeing in helicopters. They are so disruptive to nature's serenity that it makes us crazy. There's nothing worse than hiking hours into the wilderness—sweating, muddied, sore—in hopes of escaping man and machine only to have a chopper swoop down out of the sky in *Apocalypse Now* fashion, with a roar that would wake the dead. Whatever peace you were enjoying is shattered by the deafening noise. And it's not just one chopper, it's one chopper every 20 minutes. At popular sights like Na Pali, there are often more than one at a time. When you're on the ground and not in the air, it's fist-shaking time at what is jokingly called the Hawai'ian state bird.

However, we must reluctantly admit that when we finally broke down and consented to go on a helicopter tour of Kaua'i, the experience was beyond incredible—it was actually one of the high points of our stay in Hawai'i. So here's a real dilemma: to go or not to go. There are good arguments on both sides. On the one hand, we relish the peace and quiet of a pristine valley. On the other hand, the ability to see places that we would not have been able to see any other way tipped the scales. Ultimately, of course, the decision rests with you.

Let us describe your average chopper experience. Begin by demanding the front seat(s) next to the pilot. Depending on your weight, cockiness, and VIP status (as travel writers, we were given the latter), you may be able to luck out and be assigned a front seat. This is important because it allows you to see what's ahead as well as what is on your side. The worst seat is in the middle of the back, where you have to lean over a passenger to peer out the window. Wait for the next flight, if that is the case (or raise holy hell).

Once you've strapped yourself in, you don a headset that blocks out almost all sound, obliterating the din of the rotors and delivering the soundtrack for your trip, with your pilot acting as dj/tour guide. On our last flight with Will Squyres, the music was a little too Kenny G-ish for our taste, so we just tried to focus on the scenery. We've found that the musical selection varies with the companies and the pilot's own preference. Also, some pilots chatter nonstop, especially about where certain movies were filmed, which we find very tiresome. Inquire about pilot banter and music when booking. Ask for a less chatty pilot and for one who changes the music manually rather than using a preprogrammed tape. On our first helicopter tour back in the '80s, the music was awesome and the pilot—with a narrator's voice that sounded like a National Geographic special—didn't talk too much. His music selection was a combo of great epic pieces from Beethoven to Emerson, Lake, and Palmer, which made the 70-minute flight an audiovisual extravaganza. What amazed us was how the pilot could fly the bird and change tapes at just the right moment, so that when we flew out of the Waimea Canyon and over the ridge that sweeps down into the awesome Kalalau Valley, the eerie horns and strings of Richard Strauss's *Also Sprach Zarathustra* reached their crescendo as the valley came into view. The effect, even to jaded cynics like us, was mind-blowing. It was one of those moments that we wanted to freeze forever.

Anyway, after getting used to being in a helicopter again—which took us about two minutes—we relaxed and enjoyed the show. Leaving from Lihu'e airport (some companies offer departures from other parts of the island), the flight will take you over the

Mehehune (Alakoki) fishpond and the Hoary Head Ridge to the Hanapepe River valley, with so many waterfalls that you could use up all of your memory card. Don't—the best is yet to come. The pilot will "stop" the helicopter so you can take pictures and then turn it around so the people on the other side of the chopper will get a good view. Then from lush vegetation to the red canyon country, you travel over Alaka'i Wilderness Preserve (one of the largest highland swamps anywhere) and Koke'e State Park to Waimea Canyon. After hovering just off the canyon walls for a few minutes, marveling at the awesome vista, it's off you go to the Kalalau Valley. On the way, you fly over the Robinson family's hunting lodge. (The family owns Ni'ihau Island and 10 percent of Kaua'i too—now that's *owning* real estate!) As the music builds and you can't help but think of the monolith from the movie 2001: A *Space Odyssey*, the Kalalau Valley looms before you. Oh, what a feeling! And what a sight—the majestic green gothic peaks of the Kalalau Valley glowing in the afternoon sunlight.

It's about this time that the hikers who have schlepped the 11 miles into the valley look up from the beach and raise their fists. Those damn choppers, man. Here's that dilemma again. My suggestion is this: helicopters should avoid Kalalau (and many do), as there are so many other inaccessible valleys to explore. That would leave the hikers to their peace and quiet and would make possession of the valley their reward for hiking in. Fortunately most pilots are considerate, keeping their distance from the beach and avoiding flying overhead; unfortunately some aren't.

Leaving Kalalau, you fly into the smaller, inaccessible valleys, including the Valley of the Lost Tribe (a.k.a. 'Nu'alolo 'Aina—your pilot will explain its name to you) and the tiny Awa'awapuhi Valley. These are narrow and mysterious places, with remnants of old Hawai'ian homes and *taro* terraces serving as a reminder of the close and ancient relationship Hawai'ians have with their land.

By now you are beginning to slightly OD on the megadose of beauty you've been seeing, and you just want to stop for a minute and talk about it. But the whirlybird just skips down the Na Pali coast, stopping at sea-level lava arches and the spot where they filmed Jessica Lange in *King Kong* (Dino DeLaurentis's remake of the classic gorilla movie). Then come the beaches of the North

Shore, including Tunnels, Lumaha'i, and Hanalei Bay. It's common to see rainbows here. Again, scenic overload. You turn inland here and pass over the *taro* fields of the Hanalei Valley, the intensity of green getting more brilliant with every mile. By now you're headed to the innards of Mt. Wai'ale'ale, considered one of the wettest spots on earth. It is also one of the high points of this voyage. Mt. Wai'ale'ale is an extinct volcano with a collapsed face (age will do that to anyone), so you can fly right into the crater. As the mountain is one of the highest points on Kaua'i (5,148 feet), it is almost always in the clouds. flying into the crater is an extraordinarily ethereal experience. We've never been in a place like this before. Imagine a huge oval, steep-sided cavern that is open at the top and shrouded in mist. Water cascades down its flanks like hundreds of pearl strands. Surrounded by waterfalls, you feel like you're in the earth's womb. For this sensation alone, the helicopter ride is definitely worth it.

After flying out of the crater, your senses are so buzzed that you are approaching catatonia, and that music (or pilot chitchat) just won't quit. The rest of the trip is not as exciting, as you fly over Wailua and back to Lihu'e, although *Fantasy Island* fans (are there any?) will recognize the Wailua Falls from the show's opening credits. When you're finally back on your feet and out from under the rotors, you'll find yourself mouthing clichés about how beautiful everything was. Then, after the helicopter has refueled, the next group hops on, and off they go.

Well, have we encouraged you? Probably. But you've got to have a conscience about this before you go, and then maybe write a letter to the governor afterward, saying that helicopters should be restricted to areas inaccessible to man, so that both hikers and heli-sightseers can enjoy the environment without antagonism.

There are several outfits on Kaua'i that can take you up, up, and away. As helicopters are highly tuned machines and flying them requires a lot of expertise, especially above Kaua'i, safety should be a major factor in choosing a tour. Select a company that carries a Federal Aviation Regulation Part 135 certificate from the FAA–the most stringent maintenance and qualification program available. Make sure this covers the company, the helicopters, and the pilots. The FAA Part 135 certificate also allows qualified pilots to travel

beyond 25 miles from their departure point. As a number of the scenic attractions are beyond 25 miles, this is very important. At press time, these companies passed this muster: Will Squyres, Jack Harter, 'Ohana, Air Kaua'i, and Island Helicopters.

Tour prices are on the high side due to the understandably outrageous cost of operating a fleet of passenger helicopters. Just imagine the insurance premiums! Tours will run between $100 and $250, depending on the outfit and the length of your trip. Opt for the longest or grandest tour available, even though it costs more, as the island demands at least an hour in the air to see it properly. Check out discount coupons and/or activity brokers, as both can lead to significant dollars off. However, be sure that the trip is with a reputable company and at least 75 minutes long.

Helicopter Tour Operators

Will Squyres Helicopter Tours, P.O. Box 1770, Lihu'e, Kaua'i, HI 96766. Toll-free: 888-245-4354. Local: 808-245-8881.
Web site: www.helicopters-hawaii.com
E-mail: squyres@aloha.net

Will Squyres uses a six-passenger American Eurocopter ASTAR 350 with custom bubble windows for maximum viewing. Will Squyres is FAA Part 135 certified and they have a perfect flying record. All flights depart from Lihu'e Airport daily, starting at 8 A.M. with the last flight at 4:45 P.M. Their grand tour, Kauai Grandeur, costs $149/person and lasts 55 to 60 minutes.

Jack Harter Helicopters, P.O. Box 306, Lihu'e, HI 96766. Toll-free: 888-245-2001. Local: 808-245-3774.
Web site: www.helicopters-Kauai.com
E-mail: jharter@aloha.net

Jack Harter has two helicopters, a four-passenger Bell Jet Ranger and a six-passenger Eurocopter ASTAR 350. The Bell Jet has large openable windows, which are great for picture taking. Jack Harter is FAA Part 135 certified and they have had a perfect flying record for 37 years. Due to their great safety record they are also allowed to fly down to 500 feet above sea level. Their special feature is a two-way headphone-intercom system—great for asking all those ques-

RUM & REGGAE'S HAWAI'I

tions or telling the pilot to stop in midair so you can take pictures. Jack Harter offers two trips, the 55-to-60-minute trip for $165/person or the 90-to-95-minute trip for $235. Jack Harter is the only helicopter company that offers a tour of this length. You will fly at lower speeds, go deeper into the valleys and canyons, and make more turns, setting up incredible photo op's, than with the other outfits. It's well worth the extra money.

Air Kaua'i, 3651 Ahukini Road, Lihu'e, HI 96766. Toll-free: 800-972-4666. Local: 808-246-4666, fax 808-246-0101.
Web site: www.airkauai.com
E-mail: info@airkauai.com
Air Kaua'i utilizes the six-passenger Eurocopter ASTAR 350, featuring special almost-floor-to-ceiling glass windows, air conditioning, and the unique Bose Acoustic Noise Cancellation Stereo Headset with two-way communication. They are also FAA Part 135 certified and have a perfect flying record. They depart from Lihu'e Airport starting at 8:45 A.M., with the last flight at 5 P.M. Their deluxe tour cost $195/person.

'Ohana Helicopter Tours, 3222 Kuhio Highway, Suite 4, Lihu'e, HI 96766. Toll-free: 800-222-6989. Local: 808-245-3996, fax 808-245-5041.
Web site: www.ohana-helicopters.com
E-mail: info@ohana-helicopters.com
'Ohana Helicopter Tours utilizes the Eurocopter ASTAR 350. They are FAA Part 135 certified. Their grand tour, called the Maile Tour, costs $186/person and runs for 65 to 70 minutes.

Island Helicopters Kaua'i, P.O. Box 831, Lihu'e, HI 96766. Toll-free: 800-829-5999. Local: 808-245-8588, fax 808-245-6258.
Web site: www.islandhelicopters.com
E-mail: fly@islandhelicopters.com
Island Helicopters flies both the Bell Jet Ranger III and the Eurostar ASTAR 350. Both are equipped with state-of-the-art CD stereo systems and two-way radio communication. Island Helicopters is FAA Part 135 certified and has had a perfect flying record for the past 21 years. Their Kauai Grand Deluxe Tour costs $196.50/

314

person and takes 55 to 60 minutes. As a bonus you get a free video-tape of their standard trip (one per person or couple).

Hawai'i Helicopters, Princeville Airport, Princeville, HI 96714. Toll-free: 800-994-9099. Local: 808-826-6591.
Web site: www.hawaii-helicopters.com
Hawai'i Helicopters is one of the few companies that fly from Princeville. Their Garden Isle Deluxe Tour costs $179/person for a 60-minute flight. Departure times start at 8 A.M. and the last flight is at 5 P.M. Hawai'i Helicopters is FAA Part 135 certified.

Ni'ihau Helicopters, P.O. Box 370, Makaweli, HI 96769. Local: 808-335-3500, fax 808-338-1463.
Here's one of the very few opportunities to see—and actually set foot on—unspoiled and undeveloped Ni'ihau. This is more of a cerebral trip than audiovisual entertainment. There are tours with one or two stops on remote parts of the island, and also one that includes Ni'ihau and the Na Pali coast. Prices range from $338/person in a group of four to $250/person in a group of six. A private charter costs about $1,350 per hour. The tour last about three hours: one hour of flying time and two hours exploring the beaches, snorkeling, swimming, or just enjoying your time on the island.

Horseback Riding
Itching to get in the saddle? Five stables on Kaua'i cater to the traveler. There are stables at three resort areas. Here are the choices:

The North Shore

Princeville Ranch Stables (Po'oku Stables, Inc.), P.O. Box 888, Hanalei, HI 96714. Local: 808-826-6777 or 826-7473, fax 808-826-7210.
Web site: www.kauai.net/kwc4
E-mail: pstable@aloha.net
Founded in 1978 and originally called Po'oku Stables, Princeville Ranch Stables is located on the North Shore between the Princeville Resort and the airport. They feature private rides and horsemanship programs (two to three hours for $115 to $160/per-

son), as well as waterfall picnic rides (four hours for $110/person), Anini Bluff/Beach rides (three hours for $100/person), country rides (one and a half hours for $55/person), and cattle drive rides (about two hours for $125/person). If you're visiting in summer, check out the Hanalei Stampede, one of the biggest rodeos in the state.

Silver Falls Ranch, P.O. Box 692, Kilauea, HI 96754. Local: 808-828-6718, fax 808-828-2829.
Web site: www.hawaiian.net/~sfr/
E-mail: sfr@hawaiian.net
Featuring quarter horses, the ranch is located in Kilauea at the foot of Mt. Namahana. Silver Ranch offers private lessons and rides by appointment. Group rides include the Greenhorns' Trail Ride for beginners (one and a half hours for $60/person), a Hawai'ian Discovery Ride (two hours for $75/person), and the Silver Falls Ride, which includes swimming and a picnic (three hours for $99/person).

The Coconut Coast

Esprit de Corps Riding Academy, P.O. Box 269, Kapa'a, HI 96746. Local/fax: 808-822-4688.
Web site: www.kauaihorses.com
E-mail: riding@kauaihorses.com
Besides private rides and riding lessons (30 to 60 minutes for $35 to $55/person), this stable offers something a little different than the normal trail ride. The Fast Half Ride is mainly trotting and cantering (three hours for $99/person). We like that! Other rides are the Wow Ride, offering increasingly better views during the five-hour journey ($250/person), and the All Day Adventure Ride, which is the Wow Ride plus a stop at a mountain swimming hole with lunch (eight hours for $300 to $350/person).

Keapana Horsemanship, 5648 Keapana, Kapa'a, HI 96746. Local: 808-823-9303.
Web site: www.keapana.com/horse.htm
Offering private lessons, Western and English tack, flexible departure times, and rides with all gaits, this stable conducts rides

through the Keapana Valley. Prices are $50/hour, $100/two hours, and $165/three or more hours.

Po'ipu

CJM Country Stables, 1731 Kelaukia Street, Koloa, HI 96756. Local: 808-742-6096, fax 808-742-6015.
Web site: www.cjmstables.com
E-mail: cjm@aloha.net

Located on the South Shore and convenient to those staying in the Po'ipu area, CJM conducts three types of rides daily, usually into the Maha'ulepu Valley area. The Secret Beach Breakfast Ride lasts three hours and includes an hour stop on a beach for continental breakfast ($75/person); the Hidden Beach Ride goes through ranch land and shoreline and lasts two hours ($65/person); and the Beach, Swim, Picnic Ride lasts almost four hours–one and a half hours on horseback–and includes a deli-style lunch ($90/person). Instruction is also available.

Biking

If you're a serious biker, Kaua'i offers a coastal two-lane road with wide shoulders, good for cyclists. This is also the major highway, however, so there will always be lots of cars. You cannot circumnavigate the island, as the road is interrupted by the Na Pali coast. If you land in Lihu'e and intend to bike the island, you will be situated almost exactly in the middle of the island's highway and will have to backtrack both ways. To compound this, the interior of the island is virtually inaccessible to bikers, with the exception of Waimea Canyon, a grueling but scenic uphill climb to 4,000 feet above sea level and the Koke'e Lodge. Kaua'i Coasters offers a downhill ride from the top of the canyon to the coast, lasting four hours.

The North Shore

Pedal & Paddle, P.O. Box 1413, Ching Young Village, Hanalei, HI 96714. Local: 808-826-9069.
Web site: www.pedalnpaddle.com

Bike and boat rentals are available here for those staying on the

North Shore. They have single-speed beach cruisers for $10 a day/$30 a week, tandem bikes for $10 a hour/$5 each additional hour, and Kona mountain bikes for $20 a day/$80 per week. All bikes come with helmet and locks at no extra charge. Open daily from 9 A.M. to 5 P.M.

The Coconut Coast

Kaua'i Cycle and Tour, 1379 Kuhio Highway, Kapa'a, HI 96746. Local: 808-821-2115, fax 808-821-0385.
Web site: www.bikehawaii.com/kauaicycle
 This outfit offers 24-hour mountain bike rentals for $20 and info on where to ride. Kaua'i Cycle also conducts a Blue Hole Tour to the interior, near the Mt. Wai'ale'ale crater, which includes waterfalls and swimming holes ($75/person). Open Monday through Friday 9 A.M. to 6 P.M., Saturday to 4 P.M., closed on Sunday.

Kaua'i Coasters, P.O. Box 3038, Lihu'e, HI 96766. Local: 808-639-2412.
Web site: www.aloha.net/~coast/index.htm
 This company offers a four-hour 12-mile downhill trek through the Waimea Canyon (plus continental breakfast) for $65/person. It's easy and very scenic. Don't expect a lot of speed—the descents are very controlled. We find this a tad too slow for us, but we like living dangerously, so . . .

The South Shore

Outfitters Kaua'i, 2827A Po'ipu Road, (P.O. Box 1149), Po'ipu Beach, HI 96756. Local: 808-742-9667 or 742-7421, fax 808-742-8842.
Web site: www.outfitterskauai.com
E-mail: info@outfitters.com
 This is a complete bike and kayak shop in Po'ipu that rents mountain cruisers for $20/day, Specialized mountain bikes with front-suspended handlebars for $25/day, ground-control FSR full-suspension bikes for $33/day, kids' mountain bikes (20-inch & 24-inch) for $20/day, regular road touring bikes for $30/day, and Trail-a-bikes for

$15/day (baby seats are $5/day). The company offers multiday discounts and guided tours too. Open daily from 8 A.M. to 5 P.M.

Kayaking

The sport of kayaking has exploded on Kaua'i's coast and its three major rivers—the Hanalei River on the North Shore, and the Wailua River and the Hule'ia River on the Coconut Coast.

Kayak Adventures, P.O. Box 3184, Princeville, HI 96722. Local: 808-826-9340.
Web site: www.extreme-hawaii.com/kayak
E-mail: kayaking@aloha.net
Kayak Adventures offers three different kayaking guided tours. The River Tour costs $80/adult and $40/kid aged 12 and under. The Safari Paddle & Snorkel Tour is river and ocean kayaking along with ocean snorkeling, and costs $65/adult and $35/kid aged 12 and under. On the Ocean Tour you will swim in underwater caves, ocean-kayak, and snorkel. The cost is $85/adult and $40/kid aged 12 and under. They use Malibu Two (sit-on-top) ocean kayaks. In addition they provide backrests, paddles, *tabis* (protective footwear), drinks, seasonal fruit, and snorkeling equipment. Open daily 7 A.M. to 10 P.M.

Kayak Kaua'i, P.O. Box 508, Hanalei, HI 96714. Toll-free: 800-437-3507. Local: 808-826-9844 or 822-9179, fax 808-826-7378.
Web site: www.kayakkauai.com
E-mail: info@kayakkauai.com
Kayak Kaua'i runs the gamut when it comes to kayaking trips. They offer everything from guided and self-guided single-day ocean or river kayaking trips to multiday hiking and paddle trips, all of which can be customized.

Kaua'i Waterski, Kayak, & Surf, 4-356 Kuhio Highway, Kapa'a, HI 96746. Toll-free: 800-344-7915. Local: 808-822-3574.
E-mail: surfski@aloha.net
Kaua'i WK&S uses Hobie and Cobra kayaks. They offer self-guided tours that cost $45 for a double and come with detailed

instructions and maps. They also offer a five-hour guided trip that includes breakfast and lunch and costs $82/person. The shop is open Monday through Saturday 8 A.M. to 7 P.M., Sunday 9 A.M. to 6 P.M.

Outfitters Kaua'i, 2827A Po'ipu Road, (P.O. Box 1149), Po'ipu Beach, HI 96756. Local: 808-742-9667 or 742-7421, fax 808-742-8842.
Web site: www.outfitterskauai.com
E-mail: info@outfitters.com

Outfitters Kaua'i offers one of the most strenuous ocean kayaking trips around, the Na Pali Coast Sea Kayak Tour. Leaving Po'ipu at 6:45 A.M. for a 90-mile drive up to Ha'ena, you then board a two-man kayak and begin your ocean trip. After kayaking for about an hour, there's a break at the Na Pali sea caves. The trip continues along the Na Pali coast and beyond for 11 miles, breaking for lunch on a secluded beach. After lunch, four more miles remain to the put out place (Waimea). With a brief van ride to Po'ipu, you will have circumnavigated the island (the only way to do this). The cost for this tour is $145/person, and plenty of warnings are given as this trip is not a pleasure cruise. It is hard work—tons of fun, but strenuous at the same time. For those who seek a bit of an easier trek, they also offer a Jungle Stream Waterfall Tour that costs $82/person. In addition, they offer self-guided tours and rentals.

Wailua Kayak & Canoe, 4-369A Kuhio Highway, Kapa'a, HI 96746. Local: 808-821-0015, fax 808-821-2123.
E-mail: wkc@aloha.net

This location right next to the Wailua River makes for very easy launching of your kayak—no loading, lugging, or carrying the kayak on top of your car. WKC offers kayak rentals for self-guided trips and several guided tours. Prices range from $25 for single kayak rentals to $80 for a five-hour guided tour, lunch included.

Other Things to Do
≈ **Golf**
≈ **Tennis**
≈ **Beaching**
≈ **Windsurfing**
≈ **Scuba**
≈ **Cerebral stuff**

Golf

The Garden Isle is also the Golfing Isle, thanks to the Princeville Resort. One of the hubs of the Hawai'ian golfing scene, Princeville showcases *Golf Digest's* number-one-rated golf course in Hawai'i, the Prince Course. If your plans take you to Kaua'i, it would be a sin not to play at Princeville, what with four courses totaling 45 holes. Other golf options on the island include the excellent Po'ipu Bay Golf Course (home of the PGA Grand Slam of Golf), Kiahuna in Po'ipu, the Kaua'i Lagoons courses, and the superb Wailua municipal course.

Princeville Makai and the Prince Golf Courses, P.O. Box 3040, Princeville, HI 96722. Toll-free: 800-826-1105. Local: 808-826-3580 (Makai), 808-826-3240 (Prince).

Makai Course
27 holes—Par 109

Woods: 9 holes—Par 37
Championship Tee (blue): 3,445 yards
Regular Tee (white): 3,208 yards
Ladies' Tee (red): 2,829 yards

Ocean: 9 holes—Par 36
Championship Tee (blue): 3,401 yards
Regular Tee (white): 3,058 yards
Ladies' Tee (red): 2,766 yards

Lake: 9 holes—Par 36
Championship Tee (blue): 3,456 yards
Regular Tee (white): 3,149 yards
Ladies' Tee (red): 2,714 yards

Rating Combinations:

	Ocean/Woods	Ocean/Lake	Lake/Woods
Blue	72.9	73.2	72.5
White	70.4/75.4 ladies	70.5/75.2 ladies	70.1/75.3 ladies
Red	67.0/70.4 ladies	66.9/69.9 ladies	66.3/69.6 ladies

Prince Course
18 holes—Par 72
Championship Tee (black): 7,309 yards, 75.3 rating
Championship Tee (blue): 6,960 yards, 73.7 rating
Regular Tee (white): 6,521 yards, 71.7 rating
Bogie Tee (gold): 6,005 yards, 69.3 rating
Ladies' Tee (red): 5,338 yards, 72.0 ratings

As you can see, there is a helluva lot of golf to choose from at the Princeville Resort. The Makai course is the site of the annual Women's Kemper Open. There are two clusters of courses: the Makai and Prince courses. The Makai courses have consistently ranked in *Golf Digest*'s Top 100 Courses in America for the past 16 years. All told, there are at least four different combinations for 18 holes: Ocean/Woods, Lake/Ocean, Woods/Lake, and Prince. In addition to the variety of golf available, the scenery on the North Shore of Kaua'i is absolutely stunning. This is truly one of the world's most spectacular golf settings. Designer Robert Trent Jones, Jr., has responded admirably to the challenge by creating courses that match the area's beauty. There is a lot of development around the Makai and Prince fairways (houses and condos), however, so some of his efforts seem to have been in vain (although the Prince course is truly magnificent). Nevertheless, the courses are still quite lovely. The Makai Course has three orientations—ocean, forest, and lakes. The Prince Course draws elements from all three. Weather can be a factor here, as this is the windward side and stiff trade winds and frequent showers are a way of life. Usually the showers pass quickly and the sun shines again. But this is tropical weather, so be prepared for any kind of conditions. The rain does keep everything lusciously green and fragrant.

One of the best things about the Makai course is its variety. You can spend a week on the course and never be bored. The Ocean nine are our favorite, with some classic and unique holes, particularly the third and seventh. From the tee, the third drops down 160 yards over a pond to the green—with Hanalei Bay, the "Bali Hai" *pali*, and, unfortunately, the Princeville Hotel as a backdrop. On the seventh there is a raging surf hole, with the tee on one side of a cove and the pin on the other. The distance holes are the second (610 yards) and fifth (519 yards), made easier with the help of the trades. Some elevated greens and plenty of bunkers (40) keep the course challenging.

The Woods Course brings you through stands of pine, silver oak, and eucalyptus on long, narrow fairways. One of Princeville's hardest holes is the Woods' sixth, a dogleg 400-yard-plus par 4 into the trade winds. There are two water hazards—ponds—on the fourth and the ninth holes. The fourth is a pretty tough par 4 with the pond totally guarding access to the green. There are four doglegs, one long par 5 of about 500 yards on the third hole, and 46 bunkers.

The Lake Course has three lakes as its focus, on the first, eighth, and ninth holes. The first hole, a par 4, has a lake along the left side of the fairway—a hooked shot to the left will be in the drink. The eighth hole, another par 4, has a lake guarding the green, tempting the player to overpower the ball in order to clear it. The ninth hole is the best, with a tee shot over water, a fairway drive along the water, and a pitch shot over water to the pin—a fun par 5. There are three doglegs, including a double on the ninth, and 29 bunkers.

Rates for Princeville Hotel guests for the Makia course, including greens fees and shared cart, run $55 for 9 holes and $95 for 18 holes. Rates for the general public are $120.

The Prince Course, with one of the toughest front nines in Hawai'i, has built an intimidating reputation. These are serious golfer's links, as only those with a handicap of 12 or less can use the championship tees. (There are five tee options to allow for different levels of expertise.)

Robert Trent Jones, Jr., has designed some very distinct holes here. Each one has its own twist. The fourth hole, the "Eagle's Nest," tees off 223 feet above the fairway with the 'Anini Stream guarding the green. The fifth hole has a waterfall as a backdrop for the pin. The water comes from a tunnel built at the end of the 19th century by Chinese laborers—it's a beautiful setting. The sixth hole keeps up the challenge with a par 4 over two ravines and six huge bunkers (34 on the entire course). The eighth hole has a 200-yard lateral water hazard on the right side of the fairway and green. By the end of the front nine you're exhausted, and there are another nine to come. The tenth hole, with its long reach to the green, is shaped like a question mark that wraps around a tropical ravine. The 12th hole is a breathtaking par 4 from a tee perched 100 feet above the fairway to a green set in an amphitheater of ferns, tropical foliage, and the 'Anini Stream. The 16th hole may be one of the longest par-4 375 yards in the world, so play two or three clubs above normal. Just when you think you are done, you come to the 18th hole, a long and exhausting par 4 that plays uphill and against the trades. Good luck!

Rates for Princeville guests for the Prince course, including greens fees and shared cart, run $110 for 18 holes. If you're not a guest of the Princeville Resort, rates run $165. Call for tee times.

Wailua Municipal Golf Course, 3-5350 Kuhio Highway, Lihu'e, HI 96766. Local: 808-241-6666.

18 holes—Par 72
Championship Tee (blue): 6,981 yards, 73.3 rating
Regular Tee (white): 6,000 yards, 71.3 rating
Ladies' Tee (red): 5,974 yards, 73.4 rating

Wailua is considered by many to be among the best courses in the state, and it is certainly the best municipal course; a visit to Kaua'i would be incomplete without playing here. The setting is marvelous—a seaside stretch with some of the nicest beaches on this side of the island. Groves of coconut palms and ironwood pines line the fairways, and it's not unheard of to stop for a swim after the front nine.

KAUA'I

Challenge abounds on this course. The toughest holes are the 2nd and 12th, the former due to its proximity to the surf and the latter due to the 400-yard drive directly into the trade winds. Four greens front the ocean—the 1st, 2nd, 14th, and 17th holes—making the course one of the most scenic in the state. The first and second fairways also run alongside the beach, the waves crashing in just steps away from the green. Water hazards come into play on the 4th, 5th, 10th, 11th, 12th, and 13th holes. For distance, there are four holes over 500 yards, and the trades are a major factor on this course. There are 12 doglegs and 39 bunkers to keep you honest.

All in all, this is a helluva course—and the rates are ridiculously low, making Wailua the best deal in Hawai'i. Greens fees and shared cart rates are $25 weekdays and $35 on the weekends. Call for tee times and book ahead; this course is very popular. At press time, the course was undergoing some renovations, so call beforehand to check on any changes.

Kaua'i Lagoons Golf Club, 3351 Ho'olaulea Way, Lihu'e, HI 96766. Toll-free: 800-634-6400. Local: 808-241-6000.

Kiele Course
18 holes—Par 72
Championship Tee (gold): 7,070 yards, 73.7 rating
Championship Tee (blue): 6,674 yards, 71.4 rating
Regular Tee (white): 6,164 yards, 69.1 rating
Ladies' Tee (red): 5,417 yards, 70.6 rating

Mokihana Course
18 holes—Par 72
Championship Tee (gold): 6,960 yards, 73.1 rating
Championship Tee (blue): 6,578 yards, 70.9 rating
Regular Tee (white): 6,136 yards, 68.8 rating
Ladies' Tee (red): 5,607 yards, 71.8 rating

The Kaua'i Lagoons courses were designed by Jack Nicklaus. The Kiele course is meant for the serious golfer, spread over 262 acres and designed with major spectator tournaments in mind (the 1991 PGA Grand Slam of Golf was held here). The Mokihana course is tailored more toward the recreational golfer, with more forgiving fairways for beginner and occasional players.

The Kiele course is indeed for the serious golfer. Ask at the golf shop for the course description—it will give you some good pointers. Every hole has its own little secret to success. The fifth hole is one of the toughest par 3s you will ever play. The tee is over a mango, guava, plum, and schefflera forest to the course's largest green. The tenth hole, a long par 5, could hurt your ego. The 13th hole was voted one of Hawai'i's top ten golf holes, a very picturesque but demanding par 3. The 16th is the signature hole on the Kiele course, a very dramatic par 4 from start to finish.

The Mokihana has been rated by *Golf Magazine* as one of the ten most playable courses in America. Again, ask for the course description. This course tends to be more open and generous than Kiele. The ninth hole is a fun downwind par 5; if you tee it high, you have a great chance to make a birdie. The 12th hole is a par 5 that demands some strategy in playing. The 16th hole is a treacherous par 5; lay up short by 13 guarding bunkers and you will be in a good position to attack the green. The 18th hole is long and demanding, so concentrate.

Rates for greens fees and shared carts for the Kiele course are $115 for Marriott guests, $125 for other resort guests, and $150 for the general public. For the Mokihana course the rates are $75 for Marriott guests, $85 for other resort guests, and $100 for the general public.

Po'ipu Bay Golf Course, 2250 Ainako Street, Koloa, HI 96756. Toll-free: 800-858-6300. Local: 808-742-8711.

18 holes—Par 72
Championship Tee (gold): 6,959 yards, 73.4 rating
Championship Tee (blue): 6,499 yards, 71.1 rating
Regular Tee (white): 6,023 yards, 68.9 rating
Ladies' Tee (red): 5,241 yards, 70.4 rating

Home of the PGA Grand Slam of Golf since 1994, the Po'ipu Bay Course is another Robert Trent Jones, Jr., masterpiece. This 210-acre course is built on ancient Hawaiian sites. It features 86 bunkers filled with white sand imported from Australia and Idaho, and 11 water holes. With ocean holes/tees, cliffs, and other natural obstacles working in tandem with Kaua'i's rugged scenery and the wonderful Po'ipu sun, this is a very challenging yet scenic course, and shouldn't be missed.

Rates for greens fees and shared carts are $110 for Hyatt guests and $150 for visitors.

Kiahuna Golf Club, 2545 Kiahuna Plantation Drive, Po'ipu, HI 96756. Local: 808-742-9595.

18 holes—Par 70
Championship Tee (blue): 6,366 yards, 69.7 rating
Regular Tee (white): 5,650 yards, 66.5 rating
Ladies' Tee (red): 4,886 yards, 67.1 rating

Kiahuna, the original golf course in the Po'ipu resort area, now lives under the shadow of its more famous sister, the Po'ipu Bay course. Also designed by Robert Trent Jones, Jr., Kiahuna's course has gentle fairways and is reminiscent of Scottish links-type courses. There is enough challenge here to keep most golfers happy—although Kiahuna's demands don't equal those of the Princeville or Po'ipu Bay courses. Novices and occasional golfers will be comfortable here. Some interesting Hawai'ian archaeological and geological sites dot the course, including irrigation aqueducts, the foundations of a house, stone walls, and two lava tubes.

The course itself has its fair share of water hazards (7), doglegs (11), and bunkers (63). The 2nd, 8th, and 15th holes are the hardest, where water hazards, elevated greens, and crosswinds are major factors. This is not a power-hitter's course, as there are only two holes over 500 yards.

Rates for greens fees and shared cart are under $75. Call for tee times.

Tennis

There are some excellent tennis centers on the Garden Isle to complement the tremendous golf, beach, and hiking options. Kaua'i has the only clay courts in the Pacific Basin, at the Coco Palms resort, but that resort is closed for the time being. Other tennis destinations include the Hanalei Bay Resort, Princeville, the Kaua'i Marriott, the Kiahuna Plantation, and the Hyatt Regency Kaua'i. Remember that the sunniest, driest weather is found in the Po'ipu area; the wettest is on the North Shore.

Tennis Centers

The North Shore

Hanalei Bay Resort, P.O. Box 220, Hanalei, HI 96714. Local: 808-826-6522.

With eight tiered, nonlighted Laykold courts in one of the most picturesque settings in the world, Hanalei Bay is Kaua'i's biggest tennis scene. The courts are situated in such a way as to provide views of the bay and the *pali*. Seven of the 11 courts are partitioned off to keep other peoples' balls and plays from intruding on your concentration. The courts are open from 9 A.M. to 10 P.M., and cost $3/hour for guests and $6/hour for the general public. The resort is part of the Princeville complex, so there is some superb golf to be had here too.

Princeville Tennis Gardens, Princeville Resort, Hanalei, HI 96714. Local: 808-826-9823.

At the Princeville Golf Club there are six Plexi-pave courts, open from 8:30 A.M. to 6 P.M. The tennis staff conducts clinics and tournaments and provides instruction on a private and group basis. There is a pro shop, and the Princeville Makai golf course is courtside for your convenience. The fee is $12/hour for guests and $15/hour for the general public.

The Coconut Coast

The Spa and Tennis Club at Kaua'i Lagoons, Kaua'i Marriott, Kalapaki Beach, Lihu'e, HI 96766. Local: 808-246-2414.

This megaplex of a resort has an excellent tennis facility in addition to its two 18-hole golf courses. There are seven Plexi-pave courts, plus a lighted stadium that seats 650 people and a fully

equipped pro shop. Instruction, matches, and partner pairing are available. The fee is $20 for all day.

The South Shore

Kiahuna Tennis Club, 2290 Po'ipu Road, (P.O. Box 78), Koloa, HI 96756. Local: 808- 742-9533.

Located on the sunny southern side of Kaua'i in Po'ipu, Kiahuna offers ten Plexi-pave courts, plus a pool, a pro shop, and a very good breakfast and luncheon spot called Joe's Courtside Café. Instruction, clinics, and tournaments are available. These courts are not lighted. Rates for non-guests are $10 per person per day. Open 7:30 A.M. to 6 P.M.

Hyatt Regency Kaua'i, 1571 Po'ipu Road, Koloa, HI 96756. Local: 808-742-1234.

The Hyatt has four nonlighted hard courts. Cost is $20 per hour for guest and the general public. Private instruction with the tennis pro is $50 per hour.

Recommended Public Courts

With all of the superbly maintained private tennis clubs available for really just a pittance, why play on the more mediocre public courts? Probably because all the public courts are free. Here are a couple of suggestions. Otherwise, call 808-241-6670 for a complete listing.

Wailua Park
Four hard courts, lighted.

Koloa Park
Two hard courts, lighted.

Beaches

There is no question that Kaua'i is one of the most beautiful islands in the Hawai'ian chain. The sensual vegetation and the majestic *pali* (steep, fluted mountains) of its North Shore overwhelm you.

The sight of the two together is breathtaking. View it all from a deserted beach, and you know this is about as close to paradise as any human can be, in this dimension anyway.

There are four primary beach areas on the island: the North Shore, the Coconut Coast (Wailua–Kapa'a), the South Shore (Po'ipu), and the Southwest Coast. Without doubt the most beautiful beaches are on the lush North Shore, and on the parched southwestern side of the island—where the high dunes of Barking Sands Beach stretch to the *pali* cliffs of Polihale. The Po'ipu beaches are slowly recovering from the wrath of Hurricane Iniki, which washed away several area beaches in 1992. Despite the destruction, the Po'ipu area still has some small, lovely cove beaches. The Wailua–Kapa'a beaches, while pretty in their own right, aren't quite up to the standard of the beaches on the other coasts.

The North Shore

This is the place where fantasies of the South Pacific can come true (even though you are really in the *North* Pacific). Stretching from Anahola in the east to the awesome beauty of the Kalalau Valley in the west, there's a little piece of heaven for everyone.

The Na Pali Coast

Kalalau, Hanakapi'ai, and Ke'e Beaches

Probably the ultimate Hawai'ian beach experience is at Kalalau, situated 11 long miles down the rugged and totally awesome Kalalau Trail from where the road ends at Ke'e Beach. (For more information on hiking and camping on this part of the coastline, see The Na Pali coast, earlier in this chapter). Here is a beach where you can be completely naked all the time if you want, living out your fantasies of being a shipwrecked castaway (although chances are you *will* be parading around in front of other castaway wannabees).

Sadly, there are constant reminders of the encroaching outside world. While the Hawai'ian state bird, the *nene,* is flightless and an endangered species, the noisy other "state bird"—the helicopter—is definitely thriving, hovering above the coast to show off the island's beauty to tourists. In general they tend to stay away from the beach itself, preferring to explore the upper reaches of Kalalau and the inaccessible neighboring valleys. There are also several sightseeing boats and the more rugged Zodiacs plying the coast from Ha'ena beachheads. There will inevitably be others like yourself at the beach who are seeking a similar experience. But the beach is big enough, and the spirit of the valley powerful enough, that it will still be ultimately fulfilling.

There are actually three beaches along this coast, beginning at the parking lot at Ke'e Beach at Ha'ena State Park and ending at the beach at Kalalau. (And if you're on a boat or kayak, many more beaches are accessible beyond Kalalau.) The half-mile-long strip of golden sand, framed by one of the most stunning mountain settings that you will ever see, is Kalalau. To the west, the mountains shoot up several thousand feet, like the spires of some giant gothic cathedral, an impregnable fortress where man can go no farther. To the south, the valley rises up to a wall of verdant *pali* adorned with a lace of waterfalls. To the east, pinnacles soar in front of the plateau where the thousand-year-old Kalalau Trail leads back to civilization.

At the western end of the beach, there is a waterfall for rinsing off the saltwater or just refreshing yourself. Just a bit farther west, several caves provide protection from the rain and privacy for your own reenactment of Lina Wertmüller's *Swept Away*. Some people sleep in them; others bring tents or tarps and pitch them on the level sliver of land just above the beach. The state has installed a solar-powered toilet, which smoothes out one of the coarser edges of roughing it. The available water must be purified or boiled. Those who are lucky enough to spend a few days here (the maximum allowed by the state is five) come out rejuvenated and enriched.

The other beaches on the Na Pali coast are easily reached by the day-tripper. Those who are adventurous as long as there is a bed waiting for them at the end of the day can take the one-hour hike to Hanakapi'ai Beach. It's not a hard hike, although steady climbing is involved up and down a well-worn and frequently muddy trail (especially in winter). This hike is an excellent Na Pali coast sampler, providing some breathtaking views of the coastline and the cloud-enshrouded peaks. To reach the beach, you must cross a fairly lively stream. It isn't especially difficult, particularly if you don't mind getting your feet wet. Be advised, however, that the water can rise *rapidly*. If it has been raining for any length of time, heed the warning signs and stay on high ground if you see the water level increase—it can rise in a matter of minutes to the point where the stream is impassable and dangerous. Once you've made it across, you'll have to scramble over some small, loose rocks to get to the sand. A huge cave dominates the western end of the beach, while the stream that you crossed forms several cool freshwater natural Jacuzzis for rinsing and playing. In the winter the surf here can be deadly, and several signs remind you of strong swimmers who have been swept out to sea. In summer, the surf tends to be calmer and safer. But at any time be careful—this is one of the most dangerous beaches on the island!

While there can easily be 50 people here on a nice day, the attitude is fairly carefree, and occasional nude sunbathers or topless women dot the beach and surf. Ambitious hikers can walk three miles inland at Hanakapi'ai to see some of the biggest waterfalls in the state. Again, watch the weather. Portable toilets are available at the beach.

The last beach of the Na Pali trio, Ke'e Beach, sits at the trailhead of the Kalalau Trail. While it is occasionally crowded, this beach is nice for three reasons. The first is that the swimming here, in most weather conditions, is excellent due to the protection offered by an extensive coral reef. The reef has created a calm lagoon that's terrific for snorkelers and kids. Second, one of Hawai'i's most sacred *heiau* (temples), Kaulu O Laka, is a short walk away. It is said that this is where hula originated. If you do venture up to see the temple—it's on the western end of the beach below the Kalalau Trail—please treat it with the greatest respect. And finally, the beach is only seconds from your car, and who wants to lug a cooler a few miles anyway? You can escape most of the crowd by simply walking to the right (east) and around the corner. Restrooms/picnic area.

Ha'ena

Tunnels. Nicknamed by surfers for its nice "zipper" tubes, this gorgeous long crescent of golden sand is one of the most scenic in the state. The views of the mountains to the west are both

breathtaking and evocative of a South Seas fantasy. Swimming and snorkeling are excellent *when* the sea is calm. Tunnels is also the best advanced windsurfing spot on Kaua'i. It is located just after mile marker eight on Route 560—turn right at the tree with the red stripe, and park. No facilities.

Lumaha'i. Situated about halfway between Ha'ena and Hanalei, this beach is located off Route 560 near the five-mile marker (just look for parked cars). It's a short but steep walk down to this pretty little golden-sand beach surrounded by a wall of lava and lush tropical vegetation. The swimming is safest here in summer; but use caution at all times as this too is one of the most dangerous beaches on Kaua'i. Lumaha'i had its 15 minutes in the spotlight when it was the setting for the "Wash That Man Right Out of My Hair" scene in the film *South Pacific*. No facilities.

Hanalei/Princeville

Hanalei Bay/Wai'oli Beach Park. This vast and super-scenic bay, in the shape of a half-moon with the town of Hanalei in the middle, is a favorite summer anchorage for yachts from all over the world. Swimming is best during summer on either side of the pier (near the eastern end) or by the pavilion. Restrooms/ showers/picnic area/lifeguard.

Hideaways. This little stretch of beach in the Princeville Resort is directly below the Pali Ke Kua condos. It's never crowded, and the swimming/snorkeling can be quite good if the seas are calm (we're beginning to sound like a CD skip regarding sea conditions, but you can *not* let your guard down for a second when it comes to the powerful Pacific). If you're staying in Princeville, spend a day or two here. The public access is next to the Pu'u Po'a condos tennis courts. There's also a private access (and a better path) through the Pali Ke Kua condos.

Kilauea

'Anini Beach County Park. A long reef protects this beach and makes it ideal for swimming (and for kids). The calm water allows for superb snorkeling. As the beach is fairly long, you should be able to find some space for yourself (the beach is popular with campers). Try the area in front of the polo field. 'Anini is reached by taking Highway 56 west from Kilauea and turning right on the western road to Kalihiwai just before the Princeville Airport (past the 25-mile marker and over the bridge), and then bearing left on 'Anini Road. Restrooms/ showers/picnic area.

Kalihiwai Beach. Everyone loves this beach, one of three that locals like to keep to themselves (the other two are Secret Beach and Rock Quarry). The Kalihiwai Stream provides freshwater pools as it flows by. Use the eastern Kalihiwai road (just east of the 24-mile marker). No facilities.

Secret Beach. If we were in advertising and wanted to sell a beach, this is what we would call it. This beautiful, hard-to-reach beach (actually called Kauapea Beach) is a long, secluded golden band bordered by cliffs. Its inaccessibility makes it Kaua'i's premier nude beach. There are shade trees and freshwater springs in the cliffs for rinsing off the salt. To the north (right) rises the rock promontory and spire of the Kilauea Lighthouse (terrific photo ops). Swimming and snorkeling are good on calm days only. Use the eastern Kalihiwai road (just east of the 24-mile marker) and turn right onto the first dirt road; drive until you see the end, and park with the other cars. A trail will lead you to the beach (about a 12-minute walk). No facilities.

Rock Quarry (Kahili Beach). Located in Kilauea Bay this is favorite spot with surfers and locals. This small and pretty beach gets its name from the quarry on its right side. The swimming is good in summer, although as you would on other North Shore beaches, be careful and use common sense. Rock Quarry is reached by taking Kuhio Highway (Highway 56) north toward Kilauea, then taking Wailapa Road almost to its end, following a dirt road to the end, where you will see other parked cars. No facilities.

The East Coast
Kapa'a, Wailua, and Li'hue area

Most hotels are in this area. Unfortunately, the beaches aren't quite as nice as elsewhere on Kaua'i. Lydgate is the only one that gets good reviews.

Kealia Beach. Right on Kuhio Highway (Highway 56), this is a consistent and popular surfing spot, with good rights and lefts near the seawall. A fun place to watch the surfers.

Lydgate State Park. Families with small kids will love this beach park set in front of the Holiday Inn SunSpree resort right off of Highway 56. Two man-made seawater lagoons, enclosed by lava rock boulders, make for very safe swimming (the smaller, shallower one is for kids). Snorkeling in the big lagoon is great because everyone feeds the plentiful fish and the lagoon provides protection from predators. Restrooms/picnic area/playground/showers/lifeguard.

Cemeteries (Nukoli'i Beach Park). A very long and beautiful golden-sand beach that parallels the Wailua Golf Course, this is definitely one of the prettiest beaches in the area. The swimming is not very good, with shallow water and several reefs, but the snorkeling can be okay when the water is calm. To reach the beach from Highway 56, take the dirt road toward the water at the southern end of the golf course and drive to the end. No facilities.

Running Waters. Until the 1980s, this undeveloped area of two sandy coves was a favorite place for locals. Now it is part of the Kaua'i Lagoons megaplex, although by law there is public beach access and parking. If you're staying at the Marriott, try to tear yourself away from its Roman spa (the pool) and shuttle yourself over to this beach. Hotel facilities.

Kalapaki Beach. Now overwhelmed by the huge Kaua'i Marriott, Kalapaki is surprisingly uncrowded—most guests apparently prefer the pool (we *hate* to admit that we would too). The view from here is dramatic, especially if one of the cruise ships is in port. Otherwise, the huge grain building and the Nawiliwili Harbor jetty remind you that you're in Kaua'i's main harbor. The beach sometimes gets good waves for bodysurfing. Restrooms/beach bar/restaurant/water sports.

The South Shore

Po'ipu

Brennecke's Beach. There was a lot more to this beach before Hurricane Iniki rearranged its face, strewing lava boulders everywhere. Sunbathing here is rather claustrophobic. Still, this is one of the best boogie-boarding and bodysurfing beaches on the island, though you'll have to elbow your way in for a spot. It's located just east of Po'ipu Beach Park along the Po'ipu Road; it's the beach with all the people bobbing in the waves. Facilities next door at Po'ipu Beach Park.

Po'ipu Beach Park. This is a very popular beach of two golden-sand crescents that are separated by a sandy peak in the middle. Its proximity to the many condos and hotels that don't have beaches attracts visitors, and its sunny weather attracts locals, making it the most crowded beach on the island. It is reached by taking the Po'ipu Road. The western crescent fronts the condos of the Kiahuna Plantation, and at its end sits the restored Sheraton. We think this is the best swimming and sunning beach in Po'ipu and we love the huge lawn/common of the Kiahuna Plantation. Restrooms/showers/picnic area/restaurants and bars (across the street).

The Southwest Coast

This is the driest part of the island, where Waimea Canyon earns its reputation as "the Grand Canyon of the Pacific." It's hard to believe that several hundred inches of rain fall just a few miles from here. All this dry weather means sunshine—lots of it. Make sure you have plenty of beverages and sunscreen before spending a day here.

Barking Sands. The high dunes of this beach, dotted with beach grass and bordered by fields of sugarcane, are reminiscent of the big dunes on East Coast beaches (minus the sugarcane, of course). And it goes on for miles. Unfortunately, this is also part of the Barking Sands Pacific Missile Range, making some of it off-limits. You can gain access, however, if you check in at

the front gate. If maneuvers are on, it would certainly be an intriguing afternoon at the races. Most of the time, however, you should have the beach to yourself. Swim with caution—and bring water. It gets *very* hot and *very* sunny. To reach it, follow Route 50 west of Kekaha to the main entrance of the base. No facilities.

Polihale State Park. This is one of Kaua'i's most spectacular beaches, although it doesn't look as if belongs on the island. The view of the dunes south toward Barking Sands reminds us more of outer Cape Cod or New York's Hamptons than Hawai'i. If you look in the opposite direction, you'll see the huge, parched *pali* that signal the abrupt end to the Na Pali coastline. The combination is very striking—as are the sunsets from the western edge of Hawai'i. The beach goes on forever, and there's lots of space for privacy. It's definitely worth the drive from wherever you're staying. As with Barking Sands, bring refreshments (especially water). Don't leave anything valuable in the car here, as this is a notorious rental-car break-in spot. Restrooms/showers/picnic area.

Windsurfing

The windsurfing industry on Kaua'i is not nearly as developed as that on Maui or O'ahu because conditions are less favorable here. Severe currents, treacherous reefs, and lots of rocks add up to a less-than-pretty picture for most boardsailors. Only experts can access the best sailing spots, where wind and swell meet. While we wouldn't recommend Kaua'i for a windsurfing vacation, there are some good options on the Garden Isle should you decide to go windsurfing for a day or two. For beginners, Nawiliwili Harbor and Kalapaki Bay are sheltered, with steady light-to-moderate winds. 'Anini Beach County Park on the North Shore and Port Allen on the South Shore are also good for novices. Intermediates and experts should head for Tunnels Beach on the North Shore and Salt Pond and Maha'ulepu Beach on the South Shore.

Three recommended windsurfing operations provide rentals, sales, and/or lessons. Two are located on the North Shore, and one is on Kalapaki Bay (near the Kaua'i Marriott).

Equipment and Instruction

'Anini Beach Windsurfing, P.O. Box 1602, Hanalei, HI 96714. Local: 808-826-WIND (9463).

Instruction is available for all levels (from beginner to wave expert) at this outfit as well as BIC, Fantasy, Hifly, Neil Pryde, Newman Kaua'i, and Hi Tech rentals. Instructions are given at 9 A.M. and 1 P.M., last three hours, and cost $65.

Sea Star Kauai-Windsurfing, 3720 Papalani, Kalaheo, HI 96741. Local: 808-332-8189.

High-performance windsurfing and kitesurfing gear is sold here.

Windsurf Kaua'i, P.O. Box 323, Hanalei, HI 96714. Local: 808-828-6838.

Beginner I and II windsurfing lessons are conducted on 'Anini Beach. Lessons are three hours long, cost $75 (including all equipment), and are given at 9 A.M. and 1 P.M. for Beginner I, at 10 A.M. and 2 P.M. for Beginner II. Rentals are also available here: $25/hour, $50 for a half day, and $75 for a full day.

Scuba

Kaua'i is a remarkably beautiful and striking island. There is so much to see and do here that you would hardly think of diving as a major attraction, and while it may not be, the diving, mostly along the South Shore except in summer, is remarkably good. If you are going to Kaua'i, you should not miss the opportunity to dive. Keep in mind that the diving is more vulnerable to weather conditions, due to Kaua'i's exposed position in the chain and its round shape, than it is on the other Hawai'ian islands.

An abundance of tropical fish and various lava formations make up for a relatively spare coral scene. (Kaua'i's cooler water and more northern location inhibit the kind of coral growth that you see on the Big Island.) Still, you won't be disappointed—particularly with everything else there is to do here.

KAUA'I

Here's Where to go Diving:

General Store. There's lots to see here, and deep water too. The dive is 65 to 80 feet. Located on the South Shore west of Po'ipu, this boat dive is a horseshoe-shaped area with caverns on both sides lined with flat coral. Schools of butterfly fish follow you around, hoping that you'll get close enough to the egg sacks of the sergeant majors. (Your presence scares away the mother standing guard, allowing the butterfly fish a veritable feast on the eggs.) The walls of the horseshoe contain lots of *pakas* (holes) that harbor all kinds of creatures, including shrimp, lobster, squirrelfish, and bigeyes. General Store is also the site of an old steamship wreck, where five anchors on the bottom are evidence of a struggle to anchor the vessel in some very stormy weather.

Sheraton Caverns. The most popular boat dive in Kaua'i is a series of adjacent lava tubes off the Sheraton Kaua'i in Po'ipu. This is a moderate dive, with depths to 60 feet. Lots of turtles and tropical fish are here. Dolphins, morays, and whales are often sighted here, too.

Koloa Landing. Located on the South Shore, this is a consistent shore dive year-round when conditions on other parts of the island are bad. A popular spot for novices, it's shallow (10 to 40 feet) and has tons of tame fish that love being fed, especially if you're offering frozen peas. This is an excellent place for night diving.

Ni'ihau. If conditions permit, you can boat 20 miles across the channel to the north shore of Ni'ihau and Lehua islands. As this is rarely dived, the terrain is pristine and the fish are inquisitive. The islands' position in the open Pacific makes this area a haven to pelagic fish from all over. Boat dives are run here only occasionally, so be sure to ask when you arrive.

Cannons and Tunnels. These are two virtually identical shore dives off Ha'ena Beach Park on the North Shore. This wall dive to 60 feet, through caverns, lava tubes, and plate coral, can be done only in the summer months.

Dive Operations

Bubbles Below, P.O. Box 157, Ele'ele, HI 96705. Local: 808-332-REEF (7333).
Web site: www.bubblesbelowkauai.com
  While the name is a tad too cutesy for us, this is a reputable dive operation specializing in boat dives for certified divers only. It owns a 35-foot Kalmanu dive boat and takes a maximum of six to eight divers per trip. A half-day, two-tank boat dive costs $100/person. Since they don't have a storefront, you can basically call any time during the day. They suggest not too early in the morning!

Fathom Five Divers, 3450 Po'ipu Road, (P.O. Box 907), Koloa, HI 96756. Toll-free: 800-972-3078. Local: 808-742-6991.
Web site: www.fathomfive.com
  Based in Koloa, this friendly operation is a PADI five-star facility. Fathom five also specializes in dive packages with local Po'ipu accommodations, be it hotel, condo, or house. This operation also offers half- and full-day charters, leaving in the early morning. Dives accommodate no more than six people. A half-day, two-tank boat dive costs $90/person. Open 7:30 A.M. to 6 P.M.

Ocean Odyssey, 4331 Kawai Beach Drive, (P.O. Box 807), Kapa'a, HI 96746. Local: 808-245-8681.
  Located at the former Outrigger Kaua'i Beach just north of Lihu'e, Ocean Odyssey is run by Terry Donnelly, a devoted fan of Bugs Bunny and an experienced underwater juggler, who also has an impressive list of diving and seamanship credentials. A half-day, two-tank boat dive costs $105/person. Open 7:30 A.M. to 9 P.M.

Ocean Quest Water Sports Co., 1672 Kauhale, Kapa'a, HI 96746. Local: 808-822-3589.
Web site: www.oceanquest.net
  Ocean Quest offers PADI and NAUI certification as well as introductory dives. Diving the North Shore is their specialty. A half-day, two-tank boat dive costs $95/person. These guys are a dive operation only and do not have a storefront.

Mana Divers, P.O. Box 1137, Koloa, HI 96756. Local: 808-742-9849.
Web site: www.manadivers.com

This PADI operation is located on the South Shore and limits the number of divers to four to five per instructor. A half-day, two-tank boat dive costs $110/person. Open 7 A.M. to 7 P.M.

Dive Kaua'i, 4-976 Kuhio Highway, Kapa'a, HI 96746. Local: 808-822-0452.
Web site: www.divekauai.com

A PADI five-star facility and Kaua'i's only Enriched Air IDC Dive Center. Dive Kaua'i also has a 28-foot dive boat called the *Kulia*. A half-day, two-tank boat dive costs $115/person, equipment included. Open Monday through Saturday 8 A.M. to 5 P.M., Sunday 9 A.M. to 3 P.M.

Cerebral

Kaua'i is many things, but one thing it is *not* is a bastion of intellectual activities. On the other hand, its staggering beauty is in itself contemplative, so who needs more stimuli for thinking anyway? And for those people who think golf is a mental exercise, the Princeville mega-golf complex (see the Golf section) will certainly test your nerves in that department. Still, given its tremendous natural wonders, such as the Na Pali Coast and Waimea Canyon, you should probably plan a visit to the Garden Isle to be close to nature. If you really want a cerebral holiday, then head for the Big Island or O'ahu.

There are, however, a few items of interest on the Kaua'i menu. A good museum, some fine art galleries, a sacred *heiau*, a wonderful botanical garden, and some excellent examples of missionary homesteads are the offerings. Otherwise, bring a good book or your mantra.

Museums

The Kaua'i Museum, 4428 Rice Street, Lihu'e, HI 96766. Local: 808-245-6931.

Consisting of two buildings, this is a small but significant museum of Kaua'i's cultural and natural history. There are several galleries with Hawai'ian artifacts and artwork, old photographs, and informative displays on the natural and ethnic development of Kaua'i, plus current exhibitions. It won't take long to see it all, but you will learn, and probably retain, a few things about the island of Kaua'i. There is also a good gift shop with some great Hawai'iana books and maps, along with some terrific groovy souvies, such as baskets, Ni'ihau shells (considered the best of the islands'), local crafts, and woodenware.

The museum is open Monday to Friday from 9 A.M. to 4:30 P.M. and Saturday from 9 A.M. to 1 P.M.; closed Sunday and major holidays. Admission is a suggested donation of $5/adults, $1/kids aged 6 to 12; kids aged five and under are free.

Other Sights

The National Tropical Botanical Garden:

Allerton Garden, Spouting Horn, Lawa'i, HI 96765. Local: 808-742-2623.

Located on the southern coast in Lawa'i, across the street from Spouting Horn Park and just a short drive from Koloatown, this 100-acre garden was once Queen Emma's retreat and is filled with landscaped gardens, outdoor "rooms," sculptures, pools, flowing water, huge Moreton Bay fig trees, and of course tropical flowers—many of them on the endangered list. Garden tours (two and a half hours) are guided, cost $30/person, and are conducted Tuesday through Saturday at 9 A.M., 10 A.M., 1 P.M., and 2 P.M. Reservations required.

McBryde Garden, Spouting Horn, Lawa'i, HI 96765. Local: 808-742-2623.

This is a 186-acre garden of endangered and rare species situated next to the Allerton Garden. Founded in 1964 by congressional charter but supported privately, it is the country's only tropical plant research station. Here you can see lily pads the size of trampolines and such unusual species as wild ginger, *jatropha,* and strawberry bananas. Along part of this tour you can view the Allerton house and Queen Emma's summer cottage, though neither is

open for actual tours. The garden is open to the public by guided tour only (two and a half hours), Monday at 9 A.M. and 1 P.M., Tuesday at 1 P.M. Admission is $30/person and reservations are required.

Limahuli Garden, Route 560, Ha'ena, HI 96714. Local: 808-826-1053.

Set on 17 acres at the base of towering *pali*, this very lush garden has beautiful tropical vegetation and flowers as well as the ruins of ancient Hawai'ian villages and *taro* fields. It's very serene. Guided tours run between two and two and a half hours, cost $15/person, and require reservations. Self-guided tours last between one and one and a half hours and are $10/person. Open Tuesday through Friday and Sunday from 9:30 A.M. to 4 P.M.

Kaulu Paoa Heiau/Kaulu o Laka Heiau. End of Route 560, Ke'e.

Said to be the birthplace of hula, these *heiau*, situated just a short walk from Ha'ena State Park, are among the most sacred in the Hawai'ian culture. Legend has it that Pele danced here and fell for the high chief Lohiau, who was one of the drummers. Their love, however, was never consummated; a series of obstacles that will sound familiar to *Romeo and Juliet* fans blocked their way. Thinking that he would never see Pele again, Lohiau killed himself. When Pele's sister, Hi'iaka, was sent to bring him back to Pele on the Big Island, she brought him back to life (gods can do that sort of thing). As it turns out, the handsome young chief fell in love with Hi'iaka, and she for him. Needless to say, Pele was upset. So upset, in fact, that her fires still rage today. The moral of the story is twofold: Never send a more attractive sibling or friend to retrieve an *amour*—do it yourself. And don't *ever* anger Madame Pele. She holds grudges for eternity.

Nestled under the steep pali where the Na Pali Coast begins, these *heiau* occupy one of the most stunning settings in Hawaii. The three-platform lower *heiau* is a temple dedicated to Lohiau's friend Paoa. The upper *heiau*, where Pele danced, is a slim platform and is dedicated to the hula goddess Laka. Halau Hula (a cross between a school and a temple) today occasionally continues the tradition of dancing here. If you're lucky enough to see a *halau* there, you are witnessing a very special event.

Both *heiau* can be reached by taking Route 560 to its end in Ke'e and then walking west along the beach (not on the Kalalau Trail) until you see the stone platforms. *Please treat these sites with the utmost respect; they are precious to Hawai'ian culture.*

Missionary Homesteads

Like it or not, the missionaries were an integral part of Hawai'ian history, even though their attempts to make good Christians out of the local population almost destroyed the Hawai'ian culture. Every island contains overwhelming evidence of their influence, from preserved homesteads to the dominance of the "Big Five" companies (Hackfield, Brewer, Davies, Castle & Cook [Dole], and Alexander & Baldwin) in land ownership and business (the families' ancestors were missionaries). On Kaua'i, there are two excellent examples of the missionary past; the Waioli Mission House and the Grove Farm Homestead.

Waioli Mission House, P.O. Box 1631, Lihu'e, HI 96766. Local: 808-245-3202.

This fine relic of the missionary days is located in Hanalei on Kuhio Highway. A hybrid of antebellum and New England architectural styles, the Waioli Mission House was built in 1837 out of native *ohia* wood and coral stone (for the chimney). It is filled with memorabilia and period pieces. With its signature double-decker verandah in front, the house looks pretty much the way it did when the Wilcox family lived in it. A visit here takes you back to another century. Open Tuesday, Thursday, and Saturday, 9 A.M. to 3 P.M. Admission is by suggested donation.

Grove Farm Homestead Museum, P.O. Box 1631, Lihu'e, HI 96766. Local: 808-245-3202.

One of Kaua'i's original sugar plantations, Grove Farm was bought by a son of the Wilcox family (of Waioli Mission House fame). The plantation is still in operation today, although it outgrew its original buildings years ago. Today these buildings have been turned into an interesting museum, representing one of the best preservations of 19th-century plantation life in the state. There is a

two-hour tour, conducted Monday, Wednesday, and Thursday at 10 A.M. and 1 P.M.,—which, as it happens, is the only way to see the joint. You must have reservations, so be sure to call well in advance. Admission is a suggested donation of $5/adults and $2/kids.

Art Galleries

There are several galleries where you can find artwork by artists from or living in Hawaii. Among the better ones:

Artists Gallery of Kauaʻi, 5-5190 Kuhio Highway, Hanalei, 826-6441.
Handcrafted art of Hawaii. Open daily from 10 A.M. to 6 P.M.

Avanas at Hanalei, Ching Young Shopping Center, Hanalei, 826-6867.
An eclectic little shop located in the back of the shopping center. Full of incense, buddha figures, and imported arts from Asia, and showing a few pieces of artwork by local artists.

Kauaʻi Museum, 4428 Rice Street, Lihuʻe, 245-6931.
Local artisans' work is for sale here. Open Monday through Friday 9 A.M. to 4 P.M., Saturday 10 A.M. to 4 P.M., closed Sunday.

Kilohana Galleries, 3-2087 Kaumualiʻi Highway, Lihuʻe, 245-9352.
Hawaiian artists, Niʻihau shell leis, scrimshaw, and Hawaiʻian stamps and coins. Open Monday through Saturday 9:30 A.M. to 9:30 P.M., Sunday until 5 P.M.

Bookstores

Need something of substance to read? Try the following:

Borders Books & Music, Kukui Marketplace, 4303 Nawiliwili Road, Lihuʻe, 246-0862.
Open Monday through Saturday 8:30 A.M. to 10 P.M., Sunday until 8 P.M.

Waldenbooks, Kauaʻi Village, Kapaʻa, 822-7749.
Open Monday through Saturday 9 A.M. to 8 P.M., Sunday until 5 P.M.

Where to Stay

Hats off to government of the County of Kaua'i! It is determined to keep the island as unspoiled as possible while it weathers the swelling tourism tsunami. Having seen what the lack of planning hath wrought on Maui, Kaua'i developed zoning laws that limit buildings to "no taller than the tallest palm tree," actually four stories. No more mega-structures can be built—a relief to lovers of the land. Preexisting big structures remain, but that's it for high-rises.

There are three resort areas on Kaua'i—the North Shore, the Coconut Coast, and Po'ipu. Each has distinct characteristics. The North Shore, with the 11,000-plus-acre Princeville complex as its centerpiece, wins hands-down as the most beautiful resort area not only on the island but in all of Hawai'i. It has the prettiest beaches on the island and the best golf courses. However, due to its location on the windward side, it also has the wettest weather—a drawback for some—especially in winter (the rainy season). It doesn't rain all the time here (average annual rainfall is 85 inches), but frequent showers brought in by the trade winds are normal. The upside of this is verdant vegetation and slightly cooler temperatures. During the drier summer months, the North Shore is a very popular destination.

The Po'ipu area has much sunnier and drier weather (average annual rainfall is 36 inches), making it very popular in the wetter winter months for those who want to be sure they get a tan. The beaches are small, though, and not nearly as nice as those on the North Shore. Many hotels were demolished by Hurricane Iniki (a category 4 tempest) in 1992 and some, like the fabled Waiohai, have yet to be rebuilt. The area itself is crowded with development due to the favorable weather conditions (except for the occasional hurricane). Also on the South Shore is the Waimea area, home of the tiny but wonderful Koke'e Lodge, situated at the top of Waimea Canyon, and the Waimea Plantation Cottages, located on the water.

The Lihu'e-Wailua-Kapa'a area, dubbed the "Coconut Coast," was the original resort area on Kaua'i and the home of the now defunct Coco Palms resort—the setting for Elvis's *Blue Hawai'i*. Age has taken its toll; today this is the most commercial and least

desirable part of the island. By Kaua'i standards, the area is not particularly appealing and the beaches are for the most part okay at best. We don't mean that it is not pretty; it's just that the North Shore is even prettier and the South Shore has better weather. There are several big hotels and resorts on the Coconut Coast, including the Kaua'i Beach, Aston Kaua'i Coast Resort, the Holiday Inn SunSpree Resort, and the Kaua'i Coconut Beach Resort. Right in Lihu'e is the Kaua'i Marriott Resort and Beach Club. Originally the Westin Kaua'i, one of the "fantasy resorts" built by Chris Hemmeter in the 1980s, it was controversial from the get-go. Now run by Marriott and toned down somewhat, this time-share and hotel property is still a sight to see, especially the Roman-inspired pool area. Many package deals will put you on the Coconut Coast. Since it is centrally located, both North and South Shore beaches are within an hour's drive. The money you save may compensate for the compromise in beauty, aesthetics, or weather.

So what area should you stay in? Well, we'd recommend the North Shore, simply because it is so beautiful. If the thought of occasional rain scares you, then we suggest Po'ipu during the winter months (December, January, and February), when the odds for bad weather on the North Shore are greater. Whatever you decide, make a point to spend at least one night at Koke'e. If you have two weeks, a nice alternative would be to spend equal amounts of time on the North Shore and Po'ipu.

The North Shore

Princeville

The Princeville Hotel, 5520 Ka Haku Road, (P.O. Box 3069), Princeville, HI 96722. Toll-free: 800-325-DLUX (3589). Local: 808-826-9644, fax 808-826-1166. Rooms and suites: 252.
Web site: www.princeville.com

Now part of "The Luxury Collection" of Starwood Hotels, this is still one of the best hotels on Kaua'i (the other is the Hyatt). It helps that it sits on a bluff in one of the most stunning settings in the world and is also part of one of the foremost golf destinations in the Pacific. These facts would definitely tilt us toward Princeville if we had to choose. So what if it rains occasionally!

The hotel's design allows for a view from most rooms—and a fabulous one at that—of Hanalei Bay and the dramatic *pali* rising behind. The guest rooms themselves are average in size but nicely appointed with light wood furnishings, pale-toned fabrics, and berber carpeting. Louvered shutters provide privacy, although we feel the best thing about the rooms is the view. Junior suites are more grand, with king-size beds, a pop-up TV/VCR (raised and lowered by the touch of a button), and a Jacuzzi in a swank marble bath with large dual vanities. All rooms and suites have 24-hour room service, feather pillows (a nice touch), coffeemaker, iron/board, mini-bar, dataports on phones, safe, and bath windows that switch from opaque to clear at the touch of a button. A coin-op laundry room is a welcome convenience.

All that glitters isn't gold, however. Most rooms do not have lanais. To give each room its view, the hotel is spread out, from the top of a cliff down to the bay. If you're on the top floor, it will take about ten minutes to get to the pool and the beach; you will have to walk a lot and ride two elevators. The pool itself is average, but the ocean and beach are steps away—and the chaises are comfortable. There is a Jacuzzi, a snack bar, and fitness and water-sports centers at the pool level. We were a tad unsure about the décor of the public areas (although the halls are nicely done in green colonial wallpaper). With the exception of the halls, it seems rather over the top. The spacious lobby is adorned with gilt-tipped columns, white, black, and red marble-patterned floors, seating areas of Louis XVI–style furniture, a large fountain/pool in the center, Hawai'ian and Baroque art, and gilt mirrors on the walls; there's a huge fountain with an equally large statue at the outside *porte cochère*.

There are two terribly expensive restaurants in the hotel—La Cascata (the hotel's signature restaurant, serving Italian cuisine) and Cafe Hanalei (serving all meals and featuring a popular Sunday brunch)—so be prepared or go out to eat in Hanalei if you don't want to spend an arm and a leg. The Living Room in the main lobby serves high tea, cocktails, and dessert. The Beach Restaurant and Pool Bar serves salads and sandwiches all day.

Rates are **Wicked Pricey** and up.

Hanalei Bay Resort, 5380 Honoiki Road, Princeville, HI 96722. (Mailing address: P.O. Box 220, Hanalei, HI 96714.) Toll-free: 800-827-4427. Local: 808-826-6522, fax 808-826-6680. Units: 200. Web site: www.hanaleibaykauai.com

Recently acquired by Quintus Resorts, a "vacation ownership" (i.e. time-share) company, this 22-acre resort of hotel rooms (with fridge), studios with kitchenettes, and one-, two- and three-bedroom suites with kitchens sits adjacent to the Princeville Resort and shares the same stunning setting (although it's not as high up on the bluff). The Hanalei Bay also has a good tennis facility (eight Plexi-pave courts) and all that the Princeville Resort has to offer (golf and the Princeville Health Club & Spa). While we are always suspicious of time-share resorts, this one seems pleasant enough and a good place for families.

The décor of rattan furnishings, wall-to-wall carpet, and subdued tropical colors is comfortable. All rooms and suites have daily maid service, lanais, cable TV, phones, coffeemaker, safe, and fridge (or more, depending on room category). Suites also have washer/dryers. There are two pools, including one with a sandy beach for kids, and a man-made cascade running through the property. Also for parents with their kids, a baby-sitting service is available. The resort has an open-air restaurant called Bali Hai and a bar, the Happy Talk Lounge.

Rates are **Pricey** and up.

Princeville Condos

There are over ten condo properties to choose from in the Princeville Resort area alone. To complicate matters, several different management companies operate them. In many cases, more than one management company has its claws into a particular condo complex. The result is that prices and quality of the service/maintenance may vary slightly. By far the biggest manager, representing the most properties, is **Hanalei Aloha Rental Management** (also called Hanalei Vacations), 5-4280 Kuhio Highway, Princeville Shopping Center, Princeville, HI 96722. Toll-free: 800-487-9833. Local: 808-826-7288. Web site: www.800hawaii.com.

But there are a slew of others, including **Hanalei North Shore**

Properties (800-488-3366), **Kauai Paradise Vacations** (800-826-7782), and **Pacific Paradise Properties** (800-800-3637).

What a mess! Where should you stay? Whom should you call? Relax, we've straightened it all out for you. First of all, there is not much, if any, difference in price between those units on the water and those on the golf course. Hands down, staying on the water wins. Having flown thousands of miles to be in the tropics and breathe the ocean air, you should be able to step out on your lanai and watch the humpbacks go by and hear the raging surf below, rather than dodge golf balls. There are five properties (besides Hanalei Bay Resort) where you can do this. They are listed below, along with the proper numbers to call. Remember that units are usually owner-decorated, so hope for tasteful décor but expect nothing.

Pu'u Po'a, P.O. Box 1109, Hanalei, HI 96714. Local: 808-826-9602.

With a dramatic architectural flair of white, glass block, and green-tiled roofs, this multi-tiered complex features two-bedroom units, all with incredible ocean views (try to get one facing "Bali Hai"). Each has two baths, two lanais, a spacious living room, washer/dryer, and a fully equipped kitchen (dishwasher, microwave, coffeemaker, toaster, etc.). Most units also have TV, VCR, and CD player (although be sure to ask). There is a pool, and maid service is available every third day. It's also just a short walk down to a small but quiet sandy beach called Hideaways (the best access to this beach is through the Pali Ke Kua complex next door). Guests may use all the amenities of the Princeville Resort.

Rates are *Not So Cheap* and up (about $1,015/week and usually rented by the week).

Pali Ke Kua, P.O. Box 889, Hanalei, HI 96714. Local: 808-826-9066.

These attractive and spacious units offer probably the finest views in Princeville condo-land, being situated out on a point. One- and two-bedroom suites are available here, with full kitchens, washer/dryer, and lanai. It's a short walk down the complex's concrete path to the secluded and sandy Hideaways beach. There is a bar and a restaurant, the Beamreach, as well as a pool and Jacuzzi on the premises. Maid service comes midweek. Guests have access

to the amenities of the Princeville Resort.

Rates are **Not So Cheap** and up.

Ali'i Kai I, P.O. Box 1109, Hanalei, HI 96714. Local: 808-826-6002.

Two-bedroom, two-bath units front the ocean here. Each unit has a fully equipped kitchen and a washer/dryer. In the ocean units, the bedroom, bathroom, living room, and lanai are all oceanfront. Maid service is available on request. There is a pool and tennis courts, plus guests have privileges to all amenities at the Princeville Resort.

Rates are **Cheap** and up.

The Cliffs, P.O. Box 1109, Hanalei, HI 96714. Local: 808-826-6106.

This is a large complex of several buildings, with one- and two-bedroom units on the bluffs. Most units have telephone, cable TV, VCR, stereo, private lanai, fully equipped kitchen, washer/dryer, and ceiling fans. There is a small pool, four tennis courts, Jacuzzis, and maid service (an extra). Not all buildings face the ocean. Guests have access to all of the amenities of the Princeville Resort.

Rates are **Cheap** and up.

Sealodge, P.O. Box 1109, Hanalei, HI 96714. Local: 808-826-6751.

A view of the cobalt-blue Pacific from high up on the bluff is the highlight of this cheaper condo alternative. There are one- and two-bedroom units, with two pools, and maid service on request. The bedrooms, living rooms, dining rooms, and lanais all have ocean views. All units come with a full kitchen, and some have a washer/dryer.

Rates are **Cheap** and up.

Hanalei and Ha'ena

Hanalei Colony Resort, P.O. Box 206, Hanalei, HI 96714. Toll-free: 800-628-3004. Local: 808-826-6235, fax 808-826-9893. Units: 52.
Web site: www.hcr.com
E-mail: aloha@hcr.com

Probably one of the best deals for waterfront condos on the North Shore, this five-acre property of two-story buildings and well-tended grounds sits on a very pretty beach in Ha'ena. With the sound of the surf and the trades constant, those longing for a romantic spot that doesn't break the bank should be happy here. Besides the roar of the ocean, it's very quiet in these parts since there are no phones or TVs (except for those guests who can't part with their cell phones—okay, we're projecting, we kept our cell phone on all the time). Each clean and spacious unit has two bedrooms, a large lanai, a fully equipped kitchen with microwave, blender (very key), toaster, and coffeemaker (no dishwasher, though). All are furnished comfortably, and while they aren't the pinnacle of luxury, they are perfectly pleasant. Wall-to-wall berber carpet, rattan furnishings with tropical print fabric, and faded Hawai'ian prints on the walls round out the décor. Being right on the ocean, things can get a tad damp (but our tired and not-so-youthful skin felt so good). Groups of more than a couple should note that louvers, not solid wood doors, separate the bedrooms from the living areas. Our favorite units are on the second floor, right on the water.

There is a small pool and hot tub by the road. The beaches around the HCR are fairly coral-bound, so the best beach for swimming is about a mile away. Maid service is every third day (or daily if requested), and a coin-op laundry is located by the pool. A large barbecue pit sits in the middle of the property. The staff is very friendly and helpful—thankfully, since we experienced a quasi-embarrassing credit card glitch (the c.c. company's mistake, of course!). There is a tiny convenience store called the Steam Vent Café attached to Surt's restaurant (the former Charo's and overpriced). Hanalei is a scenic 15-minute drive away (over seven single-lane bridges).

Rates are *Pricey* and up.

Hanalei Properties, P.O. Box 748, Hanalei, HI 96714. Local: 808-826-6111.
Web site: www.bestofhawaii.com/hanalei
E-mail: HanaleiBay@aol.com

Carolyn Barnes is the owner of three properties in the Hanalei area, thus making this kind of a mini-empire. This was a great find for us, and should you decide to stay at one of Carolyn's places, let her know we sent you.

KAUA'I

Hanalei Plantation Guest House, about a mile outside of town on the west side of Hanalei Bay.

We were very pleasantly surprised to discover this new, welcome addition to the North Shore lodging scene. In this pretty Hawai'ian-style building across the road from the beach, there are four well-kept efficiency units that are so clean we wouldn't hesitate to eat something we dropped on the floor (shoes are not allowed inside). Owner Carolyn Barnes wouldn't have it any other way. Best of all, the price is right.

Each unit has a small lanai in front, cable TV, phone, wet bar, fridge, microwave, and coffeemaker. Baths are large, with separate loo and large vanity. While there is no A/C, there is a ceiling fan over the king-size bed. Furnishings are bamboo and rattan and include a desk and lots of shelves. Our only criticism is the somewhat too-vivid-for-our-taste green floral wall-to-wall carpet. There is an "enclosed" outdoor shower—a definite plus—although it is somewhat oddly placed right on the front lawn. A very substantial continental breakfast is included, with smoothies, coffee, homemade breads, and waffles or pancakes.

Rates are *Not So Cheap*. No credit cards accepted, prepayment only.

Bed, Breakfast, and Beach, 2 blocks from downtown Hanalei, 125 yards to the beach and public access.

Another part of the Carolyn Barnes empire is this cute four-room bed-and-breakfast set in a three-story house right in a residential neighborhood of Hanalei. It's also just down the road from the Hanalei Bay Beach Park—a fine beach. All rooms have a private bath, TV, and some sort of fan. Rooms on the first floor have their own private entrance. There is a nice common living room with parquet floors and wall-to-wall carpet. We found the décor here a tad on the kitschy side, with lots of tchotchkes and stuffed animals on display. But hey, most of the rooms are under $100, so who are we to complain? There are four outdoor showers on the premises, which are a great asset. The same style breakfast that is offered at the Hanalei Plantation Guest House is served here on the spacious second-story lanai (smoothies, coffee, homemade breads, and waffles or pancakes).

Rates are **Cheap** and up. No credit cards accepted, prepayment only.

Tutu's Cottage, 1/2 block to the beach, 1/2 block to downtown Hanalei.

She's just all over town, and thankfully so, as we adore this little cottage (and no, Carolyn didn't pay us to plug her properties!). It has a small living room and a small but full kitchen (no dish-washer), one bath, two bedrooms (a king-size bed in the master and one double in the second bedroom) and will sleep up to four. The décor features hardwood floors and rattan/pine furniture. Best of all is the private outdoor shower in the well-kept backyard (starring a banana tree and red-leaf ti plants), which faces a pretty meadow and the distant mountains. The beach park and the restaurants/shops of Hanalei are just down the street.

Rates are **Not So Cheap**. No credit cards accepted, prepayment only.

The Coconut Coast

Lihu'e to Kapa'a

While some may disagree with us (mainly certain resort opera-tors), the Coconut Coast is the "mass market" tourist area of the Garden Isle. A string of large tour-package resorts and properties lines the coast (Po'ipu also has a lot of resorts, but they are, with a few exceptions, more upscale). Don't misunderstand us—while we may sometime sound like it, we are *not* snobs! You don't have to spend a fortune to have a great time (see some of the North Shore places we recommend above). It's just that the area makes us *feel* like a tourist, and you should know by now how we loathe that label. The main road, Highway 56, gets jammed with cars during the day due to the shopping plaza/center and other stoplights. For us, Kaua'i is not about traffic, strip mall developments, or charm-less resorts. If you do elect to stay at one of the resorts, be sure to look for package deals, as they can be steeply discounted. Note that there are a number of bed-and-breakfasts in inland residential areas that provide an alternative. Contact www.gonativehi.com or

www.bandb-hawaii.com for more information. That said, here are some of your resort choices:

The Kaua'i Marriott Resort and Beach Club, Kalapaki Beach, Lihu'e, HI 96766. Toll-free: 800-228-9290. Local: 808-245-5050, fax 808-245-5049. Units: 345.
Web site: www.marriotthotels.com

Formerly the much-talked-about Westin Kaua'i, this was bought by Marriott in 1993 and fortunately they have toned it way down. Once an odd combination of Roman grandeur, Vegas tackiness, and Oriental refinement, it seems to have shed most of the Vegas element and has tried to add more Hawai'ian style. To a degree, it has succeeded (e.g., Hawai'ian names are now used for all parts of the resort). Now part hotel, part time-share, this behemoth lives on.

A long escalator takes you down to where doors sweep open to a very large garden and koi pond to your right and the main lobby down a few steps to your left. Beyond the lobby, the Romanesque pool area emerges. Left untouched since the Westin days, it's still the most outrageous pool we have ever seen. One of the largest pools in the state at 26,000 square feet, there is an island in the middle, connected to the "mainland" by a footbridge. Gargoyles gush water from five points on the island. Rimming the perimeter are chaises. On one end of the pool, columns rise up in Roman majesty. Under each cluster of pillars, there is a huge Jacuzzi—five of them, in fact. They are open all night—one of the best features of this hotel. The Jacuzzi/column clusters are separated by waterfalls. On the mezzanine, a reflecting pool, with Oriental vases appearing to float motionless in the middle, forms the top of the waterfalls. It's interesting to note that the pregnant pillars that line the courtyard and pool are made of fiberglass, not marble, and have been filled with sand. In the Westin days, people used to tap on them and hear a hollow sound, so the sand was Westin's response to too much tapping. It's a wonderfully decadent scene. On the other side of the pool is a lawn leading to pleasant Kalapaki Beach. Behind all this, the towers of the Kaua'i Marriott soar above, having somehow escaped the new zoning laws on building height.

The hotel has 345 rooms, so there are many options for accommodations, including 11 luxury suites. The standard rooms are of average size but are tastefully appointed and have an understated elegance that is Marriott's touch. All have lanais and wall-to-wall carpet. Rattan furnishings with tropical prints are comfortable and pleasant. Rooms come with king-size or two double beds, a fridge, iron/board, cable color TV (with HBO), coffeemaker, safe, and dual-line phones with dataport and voice mail. There are five restaurants/bars on site as well as a fitness center and coin-op laundry.

On the plus side, the hotel is adjacent to Kaua'i Lagoons, a lush 750-acre complex that includes The Kaua'i Lagoons Golf Club and The Spa and Tennis Club at Kaua'i Lagoons. The Kaua'i Lagoons Golf Club boasts two 18-hole Jack Nicklaus golf courses (the Kiele and the Mokihana). The Spa and Tennis Club at Kaua'i Lagoons features an excellent tennis park (seven courts) and a superb health spa. The spa, segregated by sex, offers more ancient Roman opulence, with marble, skylights, and all kinds of soothing therapies for the body—Jacuzzis, saunas, steam rooms, cold plunge pools, massage, loofas, and herbal wraps.

Rates are *Very Pricey* and up. Look for packages.

Kaua'i Beach Hotel, 4331 Kaua'i Beach Drive, Lihu'e, HI 96766. Toll-free: 888-805-3843. Local: 808-245-1955. Units: 347.

Formerly the Outrigger Kaua'i Beach, and the Kaua'i Hilton before that, this resort, located a few miles north of the airport and Lihu'e, changed hands once again in April 2000. Given the change, we not sure what's up. At press time they were open, had started renovations, and expected to be completed sometime in November. Thus, we suggest looking elsewhere for the meantime.

Aston Kaua'i Beach Villas, 4330 Kaua'i Beach Drive, Lihu'e, HI 96766. Local: 808-245-7711, fax 808-245-5550. Units: 55.
Web site: www.aston-hotels.com
E-mail: reskbv@aston-hotels.com

One of four Aston properties on the Coconut Coast, this is an all-condo beachfront property set on 13 acres and adjoined to the Kaua'i Beach Hotel (see above). It's also just two miles north of the airport. Units are housed in four-story red-roofed buildings and are either one bedroom/one bath or two bedrooms/two baths.

All feature lanais, air-conditioned bedrooms, ceiling-fanned living area, full kitchen, washer/dryer, safe, and cable TV. There is a pool with a spa, barbecue facilities, and four tennis courts. Guests can also use the restaurants, bars, and three pools of the Kaua'i Beach Hotel.

Rates are *Pricey* and up. Look for packages.

Holiday Inn SunSpree Resort, 3-5960 Kuhio Highway, Kapa'a, HI 96746. Toll-free: 888-823-5111. Local: 808-823-6000, fax 808-823-6666. Units: 216.
Web site: www.holidayinn-kauai.com
E-mail: info@holidayinn-kauai.com

Somewhere in the haze that was the '70s, we seem to remember Elton John singing about a Holiday Inn. While this has nothing to do with this Kaua'i resort, we needed something interesting to write about as all these places begin to blur into their own haze of sameness. Looking more like a medical center than a hotel and actually not on the water (it's situated on a rise behind Lydgate State Park—a great public swimming beach and facility, by the way, accessed through gates from the resort)—we wouldn't stay here as it just doesn't speak to us. All rooms and suites have a pastel décor, fridge, safe, and iron/board. There are 26 one-bedroom cabanas, which have more character and privacy. Two small pools, a fitness center, tennis court, restaurant, snack bar, lounge, and coin-op laundry round out the facilities.

Prices are *Pricey* and up. Look for packages.

Islander on the Beach, 484 Kuhio Highway, Kapa'a, HI 96746. Toll-free: 800-847-7417. Local: 808-822-7417, fax 808-822-1947. Units: 198.
Web site: www.islander-kauai.com
E-mail: islander@aloha.net

Another Aston property, this consists of eight fairly attractive Hawai'ian-style three-story buildings on six acres, located on the beach in front of the Coconut Market Place megaplex (lots of shops and two movie theaters). Rooms have a lanai and the standard tropical décor, with wet bar, fridge, safe, cable TV, and coffeemaker.

We'd suggest splurging on an oceanfront room as close to the beach as possible. There is a small pool with spa, a barbecue area, and a coin-op laundry facility.

Rates are **Not So Cheap** and up. Look for packages.

Kaua'i Coconut Beach Resort, P.O. Box 830, Kapa'a, HI 96746. Toll-free: 800-22-ALOHA (222-5642). Local: 808-822-3455, fax 808-822-1830. Units: 307.
Web site: www.hawaiihotels.com

We found this place rather lackluster and stark (and the carpets were threadbare and stained). Maybe it was the minimal landscaping or the lack or character, but something was missing (people maybe?). The beach in front is actually quite nice, though. The rooms are standard tropical fare with fridge, safe, cable TV, coffeemaker, and phones with voice mail. There are three tennis courts, a pool/spa area, and a restaurant/lounge. We wouldn't stay here (the clientele was too mainstream for us), but steeply discounted rates may appeal to some.

Rates are **Cheap** and up. Look for packages.

The South Shore
Po'ipu

The Po'ipu area is one of the most popular Kaua'i destinations because of the weather (it receives 50 percent less rainfall per year than the North Shore). Sun worshippers should opt for this, especially in winter. With this popularity has come a lot of development, with just about every inch of buildable coastline taken. Fortunately, nothing taller than four stories is allowed. While it is sunny, the beaches here tend to be smaller and not as dramatic as on the North Shore (with the exception of Polihale on the southwest coast—one of the prettiest beaches in the Aloha State). Hurricane Iniki did major damage here in 1992, including taking away some of the beaches. Another casualty is the fabled Waiohai, which at press time, was a rusting hulk. In 1999 Marriott purchased the property and in June 2000 they received approval from the Kaua'i Planning Commission to demolish the old hotel, and begin construction on what will be the Waihohai Beach Club. Fortunately, one of

Hawai'i's nicest hotels, the Hyatt Regency Kaua'i Resort & Spa, is alive and very well.

Hyatt Regency Kaua'i Resort & Spa, 1571 Po'ipu Road, Koloa, HI 96756. Toll-free: 800-55-HYATT (554-9288). Local: 808-742-1234, fax 808-742-1557. Units: 602.
Web site: www.kauai-hyatt.com

The stunning entrance to this fabulous hotel—the ocean is framed by a rectangular arch at the far end of an orchid-filled, carved-wood courtyard—makes you realize that this isn't your ordinary big resort. The design, in the renowned Hawai'ian architectural style of C. W. Dickey (he is famous for the sloping-roof design on the original Halekulani on O'ahu), harkens back to the early part of the last century. Island artwork is tastefully displayed on the walls and in various sitting areas.

Set on 50 acres on a hill overlooking Keoneloa Bay and fairly large with 602 rooms, the layout doesn't leave one with the impression that this is Kaua'i's biggest hotel (the Marriott would be bigger but most of its rooms are time-shares and not part of the hotel). This place has everything, but it doesn't hammer you on the head the way some of the other Disney/Vegas-style resorts (i.e. the Hilton Waikaloa on the Big Island) do. There is a long golden-sand beach in front and two pools—a quiet one for adults only and an "action" one for kids with a 150-foot water slide. There is also a five-acre saltwater swimming lagoon (man-made), a 25-yard lap pool at the wonderful 25,000-square-foot ANARA Health and fitness Spa (itself a reason to stay here), four Plexi-pave tennis courts, riding stables, and the Po'ipu Bay Golf Course next door, designed by Robert Trent Jones, Jr.

The rooms here match the spaciousness of the resort. At 606 square feet, they are larger than in many hotels elsewhere. The décor is understated and tasteful, with framed prints of Hawai'ian flowers on the cream-colored walls, tan berber carpet, dark cherry wood furnishings, a king-size or two double beds, and Hawai'ian quilted bedspreads. The green-and-white-tile baths, with dual marble vanities and separate loo, feature pocket doors that open up to the room. All rooms have an ample-size tiled lanai, feather pillows, ceiling fans, coffeemaker, iron/board, hair dryer, dual-line phones with dataport, and cable TV. Fridges are available on request and there is 24-hour room service.

As at all Hyatts, there is a Camp Hyatt for kids (ages 3 to 12), which is a welcome program for parents (a baby-sitting service is also available). There are six restaurants, featuring the resort's signature eatery called Tidepools, and six lounges including the Stevensen's Library Bar with billiards and nightly jazz entertainment. A Business Center is on site and even has computers with such programs as Adobe Photoshop and Quark Express. The resort has also been noted for its cultural and environmental programs. But we truly went ga-ga over the ANARA Spa (the acronym stands for "A New Age Restorative Approach"). This is what a hotel spa should be. Besides the aforementioned outdoor lap pool, there are separate facilities for men and women, each with open-air lava rock showers and sunning areas plus steam, sauna, Swiss shower, and locker room. Treatments offered include facials, loofah scrubs, herbal wraps, aromatherapy, botanical baths, hydrotherapy, and of course massage. A beauty salon puts on the finishing touches.

Rates are **Wicked Pricey** and up.

Kiahuna Plantation, 2253 Po'ipu Road, Koloa, HI 96756. Toll-free: 800-367-5004. Local: 808-742-2200, fax 808-742-1047. Units: 333. Web site: www.castle-group.com

Built on the fields of the oldest sugar plantation in the Hawai'ian territory, Kiahuna Plantation is a sprawling condo development of 42 two-story plantation-style buildings on 35 nicely landscaped acres and one of the prettiest beaches in Po'ipu. Very family-oriented, the developer thoughtfully left a "common" in the middle and along the beach, which becomes a mecca for kids throwing frisbees and such or parents barbecuing. Across Po'ipu Road is the Po'ipu Shopping Village, with a slew of restaurants and shops for diversion. Also across Po'ipu Road is the Kiahuna Tennis Club (ten clay courts), where, oddly, the resort's only pool (very small, we might add) is to be found—as is the popular Joe's Courtside Café (breakfast and lunch). Guests may also use the Sheraton tennis courts.

The units themselves are spacious and well maintained, although we were baffled by the use of fake flowers instead of fresh

ones, especially here on the "Garden Isle." Equally baffling was the lack of air conditioning, especially for the rates asked. The units are owner-decorated and thus the décor can vary widely. The one we saw had white walls and dark wood trim, wall-to-wall carpet (tiled entryway, lanai, kitchen, and bath), white louvered doors onto the large lanai with two chaises and a table for four, a complete kitchen including dishwasher and microwave, whitewashed rattan and bamboo furnishings with tan and white fabrics, a CD/tape player, two cable TVs (one with VCR), iron/board, ceiling fans, safe, hair dryer, very old tabletop phones, and a bath with separate tub/loo. There are several different grades of units, from Garden View to Ocean Front. Prices reflect the proximity to the water. Hotel amenities include daily maid service and a coin-op laundry. Note that the property is managed by two companies, Castle Resorts and Hotels and Outrigger, with the line of demarcation basically right down the middle (we're not sure why). There is an excellent Italian restaurant called Piatti's, also right in the middle.

Rates are *Pricey* and up. Look for deals on Castle's and Outrigger's Web sites.

Po'ipu Kapili, 2221 Kapili Road, Koloa, HI 96756. Toll-free: 800-443-7714. Local: 808-742-6449, fax 808-742-9162. Units: 60.
Web site: www.poipukapili.com
E-mail: aloha@poipukapili.com

We really liked this smaller (five-acre) pretty property set across Ho'onani Road from the water, next to the Sheraton. These very spacious and well-maintained condos come in one- and two-bedroom units, all with a water view. All owner-decorated units have huge living/dining areas carpeted in tan berber and furnished with wicker and tropical-motif fabrics. Wood louvers provide privacy. A CD/stereo and TV/VCR (and TV in the master bedroom) provide entertainment. We also loved the big tiled baths with separate loo. A complete white-tile-countertopped kitchen (dishwasher, microwave, toaster, but no blender) and a large lanai round out the amenities. Note that there is no air conditioning but there are ceiling fans.

The focal point of Po'ipu Kapili is a small but attractive square-cross pool and surrounding coral stone patio, which we feel would be a very pleasant place to read the latest Bridget Jones novel. While there isn't a swimmable beach in front, the Sheraton/Kiahuna beach is a five-minute walk away. There are two tennis courts, a coin-op laundry, and a small library on site.

Rates are **Very Pricey** and up.

Sheraton Kaua'i Resort, 2440 Ho'onani Road, Koloa, HI 96756. Toll-free: 800-782-9488. Local: 808-742-1661, fax 808-742-9777. Rooms and suites: 413.
Web site: www.sheraton-hawaii.com

Completely rebuilt after the fury of 1992's Hurricane Iniki hammered the place, the new Sheraton opened in 1997. Set at the western end of Po'ipu Beach, next to Kiahuna Plantation, the resort sprawls over 20 acres with a score of buildings including 11 four-story guest wings. Maybe it was the relative "newness," but we didn't get a warm, fuzzy feeling from this resort. It seemed a tad cold to us. We did like that the ocean units are indeed close to the water but thought the garden units a bit far from the action.

The rooms are nicely done with a tasteful décor that is refreshingly *not* tropical (lots of gray, green, and rust-colored fabrics), with green rattan furniture (well, okay, rattan is kind of tropical). There is a large, private gray-tiled lanai. Beds come with feather pillows—a definite plus in the battle with the facial lines. The marble and tile baths have a separate loo/tub, a double marble-composite vanity, and magnifying mirror. The rooms also have cable TV, Sony PlayStation, fridge, coffeemaker, phone with dataport, iron/board, safe, hair dryer, and robes. Room service is available from 6:30 A.M. to 11 P.M. A coin-op laundry, a decent fitness center, a beauty salon, and a children's baby-sitting program round out the amenities.

For recreation, there are two swimming pools (including one on the beach) and two kids' pools, a hot tub, a beach activities center, three tennis courts (two lighted), five restaurants/snack bars, and a lounge with nightly entertainment.

Rates are **Very Pricey** and up. Look for packages.

Embassy Vacation Resort, 1613 Pe'e Road, Koloa, HI 96756. Toll-free: 800-EMBASSY (535-0085). Local: 808-742-1888, fax 808-742-3343. Units: 212 (eventually 219).
Web site: www.marcresorts.com

KAUA'I

We were skeptical about this sprawling gray resort. Why, you ask? Well, does the term time-share mean anything to you? It's an alarming trend at several Hawai'ian resorts (we thought the time-share fad died in the mid-'80s, but no, unfortunately it lives on). A place that is converting to time-share is usually not focused on occasional visitors. Indeed, we've heard of sales presentations at the "free" breakfasts offered here. That said, the one- and two-bed-room units are so self-sufficient that you could make a sport of dodging the pitch. Families with young kids would definitely like this place.

What we liked about the Embassy was the units themselves. We found them surprisingly spacious and tasteful: white-tiled floors with wall-to-wall tan carpet, pine furniture with a Hawai'ian/colo-nial motif, Hawai'ian quilted linens, and attractively framed prints of Hawai'iana adorning the walls. There were two phones, two TVs, VCR, and full CD stereo for electronic entertainment. The com-plete kitchens had granite countertops, side-by-side fridge with ice maker, dishwasher, dual sink, toaster, coffeemaker, blender, and microwave. The bedrooms were big and featured large walk-in clos-ets. Baths had a deep tub, separate shower, dual marble vanity, and separate loo. There's even a stacking washer/dryer. We found the lanai was also a good size. All units have air conditioning and ceil-ing fans.

Outside, there is a terraced lily pond and a sand beach pool (ideal for kids), a large hot tub, lanes for swimming laps incorpo-rated into the big pool, and gas grills at poolside. A fitness center with steam and sauna rounds out the facilities.

Rates are **Wicked Pricey** and up. Look for packages.

Waikomo Stream Villas, 2721 Po'ipu Road, Koloa, HI 96756. Toll-free: 800-742-1412. Local: 808-742-7220, fax 808-742-9093. Units: 60. Web site: www.granthamresorts.com

The peaked roofs of the Waikomo Stream piqued our interest enough to check out this small resort set in dense vegetation near the Sheraton and the Kiahuna Plantation. There are 60 spacious one- and two-bedroom units, and best of all, this place is a bargain. While not on the water, Po'ipu Beach (the area's nicest) is less than a ten-minute walk away.

All units have a complete kitchen, washer/dryer, tiled lanai, koa-wood-trimmed interiors, teak cabinetry, rattan furnishings with tropical-motif fabrics, cable TV, VCR, CD player, and phone. There is no air conditioning but there are ceiling fans. Also note that there is no maid service. Two pools (a tiny one for kids), a tennis court, and several outdoor grills complete the facilities.

Rates are *Not So Cheap*.

Gloria's Spouting Horn Bed & Breakfast, 4464 Lawai Beach Road, Koloa, HI 96756. Local/fax: 808-742-6995.
Web site: www.best.com/~travel/gloria
E-mail: glorbb@gte.net

While we found this bed-and-breakfast perched on the rocky Po'ipu coastline striking, we also found the rates equally striking, especially for a B&B. Originally a one-story plantation house, it was wiped out in Hurricane Iniki and rebuilt in the style of a Polynesian long house. There are only three guest rooms (called suites here), all with private baths, all right on the water. The rooms are stunning, with very interesting furnishings made of koa, bamboo, and bent willow, depending on the room (we loved the bent willow "Love Nest" bed). Each room has a private lanai, wet bar, TV/VCR, iron/board, hair dryer, fridge, coffeemaker, blender, utensils, and phone. Baths feature a Japanese-style soaking tub (small, square, and deep), a separate shower, and bathrobes. There is no air conditioning but there are ceiling fans.

Outside, there is a private sand terrace with chaises, and a small free-form solar-heated pool. There is also a lava rock hot-water shower. Inside, there's a good video and book library. Gloria and her husband, Bob, live in the house too. While we find this place special, we couldn't help but get the feeling that we were staying in someone's home, which would make us feel a tad too responsible (and uncomfortable) for *our* vacation. But if you like that personal touch, you'll love it here. No pets, shoes, or smoking allowed inside.

Rates are *Very Pricey*. No credit cards. A three-night minimum is requested.

Garden Isle Oceanfront Cottages, 2660 Pu'uholo Road, Koloa, HI 96756. Toll-free: 800-742-6711. Local: 808-742-6717, fax 808-742-1933.
Web site: www.oceancottages.com

E-mail: vacation@oceancottages.com

These one-bedroom cottages line an inlet in Po'ipu and offer a good value, especially for waterfront. We're told the snorkeling and diving is great just off your lanai. There is also a small sandy beach within a five-minute walk. Located on a quiet side street, all cottages have lanais with gas barbecue, fully equipped kitchens (microwave and blender, no dishwasher), TV/VCR, ceiling fans (no air conditioning), wall-to-wall carpet, and wicker/rattan furnishings. While the décor isn't award-winning, it's comfortable and beachy.

Rates are **Not So Cheap**. No credit cards.

Waimea

The far side of Kaua'i is also its quietest and least traveled, with the exception of the spectacular Waimea Canyon, which Mark Twain dubbed "the Grand Canyon of the Pacific." At the end of the road is the equally spectacular Polihale beach, a great place for a picnic and sunset.

Koke'e Lodge, P.O. Box 819, Waimea, HI 96796. Local: 808-335-6061.

No one should miss an opportunity to stay here. Perched 3,600 feet above sea level at the top of Waimea Canyon, the Koke'e Lodge is actually a group of 12 cabins strung along the road in the forest of Koke'e State Park. It is owned by the state but operated by two outdoorsy couples from O'ahu who used to vacation here often and absolutely adore it. Wild chickens, called *moa* in Hawai'ian and descendants of the red jungle fowl the Polynesians brought with them, roam and crow freely about the cabins and the 4,345-acre park. At night the temperature dips to see-your-breath levels, so each cabin has a fireplace to warm your toes (firewood can be purchased at the Lodge). Obviously this is a wonderfully romantic hideaway. And the contrast to the tropical climate at sea level is marvelous. Koke'e State Park offers 45 miles of hiking trails (see Hiking in Waimea Canyon), as well as the only trout fishing in all of Hawai'i (and then only in August and September).

The cabins are rustic yet infinitely charming—that is, if you find rustic as charming as we do. "Basic" is the buzzword here, as the wood-sided, tin-roofed cabins are about as far from deluxe as you can get. Each has a fully equipped kitchen (sorry, no dishwasher), bathroom with freestanding metal shower stall (remember them?), elementary furnishings, and linens. The layouts of the cabins range from one large room that sleeps three to two-bedroom cottages that accommodate seven. The cabins are clean, relatively private, and in good working order. Our only complaint is the lack of reading lamps. The overhead lights just don't play with the romantic atmosphere. We stayed in Ohe-Ohe, which had a double bed in the living room in front of the fireplace. If you don't want to cook, the Lodge has a dining room, which offers very reasonably priced meals daily for breakfast and lunch. There is no longer a cocktail lounge, but the huge koa wood bar—a souvenir of Hurricane Iwa—is still there.

All of this for $35 to $45 per night per cottage makes the Koke'e Lodge the best deal in the Aloha State. It is also one of the most popular, especially with locals: 60 percent of the guests are from Hawai'i. With demand so high and in accordance with park rules, stays are limited to five days; thus it is key to reserve as far in advance as possible.

Rates are **Dirt Cheap**.

Waimea Plantation Cottages, 9400 Kaumuali'i Highway, (P.O. Box 367), Waimea, HI 96796. Toll-free: 800-92-ASTON (922-7866). Local: 808-338-1625, fax 808-338-2338. Units: 48.

Once the management living quarters for the old sugar plantation in town, this turn-of-the-century (that's the turn from the 19th to the 20th century) 27-acre oceanfront property with stately coconut trees is a throwback to another era. The wooden cottages line a common that extends from the main plantation house to the sea (a black-sand beach). There is also a deluxe five-bedroom Manager's Hale (house) to one side of the property and close to the beach. A good-size pool at beachside provides relief from the sun. All cottages have been updated without losing their Old World charm. Each has a front porch/lanai, complete kitchen (stove, microwave, coffeemaker, toaster; some units have a dishwasher and even a Jenn-Air cooktop–go figure!), Mission-style furniture with colorful fabrics, wood floors, cable TV, VCR, CD player,

phone with dataport and voice mail, ceiling fans (no air conditioning), and maid service every third day. There is a restaurant and a very good microbrewery (we could have stayed at the bar all day) in the main house. A coin-op laundry is also available.

Rates are **Pricey** and up.

Where to Eat

There is one area where the growth in tourism on the Garden Isle has had tremendous benefits. Are we talking heresy here? Growth and development are usually greeted with a boo and a hiss—but not here. We feel everyone would agree that when it comes to matters of the stomach, more is definitely better. And there are definitely a lot more dining options on Kaua'i than a decade ago.

The North Shore

Nowhere is the dining explosion more evident than in the quaint little village of Hanalei. There are enough options here to keep anyone satisfied for a week. Best of all, these places are much more affordable than those in more touristy areas and seemed geared to the local/seasonal population.

Bali Hai, Hanalei Bay Resort, 5380 Hono'iki Road, Princeville, 826-6522. The Hanalei Bay Resort's open-air restaurant has great views and sunsets but mixed reviews for its pricey Pacific Rim cuisine. Open daily for breakfast, lunch, and dinner. Reservations recommended. $$$$

Bamboo Bamboo, 5-5161 Kuhio Highway, Suite E101, Hanalei, 826-1177. We happened on this very attractive spot (with equally attractive waitstaff, we might add!) in the Hanalei Center and decided immediately that we had to try it. Maybe it was the wink from the bartender or the undulating hula dancer beaded doorway, we don't remember which. After a few Cosmopolitans and the Crispy Ahi Spring Rolls, we were happy campers indeed. Dinner followed, with Potato-Crusted Mahi Mahi, which was superb, as was the filet mignon. Recently opened in the former Café Luna space, it is open daily for lunch from 11:30 A.M. to 3 P.M. and for dinner from 5:30 to 9:30 P.M. Reservations suggested. $$$

Bubba's Burgers, 5-5151 Kuhio Highway, Hanalei Center, Hanalei, 826-7839. After considering Bubba's motto, "We Relish Your Buns," we decided to live less dangerously and ventured next door to have lunch at Hanalei Gourmet. Nevertheless, there seemed to always be a line for this burger shack, which uses 88-percent fat-free Kaua'i beef and relishes being rude with abandon (but with a sense of humor). If you need a burger/fry fix, look no further. And be forewarned, special orders do upset them here. Bubba's does a big groovy souvie business too. Open 10:30 A.M. to 6 P.M. There's a Bubba's in Kapa'a as well. $

Café Hanalei, Princeville Hotel, Princeville, 826-2760. This is the best (albeit expensive) place for Sunday brunch on the North Shore. The all-you-can-eat spread provides a delectable array of dishes and a lovely place to consume them—the Princeville Hotel's terrace overlooking the bay. Lunch and dinner are also served here. Reservations suggested. Open daily 6:30 A.M. to 9:30 P.M. $$$

Hanalei Dolphin Restaurant & Fish Market, Kuhio Highway, Hanalei (just west of the bridge), 826-6113.   One of the oldest restaurants on the North Shore and a tad too touristy for our taste, this popular surf n' turf spot sits along the Hanalei River and is noted for its bullfrog chorale (no, they don't sing "Bud-weis-er"). No reservations. Open daily from 11:00 A.M. to 10 P.M. $$$$

The Hanalei Gourmet, Hanalei Center, Hanalei, 826-2524. We returned several times to this eatery/bakery/gourmet take-out/bar set in an old wooden schoolhouse 'cause the food is great and we just loved sitting on the lanai watching Hanalei pass by. We suggest their salads or sandwiches for lunch and the daily fresh catch for dinner. This is also one of the few "nightlife" options (they have live entertainment) in the area. Open daily 8 A.M. to 10:30 P.M. $$$

Hanalei Mixed Plate, Ching Young Village, Hanalei, 826-7888. A local favorite for plate lunch, or what could be called "gourmet" plate lunch with an Asian twist, this take-out joint with picnic tables on the side also serves excellent sandwiches, salads, and

burgers. Definitely worth a stop! Open Monday through Saturday from 10:30 A.M. to 8:30 P.M. Closed Sunday. $

La Cascata, Princeville Hotel, Princeville, 826-2761. The premier and very pricey restaurant of the Princeville Hotel, this Italian/Mediterranean restaurant is a good special-occasion let's-get-dressed-up-for-dinner place. To enjoy its perch above the bay overlooking the *pali*, eat early and absorb the sunset views with your focaccia. Reservations advised. Open daily for dinner only, 6 to 10 P.M. $$$$

Lighthouse Bistro, Kong Lung Center, Kilauea, 828-0480. This new eatery serves more traditional Italian/Continental cuisine and features an extensive wine list. Open daily from 5:30 to 9:30 P.M. $$$$

Paradise Bar & Grill, 5-4280 Kuhio Highway, Princeville, 826-1775. Located in the Princeville Shopping Center, this is a great value, especially for lunch (don't miss their fresh fish sandwich or the crab legs). Open daily 11 A.M. to 11 P.M. $$

Pau Hana Pizza/Kilauea Bakery, Kong Lung Center, Kilauea, 828-2020. Tucked away in the Kong Lung Center on the road to the lighthouse, this is one of those places where they won't blink if you order a slice and a scone in the same breath. Try their Billie Holiday pizza (smoked ono, Swiss chard, roasted onions with Gorgonzola rosemary sauce) or their renowned sourdough breads. Open from 11 A.M. to 9 P.M. (the bakery opens at 6:30 A.M.); both are closed on Sunday. $$

Pizza Hanalei, Ching Young Village, Hanalei, 826-9494. Featuring thin whole-wheat sesame-seed-crust (or thin traditional white-crust), all-natural, homemade pizzas. Open daily from 11 A.M. to 9 P.M. $$

Postcards, 5-5075 Kuhio Highway, Hanalei, 826-1191. This cute little vegetarian restaurant (although seafood is served) set in an old wooden house has distinctly mixed reviews when it comes to the organic cuisine served and the relatively high prices charged. Vegetarians will probably be happy, but omnivores should look elsewhere. Open 8 A.M. to 11 A.M., dinner 6 to 9 P.M. Closed Monday. $$$

Roadrunner Bakery & Café, 2430 Oka, Kialuea, 828-TACO (8226). Good Mexican food on the North Shore is found in this funky café with sand floors. The attached bakery makes yummy *taro* pastries and breads. Open Monday through Friday 7 A.M. to 8 P.M., Saturday to 8:30 P.M., and for Sunday brunch from 7 A.M. to 1:30 P.M. $$

Surt's on the Beach, Kuhio Highway (at the Hanalei Colony Resort), Ha'ena, 826-0060. In the former Charo's restaurant space, the acclaimed Euro-Asian fusion cuisine here is popular with day-trippers. We were disappointed that the view of the crashing surf was obscured by salt-caked windows. Open daily for lunch from 11:30 A.M. to 4 P.M., and light dinner from 5:30 to 8:30 P.M. $$

Sushi Blues & Grill, Ching Young Village (2nd floor), Hanalei, 826-9701. The place for sushi and sashimi in Hanalei, Sushi Blues also serves wok-charred, grilled, or sautéed fresh fish, and entrées like grilled kiwi teriyaki chicken and stir-fry. Great live jazz on Wednesday, Thursday, and Sunday, blues on Tuesday, and live music and dancing on weekends make for a convivial atmosphere. Open Tuesday through Sunday 6 to 10 P.M., closed Monday. $$$

Tropical Taco, on the side of the road near the Dolphin in Hanalei, no phone. Look for the green food van. Good, cheap Mexican fare (fresh fish tacos are a "house" specialty). This is a local favorite. Open for lunch only. No credit cards. $$

Zelo's Beach House, 5-5156 Kuhio Highway, Hanalei, 826-9700. Everyone seems to rave about Zelo's, including its ample portions and its funky beachy ambience. It's always busy, the menu spans the world, and the beer and cocktail list is extensive (great martinis and margaritas). Open 11 A.M. to 10 P.M. daily. $$$

The Coconut Coast (Anahola to Lihu'e)

A Pacific Café, Kauai Village, Kapa'a, 822-0013. The original of the acclaimed restaurants by chef Jean-Marie Josselin (he has branches on O'ahu and Maui), the Pacific Rim cuisine served here is among the best on the island and in the state. Set in the unlikely location of a Safeway shopping plaza (at least parking isn't an issue), this attractive place is always packed. House spe-

cialty appetizers include Peking duck and sweet shrimp taco with a papaya ginger salsa, and foie gras in a crispy Asian wrapper with a Thai basil lime ginger glaze; for entrées, wok-charred *mahi mahi* (dolphin fish) with garlic sesame crust in a lime ginger beurre blanc sauce, and *kiawe-* (mesquite-) grilled local *ahi* (tuna) with tempura shittake mushrooms in a sweet soy miso glaze. Drooling yet? Reservations a must! Open daily for dinner only, from 5:30 to 10 P.M. $$$$

Aloha Diner, 971F Kuhio Highway, Kapaʻa, 822-3851. This is a good choice for authentic Hawaiian cuisine, including traditional plate lunch—a must-visit! Open daily for lunch from 10:30 A.M. to 2:30 P.M., dinner from 5:30 to 9 P.M. $

The Bull Shed, 4-796 Kuhio Highway, Kapaʻa, 822-3791 or 822-1655. While we ponder the wisdom of giving a restaurant a name perilously close to the term b.s., it *is* memorable. As the name hopefully implies, this is a steak (and surf n' turf) establishment. With a nice setting on the ocean, ample portions, and very good prices, this is a popular place—now in its 25th year (and over 2 million dinners served!). The prime rib is Bull's trademark. Reservations taken only for parties of six or more. Open daily for dinner from 5:30 to 10 P.M. $$$

Café Portofino, 3501 Rice Street, Nawiliwili, 245-2121. As the name implies, this is a more traditional Italian restaurant with great water views (of Nawiliwili Harbor) where you can find a very good osso bucco or shrimp scampi. Popular with locals; reservations are suggested. Open daily for dinner only, from 5 to 10 P.M. $$$

Duane's Ono Char-Burger, 4-4350 Kuhio Highway, Anahola (next to the general store), 822-9181. Great burgers are the obvious choice at this road side take-out institution, open daily from 10 A.M. to 6 P.M., Sunday from 11 A.M. to 6 P.M. There are tables outside for dining among the wild chickens. $

Duke's Canoe Club, 3610 Rice Street, Lihuʻe, 246-9599. A beach bar/restaurant located on Kalapaki Beach at the Kauaʻi Marriott, this is a very popular luncheon spot, happy hour (great *pupus*) hangout, or place to have a cocktail with the tourist crowd. The upstairs restaurant has mixed reviews (we heard more on the negative side) and service is notoriously uneven. Open daily 11 A.M. to 12 midnight, dinner served from 5 to 10 P.M. $$$

Gaylord's at Kilohana, 3-2087 Kaumoali'i Highway, Lihu'e, 245-9593. A once highly acclaimed restaurant in the old Wilcox plantation mansion (circa 1935), many claim it's not what it used to be and locals call it a tourist trap, although the ambience, especially in the evening, is quite romantic. The cuisine is best classified as "world fusion." Sunday brunch is still a favorite. Reservations advised. Open for lunch Monday through Saturday 11 A.M. to 2:30 P.M., dinner daily from 5 to 8:30 P.M., and Sunday brunch from 9:30 A.M. to 2:30 P.M. $$$$

Hamura's Saimin Stand, 2956 Kress Street (in back of BJ Furniture), Lihu'e, 245-3271. Reputed to serve the best *saimin* (Japanese noodle soup) in Hawai'i, this dive is famous among locals statewide (and a must-stop when on Kaua'i). It's also *the* scene outside after the bars close. Open daily at 10 A.M., and basically closes when the crowd goes away, sometimes not until 3 or 4 A.M. $

Hanama'ulu Restaurant & Tea House, 3-4291 Kuhio Highway, Hanama'ulu, 245-2511. Another institution on Kaua'i (it's been in the same location for over 65 years), the cuisine here is a combo of Cantonese and Japanese. The restaurant includes private garden tearooms (reservations required), a sushi bar, a teppan yaki room, and a Japanese garden with a koi pond. Open for lunch Tuesday through Friday 9 A.M. to 1 P.M., dinner Tuesday through Sunday 4:30 to 8:30 P.M., closed Monday. $$

J.J.'s Broiler, 3416 Rice Street, Kalapaki, 246-4422. Located at the Anchor Cove Shopping Center in Lihu'e, next to the Kaua'i Marriott, this surf n' turf restaurant's specialty is something called slavonic steak (filet mignon with a cream and chardonnay sauce). We recommend lunch over dinner here because it's a much better deal all around. Whatever you decide, a nice view of Kalapaki Bay adds to the occasion. Open daily from 11 A.M. to 10 P.M. $$$

Joni-Hana, Kukui Grove Shopping Center, Lihu'e, 245-5213. Great plate-lunch specials for when you're done with your Liberty House shopping. Open 9:30 A.M. to 7 P.M. $

King and I Thai Cuisine, 4-901 Kuhio Highway, Kapa'a, 822-1642.

We've heard raves about the Thai food at this unpretentious authentic restaurant. Specialties include Siam fresh basil (meat sautéed in a basil, chili, garlic, and oyster mushroom sauce), garlic shrimp, and the tricolor of curry dishes (red, green, and yellow). Open for lunch Monday through Friday from 11 A.M. to 2:00 P.M., and daily for dinner from 4:30 to 9:30 P.M. $$

Restaurant Kintaro, 4-370 Kuhio Highway, Wailua, 822-3341. This teppan yaki and sushi bar fave is consistently rated among the best for both on Kaua'i. Always packed, reservations are suggested in this pleasingly attractive space. Open Monday through Saturday from 5:30 to 9:30 P.M. $$$

L&L Drive Inn, 733 Kuhio Highway, Kapa'a, 822-8880. Looking for a cheap fast-food joint that isn't a McDonald's or Burger King? Then try an L&L, which are all over Hawai'i and offer good plate lunch and Chinese/Asian eats. Open daily 9 A.M. to 10 P.M. $

Mema Thai Chinese Cuisine, 361 Kuhio Highway, Wailua, 823-0899. This Thai-Chinese hybrid offers very good Asian cuisine, serving up the best of both worlds. Mema also has a great selection of vegetarian dishes. Open for lunch Monday through Friday from 11 A.M. to 2 P.M., and daily for dinner from 5 to 9:30 P.M. $$$

Norberto's El Café, 4-1373 Kuhio Highway, Kapa'a, 822-3362. Margaritas by the pitcher or glass—need we say more? Oh, all right, the Mexican food is this funky place is pretty decent too. Open 5:30 to 9 P.M., closed Sunday. $$

Ono Family Restaurant, 4-1292 Kuhio Highway, Kapa'a, 822-1710. This cheap breakfast and lunch diner is the place for everything from omelets to burger plates. Open daily 7 A.M. to 2 P.M. $

Papaya's Natural Foods and Café, Kaua'i Village, Kapa'a, 823-0190. You want organic and vegetarian, you got it at Papaya's. All kinds of tofu, tempeh, and hummus combos are dished out, along with fish sandwiches and tacos (why fish is considered vegetarian by so many "vegetarian" establishments baffles us, but hey, we eat meat). Organic lattes and smoothies are served up, and there's a market too. Open 9 A.M. to 8 P.M., closed Sunday. $

The South Shore (Koloa/Po'ipu to Waimea)

Beach House Restaurant, 5022 Lawai Road, Po'ipu, 742-1424.

Another venture by A Pacific Café chef Jean-Marie Josselin, the Beach House has been swept out to sea by two hurricanes and yet it still keeps coming back, and to greater acclaim each time. Josselin encores his excellent Pacific Rim cuisine and adds Mediterranean accents here, with chef Linda Yamada at the helm. Fab views of the sea from this restaurant's precarious perch make for a pretty damn good dining experience. Reservations advised. Open daily for dinner from 5:30 to 10 P.M., lounge opens at 4:30 P.M. $$$$

Brennecke's Beach Broiler, 2100 Hoone Road, Po'ipu Beach Park, Po'ipu, 742-7588. This 2nd-floor restaurant, actually now an institution, is known for its appetizers, *kiawe*-broiled fresh fish dishes, salad bar, and fabulous sunsets. Brennecke's is not fancy—in fact the décor is so minimal it isn't—but is a very popular tourist hangout. Reservations suggested. Open daily 11 A.M. to 10 P.M. $$$

Brick Oven Pizza, 2-2555 Kaumuali'i Highway, Kalaheo, 332-8561. Reputed to be the best pizza on Kaua'i by those who live there, it's also among the most expensive ($28.30 for a large mix 'n' match pie is a tad excessive). But the hordes keep coming back and if you get it to go, it's about 5 percent less for reasons unknown (maybe no dishes, no cleanup?). It's situated on the way to or from Waimea Canyon and Polihale, so it may be worth the stop, especially for the kids. Open 11 A.M. to 10 P.M., closed Monday. $$

Camp House Grill, Highway 50, Kalaheo, 332-9755. With three locations on the island (the others are in Hanapepe and Kapa'a), this dinerish family-style restaurant is a good value—a place for breakfast or burgers, fries, a frappe (New Englandese for milk shake), barbecue chicken and pork ribs, and their award-winning pies. Open daily from 6:30 A.M. to 9 P.M. $$

Casa di Amici, 2301 Nalo Road, Po'ipu, 742-1555. This old, dependable Kilauea favorite has moved to the South Shore, but they still serve up very good Italian food (including fresh pastas) and atmosphere with mostly North Shore in-the-knows. Reservations suggested. Open daily 5:30 to 9:30 P.M. $$$

Dondero's, Hyatt Regency Kaua'i, 1571 Po'ipu Road, Koloa, 742-6260. One of the Hyatt's finer restaurants, Dondero's features traditional Italian cuisine with fresh pastas and herbs from its own garden. Marble floors, tiles, and murals add to the Old World ambience. It's kinda dressy and not cheap, but it *is* at the most deluxe resort on Kaua'i, so . . . Open daily for dinner only, 6 to 10 P.M. Reservations advised. $$$$

Green Garden, Highway 50, Hanapepe, 335-5422 or 335-5528. One of the more popular restaurants on the island for locals and tourists alike, probably because it's relatively cheap. Their complete seafood dinners—*onaga* (red snapper), *ono* (wahoo), *mahi mahi* (dolphin fish), and *ahi* (tuna)—are *very* reasonably priced. While the buzz on the food is mixed, the atmosphere is casual and unpretentious, and it's always lively. Open for breakfast and lunch Monday through Friday 8:30 A.M. to 2 P.M., Saturday 8 A.M. to 2 P.M., and Sunday 7:30 A.M. to 2 P.M. Open for dinner 5 to 9 P.M. except Tuesdays, when it's closed for dinner. Got that?! $$

House of Seafood, 1941 Po'ipu Road, Po'ipu Kai Resort, Po'ipu, 742-6433. While this place has a great selection of fresh seafood, it's way too expensive (we draw the line at the $40/entrée threshold, unless it's, like, Alain Ducasse, Jean-Georges, LA's Citrus, or SanFran's Aqua). Open daily for dinner from 5:30 to 9:30 P.M. Reservations suggested. $$$$$

Joe's Courtside Café, Kiahuna Tennis Club, Po'ipu, 742-6363. Joe's is a great place for a hearty breakfast or good-size lunch that definitely won't burn a hole in your pocket. It's especially satisfying after a few lively sets of tennis. Open for breakfast from 7 to 11 A.M. and for lunch from 11 A.M. to 2 P.M. $$

Kalaheo Coffee Co. & Café, 2-2436 Kaumuali'i Highway, Kalaheo, 332-5858. Hawai'ian coffees and really good eats (including fresh pastries) and lunches make this a must-stop among gourmands, especially those keeping an eye on the budget. Open daily 6 A.M. to 3 P.M. $$

Kalaheo Steak House, 4444 Papalina Road, Kalaheo, 332-9780. Looking for a melt-in-your-mouth filet mignon at a decent price and away from the tourist crowds? Then try this casual place on the road to/from Waimea. While beef is the focus, the menu has surf, scratch, and oink, too (that's seafood, poultry, and pork). Open daily for dinner from 6 to 10 P.M. Always crowded with no reservations accepted, so plan accordingly (or call ahead). $$$

Keoki's Paradise, Po'ipu Shopping Village, Po'ipu, 742-7535. We're sorry, but this place is just *too* hokey and contrived for our taste. A real touristo trap, the food is average at best. Skip it. Open daily 11 A.M. to 11 P.M. Reservations suggested. $$$

Koke'e Lodge, 3600 Koke'e Road, Waimea Canyon, 335-6061. This is the *only* pit stop for breakfast or lunch in Waimea Canyon, outside of Waimea itself (a *winding* 25-minute drive away). They have totally changed the menu here, now specializing in vegetarian-style dishes made with home-grown produce and offering several locally made 12-grain breads. They have developed quite a reputation for this little place. Open daily 9 A.M. to 3:30 P.M. $$

Pattaya Asian Café, Po'ipu Shopping Village, Po'ipu, 742-8818. The sister restaurant of Mema Thai on the Coconut Coast, that is a tad more expensive (there aren't many choices for Thai food in these parts). If you need a curry fix, Pattaya is what we'd suggest. Open for lunch Monday through Saturday from 11:30 A.M. to 2 :30 P.M., and for dinner daily from 5 to 9:30 P.M. $$$

Piatti, Kiahuna Plantation, 2253 Po'ipu Road, Po'ipu, 742-2216. We heard nothing but accolades for chef David Abell's Pacific/Mediterranean fusion cuisine, and the menu bears out the buzz. Porcupine shrimp in shredded filo with a mango chili sauce, open fresh ravioli with arugula and fresh pumpkin, and a sugarcane pork tenderloin in a tamarind plum sauce had us salivating. Open daily for dinner from 5:30 to 10 P.M. Reservations advised. $$$$

Pizzetta, 5408 Koloa Road, Old Koloa Town, 742-8881. Pricey (over $20 for a large pie) but good thin-crust pizzas, fresh pastas, and salads are the name of the game here. Slices are also available, and there's a full-service bar for something to wash it down. Free delivery to the Po'ipu area. Open daily from 11 A.M. to 10 P.M. $$

Roy's Po'ipu Bar & Grill, Po'ipu Shopping Village, Po'ipu, 742-5000. Roy Yamaguchi is famous in the Aloha State, having made a big bang in Honolulu and now hosting his own PBS show called *Hawai'i Cooks*. One of the pioneers of Pacific Rim/Hawai'ian regional cuisine when he opened his first restaurant in 1988, he now has 17 restaurants on four Hawai'ian islands, around the Pacific Rim, and on the U.S. mainland. That said, this is a popular, lively place and is always packed. More

important, the food lives up to its reputation. Open daily 5:30 to 9:30 P.M. Reservations strongly advised. $$$$

Sueoka's Store Snack Shop, 5392 Koloa Road, Koloa (on the right side of the store), 742-1112. Koloa's favorite plate-lunch and take-out stand—daily specials. $

Tidepools, Hyatt Regency Kaua'i, 1571 Po'ipu Road, Koloa, 742-1234. The Hyatt's signature restaurant on its signature lagoon, Tidepools is a good place for that special dressy dinner to celebrate that certain someone or something (you get the point!). While we think there is better fare for the money elsewhere (the menu can be best described as gourmet surf n' turf), it's the gestalt of the food and the ambience that makes this a worthwhile splurge. Open for dinner daily from 6 to 10 P.M. Reservations advised. $$$$

Waimea Brewing Co., 9400 Kaumuali'i Highway, Waimea, 338-9733. We'd come here just to drink their yummy microbrews, but we're from the Patsy Stone School of Dining so *you'd* probably want something to eat too. Fortunately, this unassuming vintage place has great *pupus,* sandwiches, and real meals. We liked the Jawai'ian Chicken (jerk chicken) and the Kalua Pork with cabbage and sticky rice. Best of all, it's cheap! Open daily from 11 A.M. to 11 P.M. (food served until 9 P.M.) $$

Wrangler's Steakhouse, 9852 Kaumauli'i Highway (Route 50), Waimea, 338-1218. A relaxed restaurant with a Western look and serving Hawai'ian beef, it has a friendly staff and pizzas too. Open Monday through Friday for lunch from 11 A.M. to 4 P.M., for dinner 4 to 9 P.M., Saturday for dinner from 5 to 9 P.M., closed Sunday. $$

Going Out

If you're looking for steamy nightlife, then read no further and go to the O'ahu chapter. Kaua'i is a quiet place, which is part of its appeal. If having a relaxing cocktail is enough, then the Garden Isle will suit you just fine. Of course there are bars and lounges, places with live music and the occasional hotel disco, but for the most part it's B.Y.O.B. (Bring Your Own Bedmate). Kaua'i is a fabulous place for a romantic getaway, a honeymoon, an illicit tryst, or even fun with the kids. But nightlife, uh-uh.

The North Shore

Bamboo Bamboo, 5-5161 Kuhio Highway, Hanalei, 826-1177. Want a martini in an elegant tropical setting? Then head to the bar of this tony restaurant. The bar closes sometime between 10 P.M. and midnight, depending on the crowd.

The Hanalei Gourmet, Hanalei Center, Hanalei, 826-2524. Set in an old wooden schoolhouse in the center of town, this restaurant/café/bar/bakery/take-out joint has live music most nights, sports on the tube, and a convivial atmosphere. Open daily till 10:30 P.M.

Happy Talk Lounge, Hanalei Bay Resort, Hanalei, 826-6522. This is a great place for a sunset cocktail or a couple of rounds of Mai Tais. Its open-air setting overlooking the bay adds to the atmosphere.

Sushi Blues & Grill, Ching Young Village (2nd floor), Hanalei, 826-9701. The place for sushi and sashimi in Hanalei also has live jazz on Wednesday, Thursday, and Sunday, blues on Tuesday, and live music and dancing on weekends. Open until 10 P.M., closed Monday.

Tahiti Nui, Kuhio Highway, Hanalei, 826-6277. This was a favorite bar of ours, but the place seems to be a bit up in the air these days. Started by a very hip Hawai'ian woman named Louise, who was there almost all the time, Tahiti Nui has a nice, quaint bar with occasional live Hawai'ian music. The front lanai has comfortable chairs and an old-time tropical ambience. Due to its peripatetic nature, it's best to call ahead to see if anything's going on (or if it's open). It's also very close to the other Hanalei watering holes, so you can't lose.

The Coconut Coast

Club Jetty, foot of Nawiliwili County Park, Nawiliwili Harbor, Lihu'e, 245-4970. This place is probably the premier live band venue on Kaua'i. The views of the harbor and the funky-faded interior make it a must-visit. It's especially fun when the cruise ships are in. Open until 4 A.M.

Duke's Barefoot Bar, Kaua'i Marriott, Kalapaki Beach, Lihu'e, 246-9599. On the beach in Lihu'e, Duke's is a fun hangout with great *pupus* and a lively happy hour. Food is served daily until 11:30 P.M., and the bar closes at midnight.

Margarita's, 733 Kuhio Highway, Kapa'a, 822-1808. With live music on weekends from 8 to 11 P.M. and, of course, margaritas with chips and salsa, why not?

Norberto's El Café, 4-1373 Kuhio Highway, Kapa'a, 822-3362. Margaritas by the pitcher, and cheap too—what else could you want? Open daily until 10 P.M.

Park Place, Harbor Village, 3501 Rice Street, Lihu'e, 245-5775. Kaua'i's "big" disco. It's fun to see the local crowd, watch the videos, and dance under the mirrored ball. Open until 4 A.M.

The South Shore (. . . zzzzzzzzzzzzzzzz)

The Point, Sheraton Kaua'i Resort, 2440 Ho 'O Nani Road, Koloa, 742-1661. Occasional live music and pretty vistas to enjoy with a cocktail make this an interesting if mellow spot for a pop. Open 11 A.M. to midnight.

Po'ipu Beach Hotel, 2249 Po'ipu Road, Po'ipu, 742-1681. The hotel's Mahina Lounge often has great cover bands. Kick up your heels. Open until 2 A.M.

Cinema

And when you don't have the energy to make an effort but you still want to get out of the house, there are movie theaters to catch up on your film-going. Generally titles will not be as current as those on the mainland, but maybe you can find one you missed on its first go-round.

The North Shore

Kilauea Theater and Social Hall, Kilauea, 828-1722.

The Coconut Coast

Consolidated's Plantation Cinema, Coconut Marketplace, Kapa'a, 822-2324.

Kukui Grove Cinemas, Kukui Grove Shopping Center, Lihu'e, 245-5055.

Roxy Theater, 4533 Kukui Grove Street, Lihu'e, 822-0933.

Health Clubs

The Coconut Coast

Kanai Athletic Club, 4370 Kukui Grove Street, Kukui Grove Shopping Center, Lihu'e, 245-5381.

This is Kaua'i's premier health club, with an excellent free-weight room, aerobics classes, aquasize, massage, lap pool, racquetball, Nautilus steam and sauna rooms, and a Jacuzzi. Open Monday through Friday from 6 A.M. to 9 P.M., Saturday 8 A.M. to 6 P.M., and Sunday 11 A.M. to 5 P.M.

The North Shore

Hanalei Athletic Club, Princeville Resort, Princeville, 826-7333

And this is the North Shore's health club, with free weights, Nautilus, aerobics, jazz, karate, lap pool, massage, Jacuzzi, and steam rooms available. Open Monday through Friday from 7 A.M. to 8 P.M., Saturday 8 A.M. to 6 P.M., and Sunday 11 A.M. to 5 P.M.

Don't Miss

Helicopter Tour (the long version)—This is the only way to really see all of the island and to fly into the Wai'ale'ale Crater (very intense).

Afternoon Tea at the Princeville Hotel—Tally-ho to the Living Room of the Princeville Hotel for some tea sandwiches, cakes, and a fab selection of teas. Oh c'mon, why not?

Dinner at A Pacific Café—One of the best dining experiences in the state, this is the original.

Hamura's Saimin Stand—People come from all over the state for a taste of Hamura's *saimin* (Japanese noodle soup), so find out why it's so popular.

Hanalei town—It's groovy, it's fun, so check it out.

KAUA'I

The North Shore—This is probably the most beautiful place you'll ever see.

Plate lunch at Hanalei Mixed Plate—So *ono,* this is great plate lunch.

Polihale—This very long stretch of beach is one of the prettiest in Hawai'i, and never crowded.

Waimea Canyon—You gotta see the "Grand Canyon of the Pacific." It's really worth the drive!

Lana'i

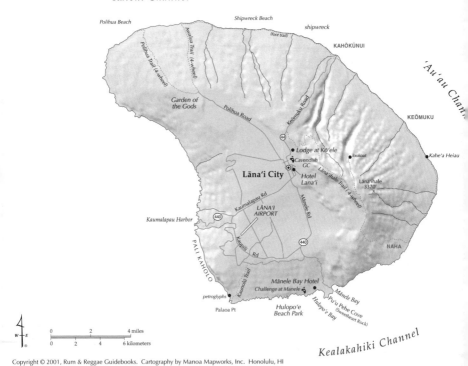

Kalohi Channel

Polihua Beach

Shipwreck Beach

shipwreck

KAHŌKŪNUI

'Au'au Chan..

Polihua Trail (4-wheel)

Awalua Trail (4-wheel)

(foot trail)

Garden of
the Gods

Polihua Road

Keōmuku Road

KEŌMUKU

Lodge at Kō'ele

lookout

Kahe'a Heiau

Cavendish
GC

Lāna'i City

Hotel
Lana'i

Lāna'ihale Trail (4-wheel)

Lāna'ihale
3370'

Kaumalapau Rd

LĀNA'I
AIRPORT

Mānele Rd

Kaumalapau Harbor

440

NAHA

440

PALI KAHOLO

Kaupili Rd

Kaunolū Trail

petroglyphs

Mānele Bay Hotel

Challenge at Manele

Mānele Bay

Palaoa Pt

Hulopo'e
Beach Park

Pu'u Pehe Cove
(Sweetheart Rock)

Hulopo'e Bay

Kealakahiki Channel

N
W—E
S

| 0 | | 2 | | 4 miles |
| 0 | 2 | 4 | | 6 kilometers |

Lana'i

Touristo Scale:
 (4)

ANA'I IS A VERY SPECIAL PLACE. Owned almost entirely
by Dole Pineapple Co. (a subsidiary of Castle & Cooke), until
1990 the island was basically one huge pineapple plantation
and hunting preserve. Then Castle & Cooke transformed its private
island from pineapple producer to a very spacious private playground for the wealthy with the development of the Lodge at Ko'ele
and the Manele Bay Hotel. There are no busloads of tourists here,
no traffic lights, no traffic, in fact, no fast-food chains. It is the
picture of small-town warmth and friendliness. Everyone waves
when you drive by—both pedestrians and other drivers— which
does not happen elsewhere in Hawai'i. We applaud Castle & Cooke
(and its subsidiary, the Lana'i Company) for keeping the lid on
development and maintaining the charm and ambience of the
island. We do miss the miles and miles of pineapple fields—there
was a certain Zen-like quality to their symmetry. When the
plantation was in operation, a siren that went off at 5:00 A.M. as
reveille for the workers, and again at 8 P.M. to signal the close of
operations for the day. After the plantation closed down, the locals
fought to keep the 8 P.M. siren. (Thank goodness they didn't keep
the wake-up whistle! You know by now how we hate getting up at
the crack of dawn.) The locals wanted to maintain the evening
whistle as a way to set their watches and to make sure the kids were
home for curfew (state law—kids 12 and under must be in by
8 P.M.). Do you know where *your* children are? Siren aside, there's
a peacefulness and serenity here that is found in very few places in

this island paradise, making Lana'i one of our favorite spots in the Aloha State.

The Lana'i Company provides for its guests, not only with luxury accommodations, but with two world-class golf courses, stables, tennis, fishing, kayaking, snorkeling, bicycling, hiking, aerobics, sporting clays, four-wheel-drive tours, archaeological walks, and Hawai'ian crafts. The scuba diving off the south coast is superb. Fortunately, there is now a dive operation on Lana'i. If it were our vacation, we'd go to Lana'i with little on the agenda except to enjoy the outdoors and maybe catch up on that pile of unread *New Yorkers*.

Lana'i is shaped like an engorged teardrop, the sixth-largest island in the chain (out of eight—the seventh, Ni'ihau, is owned by the Robinson family and the eighth, Kaho'olawe, is under the control of the U.S. Navy). Lana'i is only eight miles south of Moloka'i and nine miles due west of Maui. Located in the center of the island is Lana'i City, a picturesque little plantation town and the only community on Lana'i. It sits amid towering Cook (Norfolk) pines, nestled under a ridge of mountains. With the elevation at 1,500 feet, the temperatures are cooler and the weather is sometimes misty from the mountain clouds. Lana'i City and the island of Lana'i are a good representation what Hawai'i was all about before statehood and the tourism boom took over—even with the two resorts.

The Briefest History

While the rest of the islands were quickly populated after the arrival of the first wave of immigrants from the Marquesas, Lana'i was left alone, as it was believed to be inhabited by evil spirits. We're not sure why the Hawai'ians thought this. Perhaps the boulder-strewn north slope of the island seemed otherworldly to someone, and as spin doctors know all too well, once a rumor is started it can take on a life of its own. It wasn't until the 15th century that the island was settled, when Kaulala'au, the banished son of a West Maui chief, "drove" the demons away (he needed a place to live).

Captain Cook stopped at Lana'i on his island exploration and noticed that Hawai'ians lived, fished, and cultivated taro on the south coast. By that time, Lana'i was under the rule of the ruthless

Maui chief Kahekili. However, Kamehameha the Great of the Big Island had other ideas and defeated Kahekili's heirs in 1795. Lana'i would hence be part of the Kingdom of Hawai'i, followed by the brief tenure of the Republic of Hawai'i and finally annexation by the U.S.A. in 1900. New England missionaries (read: the Castles and the Cookes) arrived on Lana'i in 1835 and "colonized" the island for a variety of agricultural uses, including cattle ranching, sugar cane, and finally pineapples.

Lana'i: Key Facts

LOCATION	Lana'i City: Longitude 20°50' N, latitude 156° 55' W
SIZE	140 square miles/226 square kilometers
HIGHEST POINT	Lana'ihale (3,370 feet)
POPULATION	3,193 (2000 Census)
TIME	Hawai'ian Standard (year-round): 2 hours behind LA, 5 hours behind New York, 10 hours behind London
AREA CODE	808
AIRPORTS	Lana'i Airport
MAIN TOURIST AREAS	Hulopo'e Beach Park, Lana'i City
TOURISM INFO	The Lana'i Company, Inc., 808-565-3924

Focus on the Lana'i: Relaxing at the Ko'ele Lodge

While golf may be the *raison d'être* for many who travel to Lana'i, we would adore coming here just to unwind and enjoy the Ko'ele Lodge. Nestled at an elevation of 1,600 feet under the spine of the ridge of low mountains capped by Lana'ihale, the Lodge is our choice for headquarters of a Lana'i holiday. The altitude and the mountains provide a cooler and lusher alternative to parched and hot Manele Bay, and the Lodge itself has a lot more character than the more generic Manele Bay Hotel. We also love being able to stroll into Lana'i City and get a plate lunch at the Blue Ginger Café. And call us crazy (you wouldn't be the first), but we went postal over the Executive Putting Course (what we would call miniature golf, but that label may sound too plebeian for some establishments). It is *so much fun* and right next to the Lodge. You don't have to be a golfer to enjoy this activity.

There are many other ways to relax at the Lodge. A wraparound lanai provides comfy chairs for curling up with a book while watching the occasional passerby for diversion. Speaking of reading, the library here has a decent selection of books should you have forgotten to pack one or finished yours before anticipated, and the music room provides classical music on CD and a Steinway grand piano. The Lodge's two dining rooms, while not at all cheap, serve excellent food. The huge stone fireplace in the Great Hall takes the chill off the Lana'i City nights. Afternoon tea, a somewhat foofy and pretentious deluxe hotel practice, is more casual and enjoyable here. We reminded ourselves that the Hawai'ian monarchs and their courts where Anglophiles, so, a British-style tea in Hawai'i is not as preposterous as it sounds. And what the hell, it's free. We admit that we enjoyed it . . . twice! If tea isn't your bag, the bar is in the next room (and we do *love* our "cups"). There is a good-size pool, a health club, an orchiderie called the Orchid House, and a pond in back surrounded by giant banyan trees. Those who want the beach can take the regularly scheduled shuttle to the Manele Bay Hotel, where guests have privileges. The only thing that we would lose is the candy-striped carpet in the guest rooms. It drove us to distraction!

Other Things to Do

- ≋ **Golf**
- ≋ **Lana'i Art Program**
- ≋ **Scuba**
- ≋ **Horseback riding**
- ≋ **Tennis**
- ≋ **Sporting clays**
- ≋ **Archery**
- ≋ **4-wheeling**
- ≋ **Kids**

Golf

The Lana'i Company has built two world-class 18-hole golf courses on the island, the Challenge at Manele and the Experience at Ko'ele. Despite being rather gratuitously named, these courses are superb and have won accolades from that affected travel rag *Condé Nast Traveler* and other magazines. Each offers the duffer a different game. Manele is an ocean course, with sea views from every hole and little room for mistakes. Ko'ele is a verdant upcountry course with lots of hilly and wooded terrain dotted by water hazards.

The Challenge at Manele, Manele Bay Hotel, P.O. Box 310, Lania'i City, HI 96763. Local: 808-565-2222.

> 18 holes—par 72
> Nicklaus (black): 7,039 yards, 73.3 rating
> Championship (gold): 6,684 yards, 71.6 rating
> Tournament (blue): 6,310 yards, 69.8 rating
> Resort (white): 5,874 yards 67.8/73.2 rating
> Forward (red): 5,024 yards, 64/68.8 rating

Opened on Christmas Day 1993, this Jack Nicklaus–designed links-style course is tough and unforgiving. Carved out of 100 acres of rock on the hot and dry south side and over 7,000 yards long (from the Championship tee), there are several cliff-to-cliff over-the-ocean holes. The signature hole, the par-3 12th, is a 200-yard tee-off over the Pacific to the green. Bill Gates got married to Melinda here (the hotel delayed opening the tee until after the wedding so the grass would be perfect), and the Queen of Malaysia got a hole in one (Malaysia is a constitutional monarchy). The 15th hole is a par 5 into the trades onto a well-guarded green. The 17th hole is another sea obstacle course, and at 347 yards, many consider it one of the toughest anywhere. If you can master this baby, you're pretty damn good! Greens fees are $150 for guests and $205 for non-guests. Reservations are required, but you can book up to 90 days in advance.

The Experience at Ko'ele, The Lodge at Ko'ele, P.O. Box 310, Lana'i City, HI 96763. Local: 808-565-4653.

18 holes—Par 72
Tournament (black): 7,014 yards, 73.3 rating
Championship (blue): 6,628 yards, 71.5 rating
Resort (white): 6,217 yards, 69.7 rating
Forward (red): 5,425 yards, 66.0 rating

The first 18-hole course on Lana'i, the Experience was designed by Greg Norman and Ted Robinson and opened in 1991. In contrast to the dry ocean surroundings (not an oxymoron) at Manele, the lush, green bent-grass fairways of Ko'ele have waterfalls and lakes dotting the course. The two 512-yard par 5s are a power-hitter's dream. The course is cooler and a tad more forgiving (except the signature 17th hole, which drops 200 feet from the tee, and the 18th, with its ball-swallowing water hazard before the green). Large custom homes line some of the fairways. Greens fees are $145 for guests, $200 for non-guests. Reservations are required, but you can book up to 90 days in advance.

Cavendish Golf Course, P.O. Box 862, Lana'i City, HI 96763. No telephone available.

9 holes—par 36

This nine-holer was designed by E. B. Cavendish, a superintendent of factory guards, for the Dole Company management back in the old pineapple days. Despite its size (3,071 yards), it's a tough course. Cavendish has a flat layout with long, straight fairways. The finishing hole may be the toughest on the course, featuring an elevated green and particularly strong trades. An enjoyable aspect of this course is the fact that it is so uncrowded—the golfer could even end up playing the course alone. This is the state's only free course (for residents). Obviously it's a popular weekend recreation for locals. Donations suggested for non-residents. Hey, you can't beat the price.

Lana'i Art Program

The Lana'i Art Program, (P.O. Box 701), 339 Seventh Street, Lana'i City, HI 96763. Local: 808-565-7503.

Located in Lana'i City in several converted Dole plantation buildings, this is a novel program for residents and visitors alike. There is a gallery, studio space, pottery barn (not the store), woodworking shop, and photo darkroom. There are classes in painting, ceramics, pottery, cabinetry, photography, and more. The cost is $60 per person for a one-on-one private session, or you can join a group if one is available.

Scuba

Maui's Trilogy Ocean Sports, P.O. 1119, Lahaina, HI 96767. Toll-free: 888-MAUI-800. Local: 808-661-4743.
Web site: www.sailtrilogy.com

Scuba diving (and snorkeling excursions) are now available through Trilogy Ocean Sports. This is great news, as some of Hawai'i's best dive sights are off the south coast of Lana'i. Both introductory and two-tank boat dives are offered. Contact the concierge at the Manele Bay Hotel or at the Lodge at Ko'ele, or book directly at the above address. The Discover Scuba intro dive is $170 and the Lana'i Adventure Scuba (8:30 A.M. to 12:30 P.M.) is $160 per person (certified divers only).

Horseback Riding

The Stables at Ko'ele, (P.O. Box 310), Lana'i City, HI 96763. Local: 808-565-4424.

Trails rides of all persuasions are available at the Stables, with both Western and English saddles. Advanced riders should opt for private rides for a faster pace. With lots of varied terrain and land to explore, this is a fun option. There is a daily group ride at 9 A.M., and scheduled private rides at 9:30 A.M., 1:30, and 2 P.M. Costs start at $40 per person for a one-hour ride. Your best bet is to call the concierge at the Lodge to see what is scheduled for the day.

Tennis

The Manele Bay Hotel and the Ko'ele Lodge have excellent tennis play available, with Peter Burwash International instruction and clinics at both. Manele has six Plexi-pave courts, and Ko'ele has three (none are lighted). Tennis clinics are available Tuesday through Saturday, and offer courses like "Groovin' Groundstrokes," "Vicious Volleys," and "Smokin' Serves." (Our eyes are rollin'!) Clinics are $25 per person and run from 9 to 10 A.M. All tennis courts are open daily from 6:30 A.M. to 5:30 P.M.

Sporting Clays and Archery

Both sporting clays (where you shoot launched clay discs out of the air with shotguns) and archery are offered (along with instruction if desired) at Lana'i Pine Sporting Clays, located a 10-minute shuttle ride from the Ko'ele Lodge. Rates for archery are $45 per hour (equipment included). Rates for clay shooting start at $85 for 50 targets. Open daily from 9 A.M. to 2 P.M.

4-Wheeling

Jeeps are available to rent from **Lana'i City Services,** 1036 Lanai Avenue, Lana'i City, HI 96763. Local: 808-565-7227. Cost is $129 per day. The northern half of the island has miles of interesting dirt roads, including one through the "Garden of the Gods" and the Munro Trail, which follows the mountain spine above Lana'i City. With 4WD, you can also visit Shipwreck Beach, on the northern coast, which is always empty.

Kids

The Pilialoha Children's Program offers all kinds of activities for kids ages 5 to 16. Parents will love this, as well as the baby-sitting and day-care services. After all, vacations are meant to be enjoyed by all! Rates are $40 for a half-day program (9 A.M. to 12:30 P.M. or 11:30 A.M. to 3 P.M.), $60 for a full day (9 A.M. to 3 P.M.), and $55 for an evening (5 to 10 P.M., Friday and Saturday only). There are discounts for more than one child.

Where to Stay

It used to be that the only place to stay was the Hotel Lana'i, an 11-room wooden bungalow in the heart of Lana'i City that was used for executives and guests of the Dole Pineapple Company. The Hotel Lana'i is still around, but it's dwarfed by the 250-room Manele Bay Hotel and its older and more petite sister, the 102-room Lodge at Ko'ele. Given that there are 89,000 acres of Lana'i, that's 245 acres of land per room—lots of breathing space.

Those who want any semblance of a community should opt to stay at the Lodge at Ko'ele or at the Hotel Lana'i because Lana'i City, while tiny, does allow the visitor to get off the resort grounds and mix with the locals. We like the climate of Lana'i City, too—a lot cooler and greener than the parched south side of the island. Dining options are also slightly better here. Looking for nightlife? One word: O'ahu.

Lana'i City

The Lodge at Ko'ele, P.O. Box 310, Lana'i City, HI 96763. Toll-free: 800-321-4666. Local: 808-565-7300, fax 808-565-4561. Units: 102 rooms and suites.
Web site: www.lanai-resorts.com

We droned on (or drooled on—you decide) about the Lodge in the Focus on Lana'i section earlier in this chapter. Read that first and then read on. This resort is located in what probably is one of the most beautiful spots on Lana'i (and one of the most sacred). Much to the chagrin of island residents, a church had to be moved to accommodate the resort (but it was restored by the Lana'i Company).

With the exception of the candy-striped carpet (designed by Castle & Cooke chairman David Murdock — hey Dave, stick to running the company and leave the decorating to decorators), we adore the Lodge's rooms. There's an appropriate pineapple motif throughout the Lodge, including a large pineapple mural on the front portico. We found the rooms to be spacious and very comfortable. Of note are the window sofa-seats, our favorite reading spot in the room. Four-poster king-size beds (with hand-painted headboards), country pine and wicker furniture, light blue walls, and blue upholstery are accompanied by a TV/VCR, mini-bar/fridge, ceiling fans, iron/board, safe, his-and-her bathrobes, dataport phones, and a large lanai. We even had a Murphy bed in our space, and it was surprisingly comfortable. Baths are ample-size, with white and blue tiles, a blue granite vanity, magnifying mirror, hair dryer, a deep tub/shower, and a separate loo.

Rates are *Ridiculous* and up.

Hotel Lana'i, 828 Lana'i Avenue, Lana'i City, HI 96763. Toll-free: 800-795-7211. Local: 808-565-7211, fax 808-565-6450. Units: 10 rooms and Manager's Cottage.

Resembling an old wooden hunting lodge (with red tin roof), this wonderful 11-room hotel is one of our favorite lodgings in Hawai'i. Built in 1923 by James Dole to house his execs, it still has the air of a venerable rustic inn, and its excellent restaurant, Henry Clay's Rotisserie, a roaring fire, and a feeling of aloha add to its appeal. The rooms are simple, with high ceilings, big casement windows, phones, alarm clocks, ceiling fans, and lots of the "c" words: charm and character. Each has a small private bath, and Room 10—a corner room—has a little lanai/entrance where you can sit and watch time go by. Room 6 has a four-poster bed. There are 125 Cook pines on the grounds (a pinecone-collector's dream).

Rates are *Cheap*.

Manele Bay

The Manele Bay Hotel, P.O. Box 310, Lana'i City, HI 96763. Toll-free: 800-321-4666. Local: 808-565-7700, fax 808-565-2483. Units: 250 rooms and suites.
Web site: www.lanai-resorts.com

We don't know what it is about the Manele Bay Hotel, but we've never really glommed onto this place. It seems a tad to contrived for us, and there are other oceanside resorts with more panache in the Aloha State. Perhaps it's the gawd-awful carpeting in the lobby, Kailani Terrace, and elevators (D.M. take note). Or maybe we just don't *understand* the John Wullbrandt Asian-motif murals adorning the walls. In any event, we feel Manele's approach is as subtle as a sledgehammer. The term *nouveau riche* comes to mind. A Calvin Klein minimalist redecoration would just do wonders for this hotel.

Perched at the end of and just above Hulopo'e Beach—the best beach on Lana'i— this is the choice for those who want ocean, beach, and great golf. The beach is open to residents and visitors staying on Lana'i (and to the dive groups from Maui's Trilogy Excusions). The Manele is on the sunny dry side of the island, with a western exposure and fabulous sunset views. There's a good-size pool with hot tub, the full-service Spa at Manele Bay, five different themed courtyard gardens, two very fancy and expensive restaurants, and the Hale Aheahe Lounge (serving daily until I A.M.—a plus). Regularly scheduled shuttle service takes guests to Lana'i City and Ko'ele.

Rooms and suites feature colonial and Asian-style furnishings, yellow or peach-colored walls with matching floral upholstery, bright wall-to-wall carpeting, terra-cotta-tiled lanais with louvered shutters, four-poster or mahogany king-size bed or two double beds, TV/VCR, safe, iron/board, phones with dataport, mini-bar/fridge, his-and-her robes, and lots of closet space. The white marble baths are good-size with marble double-vanity, separate shower/tub, and separate loo.

Rates are **Wicked Pricey** and up.

Where to Eat

In keeping with the small-is-beautiful philosophy of Lana'i, there are not many dining choices here. Fortunately, there are a few offerings in Lana'i City, where dining out is more casual and a helluva lot cheaper than at Manele and Ko'ele. We're starvin' Marvin, so let's go eat!

Lana'i City

Henry Clay's Rotisserie, Hotel Lana'i, 828 Lana'i Avenue, Lana'i City, 565-7211. One of the best things to happen to Lana'i is Henry Clay's, cookin' up a brew of Cajun aloha. The cuisine is a fusion of New Orleans, American, and Hawai'ian regional flavors, although the pepper element definitely prevails. Chef

Clay, trained at the Culinary Institute in Hyde Park, N.Y., makes his bayou roots clear with dishes like Rajun Cajun Clay's Shrimp, Louisiana-Style Ribs, and Lobster and Seafood "Almost Grandma's" Gumbo. If your don't like chile pepper, bring your fire extinguisher or opt for the Catch of the Day or the Gourmet Pizzas. Reservations advised. Open daily from 5:30 to 9 P.M. $$$$

The Lodge's Formal Dining Room, the Lodge at Ko'ele, 565-7300. Everything here is superlative: the food, the portions, the fancy space with fireplace, *and* the prices. Don't be surprised to see entrées well into the $40 range. We were stuffed after the appetizers! Who can eat these kinds of portions? We rolled out with that "I can't believe I ate the whole thing" feeling. Problem was, the food was so tasty we couldn't waste it and the "doggy bag" idea just wasn't going to work for us (we were leaving the next day). Chef Andrew Manion-Copley's American Rustic cuisine utilizes local meats, seafood, and produce. Our adorable waitron talked us into venison, and it *was* excellent. Other faboo dishes include roasted rack of Colorado lamb and pan-roasted Maine lobster. Reservations strongly advised. P.S. Even though it says "formal," black tie is not required—just a jacket for men (and they can lend you one if you didn't bring your blue blazer). Open daily from 6 to 9:30 P.M. $$$$$

The Terrace Room, the Lodge at Ko'ele, 565-7300. At the northern end of the Great Room and spilling out onto the lanai (on Lana'i — hey hey) is the Terrace, offering lighter American Rustic fare in a more casual environment and a somewhat reduced pricing structure than the Formal Dining Room. Under the direction of chef Andrew Manion-Copley and coming from the same kitchen, the offerings are what you'd expect from this place: very good and too much. For dinner try the barbecued veal chop on herb mashed potatoes or the seared Atlantic salmon on crushed fingerling potato cake. Open for breakfast from 6 to 11 A.M., lunch from 11 A.M. to 6 P.M., and dinner from 6 to 9:30 P.M. Reservations suggested for dinner. $$$$

Blue Ginger Café, 409 7th Street, Lana'i City, 565-6363. This family and local-style joint is *da place* for plate lunch on Lana'i as well as one of those hearty, artery-clogging Hawai'ian-style breakfasts. We love the casual local ambience of the Blue

Ginger (we could lose the fluorescent lighting but, who's complaining?). Open daily from 6 A.M. to 9 P.M. $

Pele's Other Garden, 811 Houston, Lana'i City, 565-9628. This is a multi-function food source: a gourmet deli serving great sandwiches and pizza for lunch, and an Italian-style bistro serving big portions of spaghetti and meatballs or bow-tie pasta with prosciutto for dinner. There is also a health-food store stocked with natural foods, vitamins, herbs, and much more. Open Monday through Saturday, for lunch from 9:30 A.M. to 3 P.M., dinner from 5 to 9 P.M. Lunch $, Dinner $$$.

Manele Bay

Ihilani Restaurant, Manele Bay Hotel, 565-7700. Chef Edwin Soto, formally the executive chef at the Lodge at Ko'ele, is now in charge at Manele and added some of his signature dishes to the French and Mediterranean cuisine at Manele's mauve and etched-glass bistro. Of particular interest are the pan-roasted Lana'i venison loin and the braised beef short ribs. Open for dinner only, Tuesday through Saturday, 6 to 9:30 P.M. Jackets are optional; reservations required. $$$$$

Hulupo'e Court, Manele Bay Hotel, 565-7700. Hawai'ian regional seafood is the main feature of this more casual, seaside-view restaurant. Try the citrus grilled tiger prawns or the tropical paella for two. Open daily for breakfast from 7 A.M. to 11 A.M. and for dinner from 6 to 9:30 P.M. $$$$

The Pool Grille, Manele Bay Hotel, 565-7700. Burgers, sandwiches, and light fare are served by the pool. Open daily for lunch only, from 11 A.M. to 5 P.M. $$

Challenge at Manele Clubhouse, Manele Bay Hotel, 565-7700. Overlooking the links of the Challenge course with views of the ocean, this is a relaxed place with a casual menu and reasonable prices. Open daily for lunch from 11 A.M. to 5 P.M., and for dinner Thursday through Monday from 5:30 to 9 P.M. &

Going Out
B.Y.O.B. (Bring Your Own Bedmate!)

Don't Miss

Executive Putting Course—Eighteen holes of miniature golf in a beautiful setting next to the Lodge at Ko'ele. We could (and did) play this for hours (and it's not far from the bar).

Henry Clay's Rotisserie—A unique Lana'i and Hawai'ian dining treat, with plenty of Cajun spice. *Enjoy!*

The Challenge and Experience—Any golfer worth his weight in lost and errant balls will tackle these two masterpieces without a major increase in blood pressure.

Afternoon Tea at the Ko'ele Lodge—Yummy treats to swill with fine tea. It's free, and an old tradition from the days of the Kingdom.

Diving off Lana'i—With excellent lava formations and plenty of marine life, Lana'i's relatively pristine underwater scene is well worth going down for (we know, we ended the sentence with a preposition, but it just works here, so get off our back!).

Moloka'i

Touristo Scale:

🐷 🐷 🐷 (3)

WEDGED BETWEEN THE DESTINATION colossi of O'ahu and Maui is the still unspoiled island of Moloka'i. Like Cinderella, she has been considered the ugly stepsister of her powerful neighbors. However, the whereabouts of her glass slipper has long been known to Hawai'i residents and should be discovered by the adventurous traveler, as this integral part of the Aloha State necklace is a gem of natural beauty and Hawai'iana. On Moloka'i there are no 7-11's or Wal-Marts. The island doesn't even have a stop light. That's right, not even a stop light. What it does have are 3,000-foot seaside cliffs on its north side, unspoiled and lush valleys adorned with waterfalls along the north and east coasts, a long stretch of undeveloped golden sand on the west coast, one of the world's most beautiful yet tragic places in the leper colony of Kalaupapa, and miles and miles of ranch land.

Tourism has not really taken hold here, and past and present efforts by the island and the state have had mixed results. The natural beauty of Moloka'i is often overlooked because the other, bigger neighbor islands offer such a huge diversity and variety of tourist facilities. The Moloka'i airport can accommodate only small inter-island jets, limiting the number of arrivals. In addition, many residents of the state see Moloka'i as the last preserve of the old Hawai'i, and a battle rages in the media, particularly on O'ahu, between those who want to keep Molokai as it is and those who see the need for jobs for island residents. We believe it is up to the residents of Moloka'i, not the armchair quarterbacks on O'ahu and elsewhere, to decide what they want. If they want to maintain the status quo, so be it. If they want jobs, which means development, then that is their choice. We believe everyone should have the opportunity to put food on the table and get a good education. There exists a Moloka'i plan, specifically designed to prevent the rape of the land. Somewhere between the present state and extensive development is probably where the island's future lies. Be that as it may, now is a great time to see a piece of authentic Hawai'i, and it's on Moloka'i.

A Brief History

Like its position in the shadows of Maui and O'ahu, Moloka'i has been a minor player in the role of Hawai'ian history. Usually ruled in the past by the king of Maui, Moloka'i doesn't really have a history of being on its own.

The fifth-largest in the Hawai'ian chain (260 square miles), the island was formed about one and a half million years ago by volcanoes when Moloka'i sat on the magma hotspot that's now under the southeast coast of the Big Island and the Lo'ihi Seamount (currently about 3,000 feet below sea level). The last volcanic eruption occurred about 340,000 years ago. There are no active or dormant volcanoes left on the island.

Originally settled by two migration waves from the Marquesas and Society (Tahiti) Islands in the 8th and then the 12th and 13th centuries, the Hawai'ian Islands were left in isolation from the outside world until the arrival of Captain Cook's expedition in 1778 at Kaua'i. At that time, Moloka'i shared the language and customs of the other Hawai'ian Islands and was ruled by the ruthless and powerful chief of Maui, Kahekili. Contact with neighboring Hawai'ian islands was limited to periodic conquests, defeats, and occasional trading. Within a year of Cook's first contact on Kaua'i, disease, especially venereal diseases, brought by the Europeans had spread to all of the islands.

It was inevitable that the rivalry between Hawai'i's most powerful chiefs would come to a head. Both Kahekili and Kamehameha tapped into the white man's technology, making deals for guns and other support from various British and American traders and mer-

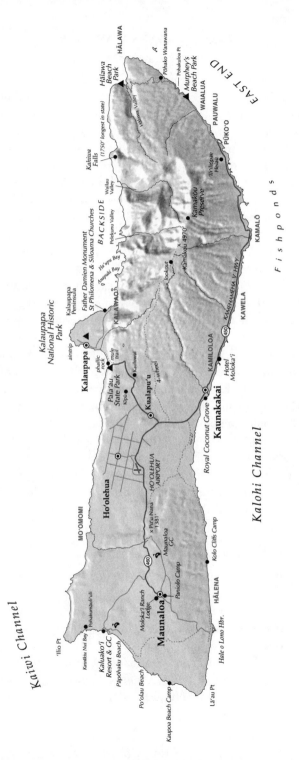

Moloka'i

Kaiwi Channel

'Ilio Pt

Kanaliku Nui Bay
Pohakumauli'uli

MO'OMOMI

Kaluako'i
Resort & GC
Papohaku Beach

Po'olau Beach

Kaupoa Beach Camp

La'au Pt

Hale o Lono Hbr.

HĀLENA

Kolo Cliffs Camp

x Pu'u Nana
1381

Maunaloa
GC

Paniolo Camp

Moloka'i Ranch
Lodge

Maunaloa

460

Ho'olehua

HO'OLEHUA
AIRPORT

Kalohi Channel

Kalaupapa
National Historic
Park

airstrip

Kalaupapa

phallic
rock

mule
trail

Pala'au
State Park

Kipu

Kualawai

Kualapu'u

4-wheel

Kalaupapa
Peninsula

KALAWAO

Father Damien Monument
St Philomena & Siloama Churches

'Ili'ili'opae Bay
Oloupena Bay

lookout

Ha'upu Valley
Pelekunu Valley

BACKSIDE

Kahiwa
Falls
(1750' longest in state)

Waikolu
Valley

Kamakou
Preserve

x Kamakou 4970

Kalupapa

lookout

Royal Coconut Grove

Kaunakakai

Hotel
Moloka'i

KAMILOLOA

450

KAMEHAMEHA V HWY

KAWELA

KAMALŌ

'Ili'ili'opae
Heiau

PUKO'O

Wailau Valley

PAUWALU

WAIALUA

Murphey's
Beach Park

Pohakuloa Pt

Pohako Wananana

EAST END

Hālawa Valley

Hālawa Beach
Park

HĀLAWA

Fishponds

Copyright © 2001, Rum & Reggae Guidebooks. Cartography by Manoa Mapworks, Inc. Honolulu, HI

0   2   4   6   8 miles
0 2 4 6 8 10 12 kilometers

N
W   E
S

cenaries. The more guns and cannons a chief had in his forces, the more success he would have in battles. However, Kahekili died of natural causes in 1794, leaving his half-brother Ka'eokulani of Kaua'i and his son Kalanikupule in charge of his empire. Of course egos battled, and to make a long story even longer, Kalanikupule prevailed. However, Kalanikupule made a grave error in judgment when he killed an English captain on O'ahu, William Brown, and tried to commandeer his ships and men to sail to the Big Island and fight Kamehameha. Unsuccessful and humiliated, he was now without the white man's guns and support. In 1795, Kamehameha, sensing weakness, set out from the Big Island and conquered Maui, Lana'i, and Moloka'i, and headed on to O'ahu and eventually defeated Kalanikupule. After this battle, O'ahu became part of the Hawai'ian Kingdom under the rule of Kamehameha the Great. Kaua'i peacefully, if reluctantly, joined the kingdom in 1810. The unification of Hawai'i was complete.

Moloka'i remained, and some say it still is, a backwater of Hawai'i. The island would become infamous as the location of one of the world's last leper colonies (see Focus on Moloka'i later in this chapter). Ranching and fishing were the economic mainstays of the island and remain major players in Moloka'i's economy today. Tourism is beginning to make inroads but is light-years behind what's found on the neighboring behemoths. Statehood (since 1959) hasn't changed much on the island either. In fact, Moloka'i has been losing population with every census, mainly due to economic factors (i.e. no jobs).

Moloka'i: Key Facts

LOCATION	Kaunakakai: Longitude 21°6' N, latitude 157°1' W
SIZE	260 square miles/420 square kilometers
HIGHEST POINT	Kamakou (4,970 feet/1,515 meters)
POPULATION	7,404 (2000 Census)
TIME	Hawai'ian Standard (year-round): 2 hours behind LA, 5 hours behind New York, 10 hours behind London
AREA CODE	808

MOLOKA'I

AIRPORTS Ho'olehua Airport

MAIN TOURIST Moloka'i Ranch, Kaluako'i, Kalaupapa
AREAS

TOURISM INFO www.visitmolokai.com, www.molokai.com

Focus on Moloka'i: Kalaupapa

Kalaupapa, which means "flat reef" in Hawai'ian, is a low peninsula that juts out from the immense cliffs on the northern coast of Moloka'i. Surrounded by water on three sides and the cliffs on the fourth, it's one of the most isolated and inaccessible spots in Hawai'i. So when leprosy appeared in the islands in the 19th century, brought here by the traders and *haoles*, King Kamehameha V decided that this was the ideal place to sequester its victims from the general populace. In short, he made Kalaupapa a leper colony. Today it is still populated by people who suffer from the disease, though of course they're no longer quarantined.

Leprosy, or Hansen's disease as it is called today, is a degenerative bacterial nerve disorder. It causes painful open sores on the skin and lack of feeling in the extremities. Loss of fingers, limbs, noses, and so on results from constant injury and infection to nerveless body parts. Steady and repeated exposure to the open sores allows the bacteria to invade cuts or abrasions on a healthy person, causing the disease to spread. In times past, little was known about the disease except that it was contagious and disfiguring. Up until almost the middle of this century, lepers truly were "untouchables." Fear of the disease, a scourge for thousands of years, made quarantine absolute and medical care minimal at best. Very few people would get close enough to really help. The treatment of these victims is one of the darker chapters in human history.

The story of Kalaupapa's first settlers is a small but telling part of the tale. In 1865, by the king's decree, men, women, and children with leprosy were forced from their homes onto a ship where they were cruelly isolated. The crew would not go near them, and at the journey's end the lepers, many gravely ill, were either dumped on an island 200 yards offshore or into the water (some compassionate captains rowed them close to shore). Those who made it to shore found no human settlement, and took refuge in caves. Basically, they had been brought there to die, but somehow they managed to hang on. More and more sufferers were brought in. Eventually missionaries arrived to help, building the Siloama Congregational Church and establishing the community of Kalawao in 1866. Then came Father Damien, a Roman Catholic priest from Belgium, who built St. Philomena Church and became the saintly leader of the lepers until he finally contracted the disease himself and died, 16 years after his arrival. But his tremendous efforts on behalf of the community improved conditions and established hope for those who had lived without it.

As the disease spread, victims continued to arrive. Another community, Kalaupapa, was established on the calmer and drier lee side of the peninsula, where conditions were more comfortable. At one point there were over a thousand people living there. Medical personnel increased and health care improved, as did communication and support from the outside world. Houses were built, along with stores, schools, and a movie theater.

In 1940 a Louisiana doctor developed a drug program to control the disease. It didn't reach Kalaupapa until 1946. In its experimental stage, many patients died of kidney failure from toxic high doses. By 1969 the disease was at last considered under control, and the quarantine was finally lifted. Some people left, but many decided to stay. Kalaupapa was, after all, their home—it was where they were comfortable. Today there are fewer than 100 residents left on the peninsula, which is now a National Historic Site administered by the U.S. Park Service.

Kalaupapa is truly one of the most stunning places in Hawai'i, if not the world. The view from the eastern side of the peninsula, where the original settlement of Kalawao was located, is breathtaking. So is the view of the three valleys that unfold onto the peninsula and its leeward beaches. Had this area not had such an unfortunate past, it would probably be the premier resort destination in the islands.

A visit to Kalaupapa is a very poignant experience. Parallels between the tragic lives of these victims and the lives of victims of other little understood and widely feared diseases, such as AIDS, are inescapable. Isolation and quarantine are convenient solutions to assuage the fear and loathing of ignorant people. Those in favor of such drastic steps should come here to listen to the Kalaupapa stories and feel the added suffering that a frightened society placed on those already in such pain. Kalaupapa should be a lesson to humanity.

Seeing Kalaupapa may lead to a guilt trip by association. Don't let this discourage you, however, as it is well worth your time and provides a counterpoint to the otherwise pleasant surroundings of the islands. It will get the mind working again, too.

There are several ways to see Kalaupapa. You can fly in to its airfield, hike down (with permission) and back, or arrive by boat. We think the best way is by mule. That's right, mule. You might think it sounds hokey, but the Moloka'i Mule Ride is an exciting and appropriate way to enter and exit the peninsula. The excitement comes from the trail's physical characteristics—it's a steep three-mile route that takes you from 1,700 feet to sea level. It clings to the side of the massive cliff and takes you around 26 switchbacks. You'll get firsthand validation of the truth behind the old phrase "as surefooted as a mule" on this trail. It is amazing how the mules are able to find the right spot to stop on this slippery and very rocky trail. For many years the trail and the mules were the only direct way into or out of the rest of the island (the roundabout way was by boat).

Not everyone will be able to ride the mules. The ride is one and a half hours of bumps and grinds *each way*. Those with back problems are better off flying. And if you weigh over 225 pounds, the mules cannot accommodate you. If you have any health problems as determined by "yes" answers on the Mule Ride company's medical questionnaire, you will be excluded for insurance reasons. (So either answer "no" and mean it or use another means for getting there.) The mule skinners (guides and handlers) will match you up with an animal corresponding to your riding experience. To us, all the mules are the same—stubborn. The skinners, who accompany the trip, ensure that recalcitrant mules move along with the rest of the group. Be sure to bring your camera; there are vistas galore on the trip down and on the peninsula.

The mule ride and tour lasts about seven hours (from 8 A.M. to 3:30 P.M.). The cost is around $150 per person and includes lunch. Reservations are essential, as the tour fills up fast and has a limit of

18 people per day. Since you will be riding, be sure to wear pants, sensible shoes, and clothes that can get splattered with muddy water. (The rear hooves of the mule in front don't give a damn where they splash. We got splattered with mud that forever stained our new groovy souvy T-shirts.) A jacket or light cover-up is a good idea (there are ponchos on your saddle should it start to rain), and bring plenty of film; there may be none available in Kalaupapa (we've entered the digital age ourselves, so film is a thing of the past for us).

Regardless of which mode of transportation you use, all visitors to Kalaupapa must take the guided tour offered by Damien Tours (included in the mule ride). Unless you are the guest of a resident, you cannot wander around the town unsupervised (the law exists to protect the residents' privacy). In addition, the health department prohibits children under 16 from entering the settlement. The tour van will meet you at the bottom of the trail, at the airport, or at the dock. You'll get a quick drive through Kalaupapa, where you will see the fire station and the center of town, including the defunct movie theater (due to the advent of the VCR and Direct TV). It's strangely quiet as you pass through; signs of life are few and far between. Probably most residents know the tour times and stay out of sight then. Many visitors harbor a morbid curiosity to see exactly what a leper looks like—expecting deformed human figures to be lurking about—and are surprised to find that most of the drivers are lepers.

The tour spends most of its time at the old Kalawao settlement. There are two very scenic churches here—the original Siloama Congregational Church, built by the Protestant missionaries before Father Damien arrived, and St. Philomena, which is much revered by the residents of Kalaupapa (as is Father Damien). Lunch is served (for those on the mule ride only—otherwise bring your own) at a picnic spot that is one of the most incredible sites in Hawai'i. This area is under the auspices of the National Park Service. Someday, when all of the patients have moved away or died, the entire peninsula will be a national park.

For more information on both the mule ride and Damien tours (the Damien tour is included in the cost of the mule ride), contact:

Moloka'i Mule Rides, Inc., P.O. Box 200, Kaulapu'u, HI 96757-0200. Toll-free: 800-567-7550. Local: 808-567-6088, fax 808-567-6244. Web site: www.muleride.com

Damien Tours, P.O. Box 1, Kalaupapa, HI 96742. Local: 808-567-6171.

Other Things to Do

≋ **Beaches**
≋ **Mountain Biking**
≋ **Hiking**
≋ **Kayaking**
≋ **Horseback Riding**
≋ **Golf**
≋ **Snorkel and Scuba**
≋ **Cerebral Stuff**
≋ **Other Sights**

Beaches

In Hawai'i it is rare to find a beach that's not only beautiful but also deserted and undeveloped. On Moloka'i, there are several. Here you can enjoy a sandy cove all to yourselves and the longest beach in the islands—both are within walking distance of the Kaluako'i Resort (for parking) on the west end. There are also some very pretty small beaches on the road to the east end that are cooled by the trade winds.

The West End

While the most spectacular beaches on Moloka'i are the beachheads of the very hard-to-reach valleys of the northern coast (the "back side"), the beaches on the western end of the island are also quite stunning and easily accessible. It is possible to spend a week here and enjoy a different deserted beach every day. If you're staying at Kaluako'i, these beaches are minutes away from your condo. Guests of the Moloka'i Ranch are only a short drive away from the west end's long strands and also have a small beach at its Kaupoa Beach Village site.

Please note: As you should on most Hawai'ian beaches, exercise caution when swimming here, especially during the winter, as surf and current conditions can sometimes be dangerous. Use your common sense, and wear fins to give you that extra horsepower that may be needed.

Kepuhi Bay. The Kaluako'i Resort's main beach is also the best place for surfing. (Dixie's—near Rocky Point—runs a close second.) Kepuhi is split in half by the hotel and a rocky midsection, with the best sunning and swimming spots on the southern half and the best surfing on the northern half. On the surfing part of Kepuhi Bay, there are two reefs. The biggest waves form on the left side, where rocks and coral earn it the name "Boilers." The right side has smaller waves and is appropriately called "Baby Right." If you didn't bring your board, a beach rental shop provides rather basic body-boards, as well as snorkels, masks, and fins. Be sure to ask about conditions and the bottom so you'll be aware of the strong currents and coral patches. The waves can break fairly well here. Kepuhi is the most crowded beach at the Kaluako'i, which means that there may be six other people sharing it with you. As they do at other resorts, many people prefer to be on a chaise longue at the sand-free condo pool. This keeps the beaches very uncrowded, a boon for beach-goers. No facilities.

Papohaku Beach. A two-mile stretch of golden sand that is considered one of the top ten beaches of Hawai'i, this is the longest beach on Moloka'i. Situated south of the Kaluako'i Resort, Papohaku offers no hotels, condos, or houses—just *kiawe* (mesquite) trees. You can take long walks and relish the solitude. At the northern end, which borders the Kaluako'i Resort's (currently defunct) golf course, is Papohaku Beach Park, with parking, restrooms, and showers available. (Take the first right—clearly marked—after the entrance to the hotel.) However, the best swimming is found on the southern end, where the bottom is the sandiest. (Take the third right along the Kaluako'i Road south of the entrance to the hotel.) In other areas, you will have to watch out for occasional coral shelves along the shore break. But there is lots of sand and virtually no one on the beach. It's easy to find a place where you can be left to your own devices. Restrooms/showers/picnic area.

As with all the west coast beaches, you must use your own judgment before taking the plunge, because the currents are strong and there are no lifeguards on duty. So if it looks too rough, don't go in. If you do get caught in a rip, swim perpendicular to the direction of the current (usually parallel to the shoreline) and you will eventually get out of it. If you try to fight it, you will just tire yourself quickly. Again, fins make sense when swimming in these waters.

Po'olau Bay. Apparently this is Moloka'i's de facto nude beach, although when we were there, no one was on the beach, so we couldn't tell. But a reliable source informs us that it is, so try it and see what shakes. Po'olau is reached by taking Kaluako'i Road south to Pohakuloa Road. Turn right here and take the second access road on the right (just after Kulawai Place). No facilities.

Dixie Maru Beach. This sandy cove is the other good surfing spot and a favorite with locals. The waves can break nice and clean off the rocky point on the left. The swimming is good here, too. Watch out when crossing the washout on your way to the beach; if it looks at all wet, you will squish around in a red clay mud. Stay to the far right and you will be okay. Dixie is the third right south of Kulawai Road. Shower.

Pohakuma'uli'uli Beach. Try saying that word—which in Hawai'ian means "very dark rock"—five times quickly. This is a high cliff made up of what looks like very loose dark rocks that could rain down on you at any second. Fortunately, the two very pretty beaches just south of this wall of instability are out of the falling-rock zone and perfectly delightful. The beach nearest Pohakuma'uli'uli is very private and affords a fantastic view of the precipice. Be sure to stay as close to the shoreline as possible when walking by it, and by all means don't sneeze! This beach is reached by walking from the parking circle at the Paniolo Hale condos down the dirt road to the golf course fairway. Cross the fairway, and you're on the beach. Turn right, go around the small point, and you're there. No facilities.

Kawakiu Nui. This, the northernmost beach on the west end, is sandy, private, and good for swimming and snorkeling. It has lots of tidepools, which are great for kids. From the Kaluako'i Resort, it is a 35-minute walk by following the coastline (which involves some minor rock-scrambling) or the dirt road that begins at the Paniolo Hale condos and winds through Moloka'i Ranch land. This road was designated a public beach access to appease activists protesting the development of the Kaluako'i Resort. Kawakiu Nui is popular with locals on weekends. No facilities.

The Rest of Moloka'i

There are some very pretty small beaches on the southern coast west of Kaunakakai, particularly around Halena. These are accessed through the Moloka'i Ranch (check in at the Moloka'i Ranch Outfitters Center at Maunaloa), which has a shuttle that non-guests can use. There is also a public access road that will bring you to Hale O Lono Harbor, but you pretty much need a four-wheeler to made it down there.

East of Kaunakakai, there are several pretty and easily reached beaches starting at Puko'o and continuing here and there all the way to Halawa. As the road runs right alongside, these are not particularly private, but the currents are milder, due to the presence of offshore reefs, so the swimming is easier. The trade winds also keep the beaches nice and cool—perfect conditions for serious sunbathing.

Puko'o and Murphey's Beach Parks. These are the best beaches on the east end of the island. Puko'o is located at the boat harbor (built by the Army Corps of Engineers) in Puko'o. You'll find Murphey's Beach Park just after Waialua. There are others along the way that may look empty and inviting, so pull over and enjoy them if they look good. At Puko'o, the boat harbor has a sandy lagoon that's ideal for swimming. However, access here is currently a hotly contested issue between a California family trust that bought the land around the boat basin and Moloka'i residents. At press time, there were signs saying *"day use only"* and stipulating that you must get permission from the caretaker before entering. Just go in; no one should hassle you. There is one little-known beach at mile marker 22—a very quaint sandy cove. Take a look. On the other side of the Manai Canoe Club pavilion is a very pretty little beach with a great view of Lana'i and trade wind ventilation. Continuing east, Murphy's Beach Park has very good swimming, restroom facilities, trade winds, and a terrific view of West Maui. Surfers are very fond of Pohakuloa Point (a.k.a. Rocky Point), where the sets can attract locals out on their boards.

Mountain Biking

Molokai Ranch Outfitters Center, Molokai Ranch, Maunaloa, HI 96770. Toll-free: 888-729-0059. Local: 808-660-2824.
Web site: www.molokairanch.com

The opening up of the 54,000-acre Moloka'i Ranch to mountain biking has made the island a wonderful destination for this sport. There are two instructional courses, MTB 101 and MTB 102, to make riders familiar with all kinds of techniques for negotiating Molokai's terrain. There is also a Gravity Ride for downhillers, an Intermediate/Advanced Ride, a Full Day Ride by the back side's huge sea cliffs or the Mo'omomi Sand Dunes, and Night Rides. Bike rentals start at $35 a day.

Molokai Bicycle, 80 Mohala Street, Kaunakakai, HI 96748. Neighbor islands toll-free: 800-709-BIKE (2453). Local: 808-553-3931, fax 808-553-5940.
Web site: www.bikehawaii.com/molokaibicycle

Biking options outside of the Ranch are available to equipment renters at this Kaunakakai store. Rentals of both unsuspended and front-suspended bikes are available for $15 and $20 respectively for the first day. Rates decrease with longer-term rentals. Road bikes are also available at $24 for the first day. Bicycle drop-off and pick-up are available for an additional charge. A convenient airport drop-off/pick up is available for neighbor island day-trippers.

Hiking

Some of the best wilderness areas in Hawai'i are on the small bypassed island of Moloka'i. Here, on the northeast corner of the island, lie five big valleys isolated from 21st-century man. They are some of the most beautiful, pristine settings in the state: Halawa, Papalaua, Wailau, Pelekunu, and Waikolu. Unfortunately, most of this paradise is privately owned, primarily by the Moloka'i Ranch, and thus off-limits or difficult to access. However, there are a few ways you can see them. And you can drive to Halawa Valley, so you can get a glimpse there of what the valleys beyond are like.

Two very different hikes easily available to the traveler will take you into Moloka'i's wilderness. The first, Halawa Valley, is a gentle, although muddy, trail that leads you up to the 250-foot Moa'ula Falls and a great pool for swimming. The second, the Wailau Trail, is very difficult, long, and rugged. It is maintained by the Sierra Club, and you must secure permission to access the trail from (call Pearl Petro at 808-558-8113). You should call well in advance of your trip as you will need to send her information about when you want to use the trail. Her address is P.O. Box 125, Kaunakakai, HI 96748. If you are a serious backpacker, this may be appealing. Otherwise, you may want to go to Halawa in the padded luxury of your rental car.

Nature Conservancy of Hawai'i, Kamakou Preserve, P.O. Box 220, Kaulapu'u, HI 96757. Local: 808-553-5236, fax 808-553-9870.

The Nature Conservancy operates this 2,774-acre preserve tucked away at the end of a four-wheel-drive road (Maunahui Road); it encompasses several climate zones, from summit rain forest to dry shrubland. There are over 250 kinds of native Hawai'ian plants here, 219 of which are found nowhere else except in Hawai'i. The preserve is also a bird sanctuary, where you might be able to see the very rare 'olomao (Moloka'i thrush) or the *kakawahie* (Moloka'i creeper) and the red 'iiwi and green *amakihi*, or the more common *apapane* and *pueo* (Hawai'ian owl).

To visit Kamakou, first call the preserve manager at the number listed above for road conditions and other pertinent information. Then take Route 460 and turn off on the Forest Reserve jeep road about a half mile south of the junction of Routes 460 and 470.

Remember that you must have four-wheel drive. Once you arrive at the Wailoku Lookout (about 45 minutes), register at the Visitor Check Station (groups of eight or more must give advance notice). You are asked to stay on the trails and roads, and even there you should tread lightly to help preserve this unique sanctuary of endemic Hawai'ian wildlife.

Halawa Valley

Halawa Falls Cultural Hike, (P.O. Box 863), Kaunakakai, HI 96748. Local: 808-553-4355, fax 808-567-6244.
E-mail: pilipo@visitmolokai.com

Tucked away at the end of the road in eastern Moloka'i are this very pretty valley, reminiscent of the grander Waipi'o Valley on the Big Island, and the scenic Moa'ula Falls. Certainly, if you're on Moloka'i for any length of time, you shouldn't miss Halawa. It used to be that you could just park at the trailhead and hike in on your own. However, those old spoilers, liability and insurance, have ended that freedom because the owners of the land that the trail traverses felt too vulnerable in today's litigious society. But you can still hike to Halawa with Pilipo and Kawaimaka—two local men from Moloka'i. They know the area like the back of their hands and will take you to the falls. Fees are $25 per person. A light lunch is provided. You are asked to bring snacks, sunscreen, insect repellent, and water (leave that thong at home!). Hikers meet at 8:30 A.M. in Kauanakakai and return around 4 P.M.

The hike itself is about five miles round-trip (about two to three hours each way) and fairly easy. As we said earlier, the trails are very muddy, partly due to the use of the hiking trails for horses. The hoof-pounding, combined with frequent rainfall, just makes for a muddy mess.

Along the way, you will see foundations of Hawai'ian *halau* (houses) and *taro* terraces, some of which date back to A.D. 650. You will also see lots of *kukui* nut, mango, Java plum, and *'ulu* (breadfruit) trees. You must cross the Halawa Stream twice. Once at the lower falls, there is a large pool of clean water for swimming. It is shallow at first but gets deeper as you head for the falls. Looking up from the edge of the pool, you can see the peak of the upper

falls cascading into another pool that is out of sight. It's a delightful spot to just sit and enjoy.

A word of caution: During heavy rains or when the level of the
river and falls has increased noticeably, the guides will have you
retreat to higher ground and try to get as far away from the falls as
possible. Obviously, hikes will not be conducted if it has been raining heavily.

Before leaving the Halawa Valley, be sure to check out the black-
sand beach. It's easy to reach with your car (just follow the road to
the water) and is a great spot for surfing and swimming (not too far
out, please—remember those currents). The freshwater stream
emptying into the bay is very refreshing.

Other Areas

**Historical Hikes West Moloka'i, Moloka'i Ranch Outfitters
Center**, Moloka'i Ranch, Maunaloa, HI 96770. Toll-free: 800-274-
9303. Local: 808-660-2825, fax 808-552-2773.

These hikes, from two to six hours in length, are a great way to
see the vast Moloka'i Ranch and learn some interesting things too.
From the dramatic sea cliffs of Moloka'i's back side (north coast) to
the shallow coral reefs of the south, there are hikes of varied terrain
for novice through advanced hikers. Rates are from $50 to $125.

Kayaking

The northeastern coast of Moloka'i, from Halawa Valley to the
Kalaupapa peninsula, is one of the most stunning places in the
world. Also known as the "back side," this is where you'll find some
of the world's tallest sea cliffs and waterfalls (up to 4,000 soaring
feet high-and another 4,000 plunging feet down), as well as the gorgeous valleys discussed above. Seeing it, even from a plane, is a
most profound experience. From a kayak the experience is even
better. The sheer walls of the coast, laced with waterfalls, the green
of these valleys of Eden, and the mountains beyond them make the
entire scene pretty damn incredible.

The calm sea months of May through September are the best
(and really the only) time to explore this dramatic heaven. There

are a couple of outfits that do kayak rentals: **Go Bananas**, out of O'ahu (808-737-9514), **Moloka'i Outdoor Activities**, located in the lobby of the Hotel Moloka'i (808-553-4477), and **Moloka'i Ranch Outfitters Center**, (808-660-2824).

Horseback Riding

Moloka'i Ranch Outfitters Center, Moloka'i Ranch, Maunaloa, HI 96770. Toll-free: 888-729-0059. Local: 808-660-2824.

If you are a recreational rider, Moloka'i has lessons, cattle drives, and trail rides available through the ranch. Rates start at $80 per person per ride.

Golf

Moloka'i, almost forgotten as a golf destination amid its competitive neighbors to the east and west, had two golf courses until January 2001. That's the date when the island's best (and only 18-holer)—the Kaluako'i Golf Course—was closed when the Kaluako'i Hotel & Golf Course went bankrupt. It was on the block at press time and could reopen someday. Until that time, the only option is the nine-hole Ironwood Course.

Ironwood Hills Golf Course, Kala'e, (P.O. Box 182), Kualapu'u, HI 96748. Local: 808-567-6000, fax 808-567-6622.

9 holes-par 35
3,088 yards

This public course is located at 1,200 feet above sea level on the breezy northern coast. It was built in 1938 for Scottish plantation workers, and for years was the only golf option until Kaluako'i was opened. Now it is the only option once again.

While there are no water hazards on the course, the hilly landscape, steady trade winds, slim and tree-studded fairways, and tiny and fast greens provide a good challenge. The toughest holes are the fifth, a 460-yard par four, and the ninth, a 410-yard par four. Both play into the wind. Those golfers who don't like wind factors should tee off before the trades reach their peak velocity in the afternoon. There is a driving range and a pro shop/café at Ironwood. Golfers can walk the course or rent carts. Greens fees are what we call cheap. If you want to do 18 holes, the cost is only $14.

Snorkel and Scuba

Bill Kapuni's Snorkel & Dive, Box 1962, Kaunakakai, HI 96748.
Toll-free: 888-553-9867. Local: 808-553-9867.
E-mail: kapuni@molokai.aloha.com

There is one small dive operation on the island, run by, you guessed it, Bill Kapuni (a local *and* pure-blooded Hawai'ian—a rarity). While we haven't gone diving with him, he is a PADI instructor. He also does snorkel trips. Rates are $95 for a two-tank dive and $65 for snorkel trips. Bill's dives are mostly in the morning, as that is when the conditions are best. He offers only boat dives.

Cerebral Stuff

Ili'ili'opae Heiau. Located east of Kaunakakai just off Route 450, this is one of the largest *heiau* in the state. About the size of a football field and surrounded by dense vegetation, this *heiau* was a temple of human sacrifice (a *luakini*), and one that was much feared throughout the islands as a center of sorcery. *Kahunas* (priests) from all over Hawai'i came here to study the "dark side" of Hawai'ian religion. According to legend, wicked *kahunas* sacrificed nine sons of a local fisherman here. The father appealed to the shark god Kauhuhu, who avenged the sacrifice by flooding the temple and sweeping the evil priests out to sea, where they were eaten by sharks (there is justice in Hawai'ian legends). Legend also claims that the temple was built in one night by those tireless little people, the *Menehunes*, who formed a chain from the Wailau Valley and passed each stone hand over hand. Their reward (appropriately enough) was shrimp.

To visit Ili'ili'opae, you should get permission from a very nice woman named Pearl Petro (808-558-8113), as it sits on her property. That done, drive east from Kaunakakai on Route 450. You will pass

Mapulehu Mango Grove on the right and then will cross a bridge. Immediately past the bridge on the left is a green wooden gate. Park by the hydrant and telephone pole a bit farther down the highway (if you've reached the store you've gone too far). Return to the gate, walk around it, and hike back into the valley on the dirt road as far as the house on the right. Turn left on the trail leading into the woods and you will see the *heiau*.

Where to Stay

In keeping with the low-key character of this very mellow island, there are not a helluva lot of choices for accommodations, as one finds on Moloka'i's neighbors to the east and west—Maui and O'ahu. This makes decision-making very simple. You can stay at the Moloka'i Ranch, the Kaluako'i Resort with its two condo-resorts (the Hotel and Golf Course have been closed until further notice), or in Kaunakakai at the rather funky but cheap Hotel Moloka'i. The finest lodgings and beaches are located on the western end of Moloka'i.

The Moloka'i Ranch, which dominates the western end of the island, has finally opened its doors to visitors and tourism (and for some of the state's residents, controversial development and a shift in the status quo). Headquartered in the sleepy, windswept, up-slope village of Maunaloa, the Ranch has built a wonderfully luxurious hotel called the Moloka'i Ranch Lodge and several rustic "camps" throughout the Ranch's land. The Kaluako'i Resort, also on the western end of the island, sits on Moloka'i's prettiest beach. Kaunakakai, located in the middle of the south coast, is the major town on Molokai—which is to say there is a main street with some really funky stores and restaurants, a bank (with ATM), an old-fashioned supermarket, and the famous Kanemitsu Bakery, where over 1,000 loaves of Moloka'i bread, a Hawai'ian fave, are baked fresh daily and shipped throughout the state. This is an authentic town, not a creation of cutesy boutiques for tourists. Even in the year 2001, there is still no traffic light in town—or on the island. We feel that if one is ever proposed, the uproar will be as loud and ferocious as a tsunami. Moloka'i is pretty much a still-life, so if it's real

Hawai'i you're looking for and you're watching your dollars, stay at the Hotel Moloka'i, which is minutes from the center of town and located on the water overlooking Lana'i. Keep in mind that it can get hot and still in Kaunakakai, as it is located in the lee of the mountains, so the trades can't do their cooling thing as they do elsewhere. But Kaunakakai's location will allow you to explore more of Moloka'i than you would if you were comfortably ensconced in west end digs (unless your agenda is, of course, to be comfortably ensconced, period).

The Moloka'i Ranch

The Ranch, as it is locally known, is no small potato. At 54,000 acres, it is Hawai'i's second-largest privately held property (the Parker Ranch on the Big Island is almost five times the size). Still a working cattle ranch of about 2,000 head, the Moloka'i Ranch branched into the tourist biz in 1996. As we said at the beginning of this chapter, a battle has been raging regarding tourism development on Moloka'i. At center stage of this debate is the Ranch and its vast lands. Some residents of Hawai'i, particularly from the metropolis of Honolulu, see Moloka'i as the last preserve of what was "old Hawai'i." But anyone who visits Moloka'i, or studies its emigration statistics (it is the only major Hawai'ian island to lose population), will realize that jobs are needed here. We will state again that we feel it is up to the residents of Moloka'i to decide for themselves what kind of future they want. Democracy, and not democratic elitism, is the American way and one of the *few* good legacies that we have forced on this mid-Pacific paradise.

The Ranch offers two places to stay: the luxurious Lodge and the more primitive (yet still deluxe) Kaupoa Beach Village. Two other areas, the Kolo Cliffs (with its ropes course) and the Paniolo Village were available for large groups at press time.

The Lodge at Moloka'i Ranch, P.O. Box 259, Maunaloa, Moloka'i, HI 96770. Toll-free: 877-726-4656. Local: 808-660-2722, fax 808-660-2724. Units: 22 rooms and suites.
Web site: www.molokai-ranch.com

We adore The Lodge and wished we could have stayed longer

(next time we hope to do just that). Perched on a windswept hill at 1,100 feet in Maunaloa town, the Lodge opened for guests in the fall of 1999. With a rustic and luxurious charm (not an oxymoron) and without trying too hard, the Lodge has provided Molokaʻi with its first truly comfortable and welcoming small hotel. It's a much smaller and more *intime* version of Lanaʻi's Koʻele Lodge (minus the golf courses and that striped carpet).

The Lodge is right in the village of Maunaloa, with fabulous views west and south of the Kaiwi and Kalohi Channels. Sunsets here are faboo, especially with a cocktail at the Paniolo Lounge and Pool Bar. Opposite the Lodge is the Molokai Ranch Outfitters Center, which offers enough to keep even the most restless vacationer happy—including excellent mountain biking, horseback riding, and ocean kayaking (see Other Things to Do for more info). A free-form heated pool with comfy chaises and hardly a soul at its edge faces the sea in front of the lodge. Guests who want to use the beach can take a shuttle to Kaupoa Beach Village (about a 20-minute ride through the Ranch's cattle lands—lunch is available at the beach). Inside, there is an airy great room with a huge stone fireplace and plenty of places to relax, read, or stretch out. A library on the mezzanine overlooks the room. Hula from some of the island's (and state's) best hula *halau* are presented several nights during the week—a real treat in such a warm and cozy setting. A billiard room near the bar and a well-equipped fitness center and massage/spa area downstairs are great options for diversion and well-being. The Dining Room is Molokai's finest (and most expensive) place to eat. The Paniolo Lounge is more informal and cheaper. Up the street in Maunaloa town is another Ranch property and dining option called The Village Grill.

The guest rooms are magnificent. In keeping with the rustic western lodge décor, earthy tones prevail, with rough-hewn and "distressed" furnishings and what we would describe as a futon-ish yet comfortable TV-lounge area, all with berber wall-to-wall carpet. We especially loved the bed quilts, each one handmade and unique. Our only criticism is that we missed having soft feather pillows for the king-size beds, as foam pillows, while more efficient for hotel use, just don't cut it when it comes to luxury and high prices. (We fondly recall the "Pillow Menu" at the Cotton House on Mustique.) The spacious baths have a claw-foot tub, separate shower, separate loo, terra-cotta-tiled floor, and pedestal sinks. Slippers and thick white terry robes with the Moloka'i Ranch logo are provided for guests (the robes are superb—we bought one). The private lanai and windows have screens (there are bugs) so you can sleep with fresh air (the night temps here are cooler due to the altitude). A wet bar, fridge, safe, and phone with hi-speed dataport round out the room amenities.

Rates are **Wicked Pricey**.

Kaupoa Beach Village, P.O. Box 259, Maunaloa, HI 96770. Toll-free: 877-726-4656. Local: 808-660-2722, fax 808-660-2724. Units: 40 bungalows.
Web site: www.molokai-ranch.com

Located in the southwest corner of Moloka'i, with tidal pools in front and a small sandy beach just to the north, Kaupoa is a great place for those who want quiet beachside living in total isolation (no cities, mega-hotels, condos, or tour buses here). The only people you will see besides other guests and staff are local fishermen. Each "bungalow" sits on a wooden platform, is made of canvas, with tan walls and dark green roof, and shares a deck with another unit (the shared deck units are perfect for two couples or families with kids). If there is only one couple, the other unit stays empty for privacy (thank God!). Remember, the walls are canvas—bedroom screamers take note or be subject to the looks of others. Inside there are rough-hewn wooden queen-size beds over straw mats and red-painted wood floors. There is footlocker with a lock and key for personal items, a beverage cooler, solar-powered lights (with one-hour auto shut-off), and a ceiling fan. There are outlets for cell phone recharging and laptops (after all, this *is* the 21st century). The bath is open to the sky (the self-composting loo is covered) with necessary, but annoying to us, spring-loaded hot- and cold-water conservation faucets. Be sure to request a bungalow away from the generator (with all the land the Ranch has, why not relocate the generator far enough away from the Village so no one can hear it?). All bungalows have daily maid service.

All meals are available at the Village's Dining Pavilion & Bar. Guests also have privileges at the Lodge and the Village Grill. There

is an activities desk at the Village and regularly scheduled shuttle service to the Lodge and Maunaloa town. A "great lawn" has horseshoes and croquet, and hammocks are strung about the property.

Rates are **Very Pricey**.

Kaluako'i Resort

Once the premier resort property on Moloka'i (the Moloka'i Ranch has usurped that title), this 6,800-acre parcel is situated in a striking leeward landscape on the dry and windswept western end of the island. The resort consists of the Kaluako'i Hotel & Golf Course (which has been closed until further notice) and the Paniolo Hale and Ke Nani Kai condo-resorts. We are not surprised that the Kaluako'i Hotel is closed. When we visited last year, we were appalled at its condition. We are surprised that the golf course was closed, however, as it is the island's only 18-holer and is highly praised. We assume money (or lack of it) is involved, and that the several management and ownership changes have not helped either. At press time, the Hotel & Golf Course was on the block. All three properties are clustered on Kepuhi Bay, although the closed hotel has the primo location.

Paniolo Hale, P.O. Box 190, Maunaloa, HI 96770. Toll-free: 800-367-2984. Local: 808-552-2731, fax 808-552-2288. Units: 18. Web site: www.paniolohaleresort.com

Attractive and architecturally stimulating on the exterior, Paniolo Hale is our preferred choice for accommodations at the Kaluakoi Resort. We like the design with its screened porches (*lanai* don't have screens) that are a boon to insectophobes. While the mosquito population isn't horrendous here, it's always comforting to know that you are protected from the army of night-flying creatures, particularly if you like to read outdoors. We also like the tree canopy at the resort. The shade keeps the condos cool and provides lots of greenery in an otherwise parched environment.

The units come in three sizes: studios and one- and two-bedroom. All have oak floors and beamed ceilings. Like most condo resorts, these are owner-decorated, so you hope for everything and expect nothing regarding décor. Nevertheless, they are comfortable and quiet, being surrounded by the fairways of the golf course. Each unit has cable TV, washer/dryer, and a fully equipped kitchen with dishwasher, microwave, and ice maker (very key!). There is a pool, a paddle tennis court, weekly maid service, and, of course, the the tennis courts, and beaches of the resort.

Rates are *Not So Cheap* to *Very Pricey*.

Ke Nani Kai, (P.O. Box 126), Kaluako'i Resort, Maunaloa, HI 96770. Toll-free: 800-888-2791. Local: 808-552-2761, fax 808-552-0045. Units: 120.
Web site: www.kenanikai.com
Located on the grounds of the Kaluako'i Resort's defunct golf course (between the 8th and 17th fairways), these attractive one- and two-bedroom condos are now a time-share club with rentals available to non-club members throughout the year, depending on availability. Units are comfortably furnished in standard condo style (i.e., owner-decorated with some restraint from the managing company, so you're never quite sure what to call the décor—probably the best term is uninspired). They have a complete kitchen with dishwasher and ice maker, and washer/dryer, cable TV, direct-dial phones, two tennis courts, a good-size pool, and a Jacuzzi.

Rates are *Not So Cheap*. Look for deals in the Web site.

Kaluako'i Hotel and Golf Club, P.O. Box 1977, Maunaloa, HI 96770. Toll-free U.S. mainland: 888-552-2550, Hawai'i: 800-435-7208. Local: 808-552-2555, fax 808-435-7208.
Web site: www.kaluakoi.com
Badly in need of a facelift and looking very weathered, at press time the Kaluako'i Hotel & Golf Club was closed until further notice and was for sale.

Kaunakakai

The "greater Kaunakakai metro area" is a town of about 6,000 people. There is only one lodging we would recommend, the Hotel Moloka'i, and only for those who are on a tight budget or looking for a taste of local Hawai'ian style—a Moloka'i attribute. Those craving the slickness and pampering of the luxury resorts will not be happy here. Accommodations are simple, clean, and down-to-earth. What they lack in style they make up for in character—that savior of the small-time operation. The hotel is well integrated into the community, as the bar at Hotel Moloka'i is popular with locals.

Hotel Moloka'i, P.O. Box 1020, Kaunakakai, HI 96748. Toll-free U.S./Canada: 800-367-5004, Hawai'i: 800-272-5275. Local: 808-553-5347, fax 808-596-0158. Units: 45 rooms.

The Hotel Moloka'i, now part of Castle Resorts & Hotels, is a funky place. Try to visualize a medley of Polynesian and '60s A-frame/ski chalet architectural styles, and then place it right on the Kalohi Channel, and you can begin to imagine what this place looks like. There is a small pool at the water's edge—the shallow coral reef makes conditions unfavorable for swimming—and a restaurant on a lanai with good, hearty fare, some terrific waitresses, and wonderful views of Lana'i. The cocktail lounge keeps a drink within reach and offers Hawai'ian slack-key jam sessions on Sunday afternoons.

Rooms continue the funky Tahitian motif with woven straw mat walls and green "turf" carpeted lanais. Standard rooms are small and the baths very simple—all with a kind of rustic tackiness which can be endearing to some (and irritating to others). We recommend the hotel's Oceanfront and Deluxe categories—the extra money here is worth it. Remember, this place is not luxurious by any means. Only two units have A/C, so be sure to ask for it if it's important to you.

Rates are **Cheap** and up.

Where to Eat

Uh-oh, trouble ahead in this department. If you are a gourmand, you will either eat every meal at the Moloka'i Ranch or experience heavy withdrawal symptoms on Moloka'i. With the exception of the Ranch's Lodge and Village Grill, the food is okay at best. There are also a few small local restaurants in "beautiful downtown" Kaunakakai and one upland.

Maunaloa

The Lodge at Moloka'i Ranch, Maunaloa, 808-660-2725. There are two options here. The Maunaloa Dining Room—the only "fancy" restaurant on the island—is a beautiful space of soft tones, light woods, and a verandah (lanai) with views (during the day) to die for. The cuisine is a fusion of Hawai'ian regional and steak-house fare, and diners are often treated to hula dancing expositions. The Paniolo Lounge has pupus, sandwiches, great sunset views, and of course the bar. The Maunaloa Dining Room (appropriate resort attire, please) is open daily for breakfast from 7 to 10 A.M., lunch from 11 A.M. to 1:30 P.M., and dinner from 6 to 9 P.M. Reservations suggested. $$$$$ The Paniolo Bar is open daily from 10 A.M. to 10 P.M. $$

The Village Grill, Maunaloa, 808-552-0012. This casual restaurant has reasonably priced fare (fresh fish and Ranch beef), cooked on a Stonegrill grill. The atmosphere has a strong ranch feeling to it and the fully stocked bar adds to the fun. The Village Grill has excellent take-out plate lunches during the week. Open Monday through Friday for take-out plate lunch from 11:30 A.M. to 1:30 P.M. and daily for dinner from 6 to 9 P.M. Reservations suggested. $$$

KFC Express, next to the Maunaloa Town Cinema, Maunaloa, 808-552-2625. While we normally wouldn't even *think* of mentioning an international fast-food, chain, we do here because it is the only one on Molokai and, given the options on this sleepy island, an alternative. We hope this will be the only outpost of these ubiquitous chains. Open daily from 11 A.M. to 8 P.M. $

Kaunakakai

Kanemitsu Bakery, Ala Malama Avenue, Kaunakakai Town, 808-553-5855. This is the home of Moloka'i bread, which is revered throughout the islands (we're not quite sure why, as it seems like Wonder Bread to us, but, as they say, different strokes. . .). If you are visiting from neighbor islands, it is an unwritten law that you return with Moloka'i bread or else. So you should at least buy a loaf. With all this baking going on (they make over 1,000 loaves a day), the breakfasts here are great. Open from 5:30 A.M. to 8 P.M., closed Tuesday. $

Hotel Molokai, Kaunakakai, 808-553-5347. This is the best restaurant in town (well, actually it's two miles east of town). Their specialty is fresh seafood caught locally and prepared simply (usually broiled). The service is very cordial and the setting, on a lanai at water's edge, is wonderful. Open daily from 7 to 10 A.M. for breakfast, 11 A.M. to 2 P.M. for lunch, and 5 to 9 P.M. for dinner. $$$

Outpost Natural Foods, just off Ala Malama (opposite the State Building), Kaunakakai Town, 808-553-3377. This is a natural-foods store that has a vegetarian lunch bar, sandwiches, and fresh produce for sale. Open Sunday through Thursday from 9 A.M. to 6 P.M., Friday from 9 A.M. to 3:30 P.M., closed Saturday. $

Moloka'i Pizza Café, Kamehameha V Highway, Kaunakakai Town, 808-553-3288. The only pizza joint on the island, this air-conditioned, family-style place has been around since 1992 and also offers sandwiches, chicken, ribs, and fresh seafood dinners. Open Monday through Thursday from 10 A.M. to 10 P.M., Friday and Saturday from 10 A.M. to 11 P.M., and Sunday from 11 A.M. to 10 P.M.

Kualapu'u

Coffees of Hawai'i, Kualapu'u, 808-567-9241. Need a good Java fix? This is da place. Home of Moloka'i's only espresso bar (of heavenly Moloka'i coffee), this light breakfast and lunch spot serves pastries and sandwiches (besides coffee in various *au courant* forms). Open Monday through Saturday from 7 A.M. to 4 P.M. Closed Sunday. $

Going Out

Whoa! Nightlife on Moloka'i? Fuhgeddaboutit. There are two watering holes to note for a sunset cocktail and occasional entertainment. The Hotel Moloka'i (553-5347) is the local gathering place and often has music. The Paniolo Lounge (660-2725) is your option on the west end of the island. Your best bet is to bring your own entertainment or consult the *Moloka'i Dispatch* for any local happenings.

Don't Miss

Kalaupapa via the Mule Ride—One of Hawai'i's darker moments, the founding of the leper colony of Kalaupapa is a reminder of how cruel humans can be, and a lesson. The spectacular setting seems at odds with it all. The Mule Ride is part of the experience.

The Phallic Rock—A natural monument to fertility, it's shaped like a squat version of its namesake (with attachments). Ancient and modern Hawai'ian women would leave leis, flowers, or offerings here when getting pregnant became difficult (no one ever thought that it could be the man who was shooting blanks). The Rock is located a short walk from the parking lot of the Pala'au State Park.

The Lodge at Moloka'i Ranch—A welcome and much-needed addition to the island's lodging options. Do check out this small and very luxurious hotel on its breezy slope.

Hawai'ian Words, Pronunciations, and Definitions

A T FIRST SIGHT, Hawai'ian words look unpronounceable to the *haole*—a veritable sea of tongue-twisters. But once you learn about the language, it's really quite simple. There are twelve letters in the Hawai'ian alphabet: five vowels (a, e, i, o, u) and seven consonants (h, k, l, m, n, p, w). Vowel phonics are constant. An *a* sounds like "ah," an *e* like "ay," an *i* like "ee," an *o* like "oh," and a *u* like "oo." Combined vowels of *ai* and *ae* are pronounced "eye"; *au* and *ao* as "ow," and *ei* as "ay." If there is a backwards apostrophe, called an okina, it indicates a glottal stop and a separation of syllables. When two vowels other than the combinations above are together, they are pronounced separately. Thus the city of 'Aiea (the only city in the U.S. whose name is made up of only vowels) is pronounced "eye-ay-ah," while La'ie is pronounced "la-ee-ay." A *w* sounds like a v except at the beginning of the word. Get it?

Listed below are some of the more common or useful Hawai'ian words and their phonetic spelling. Most are words used in the text or commonly encountered. There are many more words we had to leave out, but once you get the hang of it, you'll be able to figure out how to pronounce any word you see. Have fun!

Hawai'ian	Phonetic	Definition or Location
A		
'a'a	AH-ah	rough lava flow
A'alapapa	ah-ah-la-PA-pa	street in Kailua, O'ahu
'ahi	AH-he	yellowfin tuna

ahu	AH-hoo	a small manmade pile of lava rocks left as tribute or trail marker
Ahu'ena	ah-hoo-AY-nah	restored heiau in Kailua Kona, Big Island
Ahui	ah-HOO-ee	street in Honolulu
'Aiea	eye-AY-ah	town on O'ahu
'aina	EYE-nah	the land
Aina Haina	EYE-nah HIGH-nah	neighborhood of eastern Honolulu
Akaka	ah-KAH-kah	falls and park on the Hamakua coast, Big Island
akamai	AH-kah-my	smart
aku	AH-koo	skipjack fish
'Alalakeiki	ah-lah-LAH-kay-kee	the channel between Maui and Kaho'olawe
Ala Moana	ah-lah moh-AH-nah	major boulevard and shopping center in Honolulu
Ala Wai	AH-lah weye	the canal that separates Waikiki from Honolulu
'Alenuihaha	ah-lay-noo-ee-HAH-hah	the channel between Maui and the Big Island
ali'i	ah-LEE-ee	Hawai'ian nobility
aloha	ah-LOH-hah	welcome, love
aloha'oe	ah-LOH-hah OH-ay	I love you
amakihi	ah-mah-KEE-hee	small, green Hawai'ian honeycreeper (bird)
ami	AH-mee	pelvic rotation in the hula
'Anaeho'omalu	ah-nigh-HOH-oh-MAH-loo	beach and historic fishpond near Waikoloa, Big Island
Anahola	ah-nah-HO-lah	village on Kaua'i
'Anini	ah-NEE-nee	beach park on the north shore of Kaua'i
'apapane	ah-pa-PAH-nay	Hawai'ian honey-creeper (bird)
'a'u	AH-oo	marlin
'auana	ow-AH-nah	term used to describe modern hula
'Au'au	OW-ow	the channel between Maui and Lana'i
'awa	AH-vah	milkfish

Awaʻawapuhi	ah-vah-ah-vah-POO-hee	trail and valley on the Na Pali cost, Kauaʻi

B

brah	brah	(Pidgin) pal, buddy

D

da kine	dah kein	(Pidgin) the term used when you can't remember a specific word or are just too lazy to use it

E

ʻEhukai	ay-HOO-kigh	famous beach park opposite the Pipeline on Oʻahu
ʻEwa	AY-vah	town on the western end of Oʻahu that is frequently used to denote west on Oʻahu

H

Haʻena	HAH-ay-nah	village on north shore of Kauaʻi
Haipuaʻena	high-poo-ah-AY-nah	stream and falls on the Hana Highway, Maui
halau	hah-LAU	long house, often used to denote a hula troupe
Halawa	HAH-lah-vah	valley in eastern Molokaʻi
hale	HAH-lay	house
Haleakala	hah-lay-AH-kah-lah	Maui's dormant vocano and highest point
Haleʻiwa	hah-lay-EE-vah	town on north shore of Oʻahu
Halemaʻumaʻu	hah-lay-ma-OO-MAH-oo	crater in Volcanoes National Park, Big Island
Hamakua	HAH-MAH-koo-ah	the northeastern coast of the Big Island
hana hou!	hah-nah HO!	one more time!
Hanakaʻoʻo	hah-nah-kah-OH-OH	point on West Maui
Hanakapiʻai	hah-nah-KAH-PEE-eye	stream, falls, and beach on the Na Pali coast
Hanalei	HAH-nah-lay	town on the north shore of Kauaʻi

Hanapepe	hah-nah-PAY-pay	town on the south shore of Kaua'i
haole	HOW-lee	Caucasian
hapa	HAH-pah	half
hapai	hah-PIE	pregnant
Hapuna	hah-POO-nah	beach park on the Kohala coast, Big Island
hau	how	a hibiscus tree
Haunauma	how-NOW-mah	marine park and beach on O'ahu
Hau'ula	how-OO-lah	village on the windward side of O'ahu
Hawai'i	hah-VIGH-ee	world's paradise and also the official name of the Big Island
Hawi	HAH-vee	town on the Kohala peninsula, Big Island
heiau	hay-EE-ow	Hawai'ian temple
Hi'ika	hee-EE-kah	Pele's younger sister who, in legend, ran off with Pele's lover, Lohiau; also a crater in Volcanoes National Park, Big Island
Hilo	HEE-loh	largest city and county seat of the Big Island
holoholo	hoh-lo-HOH-loh	to go out
Holualoa	HOH-loo-ah-loh-ah	village in Kona, Big Island
hono	HOH-noh	bay
Honoka'a	HOH-noh-KAH-ah	town on Hamakua coast, Big Island
Honokohau	HOH-noh-koh-HOW	boat harbor in north Kona, Big Island
Honolua	HOH-noh-LOO-ah	famous surf break on west Maui
Honolulu	HOH-noh-loo-loo	Hawai'i's capital and largest city, located on O'ahu
Honomu	hoh-NOH-moo	village on the Hamakua coast, Big Island
Ho'okena	hoh-oh-KAY-nah	beach park in south Kona, Big Island
Ho'okipa	ho-oh-KEE-pah	beach park on Maui, famous for its surfboarding
howzit	HOW-zit	(Pidgin) hi, how's it going?

Hualalai	hoo-ah-LAH-leye	third-highest peak on the Big Island
huhu	HOO-hoo	pissed off
hui	hoo-ee	club
Hule'ia	HOO-lay-ee-ah	stream on Kaua'i
Hulihe'e	hoo-lee-HAY-ay	summer palace of Hawai'ian royalty in Kailua-Kona, Big Island
huli huli	HOO-lee HOO-lee	barbecued
Hulopo'e	hoo-loh-POH-ay	best beach on Lana'i
humuhumunu **kunukuapua'a**	HOO-moo-hoo-MOO-noo koo-noo-KOO-ah-poo-AH-ah	the state fish

I

'Iao	EE-ow	park in west Maui
'iiwi	ee-EE-vee	scarlet Hawai'ian honeycreeper (bird)
iki	**EE-kee**	small
Ili'ili'opae	ee-lee-ee-lee-OH-pie	largest heiau on Molaka'i
imu	EE-moo	underground oven
'Iolani	ee-oh-LAH-nee	name of only royal palace in the U.S. and of a private secondary school, both in Honolulu
Iwa	EE-vah	famous hurricane of 1982

K

Ka Lae	KAH lie	southernmost point on the Big Island, and of the U.S.
Ka'a'awa	kah-ah-AH-vah	village on the windward side of O'ahu
Ka'ahumanu	kah-ah-hoo-MAH-noo	Kamehameha the Great's strong-willed queen, Hawai'i's first feminist
Ka'ala	kah-AH-lah	highest point on O'ahu
Ka'anapali	kah-ah-nah-PAH-lee	resort area on west Maui
Kahala	kah-HAH-lah	posh neighborhood of Honolulu
Kahalu'u	kah-hah-LOO-oo	village on windward side of O'ahu

kahiko	kah-HEE-ko	ancient term for traditional hula
kahili	kah-HEE-lee	feathered staff carried by Hawai'ian royalty
kaholo	kah-HOH-loh	the key sidestep in hula
Kaho'olawe	kah-hoh-oh-LAH-veh	off-limits island controlled by the U.S. Navy; previously used for target bombing
Kahului	kah-hoo-LOO-ee	largest town on Maui
kahuna	kah-HOO-nah	a Hawai'ian priest
kai	kigh	the sea
Kaihalulu	kigh-hah-LOO-loo	bay in Hana, Maui
Kailua	kigh-LOO-ah	tony suburb of Honolulu, on the windward side of O'ahu
Kaimana	kigh-MAH-nah	beach park in Waikiki
Kaimuki	kigh-moo-KEE	neighborhood of Honolulu
Kaiwi	KIGH-vee	the channel between O'ahu and Moloka'i
Kalakaua	kah-lah-KOW-ah	the last king of Hawai'i, known as the Merrie Monarch
Kalalau	kah-lah-LOW	the trail along the Na Pali coast
Kalaniana'ole	kah-lah-ne-ah-nah-OH-lay	the highway from Kahala to Kailua on O'ahu
Kalapaki	kah-LAH-pah-KEE	the beach at the Kaua'i Marriot
Kalapana	kah-lah-PAH-nah	village on the Puna coast wiped out by lava flows
Kalaupapa	kah-low-PAH-pah	the famous leper colony and peninsula on Moloka'i
Kalawao	kah-lah-WOW	the first leper settlement on Moloka'i
Kalihi Wai	kah-LEE-hee weye	village on the north shore of Kaua'i
Kalohi	kah-LOH-hee	the channel between Moloka'i and Lana'i
kalua	kah-LOO-ah	baked in an imu
kama'aina	kah-mah-EYE-nah	native-born, literally "child of the land"
Kamehameha	kah-MAY-hah-MAY-hah	the chief who unified Hawai'i in 1795, became its first king, and founded a dynasty bearing

		his name; a major highway and esteemed school on O'ahu bear his name
Kanaha	kah-NAH-hah	a beach park on Maui that is a major windsurfing site
Kanaloa	kah-nah-LO-ah	the god of the dead
kane	KAH-nee	man or men
Kane	KAH-nay	the god of life
Kane'ohe	kah-nay-OH-hay	a suburb of Honolulu on the windward side
Kaohikaipu	kah-oh-hee-KIGH-poo	small island off of Makapu'u Beach, O'ahu
Kapa'a	kah-PAH-ah	town on the eastern side of Kaua'i
Kapahulu	kah-pah-HOO-loo	major avenue in Kaimuki, Honolulu, O'ahu
kapu	KAH-poo	taboo; keep out
Ka'u	KAH-oo	the southeastern district of the Big Island
Kaua'i	kow-WEYE-ee	the "Garden Isle," the oldest of the major Hawai'ian islands
Kauapea	kow-ah-PAY-ah	beach on the north shore of Kaua'i
Ka'uiki	kah-oo-EE-kee	landmark hill in Hana, Maui
kaukau	KOW-kow	food
Kaulu o Laka	KOW-loo oh LAH-kah	one of the most sacred heiau in Hawai'i, where hula originated-located on the north shore of Kaua'i
Kaulu Paoa	kow-loo pah-OH-ah	part of the same heiau as Kaulu o Laka
Kaunakakai	kow-nah-kah-KIGH	the major town on Moloka'i
Kauna'oa	kow-nah-OH-ah	the beach at the Westin Mauna Kea
Kaupo	KOW-po	the trail and valley leading from Haleakala to the sea at Kaupo on the south side of Maui
Kawaihae	kah-weye-HIGH	the major shipping port on the western shore of the Big Island, located in Kohala

Kawaikini	kah-weye-KEE-nee	the highest point on Kaua'i
Kawailoa	kah-weye-LOH-ah	beaches on Kaua'i and O'ahu
Kawakiu Nui	kah-wah-KEE-oo noo-ee	bay and beach on the west end of Moloka'i
Kea'au	kay-ah-OW	town in the Puna district, Big Island
Kealaikahiki	kay-ah-lie-kah-HEE-kee	the channel between Lana'i and Kaho'olawe
Kealakekua	kay-ah-lah-key-KOO-ah	town and bay in Kona, Big Island, and the site of Captain Cook's demise, several heiau, and a marine park
Kealia	key-ah-LEE-ah	beach on eastern Kaua'i known for its surf break
Ke'anae	KEY-ah-nigh	scenic point on the Hana Highway, Maui
Keauhou	KAY-ow-hoh	town south of Kailua-Kona, Big Island
Ke'e	KAY-ay	the beach at the trailhead of the Kalalau Trail on the north shore of Kaua'i
Ke'ehi	kay-AY-hee	lagoon, marina, and beach park in Honolulu
Kehena	kay-HAY-nah	village on the Puna coast, Big Island
keiki	KAY-kee	children
Kekaha	key-KAH-hah	town on the southwest coast of Kaua'i
Keolu	key-OH-loo	the hills in Kailua, O'ahu
Keomuku	kay-oh-MOO-koo	beach and road on the north east shore of Lana'i
Kepuhi	kay-POO-hee	points on Kaua'i and O'ahu
Kewalo	kay-WAH-loh	basin in Honolulu and site of Point Panic, a famous summer surf spot
kiawe	kee-AH-vay	mesquite trees
Kihei	KEE-hay	major town on east Maui
Kilauea	kee-low-WAY-ah	the active volcano on the Big Island and a village on Kaua'i
Kipahulu	kee-pah-HOO-loo	village on the south coast of Maui where Charles Lindbergh is buried

Ko'ele	koh-AY-lay	village on Lana'i
Kohala	koh-HAH-lah	northwestern district end peninsula of the Big Island
Koke'e	ko-KAY-ay	the state park at the top of Waimea Canyon, Kaua'i
kokua	koh-KOO-ah	help
Koloa	koh-LOH-ah	town on the south shore of Kaua'i
kona	KOH-nah	leeward
Kona	KOH-nah	the southeastern districts (north and south) of the Big Island
Ko'olau	KOH-oh-low	ridge of mountains on O'ahu
Ku	koo	the god of war, who demanded human sacrifice
Kualoa	koo-ah-LOH-ah	regional park on the windward side of O'ahu
Kuhio	koo-HEE-oh	a Hawai'ian prince from Kaua'i and first congressional delegate of Hawai'i, whose name adorns several roads, centers, and buildings
kukui	koo-KOO-ee	candlenut tree
Kukuihaele	koo-KOO-ee-hah-AY-lay	village at the entrance to the Waipi'o Valley, Big Island
kumu hula	koo-moo HOO-lah	hula master/teacher
Kumukahi	koo-moo-KAH-hee	easternmost point of the Big Island

L

lae	lie	point or cape
Lahaina	lah-HEYE-nah	the major town on west Maui, previously the chief whaling port of Hawai'i and the capital until 1845
La'ie	LAH-ee-ay	Mormon town on the windward side of O'ahu
lanai	lah-NIGH	porch, veranda, or balcony
Lana'i	lah-NAH-ee	once nicknamed the "Pineapple Isle," as it was a huge pineapple plantation; it is almost entirely owned by Castle

433

		and Cooke, Inc., and now boasts two luxury resorts as well as the landmark Hotel Lana'i
Lani Kai	lah-nee KIGH	very toney neighborhood of Kailua, O'ahu
lau hale	lau HAH-lay	traditional Hawai'ian straw weave
Lawa'i	lah-WAH-ee	village on the south shore of Kaua'i and home of the Pacific Tropical Botanical Garden
lei	lay	flowers, leaves, or shells worn in a garland placed on the shoulders
Lihu'e	lee-HOO-ay	the largest town and the county seat of Kaua'i
like beef?	like beef?	(Pidgin) Wanna fight about it?
Likelike	LEE-kay-LEE-kay	named after a Hawai'ian princess, this is one of the two freeways to the windward side of O'ahu from Honolulu
loa	LOW-ah	long
Lohiau	loh-HEE-ow	Pele's lover; he ended up with her younger sister, Hi'ika
lua	LOO-ah	crater or pit; also bathroom
luakini	LOO-ah-KEE-nee	heiau of human sacrifice
luau	LOO-ow	Hawai'ian feast
Lumaha'i	loo-mah-HAH-ee	beach on the north shore of Kaua'i

M

Ma'alaea	mah-ah-lah-AY-ah	harbor, beach, and bay on the southern side of the Maui isthmus
Ma'alehu	mah-ah-LAY-hoo	village on Moloka'i
mahalo	mah-HAH-lo	thank you
Maha'ulepu	ma-ha-oo-LAY-poo	beach on the south shore of Hawai'i
mahi mahi	MAH-hee MAH-hee	dolphin fish
mahu	MAH-hoo	gay, although often used to describe transvestites

maile	MY-lee	fragrant vine often used in lei-making
Makaha	mah-KAH-hah	town on the leeward side of Oʻahu
Makahoa	mah-kah-HOH-ah	points on Kauaʻi's north shore and Oʻahu's windward side
makai	mah-KEYE	toward the sea
Makapuʻu	MAH-ka-POO-oo	beach park and point on Oʻahu's windward side
Makawao	mah-kah-WOW	town in the Upcountry part of Maui
Makena	mah-KAY-nah	village and golf course on central Maui
Makiki	mah-KEE-kee	neighborhood in Honolulu
Makua	mah-KOO-ah	village and valley on Oʻahu's leeward side
Malaekahana	MAH-ligh-kah-HAH-nah	state recreation area and beach on Oʻahu's windward side
malihini	mah-lee-HEE-nee	foreigner, newcomer, tourist
mana	MAH-nah	supernatural spirit
Manana	mah-NAH-nah	island off of Waimanalo, also known as Rabbit Island
Manele	mah-NAY-lay	bay on southern Lanaʻi
Manoa	mah-NOH-ah	valley and neighborhood of Honolulu
Maui	MOW-ee	nicknamed the "Valley Isle," this is the second-largest island in the chain
mauka	MOW-kah	toward the mountains
mauna	MOW-nah	mountain
Mauna Loa	MOW-nah LO-ah	meaning "long mountain," the second-highest peak on the Big Island and in Hawaiʻi and a dormant volcano
Mauna Kea	MOW-nah KEY-ah	meaning "white mountain," the highest peak on the Big Island
Maunalua	MOW-nah-LOO-ah	the bay facing the Kahala and Hawaiʻi Kai neighborhoods of Honolulu

mele	MAY-lay	song or chant; also merry
Mele Kalikimaka	MAY-lay kah-LEE-kee-MAH-kah	Merry Christmas
menehune	may-nay-HOO-nay	the legendary little people who would build walls, heiau, and fishponds in one night
Miloli'i	MEE-lo-LEE-ee	beach park and village in south Kona, Big Island
moana	moh-AH-nah	the ocean
Moa'ula	moh-ah-OO-lah	stream and falls in Halawa Valley, Moloka'i
moi	MOH-ee	threadfin fish (kingfish)
Mo'ili'ili	MOH-ee-lee-EE-lee	neighborhood of Honolulu
Mokapu	MOH-kah-poo	peninsula on O'ahu's wind-ward side and location of Marine Corps Air Station
moke	moak	(Pidgin) tough local guy
Mokoli'i	moh-ko-LEE-ee	island off Kualoa Point on O'ahu's windward side, commonly known as "Chinaman's Hat"
moku	MOH-koo	island or district
Moku 'Auia	MOH-koo ow-EE-ah	island off of La'ie, O'ahu, known as Goat Island
Moku Lua	MOH-koo-LOO-ah	islets off of Lani Kai, O'ahu
Moku'aikaua	MOH-koo-eye-KOW-ah	church in Kailua-Kona, Big Island
Mokule'ia	MOH-koo-lay-EE-ah	village and surf break on the north shore of O'ahu
Moloka'i	moh-loh-KAH-ee	nicknamed the "Friendly Isle", the fifth-largest in Hawai'i
Molokini	moh-loh-KEE-nee	the crescent-shaped islet off of east Maui

N

Na Pali	NAH-pah-lee	the undeveloped northwestern coast of Kaua'i, a state park
Na'alehu	NAH-ah-LAY-hoo	town in the Ka'u district of the Big Island
Napili	nah-PEE-lee	village and point on west Maui

Napo'opo'o	NAH-poh-oh-POH-oh	village in south Kona, Big Island
Nawiliwili	NAH-wee-lee-WEE-lee	harbor at Lihu'e, Kaua'i
nene	NAY-nay	the Hawai'ian goose, the state bird
Ni'ihau	NEE-ee-how	the seventh-largest Hawai'ian island, privately owned by the Robinson family of Kaua'i, home to about 250 native Hawai'ians and off-limits to the public
nui	NOO-ee	large or big
Nu'uanu	noo-oo-AH-noo	the name of a street, stream, and valley in Honolulu

O

O'ahu	oh-AH-hoo	nicknamed "the Gathering Place," the third-largest and most populous of the Hawai'ian islands
ohana	oh-HAH-nah	family or relative
'O'heo	oh-HAY-oh	the gulch on Maui where the "Seven Sacred Pools" are located
'o'io	oh-EE-oh	bonefish
'olomao	oh-loh-MAH-oh	Moloka'i thrush
Olowalu	oh-loh-WAH-loo	village on west Maui
ono	OH-noh	excellent, superb, delicious; or wahoo (king mackerel) fish
opihi	oh-PEE-hee	shellfish delicacy

P

pahoehoe	PAH-ho-ay-HO-ay	smooth lava flow
Pa'ia	pah-EE-ah	town in central Maui
pakalolo	pah-kah-LOH-loh	pot, marijuana
pali	PAH-lee	cliffs
paniolo	pah-nee-OH-loh	Hawai'ian cowboy
Papalaua	PAH-pah-LAU-ah	falls on Moloka'i
Papohaku	pah po-HAH-koo	best beach on Moloka'i
pau	pow	finished, no more
pau hana	pow HAH-nah	quittin' time

Pele	PAY-lay	the fire goddess, who should be referred to with the utmost respect or bad luck will come your way
Pelekunu	PAY-lay-KOO-noo	stream and bay on Moloka'i's "Back Side"
Pi'ilanihale	pee-ee-LAH-nee-HAH-lay	the largest heiau in the state, located north of Hana, Maui
Pohakuloa	PO-hah-koo-LOH-ah	the name of places on Kaua'i, Moloka'i, Lana'i, Maui, and the Big Island
Pohakuma'uliuli	Po-ha-koo-ma-OO-lee-OO-lee	cliff on the westem end of Moloka'i
poi	poy	a purplish paste made from baked mashed taro root, a staple of the Hawai'ian diet
Po'ipu	PO-ee-poo	town and resort area on the south shore of Kaua'i
Polihale	PO-lee-HA-lay	beach park on the western end of Kaua'i
pueo	poo-AY-oh	Hawai'ian owl
puka	POO-kah	hole
Puko'o	poo-KOH-oh	village and harbor on the southern coast of Moloka'i
Punahou	POO-nah-ho	the prestigious, posh, and mostly haole prep school in Honolulu
Punalu'u	POO-nah-LOO-oo	villages in O'ahu and the Big Island
Puohokamoa	POO-oh-ho-kah-MO-ah	stream and falls on the Hana Highway, Maui
pupu	POO-poo	appetizer
Pupukea	POO-poo-KAY-ah	village and famous surf break on the north shore of O'ahu
pu'u	POO-oo	hill or mound
Pu'u O'la'i	POO-oo oh-LAH-ee	cinder cone between Big and Little Beaches, Maui
Pu'u o Kila	POO-oo oh KEE-lah	lookout at Koke'e State Park on Kaua'i over the Kalala Valley
Pu'u Pehe	POO-oo PAY-hay	a towering, sheer rock off the south coast of Lana'i, also called Sweetheart Rock

Pu'uhonua o Honaunau	POO-oo-ho-NOO-ah oh ho-NOW-now	the City of Refuge in south Kona, also a National Historic Park
Pu'ukohola	POO-oo-koh-HOH-lah	a heiau on the Big Island, built by Kamehameha the Great and a National Historic Site

S

shaka	SHAH-kah	(Pidgin) the hand gesture, thumb and little finger up, meaning "take it easy" or "great, excellent"

T

t'anks, eh?	Tanks, ay?	(Pidgin) thanks a lot
tapa	TAH-pah	(Tahitian) a highly decorated cloth made from tree bark
taro	TAH-roh	(Tahitian) a leafy shrub, the root of which was the staple food of the Hawai'ians (poi is made from this) and a key agricultural product
ti	tee	(Tahitian) leaves of the ti plant are used for cooking and as offerings to the gods
tita	TEE-tah	(slang) tough local girl
tsunami	tzoo-NAH-mee	(Japanese) a tidal wave
uku	OO-koo	gray snapper fish
ula	OO-lah	red
'ulu	OO-loo	breadfruit
ulua	oo-LOO-ah	crevalle jack fish

W

Wahiawa	wah-HEE-ah-WAH	town near Schofield Barracks on O'ahu
wahine	wah-HEE-nee	women
wahoo	WAH-hoo	king mackerel
wai	weye	stream or any body of fresh water
Wai'alae	why-ah-LEYE	private country club in the tony Kahala section of

		Honolulu and the site of the Hawai'ian Open
Wai'ale'ale	WHY-ah-lay-AH-lay	an extinct volcano on Kaua'i and one of the wettest places on earth
Wai'anapanapa	WHY-ah-nah-pah-NAH-pah	a state park and black-sand beach north of Hana, Maui
Wai'anae	WHY-ah-nigh	town on the leeward side of O'ahu
Waikaloa	WHY-kah-loh-ah	resort area on the Kohala coast, Big Island
Waikane	why-KAH-nee	village on the windward side of O'ahu
Waikiki	why-kee-KEE	the famous resort strip in Honolulu and the best concentration of nightlife in Hawai'i
Waikolu	why-KO-loo	stream on Moloka'i's back side
Wailau	WHY-lau	trail over the mountains to Moloka'i's back side
Wailea	why-LAY-ah	resort area and golf courses on east Maui
Wailua	why-LOO-ah	town and resort area on eastern Kaua'i
Wailuku	why-LOO-koo	town and county seat of Maui
Waimanalo	why-mah-NAH-loh	town on the windward side of O'ahu
Waimanu	why-mah-noo	pristine valley on the Kohala peninsula, Big Island
Waimea	why-MAY-ah	town on the southwestern coast of Kaua'i; the name of the largest canyon in Kaua'i and Hawai'i; town and home of the Parker Ranch, Big Island; famous and largest surf break on the north shore of O'ahu
Wai'oli	why-OH-lee	stream through the Hanalei valley, Kaua'i
Waipi'o	why-PEE-oh	historic valley on the Kohala peninsula, Big Island
wikiwiki	WEE-kee WEE-kee	quickly, very fast

Index

Academy Shop, The, 54
Acqua, 88
Activities. *See also individual names*
Big Island, 205
by island, xxi–xxii
for children, 390
Lana'i, 386
Kaua'i, 321
Maui, 114
Moloka'i, 405
O'ahu, 22
Adventures on Horseback, 144
Ahi's Punalu'u, 84, 94
Aioli's, 284
Air Kaua'i, 314
Airline information, xx–xxi
Ala Moana Beach, 14
Ala Moana Park, 43
Alaka Noodle Shop, 284
Alan Wong's, 77
Ali'i Kai I, 351
All Star Café, 88
Allerton Garden, 342
Aloha Diner, 371
Aloha Dive Co., 217
Aloha Theater Café, 283–284
America II, 143
'Anaeho'omalu Bay, 220
Angles, 92
'Anini Beach County Park, 333–334
'Anini Beach Windsurfing, 338
Anna Bannana's, 89
Annie's Deli, 180
Antonio's, 180
Anuenue Room, 174–175
Aqua Zone, 37–38
Aquarium, 214

Archery,
Lana'i, 390
Art galleries,
Big Island, 234–241
Kaua'i, 345
Lana'i, 389
Maui, 145–146
O'ahu, 52–53
Artists Gallery of Kaua'i, 345
Artmosphere, 53
Aston at the Executive Centre Hotel, 70–71
Aston Ka'anapali Shores Resort, 153
Aston Kaua'i Beach Villas, 356–357
Aston Waikiki Beachside Hotel, 62–63
Aunti Pasto's, 77
Avanas at Hanalei, 345
Azul, 86

Ba-Le French Sandwich & Bakery, 75–76, 83
Backroads Bicycle Touring, 225
Backyards, 23
Baldwin Beach Park, 125
Bali Hai, 367
Bamboo Bamboo, 367, 378
Bamboo Restaurant & Gallery, 278
Banana Bungalow, 170
Banyan Court, 88
Banzai Pipeline, 19, 24
Barefoot Bar, 88
Barking Sands, 336–337
Barnes & Noble Booksellers, 54
Batik, 278
Bay Club, 175
Bay Terrace, 278

Beach House Restaurant, 373–374
Beaches,
Big Island, 218–224
Kaua'i, 329–337
Maui, 122–128
Moloka'i, 405–409
O'ahu, 7–14, 16–20, 21–22
Bed, Breakfast, and Beach, 353
Bellows Field Beach Park, 16
Bestsellers Hawai'i, 54
Bianelli's Gourmet Pizza & Pasta, 281
Big and Little Beaches, 126–127
Big Island, The, 4, 191–292
bars and clubs, 288–290
general sights, 242–243
history of, 192–198
key facts, 198–199
south, 223, 276–277
where to eat, 277–288
where to stay, 248–277
Biking,
Big Island, 224–225
Kaua'i, 317–319
Maui, 137–139
Moloka'i, 409
Bill Kapuni's Snorkel & Dive, 414
Billfish Bar, 288
Bird Park, 204
Bird-watching, 309
Bishop Museum, The, 45–46, 54
BJ's Chicago Pizzeria, 186
Blue Dolphin, 307
Blue Ginger Café, 394–395
Blue Planet, 14–15
Bluewater Sailing, 307

RUM & REGGAE'S HAWAI'I

Boating.
Kaua'i, 302–307
O'ahu, 32–33
Bob Twogood Kayaks
Hawai'i, Inc., 31–32
Bookends in Kailua, 55
Bookstores,
Kaua'i, 345
Maui, 146
O'ahu, 54–55
Border's Books & Music,
54–55, 345
& Cafe, 146
Boston's North End Pizza,
79, 84
Botanical gardens,
Kaua'i, 342–344
Breakwater Nightclub, 290
Breathless Nightclub, 88
Brennecke's Beach, 336
Brennecke's Beach Broiler,
374
Brew Moon, 89
Brick Oven Pizza, 374
Brothers Cazimero, 92
Brown's Beach House, 278
Bubba's Burgers, 368
Bubbies Homemade Ice
Cream, 83
Bubbles Below, 340
Bull Shed, The, 371
Buzz's Original Steak
House, 84, 94
Byodo-In Temple, 52

Café Che Pasta, 76, 89
Café Hanalei, 368
Café Navaca, 180, 188
Café 100, 285
Café Pesto, 278, 286
Café Portofino, 371
Cafe Sistina, 89
Camp House Grill, 374
Cannons and Tunnels, 339
Canoe House, 278–279
Captain Andy's Sailing
Adventure, 306
Captain Cook, 264–265,
283–284
Captain Sundown, 306–307
Captain Zodiac, 304
Carelli's on the Beach, 180
Carson's Volcano Cottages,
275
Casa di Amici, 374
Casanova's, 189
Cascade Grill and Sushi
Bar, 175

Cathedrals, 130
Cavendish Golf Course,
388
Cemeteries, 335
Chai's Island Bistro, 76, 89
Chalet Kilauea, 275
Challenge at Manele, The,
387
Challenge at Manele
Clubhouse, 395
Champa Thai, 79, 84–85
Charley's, 182, 188
Chart House, 175
Cheeseburger in Paradise,
80–81, 175, 186
Chef Mavro, 77
Chez Paul, 175–176
Chimney, 214
Chinatown, 50
Cholo's Homestyle
Mexican, 85
CJM Country Stables, 317
Cliffs, The, 351
Climate, xvii–xviii, 16, 19,
23, 27, 104–105, 139, 298,
347
Club Jetty, 378
Club Lan'ai, 143
Coaste Grille, 279
Coffees of Hawai'i, 423
Colony One at Sea
Mountain Resort,
276–277
Columbia Inn, 78
Compadres, 176, 186
Compadres Mexican Bar &
Grill, 89–90
Contemporary Museum,
The, 48
Correa Trails Hawai'i, 34
Crater Rim Road, 202–203
Cronies, 290
Cruises,
Maui, 139–141

Da Kitchen, 180
Damien Tours, 404–405
David Paul's Lahaina Grill,
176
Denny's, 281
Department of Land and
Natural Resources, 301
Diamond Head, 3, 4, 14,
24, 66–68, 82–83
Diamond Head Beach
Hotel, 68
Diamond Head Grill, 82, 90

Diamond Head Tennis
Center, 43
Disappearing Sands, 219
Dive Kaua'i, 341
Diving,
Big Island, 213–217
Kaua'i, 338–341
Lana'i, 389
Maui, 123–132
Moloka'i, 414
O'ahu, 34–38
Dixie Maru Beach, 407
Dollies, 176, 187
Dolphin Bay Hotel, 269
Dolphin Quest, 30–31
Don Ho Show, The, 86, 93
Don's Chinese Kitchen, 281
Don's Grill, 286
Donatoni's, 279
Dondero's, 374–375
Down to Earth, 78
Duane's Ono Char-Burger,
371
Duc's Bistro, 76, 90
Duke's Barefoot Bar,
378–379
Duke's Canoe Club, 88, 371
Durty Jake's, 288–289

Ed Robinson's Diving
Adventures, 132
Edelweiss, 284
Edward's at the Kanaloa,
281
Embassy Suites Maui, 154
Embassy Vacation Resort,
362–363
Esprit de Corps Riding
Academy, 316
Experience, The, 388

Fathom Five Divers, 340
Fishing, deep sea,
Big Island, 225–226
Flashbacks Bar & Grill, 289
Fort DeRussy, 11
Foster Botanic Gardens, 49
Four Seasons, 228
Four Seasons Hualalai,
254–255
Four Seasons Resort Maui
at Wailea, 161–162
Frank DeLima, 93
French Bakery, 281
Fujiya Restaurant, 182
Furasato, 81
Fusion, 92
Garden Cafe, 78

INDEX

Garden Isle Oceanfront Cottages, 364–365
Gaylord's at Kilohana, 372
General Store, 339
Gentry's Kona Marina, 226
Gerard's, 176
Germaine's Luau, 86
Giovanni's Aloha Shrimp, 85
Gloria's Spouting Horn Bed & Breakfast, 364
Godmother, The, 287
Gold's Gym, 189
Golden Arches, 213–214
Golden Chopstix Chinese Restaurant, 281
Golf,
  Big Island, 206–213
  Kaua'i, 321–327
  Lana'i, 387–389
  Maui, 114–120
  Moloka'i, 413–414
  O'ahu, 38–43
Gordon Biersch's Brewery Restaurant, 90
Grand Canyon, 130
Grand Palace Chinese Restaurant, 279
Grand Wailea Resort Hotel & Spa, 163–164
Green Garden, 375
Green Sand Beach, 224
Grill, The, 279
Grove Farm Homestead Museum, 344–345
Gym, The, 93

Ha'ena, 332–333, 351–354
Hakone, 180, 279
Halape Trail, 204
Halawa Falls Cultural Hike, 411–412
Halawa Valley, 411–412
Hale Aloha Guest Ranch, 265
Hale Vietnam, 79
Haleakala Bike Co., 138
Haleakala National Park, 134–136
Haleakala, 97, 98, 133
Hale'iwa Joe's Seafood Grill, 85, 94
Hale'iwa Surf & Sea, 20, 37
Halekulani, The, 6, 57–58
Halema'uma'u, 203–204
Hali'imaile General Store, 183–184
Hamakua Coast, , 221

Hamoa Beach, 128
Hamura's Saimin Stand, 372
Hana, 97, 98, 127–128, 170–174, 185
Hana Accommodations and Plantation Houses, 173
Hana Gion, 180
Hana Kai Maui Resort, 172
Hana Ranch Restaurant, 185
Hanakapi'ai Beach, 330–332
Hanalei, 333, 351–354
Hanalei Athletic Club, 380
Hanalei Bay, 333
Hanalei Bay Resort, 328, 349
Hanalei Colony Resort, 351–352
Hanalei Dolphin Restaurant & Fish Market, 368
Hanalei Gourmet, The, 368, 378
Hanalei Mixed Plate, 368
Hanalei Plantation Guest House, 353
Hanalei Properties, 352
Hanama'ulu Restaurant & Tea House, 372
Hanauma Bay, 12–13, 35–36
Hank's Café Honolulu, 90
Hans Hedeman Surf School, 15
Hapa's Brew House, 188
Happy Talk Lounge, 378
Hapuna Beach Prince Hotel, The, 207, 255–256
Hapuna Beach State Park, 220
Harbor House, 226, 280
Hard Rock Café–Kona, 289
Harrington's, 286
Harry's Music Store, 55
Hau Tree Lanai, 83
Havana Cabana, 90
Hawai'i Helicopters, 315
Hawai'i Kai Championship and Executive Golf Courses, 40–41
Hawai'i Opera, 86
Hawai'i State Capitol, 49
Hawai'i State Library, 49
Hawai'i Surf and Sail, 20–21, 27
Hawai'i Tropical Botanical Garden, 242–243

Hawai'i Volcanoes National Park, 199–205
Hawai'ian Island Surf and Sport, 108
Hawai'ian Watersports, 26–27
Heavenly Hana Inn, 173–174
Hee Hing, 80
Helicopter rides,
  Big Island, 245
  Kaua'i, 309–315
  Maui, 144
Henry Clay's Rotisserie, 393–394
Hi-Tech Surf Sports, 108
Hideaways, 333
Hike Maui, 136–137
Hike O'ahu with Hawai'ian Island Eco-Tours, Ltd., 30
Hiking,
  Big Island, 243–244
  Kaua'i, 299–302, 308–309
  Maui, 133–137
  Moloka'i, 410–412
  O'ahu, 27–29
Hilo, 217, 222, 229, 266–269, 285–286
Hilo Bike Hub, 225
Hilo Hawai'ian Hotel, 268
Hilo Municipal Golf Course, 212–213
Hilton Turtle Bay Golf & Tennis Resort, 71
Hilton Waikoloa Village, 228, 257–258
Historical Hikes West Moloka'i, 412
Hoku's, Kahala Mandarin Oriental, 83–84
Holiday Inn SunSpree Resort, 357
Holualoa Foundation for Arts and Culture, The, 235–236
Holualoa Town, 235
Honokohau, 218–219
Honolulu, 3, 10, 48–51, 70, 75–79
Honolulu Academy of the Arts, 46–47
Honolulu Bay, 124, 130
Honolulu Harbor, 3
Honolulu Hikes, 28–29
Honolulu Sailing Company, 33
Honolulu Symphony, 86

Honu Bar, 289–290
Honu's Nest, 286
Ho'okena Beach County
  Park, 223–224
Ho'okipa Beach Park, 103,
  110, 125–126
Ho'olulu Tennis Park,
  229
Horseback riding,
  Big Island, 225
  Kaua'i, 315–317
  Lana'i, 389
  Maui, 143–144
  Moloka'i, 413
  O'ahu, 33–34
Hotel Hana-Maui, 170–172,
  183
Hotel Hana-Maui Stables,
  143
Hotel Honolulu, 65–66
Hotel Lana'i, 392
Hotel Moloka'i, 421
Hotel Molokai, 423
House of Fountains, 161
House of Seafood, 375
Hualalai Club Grille, 280
Hualalai Golf Club, 210
Huggo's, 282
Huggo's on the Rocks, 289
Hui No'eau Visual Arts
  Center, 145–146
Hula Grill, 187
Hula's Bar & Lei Stand, 92
Hulihe'e Palace, 243
Hulupo'e Court, 395
Hungry Ear Records and
  Tapes, 56
Hy's Steak House, 81
Hyatt Reef, 130
Hyatt Regency Kaua'i
  Resort & Spa, 329,
  359–360
Hyatt Regency Maui,
  149–150
Hyatt Regency Waikiki
  Resort & Spa, 60–61

'Iao Valley, 147
Ihilani Restaurant, 395
Ili'ili'opae Heiau, 414–415
Imari, 279
Indigo, 76, 90
I'o, 176
'Iolani Palace, 48–49
Irifune, 80
Ironwood Hills Golf
  Course, 413–414
Ironwood Ranch, Ltd., 144

Island Helicopters Kaua'i,
  314–315
Island Lava Java, 282
Island Slice Tennis, 228
Islander on the Beach,
  357–358

Jack Harter Helicopters,
  313–314
Jack's Diving Locker,
  215–216
Jacque's Bistro, 182
Jacque's on the Beach,
  180–181
Jameson's by the Sea, 85,
  282
Jeep rental,
  Lana'i, 390
Jennifer's Korean
  Barbecue, 282
J.J.'s Broiler, 372
Joe's Courtside Café, 375
John Dominis, 78
Joni-Hana, 372
Jose's Mexican Restaurant,
  80
Jukebox Music & Gifts, 147

Ka'a'awa Grinds, 85
Ka'ala, 21, 42
Ka'anapali, 98, 149–155
Ka'anapali Ali'i, 155
Ka'anapali Beach, 123–124
Ka'anapali Beach Hotel,
  152
Ka'anapali Resort, 116–117
Kacho, 81
Ka'enae, 140
Kahala, 13, 24–25, 68–70,
  83–84
Kahala Mandarin Oriental,
  68–70
Kahalu'u Beach Park, 219
Kahili Beach, 334
Kaho'olawe, 129, 130, 169
Kahului, 98
Kahului Airport, 103
Kailua, 23, 72–73, 215–217,
  218–219, 228, 260–264,
  281–283
Kailua Beach Park, 17
Kailua Plantation House,
  260–261
Kailua Recreation Center,
  44
Kailua Sailboard & Kayaks,
  26, 32
Kailuana: Kailua

Beachfront Vacation
  Homes, 72–73
Kaimuki, 79–80
Kaiwi Point, 213
Kalaheo Coffee Co. &
  Café, 375
Kalaheo Steak House, 375
Kalalau Beach, 330–332
Kalani Oceanside Eco-
  Resort, 269–271, 287
Kalapaki Beach, 335
Kalaupapa, 401–405
Kalihiwai Beach, 334
Kaluako'i Hotel and Golf
  Club, 420
Kaluako'i Resort, 419–420
Kanemitsu Bakery, 422–423
Kamaole Beach Parks, 127
Kamehameha Highway, 15,
  18
Kamehameha Park, 229
Kamehameha Schools, 52
Kamuela Provision
  Company, 279
Kanaha Beach Park,
  110–111, 125
Kanai Athletic Club, 380
Kaohikaipu Island, 16
Kapa'a, 335, 354–358
Kapalua, 156–159
Kapalua Bay Hotel and
  Villas, 156–157
Kapalua Beach, 124
Kapalua Golf Club, 115
Kapalua Tennis Garden
  and Village Tennis
  Center, 121
Kapiolani Park Courts, 44
Kaua'i, 293–381; see also
  city names
  bars and clubs, 377–379
  cinema, 379–380
  Coconut Coast, 316–317,
    318, 328–329, 354–358,
    370–373, 378–379, 380
  east coast, 335
  health clubs, 380
  history of, 296–297
  key facts, 297–298
  Na Pali Coast, 298–307,
    330–332
  north shore, 315–316,
    317–318, 328, 330–335,
    347–354, 367–370, 378,
    379, 380
  south shore, 318–319,
    329, 336, 358–365,
    373–377, 379

INDEX

Southwest Coast, 336–345
where to eat, 367–377
where to stay, 346–367
Kaua'i Beach Hotel, 356
Kaua'i Coasters, 318
Kaua'i Coconut Beach Resort, 358
Kaua'i Cycle and Tour, 318
Kaua'i Lagoons Golf Club, 325–326
Kaua'i Marriott Resort and Beach Club, The, 355–356
Kaua'i Museum, The, 341, 345
Kaua'i Waterski, Kayak, & Surf, 319–320
Kaua'i Z-Tour Z, 304–305
Kaua'i Zodiac, 304
Ka'uiki Hill, 128
Kaulu o Laka Heiau, 343–344
Kaulu Paoa Heiau, 343–344
Kaunakakai, 420–421, 422–423
Kauna'oa Beach, 221
Kaupoa Beach Village, 418–419
Kawaihae Harbor Grill, 279
Kawakiu Nui, 408
Kayak Adventures, 310
Kayak and Outrigger Events, 32
Kayak Kaua'i, 319
Kayaking,
Kaua'i, 319–320
Moloka'i, 412–413
O'ahu, 31–32
Ke Nani Kai, 420
Kea Lani Hotel Suites & Villas, 164–165
Keahole Cove, 214
Kealakekua Bay, 242
Kealia Beach, 335
Keapana Horsemanship, 316–317
Keauhou, 281–283
Ke'e Beach, 330–332
Ke'ehi Lagoon Court, 44
Kehena Beach, 223
Ken's House of Pancakes, 286
Keo's Thai Cuisine, 81
Keoki's Paradise, 376
Keolu Hills, 17
Kepuhi Bay, 406
KFC Express, 422

Kiahuna Golf Club, 327
Kiahuna Plantation, 360–361
Kiahuna Tennis Club, 329
Kihei, 98, 112
Kihei Café, 181
Kihei Prime Rib & Seafood House, 181
Kilauea, 333–334
Kilauea Bakery, 369
Kilauea Iki Trail, 204
Kilauea Lodge & Restaurant, 272, 287
Kilohana Galleries, 345
Kimo's, 177
Kincaid's Fish Chop and Steakhouse, 78
King and I Thai Cuisine, 372–373
King Kamehameha Luau, 282
King Kamehameha's Kona Beach Hotel, 261–262
Kipuka Pua'ulu, 204
Kitada's Kau Kau Korner, 184
Kiteboarding,
Maui, 113
O'ahu, 22–27
Ko Olina Golf Club, 39
Koa House Grill, 284
Kobe Japanese Steak House, 81
Kohala, 217, 220, 227–228, 229, 250–260, 278–280
Kohala Divers Ltd., 217
Kohala Na'alapa Stables, 225
Koke'e Lodge, 365–366, 376
Koko Crater, 4, 11
Koko Crater Stables, 33–34
Koko Head District Park, 44
Kokololio Beach Park, 18–19
Koloa Landing, 339
Komoda's Store and Bakery, 184
Kona, 215–217, 218–219, 228, 260–264, 281–283
Kona Art Center, 235
Kona Bali Kai, 264
Kona Brewing Co. & Brewpub, 282, 289
Kona Charter Skippers Association, 226
Kona Coast Divers, 216
Kona Country club, 211–212

Kona Inn Restaurant, 232
Kona Ranch House, 282
Kona Tiki, 262–263
Kona Village Luau, 280–281
Kona Village Resort, 258–259
Ko'olau Range, 3, 10, 16, 29, 56
Korner Pocket Bar & Grill, 289
Kua'Aina Sandwich, 85–86
Kualapu'u, 423
Kualoa Ranch & Activity Club, Inc., 34
Kualoa Regional Park, 17–18
Kuhio Beach Park, 10
Kula Lodge, 169, 184

L&L Drive Inn, 373
La Bourgoyne, 283
La Cascata, 369
La Mer, 81–82
Lahaina, 98, 159–161, 186
Lahaina Coolers Restaurant & Bar, 177
Lahaina Divers, 131
Lahaina Fish Co., 177
La'ie, 18, 25
Lana'i, 383–396
history of, 384–385
key facts, 385
where to eat, 393–394
where to stay, 391–393
Lana'i Art Program, The, 389
Lana'i City, 391–392, 393–395
Land of Oz, The, 35
Lanikai, 17, 23
Lava Trees State Monument, 244
Lawrence Lambino, 225
Leonard's, 80
Life's A Beach, 188
Lighthouse Bistro, 369
Li'hue, 335, 354–358
Liko Kaua'i Cruises, Inc., 306
Limahuli Garden, 343
Lincoln Park, 229
Links at Kuilima, The, 39–40
Liquin's Mexican Restaurant, 287
Little Bit of Saigon, A, 75
Lobster Cove, 188
Local Motion, 15

RUM & REGGAE'S HAWAI'I

Lodge at Ko'ele, The, 391–392
Lodge at Moloka'i Ranch, The, 416–418, 422
Lodge's Formal Dining Room, The, 394
Lo'ihi, 4
Longhi's, 177, 186
Lulu's, 2889
Lumaha'i, 333
Lydgate State Park, 335
Lyman Museum and Mission House, 240–241

Ma'alaea Bay, 98, 112
Ma'alaea Beach, 127
Magic Island, 14
Magic of Polynesia, 86
Maha's Café, 284–285
Mahena, 98
Mahi, 35
Mai Tai High, recipe for, xxvii
Makaha Beach Park, 21
Makaha Caves, 35
Makaha Golf Club, 42–43
Makapu'u, 16
Makawao Steak House, 184
Makena Golf Courses, 119–120
Makena Resort Tennis Club, 121
Makena Stables, 144
Makena Surf, 167
Makua Valley, 21
Makua-Ka'ena State Park, 22
Malaekahana State Recreation Area, 18
Maluaka Beach, 127
Mama's Fish House, 182–183
Mamane Street Bakery & Café, 285
Mana Divers, 341
Manago Hotel & Restaurant, 264–265, 284
Manana Island, 16
Manana Trail, 29
Manele Bay, 392–393, 395
Manele Bay Hotel, 392–393
Marco's Grill & Deli, 183
Margarita's, 379
Mariposa, 78
Marriott Ihilani Resort and Spa, 74
Mask Bar & Grill, 289

Maui, 97–190; see also names of cities
  bars and clubs, 186–187, 189
  central, 122, 124–126, 170, 182–183, 188
  gyms and health clubs, 189
  history of, 98–102
  key facts, 102
  luaus and shows, 187–189
  south, 117–120, 121, 122, 126–127, 131–132, 161–168, 180–182, 188
  upcountry, 169–170, 183–184, 189
  west, 115–117, 121–122, 123–124, 131, 149–161, 174–179, 186–187
  where to eat, 174–185
  where to stay, 148–174
Maui Brews, 186
Maui Dive Shop, 131, 132
Maui Downhill, 138
Maui Eldorado Resort, 155
Maui Hill, 168
Maui Islander, 160
Maui Marriott Resort & Ocean Club, 151
Maui Mountain Cruisers, 138
Maui Muscle Sports Club Kahana, 189
Maui Prince Hotel, 165–166
Maui Rainbow Factory, 181
Maui Tacos, 177, 181, 183
Maui Windsurf Company, The, 107
Maui's Trilogy Ocean Sports, 389
Mauka Makai Excursions, Inc., 30
Mauna Kea Beach Hotel, 227, 250–252
Mauna Kea Mountain Bikes, Inc., 224
Mauna Kea Resort, 206–207
Mauna Lani, 221
Mauna Lani Bay Hotel and Bungalows, 253–254
Mauna Lani Resort, 208–209
Mauna Loa Trail, 204–205
Maunaloa, 422
Maunalua Bay, 36

McBryde Garden, 342–343
Mekong 2, 78–79
Mema Thai Chinese Cuisine, 373
Merrie Monarch Festival, The, 229–234
Merriman's, 285
Michel's, 83
Michelangelo, 92
Mid-Pacific Country Club, The, 39
Mike Severns Diving, 131–132
Mission Houses Museum, The, 47
Missionary homesteads, 344–345
Miyako Japanese Restaurant, 83
Moana Hotel, 6
Mokoli'i Island, 17
Moloka'i, 397–424
  history, 398–400
  key facts, 400–401
  west end, 405–408
  where to eat, 421–423
  where to stay, 415–421
Molokai Bicycle, 409
Moloka'i Mule Rides, 403–405
Moloka'i Pizza Café, 423
Moloka'i Ranch, The, 416
Molokai Ranch Outfitters Center, 409, 412
Molokini, 129–130
Monolith, 130
Mo'okini Heiau, 242
Moose McGillicuddy's, 88
Moose McGillıcuddy's, 186
Murphy's Bar and Grill, 90
Murphey's Beach Park, 408–409
Museums,
  Kaua'i, 341–342
  O'ahu, 45–48
Music stores,
  Maui, 146, 147
  O'ahu, 55–56
My Island Bed & Breakfast Inn, 272–273

Na Pali Coast Hanalei, 305–306
Na Pali Explorer, 305
Naish Hawai'i, Ltd., 25–26
Namakani Paio Cabins, 276
Naniloa, The, 267–268

INDEX

Napili, 156–159
Napali Catamarans, 305
Napili Kai Beach Club, 158–159
Napili Point Resort, 159
Nature Conservancy of Hawai'i, 410–411
Nature tours,
Kaua'i, 298
O'ahu, 29
Nautilus Dive Center, 217
Neil Pryde Maui, 109
New China Restaurant, 286
New Otani Kaimana Beach Hotel, 67–68
Nick's Fishmarket Maui, 181
Ni'ihau, 339
Ni'ihau Helicopters, 315
Norberto's El Café, 373, 379
North Kona, 228, 250–260, 280–281
North Shore Boardriders Club, 21
Nukoli'i Beach Park, 335

O'ahu, 3–96; see also Honolulu; Waikiki; and other city names
bars and clubs, 87–92, 94
gyms and health clubs, 93
history of, 4–6
key facts, 7
leeward side, 21–22, 73–74
north shore, 19–21, 71, 72, 85–86
shopping, 94–95
shows, 92–93
west, 86
where to eat, 75–86
where to stay, 56–74
windward side, 15–19, 84–85
O'ahu Country Club, The, 39
O'ahu Nature Tours, 29
Ocean Concepts Scuba, Inc., 37
Ocean Odyssey, 340
Ocean Quest Water Sports Co., 340
Ocean Seafood Chinese Restaurant, 283

Ocean View Inn, 283
Odoriko, 82
Office, The, 289
'Ohana Helicopter Tours, 314
Ohana Hotels, The, 65
Ohana Keauhou Beach Resort, 263–264
O'heo Gulch, 133, 139
Old Airport State Park, 218
Old Lahaina Luau, 177–178
Ono Family Restaurant, 373
Ono Hawai'ian Foods, 80
Oodles of Noodles, 283
Orchids, 82
Orchid at the Mauna Lani, The, 227, 256–257
Oriental Express, 178
Other Side, The, 289
O'Toole's Irish Pub, 90–91
Outback Steakhouse, 178
Outfitters Kaua'i, 318–319, 320
Outpost Natural Foods, 423
Outrigger Hotels, The, 63–64
Outrigger Royal Sea Cliff Resort, 264
Outrigger Waikoloa Beach, 259–260
Outrigger Wailea Resort, 168

Pacific Café, A, 77, 175, 180, 370–371
Pacific 'O, 178
Pacific Whale Foundation, 142
Packing list, xix–xx
Pahu I'a, 281
Pa'ia, 103, 137, 140
Pali Golf Course, 41–42
Pali Ke Kua, 350
Palomino Euro Bistro, 76–77
Paniolo Hale, 419–420
Paniolo Lounge, The 290
Paolo's Bistro, 287
Papaya's Natural Foods and Café, 373
Paperbacks Plus, 146
Papohaku Beach, 406–407
Paradise Bar & Grill, 369
Park Place, 379
Parker Ranch, 243
Parker Ranch Grill, 285

Pat's Kailua Beach Properties, 73
Pattaya Asian Café, 376
Pau Hana Pizza, 369
Paul Comeau's Condos at Pat's at Punalu'u, 72
Pavilion, 280
Pearl Harbor, 3, 6, 10, 50
Pedal & Paddle, 317–318
Pegge Hopper Gallery, The, 53
Pele, 191, 199, 246
Pele's Other Garden, 395
People's Cafe, 77
Pescatore, 286
Piatti, 376
Picnic's, 137, 183
Pier Bar, The, 91
Pi'ilanihale Heiau, 147
Pine Wreck Point, 214
Pioneer Grill & Bar, 186–187
Pioneer Inn, 160–161
Pizazz Café, 188
Pizza Bob's, 86
Pizza Hanalei, 369
Pizza Paradiso, 178
Pizzetta, 376
Plane, The, 35
Plantation Inn, 159–160
Pohakuma'uli'uli Beach, 407
Point Panic, 11
Point, The, 379
Po'ipu, 317, 336, 358–365
Po'ipu Bay Golf Course, 326–327
Po'ipu Beach Hotel, 379
Po'ipu Beach Park, 336
Po'ipu Kapili, 361–362
Polihale State Park, 337
Polli's Mexican Restaurant, 184
Polo Beach, 127
Pony Express Tours, 143-144
Po'oku Stables, 315–316
Pool Grille, The, 395
Po'olau Bay, 407
Postcards, 369
Pounders, 19
Prince Court, 181
Prince Golf Courses, 321–323
Princeville, 333, 347–351
Princeville Condos, 349–350
Princeville Hotel, The, 347–348

Princeville Makai, 321
Princeville Ranch Stables, 315
Princeville Tennis Gardens, 328
Puako Beach Apartments, 260
Pukalani Country Club, 120
Pukalani Terrace, 184
Puko'o Beach Park, 408–409
Puna, 222, 223, 229, 269–271, 287
Punahou School, 52
Punalu'u Beach County Park, 224
Pu'u Po'a, 350
Pu'uhonua O Honaunau National Historic Park, 238–240
Pu'ukohola Heiau National Historic Site, 242
Pu'uomahuka Heiau State Monument, 52

Queen's Surf, 10
Queens Beach, 12

R&R's favorites, xxii–xxvi, 95–96, 190, 291–292, 380–381, 396, 424
Rabbit Island, 16
Racquet Club at Mauna Lani, 227–228
Radisson Waikiki Prince Kuhio, 62
Rainbow Books and Records, 55
Rainbow Drive-In, 80
Ramsay Galleries, 53
Records Hawai'i, 55
Red Lantern, 178
Red Lion, 88
Red Sand Beach, 127–128
Reeds Bay Beach County Park, 222
Renaissance Wailea Beach Resort, 166
Request, 147
Restaurant Kintaro, 373
Richardson Ocean Beach Park, 222
Ritz-Carlton Kapalua, 157–158
Roadrunner Bakery & Café, 369–370
Rock Quarry, 334

Roussel's at Waikoloa Village, 280, 290
Roy Ventner Studio, 53
Roy's, 84
Roy's Kahana Bar & Grill, 178
Roy's Nicolina, 178
Roy's Po'ipu Bar & Grill, 376–377
Roy's Waikoloa Bar & Grill, 280
Royal Hawai'ian Beach, The, 10–11
Royal Hawai'ian Hotel, The, 6, 7, 60
Royal Ka'anapali North Golf Course, 117
Royal Kona Resort, 228, 263
Royal Lahaina Resort, 152–153
Royal Lahaina Tennis Ranch, 122
Royal Luau, The, 82
Royal Siam, 286
Running Waters, 335
Ruth's Chris Steak House, 179

Sacred Falls State Park, 27–28
Sacred sites, Maui, 147
Saigon Café, A, 182
Sailing. See Boating
Sal's Place, 188
Salon 5, 53
Sam Choy's, 283 Lahaina, 179
Sandcastle Restaurant & Lounge, 182
Sandy Beach, 7, 10, 11–12
Sans Souci Beach, 14
Sansei Seafood Restaurant & Sushi Bar, 179, 187
Scuba. See Diving
Sea Paradise Scuba Inc., A, 216–217
Sea Star Kauai Windsurfing, 338
Sealodge, 351
Seaside, 286
Second Floor, 290
Second Wind Sail and Surf, 109
Secret Beach, 334
Seven Sacred Pools. See O'heo Gulch

Shaka Divers, 132
Shark's Cove, 36
Sharkfin Rock, 130–131
Sheraton Caverns, 339
Sheraton Kaua'i Resort, 362
Sheraton Maui, 151–152
Sheraton Moana Surfrider, The, 59
Sheraton Waikiki Beach Resort, 63
Shipley's Alehouse & Grill, 91
Shipman House Bed & Breakfast Inn, 266–267
Shipman Park, 229
Shirakawa Motel, 277
Shooter's, 290
Siam Thai, 183
Sibu Café, 283
Silver Cloud Guest Ranch, 169–170
Silver Falls Ranch, 316
Singha Thai, 82
Skiing, 246–248
Slaughterhouse, 124
Snorkeling. See Diving
South Kona, 264–265, 283–284
South Seas Aquatics, 37
Spa and Tennis Club at Kaua'i Lagoons, The, 328
Sporting clays, Lana'i, 390
Spreckelsville, 111–112, 125
Stables at Ko'ele, The, 389
Studio 7 Gallery, 236
Sueoka's Store Snack Shop, 377
Sunrise Café, 179
Sunset Beach, 7, 19–20
Surfing, O'ahu, 14–15, 20–21
Surt's at the Volcano, 287–288
Surt's on the Beach, 370
Sushi Blues & Grill, 370, 378
SushiMan, 80
Swiss Inn, 84

Tahiti Nui, 378
Tennis, Big Island, 227–229
Kaua'i, 327–329
Lana'i, 390
Maui, 120–122
O'ahu, 43–44

INDEX

Tennis Garden at Mauna Lani, 228
Terrace Room, The, 394
Teshima, 284
Tex Drive-In and Restaurant, 285
Thai Chef, 179, 182
Thai Rin, 283
Thai Thai Restaurant, 288
3660 On The Rise, 79
Thompson Ranch, 144
Three Tables, 36
Thurston Lava Tube, 204
Tidepools, 377
Tower Records, 55
Tres Hombres Beach Grill, 230
Trilogy Excursions, 142
Tropical Disc, 147
Tropical Taco, 370
Tsunami, 188
Tunnels, 332–333
Turbo Surf Bodyboarders Headquarter, 15
Turtle Bay Golf & Tennis Resort, 34
Turtle Bay Hilton & Country Club, 40, 43
Tutu's Cottage, 354
24-Hour Fitness, 93, 189

Ulua Beach, 127
Uncle Billy's Hilo Bay Hotel, 268–269
Uncle Billy's Kona Bay Hotel, 262
University of Hawai'i–Hilo, 242
University of Hawai'i–Manoa Campus, 51–52
USS Arizona Memorial, 50–51

Valley Isle, 103
Valley of the Temples, 52
Venus, 91
Village Grill, The, 422
Village Pizzeria, 179
Villas of Wailea, 167–168
Volcano Art Center, 202, 234–235
Volcano Country Cottages, 274–275
Volcano Golf and Country Club, 202, 212, 288
Volcano House, 202, 273–274, 288
Volcano Inn, 276

Volcano Village, , 201, 271–276, 287–288
Volcano Winery, 202
Volcano's Lava Rock Café, 287, 290

W, 67–68
Wai'alae Beach County Park, 13–14
Wai'alae Country Club, 38–39
Wai'anapanapa State Park, 128, 174
Waikiki, 10–14, 56–66, 80–82
Waikiki Parc, 61–62
Waikoloa Beach Resort, 209–210
Waikoloa Village Golf Club, 211
Waikomo Stream Villas, 363–364
Wailea Beach, 127
Wailea Blue (Golf) Course, 117–118
Wailea Gold and Emerald (Golf) Courses, 118
Wailea Tennis Club, 121
Wailua, 335
Wailua Kayak & Canoe, 320
Wailua Municipal Golf Course, 324–325
Wailuku, 98
Waimanalo Beach Park, 17
Waimano Trail, 29
Waimea, 266, 284–285, 365–367
Waimea Bay, 19
Waimea Bay Beach Park, 20
Waimea Beach, 7
Waimea Brewing Co., 377
Waimea Canyon, 307–309
Waimea Coffee & Co., 285
Waimea Country Lodge, 266
Waimea Park, 229
Waimea Plantation Cottages, 366–367
Waimea Valley Adventure Park, 29
Wai'oli Beach Park, 333
Waioli Mission House, 344
Waipi'o Na'alapa Stables, 225
Waipi'o Valley, 236–238, 244, 266

Waldenbooks, 55, 146, 345
Waterfalls, 140
Wave Waikiki, 88–89
West Maui Mountains, 97, 103
Westin Maui, The, 150–151
Whale watching, Maui, 141–143
What a Wonderful World Bed & Breakfast, 162–163
Will Squyres Helicopter Tours, 313
Windsurfing, Kaua'i, 337–338
Maui, 102–114
O'ahu, 22–27
Windward Dive Center, 37
Wong on Wong, 77
Woody's Island Grill, 179
Wrangler's Steakhouse, 377

Yanaghi Sushi, 79
Yokahama Bay, 22

Zaffron, 77
Zelo's Beach House, 370,
Zippy's, 79